INFORMATION-CONTROL PROBLEMS IN MANUFACTURING TECHNOLOGY

Proceedings of the IFAC Interntional Symposium
Tokyo, Japan, 17 - 20 October 1977

Edited by
Y. OSHIMA
University of Tokyo, Japan

Published for the
INTERNATIONAL FEDERATION OF AUTOMATIC CONTROL
by
PERGAMON PRESS
OXFORD · NEW YORK · TORONTO · SYDNEY · PARIS · FRANKFURT

U.K.	Pergamon Press Ltd., Headington Hill Hall, Oxford OX3 0BW, England
U.S.A.	Pergamon Press Inc., Maxwell House, Fairview Park, Elmsford, New York 10523, U.S.A.
CANADA	Pergamon of Canada Ltd., 75 The East Mall, Toronto, Ontario, Canada
AUSTRALIA	Pergamon Press (Aust.) Pty. Ltd., 19a Boundary Street, Rushcutters Bay, N.S.W. 2011, Australia
FRANCE	Pergamon Press SARL, 24 rue des Ecoles, 75240 Paris, Cedex 05, France
FEDERAL REPUBLIC OF GERMANY	Pergamon Press GmbH, 6242 Kronberg-Taunus, Pferdstrasse 1, Federal Republic of Germany

First edition 1978

British Library Cataloguing in Publication Data

IFAC Symposium on Information-Control
Problems in Manufacturing Technology, *Tokyo, 1977*
Information-control problems in manufacturing technology.
1. Automation - Congresses 2. Production engineering - Congresses
I. Title II. Oshima, Y III. International Federation of Automatic Control. Manufacturing Technology Symposium Committee IV. Society of Instrument and Control Engineers
621.7'8 T59.5 78-40164

ISBN 0-08-022015-0

In order to make this volume available as economically and as rapidly as possible the authors' typescripts have been reproduced in their original forms. This method unfortunately has its typographical limitations but it is hoped that they in no way distract the reader.

Printed in Great Britain by A. Wheaton & Co. Ltd., Exeter

IFAC SYMPOSIUM ON INFORMATION-CONTROL PROBLEMS IN MANUFACTURING TECHNOLOGY

Organized by
The IFAC Manufacturing Technology Symposium Committee
The Society of Instrument and Control Engineers

Sponsored by
The IFAC Technical Committee on Manufacturing Technology

International Program Committee
M. Terao, Japan (Chairman)
I. Kato, Japan
W. Karner, Austria
M. Mori, Japan
J. L. Nevins, USA
Y. Oshima, Japan
A. Romiti, Italy
R. Tomović, Yugoslavia
H. J. Warnecke, FRG
E. Yakubaitis, USSR

Local Organizing Committee
Y. Oshima (Chairman)
I. Kato (Vice Chairman)
T. Sata (General Secretary)
H. Akashi
T. Goto
H. Hanafusa
K. Hasegawa
Y. Hasegawa
F. Honda
J. Ikebe
Y. Ikebe
K. Matsushima
M. Mori
Y. Morita
T. Nagata
M. Nishimura
A. Nomoto
K. Okamura
S. Ozaki
K. Sato
M. Soeda
K. Sugiyama
H. Takeyama
T. Terano
M. Terao
K. Togino
Y. Umetani
K. Yonemoto

PROGRAMME

CONTENTS

FOREWORD

IFAC Symposium on Information-Control Problems in Manufacturing Technology was held in Tokyo, Japan, from 17th to 20th October 1977.
The Symposium was sponsored by IFAC Technical Committee on Manufacturing Technology and was organized by IFAC Manufacturing Technology Symposium Committee, the Society of Instrument and Control Engineers.

The purpose of the symposium was to discuss various engineering and technical problems in automation of every step of the manufacturing processes including design, machining, material handling, assembling and inspection.

1. Information-control issue associated with material processing such as numerical control and adaptive control of machine tools
2. Information-control issue associated with material handling such as robotics
3. Information-control issue associated with assembly and inspection
4. Information-processing such as CAD, pattern recognition and artificial intelligence in manufacturing processes
5. Micro-economic modeling of manufacturing automation processes

The technical programme was developed by an International Programme Committee whose members are listed on page v.
The final programme included one special lecture, two plenary session papers and forty-three technical session papers. The order of presentation of the papers was as given on pp. vii-ix in the Programme. It should be noted that the Contents is not arranged in this order because the Proceedings consist of the Preprint material together with extra material added after the production of the Preprints.

The Organizing Committee takes this opportunity to acknowledge the splendid contributions and cooperation of all of the authors and the thorough editorial and publishing services of Pergamon Press Ltd., Oxford.

MODELING AND SIMULATION OF AUTOMATED MANUFACTURING PROCESSES

H.-J. Warnecke and E. Gericke

Institut für Industrielle Fertigung, University Stuttgart, FR Germany

ABSTRACT

Increasing automation of the manufacturing process including automated information- and material-flow causes increasing complexity of manufacturing systems. In particular automation of small batch production is very complicated, as the task of automation is combined with the need for flexibility. This paper describes modeling and simulation of a production system for small batch size metalworking production with high automation and high flexibility including the aspect of stochastic technical downtimes of the machine tools. Digital simulation with an abstract system model and computerized evaluation is used as a feasible method for planning complex production systems.

INTRODUCTION

A Flexible Manufacturing System (FMS) is an integrated system of computer controlled machine tools and other work stations with an automated flow of information, workpieces, and possibly tools in such a way that automated production of a group of complex workpieces in small and medium lot sizes is possible. Since the elements of a complex production system and the performance indexes of the manufacturing process are interdependent in many regards, the planning of these manufacturing systems is a process of high complexity as well.

For planning these systems the application of analytical models becomes extremely complicated or even impossible, thus the simulation technique as an alternative planning method has to be used for the design of an FMS.

Simulation models of production systems are useful for general aspects of system design such as the basic concept of the system, type of material flow system, scheduling algorithms etc. as well as for specific questions such as number and type of machine tools and work stations, machining capacity, maximum number of parts in the system, work station and material handling system breakdowns and many other questions /1, 2/.

1. MODELING OF SYSTEMS

1.1 Original system and model

A model is an idealized representation of the components, internal relations, and characteristics of a real-life system. In this report the system to be modeled is a FMS for production of heavy non-rotatory workpieces. Transportation of parts is performed by a stacker crane. As an example a work station of such type of FMS is shown on Fig. 1. A model of

Fig. 1 . Work station of a FMS

the original system is needed, since simulation is the imitation of a real process using a model. The analysis of the models behaviour shows ways for improving the model structure by changing model parameters. These parameter changes are assumed to have a similar effect upon the real-life system. Nevertheless, there is usually a discrepancy between the performance of the model and the original system, depending on the model's accuracy and degree of abstraction and idealisation.

1.2 Physical model

Models can be classified by their type, their purpose, and their degree of abstraction from the original system. Figure 2

Fig. 2. Small scale model of a FMS

shows a small scale FMS-model, which was built for purpose of experimentation and demonstration of the material flow of the above mentioned type of a FMS /3 /. It is a functional model in so far as the flow of workpieces is actually performed. Small scale representations of parts are moved through the system, to and from work stations, stored in the central storage and transported back to the unloading area. This model is to be controlled by a process computer. It will be feasible to simulate the operation of the system under real time conditions. This way it is possible to test transportation strategies of the stacker crane, scheduling algorithms, buffer and storage capacity in two or three shift operation, maximum number of parts and pallets in the system, and after re-building the system's structure the performance indexes of system alternatives can be tested.

These models need in real time operation much time for simulation experiments and for constructing system alternatives. This type of simulation is useful in the advanced phase of system planning, when the basic structure of the FMS is found and optimisation has to be done. Furthermore this model is a useful tool for presentation a system design to a potential user.

1.3 Abstract model

The most abstract representation of a system is a model, in which the relations between system elements are expressed mathematically. Since the different states of the manufacturing system which we want to model are changing with discrete time intervals, we can represent the system performance by changing the status of the model's components. The change of a component's status within a given time interval can be performed by calculation steps, therefore a digital computer can be applied for analysing and evaluation of model experiments.

A formal abstract digital model of a manufacturing system represents the components and elements on a certain level of system hierarchy. It is not useful to model on a low level of hierarchy, e.g. modeling machine elements or a separate engine for testing the performance of a complete manufacturing system; on the other hand when a model component represents a complete subsystem, e.g. all machine tools as one model component, the model is not sensitive to particular events like a breakdown of a separate machine tool. Figure 3 shows

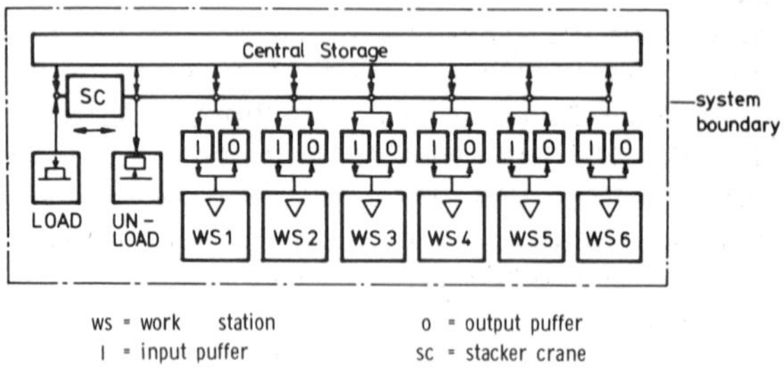

Fig. 3. Structure of an abstract FMS-model

the structure and subsystems of the FMS-model, which we used for computerized testing of the performance of different system designs. Since the digital simulation is not done in real time we can test a week's system operation within a few minutes.

2. SIMULATION

2.1 Simulation language

System simulation deals with analysing physical systems; this group of systems such as traffic systems, material flow in a plant or a production system have similar characteristics. Due to these similarities of all material and information flow systems general simulation concepts have been developed. The basic idea of these simulation systems is that mobil units enter the system, move to different stationary units, while the status of the mobil and/or the stationary units are changed, and then the units leave the system again. The separate events can be performed by standardized subroutines, which have to be interconnected and controlled by a central calender of events and a control algorithm for generating, starting, blocking, and finishing movements or status changes in the simulation system.

In order to take advantage of a ready simulation concept we applied the simulation language GPSS (General Purpose Simulation System) for our system analysis. Since we wanted a simulation system of wide applicability, we used GPSS in a into FORTRAN IV transformed version / 4 /. This version yields the possibility to write new subroutines, which are not included in the regular GPS system.

2.2 Structure of simulation model

For programming a given model structure the logical structure of the original system and the size of the programm modules and sections have to be analysed and determined. There does not exist a closed algorithm for designing a simulation model; the model's structure is influenced by the accuracy of the system analysis, by experience and by intuition of the programmer. Comparision of available simulation results with well known data of real system operation is helpful. Figure 4 shows

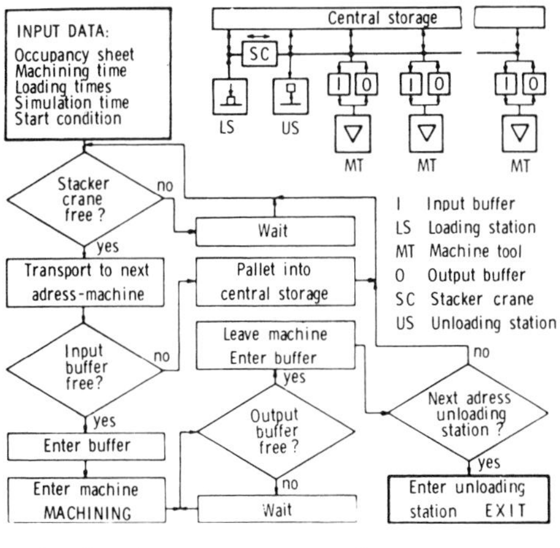

Fig. 4. Logic structure of the simulation model

the programm logic of the sequence of events in the FMS model, where the input and the output buffers of the machining stations, the central storage and the load/unload area are interconnected via a stacker crane, which is able to carry one workpiece (pallet) at a time. All parts are processed on two different machining stations.

The priority rules for the stacker crane's transportation strategy has a strong impact upon the system performance, but this problem has been discussed in other papers / 5 /.

2.3 Test of simulation model

For programm evaluation it is necessary to test the accuracy of the model and its logic structure. Programm modules should be tested separately; a relatively easy way to find faults of the model structure are test runs with extreme input data in order to generate extreme situations during the simulated process. Figure 5

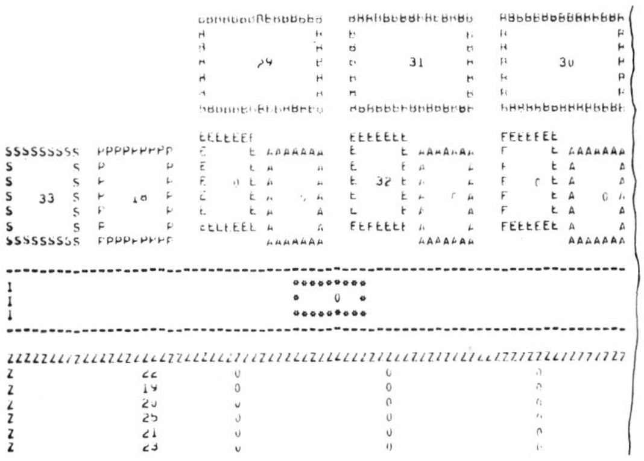

BBB = Work stations EEE = Input buffer
AAA = Output buffers SSS = Load area
PPP = Unload area *** = Stacker crane
ZZZ = Central storage

Fig. 5. Print-out of a simulation programm of a FMS

shows a graphical print-out of the simulation programm at a certain state. The numbers printed in the lay-out are the numbers of the workpieces which actually occupy the particular system component.

This type of graphical representation is useful for programm testing, for documentation and for demonstration purposes. Similar programms can be generated for computer terminal displays.

3. EVALUATION OF SIMULATION RUNS

3.1 Input data

The machining times of the workpieces are the most significant input data. Seven different groups of workpieces, characterized by their mean machining times, were tested in regard of their influence upon system performance. The number of work stations was selected as 6. The scheduling of workpieces was balanced in order to get a similar work load for all six work stations. The times for transportation and handling of parts were taken from the operation of the FMS, a part of which is shown on Fig. 1. The system operation was simulated for an 80 hour interval, i. e. two-shift operation for five days. The time unit represented in the simulation run is 30 seconds, which means: the programm's control mechanism checks and calculates the new status of the system's mobil and stationary components every 30 seconds of the real system's operation. The simulation clock stops a simulation run after

80 x 60 x 2 = 9600

simulation time units.

At the beginning of a simulation run no system component is occupied by a workpiece. Therefore we started to measure the system performance after the system had reached its steady state, which happened after about 1400 time units. The priority rules for the transportation strategy and the capacity of buffers and central storage are part of the input data as well.

3.2 Output data

The utilisation rate of the work stations is the most important output datum, since a high machine tool utilisation is prerequisite for economic operation of a FMS. The complementary output data are the through put times of the workpieces. These time intervals can be expressed by a factor, which was defined as the relation of the minimal, technical necessary through put time and the actually needed time for processing a workpiece including waiting times in buffers and storages. Among many other values the utilisation of buffers as well as the utilisation of central storage and stacker crane was measured to find system alternatives with good utilisation of all system components.

3.3 Selected results

Figure 6 shows the utilisation of the work stations and the stacker crane over the mean machining times of seven different groups of workpieces . At the machining time of ca. 38 minutes per part the work station utilisation is above 80 %, which is regarded as the minimal acceptable level for economic operation of a FMS / 6 /. At short mean machining times

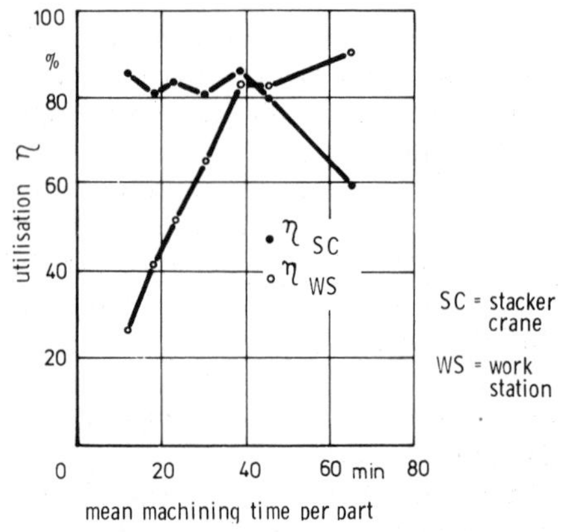

Fig. 6. Utilisation of work stations and stacker crane

the work station utilisation is low, since the time necessary for transportation and handling is reasonably high compared to the machining time of a part, so that the rate of transportation calls of parts to the stacker crane is very high and the stacker crane cannot satisfy all transportation needs.

The stacker crane's utilisation never reaches the 100 % level, since the number of pallets available is assumed to be limited, which causes some organisatorial waiting time for the pallet carrier.

A machining time of ca. 38 minutes seems to be optimal for the overall system operation under the assumed conditions, since the work stations and stacker crane utilisation are above 80 % and the maximum number of parts in the central storage is minimal (Fig. 7). This maximum number of parts is the required storage capacity. As the utilisation rate of the central storage (average value over maximum value) is minimal at 38 minutes, the through put times are minimal as well.

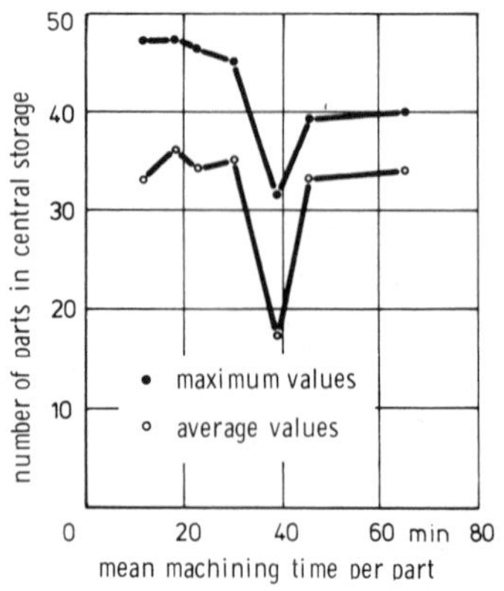

Fig. 7. Number of parts in central storage

The operation of the system with

parts of ca. 38 minutes mean machining time is reasonably good under ideal conditions, i. e. machine tool and stacker crane breakdowns do not occur.

4. BREAKDOWNS OF COMPONENTS

4.1 Classification of breakdowns

Down times of system components may have organisatorial and/or technical reasons. Since the organisatorial down times can be reduced by system internal and external measures and are supposed to be minimal in a good system design, we concentrate on techical down times.

Technical down times can be stochastic or deterministic. The deterministic technical down time such as time for preventive maintenance can be calculated and predetermined, whereas the reasons for stochastic technical down times such as malfunctions of machine tools have random character and cannot be influenced in advance. Therefore the impact of stochastic technical down times upon system performance has to be researched.

4.2 Selected results

Particular programm modules were developed to simulate stochastic technical down times of the machine tools and the stacker crane at a given frequency and with any desired distribution such as normal, exponential and others.

Figure 8 shows the machine tool utilisation under ideal and realistic conditions, i. e. breakdowns do occur. In the area of medium to long machining time the system utilisation is drastically lowered. In the range of short machining times the machine tool utilisation is under real or breakdown conditions even better than under ideal or free-of-breakdown conditions. This phenomenon seems to be contradictory to any common sense, but is to be explained as follows: In case of short machining times there are many calls for transportation from the waiting workpieces to the stacker crane. Because of the limited speed of the stacker crane only a limited number of transportation orders can be performed within a time interval. Due to the overload of the stacker crane's capacity some machine tools stand idle for some period of time. This results in a low average machine tool utilisation. As soon as a breakdown of a machine tool occurs this machine tool does not give transportation calls to the stacker crane any more, the FMS operates as if with 5 stations only. The less stations a system of this kind has, the better the average machine utilisation of the stations becomes, and this increase of machine tool utilisation of the five machines compensates the loss of machining capacity of the havaried machine. But after all the utilisation rate is too low for an economic system operation, on the other hand this effect shows what kind of situations may rise under impact of machine tool malfunction within a FMS.

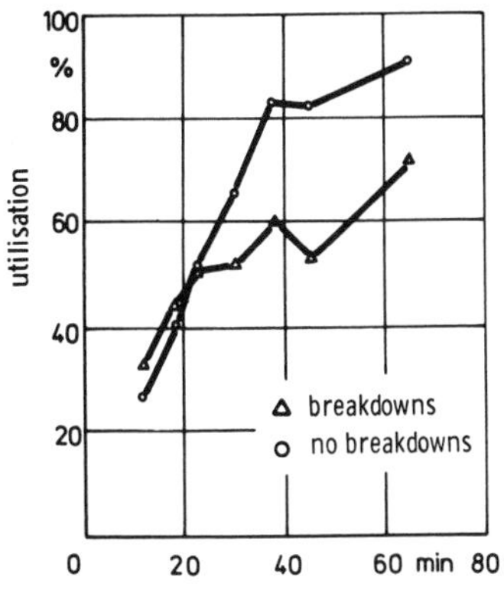

Fig. 8. Utilisation of work stations under breakdown conditions

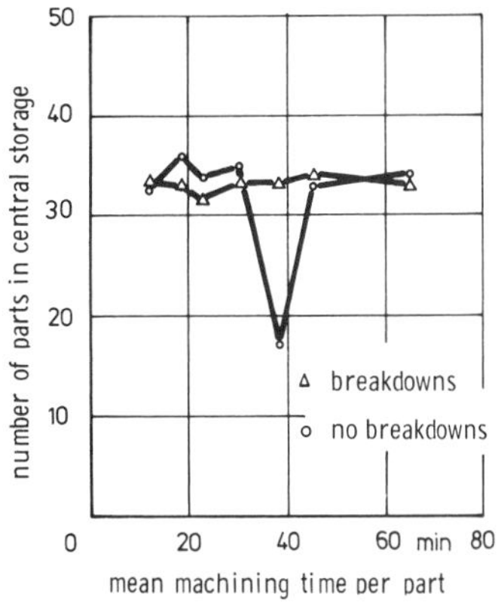

Fig. 9. Number of parts in central storage under breakdown conditions

Figure 9 shows the impact of breakdowns upon the average number of workpieces in the central storage . The characteristic of system performance at 38 minutes mean machining time has been leveled at a constant number of parts in the storage. This mean machining time is not the optimal value any more under breakdown conditions of machine tool operation.

5. CONCLUSIONS

In spite of the benefits to be expected from the installation of Flexible Manufacturing Systems such as reduction of cost per part, reduction of through put times, and increasing flexibility towards changes of the product mix the number of FMS in operation is still small. One of the main objectives against the installation of these systems is the unknown availability and reliability of a planned system. The availability has a strong influence upon the return on investment. Simulation studies are a valuable tool for researching the influence of stochastic technical down times upon system utilisation and for quantifying the production rate under reduced operation.

6. REFERENCES

/1/ H. J. Warnecke, E. Gericke, G. Vettin, Auslegung der Verkettungseinrichtungen flexibler Fertigungssysteme mit Hilfe der Simulation, Preprints 8th CIRP Seminar on Manufacturing Systems(1976).

/2/ J. J. Hughes, Simulation--Computer-aided problem solving, Proceedings of "Multi-station, digitally controlled manufacturing systems" University of Wisconsin (1977).

/3/ Several authors, Report of Sonderforschungsbereich 155 University Stuttgart (1975).

/4/ Niemeyer, G. (1972) Die Simulation von Systemabläufen, De Gruyter, Berlin - New York.

/5/ H. J. Warnecke, G. Vettin, Strategies for the organisation and control of discontinuous conveyors in flexible manufacturing systems, Preprints 9th CIRP Seminar on Manufacturing Systems (1977).

/6/ Th. Stöferle, Zielgruppen für integrierte, flexible Fertigungssysteme, VDW-Forschungsbericht 0410 (1976).

CONCEPTUAL DESIGN OF INTEGRATED PRODUCTION CENTER

F. Honda* and H. Takeyama**

**Mechanical Engineering Laboratory, 4-12-1, Igusa, Suginami-ku, Tokyo, Japan*
***Tokyo University of Agriculture and Technology, 2-24-16, Nakamachi, Koganei-shi, Tokyo, Japan*

ABSTRACT

Based upon three years' survey study on modelling of unmanned machinery factory, the conceptual design of a multi-purpose automated Integrated Production Center for batch or piecewise production, which is the core subsystem of the factory, was performed in 1976. The input of the Production Center is standardized material and the output is complete machine units or machinery of average quality up to 700 mm in size. It is aimed at a normative Production Center for the future to perform the throughout activities from material to products such as blank fabrication, machining, heat treatment, inspection, assembly, etc. The Production Center is featured by modular design of construction, convertibility of modular working units and process merger in view of function, time and space.

It has been analysed from various angles whether such an overall Production Center can be implemented by a single machine like an existing machining center, a transfer machine, or a mixed one. Apart from the aforementioned hardware, the basic idea of the Production Center is to eliminate the human participation in the production activities of the real time area to attain higher programmability, flexibility and reliability for batch and piecewise production.

INTRODUCTION

Every effort in research and development had been directed to automation in Japan. However, due to the inevitable constraints such as limited natural resources and energy and lowering rate of economic growth, the policy of industrial investment, research and development have been modified in order to adapt the foregoing constraints. Neverthless, automation is still justified in order to reduce manufacturing cost and to establish a tough structure of enterprise against serious economic recession and steep rise of labour cost. Increased energy consumption accompanied with automation is to be solved by centralizing or integrating manufacturing activities.

Existing machining centers which originated from the system concept have been very much appreciated in industry especially for batch production of products of appropriate shape, but it is not the final solution. There must be a more suited pattern of machine tool for each production mode which is the function of lot size, shape of product, size or weight of product, required accuracy of product, etc. In order to rationalize batch and piecewise production which plays an extremely important role in the national output, the greatest effort has been devoted to investigation of a normative pattern of machine tool as an element of production system and a normative pattern of the system itself. An ideal mode of production for batch and piecewise production will give a revolutionary impact even to mass production which leads to drastic reduction of lead time and higher flexibility. Then the following equation will hold as the ideal state:

$$\Sigma \text{ Piecewise Production} \rightleftarrows \text{Mass Production}$$

On the basis of such the philosophy, the National Big Project has started from 1977 as a seven year program to create a normative model of Integrated Production Center covering blank fabrication, machining and assembly which will be adaptable to batch and piecewise production. The total budget is approximately 15,000,000,000 yen for seven years.

Prior to this program survey and design study was conducted for four years (1973 ~ 1976), and for the early three years the conceptual design of an unmanned machinery factory was completed and for the last year, 1976, the subsystem of the factory, so-called Integrated Production Center, was intensively designed so that the National Big Project can be smoothly started. Although it has not reached a conclusive conceptual design, it has yielded a valuable guideline for the Big Project.

DESIGN SPECIFICATION OF INTEGRATED PRODUCTION CENTER

Products to be manufactured. Fundamental machinery units such as speed-changing gear box, pump, compressor, engine, control valve, etc. up to 700 mm in size.

Type of production. Order making by piecewise and batch production of which lot size ranges 1 to 30.

Type of process. Blank fabrication, machining, assembly and service activities involved.

Inputs from outside. Tools, jigs and fixtures, standard parts such as bolts and nuts, springs, O-rings, washers, keys, etc., smaller parts than 100 mm, and standard sheet, bar and block material.

Machining and assembling accuracy. Rougher than I. T. 7 except for mating parts of I. T. 6 ~ 7.

Clarification of human functions. Planning, altering and modifying of engineering and management programs, developing and introducing of new technologies, integrating of know-how, trouble shooting, etc.

Extent of automation. All activities except for human functions described above and all activities in the real time area are to be fully automated.

Flexibility. To aim at an Integrated Production Center for dealing with approximately 70 % of ordinary machinery smaller than 700 mm in the market, the rest (approximately 30 %) counting for special processings inherent in individual products, processings of extremely high accuracy, smaller parts than 100 mm, etc. as described before.

Promotion of process merger. To combine, delete or centralize processes and operations in view of function, space and time.

Date of development and commercialization. To be developed in the earlier part of 1980's and commercially utilized in the middle part of 1980's.

SIGNIFICANCE OF PROCESS MERGER

Process merger is one of the most important target of the project. Conventionally the activities of blank fabrication, machining and assembly have independently functioned in a production system. Since products are to be manufactured in a closed system, the Integrated Production Center, process merger in view of function, space and time, as shown in Fig. 1, seems to be advantageous in production cost, production control and required parts accuracy. Furthermore, this concept has a possibility to lead to a new image of "Production tool".

Process merger is defined as collective execution of plural processes or operations in time and / or space domains. Here the space domain denotes the coordinates of both workpiece and machine. Following after each workpiece a standard process sequence can be described by a block diagram shown in Fig. 2 taking the time axis from left to right. Here □ denotes a principal process activity such as blank fabrication, machining, assembly and material treatment, and ○ denotes an auxiliary activity such as work transfer, inspection, etc. Starting from the standard sequence in Fig. 2, conceivable types of process merger will be classified into A, B, C and D as shown in Fig. 3 by deleting or combining principal and auxiliary processes.

The benefits of process merger consist of primary and secondary ones. The primary benefit is direct reduction of processing time or deletion of processes themselves, and the latter the macroscopic effect such as reduction of inventory cost and easiness of production control resulted from less causes of disturbances or unbalances in production.

Fig. 4 shows the comparison between conventional and process-merged process plannings when manufacturing a speed changing gear box of two parallel shafts. The simulation for several products has revealed that the gross production time can be reduced averagely down to one third by process merger. This has been verified by an existing example, B. T. M. (Boring, Turning and Milling) COMPLEX developed by a bulldozer manufacturer, although the process is confined to only machining. With horizontal movement of the ram (X), cross movement of the rotary table (Y), vertical movement of the ram (Z) and indexing movement of the rotary table (C), turning, milling, boring, drilling and tapping can be performed in one chucking of workpiece, and five surfaces of a cubic workpiece can be machined. The statistics indicates that the average proportion of net machining time to non-machining time for ordinary machinery parts in small lot production is down 30 % very often, but with the aforementioned machine it reaches up 70 % approximately. Fig. 5 shows the comparison of production cost with such the integrated machine and conventional machines.

The concept of process merger must affect the machine tool design, and the ultimate machine will be a working center in which blank fabrication, machining and assembly can be performed at one station. To what extent mechanical and functional integration is justifiable depends upon the following questions:

(1) How far is the mechanical and functional integration allowed economically?
(2) To what extent can high working load and high working accuracy coexist?
(3) To what extent can high temperature or severe environment and high working accuracy coexist?
(4) What is the dimensional range of workpiece to be covered?
(5) To what extent can the modular units and structures of machine be commonly utilized?

Unfortunately there have been no reliable data to answer the above questions. Concerning (2) and (3) a trial plot is shown in Fig. 6, in which the motor power is directly related to the working load and indirectly to the heat generated. Summarizing experiences and rough data obtained so far, the structure of a possible Production Center will consists of at least the following capsules and subsystems:

Blank fabrication capsule. The capsule is one machine in which limited plastic forming such as free forging, building-block die forging, roll bending, helical roll forming, spinning, etc. and some kinds of machining can be performed.

Machining and assembling capsule. The capsule is to be implemented into one machine so that cutting, grinding, assembling, welding and local heat treatment can be performed randomly by automatically changing tools and units.

Deburring and cleaning capsule.

System of material transfer between capsules and subsystems.

Control system.

SOFTWARE

For higher flexibility and programmability the quantity and type of products, and even the mode of production must be able to be changed primarily by software with a flexible hardware construction. On the other hand the burden of software becomes heavier in accordance with (Freedom of hardware) X (Automation level of software). Considering the limitation of software cost and human functions aforementioned there must be an optimal software size for a specific production system.

Concept of Software Design

There are two phases of software in a production system; one is the software for production planning and control and the other the technological one. The former is to be designed as the image of real hardware and factory system, whereas the latter can be developed as a general purpose program, and also existing general purpose programs can be built-in for the respective technological activities in a specific production system. Since a closed Production Center to cover blank fabrication to assembly is to be newly designed, and furthermore process merger is to be realized, the most consistent and compatible program covering all activities involved is desirable. But this is a gigantic task. Now let us explain the design concept of technological software for the Integrated Production Center.

Process Planning

Based upon the input data of product design written in a specific language, the product will be disintegrated into constituting parts, and finally the process sequence will be generated.

Since there has not been an automatic process planning system to cover blank fabrication, machining and assembly and to meet process merger of them, a completely new system has to be developed.

Operation Planning

Each process such as blank fabrication, machining and assembly is disintegrated into required operations to arrange the operation sequence.

Control of Tool Path and Working Conditions

In the software for the Integrated Production Center even the geometrical description of workpiece is not easy because it will change from time to time, for instance, when a subassembled workpiece is to be machined. Therefore, even the software for machining should be reformed on the basis of a new concept. Especially no general purpose software for assembly has been developed yet. Conceivable ways of control for assembly are numerical control, sensory control and play-back control. The most promising one will be numerical control assisted by sensory feedback.

Because the operations performed in the Integrated Production Center are extremely complex, it is difficult to identify the status of workpiece in process by means of the data generated by a conventional N/C software, this being especially the case with when processing subassembled workpieces. This will necessitates a data base which holds the data concerning work geometry, function, accuracy and relative coordinates of parts being built up into a product. Based upon such the special data base the process and operation sequences can be planned, and the consistent working programs can be generated by means of the respective softwares such as APT or the like.

On the other hand, in the real time operations of assembly and inspection, especially, the programs of machine control should be modified by the feedback signals from the sensors.

EXAMPLE OF DESIGN

Several machine tool builders and users participated in the preliminary project and each independently worked out the conceptual design of the Integrated Production Center assuming the most adequate products individually, although unfortunately blank fabrication was not included. One example is the TRIANGLE Production Center as shown in Fig. 7, in which machining, assembly and inspection for blocky workpieces can be performed by automatically changing tools and working units of modular structure. Another example is the SUPER BOX Production Center capable of machining, assembly and inspection of blocky workpieces.

This is characterized by higher rigidity for the machine weight because of box structure as shown in Fig. 8. The CIRCULAR Production Center including blank fabrication proposed by the author is shown in Fig. 9.

REFERENCE

Report on Modeling of Unmanned Machinery Factory, Sponsored by the Ministry of International Trade and Industry, Association of Mechanical Technology, March, 1977.

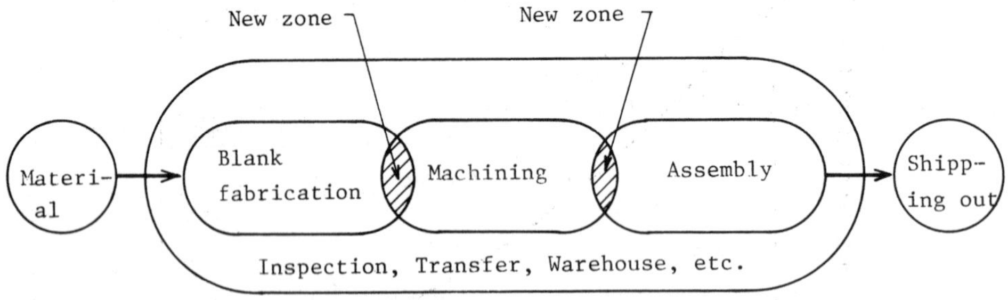

Fig. 1 Concept of process-merged Production Center

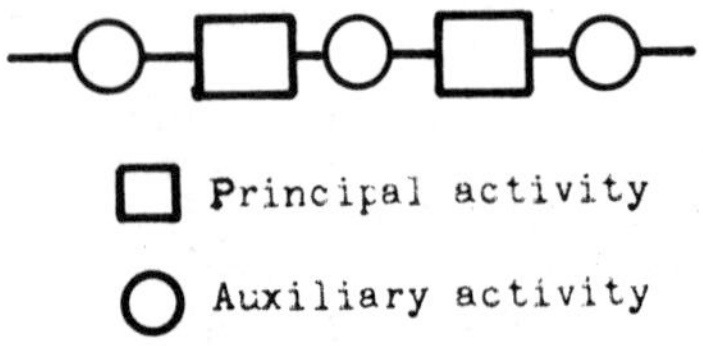

Fig. 2 Standard process sequence

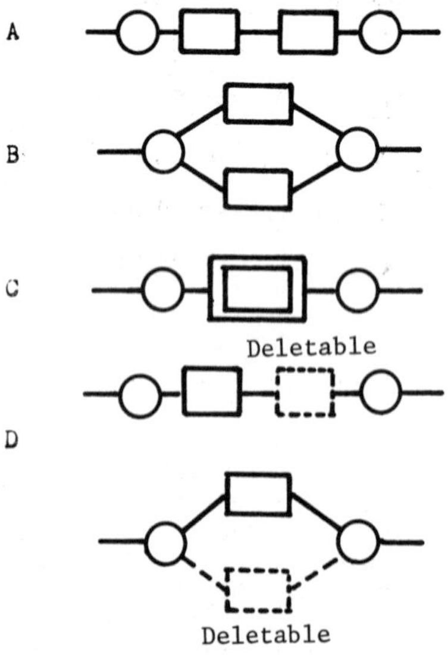

Fig. 3 Four types of process merger

Parts	Geometry	Process Sequence Conventional New	Type
Cover	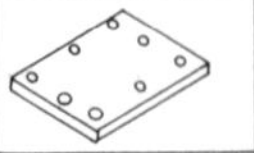	M-○-D ⇒ M·D (AAA)	A + B
Gear case (1)	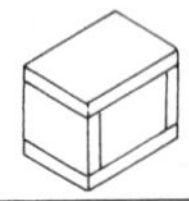	A-○-W-○-WF ⇒ A·W·WF (EAE)	A
Gear case (2)	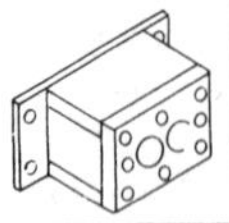	A'-○-B-○-R ⇒ A.B.R (EAE)	A
Shaft		L-○-MS ⇒ L.M.S (AAAA)	A + B
Gear	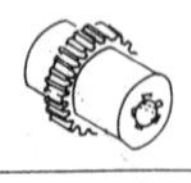	Gi-○-Q ⇒ Gi.Q (AAA)	A
Boss		L-○-D ⇒ L.D (AAAA)	A + B

A: Edge preparation, A': Bolt hole machining, B: Boring, D: Drilling, Gi: Internal grinding, L: Turning, Q: Broaching, R: Disassembly, W: Welding, WF: Weld finishing, ○ : Transfer

Fig. 4 Example of process merger (Speed changing gear box)

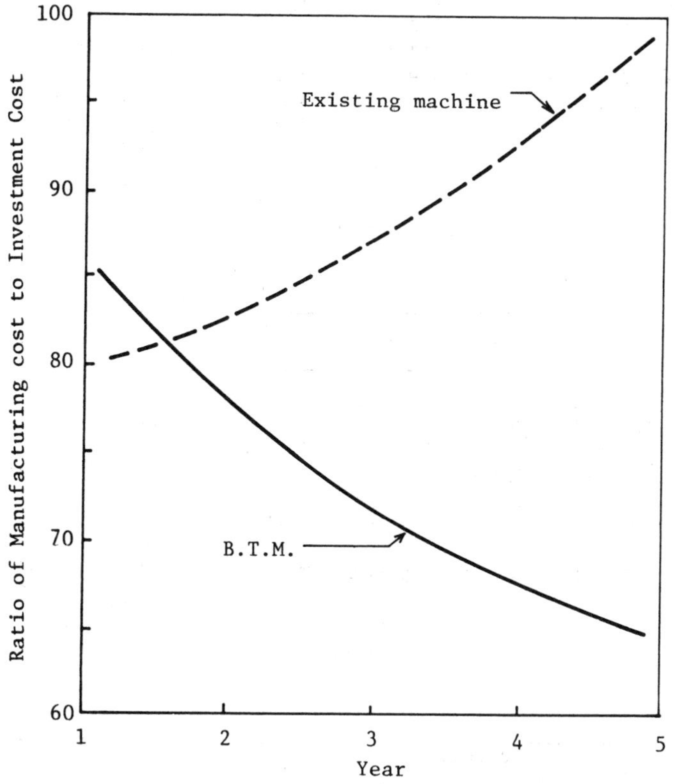

(Rise of labour cost: 10%)

Fig. 5 Comparison of production cost between B.T.M. and existing machine

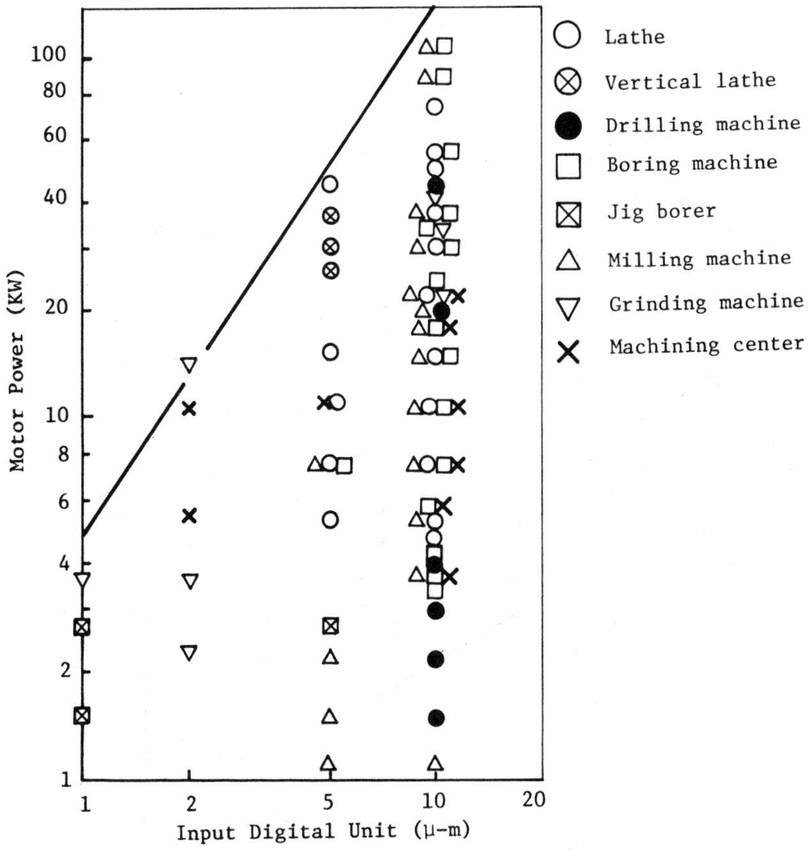

Fig. 6 Relation of motor power and input digital unit

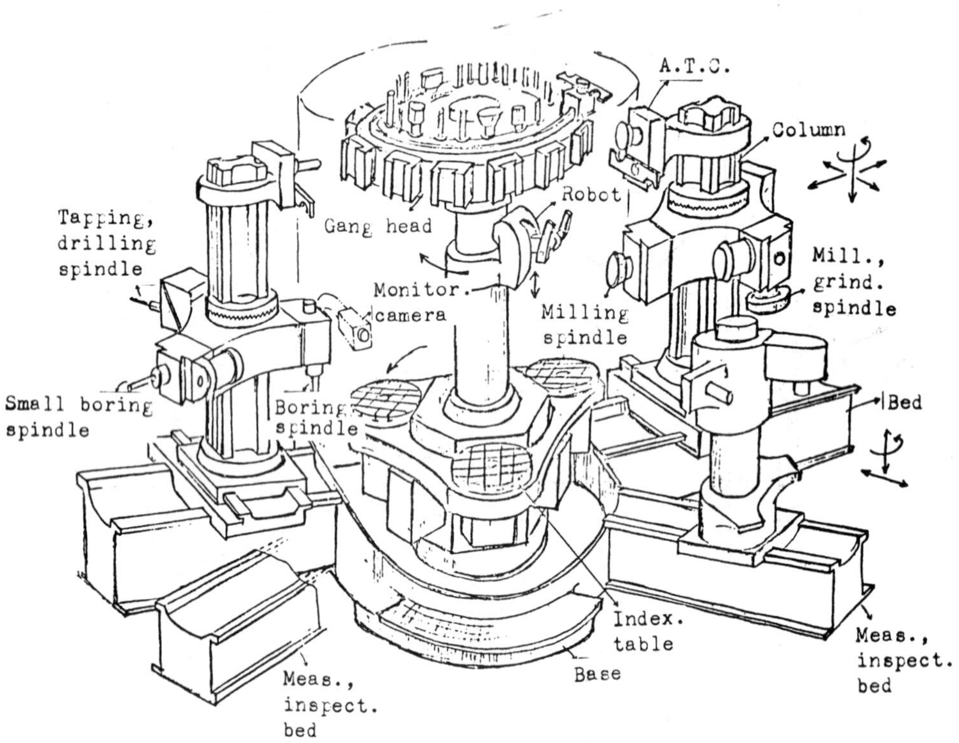

Fig. 7 TRIANGLE Production Center for cubic workpieces

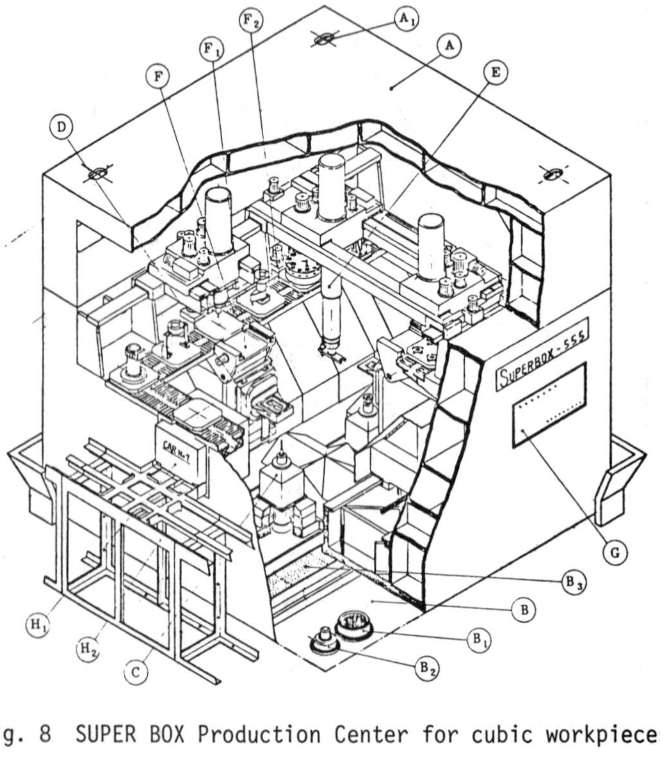

Fig. 8 SUPER BOX Production Center for cubic workpieces

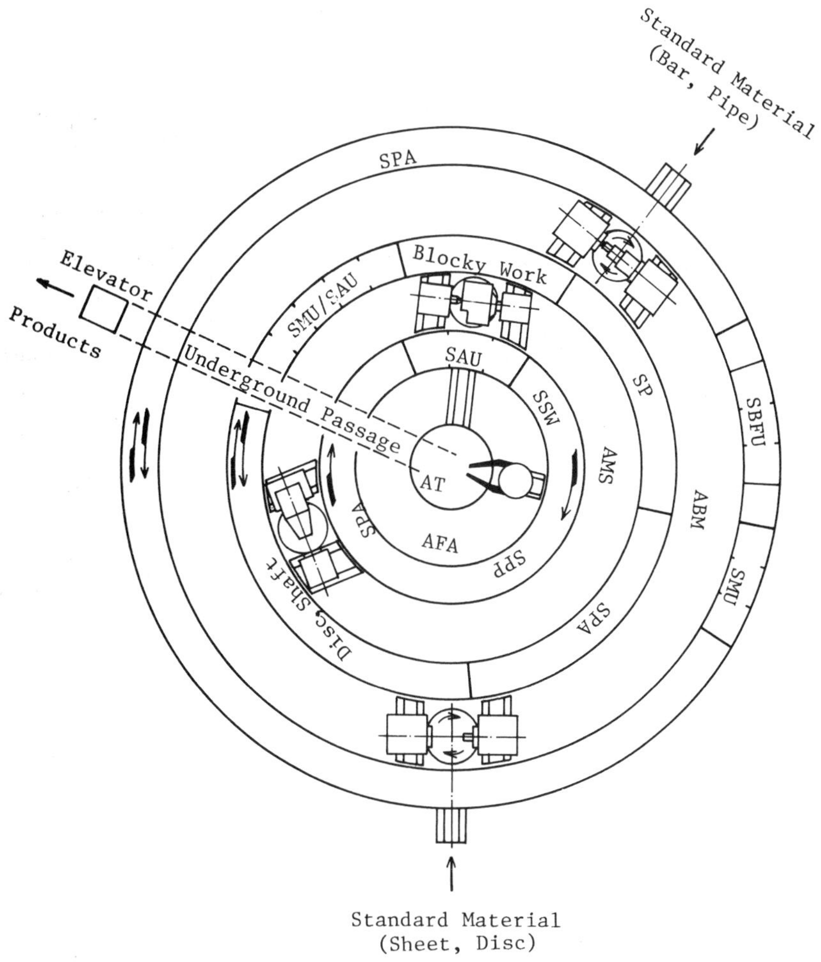

ABM: Area of Blank Fabrication and Machining
AMS: Area of Machining and Subassembly
AFA: Area of Final Assembly
AT: Assembling Table
SBFU: Storage of Blank Fabrication Units
SMU: Storage of Machining Units
SP: Storage of Parts
SPA: Storage of Pallets
SSW: Storage of Subassembled Works
SPP: Storage of Purchased Parts
SAU: Storage of Assembling Units

Fig. 9 CIRCULAR Production Center

RESEARCH ISSUES FOR AUTOMATIC ASSEMBLY

J.L. Nevins, D.E. Whitney *et al.*

Charles Stark Draper Laboratory, Cambridge, MA

ABSTRACT

The research issues currently being explored world wide will be discussed. The work falls under two main headings namely, a) parts mating phenomena-quantitative descriptions of what happens when parts interact during the assembly process, the kind of information available, its quality etc. b) programmability-the capability of a machine to be taught a new task rather than being built specifically to do the task.

Exploration of the parts mating question requires investigation into geometric, force-friction, and logical test characteristics of the mating process, involving the generation of and the carrying out of very precise experiments to examine hypothesis. Programmability issues include the analysis of manufactured products to determine kinds of tasks, statistics of their occurence and geometric requirements on the placing and alignment of parts; and the general economic modeling and comparison of manual assembly, assembly by special machines and assembly by programmable machines.

INTRODUCTION

Today there are two principal ways of assembling things, by people (Fig. 1) and by specially designed machines, Fig. 2. The present machines are mechanically driven with fixed sequence and fixed motion strokes. Each workstation represents the extreme in specialization and is designed to perform one operation (insert, fasten, check, etc.) on one part. No sensing is performed to either monitor or guide the assembly process. Part jams due to part variation are quite frequent-at the maximum they could cause the machine to be down as much as 35% of the time. The machines are one of a kind and thus expensive. They are also difficult to alter. This means that they must run continuously for several years to pay for themselves and thus are best suited to products made in large quantities with minimum

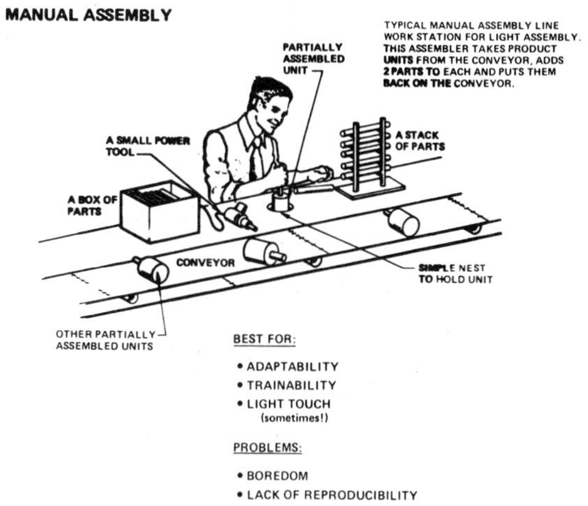

Fig. 1

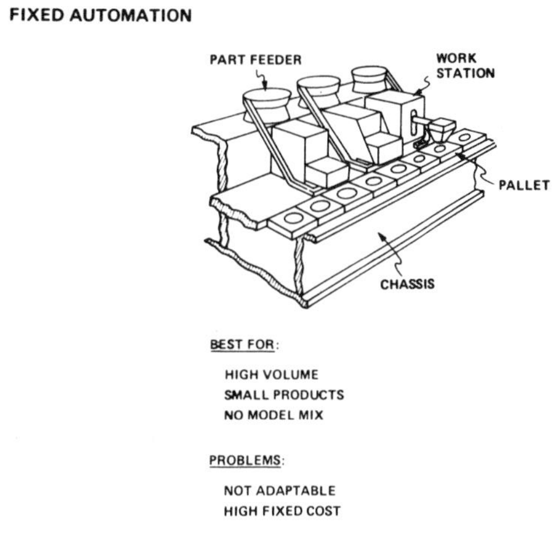

Fig. 2

style variations or evolving design changes. The machines also have difficulty with close clearance insertions and handling of flexible parts. Most assembly, however, is performed in batches on products with wide style variations. Thus current machines are not generally applicable to a wide range of assembly problems. People are the only alternative and they, too, have certain limitations.

People represent the opposite extreme in flexibility. They can easily adapt to changes in product, product design, or model mixes, and require much less in the amount and accuracy of the tools and fixtures which aid them. However, too much variety in model mix, too much tedium or specialization in the work, or fatigue can cause people to make "assembly errors" using the wrong part, leaving a fastener too loose, scratching a fine surface, and so on. As a partial remedy much work is currently being put into redesign of jobs and working conditions to improve what might be called the psychological environment of the work place.

Since 1972 the Draper Laboratory with NSF support* has been exploring a third alternative called adaptable-programmable assembly machines. An adaptable machine is one that can respond in a sensible fashion to the normal variation between manufactured piece parts. A programmable machine is one that can be reprogrammed to handle a variation in a product without the necessity of rebuilding or extensively modifying the machine.

The foundation for this work is called the force-vector-assembler concept**. (Fig. 3) (Reference 1). The idea was

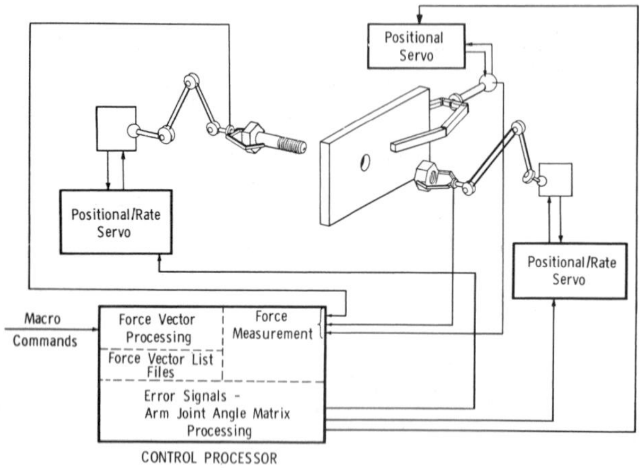

Fig. 3. Force Vector Assembler - Block Diagram

*NSF Grant No. ATA 74-18173-A01,GI-43787, GI-39432X and GK-34094.

**Concept developed during work supported by the AEC-NASA Space Nuclear Systems Office (SNSO), Contract No. SNPN 54.

first tested by one of our students (Ref. 2) using the first of a series of six-dimensional sensor arrays constructed (References 3 and 4). In mid 1972, a 1/2 inch peg was successfully inserted into a hole with a 0.0005 inch clearance (Ref. 2). This was a very fragile demonstration using a hybrid mode where the operator did the gross positioning while the fine positioning (the actual insertion) was done with a simple computerized control algorithm. It did indicate, however, that another kind of approach, differing from that being followed by the artificial intelligence research community, was possible. The approach is based on analyzing the information available during the mating of parts and then constructing control algorithms to successfully cause part mating in the presence of the errors stated above.

RESEARCH APPROACH

Research Philosophy

The early phase of work was spent defining the system architecture of assembly machines based on the prior work and point of view. (Ref. 5) The problem addressed was that of systematically analyzing the assembly problem with the goal of defining the performance needs of machines which could attack batch assembly with heavy model mix. Prior work in artificial intelligence laboratories had indicated that computer controlled arms and accompanying TV "eyes" might be relevant. No systematic analysis of the problem had been undertaken, to our knowledge, although there were reports of hardware construction activity at industrial laboratories in the U.S. and abroad. The result of our study was a proposed system architecture for a machine which was programmable (i.e. could be taught a number of tasks) and adaptable (i.e., contained force-torque sensing to aid it in slightly modifying its trajectories during actual assembly).

Underlying this work were several basic assumptions:

1. For truly mass production assembly of identical items, special purpose one of a kind assembly machines were probably preferable, given that they were economically and technically feasible on a case basis.

2. Outside special automation's range of applicability, there existed at that time no alternative except to utilize people for assembly; interest in reducing the dependence on people combines the desires to relieve people of boring or hazardous work, reduce labor costs, reduce nonreproducible

factors such as fatigue or judgement or, in the case of Europe and Japan, compensate for labor shortages.

3. The performance of any machine is governed by the quality of its components and the consistency of the object matter on which it operates; this is true equally of special purpose automation and programmable manipulators; the research problem was then to provide a scientific base of analytical models and experimental verification from which the actual performance requirements of assembly machines could be predicted.

On the basis of these assumptions, and the prior force-vector teleoperator experiments, three decisions were made: First, it was deemed promising to investigate machines organized around force-torque data obtained from a sensor located near the interface where parts are being assembled. The logic behind this decision was that the accumulation of errors in parts, jigs and manipulators would require fine modifications to the assembly motions. Futhermore, of possible means for detecting the need for such modifications, direct sensing of contact forces was the best because it offered a system with minimum control parameters and hence less computational overhead. (Vision was ruled out as not having access to the extremely small deformations involved either because of actual occlusion- you can't look conveniently into a hole you are trying to insert something into - or because of the system and computational complexity required to get the necessary resolution).

Second, since the process of assembling things was not understood in any kind of quantitative way, it was decided that the research would need to find ways of classifying assembly tasks, the parts to be assembled, the devices which would do the assembly, and the information and strategies to be utilized. What was sought was what could be termed a minimum parameter method for describing the assembly task, a method that required minimum information from the assembly interface and therefore required minimum computer processing to achieve the necessary fast control loops for economically viable systems.

Third, based on the laboratory's historical role as a bridge between science and engineering *it was planned to include industry representatives in the research team so that the work would be relevant to actual industry situations and so that a start could be made toward transferring the research results to industry. General Electric Co. Corporate R&D Center and Unimation, Inc. (maker of the Unimate) initially agreed to join the team. Later the Ford Motor Co. joined the endeavor.

Thus our goals were, in summary:

1. Establish a scientific base for the field of assembly and test the developed hypotheses by reproducible experiments carefully specified as to the performance requirements of the experimental hardware and of the test objects being assembled.

2. Investigate the usefulness and implications of force-torque sensing or the general role of sensors in closed loop assembly devices that can respond to perceived changes at the assembly interface.

3. Develop industrial technology transfer mechanisms.

Research Areas

The research areas have two principal thrusts, namely:

a. part mating studies

b. assembly systems and programmability studies

A. Part Mating Studies

The purpose in using force feedback is to aid assembly in the presence of errors. These errors are positional in effect although they have many causes, and result in the parts being out of position with respect to each other when assembly mating begins. Figure 4 shows the wide range

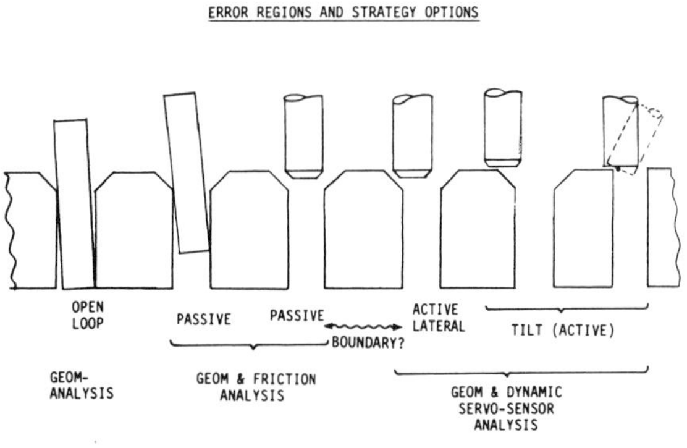

Fig. 4

*See "The Working Laboratory: A Bridge Between Science and Engineering", by R.A. Duffy, President of the Charles Stark Draper Lab, CSDL Report No. P-050, March 1974.

The upper part of Fig. 5 illustrates the prime problem for assembly, namely, that during an insertion process a peg needs to be steered so that it will contact only one side of the mating hole until it reaches the bottom of the hole. If it does not then two-point contact will occur that can lead to "jamming" or "wedging" thus preventing proper assembly. Thus, if two-point contact can be avoided until the peg reaches the bottom of the hole then the assembly process (whatever it is) can be viewed as a success. Conventional fixed automation assembly machines are carefully built and tuned over an extended time and provided with rigid jigs and part guides in the hope that errors can be kept so small that two-point contact can be avoided for most parts.

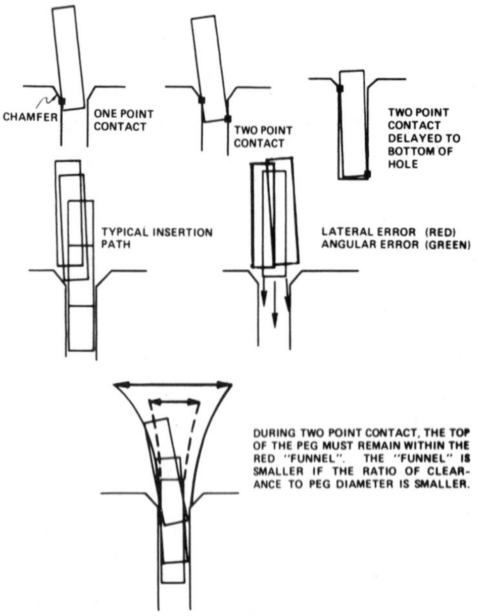

relationship between parts (Fig. 6) the classification of parts according to their size and their geometric characteristics (Fig. 7), and descriptions of the force-friction events during the mating process including the determination of the ratios between the applied forces and moments to avoid "jamming" during mating (Fig.'s 8a and 8b). Figure 9 illustrats an every day task that involves "wedging" and "jamming".

PEG IN HOLE GEOMETRY

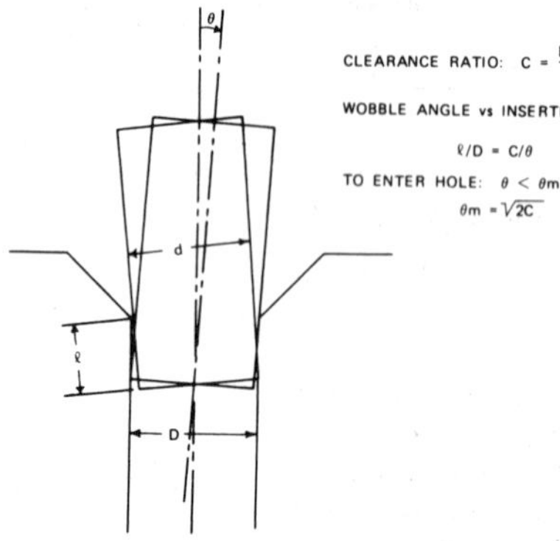

CLEARANCE RATIO: $C = \frac{D-d}{D}$

WOBBLE ANGLE vs INSERTION DEPTH:

$\ell/D = C/\theta$

TO ENTER HOLE: $\theta < \theta_m$

$\theta_m = \sqrt{2C}$

Fig. 6

Fig. 5

Fig. 7

However, parts vary from one to the next and cannot be gripped or held exactly the same way each time. Motion devices too cannot exactly reproduce the same motion path. Errors will occur and the parts may jam. Fixed jigs are also incompatible with the batch assembly environment. If the errors can be kept small, perhaps it will suffice to hold the parts compliantly (this is called passive compliance - See Fig. 4). If the errors are large, sensor based force feedback or even vision may be necessary. Just which technique (fixed jigs, compliance, sensors, visions) would be needed in which instance was a major question in this research.

To study and classify these problems detailed indepth analytical studies were made of the sources of these errors (Ref. 5 and 6), the geometric

WHERE

F_x, F_r, M — APPLIED FORCES AND MOMENT RESOLVED AROUND LOCATION (0)

T_1, T_2 — REACTION FORCES AT THE CONTACT POINTS

ℓ — PENETRATION DEPTH

θ — MISALIGNMENT ANGLE

μ — COEFFICIENT OF FRICTION

ASSUMPTIONS

- LOW SPEED, QUASI STATIC ANALYSIS, INERTIA FORCES ARE CONSIDERED TO BE SMALL.

- STATIC AND DYNAMIC COEFFICIENT OF FRICTION ARE ASSUMED EQUAL. THIS RESTRICTION CAN EASILY BE REMOVED.

- RIGID PEG AND HOLE. THE DEFORMATION OF THEIR GEOMETRY IS ASSUMED SMALL.

- PERFECT CONTROL OF APPLIED FORCES. THIS REQUIRES A PERFECT READING OF FORCES AND MOMENTS, MEASURED AT THE TIP OF THE PEG, AND AN INFINITE RESOLUTION IN THE POSITION CONTROL. THESE CONSTRAINTS CAN BE MODIFIED FOR DESIGN PURPOSES.

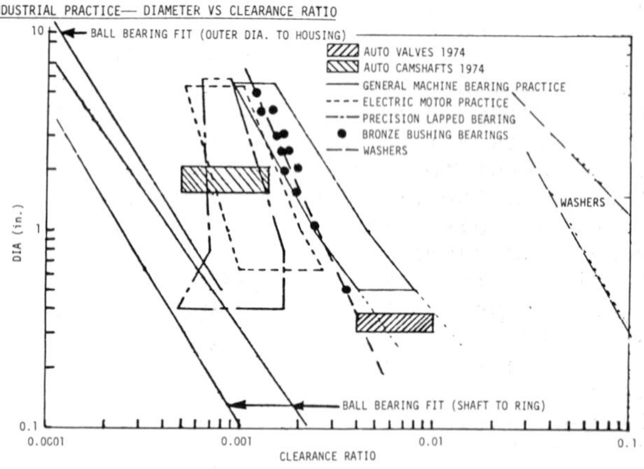

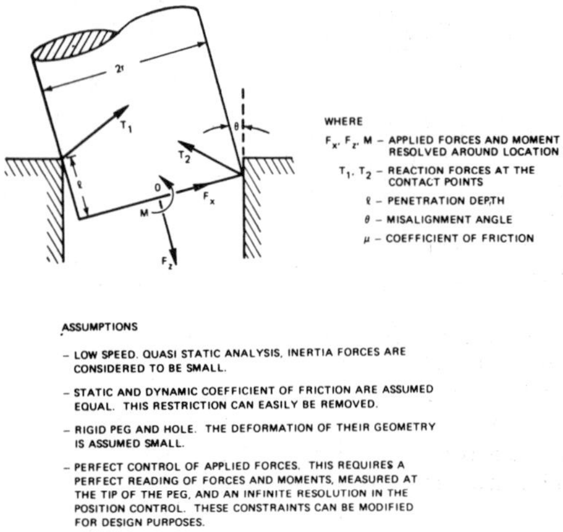

Fig. 8a. Force-Friction Assumptions

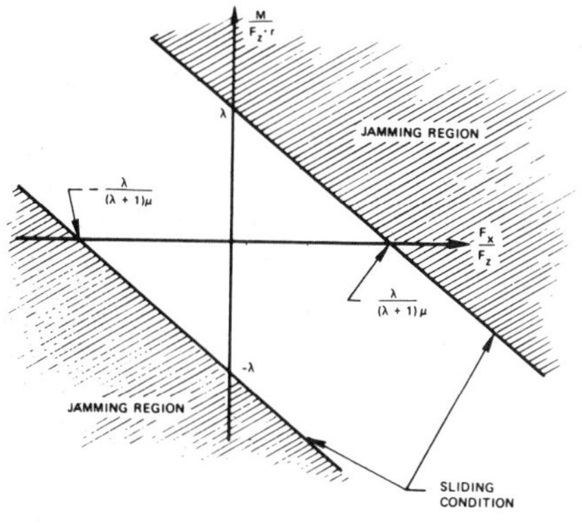

$$\frac{\dfrac{M}{F_z r}}{\lambda\,\text{sign}(\theta)} + \frac{\dfrac{F_x}{F_z}}{\dfrac{\lambda}{(\lambda+1)\mu}\,\text{sign}(\theta)} \le 1$$

SLIDING CRITERIA FOR THE REGION $\lambda > 1$ OR $\dfrac{\ell}{D}$

WHERE $\lambda = \dfrac{\ell}{2r\mu}$

Fig. 8b. Required Conditions on Axial
Forces (F_z), Lateral Force (F_x), and
Moment at Tip of Peg to Avoid Jamming.

The result of the geometric analysis
was an understanding of the variables
which determine the difficulty of a
simple chamfered peg-hole insertion.
Additional study in later years showed
that these results could be reliably
related to assembly of particular industrial items such as valve stems,
bearings and washers. (Fig. 7)

Analysis and experiments on friction
and jamming (Ref. 6,7) revealed that
jamming is a two-phase phenomenon. If
parts first touch with two-point contact when the peg is only slightly
into the hole then the parts can
wedge and cannot be pushed together
further. If two point contact occurs
when the peg is deeper into the hole,
assembly can continue if the applied
insertion force vector points the
wrong way. Figure 8b shows the relations between applied force vector
components in order that jamming not
occur. Thus jamming can be overcome,
if it occurs, by redirecting the applied force vector. Wedging cannot
be overcome. It can be made to occur
deep enough in the hole, which requires limiting the allowable error
between the parts as insertion begins.

The first friction experiments(Fig.10)
(Ref.6) showed that, when parts are
wedged, it is impossible to determine
from force sensor readings how to re-
orient them to continue assembly. Experimental evidence on jamming did
not exist, and it was not known if
the moments needed for active force
feedback steering would be measureable
in the presence of friction. In addition, it was not known if engineered
compliances could be designed which
would automatically prevent jamming.

To investigate these points, a simple

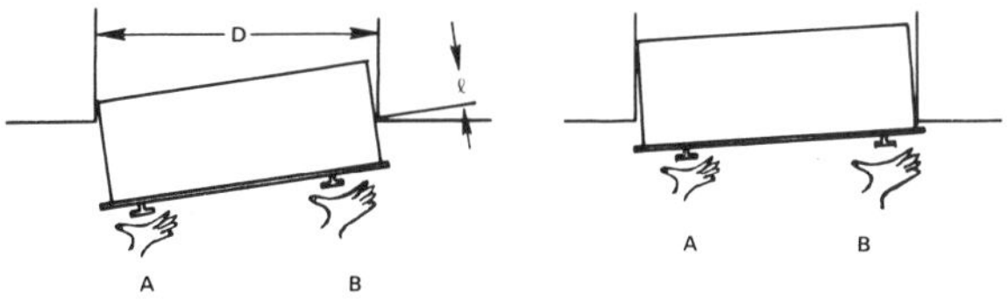

THE DIFFERENCE BETWEEN WEDGING AND JAMMING. AT THE LEFT, A
DRESSER DRAWER HAS BECOME WEDGED. WEDGING INVOLVES DE-
FORMING THE DRAWER AND LITERALLY LOCKING IT INTO THE DRES-
SER. THEORY SHOWS THAT WEDGING CAN OCCUR ONLY IF TWO POINT
CONTACT FIRST OCCURS WHEN THE RATIO ℓ/D IS VERY SMALL. RE-
GARDLESS OF WHETHER ONE PUSHES AT A OR B, THE DRAWER WILL NOT
ADVANCE, AND IS SAID TO BE WEDGED. THERE IS NO REMEDY EXCEPT
TO PULL IT OUT AND START AGAIN. IF ℓ/D IS LARGER THAN THE FRIC-
TION COEFFICIENT μ WHEN TWO POINT CONTACT FIRST OCCURS, THEN
WEDGING CANNOT OCCUR, IN THEORY. THIS IS SHOWN AT THE RIGHT.
WHILE PUSHING AT B WILL DO NO GOOD, PUSHING AT A WILL ADVANCE
THE DRAWER AND BREAK THE TWO POINT CONTACT. THE DRAWER IS
SAID TO BE JAMMED. PUSHING AT A CHANGES THE DIRECTION OF BOTH
THE APPLIED FORCE AND APPLIED MOMENT. THEORY HAS BEEN DERIVED
WHICH SHOWS EXACTLY HOW TO REARRANGE APPLIED FORCE AND
MOMENT TO ELIMINATE JAMMING. THE RCC WAS DESIGNED TO APPLY
FORCES TO THE PEG IN ACCORDANCE WITH THIS THEORY.

Fig.9. An Everyday Task Involving
"Wedging" and "Jamming"

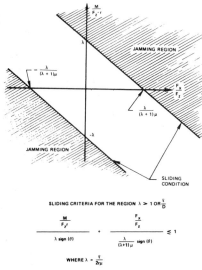

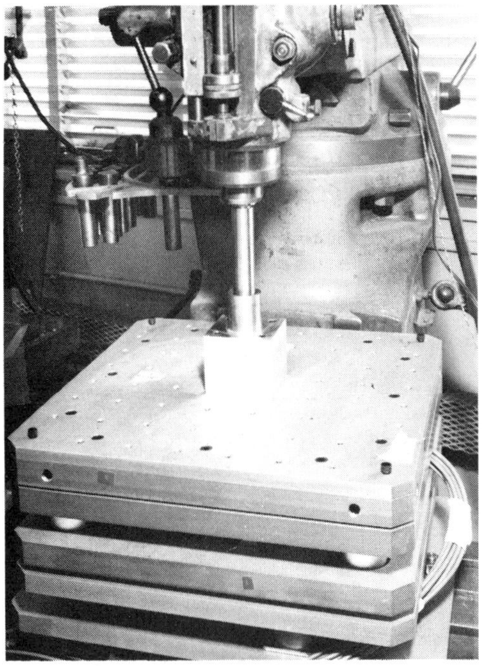

Fig.10. First Friction Experiments
Using Accurately Machined Parts

compliance device was designed and
tested experimentally. Fig. 11 also
shows a small, accurate, and stable
force sensor designed to improve on
the pedestal sensor used in the first
experiments(Fig.9)(Ref 4). A series
of chamfered test pegs and holes was
made. The apparatus was mounted in a
milling machine so that particular
lateral and angular errors could be
accurately imposed.

The result of this experiment was a
wealth of clean, repeatible force versus position data which showed that

1)the geometric analyses were correct

2)jamming was avoided where the theory
predicted it would be avoided

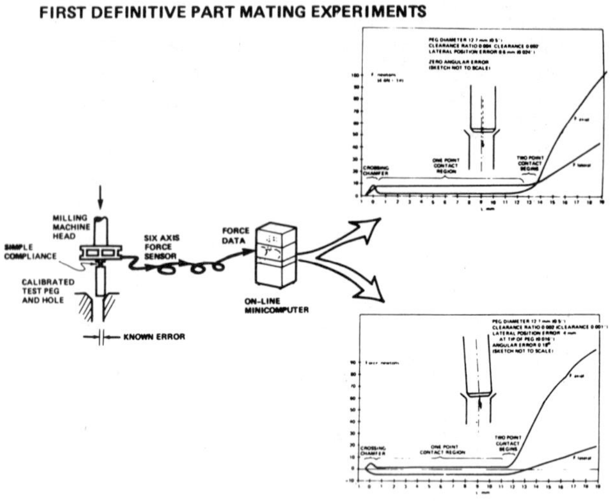

Fig.11.Schematic of First Definitive Part Mating Experiments

3)moments clear enough to guide a force feedback strategy were easily detected.

4)close clearance assembly tasks could be accomplished with a simple compliance if the errors were not too large

A schematic of the experiment and examples of the data obtained are shown in Fig. 11. As far as we know these are the first definitive part mating experiments.

The particular compliance used in the experiment was not a good candidate for assembly of pieces with close clearances in the presence of large positional errors, because it exerted too much force laterally on the peg after two point contact occurred. The excessive force is caused by the lateral stiffness being too large. Also, due to the lateral stiffness,a moment is exerted about the peg's tip almost exactly proportional to the product of the lateral force exerted and the distance from the compliance to the tip. It was then proved mathematically that a compliance device in which this distance was zero would automatically allow assembly without jamming. Although, the compliance device or mechanism cannot be located at the tip it must nevertheless allow the peg to rotate about its tip rather than about its top, where the compliance device must still be located. Fig. 12 shows the behavior of the simple compliance and the desired behavior of a compliant device. This desired behavior can also be produced by the use of the active force feedback technique, which can be thought of as synthesized compliances.

Shortly after these experiments a compliance device having the desired properties was invented. It is shown in

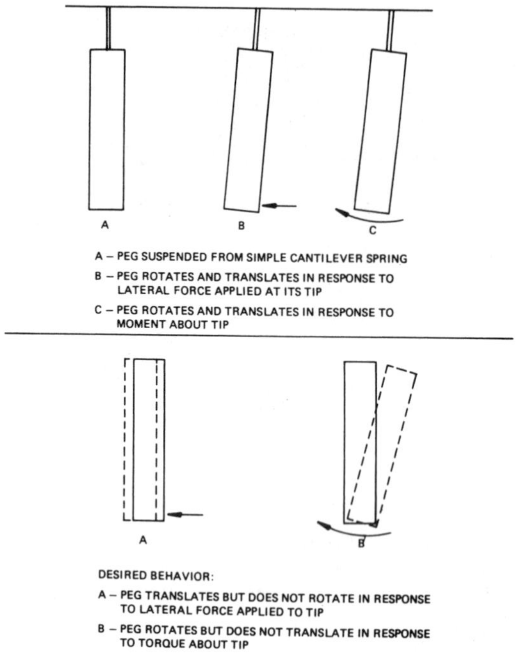

Fig.12.Behavior of Simple Compliance and Desired Behavior

Fig's 13,14 and 15* and it is called Remote Center Compliance (RCC). See Ref's 8,9 for detailed descriptions. In experimental tests on a milling machine and on a computer controlled robot arm, assembly tasks have been accomplished with large initial errors which were previously difficult or impossible except with special fixtures and guides.We routinely insert bearings 1.6" (40mm) in diameter into holes with 0.0007" (1/70mm) clearance in 0.2 seconds. (Fig. 15 and 20) The stickiness of this task cannot be appreciated unless one tries it with his own hands. Many industrial firms are keenly interested in exploiting these devices.

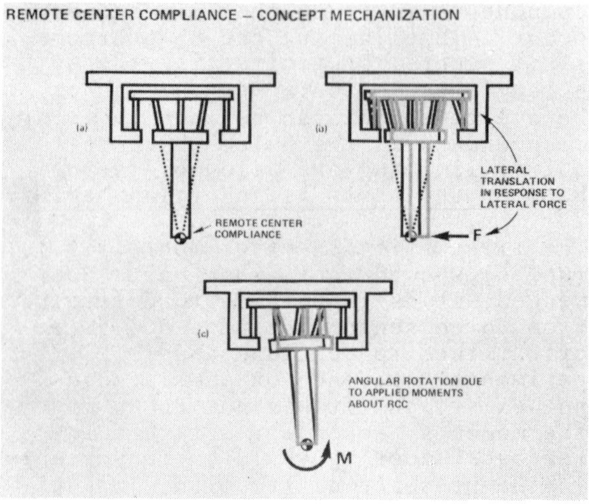

Fig. 13

*Patents have been applied for the RCC and the wrist force sensor.

Fig. 14. Remote Center Compliance-Concept Model

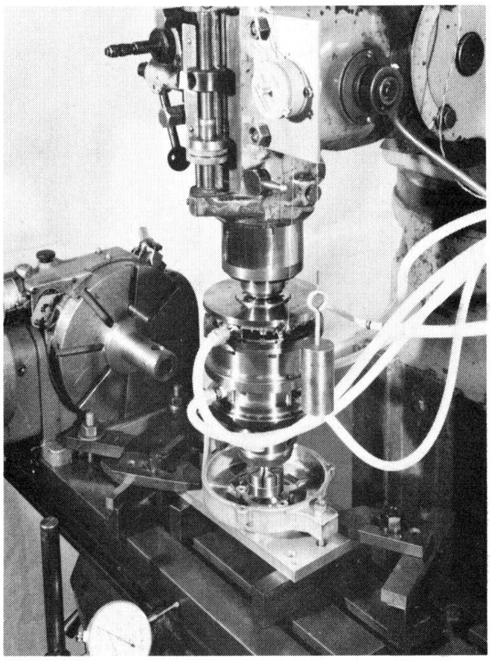

Fig.15. Advanced Model of Passive Compliance System Inserting 1.6 inch (40mm) Diameter bearing into Housing with a 0.0007 inch (1/70mm)clearance

In addition to the invention of the force sensor and the RCC, an additional part mating aid was developed. It consists of the addition of modern control and estimation theory to the interpretation of force feedback signals. Using active force feedback to maintain contact between parts, a control system and Kalman filter attempt to deduce the relative position error directly from readings of the position sensors on the motion device's joints. These sensors do not give any direct information about the error since at best they measure the position of one of the parts, telling nothing about the position of the other. A sequence of such measurements, taken while the parts move while in contact, can be used to determine the error. This technique was demonstrated using an industrial manipulator and oversized plastic pieces to overcome the performance limitations of the experimental equipment. (Ref. 7)

B. Assembly System and Programmability Studies

The design of programmable assembly systems requires that choices be made between technically feasible alternatives. The correct part mating technique must be chosen for each task. A product to be assembled must be analyzed to determine what tasks it presents. The required production volume of the product will determine how much equipment is needed to assemble product units at what rate. Many traditional techniques exist for analyzing manual assembly, such as time studies, but there existed no methods for designing programmable assembly systems when this research began.

To approach this problem, we studied many industrial products to determine statistics of the presenting tasks. We found that single insertion tasks are the most common, and that many products are stacks in the sense that most of the parts arrive from one or at most two directions. These results are indicated in Figures 16,17a, b and 18. Ref. 10 contains the details. The task statistics tell us which tasks should be studied first. The arrival direction statistics tell us that motion devices with fewer than six independent motions can assemble portions of many products and all of some products. Further, if a "robot assembly line" is built, with a series of workstations sharing the work, then the motion device at each station may be rather simple, since it will have only a few tasks to perform. If one motion device must assembly the entire product then it is more likely to need six axes of motion.

When is an assembly line the most appropriate and when should one station assembly the entire product? How much money can one justify paying for such a line or station and what must its performance specifications be in terms of size, speed, strength and accuracy? A first step in answering these questions has been taken with the development of an economic-technological model of programmable assem-

Product	Number of Parts	Longest Dimension of the Largest Family Member
Electric Timer Cover Subassembly*	7	4.5"
Electric Timer Case and Final Assembly*	18	4.5"
Refrigerator Compressor Family	26	10"
Bicycle Coaster Brake	15	6"
Transformer Electric Bushing Family	6 to 8	10"
End Cap Subassemblies for Small Induction Motors	29	7"
Induction Motor Main Body Subassembly and Final Assembly	21	15"
Electric Jigsaw	58	12"
Toaster Oven	41	15"
Automobile Alternator Family**	17	8"

*Currently assembled automatically.
**Currently assembled by a mixture of manual and automatic workstations.

Products Analyzed for Task Statistics

Fig. 16

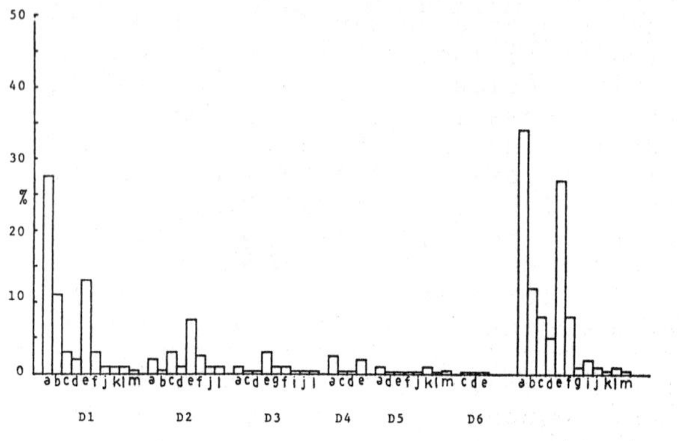

Relative Task Frequency Data Summarized for Ten Product Items

Fig. 18

OPERATION IDENTIFICATION	OPERATION DESCRIPTION	EXAMPLE OCCURRENCES
a	simple insertion or placement of part	peg in hole, part into fixture
b	stage insertion or push and twist	gear meshing or key way alignment
c	multiple insertion or alignment	placing cylinder head gasket over multiple studs
d	perpendicular insertion	retracting a spring loaded retainer prior to insertion of retained part
e	screw insertion	screw into nuts
f	interference insertion	press fits
g	part removal	removal of temporary locating pins

Assembly Tasks Encountered in Ten Product Items

Fig. 17a

OPERATION IDENTIFICATION	OPERATION DESCRIPTION	EXAMPLE OCCURRENCES
h	test operation	compression check on a compressor pistor
i	flip operation	reorient product to allow access to assembly directions or to obtain aid of gravity
j	part placement and hold	required when parts fit too loosely to support themselves
k	crimp operation	sheet metal parts
l	release hold	remove support of loose fitting parts after permanent supports have been installed
m	weld or solder	wires onto motors

Fig. 17b

bly, fixed automation assembly and manual assembly. By "economic-technological" is meant that the model attempts to combine estimates of both cost and technical performance of the system's components in one set of equations which predict the cost of assembly by each technique. The investment in capital equipment and tooling, based on the amount of work required to assemble one product unit, is included in the model. The result is a set of equations into which one can put any assumptions concerning labor or equipment costs. Curves such as those in Fig. 19 can then be drawn, indicating a mid-range production volume below mass production where programmable assembly systems have economic promise. Examination of the equations themselves also yields valuable insights. In particular it can be shown that unit assembly cost by programmable techniques is affected by the product of the station's capital cost (exclude tooling) and the time the station takes on the average to add one part to the product. This means that a station which is twice as fast and twice as costly is economically no better. The model allows many such tradeoffs to be investigated, of which only a few have been studied so far. See Ref. 11 for many additional studies.

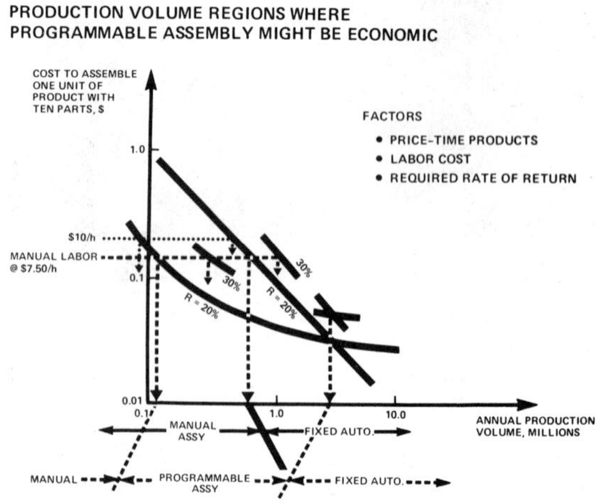

Fig. 19

Aside from the above design issues, there are many thorny control issues involving computer hardware and software and methods by which the system is taught to do its tasks. We have recognized two parts to this problem: the part mating strategies and the task sequence control, the latter including timing, interlocks between motion device and feeder, monitoring the process for success or failure, man-machine communication, etc. This division of the problem is complicated by the fact that part mating strategies may be carried out by hardware items, such as the RCC, while the controller merely monitors. Also the arrangement of mini or micro computers to control a line of arms and feeders could take many forms. The many sequences in which a product's geometry permits assembly to occur also lends richness to the problems.

We have made a first step into these areas with the above studies and by the construction of a single arm programmable system test bed (Fig. 20) This system is composed of a 4-axis electric arm, an advanced model of the RCC, and force-sensor arrays with the entire system controlled by a single mini computer. A micro computer is used for processing the force sensor. A detailed description of the system including the software control system can be found in Ref.'s 12 and 13.

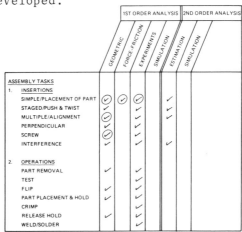

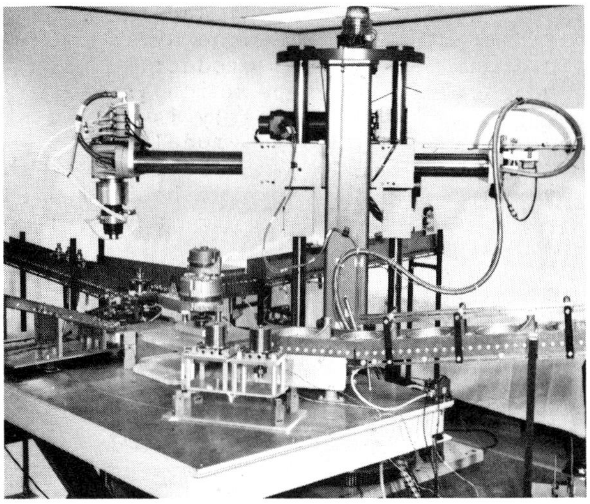

Fig.20.Programmable Research-Test Bed

CONCLUSION

In summary, it has been shown that assembly research can be divided into two principal areas: part mating and programmability. Great strides have been made in developing a scientific methodology for part mating in the last year or so, definitive reproducible experiments have been performed and unique devices and solutions have been created based on the developed knowledge base. Much however, remains to be done. Figure 21 uses the task list of Fig. 17 to indicate the limited exploitation that has occurred and how much needs to be done.

Programmability stands about where part mating was several years ago. Enough studies have been done to illuminate areas that should be examined and a high quality piece of experimental equipment has been built (Fig. 20) capable of examining research issues and hypotheses as they are developed.

	1ST ORDER ANALYSIS				2ND ORDER ANALYSIS	
ASSEMBLY TASKS	GEOMETRIC	FORCE-FRICTION	EXPERIMENTS	SIMULATION	ESTIMATION	SIMULATION
1. INSERTIONS						
SIMPLE/PLACEMENT OF PART	(✓)	(✓)	(✓)		✓	
STAGED/PUSH & TWIST	✓		✓		✓	
MULTIPLE/ALIGNMENT	(✓)		✓		✓	
PERPENDICULAR	✓		✓			
SCREW	(✓)		✓			
INTERFERENCE	✓		✓		✓	
2. OPERATIONS						
PART REMOVAL	✓		✓			
TEST			✓			
FLIP	✓		✓			
PART PLACEMENT & HOLD	✓		✓			
CRIMP			✓			
RELEASE HOLD	✓		✓			
WELD/SOLDER			✓			

✓ – PRINCIPLE RESEARCH TOOL
(✓) – RESEARCH COMPLETED

Fig.21.Part Mating Research Areas by Assembly Task List

REFERENCES

1. Nevins, J.L. and Whitney, D.E., "The Force Vector Assembly Concept" presented at the first CISM-IFTOMM Symposium on Theory and Practice of Robots and Manipulators,Udine,Italy, Sept. 5-8,1973.

2. Groome, R.C.,"Force Feedback Steering of a Teleoperator System,", SM Thesis, MIT Aeronautics and Astronautics, Aug 1962 and published as Charles Stark Draper Lab Report No. T-575.

3. "Annual Progress Report No. 2 for the Development of Multi-Moded Remote Manipulator Systems",Charles Stark Draper Lab Report No. C-3901 January 1973.

4. Watson, P.C. and Drake, S.H., "Pedestal and Wrist Sensors for Automatic Assembly", presented at 5th International Symposium on Industrial Robots, Chicago, Ill, Sept. 1975 and published as CSDL report no. P-176

5. Nevins, J.L., Whitney,D.E. and Simunovic, S.N., "System Architecture for Assembly Machines," CSDL report no R-764, November, 1973.

6. Simunovic,S.N."Force Information in Assembly Processes," presented at the 5th International Symposium on Industrial Robots, Chicago,Ill September, 1975.

7. Simunovic, S., Ph.D. Thesis in progress.

8. Watson,P.C.,"A Multidimensional System Analysis of the Assembly Process as Performed by a Manipulator", presented at the 1st North American Robot Conference Chicago, Ill, Oct. 1976.

9. Drake, S.H., Ph.D., Thesis in progress

10. Kondoleon, A.S., "Application of Technological Economic Assembly Techniques to Programmable Assembly Machine Configurations," SM Thesis, MIT Mechanical Engineering Dept. May, 1976.

11. Lynch, P.M. "Economic-Technological Modeling and Design Criteria for Programmable Assembly Machines," Ph.D. Thesis, MIT Mechanical Engineering Dept, June 1976.

12. Spencer, R.M.,"High Level Control of Reprogrammable Automatic Assembly Machines," SM Thesis, MIT Dept of Electrical Engineering Sept. 1975.

13. Nevins, J.L.,Whitney, D.E., et.al. "Exploratory Research in Industrial Modular Assembly", CSDL Report No. R-996, Aug. 1976.

ACKNOWLEDGEMENTS

The work reported in this paper was performed by the following people, in addition to the named authors: B. Bachman, H.J. Doherty, S.H. Drake, R.C. Groome, M.A. Jilani, D.L. Killoran, A.S. Kondoleon, P.M. Lynch, D.S. Seltzer, S.N. Simunovic, R.M. Spencer, S.J. Wang, P.C. Watson, and A.E. Woodin.

ON—LINE SYSTEM FOR MEASURING THICKNESS OF ULTRA-THIN NON-METALLIC LAYER ON STRIP SURFACE

A. Izumidate*, H. Yamamoto*, S. Shiki*, Motomura* and Y. Nomura**

Nippon Steel Corporation, 1-1-1, Edamitsu, Yawata-Higashi-ku, Kitakyushu-shi, Fukuoka, Japan

ABSTRACT

Nippon Steel Corporation has developed an advanced instrumentation for automatic coating control at Yawata Works. It is designed primarily for measuring the thickness of ultra-thin oil layer or hydrated chromium oxide layer on electroplated steel strip for can-making. These layers have thicknesses ranging from 2 to 20 nm, small mass and transparent or translucent appearance.

Based on the principle of ellipsometry, the new film thickness measuring system is already in service on processing lines at NSC.

It has a measuring accuracy of 0.015 g/BB for oil film on electrolytic tin plate in the coating weight range of 0.10 to 0.30 g/BB and 1.3 mg/m^2 for hydrated chromium oxide film on tin-free steel in the coating weight range of 5 to 25 mg/m^2.

INTRODUCTION

Used mainly for can-making, electrolytic tin-plate (ET) and tin-free steel (TFS) are produced at an annual rate of 15 million tons worldwide. Every indication is that world output of these can-making materials will continue to rise in the future.

Aside from general mechanical properties, they are required to have rust-resistance, corrosion-resistance, printability, lacquerability and good appearance. To economically produce steel sheets with such characteristics, electrolytic tin plate and TFS of thickness from 0.20 to 0.50 mm are manufactured by electro-plating or coating extremely thin films on both sides of mild steel strip. The protective film of ET consists of a 2 to 8 nm thick oil film, 10 to 30 nm oxide film, 0.4 to 1.5 μm plated tin layer and 50 to 100 nm Fe-Sn alloy layer, from outer to inner. TFS, on the other hand, uses chromium instead of tin for reduced production costs and its coated film consists of an outermost layer of 4 to 5 nm thick oil film, an intermediate layer of hydrated chromium oxide film with thickness of 20 to 40 nm and an innermost layer of 10 to 20 mm thick metallic chromium. Unless these film thicknesses are controlled within a preset tolerance, waste of materials will result.

For this reason, great importance is attached to the high-accuracy control of film thickness at ET and TFS manufacturing plants.

There have for many years been increasing demand from ET and TFS manufacturers for such an automatic process control system as permits continuous

---

* Electrical Automation & Instrumentation Office, Plant Engineering & Technology Center

** Coating Technical Section, Yawata Works

monitoring and recording of variation in film thickness without interrupting the process. As for plated tin layer and metallic chromium layer which consist only of metals with a comparatively large mass, continuous measurement of film thickness has already been successfully accomplished by using a fluorescent X-ray thickness gauge.

So far as such non-metallic films as oil film, oxide film and hydrated chromium oxide film are concerned, however, the conventional practices of thickness measurement of these films have been too time-consuming because all of them consist of off-line measurement of test pieces sampled from finished coils and output data of the off-line measuring center are fed back to the production line to control operating conditions of the processing line.

At the off-line measuring center, inspectors have to remove each of the non-metallic film components one by one from each sample piece of a given size before measurement. A hydrophil balance test or an ellipsometer with a de-oiling device is usually employed to measure the thickness of oil film. Measurement of the oxide film thickness is done by the method of coulometric determination. The coating weight of hydrated chromium oxide, which can dissolve in hot caustic soda, can be determined by the change in the amount of chromium between before and after dissolution, and recently the method of fluorescent X-ray analysis has also been used for this purpose.

Taking advantage of the fact that all of these non-metallic films are transparent or translucent, the authors of this paper have successfully developed a technique for on-line continuous measurement of the thickness of these non-metallic films using ellipsometry.

This paper provides an outline of the development and major benefits obtained by Yawata Works from the use of the new system. An on-line oil film thickness gauge using the system is in service at the ET line at Yawata Works and a prototype hydrated chromium oxide film thickness gauge has been in operation at the TFS line of the same works for more than 12 months.

THEORETICAL BACKGROUND

Many studies on optical aspects of thin superficial film on metal have already been reported. (Ref. 1)

To sum up these, the relationship between variations in film thickness and ellipticity is essentially expressed by Formula (1):

$$\tan\psi\,\exp(i\Delta) = \frac{r_{IP} + R_{IIP}\exp(-ix)}{1 + r_{IP}R_{IIP}\exp(-ix)} \times \frac{1 + r_{IS}R_{IIS}\exp(-ix)}{r_{IS} + R_{IIS}\exp(-ix)} \qquad (1)$$

Where ψ indicates the azimuth, Δ the phase difference measured on a metal with a thin, superficial, transparent film. The expressions x, r_{IP}, r_{IS}, R_{IIP}, R_{IIS} are determined by the formulae.

$$x = \frac{4\pi}{\lambda} n_1 d\cos\phi_1 , \qquad n_1\sin\phi_1 = \sin\phi_0 \qquad (2)$$

$$r_{IP} = \frac{n_1\cos\phi_0 - \cos\phi_1}{n_1\cos\phi_0 + \cos\phi_1} \qquad r_{IS} = \frac{\cos\phi_0 - n_1\cos\phi_1}{\cos\phi_0 + n_1\cos\phi_1} \qquad (3)$$

$$R_{IIP} = \frac{N_2\cos\phi_1 - n_1\cos\Phi_2}{N_2\cos\phi_1 + n_1\cos\Phi_2} \qquad R_{IIS} = \frac{n_1\cos\phi_1 - N_2\cos\Phi_2}{n_1\cos\phi_1 + N_2\cos\Phi_2} \qquad (4)$$

$$N_2^2 = n_2^2(1 - k_2^2) - i\cdot 2n_2^2 k_2\cos\phi_2 , \qquad N_2\cos\Phi_2 = \sqrt{N_2^2 - \sin^2\phi_0} \qquad (5)$$

$$n_2^2 = \sin^2\phi_0 \left\{ 1 + \frac{\tan^2\phi_0\cos^2 2\overline{\psi}}{(1+\sin 2\overline{\psi}\cos\overline{\Delta})^2} \right\} \qquad (6)$$

$$k_2 = \tan\phi_0\sin 2\overline{\psi}\sin\overline{\Delta} \Big/ \sqrt{(1+\sin 2\overline{\psi}\cos\overline{\Delta})^2 + \tan^2\phi_0\cos^2 2\overline{\psi}} \qquad (7)$$

$$\cos\psi_2 = \tan\phi_0\cos 2\overline{\psi} \Big/ \sqrt{(1+\sin 2\overline{\psi}\cos\overline{\Delta})^2 + \tan^2\phi_0\cos^2 2\overline{\psi}} \qquad (8)$$

Where d denotes the thickness of the film, n_1 its refractive index, and N_2 the complex refractive index of a metal. $\bar{\psi}$ indicates the azimuth, $\bar{\Delta}$ the phase difference measured on a clean metal surface. These formulae also include the angle of incidence ϕ_0 of monochromatic light having the wave length λ.

Since Formula (1) involves complex numbers, which make computation time-consuming, Drude-Tronstad's formulae (9) and (10) are very often applied provided that the thickness d of the transparent film is 10 nm or less.

$$\Delta - \bar{\Delta} = - \frac{4\pi d}{\lambda} C_1 \tag{9}$$

$$2\psi - 2\bar{\psi} = \sin 2\bar{\psi} \cdot \frac{4\pi d}{\lambda} C_2 \tag{10}$$

where

$$C_1 = \frac{\cos\phi_0 \sin^2\phi_0 (n_1^2-1)}{(\cos^2\phi_0-a_1)^2 + a_2^2} \left[(\cos^2\phi_0-a_1)\left(\frac{1}{n_1^2} - a_1\right) + a_2^2\right] \tag{11}$$

$$C_2 = \frac{\cos\phi_0 \sin^2\phi_0 (n_1^2-1)}{(\cos^2\phi_0-a_1)^2 + a_2^2} \left[n_1^2 a_2 \left(\frac{1}{n_1^2} - a_1\right) - (\cos^2\phi_0-a_1)a_1\right] \tag{12}$$

$$a_1 = \frac{4n_2^6 k_2^2 (1 - k^2) \cos^2\phi_2}{a_3 \{\sqrt{a_3}+n_2^2(1-k_2^2)\}} \tag{13}$$

$$a_2 = \frac{8n_2^6 k_2^3 \cos^3\phi_2}{a_3 \{\sqrt{a_3}+n_2^2(1-k_2^2)\}} \tag{14}$$

$$a_3 = n_2^4(1 - k_2^2)^2 + 4n_2^4 k_2^2 \cos^2\phi_2 \tag{15}$$

When formulae (13), (14) and (15) are substituted by formulae (6), (7) and (8), the right sides of the formulae (11) and (12) represent a complex function of independent variables ϕ_0, n_1, $\bar{\Delta}$ and $\bar{\psi}$. If the refractive index n_1 of the substance which comprises the film is known, however, the film thickness d can be obtained even from formula (9) alone by directing monochromatic light having the wavelength λ to the film at the angle of incidence ϕ_0 and measruing Δ, $\bar{\Delta}$, ψ and $\bar{\psi}$.

METHOD OF CONTINUOUS MEASUREMENT

The present system consists basically of a combination of approximation of Formula (11) with a linear polynominal, an ellipsometer which is capable of on-line continuous measurement of Δ, $\bar{\Delta}$, ψ and $\bar{\psi}$ and a compensation method suitable for each process.

Simplification of Formula

For the transparent oil film, the expression (9) is converted to:

$$\frac{\lambda}{4 \times 360^\circ} \times \frac{(\bar{\Delta} - \Delta)^\circ}{d} = C_1 \tag{16}$$

and approximated:

$$C_1 \cong c_0 + c_1(\Delta^\circ-120^\circ) + c_2(\bar{\Delta}^\circ-120^\circ) + c_3(\psi^\circ-36^\circ) + c_4(\bar{\psi}^\circ-36^\circ) + c_5(n_1-1.46) + c_6(\phi_0{}^\circ-70^\circ) \tag{17}$$

Then, the coefficient c_i ($i = 0 - 6$) is obtained by the multiple linear regression method. To cover sufficiently the measuring range, conditions given in this approximation are: $\lambda = 546$ nm, $\phi_0 = 68 - 71^\circ$, $\bar{\Delta} = 114 - 125^\circ$, $\bar{\psi} = 33 - 39^\circ$, $n_1 = 1.43 - 1.46$ and $d = 1 - 10$ nm, Δ being the value obtained from formula (1). The use of formula (1) made in this case is aimed at obtaining higher accuracy of approximation. The multiple linear regression is accomplished by using the expression (17) which uses as dependent variables the above-stated values substituted for the left side of expression (16).

As a result of this multiple linear regression, expression (18) below is obtained and the multiple correlation coefficient γ_m is found to be 0.996.

$$C_1 = 1.062 + 0.0038\,(\Delta^\circ-120^\circ) + 0.0065\,(\bar{\Delta}^\circ-120^\circ) - 0.034\,(\psi^\circ-36^\circ) + 0.028\,(\bar{\psi}^\circ-36^\circ) + 1.42\,(n_1-1.46) + 0.058\,(\phi_0{}^\circ-70^\circ)$$

$$= 1.062\left\{\begin{array}{l} 1.000 + 0.0036\,(\Delta^\circ-120^\circ) + 0.0061\,(\bar{\Delta}^\circ-120^\circ) \\ \quad - 0.032\,(\psi^\circ-36^\circ) + 0.026\,(\bar{\psi}^\circ-36^\circ) \\ \quad + 1.333\,(n_1-1.46) + 0.054\,(\phi_0{}^\circ-70^\circ) \end{array}\right\} \tag{18}$$

Also, under the conditions as above-given, C_1 obtained from expression (18) can be well approximated as shown in expression (19) below:

$$\left| \left\{\frac{546}{4\times 360^\circ} \times \frac{(\bar{\Delta}-\Delta)^\circ}{d} - C_1\right\} \Big/ \left\{\frac{546}{4\times 360^\circ} \times \frac{(\bar{\Delta}-\Delta)^\circ}{d}\right\} \right| \leqq 0.02 \tag{19}$$

Hence, the thickness of oil film d can be obtained from expression (20) below using expressions (16) and (18):

$$d = \frac{\lambda}{4} \times \frac{(\bar{\Delta}-\Delta)^\circ}{360^\circ} \Big/ 1.062\left\{\begin{array}{r} 1.000+0.0036(\Delta^\circ-120^\circ)+0.0061(\bar{\Delta}^\circ-120^\circ) \\ -0.0032(\psi^\circ-36^\circ) \\ +0.026(\bar{\psi}^\circ-36^\circ)+1.333(n_1-1.46) \\ +0.054(\phi_0{}^\circ-70^\circ) \end{array}\right\} \tag{20}$$

Our actual observations of the ET line at Yawata Works are that $\psi - \bar{\psi} \leqq 0.5^\circ$; $\bar{\psi} \cong 36^\circ$; $n_1 = 1.44$ and $\phi_0 = 69.3^\circ$, and what is generally accepted in the trade as the relation between the coating weight m (g/B.B.; 1 B.B = 2 × 14" × 20" × 112 sheet = 40.464 m^2) and the thickness of oil film is : m_0 (g/B.B.) = 0.04 d (nm). Then, the authors rearranged expression (20) by using 36.5°, 36°, 1.44 and 69.3° as typical values of ψ, $\bar{\psi}$, n_1 and ϕ_0, respectively, and 546 (nm) as the wavelength λ, and obtained the following expression (21):

$$m_0\ (\text{g/B.B}) = \frac{5.837\,(\bar{\Delta}-\Delta)^\circ}{-100 + 2.494\bar{\Delta}^\circ + 1.472\Delta^\circ} \tag{21}$$

As for the hydrated chromium oxide film which is translucent, necessary coefficients are determined experimentally assuming that the coating weight of the hydrated chromium oxide film m_x (mg/m^2) will be approximately obtained from expression (22). Because the refractive index of hydrated chromium oxide itself is not yet known, the manufacturing process used is such that of $\bar{\Delta}$ and $\bar{\psi}$, cannot be measured and it is empirically known that the coating weight of hydrated chromium oxide film is proportional to Δ.

$$m_x(mg/m^2) = A\Delta + B \tag{22}$$

The applicability of expression (22) is demonstrated by the fact that if the coating weight m_x is 5 to 25 mg/m^2, a range fully covered by the TFS quality data collection system at Yawata, the coefficients A and B vary depending simply on the type of surface finish applied, rough or bright.

Automatic Ellipsometer

To meet the requirement for on-line continuous measurement of the phase difference Δ, $\bar{\Delta}$ and azimuth ψ, $\bar{\psi}$, an automatic ellipsometer (AEM) has been developed by NIPPON KOGAKU K.K., a leading manufacturer of optical instruments. (Ref. 2)

Featuring quick response (1 sec. or less/5 degrees), an automatic gain control circuit which can meet varying reflection factors at various points being measured, a correction circuit which compensates for output errors (phase difference and azimuth) caused by strain in optical elements due to the change in the atmospheric temperature and a compact detecting head (about 500 mm cube), the automatic ellipsometer is the first of its kind that can be used for on-line measurement of film thickness.

Figs. 1 and 2 show the optical arrangement of AEM and block diagram of the control and display unit, respectively.

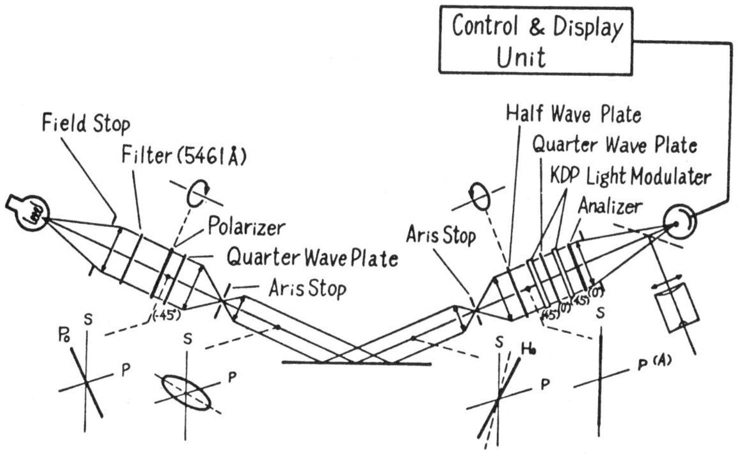

Fig. 1 Optical arrangement of the automatic ellipsometer.

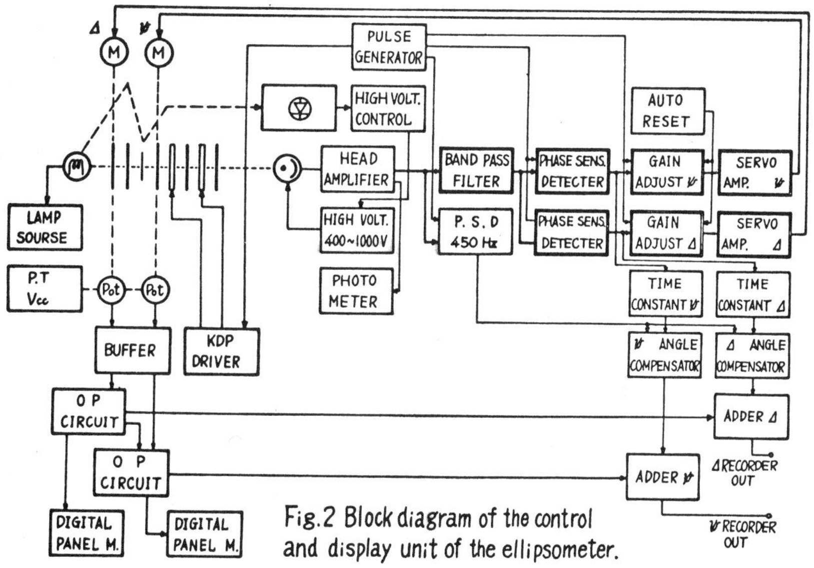

Fig. 2 Block diagram of the control and display unit of the ellipsometer.

Method of Compensation for Various Processes

An electrostatic oiler is used to apply an ultra-thin oil film to steel sheet. Oiled electrolytic tin plate is, while in contact with conveyor rollers, fed to the delivery side of the processing line, where it is processed into sheets or coils. This means that the coating weight of the finished sheet or coil is inevitably less than that of the ET strip immediately after being oiled due to contact with conveyor rollers. The data on the quality of electrolytic tin plate produced at Yawata Works indicate that change in the operating conditions of the electrostatic oiler produces only a gentle curve of variation in the coating weight of the oil film of finished products at the delivery side of the production line as shown in Fig. 3. So, we attempted an analogue simulation and, as a result, found that an output signal through a second-order lag filter shows a good correspondence to a change in the coating weight of oil film of finished products.

No compensation is necessary as to the coating weight of hydrated chromium oxide because it will not vary after measurement.

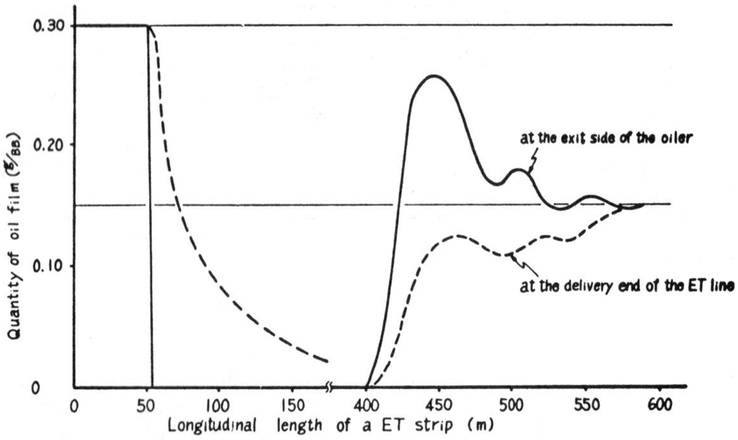

Fig. 3 The relation between quantity of oil film on ET sheet surfaces at the exit side of the oiler in the ET line and it at the delivery end of the ET line.

Measuring System

The coating weight measuring systems the authors herein propose are illustrated in Figs. 4 and 5.

Fig. 4 shows the system which is designed for on-line continuous measurement of the coating weight of extremely thin oil films in the range under 0.35 g/B.B. Fig. 5 illustrates the system intended for on-line continuous measurement of the coating weight of hydrated chromium oxide on TFS.

In Figs. 4 and 5, the solid lines represent a continuous flow data and the dashed lines a flow of off-line data for system checking use.

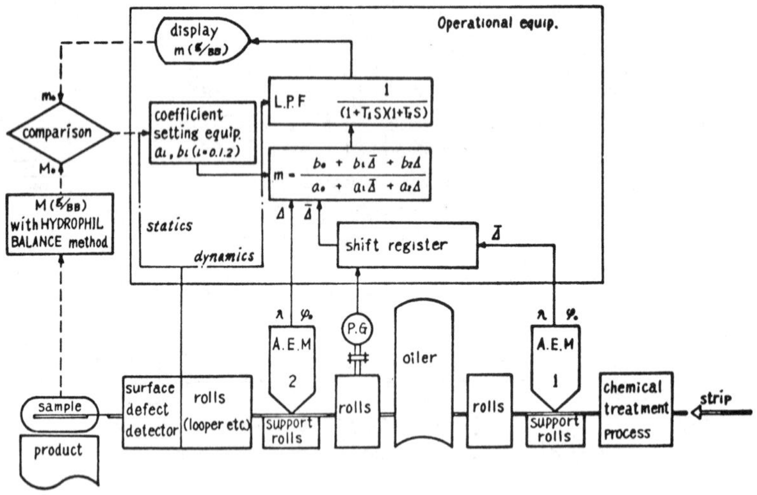

Fig. 4 The proposed measuring system for quantity of oil film in a ET line.

The results of measurement made using the measuring systems in Figs. 4 and 5 are presented in Figs. 6 and 7, respectively.

As is evident in Figs. 6 and 7, these measuring systems show accuracies as high as 0.015 g/B.B. for oil film in the coating weight range from 0.10 to 0.30 g/B.B., and 1.3 mg/m^2 for hydrated chromium oxide with coating weight 5 to 25 mg/m^2.

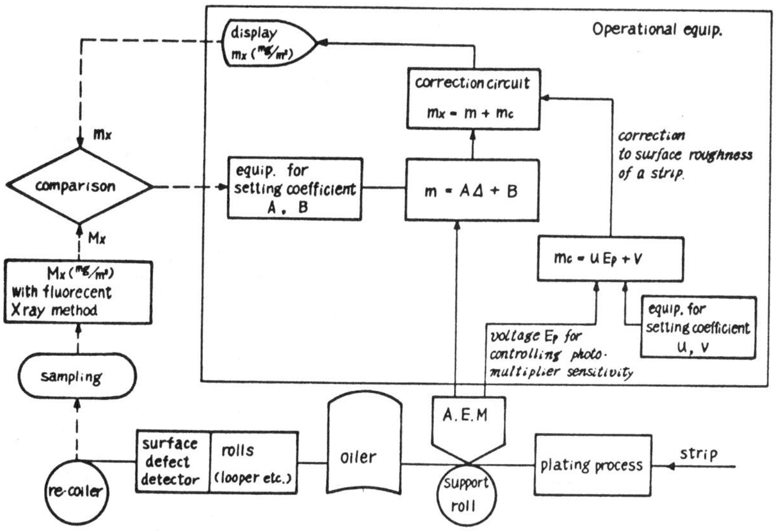

Fig.5 The proposed measuring system for quantity of hydrated chromium oxide in a TFS line.

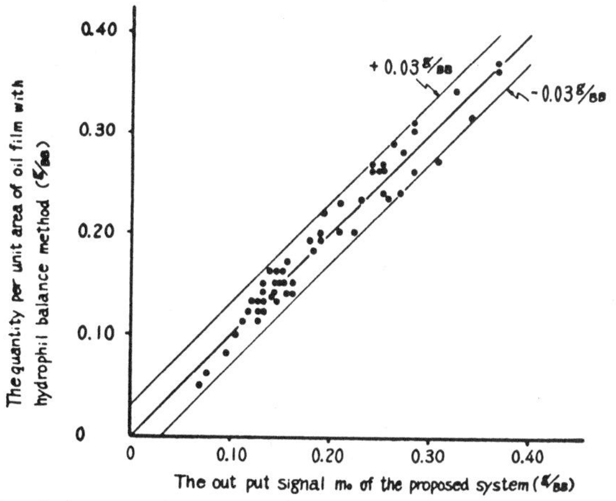

Fig.6 A result of making a comparison between the out put signal of the proposed system and quantity per unit area of oil film with a current hydrophil balance method at YAWATA WORS.

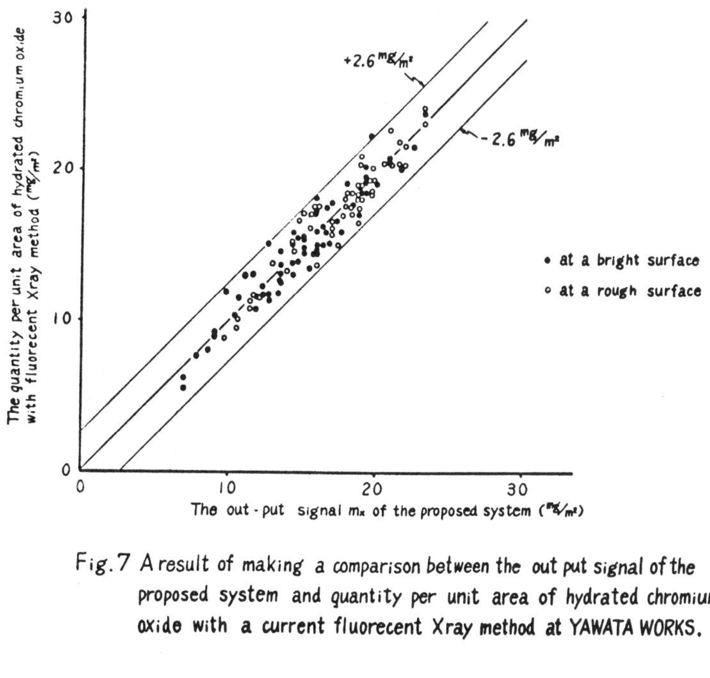

Fig.7 A result of making a comparison between the out put signal of the proposed system and quantity per unit area of hydrated chromium oxide with a current fluorecent Xray method at YAWATA WORKS.

CONCLUSION

NSC has succeeded in developing ellipsometry-based instrumentation systems that enable on-line continuous measurement of the oil coating weight of ET (0.10 to 0.30 g/B.B. or 2 to 8 nm in thickness) and the coating weight of hydrated chromium oxide of TFS (5 to 25 mg/m^2 or 20 to 40 nm in thickness), jobs which were previously considered possible only off line.

Data gathered to data indicate high accuracy of the systems, 0.015 g/B.B. for the oil film version and 1.3 mg/m^2 for the system for hydrated chromium oxide. The authors believe that the exceptionally high accuracy is a result of the combination of efforts directed to the clarification of characteristics of each coating or process parameter, on the one hand, and the automatic ellipsometer, on the other.

We are also confident that with the advent of these measuring systems, a comprehensive automatic control of film thickness applicable to ET and TFS production lines will be made possible in the not-so-distant future.

ACKNOWLEDGEMENTS

The authors would like to express their sincere appreciation to Messrs. Saburobei Tanaka, Teruo Sato and Yoshikiyo Onoue for kind collaboration in the experiements and data arrangement, to Messrs. Mitsuo Kama and Hidejiro Asano for their guidance, and to Mr. Toshiyuki Kasai* for the development of the Automatic Ellipsometer.

REFERENCES

1. Passaglia E, Stromberg R. R., Kruger J. (1964) Ellipsometry in the Measurement of Surfaces and Thin Films Symposium Proceedings Washington 1963, National Bureau of Standards Miscellaneous Publication 256

2. T. Kasai, High-speed automatic ellipsometer for industrial uses, Rev. Sci. Instrum. 47, 1044 - 1048 (1976)

* Reserch Laboratories, Nippon Kogaku K.K.

PRACTICAL APPLICATION OF DIAGNOSTIC SIGNATURE ANALYSIS TO TESTING OF ROTATING MACHINES

T. Usami*, T. Koizumi*, T. Inari and E. Ohno****

**Manufacturing Development Laboratory, Mitsubishi Electric Corporation, Amagasaki, Hyogo, 661, Japan*
***Central Research Laboratory, Mitsubishi Electric Corporation, Amagasaki, Hyogo, 661, Japan*

SUMMARY

Up to this time, it has been difficult to recognize defects of machine and equipment by automatic system instead of skilled human sensors. Now authors have developed the new art which can catch the specific features of acoustic signal from rotating machines using diagnostic signature analysis. As a result, the automated inspection and diagnosis of the rotating state of motors have become possible. For the diagnostic analysis, the pattern recognition technique composed of signal averaging and normalization method is used. Especially, the statistical classifications using a characteristic function and an estimated function have proved their usefulness. A practical inspection equipment based on this analysis for rotating machines has been developed and tested in one of our plants. This statistical methods can be also applied to the preventive maintenance and automatic diagnostic system for other kinds of machines, tools and various kinds of plants.

1. INTRODUCTION

In most mass production lines of small rotating machines, products are often tested by human inspectors who have superior ability of sensing and recognition. The signals to be detected are normally so small in comparison with the total noise from the machine that only specially trained experts can identify them. However, their test result depends on human factors such as individual and day-by-day fluctuations even for the same inspector. In order to improve the reliability and repeatability of the test results as well as the productivity of testing, human factors have been expected to be replaced by automated system not depending on human characteristics.
Such system will be composed of a microphone connected to a mini-computer or a micro processor. The signals from rotating motors are classified to several groups such as electric hum, rotor rubbing noise, journal bearing noise, magnetic noise and others.
We apply some new statistical methods to a practical diagnostic equipment which is reported in this paper.
A new vector $\bar{S}$ is defined to express the signature of the signal in our methods. $\bar{S}$ is obtained from weighted average of the power spectrum S of the signal in frequency domain. Variance and unexpected change of power spectrum may be averaged by operation of $\bar{S}$, so the statistical characteristics of the power spectrum S can be extracted easily.
The signal from a machine described above is averaged in time domain previous to the operation of the power spectrum (F.F.T.). The time averaging is operated by synchronizing sampling intervals with the period of the revolution referring to tachopulses and summation of the waveforms of the signal. The time averaging method enhances periodic components from the background noises.
This method can be useful applied to analyzing the signature of the noise from the machines in production line. The results of the analysis are used for designing a practical diagnostic equipment, which has been tested in the actual production line.
The equipment is composed of analog and digital hybrid components including frequency filters and micro processing units. A pulse is produced when the input signal after specific filter exceeds the reference signal. When the number of the pulses becomes larger than the predetermined number within predetermined time interval, "NO GO" signal is produced. The test result in

actual production line has agreed with higher rate above ninety-five percent. Considering human factors, we have concluded that this automatic system can replace the human inspections in acoustic testing in actual production lines.

2. CLASSIFICATION OF DEFECTS

The motors to be tested, whose waveform of sound is shown in Fig. 1, are induction motors rated 50 to 200 watts having journal bearings. The motor has some defects which are described as follows.

2.1. Rotor Rubbing Defect

This defect is caused by collision or friction between a rotor and a stator, or eccentricity of the rotor. Although the rotor rubbing noise appears at every revolution, it does not appear in the definite angle. Figure 2 shows a waveform of sound noise from rotor rubbing defects. In this case, it is better to use spectrum-signal averaging rather than the time-signal averaging before diagnostic analysis.

2.2. Journal Bearing Defect

This defect is not stationary. Although it occurs randomly for each revolution, it appears in the definite angle. Most of this noises appear every 2 or 3 second. This noise is caused by journal bearing defect. Figure 3 shows a waveform of sound from journal bearing defects. In this case, analysis must be started after time-signal averaging. Thus the most reasonable method of signature analysis should be found for features of every defects.

3. ANALYSIS

The definite method of diagnostic signature analysis has not yet been established. For example, correlation function, Fourier transform, power spectrum and etc. may be applied.
In our method, the microphone with reflecter gathers and records the sound noise from machine at first. The synchronized pulses are also simultaneously recorded. The system block diagram for collecting and recording noise is shown in Fig. 4. The synchronized pulses are needed for time-signal averaging and normalization. Recorded noise becomes input data to a computer. The time-signal averaging method causes the signal appearing at the definite angle to be enhanced and the noise appearing randomly to be reduced.
The time-signal averaing method is given by

$$\overline{x}(\ell) = (1/m) \sum_{i=1}^{m} x_i(\ell), \qquad (1)$$

for $\ell = 1, \ldots, n$.

where x_i is component of waveform,

ℓ is sampling number,

m is number of waveforms.

In this case, $m=16$, $n=2^{10}=1024$.
The signal $\overline{x}(\ell)$ shown in equation (1) is input a computer. The algorithm of this analysis is shown in Fig. 5.
The noisy signal is normalized in time domain, which is called time-signal normalization. The time-signal normalization is useful for extraction of these random signals. In the time-signal normalization, input signal is quantized into n points per one revolution by extension or compression of the signal in time axis.
If our time-signal normalization is not performed in the analysis of these machines, the error which depends on slight difference of each revolution of a machine makes analysis unmeaning.
The correlation is often calculated for extraction of features in time domain. The cross correlation is given by

$$R_{x_i,y_i}(k) = \frac{1}{n} \sum_{\ell=1}^{n} x_i(\ell) \cdot y_i(\ell+k), \qquad (2)$$

where $x_i(\ell)$ and $y_i(\ell)$ are waveforms, such as

$x_i(\ell)$ is the waveform of normal sound and

$y_i(\ell)$ is waveform of abnormal sound.

In our analysis, this operation given by equation (2) is carried out after the time-signal normalization.
The cross correlation becomes a periodic function because both x and y are periodic functions. The function $R_{x,y}$ shown in equation (2)

depends on similarity between x and y.
In frequency domain, our characteristic function $\bar{S}$ and our estimated function P is defined.
$\bar{S}$ obtained by smoothing power spectrums is expressed as

$$\bar{S}(\omega_n) = \sum_{i=n}^{n+m} S(\omega_i), \qquad (3)$$

where $S(\omega_i)$ is the Fourier transform of the autocorrelation,

m is smoothing factor and determined according to each case.

P is given by

$$P = \sum_{\omega_i}^{\omega_j} \{\bar{S}(\omega_n) - \bar{S}_0(\omega_n)\}, \qquad (4)$$

where ω_i is the lower limit frequency of the remarkable spectrum band,

ω_j is the higher limit frequency of the remarkable spectrum band,

$\bar{S}_0$ is the threshold value of integrated spectrums in the remarkable band.

Finally, our estimated function P is compared with the threshold value P_0. If P is larger than P_0, the abnormal signal is represented. The results of judgement in this algorithm are shown in Fig. 6, 7, 8. The algorithm is based on some pattern recognition techniques in frequency domain. The integrated value in a remarkable frequency region is set automatically.
An abnormal sound is defined only when the integrated value is larger than the threshold value. As the result of this analysis, this method can be applied to the concept of automatic diagnostic system.

4. PRACTICAL DIAGNOSTIC EQUIPMENT

Using the principle of the statistical method, we developed a practical diagnostic equipment. The block diagram of the equipment is shown in Fig. 9.
Sound noise is collected and converted to an electrical signal by microphones. The signal is amplified and supplied to a variable bandpass filter of which bandwidth is settable at will. Certain frequency components of the signal are permitted to pass through the filter. Then, the signal is supplied to the comparator and compared with a reference signal which is externally given.
When the signal level is equal to or higher than the reference, a pulsed signal is produced from the comparator. The pulses thus produced are successively supplied to the cumulating device. When a number of the cumulated pulses becomes equal to or higher than predetermined number within a predetermined time interval, the cumulating device produces "GO" or "NO GO" signal. Both the predetermined number and time interval are set by setter at will.
Several functions are added to protect the equipment from the misoperation caused by the unexpected noises. One of the added functions is the exclusion of external noises. The microphones are arranged symetric. The external noises are drowned out and on the contrary, the signals are enhanced. The results of experiment in this arrangement are given by Fig. 10. Another added function is arrangement of other microphones to catch noises caused by plant operation. When the signal level supplied to these microphones is higher than predetermined level, the function of inspection is interrupted automatically. The interruption time of the inspection is variable and is set at will. This added function has been the most useful for exclusion of noises.
The rate of agreement with the judgement of an inspector is more than ninety-five percent as a result of these added functions. This rate is within the deviation of inspector's judgements and therefore the diagnostic equipment has been decided to introduce in our plant.
The appearance of our practical diagnostic equipment is shown in Fig. 11.

5. CONCLUSIONS

From the foregoing analyses and experiments, following conclusions can be drawn.

(1) Diagnostic signature analysis based on pattern recognition technique has been developed and a practical equipment depending on this analysis has been constructed.

(2) The statistical method based on pattern recognition technique has been especially effective in this analysis, and the characteristic function $\bar{S}$ obtained by smoothing power spectrums and

the estimated function P defined by authors can be used as the parameter for classification of machines quantitatively.

(3) The result of actual test for diagnosis of rotating motors using the practical equipment has shown high rate of agreement with the judgement performed by skilled inspectors, so that our practical equipment has been decided to introduce in our plant.

6. ACKNOWLEDGEMENT

The authors thank Dr. Keinosuke Fukunaga, Professor of Purdue University, for his many helpful suggestions.

REFERENCES

(1) R.H. Peterson and R.L. Hoffman, "A new technique for dynamic analysis of acoustical noise", IBM J. Res. Develop., 9, 205 (1965).

(2) N.J. Nilsson (1965), Learning Machines, McGraw-Hill, New York.

(3) J.B. Gibbons, "Engine Vibration Diagnostic Program for Automatic Checkout Systems for Combat Vehicles", General Electric Technical Report, June, (1966)

(4) J. Page, "Recognition of Patterns in Jet Engine Vibration Signals", IEEE Comput., Conf. Dig., 102 (1967).

(5) C.R. Trimble, "What is signal averaging", Hewlett-Packard J., 19-Apr., 2 (1968).

(6) R.B. Tatge, "Acoustical techniques for machinery diagnostics", presented at The Acoustical Society of America Conf., Ottawa, Canada, May (1968).

(7) R.L. Hoffman and K. Fukunaga, "Pattern Recognition Signal Processing for Mechanical Diagnostic Signature Analysis", IEEE Trans. Computer, C-20, 1095 (1971).

(8) J.S. Bendat and A.G. Piersol (1971), Random Data, Wiley, New York.

(9) K. Fukunaga (1972), Introduction to Statistical Pattern Recognition, Academic Press, New York.

(10) L.F. Pau, "Diagnosis of Equipment Failures by Pattern Recognition", IEEE Trans. Reliability, R-23, 202 (1974).

(11) K. Fukunaga, T. Usami and T. Koizumi, "Diagnostic Signature Analysis of Small Rotating Machines", presented at the 4th Automatic Computation and Control Milwhaukee Symposium, Milwhaukee U.S.A. April (1976).

(12) T. Usami, T. Koizumi, T. Inari and K. Fukunaga, "The Analysis of Acoustical Noise by Statistical Method", The Society of Instrument and Control Engineers conf. preprint, Tokyo, Japan, 489 (1976).

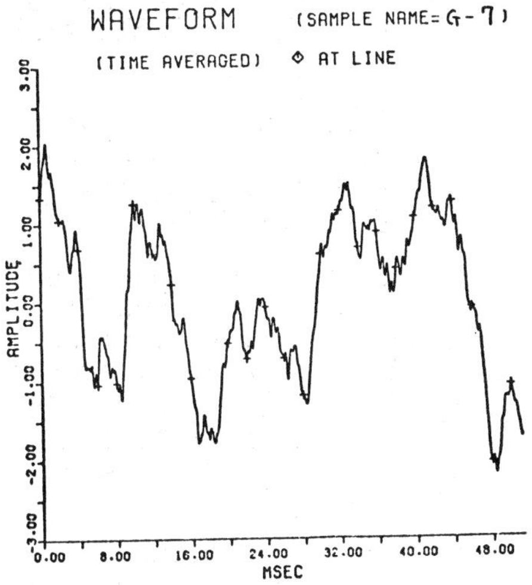

Fig. 1. Waveform of normal sound.

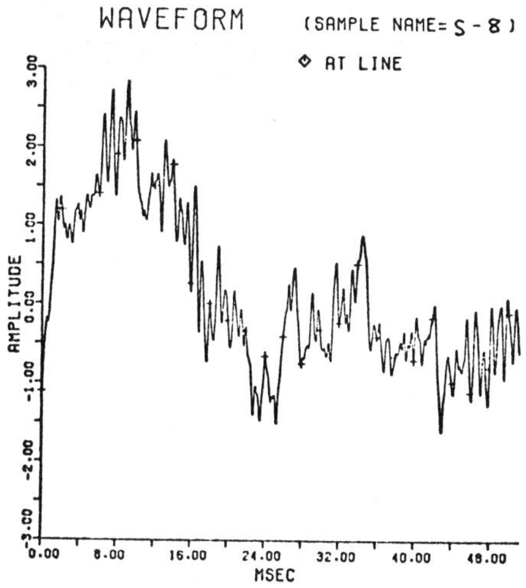

Fig. 2. Waveform of abnormal sound caused by rotor rubbing defect.

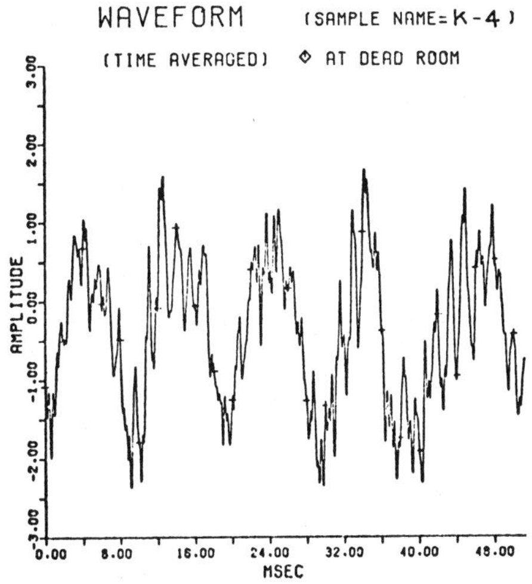

Fig. 3. Waveform of abnormal sound caused by journal bearing defect.

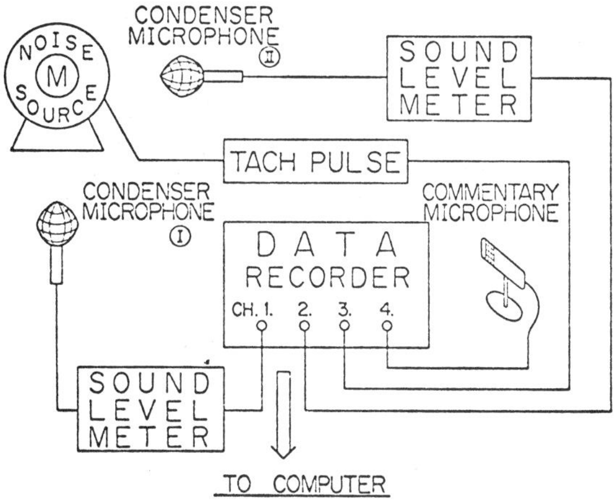

Fig. 4. System diagram for collecting and recording noise radiated from noise source.

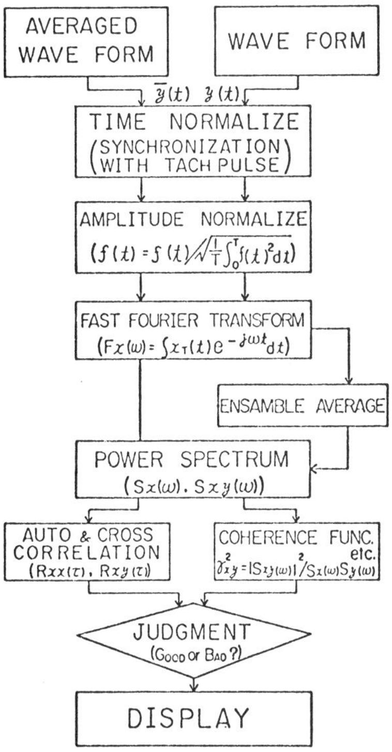

Fig. 5. Algorithm of the diagnostic signature analysis.

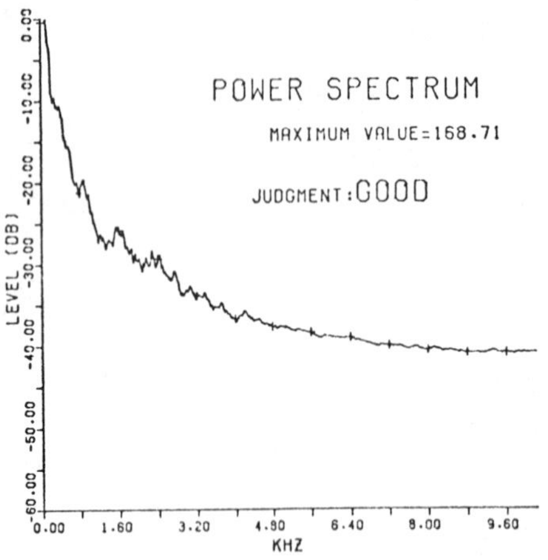

Fig. 6. Judgement on normal sound.

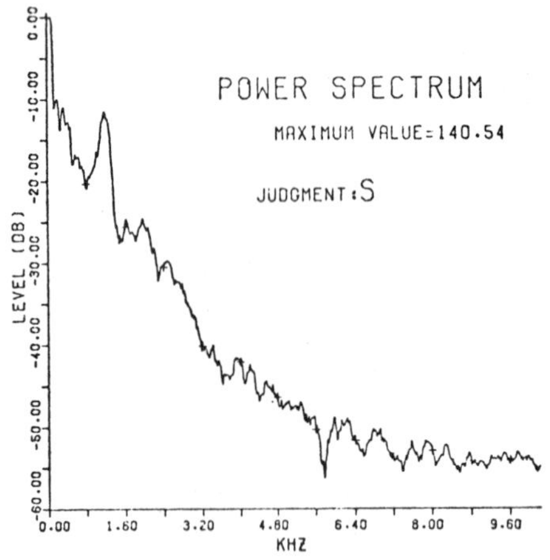

Fig. 7. Judgement on abnormal sound caused by rotor rubbing defect.

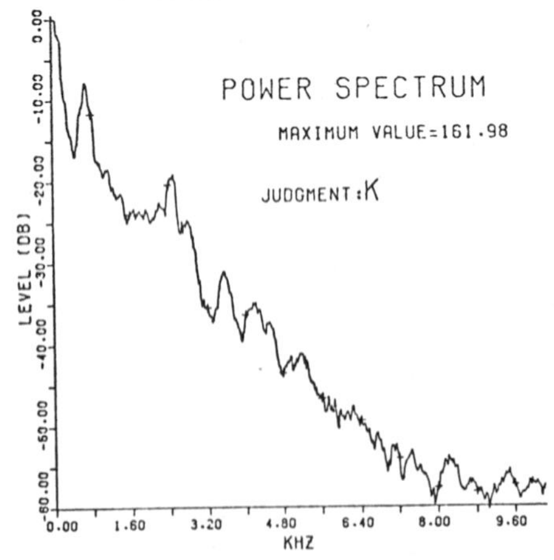

Fig. 8. Judgement on abnormal sound caused by journal bearing defect.

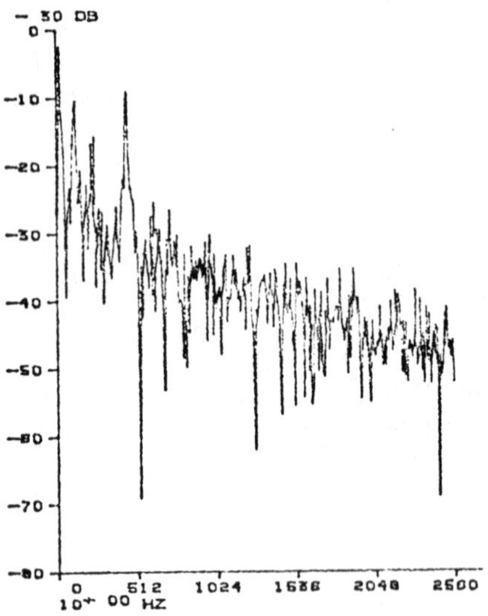

(a) Ach. Input.

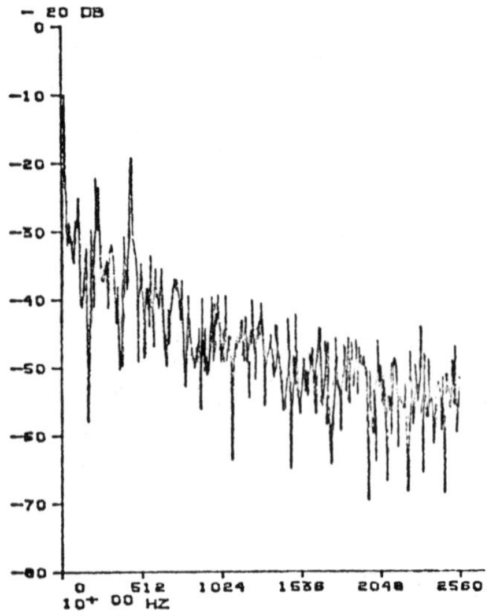

(b) Bch. Input

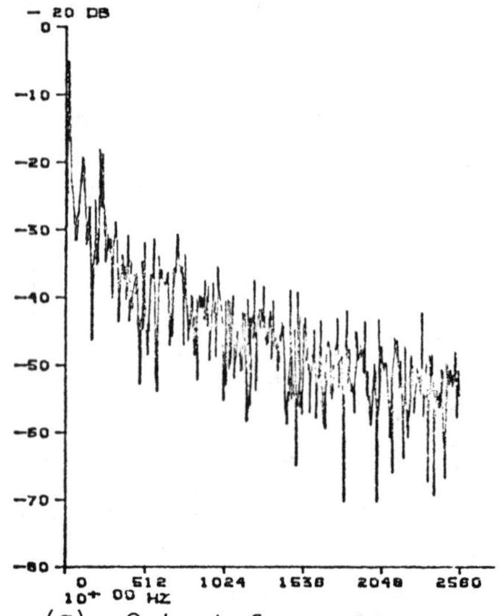

(c) Output from Adder.

Fig. 10. Phase cancellation effect in frequency domain for sinusoidal disturbance sound wave in frequency domain.

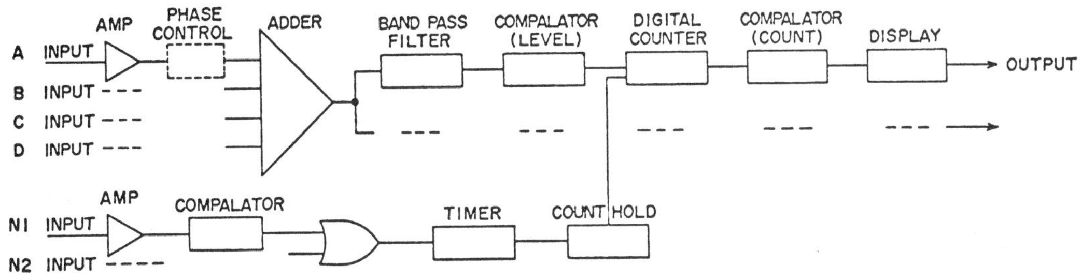

Fig. 9. Block diagram of a practical diagnostic equipment.

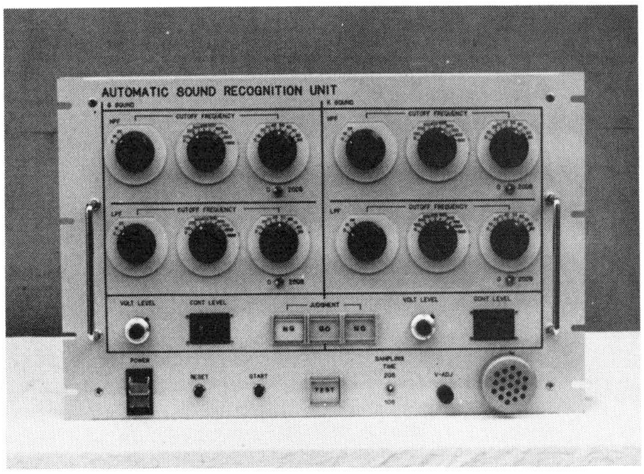

Fig. 11. The appearance of a practical diagnostic equipment.

APPLICATION OF LASER HOLOGRAPHY TECHNIQUE TO MICRO PATTERN POSITIONING IN INTEGRATED CIRCUITS MANUFACTURING

Y. Oshima*, N. Mohri* and Y. Isogai**

**Institute of Industrial Science, University of Tokyo, 7-22-1 Roppongi, Minato-ku, Tokyo*
***Fujitsu Co. Ltd. 1015 Kamiodanaka, Nakahara-ku, Kawasaki*

1. INTRODUCTION

In assembling processes of the integrated circuits (IC), the bonding process, in which electrical connections between the pads (interior terminals) of the IC mounted on the frame and the leads of the frame are done, is important. The problem of this process is how to position the IC to the desired location within the specified error (several micrometers) for wire or frame bonding.

The authors developed a photoelectric microscope for automatic positioning of the transistor pellets with pattern size of several hundred micrometers [1]. Automatic positioning of the IC is very difficult because the size of the chip, especially in case of the LSI, reaches 5 - 6 mm and the patterns involved in the chip are very complicated.

One of the most advanced bonding processes of the IC actually used at present is as follows: The IC chip is observed by an operator with a projector and the relative position of the IC chip with respect to the package is detected by adjusting an adequate portion of the IC pattern to the cross lines of the projector and then the head of the wire bonder is positioned by the command of an minicomputer which calculates the relative positions of the pads with respect to the package from the inputs of the measured data by the projector. Such a method fully utilizes the operator's function of pattern recognition which is one of the strong properties of the human beings.

Recently the laser holography technique was highly developed so as to be used for pattern recognition. The authors tried to apply this technique to automatic positioning of the micro patterns of the IC chip in order to realize a fully automatic bonding process. Our research is still now continued and several improvements have been done. This paper describes the later developments.

2. OUTLINE OF PAST RESEARCH

Fig.1 shows the principle of automatic pattern positioning by the laser holography technique [2].

An optical system for hologram making is arranged as shown in (a) of the figure. The laser beam from a He-Ne gas laser is divided into two beams by a beam splitter. The one of them is projected to a model IC chip and the other is passed through an autocollimator so as to be used as a reference beam. The reflected beam from the model IC chip is passed through a Fourier transform lens and is used as a signal beam. The Fourier transform lens means that the object and the image are spaced a focal length on either side of the lens. A photographic plate placed in the focal plane of the Fourier transform lens is exposed to both signal and reference beams. The interference fringes are recorded on the photographic plate and after development the hologram is obtained.

An optical system for generation of position signal spot is arranged as shown in (b) of the figure. The beam is projected to the IC chip to be positioned and the reflected beam after passing through the Fourier transform lens is projected to the hologram which is set at the same position with that in case of hologram making. A portion of the transmitted light is diffracted by the interference fringes of the hologram in the same direction with the reference beam in case of hologram making. The diffracted light from the hologram is passed through an inverse Fourier transform lens and an optical spot with size of several hundred micrometers is generated in the focal plane of the inverse Fourier transform lens. The position of this spot depends on the position of the IC pattern. Movement of the spot is proportional to the displacement of the IC chip in its plane. In other words, the spot represents the displacement of the IC chip. From this point we call this spot as the position signal spot. Thus we can obtain the position signal without any marking on the IC chip, which is the significant feature of this method.

Many experiments have been done to investigate the validity of this principle. The positioning accuracy obtained were $\pm$ 12 μm for translation and $\pm$ 10' for rotation. The problem of this method is that the intensity of the position signal spot is attenuated by various factors and, if things come to the worst, position detection becomes impossible. There remained more development works for improvement.

3. PRINCIPLE OF POSITION DETECTION AND ITS ANALYTICAL DESCRIPTIONS

3.1 Principle of position detection

The position signal spot by the laser holography technique is used for detection of the displacements of the IC chip in its plane (translational displacements in the x and y directions). This position signal spot is the optical autocorrelation function of the IC pattern as mentioned later in analytical descriptions. Rotational displacement of the IC chip in its place ($\Delta\theta$) results peripheral displacements of the pads to which bonding is done and moreover causes attenuation of the intensity of the position signal spot. Since the reflected beam from the IC chip is used for generation of the position signal spot, tilting of the IC chip from the reference plane causes deviation of the direction of the reflected beam and results attenuation of the intensity of the spot. Therefore, the translational displacements (Δx, Δy), rotational displacement ($\Delta\theta$) and tiltings around two axes ($\Delta\phi$, $\Delta\psi$) should be detected and controlled for positioning of the IC chip by this method (Fig.2).

In order to detect the rotational angle and tilting angles of the IC chip, the Fraunhofer diffraction pattern with a cross-line shape, obtained by projecting the laser beam normally to the IC chip and passing the reflected beam through the Fourier transform lens, is used. Each branch of the Fraunhofer diffraction pattern is detected optically by rotary scanning as described later in details. This cross-line shaped diffraction pattern is caused by the property of the IC chip that the main part of the IC patterns consists of the straight lines perpendicular to each other as shown in Photo 1.

3.2 Analysis of diffraction pattern due to reflected light from IC chip in case of normally incident light

The cross-line shaped diffraction pattern used for detection of the rotational angle and tilting angles of the IC chip is obtained by an optical system as shown in Fig.3. It is necessary to analyze the property of the diffraction pattern due to the reflected light from the IC chip.

As is well known, the light is an electromagnetic wave and is expressed as a vector wave in the mathematical descriptions. Neglecting polarization, the light is expressed as a scalar wave given by the following equation.

$$u = a\, e^{j(\omega t - kz)} \quad \cdots\cdots\cdots\cdots \quad (1)$$

where a is the amplitude, ω is the angular frequency, z is the coordinate axis of light wave propagation and k is the wave number of the light. k has the following relationships with the wavelength λ and the light velocity c.

$$k = \frac{2\pi}{\lambda}, \qquad \frac{\omega}{k} = c$$

In case of the He-Ne gas laser, these parameters are given as $\lambda = 6328\ \text{Å} = 0.6328\ \mu m$, $c = 3 \times 10^{10}$ cm/sec, $k = 10^5$ /cm, and $\omega = 3 \times 10^{15}$ rad/sec.

When the IC chip is illuminated by the laser beam, the semiconductor surface reflects the beam perfectly since the semiconductor surface is mirror finished but the spattered metal surface reflects the light diffusively. Therefore, viewing from the direction of the reflection, the semiconductor surface is bright and the spattered metal surface is dark. But viewing from the other direction, brightness and darkness are reversed.

Neglecting inversion of the phase at the reflecting surface, it is justified to regard the portions of the semiconductor as the multiple slits and to deal with the problem as diffraction by the slits.

For simplicity, let us consider an one-dimensional problem. As shown in Fig.4, the IC chip is regarded as the slits. As for the slits, the aperture function F(x) as shown by (c) of the figure is considered. As can be seen from the figure, the slits are illuminated by the light with the amplitude c(x). Here, c(x) is considered as real, but c(x) can be complex.

The essential feature of diffraction phenomena can be explained by Huygens' principle. This principle states that the propagation of a light wave can be predicted by assuming that each point of the wave front acts as the source of a secondary wave that spreads out in all directions. The envelope of all the secondary waves is the new wave front. Therefore, the problem can be solved by considering that the optical source with the amplitude c(x) F(x) is distributed on the x axis as shown in Fig.5. Thus, the diffracted light from the slits after passing through the lens L_1 produces the image on the screen spaced a focal length f from the lens as given by the following equation (See Appendix I.).

$$u(\alpha) = \int_{\Sigma} c(x)\, F(x)\, e^{-j\frac{k}{f}\alpha x}\, dx \quad \cdots\cdots \quad (2)$$

where α is the axis on the screen. Integration is done over the slits. The range of integration can be expanded to from $-\infty$ to $+\infty$ because $F(x) = 0$ outside the slits.

In case of the normally incident light, c(x) can be regarded as real and constant. Therefore, Eq.(2) represents the Fourier transform of the aperture function F(x). As for the two-dimensional problem, the equation corresponding to Eq.(2) is expressed as

$$u(\alpha) = \iint_{-\infty}^{+\infty} c(x, y)\, F(x, y)\, e^{-j\frac{k}{f}(\alpha x + \beta y)}\, dx\, dy \quad \cdots\cdots\cdots\cdots \quad (3)$$

Photo 2 shows the Fourier transform images of the IC chips.

Since the patterns of the IC chip consist of the straight lines perpendicular to each other, the aperture function can be expressed by

$$F(x, y) = \sum_{i=1}^{I} \delta(y - ax - b_i) + \sum_{m=1}^{M}$$

$$\delta(y + \frac{1}{a} x - c_m) \quad \cdots\cdots\cdots\cdots \quad (4)$$

where $\delta(x, y)$ is the Dirac's delta function. Fig.6 shows the idealized aperture function of the IC chip. Substituting Eq.(4) into Eq.(3) and performing integration, the intensity distribution of the image on the photographic plate placed in the plane of the screen is given by the following equation (See Appendix II.).

$$I(\alpha, \beta) = u^*(\alpha, \beta) \cdot u(\alpha, \beta)$$

$$= \delta(\alpha + a\beta)^2 \{I + 2 \sum_{(i,k)} \cos\beta(b_i - b_k)\} +$$

$$\delta(\alpha - \frac{\beta}{a})^2 \{M + 2 \sum_{(m,1)} \cos (c_m - c_1)\} +$$

$$2\delta(\alpha + a\beta)\ \delta(\alpha - \frac{\beta}{a}) \sum_i^I \sum_m^M \cos\beta(b_i - b_m) \quad \cdots (5)$$

where $\sum_{(i,k)}$ and $\sum_{(m,1)}$ represent the sum of all possible combinations of i, k and m, 1 when $i \neq k$ and $m \neq 1$ respectively.
The reason why the product of the conjugate complex functions $u^*(\alpha, \beta)$ and $u(\alpha, \beta)$ is taken is that the photosensitive emulsion of the photographic plate responds to the square of the magnitude of the complex amplitude $u(\alpha, \beta)$. Eq.(5) represents that the diffraction image of the IC chip is a cross-line which rotates by the angle corresponding to the rotational displacement of the IC chip and the intersection point of two crossing lines moves in accordance with the deviation of the optical axis due to the tilting angles of the IC chip from the reference plane. Thus, the diffraction image has the information concerning the rotational displacements around the three axes of the IC chip.

3.3 Analysis of detection of translational displacements by holography technique

For detection of the translational displacements of the IC chip the reflected beam from the chip is used in both cases of hologram making and generation of the position signal spot, although in these cases the incident laser beam is oblique to the IC chip as shown in Fig.7. The diffraction pattern on the hologram is different from that in case of normally incident light. Analysis of this diffraction pattern is complicated, so that for simplicity the principle of detection of the translational displacements is explained with respect to the one-dimensional problem in case of the transmitted light. As shown in Fig.8, on the photographic plate π the diffracted light by the IC chip which is placed in plane Σ with deviation x_o from the origin has the amplitude given by

$$\chi_1(\alpha) = C_1 \int F(x - x_o)\ e^{-j \frac{k}{f_1} \alpha x}\ dx \quad \cdots (6)$$

In case of hologram making the plane wave as the reference beam is projected to the photographic plate π from the direction which has angle θ with the plate normal.

The amplitude of the reference beam on the photographic plate is given by

$$\chi_r(\alpha) = C_r\ e^{-jk\alpha \sin\theta} \quad \cdots\cdots\cdots\cdots \quad (7)$$

where C_r is a constant. Eq.(7) represents that as shown in Fig.9 at point P spaced α from the origin the phase of the plane wave is lagging by

$$k\alpha \sin\theta = \frac{2\pi}{\lambda} 1 \ (1 = \alpha \sin\theta)$$

The composite amplitude $\chi(\alpha)$ in the plane π is

$$\chi(\alpha) = \chi_1(\alpha) + \chi_r(\alpha)$$

The photosensitive emulsion responds to the energy distribution $I(\alpha) = |\chi(\alpha)|^2$, which is given by

$$I(\alpha) = |\chi(\alpha)|^2$$

$$= (|\chi_o|^2 + |C_r|^2) + \chi_o^* C_r\ e^{j(\frac{x_o}{f_1} - \sin\theta)k\alpha}$$

$$+ \chi_o C_r^*\ e^{j(\sin\theta - \frac{x_o}{f_1})k\alpha} \quad \cdots\cdots\cdots\cdots \quad (8)$$

where $\chi_o = \int F(x) e^{-j\frac{k}{f_1}\alpha x} dx$ is the Fourier transform of the IC chip. Development of the exposed photographic plate results the hologram which has the bright and dark fringes proportional to $I(\alpha)$. Then let us consider the case of positioning of the IC chip which has the same pattern $F(x)$ with that while making the hologram. Assuming that the IC chip is placed with deviation x_1 from the origin, the amplitude of the diffracted light by the IC chip in the hologram plane π is given by

$$\chi_2(\alpha) = C_1 \int F_1(x - x_1) e^{-j\frac{k}{f_1}\alpha x}\ dx \quad \cdots\cdots\cdots \quad (9)$$

In this case the wave with the amplitude given by Eq.(9) is incident upon the diffracting aperture with the aperture function given by Eq.(8) and the diffracted light by the aperture after passing through lens L_2 produces the image in plane Γ
Using Eq.(2), the image is expressed by

$$L(p) = \int_\pi \chi_2(a) I(\alpha) e^{-j\frac{k}{f_2} p\alpha}\ d\alpha \quad \cdots\cdots\cdots\cdots (10)$$

where p is the axis in the plane Γ. Substituting Eq.(8) into Eq.(10), integration of the 2nd term in the righthand side of Eq.(8) results the term L_2 (p) which is expressed as

$$L_2(p) = (\text{constant}) \times \int F(x)F(x + \Delta x + \frac{f_1}{f_2} p + f_1 \sin\theta)\ dx$$

This intetegral represents the autocorrelation function and has the maximum point at

$$p = -\frac{f_2}{f_1}\Delta x - f_2 \sin\theta \quad \cdots\cdots\cdots(11)$$

where

$$\Delta x = x_1 - x_2$$

Eq.(11) shows that if $\Delta x = 0$, that is, the IC chip to be positioned is located at the same position with that in case of hologram making the optical spot appears at $p = - f_2 \sin\theta$ and the reference beam is reconstructed. If $\Delta x = 0$, the optical spot is displaced by $(f_2/f_1)\ \Delta x$ from the point $- f_2 \sin\theta$. Therefore, the position of the IC chip can be detected by picking up the displacements of the optical spot. The so-called position signal spot moves in the plane Γ in proportion to the translational displacements of the IC chip with magnification of f_2/f_1. Fig.10 shows an example of the intensity distribution of the position signal spot.

As mentioned above, in the optical system used for the experimental apparatus the incident beam to the IC chip is with obliquity 45°. The analytical treatments in this case are considerably complicated.
With respect to the light near an optical axis, however, it is ascertained from both theoretical and experimental viewpoints that the above-mentioned results are valid.
Moreover, it is verified that the rotations around the three axes of the IC chip have no effect on the location of the position signal spot. Therefore, the translational displacements and the rotational displacements of the IC chip can be detected independently.

3.4 Positioning system for translational displacements

The principle of a practical positioning system controlling the translational displacements of the IC chip is explained in the following. The table on which the IC chip is mounted is driven by two step motors in the X and Y directions respectively.
The position signal spot in the plane Γ moves in accordance with the displacements of the table. On the plane Γ two L - shaped slits as shown in Fig.11 are arranged.

The Y - directional movement of the table results the motion of the position signal spot in the q direction on the plane Γ. When the spot passes through two slits SQ_1, and SQ_2 shifted by an infinitesimal distance to each other, the recognition pulse is generated by the action of the photoelectric microscope. The Y - directional movement of the table is still continued. The recognition pulse, however, lets the reversible counter start to count the driving pulses introduced to the step motor for the Y axis. When the number of pulses counted by the reversible counter reaches the predetermined set value corresponding to ΔQ in the figure, driving of the Y step motor is stopped and at the same time driving of the X step motor is started. The X - directional movement of the table results the motion of the position signal spot in the p direction. When the spot passes through two slits SP_1 and SP_2 the recognition pulse is generated and then the X step motor is stopped. Despite of any initial position such as R_{01}, R_{02} and R_{03} as shown in Fig.11, the position signal spot, that is, the IC chip is positioned at the final position R_e.

4. DETECTION AND CONTROL OF ROTATIONAL AND TILTING ANGLES

4.1 Desired accuracy of positioning

The desired accuracy of positioning in the bonding process of the IC chip depends on several factors. At first, with regard to the translational displacements the accuracy of several micrometers is required in accordance with the size of the pads. The accuracy for the rotational displacement depends on the distance of the pad from the center of the IC chip. In case of the LSI the side length of the chip is several millimeters. In order to limit the peripheral displacement due to rotation within 1 µm, the accuracy of 0.5' is needed. The tilting angles of the IC chip have severe effect on the intensity of the position signal spot. Fig.12 shows an experimental result concerning this effect. The abscissa is the tilting angle (sec) and the ordinate is the output voltage of the detector. Reduction of the intensity depends on the pattern of the IC chip. Taking the worst case of the experimental results into account, the accuracy of the order of ten seconds will be necessary.

4.2 Principle of detection of rotational and tilting angles

The rotational and tilting angles of the IC chip are detected by rotary scanning of the Fraunhofer diffraction pattern.
The principle of this method is explained below.

As mentioned above, the diffraction pattern due to the reflected light from the IC chip in case of normally incident light is a cross-line. The intersection point of two crossing lines is on the optical axis of the reflected light and consequently moves in the image plane according to tilting of the IC chip. Therefore, the tilting angles around the two axes of the IC chip can be obtained from the position of the intersection point. Moreover, it is obvious that the rotational angle of the Fraunhofer diffraction pattern is equal to the rotational angle of the IC chip because the diffraction pattern is perpendicular to the IC pattern. Rotary scanning is done by rotating four photoelectric detecting elements around a fixed axis by means of a step motor and generating a recognition pulse when each detecting element passes through each branch of the cross-line shaped diffraction pattern. The recognition pulses are introduced to a minicomputer as the interruption pulses and the rotational angles θ_1, θ_2, θ_3 and θ_4 as shown in Fig.13 are recorded. The rotational angle of the IC chip θ and the coordinates of the intersection point x and y are obtained from

$$x = \frac{r}{\Delta}\begin{vmatrix} \sin(\theta_1 - \theta_2) & -(\sin\theta_1 + \sin\theta_2) \\ \sin(\theta_4 - \theta_2) & \cos\theta_2 + \cos\theta_4 \end{vmatrix} \cdot\cdot(12)$$

$$y = \frac{r}{\Delta}\begin{vmatrix} \cos\theta_1 + \cos\theta_3 & \sin(\theta_1 - \theta_3) \\ \sin\theta_2 + \sin\theta_4 & \sin(\theta_4 - \theta_2) \end{vmatrix} \cdots (13)$$

$$\Delta = \begin{vmatrix} \cos\theta_1 + \cos\theta_3 & -(\sin\theta_1 + \sin\theta_3) \\ \sin\theta_2 + \sin\theta_4 & \cos\theta_2 + \cos\theta_4 \end{vmatrix} \cdot\cdot (14)$$

$$\theta = \frac{1}{2}\{\frac{\pi}{2} - \tan^{-1}(\frac{\cos\theta_1 + \cos\theta_3}{\sin\theta_1 + \sin\theta_3}) + \tan^{-1}(\frac{\sin\theta_2 + \sin\theta_4}{\cos\theta_2 + \cos\theta_4})\} \cdots\cdots\cdots (15)$$

where r is the radius of the scanning circle and r = 10 mm in case of the experimental apparatus. Eqs.(12) ~ (15) are introduced as follows:

In Fig.13 the coordinates of the intersection points of the scanning circle and four branches of the diffraction pattern A, B, C and D are $A(r\sin\theta_1, r\cos\theta_1)$, $B(-r\sin\theta_3, -r\cos\theta_3)$, $C(r\cos\theta_2, -r\sin\theta_2)$ and $D(-r\cos\theta_4, r\sin\theta_4)$. The straight lines AB and CD are expressed as

$$(\cos\theta_1 + \cos\theta_3)x - (\sin\theta_1 + \sin\theta_2)y = r\sin(\theta_1 - \theta_3) \cdots\cdots\cdots\cdots (16)$$

$$(\sin\theta_2 + \sin\theta_4)x + (\cos\theta_2 + \cos\theta_4)y = r\sin(\theta_4 - \theta_2) \cdots\cdots\cdots\cdots (17)$$

Solving these simultaneous equations gives Eqs.(12), (13) and (14).

As can be seen from Eqs.(16) and (17), the inclinations of the straight lines AB and CD to the x axis are given respectively as

$$\frac{\cos\theta_1 + \cos\theta_3}{\sin\theta_1 + \sin\theta_3} \; ; \; -\frac{\sin\theta_2 + \sin\theta_4}{\cos\theta_2 + \cos\theta_4}$$

Taking the arithmetic mean of these inclinations results Eq.(15).

Let us consider the case where the preset errors namely the intial attitude errors in setting of the IC chip are very small. In this case the angles $\theta_1 \sim \theta_4$ are very small, so that Eqs.(12) ~ (15) are simplified as

$$x = \frac{r}{2}(\theta_1 - \theta_3)$$

$$y = \frac{r}{2}(\theta_4 - \theta_2) \cdots\cdots (18)$$

$$\theta = \frac{1}{4}(\theta_1 + \theta_2 + \theta_3 + \theta_4), \; \Delta = 4$$

where the second order terms of θ_i ($i = 1 \sim 4$) are neglected. In actual processes the preset errors are small enough to such an extent that Eq.(18) can be adopted.

When the attitude errors are large, the condition of normal incidence of the light can not exist and the Fraunhofer diffraction pattern deviates from a cross-line. From observation and theoretical analysis it was found that the Fraunhofer diffraction pattern in this case becomes two intersecting conic sections. The equations describing the diffraction pattern are so complicated that those application to control is not practical. Thus we consider only the case of the small attitude errors.

4.3 Conversion of variables in detection and control of attitude angles of IC chip

As shown in Photo 3 the rotary scanning mechanism for detection of the attitude angles of the IC chip consists of a driving part which is a combination of a step motor, a micrometer head and a lever and a detecting part which is composed of four photoelectric detecting elements on a rotary disc coupled with the driving part. The driving pulses to the step motor are introduced to the minicomputer and counted there. When the recognition pulses are generated at the moments of passing through the branches of the diffraction pattern, these pulses are introduced to the minicomputer as the interruption pulses. At these moments the numbers of the counted pulses are stored. The relationship between the numbers of the counted pulses (p_1, p_2, p_3, p_4) and the rotational angles (θ_1, θ_2, θ_3, θ_4) is

$$(p_1, p_2, p_3, p_4) = \lambda\,(\theta_1, \theta_2, \theta_3, \theta_4) \cdots (19)$$

λ is determined by the geometrical parameters of the driving part and $\lambda = 5 \times 10^{-6}$ rad/pulse in case of the experimental apparatus. The relationship between the coordinates of the intersection point of the cross-line shaped diffraction pattern as well as the rotational angle of the IC chip (x, y, θ) and the rotational angles (θ_1, θ_2, θ_3, θ_4) is given by

$$\begin{bmatrix} x \\ y \\ \theta \end{bmatrix} = A \begin{bmatrix} \theta_1 \\ \theta_2 \\ \theta_3 \\ \theta_4 \end{bmatrix} \cdots\cdots\cdots\cdots (20)$$

where

$$A = \begin{bmatrix} r/2 & 0 & -r/2 & 0 \\ 0 & -r/2 & 0 & r/2 \\ 1/4 & 1/4 & 1/4 & 1/4 \end{bmatrix}$$

The attitude angles of the IC chip (ϕ, ψ, θ) are given by

$$\begin{bmatrix} \phi \\ \psi \\ \theta \end{bmatrix} = B \begin{bmatrix} x \\ y \\ \theta \end{bmatrix} \cdots\cdots\cdots\cdots (21)$$

where

$$B = \begin{bmatrix} 1/2f_3 & 0 & 0 \\ 0 & -1/2f_3 & 0 \\ 0 & 0 & 1 \end{bmatrix}, \; f_3 = 179 \text{ mm}$$

Referring to Fig.14, the relationship expressed by Eq.(21) is obvious. Strictly speaking, the reflected light is expressed by the Euler's angles determined by the reflected light and the normal to the IC chip. When the tilting angles ϕ and ψ are small enough, the simplified relationship as shown by Eq. (21) is valid. As explained later in detail, the IC chip is mounted on the table supported by the gimbal which can be rotated around the vertical axis. The attitude angles of the IC chip (ϕ, ψ, θ) are controlled by three step motors. It is necessary to determine the number of the driving pulses to be introduced to each control step motor for correction of the attitude angles of the IC chip. The tilting angles around the two axes of the gimbal due to rotations of two control step motors per input pulse ν (common to two axes) and the rotational angle of the gimbal around the vertical axis due to rotation of the other control step motor per input pulse μ are given by the parameter values as

$$\nu = 4.27 \times 10^{-6} \text{ rad/pulse,}$$

$$\mu = 8.04 \times 10^{-5} \text{ rad/pulse}$$

The desired numbers of the driving pulses to be introduced to three control step motors (P_ϕ, P_ψ, P_θ) are given by

$$\begin{bmatrix} P_\phi \\ P_\psi \\ P_\theta \end{bmatrix} = C \begin{bmatrix} \phi \\ \psi \\ \theta \end{bmatrix} \quad \cdots\cdots\cdots\cdots\cdots \quad (22)$$

where

$$C = \begin{bmatrix} 1/\nu & 0 & 0 \\ 0 & 1/\nu & 0 \\ 0 & 0 & 1/\mu \end{bmatrix}$$

From Eqs.(19) ~ (22), the relationship between the desired numbers of the driving pulses to three control step motors and the stored numbers of the driving pulses is expressed as

$$\begin{bmatrix} P_\phi \\ P_\psi \\ P_\theta \end{bmatrix} = T \begin{bmatrix} p_1 \\ p_2 \\ p_3 \\ p_4 \end{bmatrix} \quad \cdots\cdots\cdots\cdots\cdots \quad (23)$$

where

$$T = \frac{\lambda}{4} \begin{bmatrix} r/f_3\nu & 0 & -r/f_3\nu & 0 \\ 0 & r/f_3\nu & 0 & -r/f_3\nu \\ 1/\mu & 1/\mu & 1/\mu & 1/\mu \end{bmatrix}$$

Fig.15 shows the conversion of the variables. With respect to the experimental apparatus P_ϕ, P_ψ and P_θ are given by Eq.(24).

$$\begin{aligned} P_\phi &= 0.0164\ (p_1 - p_3) \\ P_\psi &= -\ 0.0164\ (p_4 - p_2) \quad \cdots\cdots\cdots \quad (24) \\ P_\theta &= 0.0155\ (p_1 + p_2 + p_3 + p_4) \end{aligned}$$

In order to take the signs of the attitude angles into account, the initial position of the rotary scanning mechanism is shifted by k pulses. The number of the counted pulses smaller than k means the negative deviation and that larger than k means the positive deviation. Letting n_i be the counted pulse number and p_i be the diviation pulse number, the relationship

$$p_i = n_i - k \quad (i = 1 \sim 4)$$

exists. Using the counted pulse number, Eq. (24) is expressed as

$$\begin{aligned} P_\phi &= 0.0164\ (n_1 - n_3) \\ P_\psi &= -\ 0.0164\ (n_4 - n_2) \quad \cdots\cdots(25) \\ P_\theta &= 0.0155\ (n_1 + n_2 + n_3 + n_4 - 4k) \end{aligned}$$

4.4 Control system

Fig.16 shows the schematic diagram of detection and control of the attitude angles of the IC chip. Fig.17 shows the timing chart. When an interruption pulse is introduced to the minicomputer, a digital output DO starts to drive the step motor for rotary scanning and to rotate four photoelectric detecting elements (S_1, S_2, S_3, S_4) in the plane of the Fraunhofer diffraction pattern. When these sensors pass through the branches of the diffraction pattern, the recognition pulses are generated. The minicomputer counts the driving pulses from the driver of the step motor for rotary scanning and stores the counted pulse numbers (n_1, n_2, n_3, n_4) at the moments the recognition pulses are introduced to the minicomputer as the interruption pulses. When storage of the four counted pulse numbers is completed, the step motor for rotary scanning is stopped and the numbers of the pulses (P_ϕ, P_ψ, P_θ) to be given to the control step motors (M_ϕ, M_ψ, M_θ) are computed. As soon as the computations are completed, the control step motors are activated at the same time. The driving pulses from each driver are counted and compared with the computed results (P_ϕ, P_ψ, P_θ). Coincidence of each comparison outputs the command for stoppage of each control step motor. The minicomputer used is Mitsubishi Melcom 70, model 20 (memory : 8kw, 1 word = 16 Bits).

5. CONSTRUCTION OF EXPERIMENTAL APPARATUS

5.1 Optical system

The optical system of the experimental apparatus is shown in Fig.18 and Photo 4. The laser beam from a He - Ne gas laser (output : 50 mW) after passing through guide mirrors is introduced to beam splitter B_1. The transmitted light at B_1 after passing through guide mirrors M_3 and M_4 illuminates the IC chip in Σ plane with obliquity of 45°. The reflected light from the IC chip after passing through Fourier transform lens L_1 is introduced to photographic plate π as the signal beam. It should be noted that $\overline{L_1\Sigma} = \overline{L_1\pi} = f_1$ (focal length of lens L_1 : 70 mm). The reflected light at B_1 is turned to right at B_2 and after passing through an autocollimator consisting of lens C_1 (40 X objective lens of microscope) and lens C_2 (focal length : 150 mm) is introduced to the photographic plate π as the reference beam whose diameter is extended to 35 mm (laser beam diameter : 3 mm). After exposure of the photographic plate to both signal and reference beams, development is done and a hologram is obtained. D in the figure is a developing equipment for the fixed photographic plate. The equipment can be moved in the parallel direction with the photographic plate (Photo 5). As mentioned in the previous paper [2], the displacement of the hologram in the plane normal to the optical axis from its position while making it reduces severely the intensity of the position signal spot. The displacement of 50 μm results 6 dB reduction of the intensity. For this reason, the special developing equipment was made.

Then the hologram obtained is illuminated by the signal beam from the IC chip with the same pattern to be positioned which is placed in the plane Σ. The diffracted light by the hologram after passing through inverse Fourier transform lens L_2 and transmitted or reflected at beam splitter B_3 produces the position signal spot in Γ_A or Γ_B focal plane [Refer to Fig.18 (b).]. In the planes Γ_A and Γ_B the L - shaped slits are arranged to construct the photoelectric microscope.

On the other hand, the transmitted light at the beam splitter B_2 after passing through guide mirror M_5, prism M_6 and beam splitter B_4 is incident normally to the IC chip. The reflected and diffracted light by the IC chip after reflected at B_4 and passing through inverse Fourier transform lens L_3 (f_3 = 179 mm) produces the cross-line shaped diffraction pattern.

5.2 Driving mechanisms

The diagram of the total system is shown in Fig.19. Photo 5 shows its exterior view. The total system is mounted on the surface plate 1000 mm × 2000 mm supported by oscillation absorbers. The system consists of a He - Ne gas laser, guide mirrors, the above-mentioned optical system, an optical bench and five-axis driving mechanisms. The detailed diagram of the driving mechanisms is shown in Fig.20. The mechanisms consist of the table supported by the gimbal on which the IC chip is mounted, the attitude control mechanism and the translational displacement control mechanism.

The table has small holes used for vacuum chucking of the IC chip. The gimbal has two independent axes perpendicular to each other supported by ball bearings. The table supported by the gimbal has a rod stretched in the vertical and downward direction, to which the cross wires used for control of the tilting angles are fitted at the distance of 234 mm from the center of the gimbal. One end of each cross wire is through a coil spring fixed to the wall. The other end is fitted to the lever which is slightly rotated by a micrometer head driven by a control step motor. The lever ratio is 5 : 1. The rotational displacement of the control step motor per pulse results the translational displacement of 1 μm of the cross wire and the tilting angle of 0.8 sec of the IC chip. The gimbal and the mechanism for control of the tilting angles are mounted on the mechanism for control of the rotational angle having a horizontal rod to which the pulling wire is fitted at the distance of 143 mm from the vertical axis. One end of the wire is through a coil spring fixed to the wall. The other end of the wire is fitted to the drum rotated through a worm gear by a control step motor. The rotational angle of the IC chip around the vertical axis due to rotation of the control step motor per pulse is 17 sec. The attitude control mechanism is mounted on the X - Y table. The translational displacement control mechanism consists of two sets of control step motors, worm gears and ball nut screws. The translational displacements of the X - Y table due to rotations of the two control step motors per pulse are 0.2 μm.

5.3 Control system

The sequence of control is shown in Fig.21. At the preliminary stage the hologram is made. While making the hologram the attitude angles of the model IC chip are corrected so as to be adjusted to the reference attitude determined by the optical system. In the positioning process the attitude angles of the IC chip to be positioned are controlled and then the translational displacements of the IC chip are controlled.

6. ACCURACY OBTAINED

As for position detection utilizing the autocorrelation function image, that is, the position signal spot generated by the laser holography technique, the detection accuracy on the image plane obtained at present is ± 6 μm and in consequence the position detection accuracy for the IC chip itself is expected to be ± 2 μm. The accuracy may be improved by changing the ratio of the focal length of the inverse Fourier transform lens to that of the Fourier transform lens, but direct measurement of the final accuracy is very difficult.

The tilting of the IC chip has a severe effect on the intensity of the position signal spot. Considering the worst case as 10", the system for control of the attitude angles of the IC chip by the cross-line shaped diffraction pattern is designed. From observation of the recognition pulses it is found that the desired accuracy is satisfied.

The accuracy of the driving mechanism is disturbed by the stick-slip and the backlash. It is confirmed that the pitch error of the driving mechanism is within ± 2 μm.

7. CONCLUSION

The development research concerning accurate positioning of micro patterns such as the integrated circuits is described.

At present the total accuracy of the system is expected to be several micrometers. The limitation of the accuracy is now being investigated.

REFERENCES

[1] Y. Oshima and B.S. Chang, A micro pattern positioning system, Preprint of 4th IFAC Congress (Warszawa), T.S. 64, 17 (1969).

[2] Y. Oshima and B.S. Chang, A micro pattern positioning system utilizing laser holography, Preprint of 5th IFAC Congress (Paris), Part 1a, 11.1 (1972).

[3] J.T. Tippet, D.A. Berkowitz, L.C. Clapp, C.J. Koester and A. Vanderburgh, Jr. (1965) Optical and electro-optical information processing, MIT Press, Cambridge.

[4] G.R. Fowles (1967) Introduction to modern optics, Holt, Rinehart and Winston, Inc., New York.

[5] A.V. Lugt, The effects of small displacements of spatial filters, Appl. Optics, 6, 1221 (1967).

[6] J.C. Urbach and R.W. Meier, Properties and limitations of hologram recording material, Appl. Optics, 8, 2269 (1969).

[7] M. Sayar, D. Treves and H. Stark, Parameters and tolerances in coherent matched filtering systems, Israel Jl. of Technology, 9, 289 (1971).

APPENDIX I

Introduction of Eq.(2) expressing the Fourier transform theorem is explained below. The transmitted light at the infinitesimal region dx located at Q(x) in the IC chip can be regarded as the spherical wave emerged from the optical source with the intensity proportional to the amplitude of c(x) F(x). Referring to Fig.(I.1), the amplitude at observation point P is given by

$$u_p = \int_{\Sigma} c(x)\, F(x)\, \frac{e^{jkr}}{r}\, dx \qquad \cdots\cdots \text{(I.1)}$$

where c(x) is the amplitude of the incident laser beam, F(x) is the aperture function and r is the distance of $\overline{QP}$. The term r in the denominator of Eq.(I.1) means reduction of the amplitude of the spherical wave. Since the size of the IC chip is small enough compared with r, r in the range of integration can be regarded as constant. e^{jkr} in Eq.(I.1) is the periodical function obtained by fixing the time in Eq.(1). The interested point here is not the absolute value of the distance but the optical path length. Let us consider the case where a lens with focal length f is placed between the observation point P and the IC chip. The lens has the following property.

(1) The parallel incident light produces the focus in the focal plane regardless of the direction of the incident light.

(2) The optical path length between the point Q and the observation point P is equal to that from Q_o to P as shown in Fig.(I.2) regardless of different paths through the lens. The optical path length from Q to P is given by

$$r = QL_1P = Q_oP - Q_oT = (\sqrt{f^2+\alpha^2} + \sqrt{f^2+x_o^2} - (x - x_o)\frac{\alpha}{f}$$

Since $x_o = -\alpha$,

$$r = 2f - \frac{\alpha}{f}x \qquad \cdots\cdots\cdots\cdots \text{(I.2)}$$

is obtained, taking only the 1st order term with respect to α/f into account. Substituting Eq.(I.2) into Eq.(I.1) and omitting the constant term, Eq.(2) is obtained.

APPENDIX II

Introduction of Eq.(5) is explained in the following. Substituting Eq.(4) into Eq.(3) and regarding c(x, y) as constant give

$$u(\alpha,\beta) = c\iint\{\sum_j \delta(y - ax - b_j) + \sum_m \delta(y + \frac{1}{a}x - c_m)\}\, e^{-j\frac{k}{f}(\alpha x + \beta y)}\, dxdy$$

$$= c\sum_j \iint \delta(y - ax - b_j)\, e^{-j\frac{k}{f}(\alpha x + \beta y)}\, dxdy + c\sum_m \iint \delta(y + \frac{1}{a}x - c_m)\, e^{-j\frac{k}{f}(\alpha x + \beta y)}\, dxdy$$

$$= c\sum_j \int e^{-j\frac{k}{f}\{(\alpha + a\beta)x + b_j\beta\}}\, dx + c\sum_m \int e^{-j\frac{k}{f}\{(\alpha - \frac{\beta}{a})x + c_m\beta\}}\, dx$$

$$= c\sum_j e^{-j\frac{k}{f}b_j\beta}\, \delta(\alpha + a\beta) + c\sum_m e^{-j\frac{k}{f}c_m\beta}\, \delta(\alpha - \frac{\beta}{a})$$

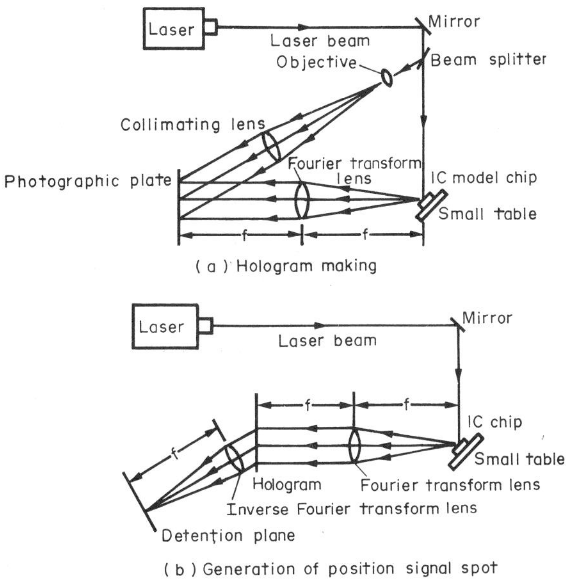

Fig.1. Principle of pattern positioning

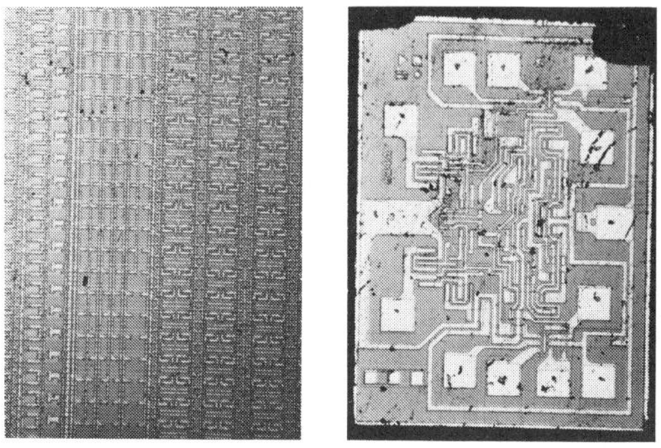

Photo 1. IC patterns

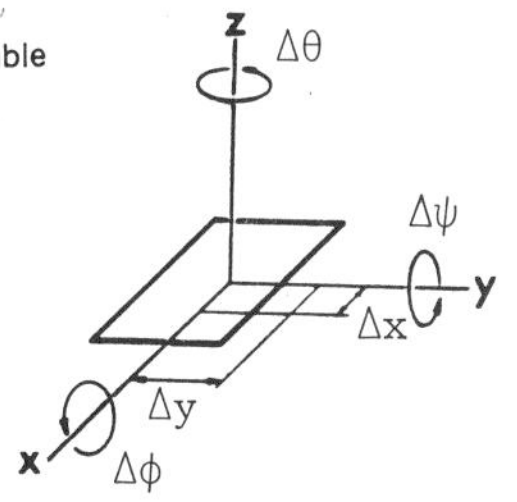

Fig.2. Displacements

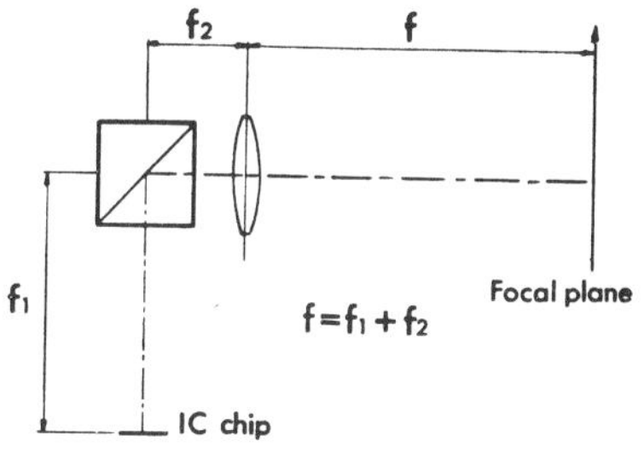

Fig.3. Attitude detection

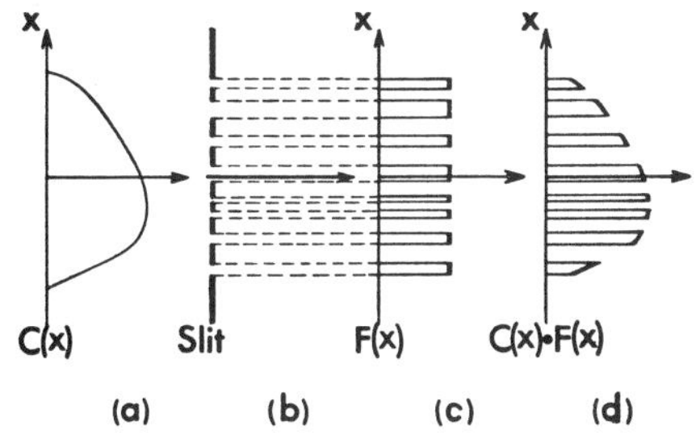

Fig.4. Diffraction by slits

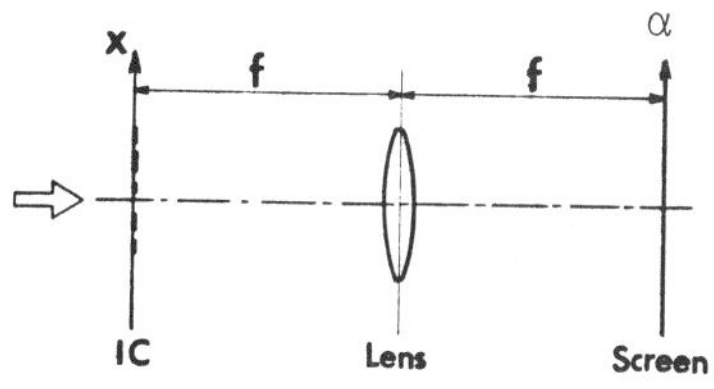

Fig.5. Fraunhofer diffraction

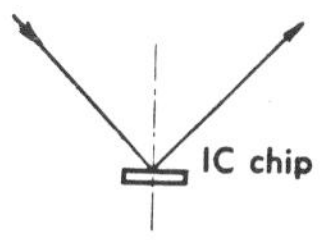

Fig.7. Oblique incidence

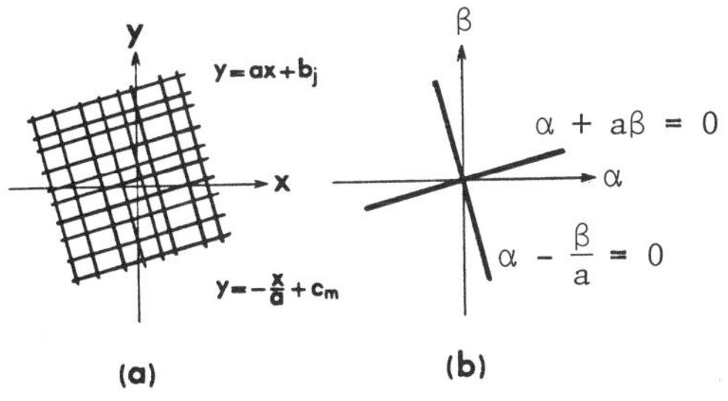

Fig.6. Idealized aperture function

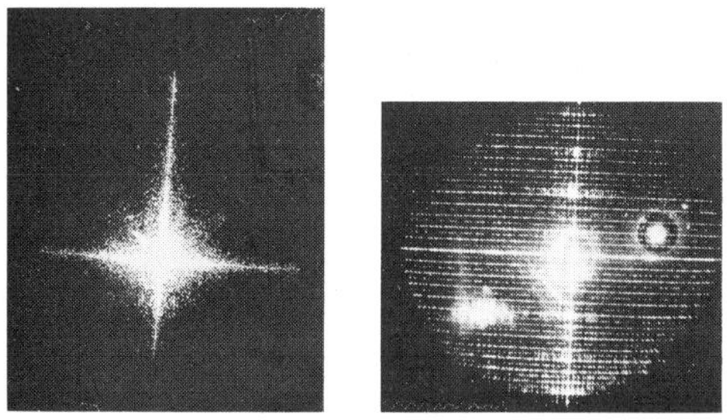

Photo 2. Fourier transform images

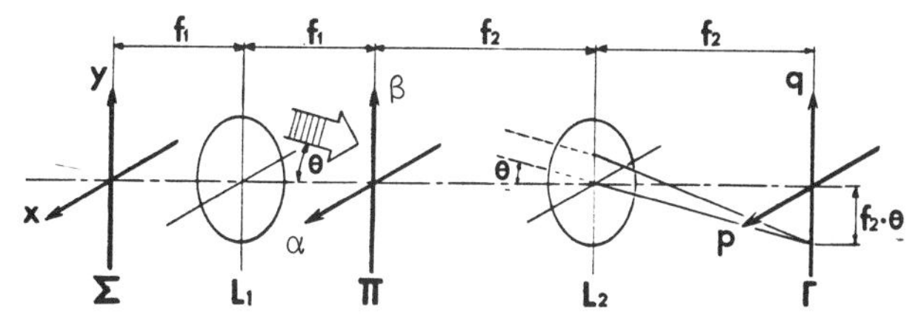

Fig.8. Detection of translational displacement by holography technique

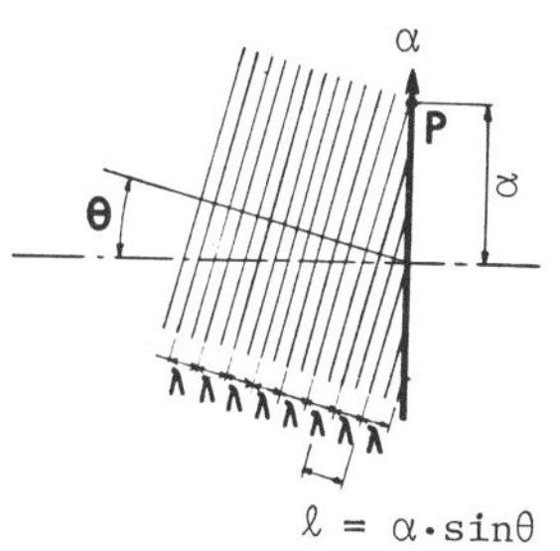

Fig.9. Reference beam

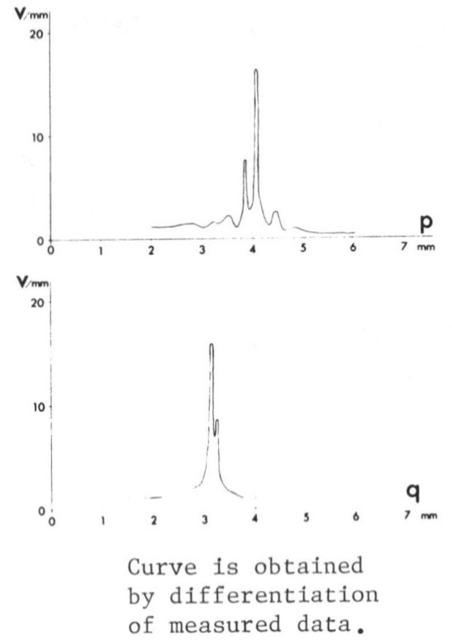

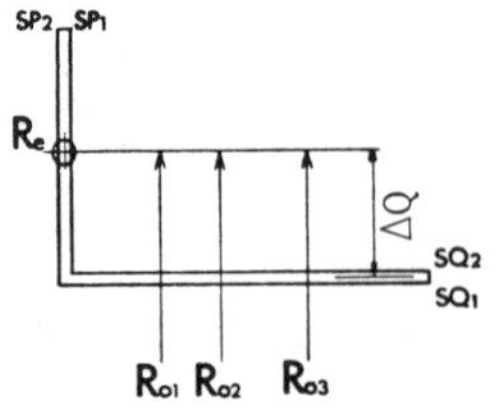

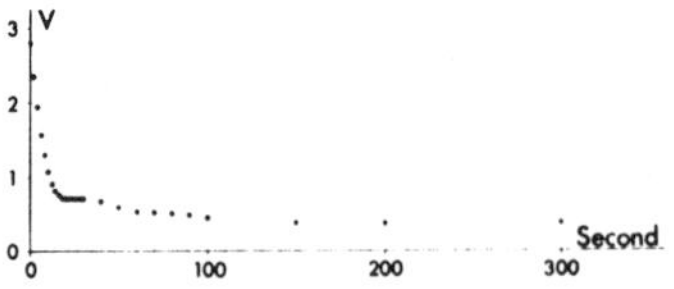

Fig.12. Reduction of intensity

Curve is obtained
by differentiation
of measured data.

Fig.10. Intensity distribution of
position signal spot

Fig.11. Positioning system

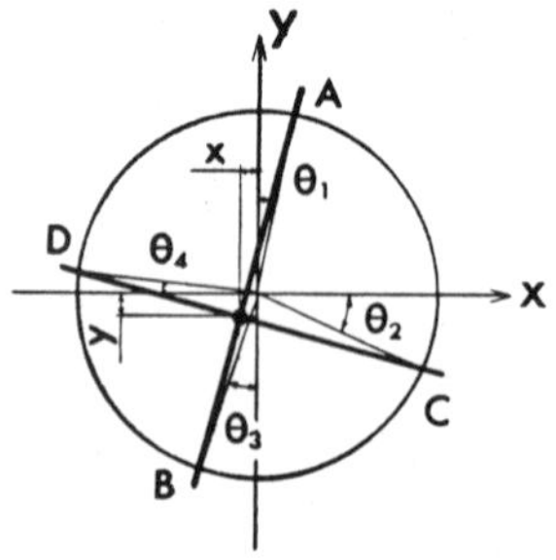

Fig.13. Rotary scanning

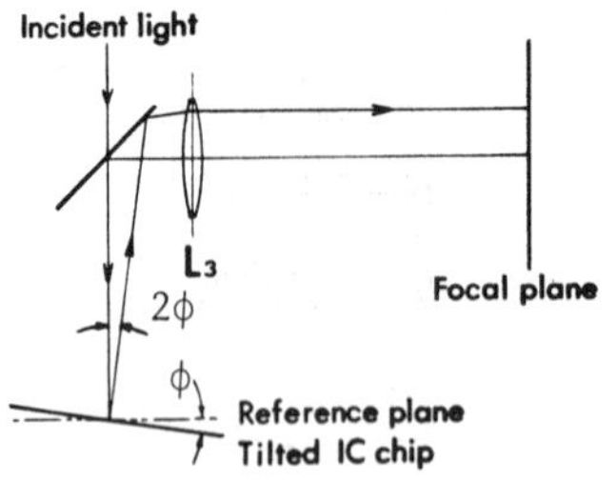

Fig.14. Reflection at IC

Numbers of counted pulses
(P_1 , P_2 , P_3 , P_4)

Rotational angle
$(\theta_1 , \theta_2 , \theta_3 , \theta_4)$

Coodinates of intersection point
and rotational angle of IC chip
(X , Y , θ)

Attitude angles of IC chip
(ϕ, ψ, θ)

Numbers of driving pulses
to control step motors
$(P_\phi, P_\psi, P_\theta)$

$$\begin{bmatrix} P_\phi \\ P_\psi \\ P_\theta \end{bmatrix} = \lambda \cdot [C \cdot B \cdot A] \cdot \begin{bmatrix} P_1 \\ P_2 \\ P_3 \\ P_4 \end{bmatrix}$$

$$T = \lambda \cdot [C \cdot B \cdot A]$$

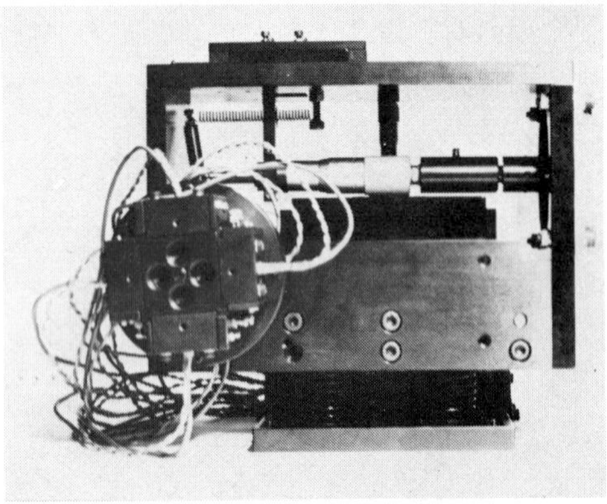

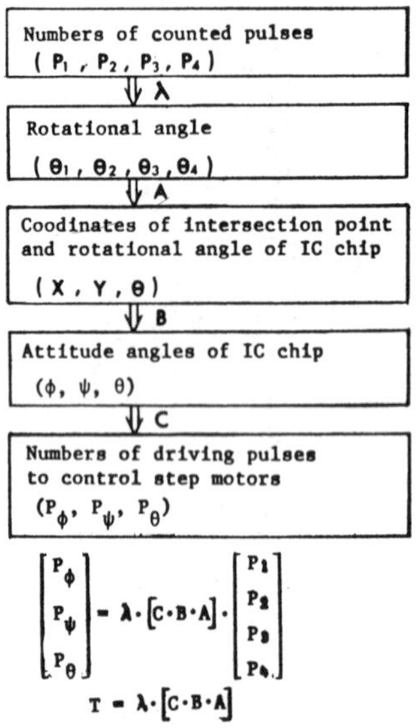

Fig.15. Conversion of variables

Photo 3. Rotary scanning mechanism

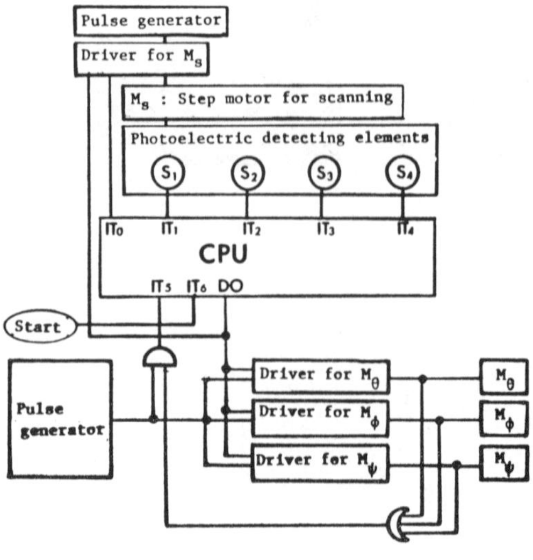

Fig.16. Detection and control
of attitude angles

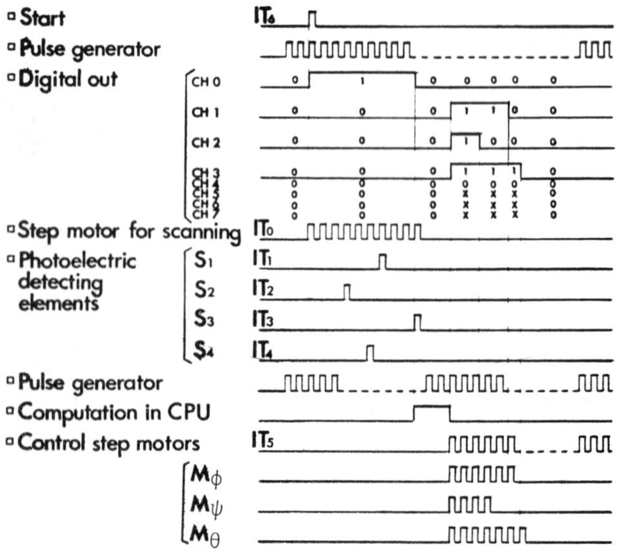

Fig.17. Timing chart

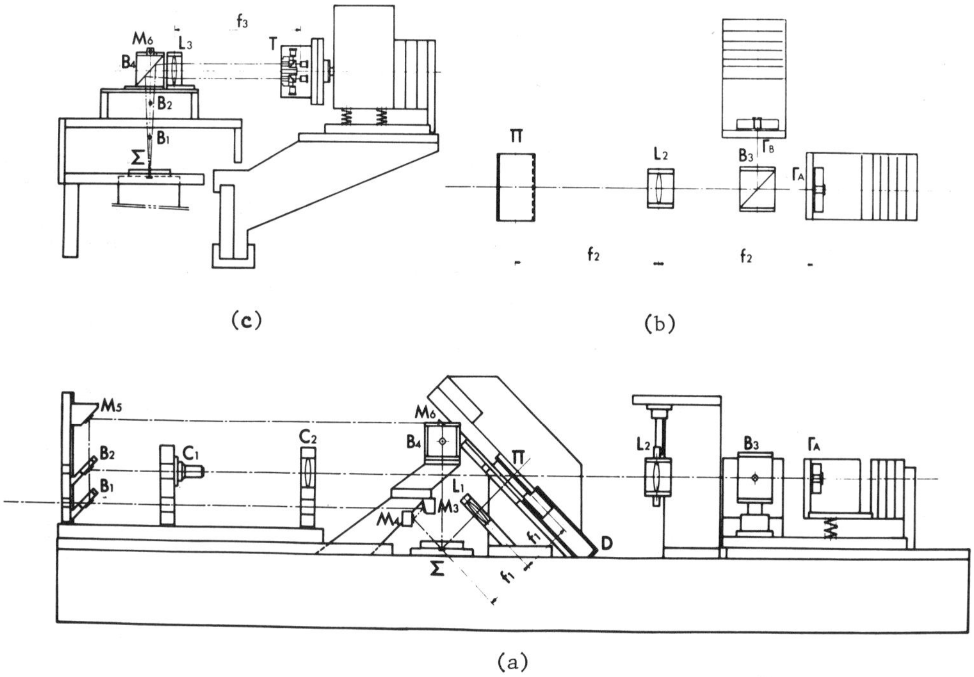

Fig.18. Optical system of experimental apparatus

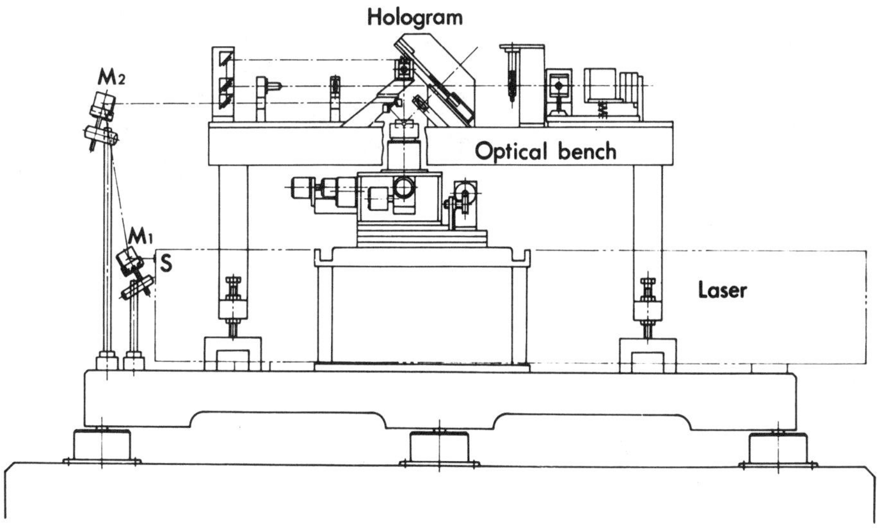

Fig.19. Total system

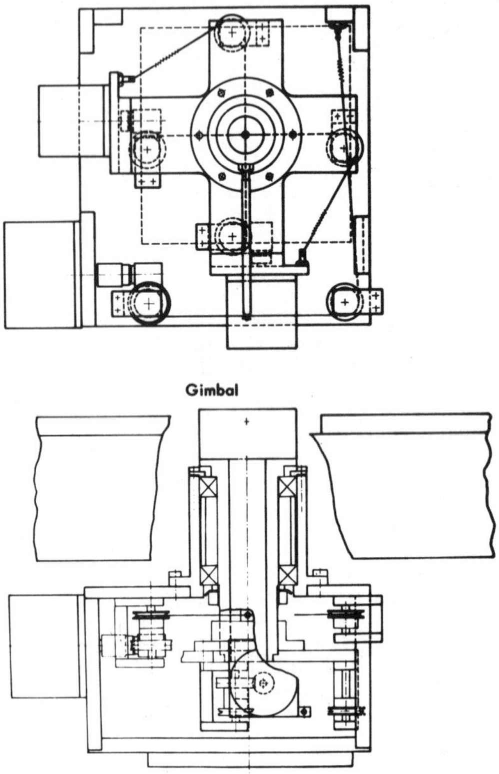

Fig.20. Driving mechanisms

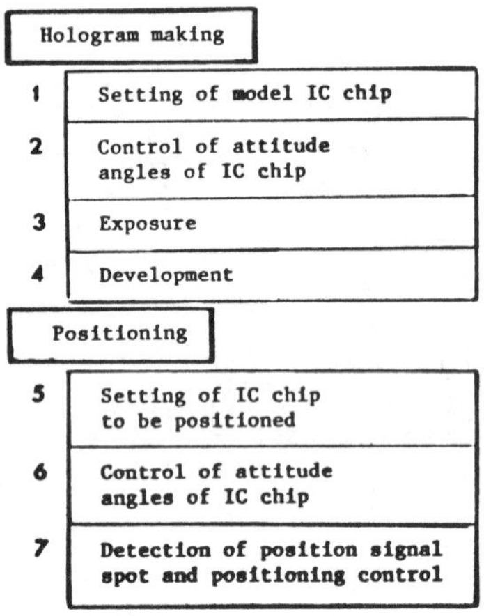
Hologram making
1 Setting of model IC chip
2 Control of attitude angles of IC chip
3 Exposure
4 Development
Positioning
5 Setting of IC chip to be positioned
6 Control of attitude angles of IC chip
7 Detection of position signal spot and positioning control

Fig.21. Sequence of control

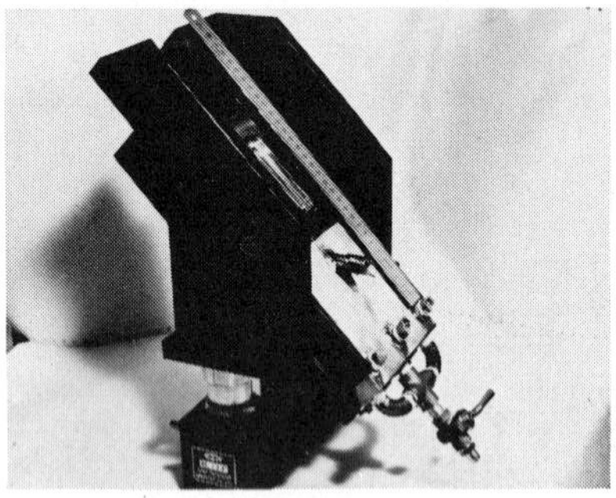

Photo 4. Developing equipment

Photo 5. Exterior view of total system

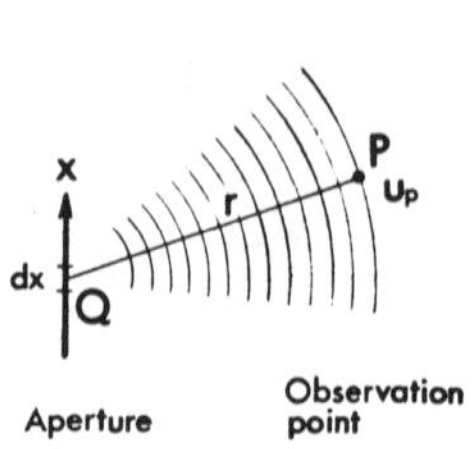

Fig.(I.1) Diffraction by aperture

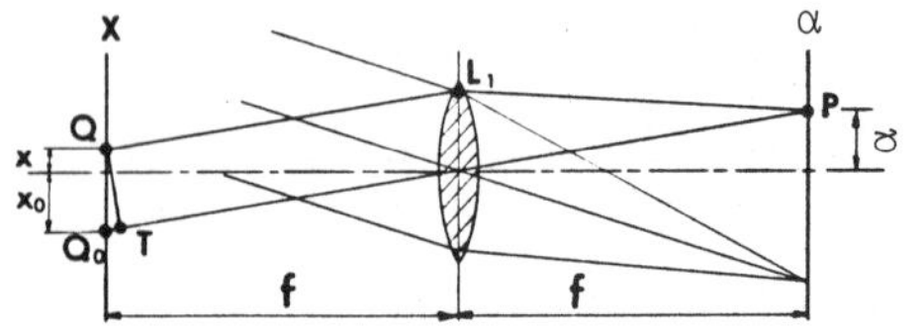

Fig.(I.2) Property of lens

PROFILE PATTERN RECOGNITION SYSTEM FOR MACHINE PARTS

H. Kono

Mechanical Engineering Laboratory, 4-12-1 Igusa, Suginamiku, Tokyo, Japan

ABSTRACT

For automated assembly and materials handling in a small lot production type of machinery shop, the pattern recognition of machine parts is inevitably required. Moreover, the processing of the pattern recognition must be executed in on-line processing. This paper deals with a newly developed methodology and related system for the automated pattern recognition of machine parts.
The pattern recognition algorithms aiming at the pattern recognition in on-line processing have been developed through the computer simulation. Also, the recognition rate, the accuracy and the limit of the pattern recognition algorithms have been assessed by means of the computer simulation. Thirty matching patterns which are symbolized referring to the sectional profile patterns of the machine parts commonly encountered in a machinery shop are stored in the minicomputer memory. The parts matching is performed in the combination of these 30 matching patterns. The developed profile pattern recognition system is featured by the capability of recognizing parts in less than 10 seconds per one parts and classifying into 100 kinds of machine parts.

INTRODUCTION

During past fifteen years, the foresighted and extensive research (Ref. 1,2,3,4,5) conducted in pattern recognition and artificial intelligence have produced numerous advanced techniques for image analysis. Intelligence robots with visual sensors have been developed and reported in several universities and research organizations (Ref. 6,7,8). The development of these robots has been aimed at the investigation of artificial intelligence. For this reason, the pattern recognition time or other processing time has not been regarded as important on the estimation of the system. Furthermore, these intelligence robots usually require a large or medium scale computer to be operated. Therefore, it will take a time for the intelligence robot to become economically feasible in practical industrial applications. Recently, several research (Ref. 9,10,11,12,13,14) aiming at the practical application in industry have been executed.
When it is planned to automate the assembly and materials handling process in manufacturing factory in which various kinds and small amount of products are manufactured, it is necessary to automate the pattern recognition of machine parts or the like. Moreover, the processing of the pattern recognition must be executed in on-line processing. The pattern recognition system with visual sensors will provide such various informations as the kinds of machine parts to be manipulated, position and direction of the machine parts on the worktable. The manipulator system applied to an industrial robot can provide more flexible operations and adaptive capabilities. Eye-Hand system cooperated both these pattern recognition capability and manipulator will operate effectively in the assembly and materials handling of machine parts.
For the purpose of developing the Eye-Hand system, the Eye system which has the pattern recognition capability of machine parts has been developed in this research. The pattern recognition algorithms aiming at the pattern recognition in on-line processing have been developed through the computer simulation.
In the developed pattern recognition process, firstly, the pattern data are sampled using a television camera in the pattern of 64x48 meshes that is 1,0 binary information. On the basis of the sampled pattern data, the pattern transformation for specifying the directional code of the contour portion around the profile pattern is executed. The directional code is classified into 7 codes, that is, horizontal, vertical, right slope, left slope, vertex, body and space.
Secondly, the corner detection is performed by tracing the transformed pattern codes. This processing is continued successively until the tracing of the contour portion is completed. The pattern matching processing to the sectional profile pattern of machine parts is decided by discriminating the number, the type and the arrangement of the corners. Thirty matching patterns which are symbolized referring to the sectional profile patterns of the machine parts commonly encountered in a machinery shop are stored in the minicomputer memory. The parts matching is performed in the combination of these 30 matching patterns. The pattern recognition algorithms (Ref. 15, 16,17,18) have been developed by using TOSBAC -3400 computer.

METHODOLOGY OF PATTERN RECOGNITION

Identification of Configuration Pattern

The profile pattern of an object is assumed as a polygon and the configuration pattern is identified on the basis of the number of the corners composed an object, the type and the arrangement of the corners.

Number of corners. Two configurations shown in Fig. 1 are identified as a square (pattern of four corners) and a hexagon (pattern of six corners) respectively. These simple configuration patterns can be classified only by the number of corners. Other two configuration pattern shown in Fig. 2 are identified as heptagons (pattern of seven corners), if the identification is performed only by the number of corners. But, as the configuration pattern shown in Fig. 2(b) has a concave portion, these two configurations are remarkably different. Therefore, it is impossible to identify these two configuration patterns as far as the identification is performed only by the number of corners.

Type of corners. The identification of configuration pattern is easily performed by adding the information of angles. The corner which has an angle of 180° or more is categorized as a concave corner. On the contrary, the corner which has an angle of less than 180° is categorized as a convex corner. Appling this methodology on the identification of configuration pattern, it will be more simple and easy to classify various kinds of patterns. Second parameter of feature extraction is the type of corners. The angle $\theta_{e,i+1}$ of the (i+1)th corner is calculated by the following equation using the angle θ_i and θ_{i+1} shown in Fig. 2(b).

$$\theta_{e,i+1}=180-(\theta_i-\theta_{i+1}) \quad (1)$$

The type of corners which composes the profile pattern is classified into 4 categories. Type 0 is the pattern of all convex corners. Type 1 is the pattern in which concave corners are arranged separately as an example of convex, concave and convex corner. This arrangement is expressed by the equation of 0-1-0. Symbol 0 and 1 represent convex and concave corner respectively. Another type 2 of corners is the pattern in which concave corners are arranged in a row as an example of convex, concave, concave and convex corner which is represented by the equation of 0-1-1-0. The last type is type 3 of corners. This type is the mixed type of type 1 and type 2 of corners. On the basis of this methodology, both configuration patterns shown in Fig. 1 are identified as the type 0 of corners. Similarly, configuration pattern shown Fig. 2(a) is identified as a heptagon with all convex corners and that of Fig. 2(b) as a heptagon with one concave and six convex corners. Therefore, configuration pattern shown in Fig. 2(a) is identified as the type 0 of corners and the other shown in Fig. 2(b) as the type 1 of corners. By adopting this parameter of feature extraction, the discrimination of these two configuration patterns may be performed.

Arrangement of corners. If more complicated configuration patterns shown in Fig. 3 are become the subject of recognition, identification is not sufficient only considering the number and the type of corners as the parameter of feature extraction. Because, E and H-shaped configuration patterns are identified as the same. Both E and H-shaped configuration patterns have 8 and 4 convex and concave corners respectively. Moreover, both patterns have type 2 of corners. Therefore, it is necessary to define another parameter of feature extraction. The third parameter is the mask number represented the arrangement of corners. The mask 1 is defined by the arrangement in which corners are arranged as concave, convex, convex and concave represented by the equation of 1-0-0-1. This mask 1 number represents the number of the convex groovy portion of the configuration pattern. Another mask 2 is defined by the arrangement of corners in the equation of 0-1-1-0. Similarly, the mask 2 number represents the number of the concave groovy portion of the configuration pattern. Accordingly, E and H-shaped configuration patterns have the number of the value 1 and 0 for the mask 1 number. These two configuration patterns are discriminated properly. Three parameters of feature extraction are proposed on the profile pattern recognition system for machine parts.

Detection of Corners

On the profile pattern recognition of machine parts, it is necessary to detect corners which composes the configuration pattern of machine parts and so on. The algorithms of the corner detection for the profile pattern recognition are developed aiming at the application to the recognition in on-line processing.

Pattern transformation. The pattern transformation for specifying the directional code of the contour portion around the configuration pattern is executed. Depending on the binary 1,0 information on the 2x2 mesh points disposed adjacent to each other of the mesh pattern, the directional code of each contour portion is defined. The 2x2 mesh points are represented in the symbol of $A_{i,j}$, $A_{i,j+1}$, $A_{i+1,j}$, $A_{i+1,j+1}$. The directional code is classified into 7 codes by the following Boolean equations. The 7 directional codes are horizontal, vertical, right slope, left slope, vertex, body and space. In the logic equations, x, + and overline as in $\overline{A_{i,j}}$ indicate logical AND, OR and NOT respectively.

$$\text{HORI}[-]=(A_{i,j}\times A_{i+1,j}\times\overline{A_{i,j+1}}\times\overline{A_{i+1,j+1}})+(\overline{A_{i,j}}\times\overline{A_{i+1,j}}\times A_{i,j+1}\times A_{i+1,j+1}) \quad (2)$$

$$\text{SLOR}[)]=(A_{i,j}\times\overline{A_{i+1,j}}\times A_{i,j+1}\times A_{i+1,j+1})+(A_{i,j}\times A_{i+1,j}\times\overline{A_{i,j+1}}\times A_{i+1,j+1}) \quad (3)$$

$$\text{SLOL}[(]=(\overline{A_{i,j}}\times A_{i+1,j}\times A_{i,j+1}\times A_{i+1,j+1})+(A_{i,j}\times A_{i+1,j}\times A_{i,j+1}\times\overline{A_{i+1,j+1}}) \quad (4)$$

$$\text{VERT}[I]=(A_{i,j}\times\overline{A_{i+1,j}}\times A_{i,j+1}\times\overline{A_{i+1,j+1}})+(\overline{A_{i,j}}\times A_{i+1,j}\times\overline{A_{i,j+1}}\times A_{i+1,j+1}) \quad (5)$$

$$BODY[*]=(A_{i,j} \times A_{i+1,j} \times A_{i,j+1} \times A_{i+1,j+1}) \quad (6)$$

$$SPAC[\ ]=(\overline{A_{i,j}} \times \overline{A_{i+1,j}} \times \overline{A_{i,j+1}} \times \overline{A_{i+1,j+1}}) \quad (7)$$

$$\begin{aligned} VERX[+]=&(A_{i,j} \times \overline{A_{i+1,j}} \times \overline{A_{i,j+1}} \times \overline{A_{i+1,j+1}}) \\ &+(\overline{A_{i,j}} \times A_{i+1,j} \times \overline{A_{i,j+1}} \times \overline{A_{i+1,j+1}}) \\ &+(\overline{A_{i,j}} \times \overline{A_{i+1,j}} \times A_{i,j+1} \times \overline{A_{i+1,j+1}}) \\ &+(\overline{A_{i,j}} \times \overline{A_{i+1,j}} \times \overline{A_{i,j+1}} \times A_{i+1,j+1}) \\ &+(A_{i,j} \times \overline{A_{i+1,j}} \times \overline{A_{i,j+1}} \times A_{i+1,j+1}) \\ &+(\overline{A_{i,j}} \times A_{i+1,j} \times A_{i,j+1} \times \overline{A_{i+1,j+1}}) \quad (8) \end{aligned}$$

Corner detection. The corner detection is performed by tracing the transformed pattern codes. Detected corners are not necessarily actual corners but include as it is called imaginary corners which do not actually exist. On the processing of corner detection, an imaginary corner is detected at first in any case. After successively analyzing the transformed pattern codes in the vicinity of the first detected corner, the direction of the edge line locus is determined on the basis of the results thereof. Simultaneously, the informations of the directional code are stored in the memory of the pattern recognition unit before proceeding the analysis in the direction of the edge locus. Where the stored locus informations are not imaginary, furthermore, the tracing is continued along the locus direction stored in the memory, in a successive manner until an imaginary corner is detected. On finding an imaginary corner, the information accumulated so far is stored with the coordinates of the imaginary corner. The operation just discussed is continued successively until the tracing of the contour portion is completed.

When the tracing is completed, the detected imaginary corners are now analyzed as to whether they could be real corners based on the informations about two adjacent directional codes. That is to say, if both sides of an imaginary corner happen to be the same code, it is apparent that the detected imaginary corner cannot be the real corner. When the coordinates of the real corners are stored in the memory, excluding the imaginary corners, the processing of corner detection is completed.

It sometimes happens that a plurarity of corners is found at extremely close positions to each other. In this case, such corners may be an identical point and must be judged accordingly. In other words, not all of the detected corners are not necessarily real. With this fact, a threshold value as to when a plurarity of closely positioned corners is judged to the identical point must be determined. Suitable degree of proximity for judging closely positioned corners to be one corner will depend on the size of a configuration pattern or an object which is identified. The threshold value can be automatically determined by the pattern recognition unit in the processing of the corner detection based on the size of the configuration pattern.

By using the coordinates of the individual corners stored in the processing of the corner detection, the approximate size of the configuration pattern can be calculated from the location of such corners and the selection of a suitable thrshold value is determined automatically. After the selection of the threshold value, the stored informations regarding the corners are examined to see whether any closely positioned corners fall within the selected threshold value. If the individual corners are sufficiently far apart, these corners are determined as real.

Separation of Inner Pattern

On the processing which separates the inner pattern from the configuration pattern to be recognized, the separator determines a first scanning line and scans the binary pattern informations from the first scanning line and counts the number of points of variance from 0 to 1 or vice versa of the binary signals on each scanning line, memorizing a N_{cmax} that is a maximum counting number of points of variance. For the separation of the inner pattern, except for the period of no variance ($N_c=0$) and the period of last variance ($N_c= N_{cmax}$), the signals in the period of variance of every even-number count are inverted from 0 to 1 while the signals in the period of variance of every odd-number count are inverted from 1 to 0. The counting of the points of variance and binary pattern informations inversion are carried out sequentially from the first ($N=1$) to the last scanning line ($N=N_{max}$), thereby converting the binary pattern informations. More particularly, on the scanning line $N=N_i$ of the binary pattern shown in Fig. 4(a), the signal inversion does not take place in the period of no variance (0), while inverting the signals in the period of first variance (1) from 1 to 0, the second variance (2) from 0 to 1, the third variance (3) from 1 to 0. The signals in the period of fourth or last variance (4) do not undergo the inversion. By sequentially repeating the conversion of the binary pattern informations at the respective scanning lines, a separated inner pattern shown in Fig. 4(b) may be obtained.

Parts Matching

Thirty matching patterns which are symbolized referring to the sectional profile patterns of the machine parts commonly encountered in a machinery shop are considered. Matching patterns are equivalent to the pattern number from 1 to 30 as shown in Table 1. The configuration pattern of the matching pattern number 7 is assumed the following model that is the sectional profile pattern of nut parts. In the same way, the matching pattern number 26 is the spline or gear parts. The trigonometry that shows the front view and the side or plane view as an illustration of parts has been adopted especially as the methodology of the matching for machine parts. Consequently, parts matching is performed in the combination of the matching patterns obtained from three perpendicular directions. These three are vertical, first horizontal and second horizontal directions. Parts matching equation P_{37} for parts number 37 is defined by the following equation. Where $P_{7,v}$ means that the recognition result in the vertical direction is matching to the pattern number 7. Also, $P_{2,h1}$ is matching to the pattern number 2 in the first horizontal direction and $P_{2,h2}$ matching to the pattern number 2 in the second horizontal direction. In the logic equation, x and + indicate logical AND and OR respectively.

$$P_{37}=(P_{7,v} \times P_{2,h1} \times P_{2,h2})+(P_{2,v} \times P_{7,h1} \times P_{2,h2}) +(P_{2,v} \times P_{2,h1} \times P_{7,h2}) \quad (9)$$

Applying this methodology to the processing of parts matching, algorithms will be greatly simlified. In this result, the capacity for memorizing matching parts is extremely little and the processing time becomes short.

SOFTWARE

The schematic block diagram of the developed profile pattern recognition algorithms is shown in Fig. 5. The profile pattern recognition algorithms are consisted of the processing of input of pattern, pattern transformation, corner detection, setting-up of threshold, discrimination of corners closely positioned, discrimination of convex and concave configuration, discrimination of inner pattern, separation of inner pattern, deletion of inner pattern discriminated and pattern analysis. Fig. 6 shows the processing of corner detection more precisely. The profile pattern recognition algorithms aiming at the pattern recognition in on-line processing have been developed through the computer simulation. TOSBAC-3400 computer with 96k words core memory has been used on the development of this pattern recognition algorithms. The performance of the developed pattern recognition algorithms is shown in Fig. 7. The curve for recognition rate vs. corner angle is referred as a characteristic curve. The parameter UM is the distance between one and another corner. The recognition limit of the corner angle exists between 225° and 315°, because the directional codes are considered only 4 directions. This character is symmetry with the 180° of corner angle. In Fig. 8, the theoretical recognition rate for various kinds of configuration patterns are compared with the experimental results which were obtained through the computer simulation. The experimental results are shown as the results obtained by the 100 trials of simulation which are changed the position and the direction of the configuration patterns. As the result, the sampling points which are necessary to recognize the profile pattern are extremely little. On the processing of the pattern analysis, such as corners coordinates, gravity center coordinates, vertexes angle, corners angle, length of sides and diameter are calculated. Simultanously, the pattern matching and the parts matching are performed based on the number of the detected corners, the type and the arrangement of the corners.

HARDWARE

The overview of the profile pattern recognition system and the conceptual sketch of the system are shown in Fig. 9 and Fig. 10 respectively. This system consists of two television cameras, a worktable, a control unit and a minicomputer PDP-11/34.

Visual Input System

Two television cameras are utilized as visual input devices in the developed system. The one (vertical camera) is fixed above the worktable in vertical direction and is used to recognize the position and orientation of the machine parts on the worktable. The other (horizontal camera) is fixed side the worktable in horizontal direction and is used to recognize the side pattern of the machine parts. The optical axis of the vertical camera is concentric with the rotational axis of the worktable. Two optical axes of the vertical camera and the horizontal camera are perpendicular to each other. These two cameras mount the zooming-up mechanisms which are automatically zooming up the profile pattern of machine parts.
One of the video outputs is selected by a switch controlled by the minicomputer. The video output signal is quantified into two 1 and 0 levels, by a comparator whose threshold level is manually adjustable into 1,000 steps. The 1 level corresponds to a dark image and 0 to a bright image. The quantified video signal is fed to a buffer register. The buffer register is a 256 (16x16) bit serial-in parallel-out shift register. Parallel outputs of the buffer register are transferred to the computer memory through the direct memory access channel. The time required to read in a complete image consisting of 256x192 meshes is 1/60 sec.. The read-in time is equal to the one flame scanning time of the television camera. Sampling mode is selected in manual. Sampling mode 1/1 is the 256x192 meshes. Sampling mode 1/2 and 1/4 are the 128x96 and 64x48 meshes respectively. On the developed profile pattern recognition system, sampling mode 1/4 is selected in general.

Lighting Method

The lighting method is important at the image information input process, as one of the processing step in the pattern recognition. Two lighting methods shown in Fig. 11 are compared. One is a shadow lighting method shown in Fig. 11(a) and the other is a reflective lighting method shown in Fig. 11(b). The experiments with respect to the two methods were conducted with a gear as a sample of the machine parts. The experimental results are shown in Fig. 12. The figures show the relationship of the threshold level permitting good quality image vs. illumination intensity, i.e. the effective zone. In the shadow lighting method, the effective zone is wide and image is little effected by the illumination intensity.
Fig. 13 shows a monitor image and a digitized data when cylinder parts and flange parts are caught by the reflective lighting method. In the reflective lighting, the image effected

strictly by the shadow produced by the illumination. Particularly, it is very difficult to illuminate the lustrous curvature surface. Therefore, the shadow lighting method is adopted in the pattern recognition system for machine parts.

Worktable Control System

The worktable has three degree of freedom of motion, that is, two liner X and Y axes and rotational θ axis. These X, Y and θ axes are operated by the electrical pulse motors. The worktable is available for controlling the position and the orientation of the machine parts and is numerically controlled through the program controlled channel connected to the minicomputer PDP-11/34. The working range of X and Y axes are ±200mm respectively and for θ axis is ±180°. The stopping motion accuracy of X and Y axes are ±0.1mm and for θ is ±0.25°. The rotational speed of θ is 60°/sec in the maxmum state.

Operation of the Recognition System

The pattern recognition process is shown in Fig. 14. In this case, a nut is caught by the shadow lighting. In the figure, (a) is a monitor image, (b) is a digitized image, (c) is a input data, (d) to (f) are recognition processes, (g) is the display of the recognition results and (h) is the display of the parts matching results. The recognition time per one direction of the machine parts is about 1 second. The typical computer running time for the zooming-up, the worktable moving and the recognition are about 4 seconds, 3 seconds and 3 seconds respectively. The programs have been written in an ASSEMBLER and FORTRAN LANGUAGE, and occupy about 20k words including data areas of 3k words for the image storage area.

CONCLUSIONS

The developed profile pattern recognition system for machine parts can be applied to not only industrial robots but also to other system such as automatic assembly machines. Particularly, on the development of the Eye-Hand system, the developed system can be applied more easily.

REFERENCES

(1) H. Freeman, Techniques for the Digital Computer Analysis of Chain-Coded Arbitary Plane Curves, Proc. of National Electronics Conf., Vol.17, (1962).

(2) L. G. Roberts, Machine Perception of Three-Dimensional Solid, Tech. Rep. No.315 MIT, (1963).

(3) A. Gozman, Decomposition of a Visual Scene into Three-Dimensional Bodies, Fall Joint Computer Conf., p291 (1968).

(4) T. Sakai, M. Nagao and S. Fujibayashi, Line Extraction and Pattern Detection in a Photograph, Pattern Recognition 1, p233 (1969).

(5) A. Rosenfeld and M. Thurston, Edge and Curve Detection for Visual Scene Analysis, IEEE Trans. on Computer, C-20, p562 (1971).

(6) Y. Shirai and S. Tsuji, Extraction of the Line Drawing of 3-Dimensional Objects by Sequential Illumination from Several Directions, 2nd. Artificial Intelligence Conf., p71 (1971).

(7) Y. Shirai, A Contex Sensitive Line Finder for Recognition of Polyhedra, Artificial Intelligence 4-2, p95 (1973).

(8) C. Rosen et al., Exploratory Research in Advanced Automation, First Semi-Annual Report, NSF Grant GI-38100X, SRI Project 2591, Stanford Research Institute (1973).

(9) Y. Tsuboi, E. Tsuda, T. Shiraishi and N. Kosaka, A Mini-computer Controlled Industrial Robot with Optical Sensor in Gripper, Proc. of 3rd. Int. Symp. on Industrial Robots, p343 (1973).

(10) H. Yoda and M. Ejiri, A Hand-Eye-System for Selection Process, Proc. 2nd. Symp. on Industrial Robots, Chubu Automations Society, (1973).

(11) M. Ejiri and H. Yoda, A Process for Detecting Defects in Complicated Patterns, Computer Graphics and Image Processing, Vol.2, p326 (1973).

(12) W.B. Heginbotham, C.J. Page and A. Pugh, Robot Research at the University of Nottingham, Proc. of 4th. Int. Symp. on Industrial Robots, p53 (1974).

(13) S. Hagihara and Y. Tsuboi et al., Automatic Assembly of Components with Flexible Wire, Int. Conf. on Production Engineering, p480 (1974).

(14) G.J. Agin, An Experimental Vision System for Industrial Application, Proc. of 6th. Int. Symp. on Industrial Robots, p135 (1976).

(15) H. Kono, Algorithms for Profile Pattern Recognition, Proc. of 13th. SICE, Japan, p503 (1974).

(16) H.Kono, Accuracy of Profile Pattern Recognition, Proc. of 13th. SICE, Japan, p505 (1974).

(17) H. Kono, Recognition Performances in Profile Pattern Recognition, Proc. of 14th. SICE, Japan, p269 (1975).

(18) H. Kono, Profile Pattern Recognition System for Machine Parts, Proc. of 15th. SICE, Japan, p455 (1976).

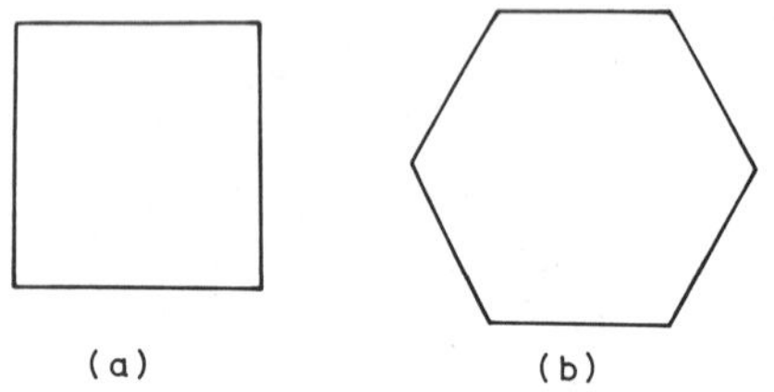

Fig. 1 Convex configuration patterns

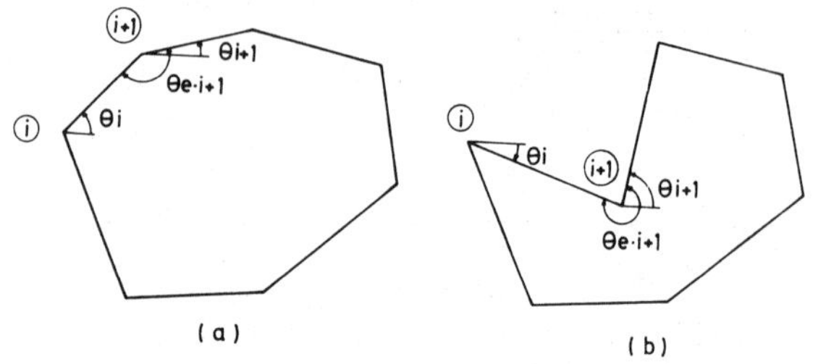

Fig. 2 Convex and concave configuration pattern

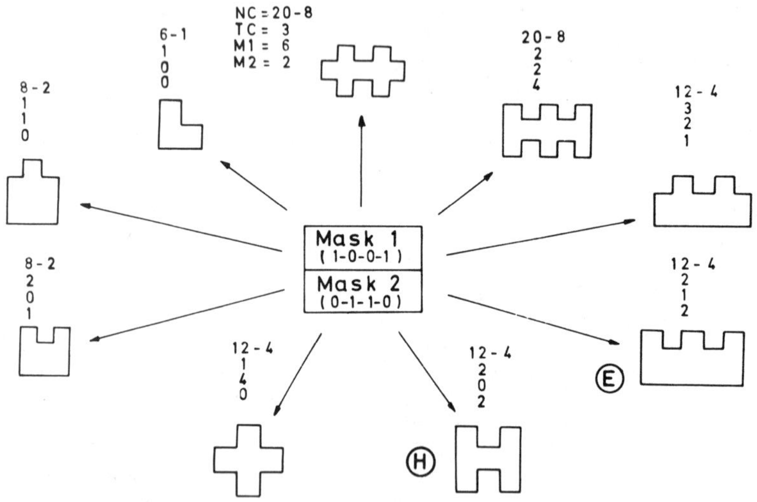

Fig. 3 Complicated concave configuration patterns

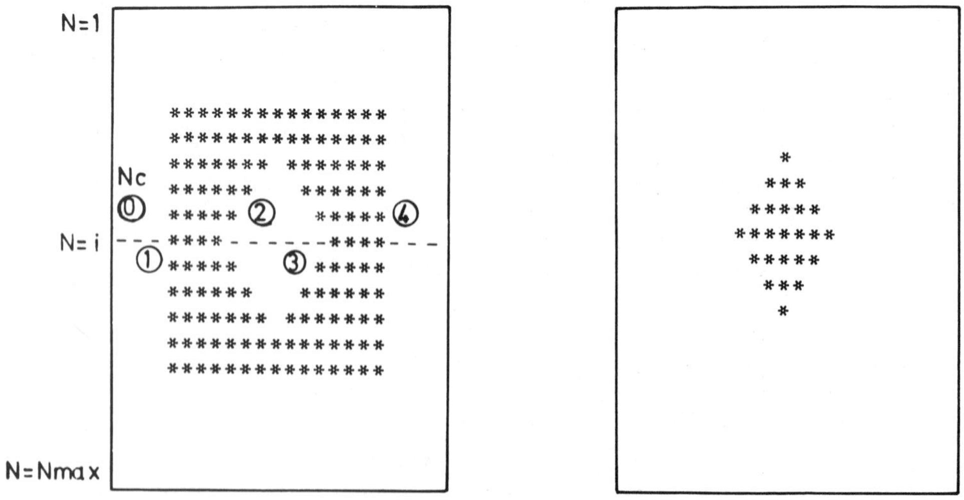

(a) Configuration pattern (b) Separated inner pattern

Fig. 4 Separation of inner pattern

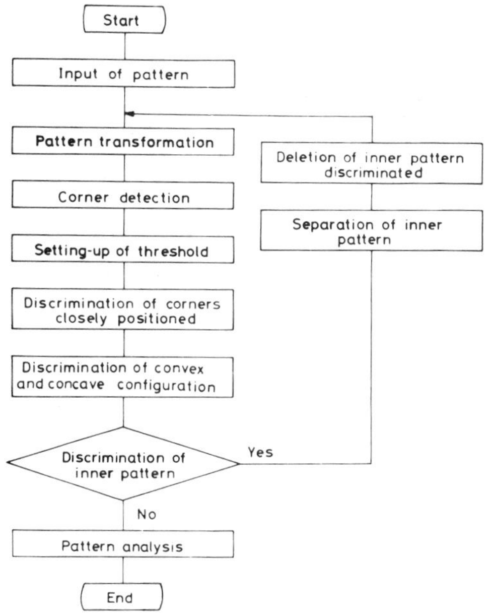

Fig. 5 Procedure of pattern recognition

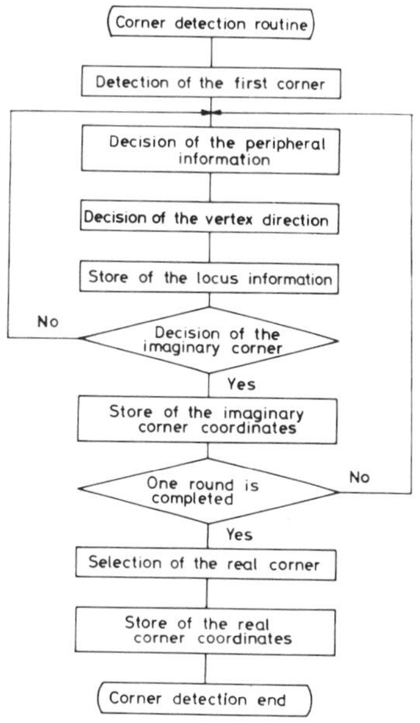

Fig. 6 Procedure of corner detection

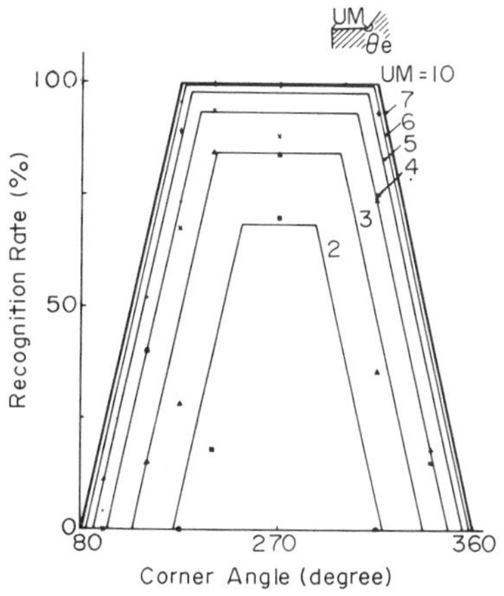

Fig. 7 Characteristics of the corner angle detection

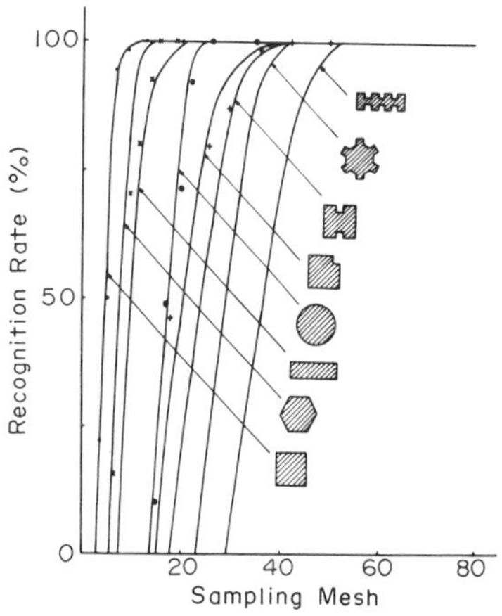

Fig. 8 Characteristics of the pattern recognition rate

Fig. 9 Overview of the system

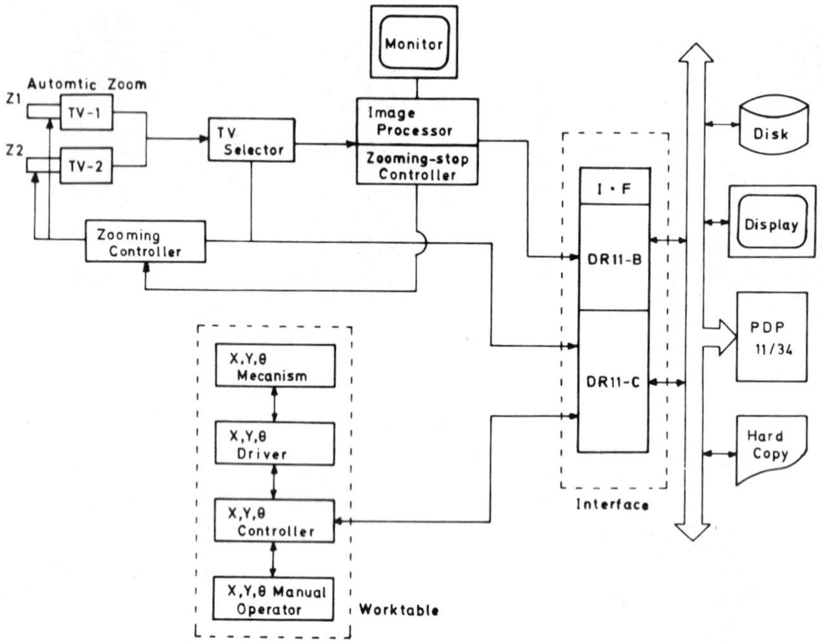

Fig. 10 Block diagram of the system

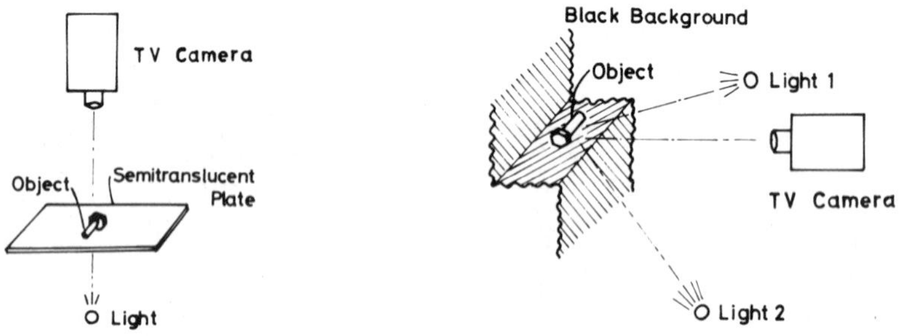

(a) Shadow lighting (b) Reflective lighting

Fig. 11 Lighting method

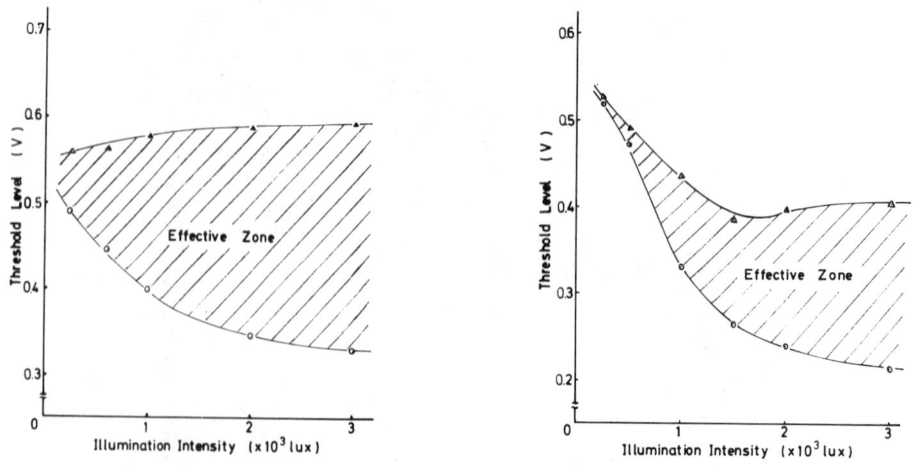

(a) Shadow lighting (b) Reflective lighting

Fig. 12 Comparision of the effective zone

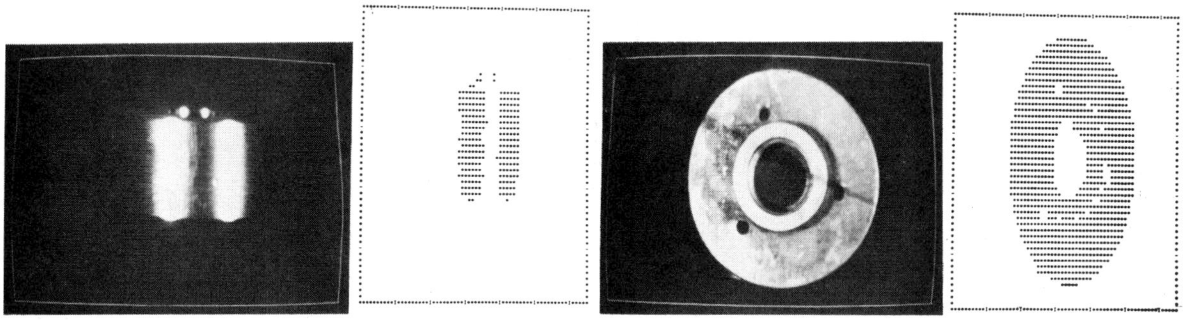

(a) Monitor image (b) Input data (a) Monitor image (b) Input data

(1) Cylinder parts (2) Flange parts

Fig. 13 Disadvantage of the reflective lighting

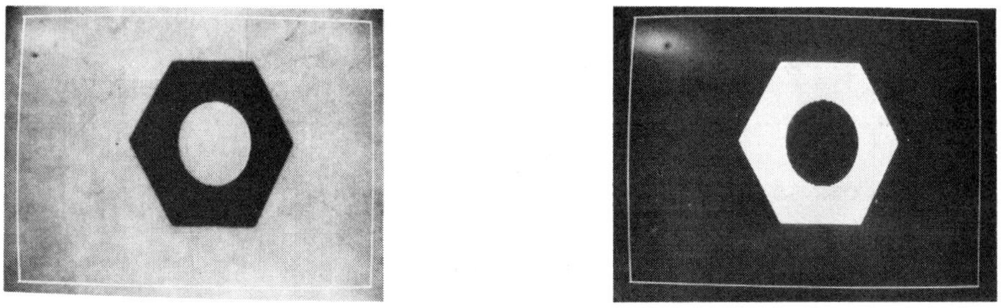

(a) Monitor image (b) Digitized image

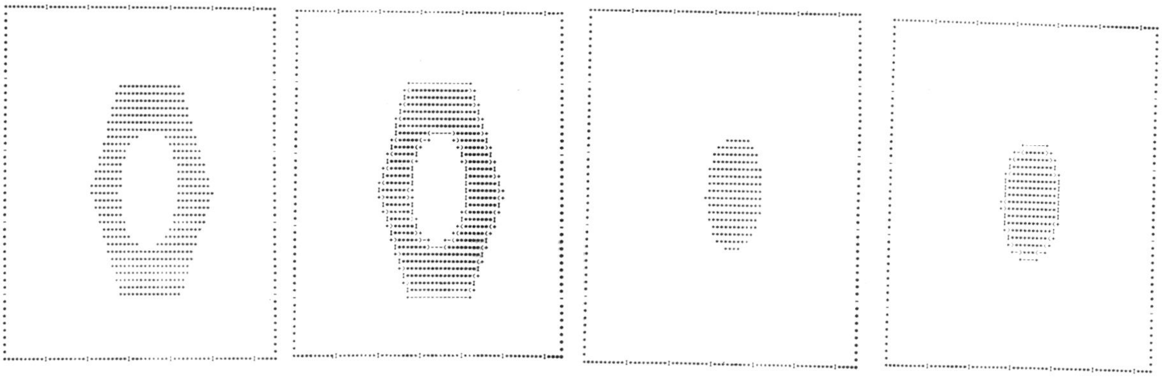

(c) Input data (d) Pattern transformation and corner detection of outer pattern (e) Inner pattern separation (f) Pattern transformation and corner detection of inner pattern

```
PLEASE INPUT START  START

   ** V  RECOGNITION **

 OUTER PATTERN=      6 CORNERS        CONVEX        SAMPLE= 32
CORNER TYPE= 0 MASK1 NUMB= 0 MASK2 NUMB= 0
 0 0 0 0 0 0
X-COR  -3.9   6.9  11.8   7.5  -3.3  -8.1
Y-COR  -7.5  -7.5   0.9  10.0  10.0   1.5
GRAVITY CENTER  XG=   1.8  YG=   1.2
THETA 180.0 119.7  65.0   0.0 -60.3-115.0
ETHET 115.0 119.7 125.2 115.0 119.7 125.2
 INNER PATTERN=  CONVEX CIRCLE * 8*  CONVEX        SAMPLE= 18
CORNER TYPE= 0 MASK1 NUMB= 0 MASK2 NUMB= 0
 0 0 0 0 0 0 0 0
X-COR  -0.9   3.9   6.9   6.9   3.3  -0.9  -3.3  -3.3
Y-COR  -3.9  -3.9  -0.3   3.3   6.3   6.3   3.3  -1.5
GRAVITY CENTER  XG=   1.6  YG=   1.2
RADIUS          R=    5.6

 * MATCHING TO PATTERN=  7 *
```

(g) Display of recognition results

```
PLEASE INPUT START  START

   ** V  RECOGNITION **

 * MATCHING TO PATTERN=  7 *

   ** H  RECOGNITION **

 * MATCHING TO PATTERN=  2 *

   ** H  RECOGNITION **

 * MATCHING TO PATTERN=  2 *

** MATCHING  TO  PARTS= 37 **

RECOGNITION END
```

(h) Display of parts matching results

Fig. 14 Pattern recognition process

Table 1 One hundred kinds of matching parts

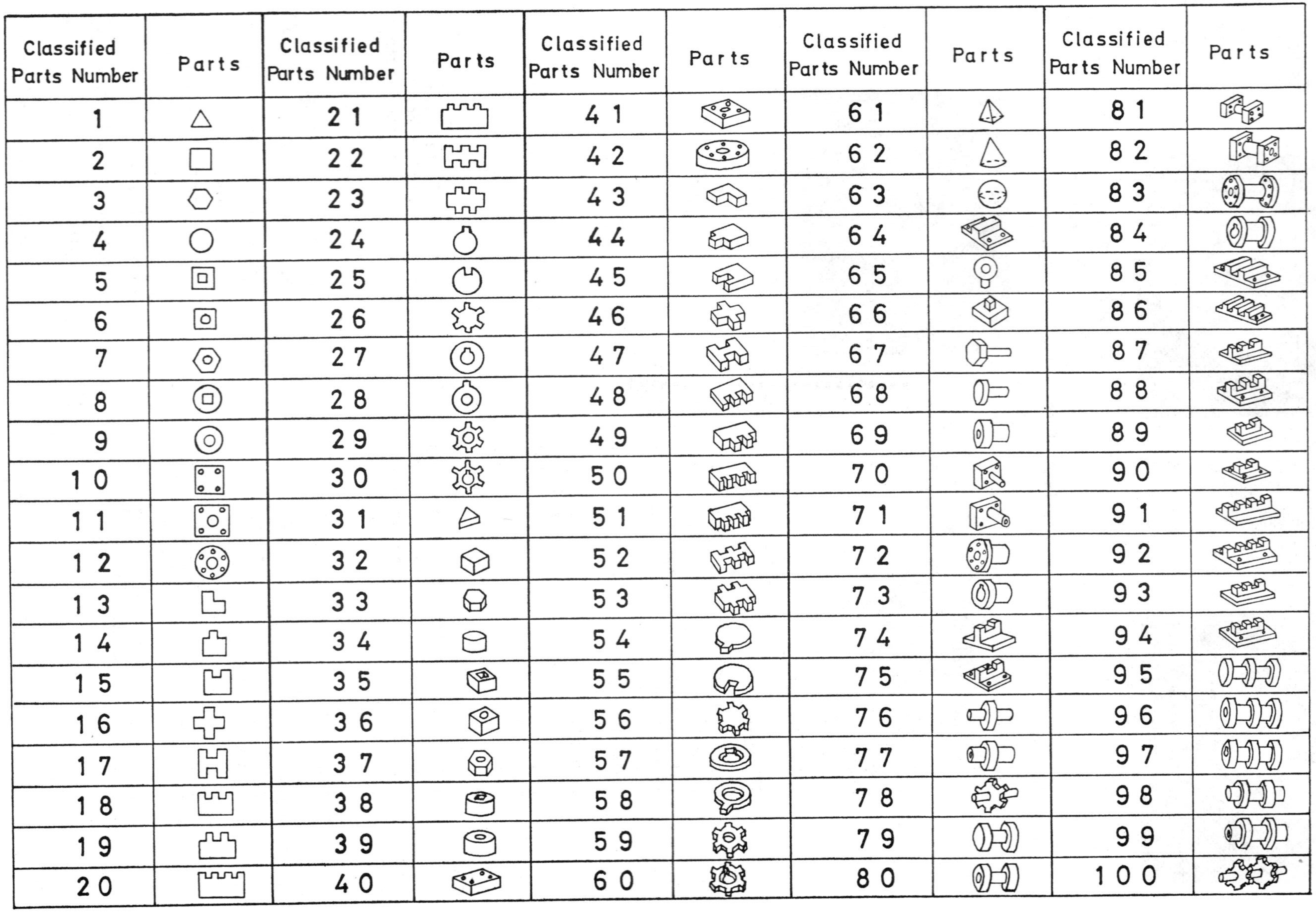

Classified Parts Number	Parts	Classified Parts Number	Parts	Classified Parts Number	Parts	Classified Parts Number	Parts	Classified Parts Number	Parts
1		21		41		61		81	
2		22		42		62		82	
3		23		43		63		83	
4		24		44		64		84	
5		25		45		65		85	
6		26		46		66		86	
7		27		47		67		87	
8		28		48		68		88	
9		29		49		69		89	
10		30		50		70		90	
11		31		51		71		91	
12		32		52		72		92	
13		33		53		73		93	
14		34		54		74		94	
15		35		55		75		95	
16		36		56		76		96	
17		37		57		77		97	
18		38		58		78		98	
19		39		59		79		99	
20		40		60		80		100	

STUDY ON AUTOMATIC VISUAL INSPECTION OF SHADOW-MASK MASTER PATTERNS

Y. Nakagawa, H. Makihira, N. Akiyama, T. Numakura and T. Nakagawa*

Production Engineering Research Laboratory, Hitachi, Ltd. 292 Yoshida-cho, Totsuka-ku, Yokohama 244, Japan
**Mobara Works, Hitachi, Ltd. 3300 Hayano, Mobara-shi, Chiba 297, Japan*

ABSTRACT

An automatic appearance inspection technique for C.P.T. shadow-mask master patterns has been developed. The system structure of the automatic inspection machine, characteristics on the pattern detection, algorithm of judgment and the experimental results are reported.

INTRODUCTION

A color picture tube (C.P.T.) has a shadow-mask at the back of its front panel. It is made of thin iron plate, on the surface of which there are many small rectangular holes arrayed in rows, and the total number of these holes is several hundred thousands per a shadow-mask.

These rectangular holes are formed by contact-exposure printing and chemical etching. For obtaining high quality of shadow-masks, it is very essential to keep high quality of a master-plate used in contact-exposure printing. The patterns on the master-plate are damaged while they are produced or used for contact-exposure printing in many times. So the master-plate should be inspected and retouched for repetitive use.

Conventionary this inspection of master patterns has been done by human eye through a magnifying glass. But it is very tedious and time-cosuming, and it is almost impossible to avoid oversights. Figure 1 shows this inspection routine by human eye in the factory, Mobara Works, Hitachi, Ltd.

The purpose of this development was to automate this routine in order to realize high speed and high reliability of the inspection and to demonstrate the economic feasibility of an automated inspection system for visual processes in C.P.T. production.

Studies on automatic pattern inspection for printed board circuits (Ref. 1), for LSI masks (Ref. 2), and hybrid circuits (Ref. 3) are known. But we cannot find precedents for applications to the C.P.T. patterns.

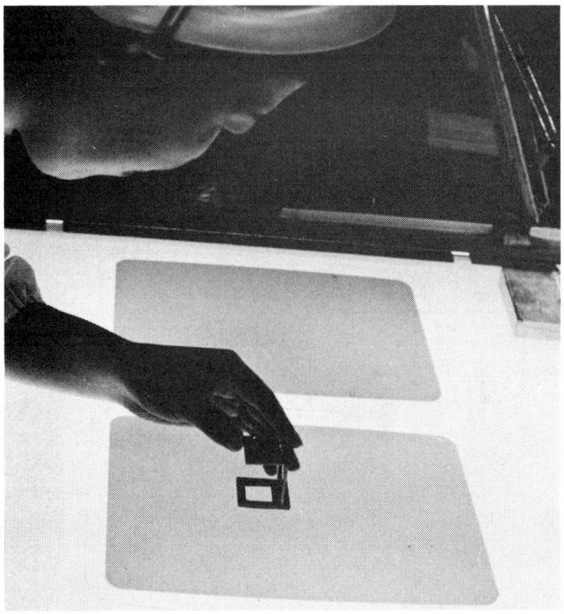

Fig. 1. Pattern inspection by human eye

CRITERIA AND EXPECTED PERFORMANCE

Master Patterns

A master pattern for shadow-masks is a dry plate, size of which is about 610x800 mm, and on its surface many stripe patterns are photo-printed within a frame line of a C.P.T. panel. Figure 2 shows the examples of the stripe patterns. There are two kinds of stripe patterns, i.e. "thick stripes" and "fine stripes" which are used for making one shadow-mask. The sizes of these stripe patterns are a little different in the sorts of C.P.T. Table 1 shows an example of the sizes, where an arrow in the width "W" of "fine stripes" means that the width is decreased from the center to the edge of a C.P.T. smoothly, that is to say "grading".

A designed stripe pattern is an exact rectangular pattern, but in real patterns there are some distortions, something like roundness of its corner, tiny unevenness of the edge line and other irregularities. Figure 3 shows the magnified photograph of the real pattern. In the automatic inspection these tiny irregularities should be tolerated.

(a) Thick stripes

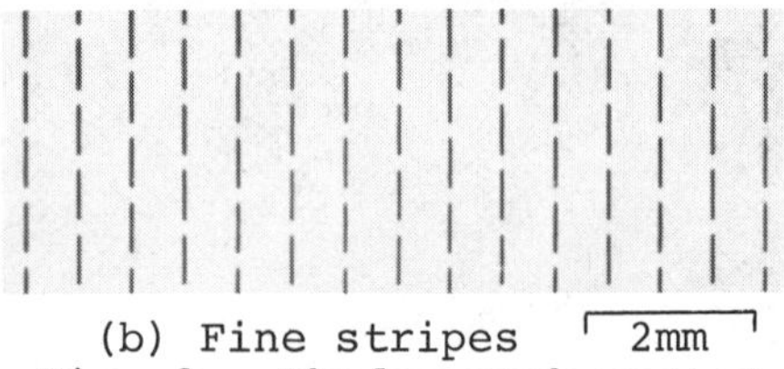

(b) Fine stripes

Fig. 2. Shadow-mask master patterns

(a) Thick stripes

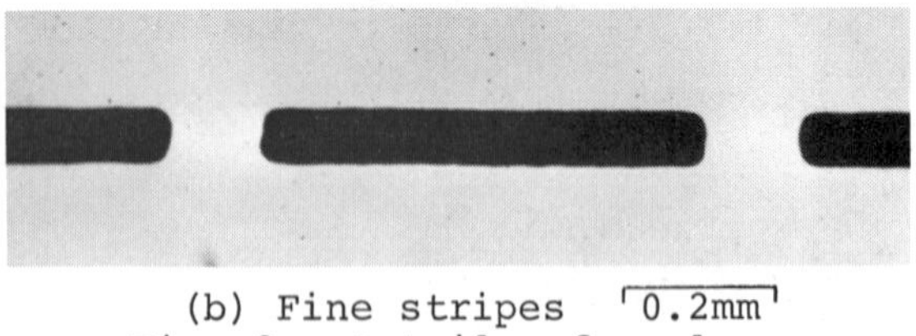

(b) Fine stripes

Fig. 3. Details of real patterns

Criteria of Inspection

Table 2 shows the criteria of the inspection, i.e. the kinds of defects and its minimum sizes to be detected. The defects can be classified to ten kinds. These defects are caused by pinholes or alien substances in the processes of pattern making, by scratches during using master-plates and by mistake of retouchment of defect patterns.

TABLE 1 Sizes of stripe patterns

	THICK STRIPES	FINE STRIPES
W	0.38	0.10 → 0.07
L	0.67	
B	0.13	
Px	0.60	
Py	0.80	

unit:mm

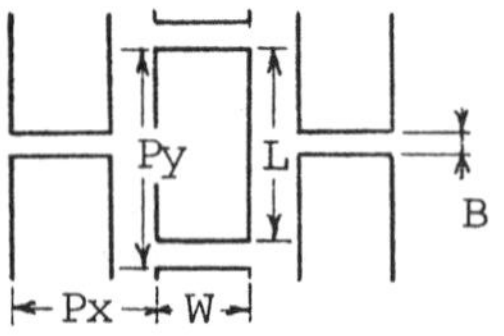

TABLE 2 Criteria of pattern inspection

No.	Name	Feature	Limit size
1	chip-1	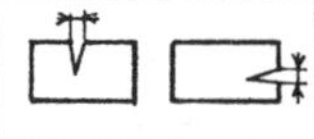	10μm
2	chip-2	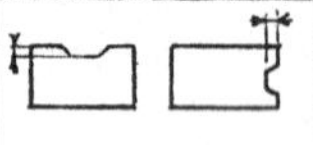	10μm
3	projection	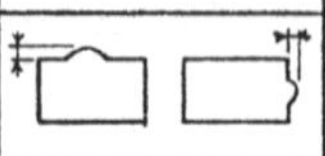	10μm
4	pinhole	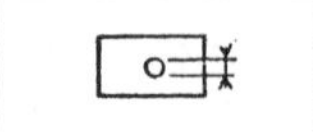	10μm
5	missed		10μm
6	too large	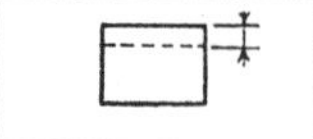	10μm
7	too small		10μm
8	dot	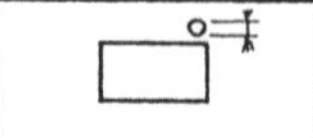	10μm
9	bridge width	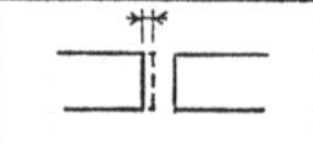	10μm
10	position error	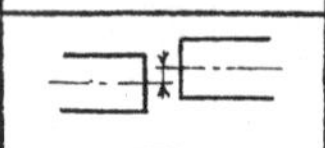	10μm

Expected Performance

In the automatic inspection the ten kinds of defects should be detected precisely.

The speed of inspection should be much higher than the visual operation. In the visual operation an operator uses a magnifying glass and checks many patterns in a visual field simultaniously. From the point of efficiency of investment, we concluded that the automatic inspection speed should be more than 800 stripe patterns per second. It is five times faster than the manual operation.

SYSTEM STRUCTURE

We considered two kinds of methods as the inspection system, i.e. a method which detects defects in an area simultaniously by applying the technique of hologram or optical Fourier transformation, and another method which inspects each pattern successively by using CCTV or other image sensors. As the result of examination, we concluded that the latter method is more practical for this inspection.

For the detector, a TV tube, solid-state image sensor or flying-spot scanner is applicable. Among them the solid-state linear image sensor has the features of small distortion, rather high speed detection and small size of detector. From these points of view, we use the solid-state linear image sensor as the detector.

Figure 4 shows the shematic structure of the inspection machine. It consists of detecting heads which include microscopes and image sensors on the real image planes, a sliding table on which a master-plate is set with the surface upward, driving motors and circuits for judgment and control. Five microscopes are arrayed transverse against the table sliding direction. Longitudinal scanning is done by moving the table to and fro. During this scanning each of the microscopes detects a row of stripe patterns respectively. Every time after the longitudinal scan is completed, the gang of microscopes is moved transverse, step by step, so as each of the microscopes can inspect a new row. Signals from the image sensors are led to circuits for judgment, and if a defect is detected, a marker is actuated to print a mark just at the back of the defect.

On the development of this automatic inspection machine, the main technical problems to be solved are the reliability of judgment and the high-speed of the inspection. They require the establishment of the high-speed and stable pattern input technique and the development of the reliable algorithm of judgment.

CHARACTERISTICS ON THE PATTERN DETECTION

Patterns are detected by the linear image sensor on the real image plane of the objective lens under the transmitted illumination. The obtained video signal from the sensor is transformed to binary signal by an adaptive thresholding. Table 3 shows the specification of the pattern detector. As the result of experiments it became apparent that its resolution is 7 μm under the conditions that the clock frequency of the sensor is 5 MHz and that the magnification of the objective lens is 10X. And in these conditions each head can detect about 200 stripe patterns per second.

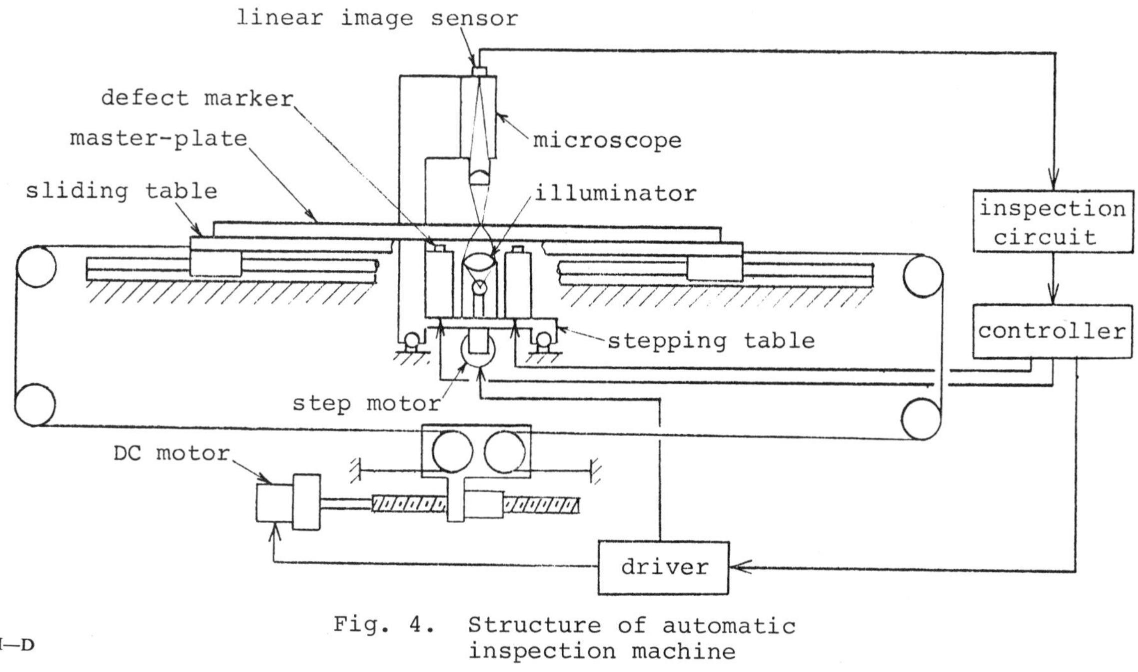

Fig. 4. Structure of automatic inspection machine

TABLE 3 Specification of detector

image sensor	RL128EC (RETICON)
number of elements	128
center-to-center spacing	50.8 μm
aperture width	25.4 μm
clock frequency	5 MHz
magnification of microscope	10 X
light source	Halogen lamp (150 watt)

ALGORITHM OF JUDGMENT

Structure

It is advantageous to apply comparative inspection between two neighboring patterns, because the difference of sizes between neighboring patterns is small, while in fine stripes the sizes of patterns change gradually along with inspection sequence. On the other hand it is essential to extract tiny defects by self-inspection of patterns, because the limit size of defects is small and is only a little larger than the detectable minimum size.

From the above points of view, we designed the algorithm of judgment, as shown in Fig. 5. After the video signal is thresholded, the obtained binary signal of patterns is divided by "pattern extraction" into "effective patterns" and "invalid patterns". Figure 6 shows this process shematically. In Fig.6 the left side neighboring patterns are neglected by "pattern extraction" which functions just when the bright, transparent area is appeared during a scan. The obtained effective patterns are judged by six methods. In these methods, "area comparison", "bridge width comparison", "maximum width comparison" and "center position comparison" are comparative inspection between a pattern just under the inspection and a correct pattern inspected just before. "Width change" and "center change" judge a pattern itself just under the inspection. The divided invalid patterns are checked by "extraction judgment" whether they are defects or neighboring stripes over the edge of the detected field. If any defects are detected, the error signal is transmitted to a defect marker.

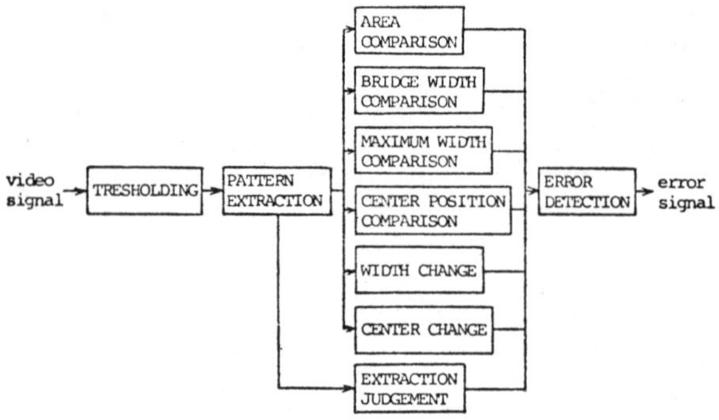

Fig. 5. Structure of judgment algorithm

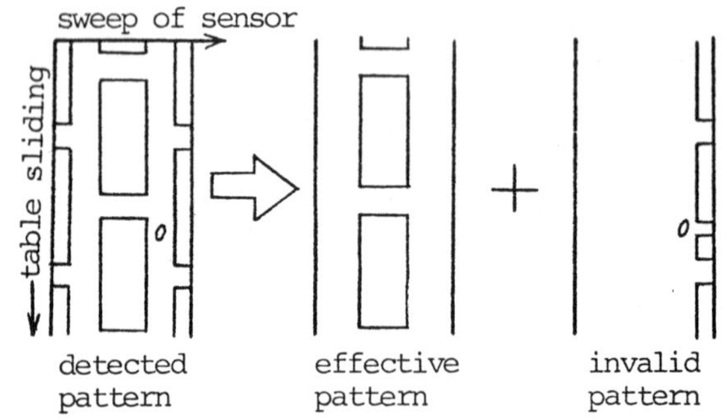

Fig. 6. Pattern extraction

Pattern Extraction and its Judgment

As realizing the pattern extraction, pattern's bit-error caused by quantization must be concidered. The top and botum of a stripe pattern are parallel to a sweep direction of the sensor. In these parts two dimensional binary pattern often causes one bit unevenness even in correct patterns. It is necessary to divide patterns referring to scans above and below not only by a scan aimed at.

Figure 7 shows a block diagram of pattern extraction and its judgement. In "pattern extraction", informations of an aiming scan and other 4 scans above and below the aiming scan are extracted by "detective mask of extraction". "Detective mask" outputs 0 or 1 as D signal respectively, according to the conditions of the mask state, as shown in Fig. 8. From the statuses of the D signal, the signal obtained 1 picture element before by "1 bit delay" and the start signal of a scan, "gate control" operates "gate 1" and "gate 2" to divide binary patterns into effective patterns and invalid patterns. To be more precise, after the start signal is sensed, when D signal is 1 and its 1 bit delay signal is 0, "gate 1" is opened, and in the next time when D signal is 1 and its 1 bit delay is 0, "gate 1" is closed and "gate 2" is opened, and thirdly when the same

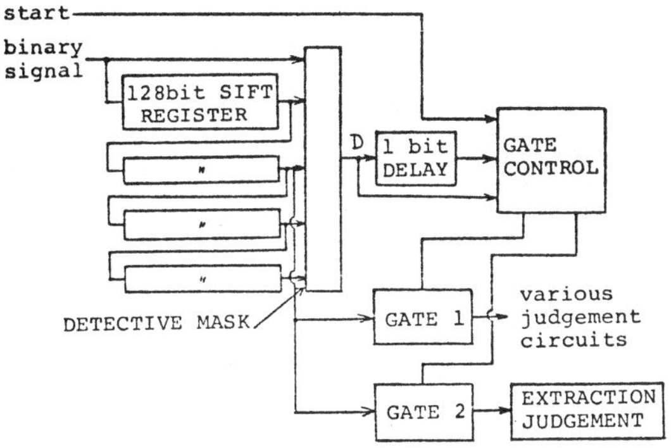

Fig. 7. Block diagram of pattern extraction

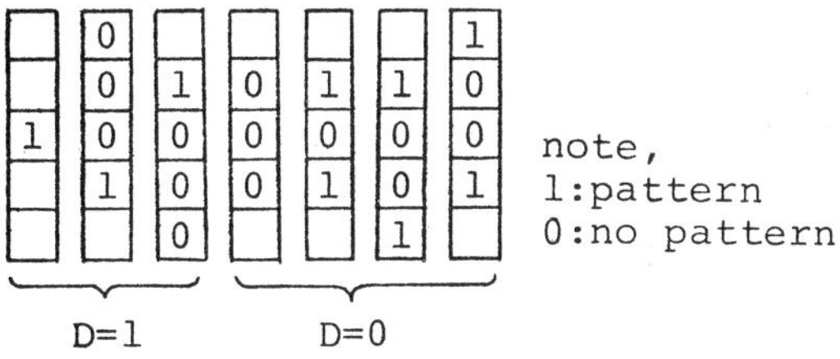

Fig. 8. Statuses of detective mask

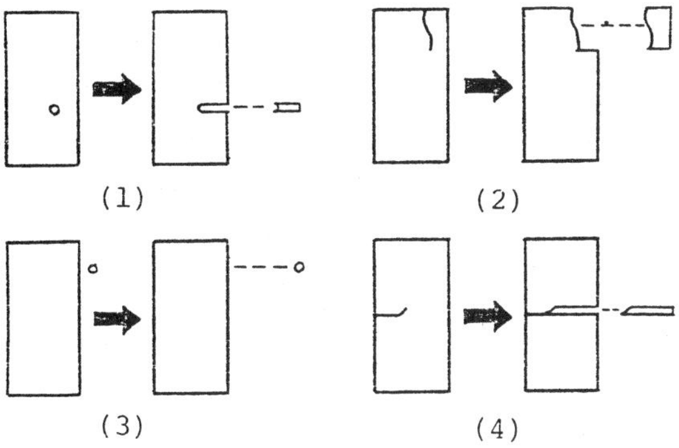

Fig. 9. Examples of pattern extraction

conditions are appeared, "gate 2" is closed. "Extraction judgment" distinguishes whether the obtained invalid patterns are over the edge of the detected field or not. If it is not, "extraction judgment" produces an error signal.

By this method, tiny defects, e.g. as shown in Fig. 9, are detected precisely, and the unevenness of correct patterns is not detected securely.

Other Judgment

Other six methods are judgments on sizes. If the conditions on judgments as follows are satisfied, the pattern is correct. In following conditions, each symbol is indicated in Fig. 10, and the subscript 0 means the value of a correct pattern judged just before. ΔS etc., are the maximum permissible limits of each value.

Area comparison. For the detection of "too big", "too small" and other big defects.

$$|S-S_0|<\Delta S \quad (1)$$

Bridge width comparison. For the detection of "bridge width" etc.

$$|B-B_0|<\Delta B \quad (2)$$

Maximum width comparison. For detection of "projection" etc.

$$|W_{max}-W_{max0}|<\Delta W_{max} \quad (3)$$

Center position comparison. For the detection of "position error" etc.

$$|C-C_0|<\Delta C \quad (4)$$

where C, C_0 are average values of each pattern.

Width change. For the detection of "projection", "chip-2", etc.

$$|W_i-W_t|<\Delta W \quad (5)$$

where except for section N.

Center change. For the detection of mixed defects of "projection", "chip-2", etc.

$$|C_i-C_t|<\Delta C' \quad (6)$$

where except for section N.

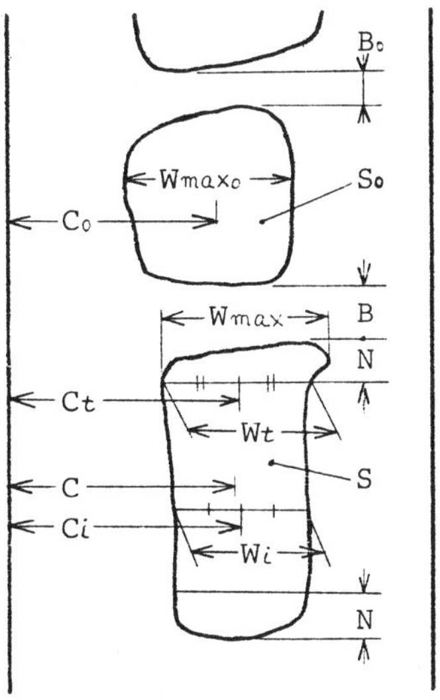

Fig. 10. Other methods of judgment

EXPERIMENTAL RESULT

In this chapter, we report the experimental results of the algorithm of judgment. In the experiment, limit size defect samples which were made precisely by photo-printing and real defect patterns were tested. The results of experiment for the real defect patterns were compared with the results of visual inspection by skilled operators.

Method of Experiment

Figure 11 shows the structure of the experimental equipment. The patterns were detected in the same conditions as in the expected real use. The driving speed of the sliding table is 19 cm/sec and the clock frequency of the sensor is 5 MHz. The obtained video signal from the sensor was thresholded and stored in a mini-computer system through a DMA interface. For judgments the patterns were processed by software. One field for detection was 128x512 picture elements, i.e. 0.64x 2.56 mm, and 3 stripes were included in a field.

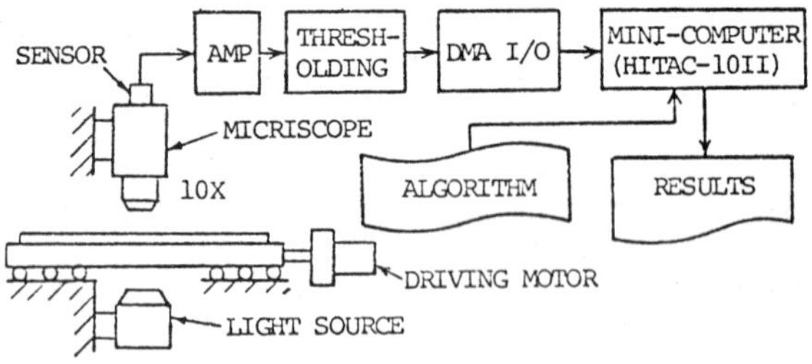

Fig. 11. Experimental equipment

TABLE 4 Experimental results for limit size samples (Fine stripes)

NO.	NAME	DEFECT DETECTION RATE (%)							
		TOTAL	PATTERN EXTR.	AREA COMP.	BRIDGE WIDTH COMP.	MAX. WIDTH COMP.	CENTER POSIT. COMP.	CENTER CHANGE	WIDTH CHANGE
0	CORRECT	0	0	0	0	0	0	0	0
1	CHIP-1	100	60	0	0	0	0	32	40
2	CHIP-2	100	50	0	0	0	0	22	50
3	PROJECTION	76	0	0	3	26	0	7	74
4	PINHOLE	100	100	0	0	0	0	0	0
5	MISSED	100	0	0	100	0	0	0	0
6	TOO BIG	100	0	89	0	25	0	0	0
7	TOO SMALL	100	0	92	0	30	0	0	0
8	DOT	100	100	0	0	0	0	0	0
9	BRIDGE WIDTH	92	0	0	92	0	0	0	0
10	POSITION ERROR	100	0	0	0	0	100	0	0
CONDITIONS OF JUDGEMENT (p.e.)				$\Delta S<122$	$\Delta B<3$	$\Delta W_{max}<2$	$\Delta C<2$	$\Delta C'<2$ N=2	$\Delta W<2$ N=2

Results of Experiment

Limit size samples. We made ten kinds of limit size defects as shown in Table 2. In the experiment, each sample was picked up 50 times, and the extraction error and the parameters of other six methods were checked. Table 4 and 5 show the results of defect detection rate for each sample in fine stripes and thick stripes respectively, in the judgment conditions that correct patterns are never misjudged as defects.

From these tables, it is easy to understand that each method of judgment acts in designed effectiveness for each defect, and that high detection rates are obtained for limit size samples.

Real patterns. The experiment was done for about 1,600 stripes which consist of about 400 defects decided by visual inspections of skilled operators and about 1,200 correct stripes picked up arbitrarily, in 8 masterplates.

Table 6 and 7 show the experimental results and its conditions of judgment. One of the tested correct patterns was apparently a defect, so it was dealt with as a defect. We found that the retouched patterns are often judged well-meaningly by the operators. And we omitted the retouched patterns in these tables. In this experiment, the results of judgment by this algorithm was coincident with the results of visual inspection, as shown in these tables. And the conditions of judgment are relaxed, as compared

TABLE 5 Experimental results for limit size samples (Thick stripes)

NO.	NAME	DEFECT DETECTION RATE (%)							
		TOTAL	PATTERN EXTR.	AREA COMP.	BRIDGE WIDTH COMP.	MAX. WIDTH COMP.	CENTER POSIT. COMP.	CENTER CHANGE	WIDTH CHANGE
0	CORRECT	0	0	0	0	0	0	0	0
1	CHIP-1	100	56	0	0	0	0	26	44
2	CHIP-2	100	50	0	0	0	0	13	50
3	PROJECTION	93	33	0	10	27	0	13	56
4	PINHOLE	100	100	0	0	0	0	0	0
5	MISSED	100	0	0	100	0	0	0	0
6	TOO BIG	100	0	48	0	70	0	0	0
7	TOO SMALL	100	0	56	0	62	0	0	0
8	DOT	100	100	0	0	0	0	0	0
9	BRIDGE WIDTH	95	0	0	95	0	0	0	0
10	POSITION ERROR	100	0	0	0	0	100	0	0
CONDITIONS OF JUDGEMENT (p.e.)				$\Delta S<200$	$\Delta B<3$	$\Delta W_{max}<2$	$\Delta C<2$	$\Delta C'<2$ N=2	$\Delta W<2$ N=2

with those for limit patterns in Table 4 and 5.

CONCLUSION

By using solid-state linear image sensor, it is possible to detect 200 stripes per second per a detecting head in the resolution of 7 μm. The algorithm, consists of "extraction judgment" etc., can detect ten kinds of limit size defects in high detection rate. As the conditions of judgment are relaxed, the results of automatic inspection are coincident with the results of visual inspection by skilled operators.

Figure 12 shows the developed automatic inspection machine for real use. This machine was verified to have the expected performance and has been used in the factory practically.

Fig. 12. Automatic inspection machine for real use

REFERENCES

(1) M. Ejiri, T. Uno, M. Mese, S. Ikeda, A process for detecting defects in complicated patterns, Comp. Graphics and Image Processing, 2, 314 (1973).
(2) T. Ito, Pattern classification by color effect method, Proc. 3rd Int. Joint Conf. on Pattern Recognition, 26 (1976).
(3) R. T. Chien, Visual understanding of hybrid circuits via procedual model, Proc. 4th Int. Conf. on Artificial Intelligence, 742 (1975).

TABLE 6 Experimental results for real patterns (Fine patterns)

	DEFECT DETECTION RATE (%)							
	TOTAL	PATTERN EXTR.	AREA COMP.	BRIDGE WIDTH COMP.	MAX. WIDTH COMP.	CENTER POSIT. COMP.	CENTER CHANGE	WIDTH CHANGE
DEFECT PATTERNS BY HUMAN EYE	100	68.8	14.5	3.6	3.6	0	18.8	23.2
CORRECT PATTERNS BY HUMAN EYE	0	0	0	0	0	0	0	0
CONDITIONS OF JUDGMENT (p.e.)			$\Delta S<130$	$\Delta B<4$	$\Delta W_{max}<3$	$\Delta C<3$	$\Delta C'<3$ N=3	$\Delta W<4$ N=5

TABLE 7 Experimental results for real patterns (Thick stripes)

	DEFECT DETECTION RATE (%)							
	TOTAL	PATTERN EXTR.	AREA COMP.	BRIDGE WIDTH COMP.	MAX. WIDTH COMP.	CENTER POSIT. COMP.	CENTER CHANGE	WIDTH CHANGE
DEFECT PATTERNS BY HUMAN EYE	100	79.0	0	0	2.2	0	15.6	18.8
CORRECT PATTERNS BY HUMAN EYE	0	0	0	0	0	0	0	0
CONDITIONS OF JUDGMENT (p.e.)			$\Delta S<250$	$\Delta B<4$	$\Delta W_{max}<3$	$\Delta C<3$	$\Delta C'<3$ N=3	$\Delta W<4$ N=5

TRANSIENT INFORMATION IN INSPECTION

Y. Morita, T. Yamaura and K. Ito

Tokyo Institute of Technology, 2-12-1 Oh-Okayma, Toklyo, 152 Japan

ABSTRACT

A high measuring accuracy and a short measuring time are required for inspection in manufacturing processes. To achieve a high measuring accuracy, multi-sensors may be used for giving the spatial average of sensing points, and to shorten the measuring time, the transient information from the sensors should be fully utilized. Another problem with inspection is noise. The inspection cannot be always reliable under contamination by noise in the processes. In the present paper, a guiding principle in designing a reliable inspection system is shown with examining the noise contamination. The authors discuss means of achieving high accuracy and short measuring time from various angles.

INTRODUCTION

Inspection in manufacturing processes involves measurement to which a high accuracy and a short measuring time are demanded despite noise contamination. The measurement cannot be always reliable if one directly applies ordinary measuring instruments without examining the noise contamination. In view of noise contamination, it can be generally said that a high accuracy results from a long measuring time, and a short measuring time spoils the measuring accuracy. So it is not easy to design an inspection system with a sufficient accuracy and requiring an adequately short measuring time. To overcome the above difficulty in the design of measuring instruments for inspection, the configuration of sensors and the method of information-processing have to be carefully contrived.

The problems are pointed out and case solutions are shown. To achieve a high measuring accuracy without spoiling the measuring time, multi-sensors are used for giving the spatial average of sensing points, and to shorten the measuring time without spoiling the accuracy, the transient information from the sensors is fully utilized.

In this paper, typical examples of the design for using multi-sensors and transient information are studied in thermometry. Some designs are compared with each other by the criterion of variances of their measured temperatures. One method is that transient signals from the multi-sensors and the low pass filters are directly sampled in equal intervals, and the sampled data are utilized. Another method is that the initial conditions of the sensors are controlled for the purpose of acquiring good transient information, and the obtained transient signals are differentiated for giving peak values which are proportionate to the temperature differences between the sensors and the object to be measured.

In both the methods, it is assumed that (1) the sensors always give signals contaminated with noise, (2) the dynamics of sensors are expressed by first-order differential equations, (3) the low pass filters for giving the average in the time domain are expressed by second-order differential equations, and the transient infomation is the transient responses of the sensors brought into contact with the object to be measured, the so-called step responses.

In conclusion, this paper shows a guiding principle in designing an inspection system in which incompatible requirements exist with respect to the accuracy, the measuring time and the reliability. The authors' numerical calculations offer a quantitative foresight in designing the system.

DESCRIPTION OF PROBLEM

Measuring Processes

In the present paper, a measuring process for inspection is illustrated by a block diagram, as shown in Fig.1. In the measuring process, it is assumed that:

(i) The variable to be measured is constant, and
(ii) The measuring instrument is a dynamical system characterized by a frequency transfer function $H(\omega)$, or an impulse response $h(t)$.

The response $h(t)$ is written by

$$h(t) = \frac{1}{2\pi}\int_{-\infty}^{\infty} H(\omega)\, e^{j\omega t} d\omega \tag{1}$$

which is known as the inverse Fourier transformation. Then the step response is given by

$$w(t) = \int_0^t h(\tau)\, d\tau \tag{2}$$

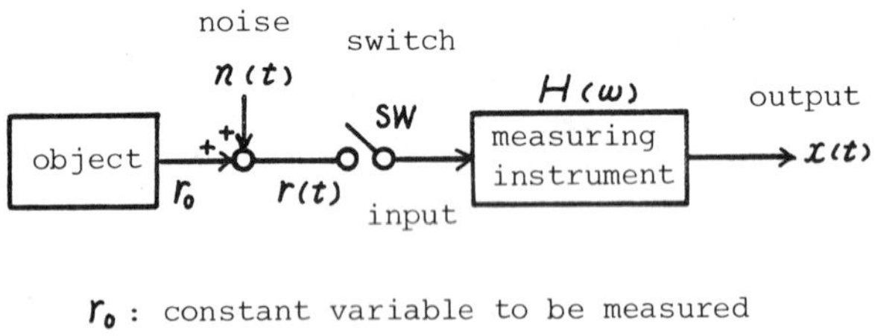

Fig.1 The block diagram of a measuring process

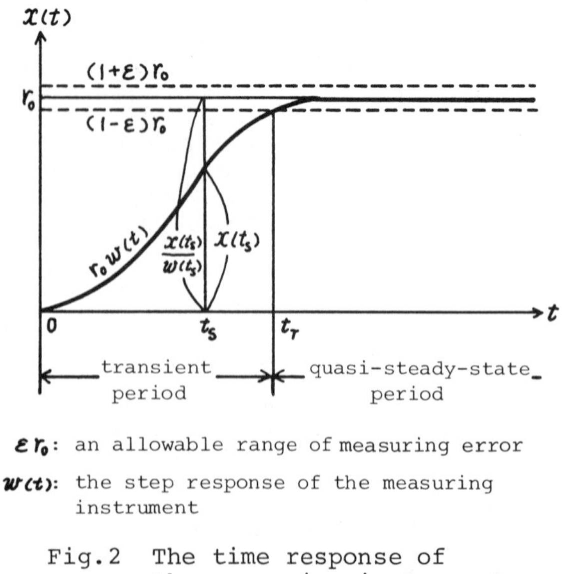

Fig.2 The time response of the measuring instrument

In general, the time response of the measuring instrument can be divided into two periods. One is the transient period and the other the quasi-steady-state period, as shown in Fig.2. The transient period is the time interval from the starting time and the settling time t_T, that is $[0, t_T)$, and the quasi-steady-state period is the time interval $[t_T, \infty)$. The settling time is defined as the time required for the response to stay within an allowable range of measuring error. In the quasi-steady-state period, it follows that

$$|1 - w(t)| \leq \varepsilon\,, \quad t \in [t_T, \infty) \tag{3}$$

An ordinary measurement without utilizing the transient information is performed in the quasi-steady-state period. The output of the measuring instrument directly gives the value of the constant variable to be measured. In this case, the minimum measuring time is t_T and the measuring error is within $\pm\varepsilon r_0$. If the noise component of the output is negligibly small, the error due to the noise contamination is also negligibly small.

Now consider a measurement utilizing the transient information. In the measurement, the output of the measuring instrument is sampled in the transient period. The sampled datum is compensated to give the value to be measured, that is $x(t_s)/w(t_s)$, as shown in Fig.2. The error due to the noise contamination is not necessarily negligibly small even if the noise component of the output is negligibly small. The reason is that when the sampled datum is compensated, the noise component of the output is multiplied by the compensating factor $1/w(t_s)$ at the same time, as shown in Fig.3.

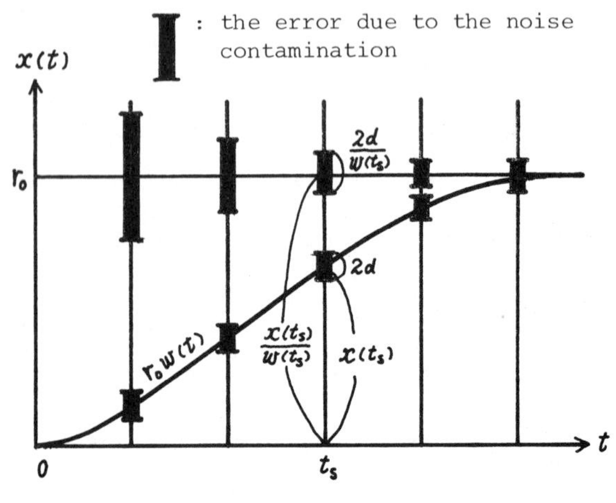

Fig.3 The error amplification accompanied with the compensation

For the purpose of improving the statistical error due to the noise contamination, there are two main ways of information processing: averaging in the time domain, and spatial averaging. The averaging in the time domain is performed using the data obtained by sampling the time response at several points. The spatial averaging is performed by using multi-sensors. The noise contamination at each sensing point is assumed to be independent of any other points. In a practical situation, the spatial average given by the multi-sensors will be a reliable bit of information for inspection.

In the case that the object to be measured is a distributed parameter system, the step response of the measuring instrument is not always fixed because of the interaction between the materials of the object and of the sensors. Let us assume that the system is linear. The step response should be expressed by $k\,w(t)$, instead of $w(t)$, where k is depended on the materials of the object to be measured and the sensors.

For this kind of measurement, the zero-derivative method has been proposed in thermometry.[5),6)] The principle of the zero-derivative method is based on a fact that if the temperature difference does not exist between the object and the sensor, no change is observed in the output of the sensor brought into contact with the object. For the purpose of realizing the several temperature differences, the initial conditions of the multi-sensors are controlled. The time responses as the output of the measuring instrument are sampled. From the initial temperatures and the sampled temperatures, the surface temperature of the object is estimated by the least-square method for the case of two unknown variables.

Formulation of the Measuring Processes

(A measuring process in which the time response is sampled)

A measuring process is formulated for averaging the measured values in the time domain by sampling the time response, as shown in Fig.4. The output $x(t)$ in Fig.4 is written by

$$x(t) = \hat{x}(t) + d(t) \tag{4}$$

where $d(t)$ is the noise component in the output $x(t)$. In (4), $\hat{x}(t)$ is given by

$$\hat{x}(t) = r_0\, w(t) \tag{5}$$

where $w(t)$ is the unit step response.

The output $x(t)$ is sampled by the multi-point sampler, and the sampled data are denoted by $x_i = x(t_i)$; $i = 1, 2, \cdots\cdots, N$ where $0 < t_1 < t_2 < \cdots < t_N$. The sampled data x_i ; $i = 1, 2, \cdots\cdots, N$ are compensated as follows:

$$y_i = a_i x_i \;;\; i = 1, 2, \cdots\cdots, N \tag{6}$$

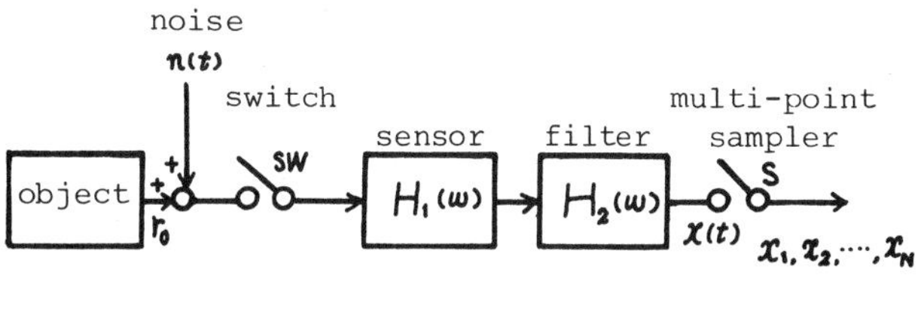

Fig.4 A measuring process in which the time response is sampled

where

$$a_i = \frac{1}{w_i} \;;\; i = 1, 2, \cdots\cdots, N \tag{7}$$

$$w_i = w(t_i) \;;\; i = 1, 2, \cdots\cdots, N. \tag{8}$$

From (4), (5), and (7), (6) is rewritten by

$$y_i = r_0 + a_i d_i \;;\; i = 1, 2, \cdots\cdots, N. \tag{9}$$

In (9), it is assumed for d_i that

$$E[d_i] = 0 \;;\; i = 1, 2, \cdots\cdots, N. \tag{10}$$

In the present paper, the estimated value of the constant variable r_0 to be measured is assumed to be given by the linear combination, as averaging in the time domain, of the compensated data y_i ; $i = 1, 2, \cdots\cdots, N$. The estimated value is expressed by

$$z = \boldsymbol{\alpha}^T \boldsymbol{y} \tag{11}$$

where $\boldsymbol{\alpha}^T$ is the transpose of $\boldsymbol{\alpha}$,

$$\boldsymbol{\alpha}^T = (\alpha_1, \alpha_2, \cdots\cdots, \alpha_N) \tag{12}$$

$$\sum_{i=1}^{N} \alpha_i = 1 \tag{13}$$

and

$$\boldsymbol{y}^T = (y_1, y_2, \cdots\cdots, y_N). \tag{14}$$

The constraint expressed by (13) gives $z = r_0$ where $n(t) = 0$.

The vector $\boldsymbol{\alpha}$ is the weight vector for $\boldsymbol{y}$, and is to be chosen so as to minimize the variance of the estimated value z under the constraint (13).

The expected value of z is given by

$$E[z] = r_0 \tag{15}$$

from (11), (9), (10), and (13). The variance of z is written by

$$\sigma_z^2 = E[(z-E[z])^2]$$
$$= E[(\sum_{i=1}^{N} \alpha_i a_i d_i)^2]. \quad (16)$$

For simplicity, the following notations are introduced:

$$v_{ij} = E[d_i d_j] \; ; \; i,j=1,2,\cdots,N \quad (17)$$

$$P_{ij} = a_i v_{ij} a_j \; ; \; i,j=1,2,\cdots,N \quad (18)$$

and the matrix $\mathbf{P}\,(N\times N)$ of which the element is P_{ij}. Using the above notations, (16) is rewritten by

$$\sigma_z^2 = \boldsymbol{\alpha}^T \mathbf{P} \boldsymbol{\alpha}. \quad (19)$$

In (19), the matrix $\mathbf{P}$ is the covariance matrix of the noise component in the compensated data y_i; $i=1,2,\cdots,N$. Then the element P_{ij} is given by

$$P_{ij} = a_i \phi_{dd}(t_i - t_j) a_j \quad (20)$$

where $\phi_{dd}(\tau)$ is the autocorrelation function of the noise component $d(t)$ in the output $x(t)$.

The autocorrelation function $\phi_{dd}(\tau)$ is given by

$$\phi_{dd}(\tau) = \int_{-\infty}^{\infty} h(\tau_1)d\tau_1 \int_{-\infty}^{\infty} h(\tau_2)\phi_{nn}(\tau+\tau_1-\tau_2)d\tau_2 \quad (21)$$

where $\phi_{nn}(\tau)$ is the autocorrelation function of the noise $n(t)$, that is

$$\phi_{nn}(\tau) = \lim_{T\to\infty} \frac{1}{T} \int_{-\frac{T}{2}}^{\frac{T}{2}} n(t)\,n(t+\tau)dt \quad (22)$$

and

$$h(\tau) = \frac{1}{2\pi} \int_{-\infty}^{\infty} H_1(\omega) H_2(\omega) e^{j\omega\tau} d\omega. \quad (23)$$

Or the autocorrelation function $\phi_{dd}(\tau)$ is given by

$$\phi_{dd}(\tau) = \frac{1}{2\pi} \int_{-\infty}^{\infty} |H_1(\omega) H_2(\omega)|^2 N(\omega) e^{j\omega\tau} d\omega \quad (24)$$

where $H_1(\omega)$ and $H_2(\omega)$ are the frequency transfer functions and $N(\omega)$ is the power spectrum of the noise $n(t)$. The power spectrum $N(\omega)$ is given by

$$N(\omega) = \int_{-\infty}^{\infty} \phi_{nn}(\tau) e^{-j\omega\tau} d\tau. \quad (25)$$

(A measuring process in which the multi-sensors are used)

A measuring process is formulated for averaging the measured values in the spatial domain by using the multi-sensors, as shown in Fig.5. The outputs in Fig.5 are written by

$$x_i(t) = \hat{x}_i(t) + d_i(t) \; ; \; i=1,2,\cdots,N \quad (26)$$

where $d_i(t)$ is the noise component in the output $x_i(t)$. In (26), $\hat{x}_i(t)$ is given by

$$\hat{x}_i(t) = (r_0 - r_i) w(t) \; ; \; i=1,2,\cdots,N \quad (27)$$

where $w(t)$ is the unit step response. The initial conditions of the multi-sensors are expressed by the references r_i ; $i=1,2,\cdots,N$ in Fig.5. The values of the references are obtained by sampling the outputs in

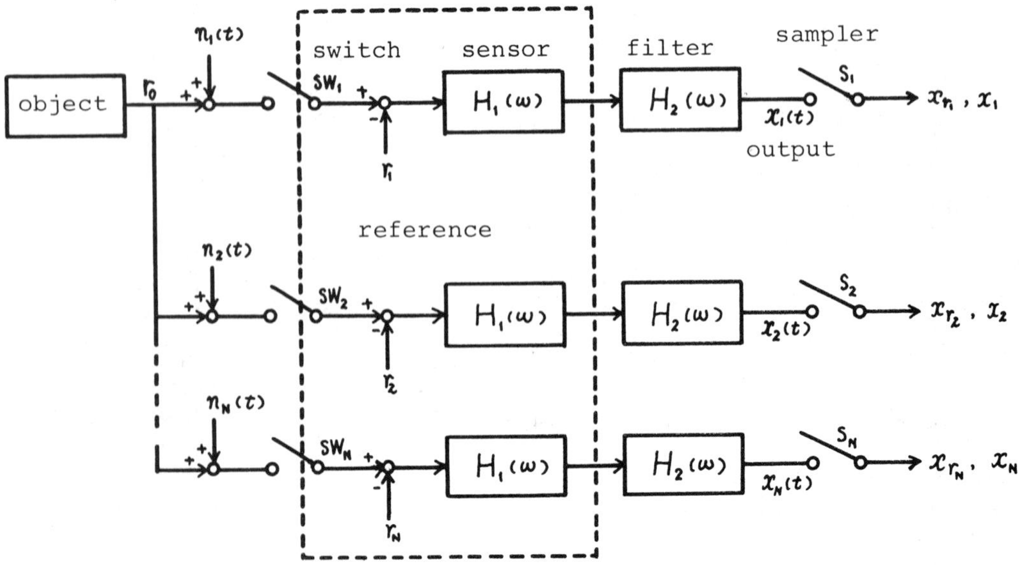

Fig.5 A measuring process in which the multi-sensors are used.

advance of the action of measurement expressed by closing the switches SW_i ; $i=1,2,\cdots,N$ in Fig.5.

The outputs $x_i(t)$; $i=1,2,\cdots\cdots,N$ are sampled by the samplers, and the sampled data are expressed by

$$x_i = x_i(t_T)\ ;\ i=1,2,\cdots\cdots,N. \quad (28)$$

The sampled data are compensated as follows:

$$y_i = a x_i + r_i\ ;\ i=1,2,\cdots\cdots,N \quad (29)$$

where

$$a = \frac{1}{w(t_T)}. \quad (30)$$

From (26), and (27), (29) is rewritten by

$$y_i = r_0 + a d_i\ ;\ i=1,2,\cdots\cdots,N. \quad (31)$$

In (31), it is assumed for d_i that

$$E[d_i] = 0,\ i=1,2,\cdots\cdots,N. \quad (32)$$

The estimated value z is expressed by

$$z = \alpha^T y \quad (33)$$

where

$$\sum_{i=1}^{N} \alpha_i = 1. \quad (34)$$

The expected value of z is given by

$$E[z] = r_0 \quad (35)$$

and the variance of z is given by

$$\sigma_z^2 = E[(z-E[z])^2] = a^2 E[(\sum_{i=1}^{N} \alpha_i d_i)^2]. \quad (36)$$

Applying the matrix notation used in (19) gives

$$\sigma_z^2 = \alpha^T P \alpha \quad (37)$$

where

$$P_{ij} = a^2 v_{ij}\ ;\ i,j=1,2,\cdots\cdots,N \quad (38)$$

$$v_{ij} = E[d_i d_j]\ ;\ i,j=1,2,\cdots,N \quad (39)$$

The element P_{ij} is given by

$$P_{ij} = a^2 E[d_i(t_T).\ d_j(t_T)]. \quad (40)$$

The formulation given in the present section is equivalent to the formulation given in the previous section by letting

$$a = a_i\ ;\ i=1,2,\cdots\cdots,N \quad (41)$$

in the variance σ_z^2 expressed by (19).

(A measuring process of the zero-derivative method)

The measuring process of the zero-derivative method is also shown in Fig.5, but it is assumed that there exists some interaction between the object and the sensors. The step response of the measuring system is expressed by $kw(t)$, instead of $w(t)$, where k is a variable which depends on the magnitude of the interaction.

The outputs in Fig.5 are written by

$$x_i(t) = \hat{x}_i(t) + d_i(t)\ ;\ i=1,2,\cdots,N \quad (42)$$

and $\hat{x}_i(t)$ is given by

$$\hat{x}_i(t) = (r_0 - r_i) k w(t);\ i=1,2,\cdots,N. \quad (43)$$

The sampled data are expressed by $x_i = x_i(t_T)$; $i=1,2,\cdots,N$ and the noise component $d_i(t_T)$ is denoted by d_i .

The sampled data are compensated as follows:

$$y_i = a x_i + r_i\ ;\ i=1,2,\cdots,N \quad (44)$$

where

$$a = \frac{1}{k w(t_T)}. \quad (45)$$

Assuming that

$$E[d_i] = 0;\ i=1,2,\cdots,N \quad (46)$$

gives

$$E[y_i] = r_0\ ;\ i=1,2,\cdots,N. \quad (47)$$

Therefore, let y_i be expressed by

$$y + \varepsilon_i = a x_i + r_i\ ;\ i=1,2,\cdots\cdots,N \quad (48)$$

and substituting (48) into (44) gives

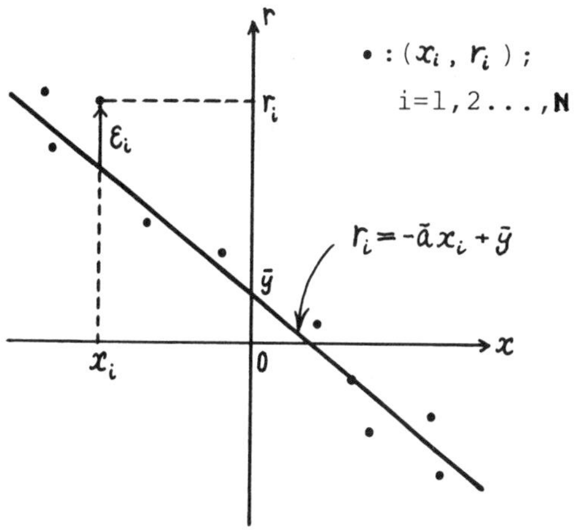

$\bar{a}, \bar{y}$: the values minimizing the criterion $J = \sum_{i=1}^{N} \varepsilon_i^2$.

Fig.6 The estimation by the least-square method

$$y + \varepsilon_i = a x_i + r_i \; ; \; i=1,2,\cdots\cdots,N \tag{49}$$

where y and a are constant.

In the present paper, the estimated value y is chosen so as to minimize the criterion

$$J = \sum_{i=1}^{N} \varepsilon_i^2 \tag{50}$$

by the least-square method, as shown in Fig.6.

SOLUTIONS

The Measuring Process in Which the Time Response is Sampled[4]

The estimated value z for the constant variable r_0 is given by (11), and the weight vector α in (11) is to be chosen so as to minimize the variance σ_z^2 under the constraint (13) and the given covariance matrix P. The optimal weight vector α^* to minimize the variance σ_z^2 is obtained by using the Lagrange multiplication. The optimal weight vector α^* is given by

$$\alpha^* = \frac{P^{-1}\mathbf{1}}{\mathbf{1}^T P^{-1}\mathbf{1}} \tag{51}$$

where P^{-1} is the inverse matrix of P and

$$\mathbf{1}^T = (1, 1, \cdots\cdots\cdots, 1). \tag{52}$$

The minimum value of the variance is given by

$$\sigma_z^{*2} = \frac{1}{\mathbf{1}^T P^{-1}\mathbf{1}}. \tag{53}$$

Assuming that the noise components $d_i \; ; \; i=1,2,\cdots\cdots\cdots,N$ are independent of each other gives

$$v_{ij} = E[d_i d_j] = 0 \; ; \; i \neq j, \; i,j = 1,2,\cdots,N \tag{54}$$

Then the optimal weight vector is given by

$$\alpha^* = \begin{pmatrix} \alpha_1^* \\ \alpha_2^* \\ \vdots \\ \alpha_N^* \end{pmatrix} \tag{55}$$

where

$$\alpha_i^* = \frac{1}{P_{ii}} \Big/ \sum_{j=1}^{N} \frac{1}{P_{jj}} \; ; \; i=1,2,\cdots,N \tag{56}$$

and the minimum variance is given by

$$\sigma_z^{*2} = 1 \Big/ \sum_{j=1}^{N} \frac{1}{P_{jj}} \tag{57}$$

If

$$P_{ii} = P \; ; \; i=1,2,\cdots\cdots\cdots,N \tag{58}$$

are assumed, then it follows that

$$\alpha_i^* = \frac{1}{N} \; ; \; i=1,2,\cdots\cdots\cdots,N \tag{59}$$

and

$$\sigma_z^{*2} = \frac{P}{N}. \tag{60}$$

The Measuring Process in Which the Multi-Sensors are Used

The optimal weight vector α^* and the minimum value of the variance are given by (51) and (53), respectively. But the covariance matrix P appearing in (51) and (53) is replaced by the matrix P of which the element is given by (40).

Assuming that the noise components $d_i(t_T) \; ; \; i=1,2,\cdots\cdots\cdots\cdots,N$ are independent of each other gives

$$\alpha_i^* = \frac{1}{v_{ii}} \Big/ \sum_{j=1}^{N} \frac{1}{v_{jj}} \; ; \; i=1,2,\cdots\cdots,N \tag{61}$$

and the minimum variance is given by

$$\sigma_z^{*2} = a^2 \Big/ \sum_{j=1}^{N} \frac{1}{v_{jj}}. \tag{62}$$

If

$$v_{ii} = v \; ; \; i=1,2,\cdots,N \tag{63}$$

are assumed, then it follows that

$$\alpha_i^* = \frac{1}{N} \; ; \; i=1,2,\cdots,N \tag{64}$$

and

$$\sigma_z^{*2} = \frac{a^2}{N} v. \tag{65}$$

The Measuring Process of Zero-Derivative Method

First the equations (49) are rewritten as

$$\begin{cases} -a x_1 + y = r_1 - \varepsilon_1 \\ -a x_2 + y = r_2 - \varepsilon_2 \\ \quad \vdots \qquad \vdots \qquad \vdots \qquad \vdots \\ -a x_N + y = r_N - \varepsilon_N \end{cases} \tag{66}$$

for the measured data (x_i, r_i); $i=1,2,\cdots\cdots,N$. For convenience, the following notations are introduced:

$$A = \begin{pmatrix} -x_1 & 1 \\ -x_2 & 1 \\ \vdots & \vdots \\ -x_N & 1 \end{pmatrix} \tag{67}$$

$$X^T = (a, y) \tag{68}$$

$$B^T = (r_1, r_2, \cdots\cdots, r_N) \tag{69}$$

$$E^T = (\varepsilon_1, \varepsilon_2, \cdots\cdots, \varepsilon_N). \tag{70}$$

Using the above notations, (66) is rewritten by

$$AX = B - E \tag{71}$$

and the criterion (50) is rewritten by

$$\begin{aligned} J &= E^T E \\ &= (AX - B)^T (AX - B). \end{aligned} \tag{72}$$

The optimal vector X^* minimizing J is given by

$$X^* = (A^T A)^{-1} A^T B. \tag{73}$$

Substituting (67), (68), (69), and (70) gives

$$y = \bar{r} + \frac{\bar{r}\bar{x} - \frac{1}{N}\sum_{i=1}^{N} r_i x_i}{\frac{1}{N}\sum_{i=1}^{N} x_i^2 - \bar{x}^2}\,\bar{x} \tag{74}$$

where

$$\bar{r} = \frac{1}{N}\sum_{i=1}^{N} r_i \tag{75}$$

and

$$\bar{x} = \frac{1}{N}\sum_{i=1}^{N} x_i. \tag{76}$$

Assuming that the noise components d_i; $i = 1, 2, \cdots, N$ are independent of each other gives

$$E[d_i d_j] = 0;\ i \neq j,\ i, j = 1, 2, \cdots, N. \tag{77}$$

Then the expected value of y is given by

$$E[y] = r_0. \tag{78}$$

The variance of the estimated value y is given by

$$\begin{aligned} \sigma_y^2 &= E[(y - E[y])^2] \\ &= \left(1 + \frac{\bar{x}^2}{\frac{1}{N}\sum_{i=1}^{N} x_i^2 - \bar{x}^2}\right) a^2 \frac{\sigma^2}{N} \end{aligned} \tag{79}$$

where

$$\sigma^2 = E[d_i d_i];\ i = 1, 2, \cdots, N. \tag{80}$$

NUMERICAL EXAMPLE

In this section, a numerical example is shown with the following assumptions (i)~(iii).

(i) The autocorrelation function of the noise $n(t)$ is expressed by

$$\phi_{nn}(\tau) = \sigma_n^2 e^{-\beta|\tau|} \tag{81}$$

or the power spectrum of the noise is given by

$$\Phi_{nn}(\omega) = \frac{2\beta}{\beta^2 + \omega^2}\sigma_n^2. \tag{82}$$

(ii) The dynamics of the sensor is expressed by

$$H_1(\omega) = \frac{k_1}{1 + j\omega T_1} \tag{83}$$

(iii) The characteristics of the filter is given by

$$H_2(\omega) = \frac{k_2}{(1 + j\omega T_2)^2}. \tag{84}$$

The unit step response $w(t)$ of the measuring system in this example is given by

$$\begin{aligned} w(t) = k_1 k_2 \Bigg[1 &- \frac{T_1^2}{(T_2 - T_1)^2} e^{-\frac{t}{T_1}} \\ &- \left\{1 - \frac{T_1^2}{(T_2 - T_1)^2} + \frac{1}{T_2 - T_1} t\right\} e^{-\frac{t}{T_2}} \Bigg] \end{aligned} \tag{85}$$

and the autocorrelation function $\phi_{dd}(\tau)$ is calculated as follows:

$$\begin{aligned} \phi_{dd}(\tau) &= \frac{1}{2\pi}\int_{-\infty}^{\infty} \left| \frac{k_1}{1 + j\omega T_1} \cdot \frac{k_2}{(1 + j\omega T_2)^2} \right|^2 \frac{2\beta\sigma_n^2}{\beta^2 + \omega^2} e^{j\omega\tau} d\omega \\ &= c_1 e^{-\frac{|\tau|}{T_1}} + (c_2 + c_3|\tau|) e^{-\frac{|\tau|}{T_2}} + c_4 e^{-\beta|\tau|} \end{aligned} \tag{86}$$

where

$$c_1 = k_1^2 k_2^2\, 2\beta\sigma_n^2 \frac{T_1^5}{2(T_1^2\beta^2 - 1)(T_2^2 - T_1^2)^2} \tag{87}$$

$$c_2 = k_1^2 k_2^2\, 2\beta\sigma_n^2 \left[\frac{T_2^3}{4(T_2^2\beta^2 - 1)(T_2^2 - T_1^2)} + \frac{T_2^3(-T_2^2 T_1^2 \beta^2 + 2T_1^2 - T_2^2)}{2(T_2^2\beta^2 - 1)^2 (T_2^2 - T_1^2)^2}\right] \tag{88}$$

$$c_3 = k_1^2 k_2^2\, 2\beta\sigma_n^2 \frac{T_2^2(-T_2^2 T_1^2 \beta^2 + 2T_1^2 - T_2^2)}{4(T_2^2\beta^2 - 1)(T_2^2 - T_1^2)} \tag{89}$$

$$c_4 = k_1^2 k_2^2\, 2\beta\sigma_n^2 \frac{-1}{2\beta(T_1^2\beta^2 - 1)(T_2^2\beta^2 - 1)^2}. \tag{90}$$

The element p_{ij} of the covariance matrix P is given by (20), that is

$$p_{ij} = \frac{1}{w(t_i)} \phi_{dd}(t_i - t_j) \frac{1}{w(t_j)}. \tag{91}$$

The optimal weight vector α^* is given

by (51) and the minimum value of the variance is given by (53):

$$\alpha^* = \frac{P^{-1} 1}{1^T P^{-1} 1} \qquad (92)$$

and

$$\sigma_z^{*2} = \frac{1}{1^T P^{-1} 1}. \qquad (93)$$

The numerical calculations are performed by letting

$$T_1 = 1.00 \text{ sec} \qquad (94)$$

and

$$\beta = 200\pi \text{ sec}^{-1}. \qquad (95)$$

The sampling time t_i is given, in this example, by

$$t_i = \frac{t_T}{N} i \ ; \ i = 1, 2, \cdots\cdots, N \qquad (96)$$

where t_T is the measuring time and N is the number of sampling points. The value of T_2 is chosen, as shown in Figs.7 and 8, to minimize σ_z^{*2} for each measuring time and each number of sampling points.

The minimum variance σ_z^{*2} for the optimal T_2^* is calculated by (93). The result is shown in Fig.9. In the calculation, the multi-sensors are taken into account under the assumption of the independent contamination of the noises, and the variance is given by σ_z^{*2} / M where M is the number of the sensors constructing the multi-sensors.

It should be noted in Fig.9 that utilizing the transient information and using the multi-sensors make it possible to design a measuring system which satisfies the demand for a sufficient accuracy and an adequately short measuring time. This is based on the equivalent relationship between the measuring time and the number of the sensors. For example, a measuring system of $t_T = 0.10$ sec and $M = 3$ is equivalent to that of $t_T = 0.40$ sec and $M = 1$ where N = 2 .

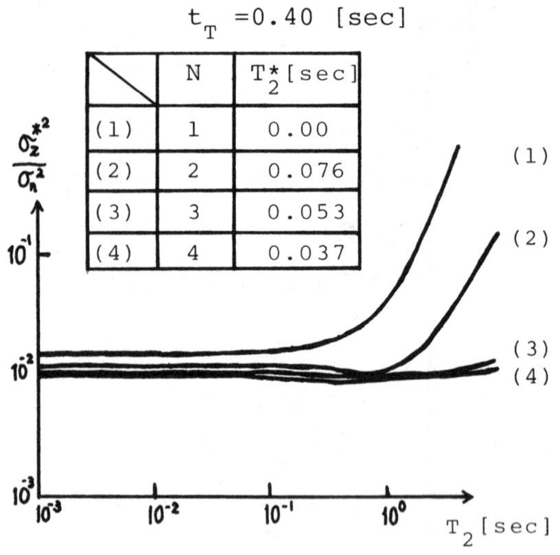

T_2^* : the optimal value of T_2

Fig.7 The relation of T_2 to the normalized variance σ_z^{*2}/σ_n^2 where t_T = 0.40 sec .

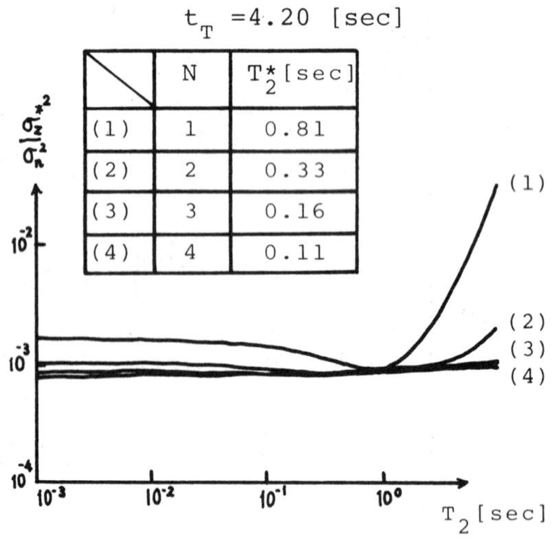

T_2^* : the optimal value of T_2

Fig.8 The relation of T_2 to the normalized variance σ_z^{*2}/σ_n^2 where t_T = 4.20 sec .

EXPERIMENTAL EXAMPLE

As an experimental example, the zero-derivative method is applied to the measurement of surface temperature. The measuring system is shown in Fig. 10. The multi-sensors are represented by an assembly of four sheathed thermocouples forming a sensing area of 4 × 8 mm^2. Two of the thermocouples are heated and simultaneously the other two are cooled by their separate base plates whose temperatures are controlled by Peltier elements.

The time constant of each of the multi-sensors is 1.0 sec. The cut-off frequency of the filter is chosen to be 5 Hz and that of the quasi-differentiator is set to be 30 Hz .

The measuring system is tested by using the instrument shown in Fig.11. The surface temperature of vinyl film is close to the water temperature because the thickness of vinyl film

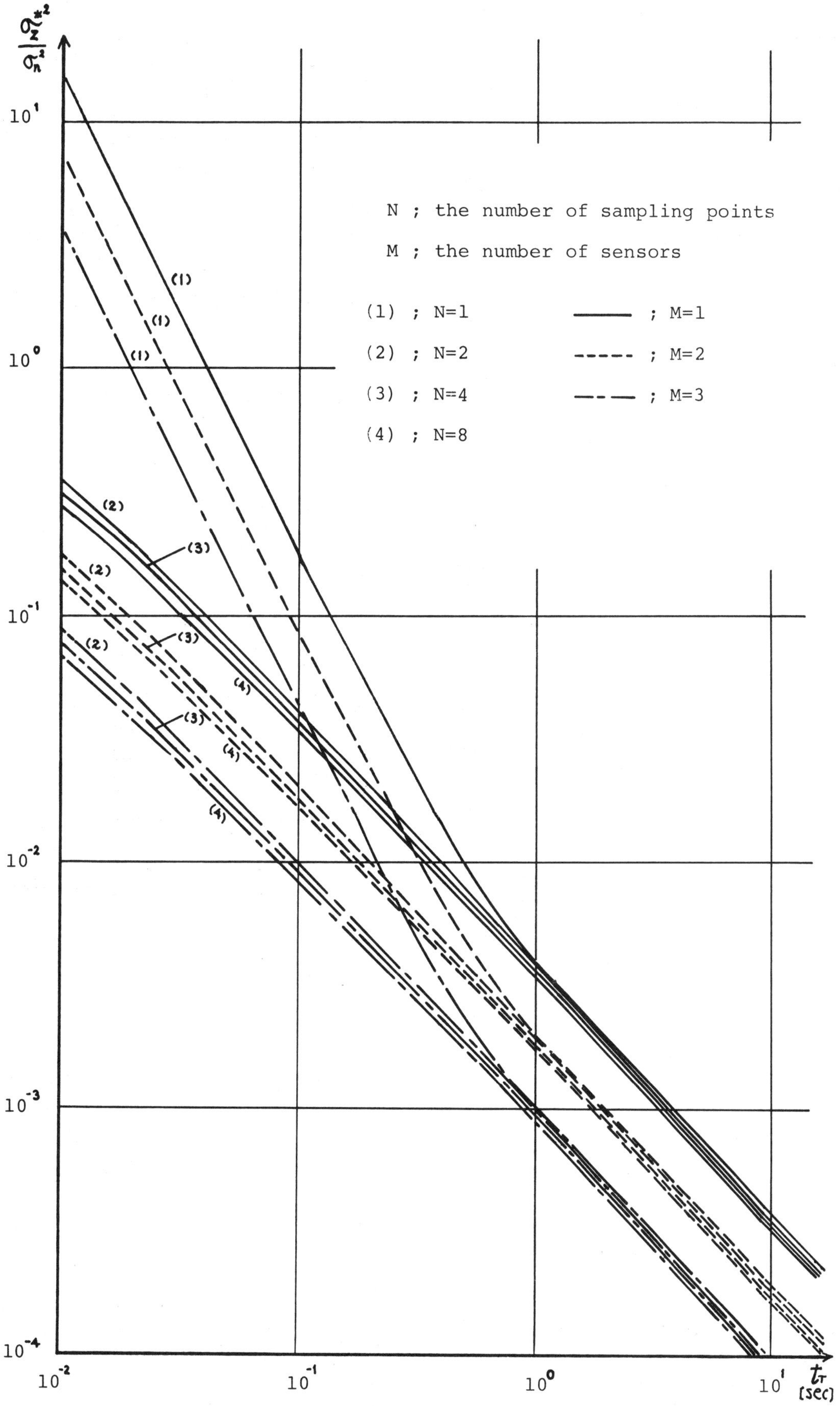

Fig.9 The relationship between the measuring time and the minimum variance.

is only 0.05 mm and water is on one
side and air is on the other side of
the film. The surface temperature is
estimated to be different from the
water temperature by less than 1 % of
the difference between the temperatures of the water and the surrounding
air.

The experimental result is shown in
Fig.12. Each measurement by the zero-
derivative method has a good repeatability and an accuracy of ± 0.1°C.
For comparison, the surface temperature is measured by a 0.1ϕ mm thermocouple and the result is also shown
in Fig.12. While the measurement by
the 0.1 ϕ mm thermocouple is dependent on the difference between the
temperatures of the water and of the
air, the system by the zero-derivative
method measures the correct surface
temperatures regardless of the temperature difference.

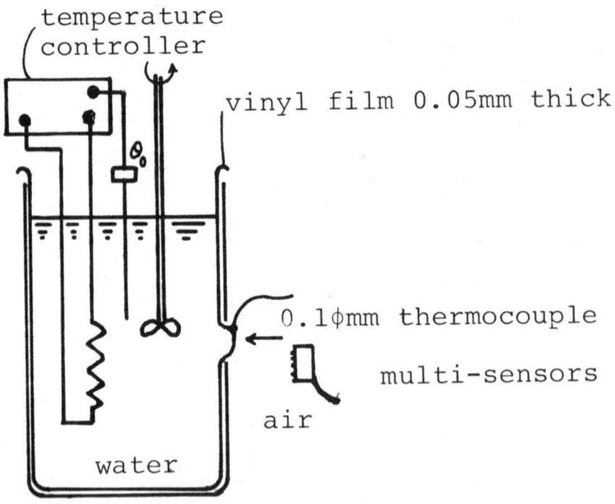

Fig.11   The experimental setup
         for testing the zero-
         derivative method.

A ; multi-sensors

B ; initial conditioners

C ; measuring subsystems

D ; data processer

(a)   the total system

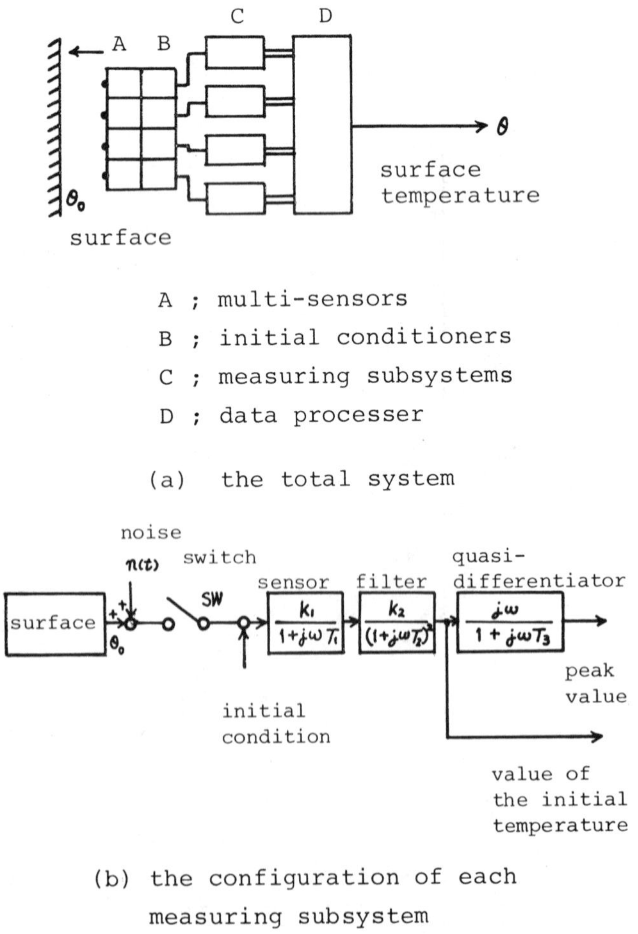

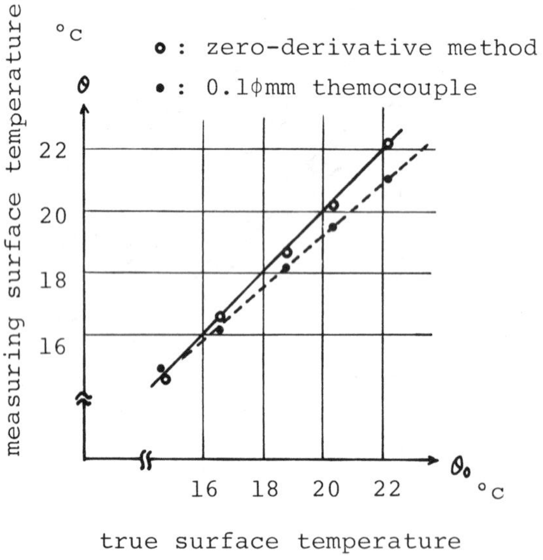

Fig.12   The experimental result
         where the air temperature
         is 15.5°C

(b) the configuration of each

     measuring subsystem

Fig.10   The measuring system
         to which the zero-
         derivative method is
         applied

CONCLUSION

In the present paper, a guiding
principle in designing a reliable
inspection system is shown with ex-
aming the noise contamination. To
achieve a high measuring accuracy,
the multi-sensors are used for giving the spatial average of sensing
points, and to shorten the measuring
time, the transient responses from
the sensors are sampled for averaging in the time domain.

As a numerical example, the measuring system is studied in which the

time responses are sampled and/or the multi-sensors are used. As an experimental example, the measuring system by the zero-derivative method is studied for measuring the surface temperature.

ACKNOWLEDGEMENT

The authors wish to thank Associate Prof. A. Kobayashi of Tokyo Institute of Technology for his helpful suggestions in this study.

REFERENCES

1) W.B.Davenport, and W.L.Root, (1958) An Introduction to the Theory of Random Signals and Noise, McGraw-Hill, New York.
2) J.S.Bendat, Mathematical analysis of average response values for nonstationary data, IEEE Trans., BME-11, 72-81(1964).
3) Y.Sawaragi, et al., (1966) Statistical Theory of Automatic Control, Corona, Tokyo.
4) A.Kobayashi, et al., Analysis of a measurement system considering correlated noises, Trans. SICE, 10-6, 662-668(1974).
5) Y.Morita, et al., Measurement of surface temperature by a zero-derivative method, Trans. SICE, 11-3, 263-268(1975).
6) Y.Morita, et al., An automated zero-derivative method for measurement of surface temperature, Trans. SICE, 13-1, 47-52(1977).

A NEW VISTA FOR INSPECTION AND EVALUATION OF MANUFACTURED GOODS

M. Ishigami*, M. Shiizuka* and Y. Morita**

**Technical Research Institute J.S.P.M.I., 1-1-12 Hachiman-cho, Higashi-Kurume-shi, Tokyo, 180-03, Japan*

***Tokyo Institute of Technology, 2-12-1 Ohokayama, Meguro-ku, Tokyo, 152 Japan*

ABSTRACT

Modern instrument technology provides us with means of acquiring lots of data about our manufactured products. Along with the convenience and possibility of judging the products more reasonably than before, a new problem seems to arise, that is, how best to make use of the power of modern instrumentation in our evaluation of a product. In the present paper, the problem is described by referring to some practical examples. A basic theoretical argument is given in a general setting of order topology.

INTRODUCTION

Any product, whether is it one of the similar thousands passing by on a conveyer belt or one assembled by hand in a shop once for all, must meet inspection and evaluation. The purpose of inspection is manifold: to compare one product with another, to discover defects at an early stage, to see if the product is made according to its specification, or to feed the inspection data back to the designer for improvement of the product.

So far no doubt has been raised against the common belief that inspection will improve the quality of a product. There has been an ever-increasing demand on the accuracy, the speed and the variety of inspection. It has been a self-accelerating development. The trend is that all products are to be inspected in process. The recent advances in IC components and computers seem to make "all products inspection" and "in process inspection" quite feasible.

With this feasibility in sight, and for the sake of increasing our knowledge about a product, we are tempted to go on endlessly. Take for example, the case of inspecting the shape of a product. There are verniered calipers and a micrometer to determine lengths, but they are not fit to determine parallelism between two planes. Nor are they suitable for showing the roundness of a cylinder. What about the angles? Speaking of planes, we have the problem of determining their surface roughness for which no final conclusion seems to exist as to how we should describe it. So it might be said that our idea about the shape remains vague and incompatible with the means of determining the shape.

It is well to point out that not only we are tempted to increase our knowledge about the product, but also we are required to execute an overall judgement based on all the data we have taken about the product. The task of an inspector is not simple, but he is very often required to make his conclusion simple. He is to select important parts of the data, weigh the importance of each part and arrive at a simple conclusion. A human mind seems to be capable of comprehending only a few simple conclusions.

In the later chapter of the present paper, a treatise is given to describe an inspection-evalution process as topologizing a set by an order relationship. The simpleness of conclusion in an inspection-evaluation process is reflected by the use of a single inequality relationship in this treatise.

The rich complexity of data gathered by the modern instruments on the one hand, the same old simplicity of mental faculty of men on the other hand, there should be a methodology that unite the both in harmony. This is what the authors try to develop in the present paper.

The application of the methodology seems promising. It can be applied to a general argument of industrial measurement. A few paragraphs before was pointed out the complexity of measuring a shape though it is but a successive measurement of lengths.

A similar argument may be made in measuring temperature. We say that the temperature of a room is such and such. But what do we mean by the temperature of a room? A mercury-in-glass thermometer placed in mid air of the room may tell us one temperature, but that is not all. An elaborate network of thermocouples may be fit into the representative locations of the room: the mid air, the walls, the ceiling, the vent, and so on. The temperature varies with time as well as with locations. If we wish to hook the thermocouples to a recorder so that we take the temperature variation with time, we may do so. But still we may not be taking the temperature of the room.

The complexity of taking data is not a problem. Nor is the speed of taking data. The cost to equip all these modern instruments may be a problem. However, it is not a new problem.

A real new problem emerging with the modern instrument technology is not so technical as it is philosophical. It is not how much, how fast or how accurately we are able to gather measured data. It is rather a problem of interpreting them. Faced with an industrial product, say a gear, we are to judge whether the gear is good, bad, of the first class or of the second class. Our technology can provide us with lots of measured data concerning the various parameters of the gear, but the final form of conclusion must be simple. The totality of gears, each of which has multi-dimensional properties, is somehow classified by one-dimensional order. Any classification of this type is based inevitably on some agreement among us, that is, on our subjectivity.

The concept of measurement held by the authors in this paper is a very general one as illustrated in Fig. 1. There is a set X to be measured. The measurer maps X into L, a set having an order relationship among its members. The measurer may be a mathematical operation, an instrument, a man or any combination of them. The map is influenced by the measurer's will or purpose. In the following chapters we shall discuss the nature of the problem, study the basic mathematics of L, show some examples of L and seek to evaluate the map $f: X \to L$.

The fact that the measurer's will or purpose comes into the picture seems to be very important. This may be explained by an example of measuring a set of students in a classroom. The

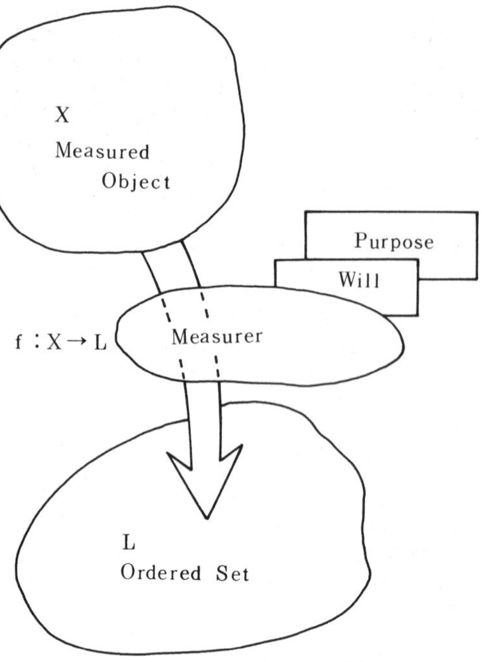

Fig. 1 The concept of measurement

set X may be written as $\{x_1, x_2, \ldots .$ $x_n, \ldots .\}$ each x_i representing an individual student. With the subscripts 1, 2, ... n, ... the set X may seem to have a map f into an ordered set L, i.e., the set of natural (or real) numbers. However, the map $f: X \to L$ may or may not represent a measurement. If, for instance, the subscripts are given only to distinguish one element from another, X may well be written as $\{\alpha, \beta, \gamma \ldots .\}$ rendering the whole set X unorderable (of course, one may still insist that it is ordered according to the Greek alphabetical order, but he is missing the point of argument). If, however, the students are subscripted according to their heights, the map $f : X \to L$ is a measurement of their heights, though it is a crudest form of measurement. The point is that unless we know why they are so subscripted we shall never know if $\{x_1, x_2, \ldots .,$ $x_n, \ldots .\}$ represents a measured set or not. Likewise, according to a measurer's purpose the map $f : X \to L$ gains or loses the meaning. To a measurer interested in the students' intelligence the order by their heights is meaningless.

Now an inspector or an evaluator takes the measured data and draws conclusions. His main job is to summarize and interpret. Some of his tasks may be expressed and discussed in the language of topology as given in the following chapters so that we may rely on the exact definitions and logics of mathematics to make our thought clear and argument straight concerning inspection and evaluation.

The will or purpose is closely related to man's subjectivity. In measurement, inspection or evaluation, the ultimate criterion is within the man. He may have the criterion inborn or brought up by training. When everybody's criterion is the same there is no trouble. But what if there are different criteria? Is every criterion equally good? Or is there a difference?

Only answer to these questions seems to lie in the consequences of these different criteria. However, there is a strong evidence that there are bad criteria and also good criteria. We seem to train ourselves to become wiser in evaluation based upon subjectivity. Some men are born wise, others are not although. More and more attention is given to those special cases of evaluation where only sensory organs of men, animals or other living creatures may be effectively used. Tastes and smells remain to be sanctuary for human inspectors in the world of instrumentation and mechanization. It is interesting to observe that after developing much mechanization to gather large amount of data concerning many factors of a manufactured product, man begins to execute his own inborn ability for judging the product. This is a new sanctuary for men.

AN ILLUSTRATIVE EXAMPLE

In the present paper, the inspection of a gear is discussed at length as an illustrative example. A gear is a manufactured product, fairly complicated in that it has many specifications. The pitch, the profile, the normal pitch, the run-out, the tooth thickness and the tooth alignment are measurable with each gear. Meshed with other gears, the angular transmission error and the power transmission loss are two important variables to note.

The long history of the use of gears and the relative importance among the standard mechanical components, each country has its own standard. There are ISO-1328, AGMA, DIN-3960, 3961, BS-3696, ΓOCT-1643-56, VSM-15535 and JIS B1702 all concerning gears. They have a common purpose to classify gears. However, their criteria are different, though not too greatly.

One important query that the authors would like raise here is on the reasonableness of these criteria. The authors are not proposing that all countries should have one common standard. Our attention should be given to a more fundamental problem of industrial classification, or product evaluation. The authors are concerned about the basic philosophy lying under the prevailing method of classification in the industry.

Take JIS (and the authors are sure that other standards are likely vulnerable). The classification is done by taking the measurement of eight variables of a gear:

1. adjacent traverse pitch error
2. difference in adjacent traverse pitch errors of two neighboring teeth
3. normal individual base pitch error
4. total cumulative pitch error
5. radial run-out
6. total profile error
7. pitch circle diameter
8. module

There are nine classes in the variables 1 through 6. The pitch circle diameter (item 7) has five to eight ranges depending upon the size of the gear. The module (item 8) has nine ranges. A gear has a range with respect to each of the items 7 and 8. Its nominal class is the lowest of its classes with respect to the items 1 through 6. (See Fig. 2).

The total cumulative pitch error may be measured from such actual measurement data as shown in Fig. 3. Notice it is only a single-valued function, a point in a function space. To classify the function, the usual practice is to take its Chebyshef's norm.

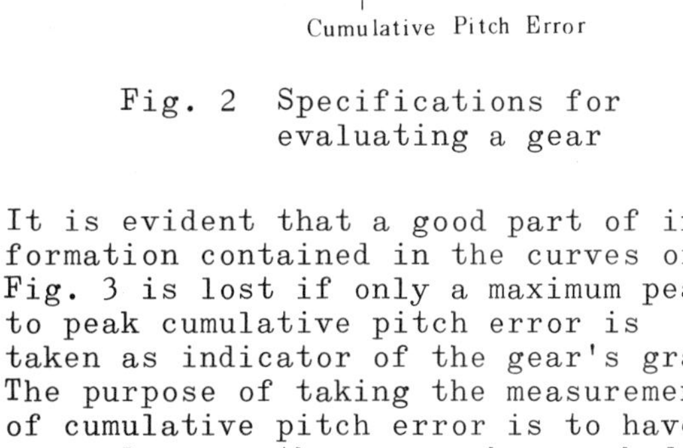

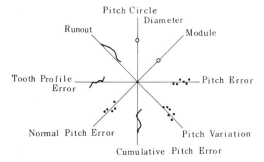

Fig. 2 Specifications for evaluating a gear

It is evident that a good part of information contained in the curves of Fig. 3 is lost if only a maximum peak-to peak cumulative pitch error is taken as indicator of the gear's grade. The purpose of taking the measurement of cumulative pitch error is to have some clues on the gear, when meshed with another gear, as to:

(1) how well it transmits an angle,
(2) how effectively it transmits power,
(3) what level of noise will be expected
(4) what amount of heat will be gen-

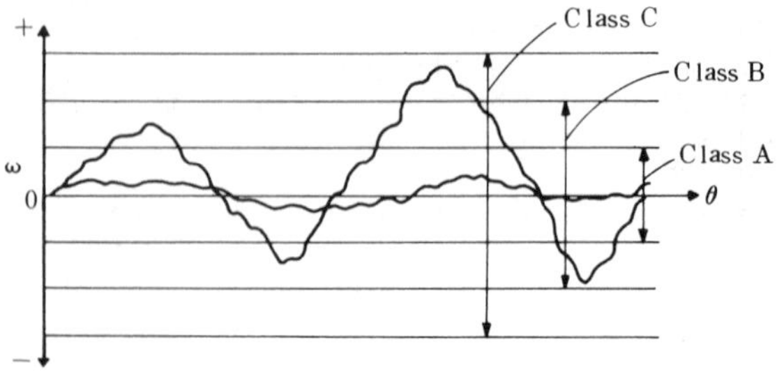

Fig. 3 Classification by Chebyshef's norm

erated.

We have not yet known exactly how many variables of the gear would properly describe its characteristics in order that we may answer the above questions (1) ~ (4). But our engineering intuition tells us that a gear should be measured in meshing with another gear if some characteristics (such as those (1) ~ (4)) closely related to meshing are sought after.

In the later chapter, we shall introduce a method to obtain the cumulative pitch error from the record of a single-flank gear meshing tester. The modern data handling technique is fully utilized. An era of highspeed computing systems, now is the time for us to take a good look again at those established standards and methods of classification made according to the obsolescent, if not obsolete, technology of old days. By the authors' method, it is easy to show the span or range in which the meshing curves lie, and to show that there is no clear-cut boundary between a first-class gear and a second-class gear.

Is it possible then to assign a logical classification in the set of manufactured gears? How does the classification relate to the vagueness of measured variables such as those in gear meshing? The authors try to answer these questions by treating them in a general setting of the fundamental theory of metrology.

THEORETICAL

The Nature of the Problem of Classification

In Fig. 3 are depicted some typical curves representing cumulative pitch errors. Our immediate purpose is to evaluate the goodness of the gear from the record. A similar situation arises with the single flank gear meshing test explained in the later chapter. We have a meshing record as shown in Fig. 4.

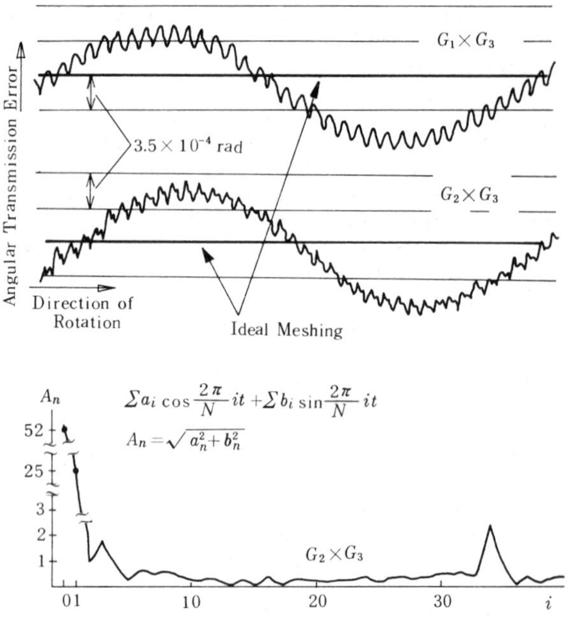

Fig. 4 Record of gear meshing and its frequency analysis

There are two records of angular transmission. One is between gear G_1 and gear G_3 ($G_1 \times G_3$) and the other is between gear G_2 and gear G_3 ($G_2 \times G_3$). The abscissa is the rotating angle of the gear and the ordinate is the angular transmission error. So, as indicated in the figures, an ideal meshing of gears is a horizontal straight line viz. zero angular transmission error at all angles.

Notice that two records in Fig. 4 are similar but not the same. We are to judge which meshing is better $G_1 \times G_3$ or $G_2 \times G_3$. Each record is only a part of long continuous output from the tester. We may apply Fourier analysis and list up all the frequency components as indicated in the lower part of Fig. 4. But the analytical result is only showing a general idea about the curve. Continuing recording we may pick another part having a little different frequency component.

In comparing two records of the tester, we may choose a suitable metric (distance) from the ideal record shown in Fig. 4 and say that the larger the metric is the less desirable the meshing becomes. The choice of the metric depends on our own subjectivity, or an agreement among us. We shall observe that even when only two factors are to be considered from our experience, the choice of the metric cannot be unique. Let X be a set of records of the tester. For a fixed $y \in X$ can be assigned two characteristics desirable for meshing. One is the amplitude of the record

(Chebyshef's metric). We shall name it A, and assume there are three classes A^+ (desirable), A^0 (median), A^- (undesirable).

The other is the high frequency component. We say that the more rugged the meshing record looks, the less desirable the meshing becomes. This characteristics we shall name B and similarly assume B^+, B^0, and B^-. Now we give an order structure to X and write it as $(X, \gtrsim)$. As is usually understood in the theory of ordered structure, for some $x, y \in X$, $x \gtrsim y$ means x is given priority over y. Both x and y have characteristics A^0B^-, A^+B^-, etc. If x has A^+B^+(denoted as $x(A^+B^+)$) and $y(A^-B^0)$, obviously $x \gtrsim y$. There may be other elements $w, v \in X$ difficult to compare, e.g. in case $w(A^+B^-)$ and $v(A^-B^+)$, as long as we place an equal weight on A and B. No unique choice of metric seems possible because A and B are qualitatively different.

This example suggests that when we describe our ordered structure $(X, \gtrsim)$, it should be as general as possible. The weak order and the simple order have been investigated to a considerable extent (1), but their axioms, the connectedness in particular, seem to be too restrictive to be useful in our industrial classification. We propose a partially ordered structure and investigate its basic properties in the next section.

A Topology Induced in the Partially Ordered Set

First we give basic definitions with respect to $(X, \gtrsim)$. For some $x,y,z \in X$,

Def. 1 x and y are comparable $\Leftrightarrow$ $x \gtrsim y$ or $y \gtrsim x$
Def. 2 $x \gtrsim y \Leftrightarrow y \lesssim x$
Def. 3 $x \gtrsim x$ ($\gtrsim$ is reflexive)
Def. 4 $x \gtrsim y,\ y \gtrsim z \Leftrightarrow x \gtrsim z$ ($\gtrsim$ is transitive)
Def. 5 $x \gtrsim y,\ y \gtrsim x \Leftrightarrow x \sim y$ ($\gtrsim$ and $\lesssim$ are antisymmetric)

The binary relation $\gtrsim$ is not excluding the possibility of a loop, namely, $x \gtrsim y$, $y \gtrsim z$, and $z \gtrsim x$ for some $x,y,z \in X$. This is inconvenient to topologize X by the partial ordering. It seems necessary to introduce the concept of negation, in one sense or another, to define $\succ$ in a partially ordered set. Thus,

Def. 6 x and y are negatively comparable. $\Leftrightarrow$ Either x NOT $\gtrsim$ y or x NOT $\lesssim$ y
Def. 7 x NOT $\gtrsim$ y $\Leftrightarrow$ y NOT $\lesssim$ x
Def. 8 x NOT $\gtrsim$ y $\Rightarrow$ $x \in \{w/w \gtrsim y\}^c$, x NOT $\lesssim$ y $\Rightarrow$ $x \in \{w/w \lesssim y\}^c$ (where the superscript c means the complement of a subset)
Def. 9 $x \succ y \Leftrightarrow x \gtrsim y$, x NOT $\lesssim$ y
Def.10 $x \prec y \Leftrightarrow x \lesssim y$, x NOT $\gtrsim$ y
Def.11 $x \gtrsim y$, y NOT $\lesssim$ z $\Rightarrow$ x NOT $\lesssim$ z
Def.12 $x \lesssim y$, y NOT $\gtrsim$ z $\Rightarrow$ x NOT $\gtrsim$ z
Def.13 x NOT $\lesssim$ y, $y \gtrsim z$ $\Rightarrow$ x NOT $\lesssim$ z
Def.14 x NOT $\gtrsim$ y, $y \lesssim z$ $\Rightarrow$ x NOT $\gtrsim$ z

From the above definitions, it is easy to prove the following propositions.

Prop. 1. $x \succ y \Leftrightarrow y \prec x$

Proof. LHS $x \succ y \Rightarrow x \gtrsim y$, x NOT $\lesssim$ y (Def. 9)
$\Rightarrow y \lesssim x$, y NOT $\gtrsim$ x (Defs. 2, 7)
$\Rightarrow y \prec x$ (Def.10) Q.E.D.

Prop. 2. $x \succ y,\ y \succ z \Rightarrow x \succ z$

Proof. $x \succ y \Rightarrow x \gtrsim y$, x NOT $\lesssim$ y (Def. 9)
$y \succ z \Rightarrow y \gtrsim z$, y NOT $\lesssim$ z (Def. 9)
LHS $\Rightarrow x \gtrsim y$, y NOT $\lesssim$ z, $x \gtrsim z$ (Def. 4)
$\Rightarrow x \gtrsim z$, x NOT $\lesssim$ z (Def.11)
$\Rightarrow x \succ z$ (Def. 9) Q.E.D.

Prop. 3. $x \succ y,\ y \gtrsim z \Rightarrow x \succ z$

Prop. 4. $x \gtrsim y,\ y \succ z \Rightarrow x \succ z$

Prop. 5. $x \gtrsim y,\ y \sim z \Rightarrow x \gtrsim z$

Prop. 6. $x \sim y,\ y \gtrsim z \Rightarrow x \gtrsim z$

Prop. 7. In a one-way comparison (when only $\succ$, $\gtrsim$ and $\sim$ are involved), the ordering polynomials are associative.

Proof. There is a definite order of strength between $\succ$, $\gtrsim$ and $\sim$ as seen in the above propositions 2 through 6 so that for example the following deduction yields the same result.

$$(x \succ y \gtrsim w) \sim v \succ t \Rightarrow x \succ t$$

$$x \succ (y \gtrsim w \sim v \succ t) \Rightarrow x \succ t$$

Prop. 8. $x \succ y \Rightarrow$ x and y are distinct elements of X.

Proof. Suppose false.

By Def. 7 $x \succ x \Rightarrow x \gtrsim x$, x NOT $\lesssim$ x.

But x NOT $\lesssim x \Rightarrow x \in \{w/w \lesssim x\}^c$ which is a contradiction to Def. 3, the reflexivity of $\gtrsim$. Q.E.D.

If there are elements of X such that $x_1 \succ x_2$ ..... $x_i \succ x_{i+1}$ ....., we know they are distinct by Proposition 8, and we can introduce a topology $\mathcal{T}$ into $(X, \gtrsim)$ by defining open sets $\{x/x \succ x_i\}$ $i = 1, 2, \ldots$ satisfying:

$$\{x/x \succ x_i\} \subset \{x/x \succ x_j\} \Leftrightarrow x_i \succ x_j \quad (1)$$

where the inclusion means a proper inclusion.
In Equation (1) $\Leftarrow$ is obvious by the transitivity of $\succ$ (Prop. 2), but $\Rightarrow$ must be defined.

Theorem 1. When $(X, \gtrsim)$ is topologized by the open sets defined by Equation (1),

$$\{x/x \gtrsim x_i\} \subset \{x/x \gtrsim x_j\} \Longleftrightarrow x_i > x_j .$$

Proof. First we show RHS $\Longrightarrow$ LHS. By Def. 9 and Def. 8,

$$\{x/x \gtrsim x_i\} \supset \{x/x > x_i\} \tag{2}$$

$$\{x/x \gtrsim x_j\} \supset \{x/x > x_j\} \tag{3}$$

$\forall x_m \in \{x/x \gtrsim x_i\}$ we have $x_m \gtrsim x_i > x_j$.

Assume $\{x/x \gtrsim x_i\} \supset \{x/x > x_j\}$.

Prop. 4 tells that $x_m > x_j$, and so we have $x_m \in \{x/x > x_j\}$ a contradiction. Therefore we must have

$$\{x/x \gtrsim x_i\} \subseteq \{x/x > x_j\} \tag{4}$$

Equations (2), (3) and (4) give $\{x/x \gtrsim x_i\} \subset \{x/x \gtrsim x_j\}$.

Next we show LHS $\Longrightarrow$ RHS. From LHS

$$x_i \gtrsim x_j . \tag{5}$$

Assume $x_j \gtrsim x_i$ at the same time, $\forall x_n \in \{x/x \gtrsim x_j\}$, we have $x_n \gtrsim x_j \gtrsim x_i$ $\Longrightarrow x_n \in \{x/x \gtrsim x_i\}$ a contradiction to the proper inclusion of LHS. Therefore we must have

$$x_j \in \{x/x \gtrsim x_i\}^c \tag{6}$$

When x_i and x_j are chosen to satisfy Equation (1), x_i and x_j must be negatively comparable. So either x_i NOT$\lesssim x_j$ or x_j NOT$\lesssim x_i$, but the latter possibility is non-existent because of Def. 8 and Equation (5). Therefore

$$x_i \text{ NOT} \lesssim x_j \tag{7}$$

Equations (5) and (7) and Def. 9 give RHS.
This completes the proof.

Q.E.D.

Theorem 2. When $(X, \gtrsim, \mathcal{T})$ is a T_0-space, it is also a T_1-space.
Proof. First the terminology is given (2).

T_0-space: $(X, \gtrsim, \mathcal{T})$ is said to be a T_0-space iff given any two distinct points $x,y \in X$, at least one point has a topological neighborhood not containing the other.

T_1-space: $(X, \gtrsim, \mathcal{T})$ is said to be a T_1-space iff given any two distinct points $x,y \in X$, each point has a topological neighborhood not containing the other.

Point of Closure: A point s is said to be a point of closure of $A \subseteq X$ if each neighborhood of s contains a point (or points) of A. The set of such points is called the closure of A and written as $\tilde{A}$.

Now, our Equation (1) defines a special topological space $(X, \gtrsim, \mathcal{T})$ in which two distinct open sets are joined by the proper inclusion. Therefore if the space is T_0, it is obvious that each topological neighborhood contains a point of X, and so any point of X is a point of closure if it is not maximum with respect to $>$.

If x_m is the maximum, $\{x/x > x_m\}$ is empty; however, since X is a T_0-space $\{x_m\}$ must be an open set, and $\{x_m\}$ is contained in every other non-empty topological neighborhood. Therefore x_m is a point of closure.

Thus we conclude if $(X, \gtrsim, \mathcal{T})$ is a T_0-space, every open set is also a closed set. Hence taking any two distinct points of X, we can find each has a topological neighborhood not containing the other.

Q.E.D.

It is suggested that if we distinguish every element of X with respect to $>$ or when X is a T_0-space our method of classification is perfect, since $(X, \gtrsim, \mathcal{T})$ becomes a linearly ordered space and all the rich results with linearity can be applied. Generally, we cannot expect $(X, \gtrsim, \mathcal{T})$ to be linearly or even weakly ordered. The less we can choose candidates for x_i's in Equation (1), X becomes the less separable or the more ambiguous with respect to $\gtrsim$. We may take the degree of separation as an indicator of the ambiguity of X. In the last chapter, we shall discuss the numerical evaluation of the degree of separation.

APPLICATION OF DATA HANDLING TECHNOLOGY TO INSPECTION — A CASE OF GEAR MESHING TEST

A Trial to Obtain Cumulative Pitch Error from the Record of Gear Meshing Tester

As was pointed out in the foregoing, the (cumulative) pitch error is one of the important specifications of a gear. A standard method of measuring the pitch error is by a gear tester operated manually to measure the pitch tooth by tooth. It takes time and skill to get a good result. Small gears are not measurable by a manual method.

In Fig. 5 is shown the principle of a gear meshing test. The driving and driven gears are mounted on two parallel shafts, each of which has the same circular grated disk. The rotating angle of each shaft is read by the grating electrically.

The angular transmission error $\Delta\theta$ is expressed as difference between the theoretical angle rotation $\theta(n+1)/n$

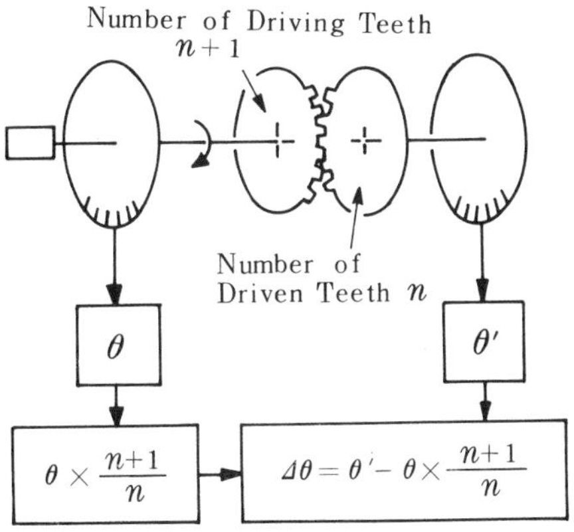

Fig. 5 Principle of gear meshing test

of the driven gear and the actual angle rotation θ' of the driven gear which has some errors in the dimensions of its teeth. Thus,

$$\Delta\theta = \theta' - \theta \frac{n+1}{n} \tag{8}$$

The level of manufacturing technology for gears today is such that each tooth is cut, ground or shaped almost identically, one tooth differing from its neighbor by perhaps 3 ~ 30 μm in its shape. This is reflected in the second harmonic component of the record shown in Figs. 4, 10 etc. We see a big undulation superimposed with a ripple-like small oscillation. The big undulation has the same period as that of one turn of the driving gear. The small oscillation is composed of generally similar peaks and valleys. The similarity is an indication of the similarity of the teeth of the gear. The first harmonic is usually thought to be caused by a run out or an eccentric mounting of the gears. The second harmonic is caused by one cycle of meshing, that is, from the moment one tooth starts engaging with a tooth of the other gear to the moment it ends engaging.

When there is no first harmonic angular transmission error between the two gears, the second harmonic component may still exist. However on the record, it will be lying along a straight line parallel to the abscissa.

Let us take the difference of the heights of two neighboring peaks of the second harmonic oscillation. We assume, and are convinced that we do so on a sound ground, that the difference is principally caused by the sum of the pitch errors or the two meshing teeth. In our experiment, the driving gear has one tooth more than the driven gear (Table 1). So if a tooth T_a of the driving gear meshes a tooth T_b of the driven gear, T_a meshes the tooth next to T_b of the driven gear after the shaft makes one turn.

TABLE 1 Gears Used in Experiment

	Module	Pressure Angle	Number of Teeth	Note	
Driving	3	20°	36	Ground	Contact Ratio: 1 approx.
Driven			35	Hobbed	

Parts of the meshing curve are shown in Fig. 6. We shall take a peak P_0 and call it the start of meshing. From P_0 to P_1 the curve is continuous and the driving gear rotates by θ_0. Let the cumulative pitch error of the driving gear during this rotation be designated as ε_{11} .

From P_1 to P_i the driving gear makes i-1 complete turns (by $2\pi(i-1)$ radian). Now if the cumulative pitch error of the driven gear from P_0 to P_1 is ε_{2i} , the angular transmission error $\Delta\theta_i$ between the two gears from P_0 to P_1 is expressed as follows.

$$\Delta\theta_i = \{\theta_0 + 2\pi(i-1) + \varepsilon_{11}\} \frac{n+1}{n} + \varepsilon_{2i} - \{\theta_0 + 2\pi(i-1)\} \frac{n+1}{n}$$

$$= \varepsilon_{11} \frac{n+1}{n} + \varepsilon_{2i} \quad (i=1 \quad n) \tag{9}$$

The error $\Delta\theta_i$ in equation (9) has the same dimension and meaning as $\Delta\theta$ in equation (8). The correspondence between the terms of equations (8) and (9) will be easily figured out.

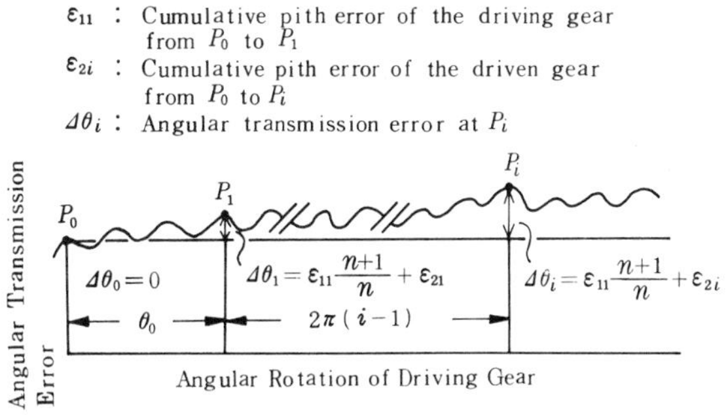

Fig. 6 Calculation of angular transmission error from the record of the gear meshing tester

Take $\Delta\theta_1$ to obtain $\Delta\theta_1 = \varepsilon_{11} \frac{n+1}{n} + \varepsilon_{2i}$

and call P_1 as the starting point for obtaining the cumulative pitch error ε_{2i} letting $\varepsilon_{21} = 0$.
Thus,

$$\varepsilon_{2i} = \Delta\theta_i - \Delta\theta_1 \tag{10}$$

Based on a similar principle, the cumulative pitch error of the driving gear can be obtained. A particular tooth is chosen on the driven gear and the same method explained by Fig. 6 can be used. The angle of rotation between P_1 and P_i is, however, (i-1) complete turns of the driven gear not of the driving gear.

Another way of obtaining the cumulative pitch error of the driving gear is to subtract ε_{2i} (Eq. (10)) from the original angular transmission error curve (Fig. 4). In fig. 13 is shown the obtained cumulative pitch error of the driving gear. The dot signifies that it has been obtained by the method shown in Fig. 6 and the cross signifies that it has been obtained by subtraction of ε_{2i} from the angular transmission error curve. There are only slight differences, for which a comment will be given shortly.

Data handling and result. The output of the single-flank gear meshing tester looks like the one shown in Fig. 7. This analogue output is

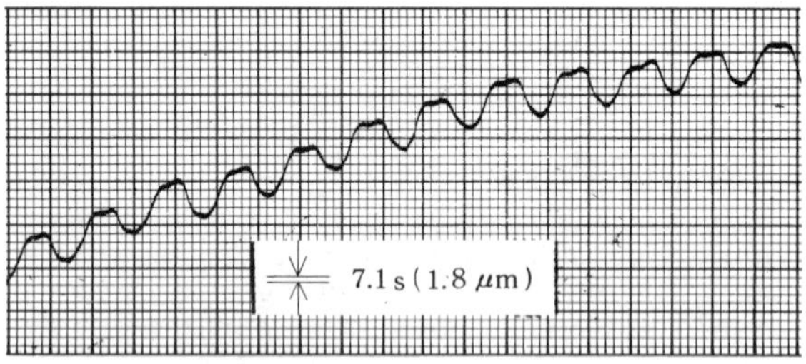

Fig. 7 Output of the single-flank gear meshing tester

converted into a digital form and then processed through a chain of computing circuit.

In Fig. 8 the general outlay of the data handling system is shown.

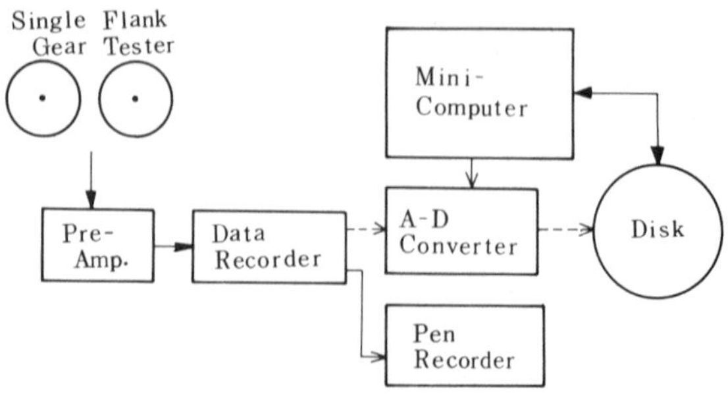

Fig. 8 The data handling system

The main flow of data handling is shown in Fig. 9.

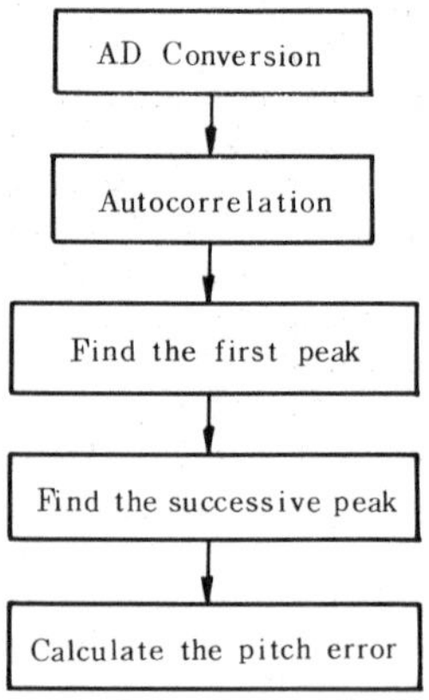

Fig. 9 Flow of data handling

The analog output from the single-flank gear meshing tester is amplified by the pre-amplifier and recorded into the data recorder in a form of magnetic tape. The recorded analogue signal is A-D converted. The minimum step for the digital output is 5mV. The digital output of the converter is expressed in the unit of circular pitch (μm). The teeth engagement is so adjusted that the number of engaged teeth of a gear is nearly one at a time. The sampling interval is twenty-one for one tooth. The digital

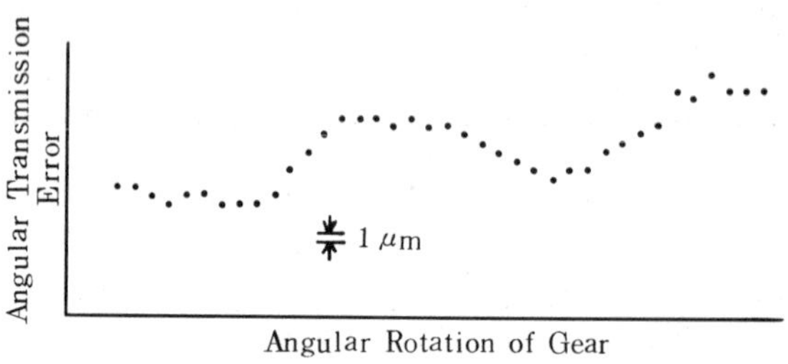

Fig. 10 Digitalized meshing curve (angular transmission error)

form of angular transmission error is shown in Fig. 10. Since the driving gear has thirty-six teeth and the driven gear thirty-five there are $36 \times 35 \times 21 = 26460$ points for one complete run of a meshing test.

In the flow of data handling, the next step is taking the autocorrelation function. This is done by a commercially available program. The purpose of this step is to determine the exact number of sampling points during a tooth's engagement cycle.

The third step of data handling is the search for a peak. A problem here is the irregularity of wave forms of the second harmonic oscillation. The number of sampling points is large enough to indicate a peak or near-peak, provided that there are not much spikes in the record. The method of locating the peak P_{i+1} next to a known peak P_i is shown in Fig. 11. The area S defined by the curve and the straight line connecting the two sampling points, one of which is P_i, is computed. The other point is taken one by one around the location estimated by the autocorrelation function. When S becomes maximum, we say that the point is P_{i+1} and finish the search.

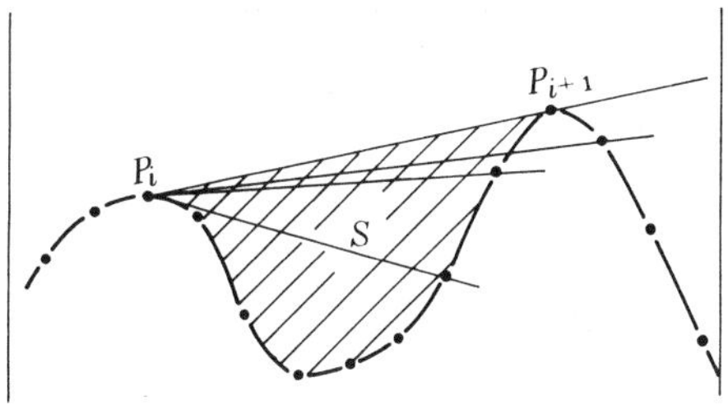

Fig. 11 Search of peak

Once P_i (i=1, 2, ..., n, ... 36) is determined, we can apply the method described in Fig. 6 and by Equations (9) and (10) to obtain the cumulative pitch error of the driven gear. We may start from any tooth and call the corresponding peak as P_1 in Fig. 6. Depending on the initial tooth the cumulative pitch error will be slightly changed.

Here the power of modern data handling technique can be made to work fully. All data taking, peak searching, calculating and printing data are automatic. Taking average is of no trouble either. In Fig. 12 we show the cumulative pitch error of the driven gear, a result of averaging ten cumulative pitch errors obtained by taking ten consecutive teeth in turn to be a starting tooth. Manually this process of getting the average is too formidable to execute.

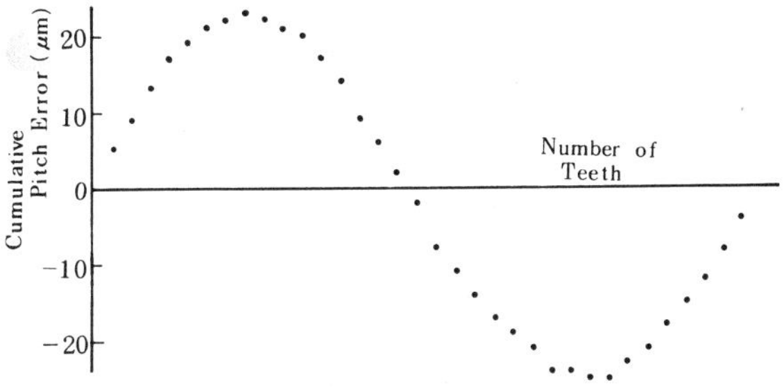

Fig. 12 Cumulative pitch error of the driven gear

Immediately after Equation (10), we showed that there are two alternative methods of obtaining the cumulative pitch error of the driving gear. In Fig. 13 are the data given by the two methods shown, one by dots and the other by cross.

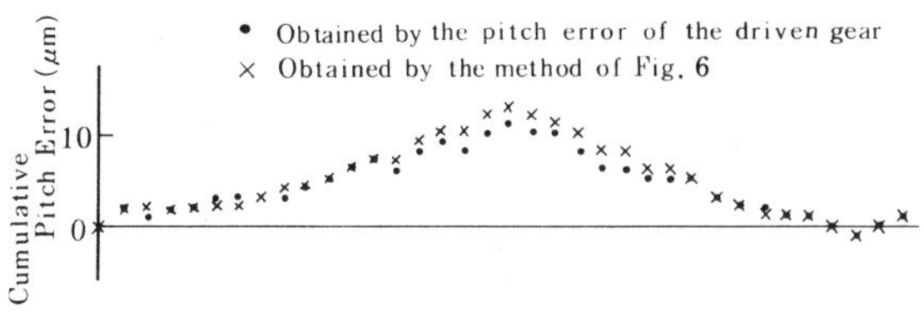

Fig. 13 Cumulative pitch error of the driving gear

The both cumulative pitch errors shown in Figs. 12 and 13 are in fair agreement with manually obtained figures. However, it should be emphasized again that the results obtained by the proposed method should contain more information about the gear than a result manually obtained. For instance, we doubt if the cumulative pitch error should be expressed by a single number (peak-to-peak) when we know how the error curve differs depending on the choice of initial tooth in taking the measurement.

EASE OF EVALUATION

The case of evaluating a record of single flank gear meshing tester was discussed already. Classifying curves of cumulative pitch error will pose a similar, but perhaps a little simpler, problem. Here we have more or less the same frequency component and we are concerned only with the amplitude of the curve.

We have pointed out that a curve may be thought of a thick belt within which the data may vary with the initial choice of tooth. Now if we have many such belts to compare in proximity, the evaluation becomes difficult. It is evident that there is no clear-cut boundary between a class and a class above it.

In our chapter THEORETICAL, we pointed out the separability as indication of ambiguity of a set X to be evaluated. If X is separable, it is easy to evaluate, so the separability is synonymous to the ease of evaluation as far as one-dimensional ordering is concerned. In the sequel, we develop a numerical argument.

Numerical Expression of Ease of Evaluation

As we have seen with $X=\{x_1, x_2, \ldots x_i \ldots\}$, we may choose x_i's satisfying Equation (1) so that the whole set may be ordered. An element $x \in X$ will have an open neighborhood of the form

$\{w/w \succ x_i\}$. If we can state further $x_j \succ x \succ x_i$, the measurement of x with respect to becomes more precise. A natural extension of this thought would lead us to map X into (0,1). Since x_i's satisfying Equation (1) are distinct points (Prop. 8), they have corresponding points on (0, 1). If we take into account that there may be elements in X joined by $\sim$ with x_i's, it is more practical to assign intervals to x_i's instead of points. Let these intervals lie on (0,1) from right to left in the order of $\succ$. Other points will have corresponding intervals lying within (0,1). We may define that a point uncomparable with any other point has the interval (0.1).

Let an interval as such have a positive length (Lebesgue measure) Δ_1 on (0,1) and the set of all points mapped into this interval be A_1. Similarly let Δ_2 define A_2, let $\Delta_3 A_3$ ... to divide X in such a way that

$$\cup A_i = X \qquad i=1, 2 \ldots.$$

$$A_i \cap A_j = \phi \qquad i \neq j.$$

Let $\triangle$ be representing all Δ_i's. What does a $\triangle$ signify? It is an indicator of measurement precision. Numerically its degree is written as a function of $\triangle$. We may derive an index of "goodness" $G(\triangle)$ of the measurement with respect to $\gtrsim$. Our engineering experience tells us that $G(\triangle)$ should possess the following characteristics.

1. G is a monotone decreasing function of $\triangle$. A narrow interval represents a good measurement.
2. $G(1) = 0$.
3. $G(n\triangle) - G(\triangle)$ is a function of n only, where n is a positive integer.

Thus we may propose

$$G(\triangle) = k \log \triangle \qquad (11)$$

where k is a negative constant, as an expression of goodness of measurement.

The contribution of the subset Y to the whole set X with respect to the goodness of measurement will be taken proportional to the measure $\mu(Y)$ of $Y \subset X$. So the index S_X representing how good a set X is measured will be expressed as:

$$S_X = \sum_X \mu(Y) \log \frac{1}{\triangle} \qquad (12)$$

taking $k = -1$.

It can be seen readily that a well separated set has a high S_X value; whereas if there is no x_i all intervals will have a length 1 rendering S_X to be zero. The length of $\triangle$ is determined by various factors, but once a rule is set, it is a matter of simple calculation to express numerically the degree of separation of the original set X.

Some Calculation of S_X We shall restrict our problem to the industrial classification and see how Equation (11) could be utilized. In Fig. 14 we show a set X is divided into two classes according to the order relationship $\succ$. If the classes are clear-cut and no ambiguity is involved at the boundary element x_i with respect to $\succ$ as in Figure 14(a) there are $X_1 = \{x/x \succ x_i\}$ and $X_2 = \{x/x \lesssim x_i\}$, for instance. Two elements belonging to X_1 need not be comparable. The same applies to X_2. The interval $\triangle_1$ corresponding to X_1 and $\triangle_2$ corresponding to X_2 are now to be determined. We may suppose $\triangle_i$ (i=1,2) is in proportion to $\mu(X_i)$ since increasing the size of a subset X_i will tend to introduce more variety among its members.

Suppose there are two distinct points x_i and x_j giving $X_1 = \{x/x \gtrsim x_j\}$ and $X_2 = \{x/x \lesssim x_j\}$ with $x_i \succ x_j$. The whole set divides into several conceivable classes, e.g. $\{x/x \in X_1\}$, $\{x/x \text{ NOT} \lesssim x_j\}$, $\{x/x \in X_1,\ x \in X_2\}$, etc. But for now let X_1 and X_2 be interpreted to roughly divide the whole set into two classes and all members of X are to be labeled as belonging to one of the following subsets: (i) X_1, (ii) X_2, (iii) neither of X_1 alone nor X_2 alone. The subset (iii) may include an element $x \in X_1$ and X_2 or an element $y \in X_1$ or X_2 and may be expressed as $(X_1, \triangle, X_2)^c$, where $\triangle$ means a symmetric difference. This interpretation is admittedly subjective, but thought to represent an aspect of classification.

As shown in Fig. 14 (b), $\triangle_1$ and $\triangle_2$ are now assigned to X_1 and X_2 to be proportional to $\mu(\{x/x \gtrsim x_j\})$ and $\mu(\{x/x \lesssim x_j\})$, respectively. The remaining subset will have $\triangle_a$. Let $\triangle_a = 1$, $\triangle_1 = p + p_a$ and $\triangle_2 = 1 - p$. The goodness of measurement calculated by Equation (11) is

$$S_X = p_a \log \frac{1}{1} + p \log \frac{1}{p+p_a} + (1-p-p_a) \log \frac{1}{1-p}$$

taking the proportaonal constant between μ and $\triangle$ as unity. Regarding S_X as a function of p and assuming p_a is constant,

$$\frac{dS_X}{dp} = \log \frac{1-p}{p+p_a} - \frac{p}{p+p_a} + \frac{1-p-p_a}{1-p} = 0$$

yields $p = \frac{1-p_a}{2}$ to give the maximum of S_X. This means a symmetric classification is the best measurement when the whole set is divided into two rough classes. Similar calculations have been made with symmetric three classes and with equal-sized n-classes as shown in Fig. 15 and Fig. 16 respectively.

In the calculations of Figs. 14, 15 and 16, the whole set is "covered" by finite classes and every element of x belongs at least one of these classes. If it belongs to two or more classes, their union is thought to be its class. This concept may be found useful when the boundary of the classes becomes fuzzy by human subjectivity or by some other reasons. The size of the class and the number of classes to cover the whole set should have optimum values according to the special conditions of the problem.

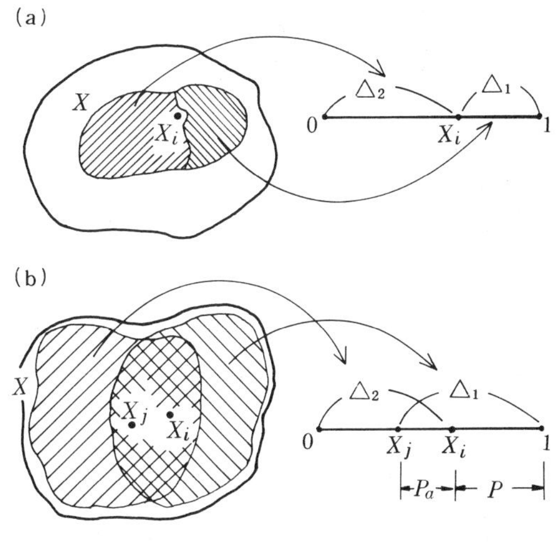

Fig. 14 Classification into two classes

The critical step in the above procedure of evaluating the classification numerically is the determination of $\triangle$. This is somehow related to our subjectivity and engineering common sense. The authors claim no justification for the theoretical ambiguity in proposing the index S_x. However, the intention of the authors may be expressed as follows.

1. When dealing with one-dimensional ordering, there may be no clear-cut boundary between two classes.
2. To express the fuzziness of such an ordering, one must have an overall evaluation of the evaluated set.
3. There are two major factors affecting the ease of evaluation. One is the sharpness of each measured value, and the other is the proportion of this measured value in the totality of the measured object.

There are other ways to formulate Equation (12) (Ref. 4). Though we have not yet tried a use of other types of summations or integrals, it will be also interesting.

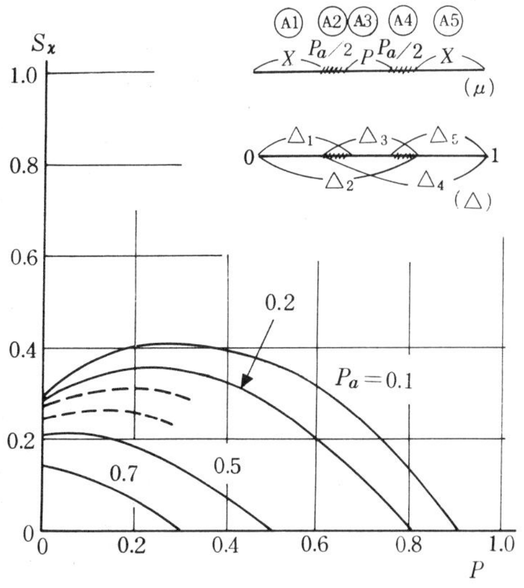

Fig. 15 Classification into three classes

CONCLUSION

In the present paper, the authors have developed a treatise to deal with inspection and evaluation in the mathematical language. The numerical argument might have been a little too far fetched, but it is a first step to arrive at a more realistic and practical method.

Practical application of the present paper may be found where complicated data of inspection pile up high waiting our summary, analysis and succinct conclusion. However, the aim of the present paper is to draw the reader's attention to the very interesting and important aspect of modern instrument technology that a mass of data gathered by instruments, how gigantic it may be, must be broken down and re-assembled to be accepted by a man's mind. This process can be discussed logically and a better, if not best, way of evaluation can be proposed. After all, man should remain a master, not become a slave of the system of instruments and mechanical data handling devices.

REFERENCES

1. Krantz,D.H., Luce,R.D., Suppes, P., and Tversky,A., (1971) Foundations of Measurement, Volume I, Academic Press, New York and London.
2. Morita,Y., Oka,Y., On a loop in fuzzy evaluation and measurement, Summary of Papers on General Fuzzy Problems Report No. 2, 87 (1976)
3. Jameson,G.J.O., (1974) Topology and Normed Spaces, Chapmand and Hall, London.
4. Ishigami,M., et al., Study on

Pattern Measurement and Data Processing, J. of Technical Research Institute JSPMI, 12, 1, 1 (1976)

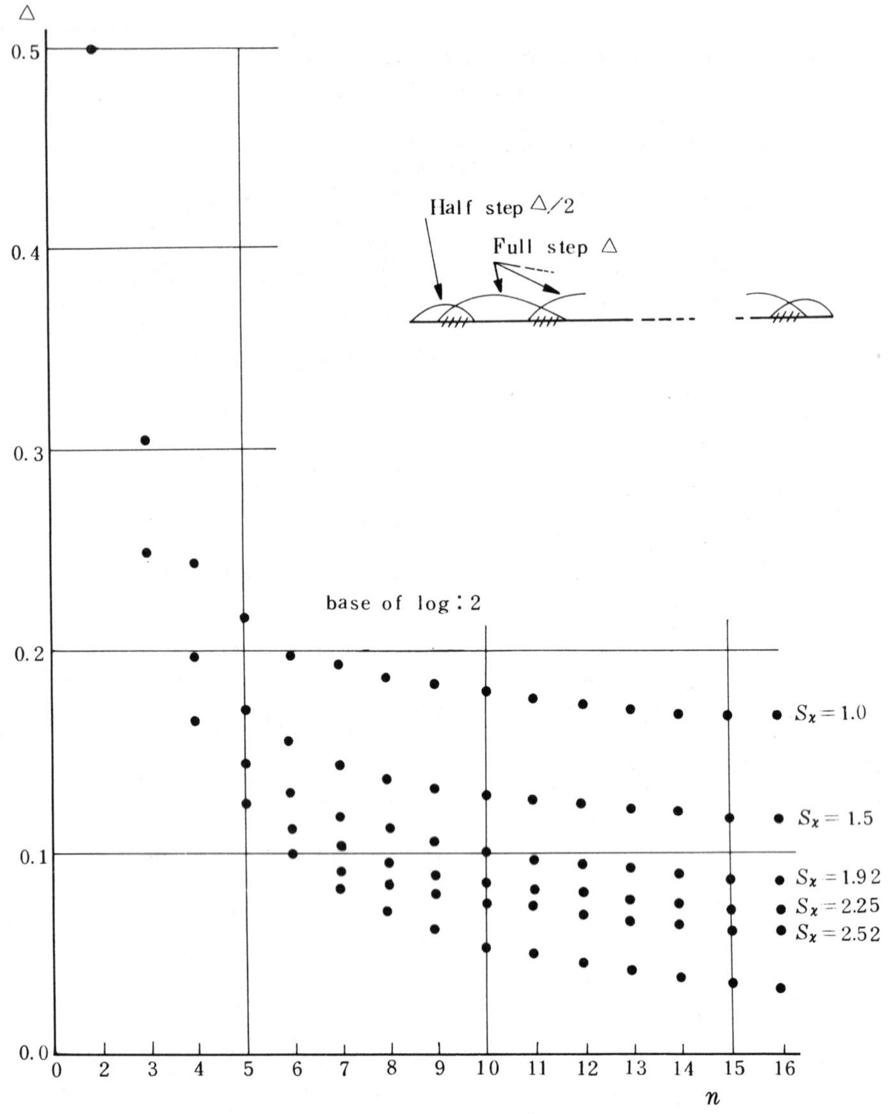

Fig. 16 Classification into n classes

STUDY ON AUTOMATIC INSPECTION OF DEFECTS ON CONTACT PARTS

A. Kuni*, Y. Ohshima*, N. Akiyama*, K. Isoda*, N. Uno and S. Hiratsuka****

**Production Engineering Research Laboratory, Hitachi, Ltd. 292 Yoshida-cho, Totsuka-ku, Yokohama 244, Japan*
***Totsuka Works, Hitachi, Ltd. 216 Totsuka-cho, Totsuka-ku, Yokohama 244, Japan*

INTRODUCTION

Automation for the appearance inspection process has been so far the following two reasons, while automation for the production process has been made a great progress. It appears difficult firstly to mechanize the excellent function of the eyes of human being, and secondly to indicate the appearance inspection criteria in terms of quantity. In addition, it seems almost impossible for the purpose of automation of inspection to change the design of products and to alter the existing criteria which is carried out through visual inspection, from the stand point that the first priority is given to production.

However, nowadays the requests from the production side for automation of appearance inspection has been greatly increased and in this connection it seems necessary to meet the demand step by step. In compliance with the requests, we developed an automatic appearance inspection device for contact points of relay switch with the aid of TV camera, and it has successfully been introduced to the production line.

This is the report on the mechanism of detective parts and its algorithm.

Contact Points of Relay Switch and their Defects

As shown in Fig. 1, 16 pairs of or total number of 32 contact points are welded on a stainless spring sheet. Dimension of a set of each pair is also shown in Fig. 1. A contact point is made of a Cu chip gilded with Au and Pd.

Fig. 2 shows an example of having defects in appearance, which will give bad effects of electrical contact when the switch is turned on, and to insulation when the switch is turned off. These defects are caused while contact points are welded on the spring, and they are roughly classified as follows:

Defects in re welding position of contact points
---- Fig. 2-(a)
Defects in re shape and surface of contact points
---- Fig. 2-(b),(c),(d),(f)
Defects in re surrounding of contact points
---- Fig. 2-(e),(f)

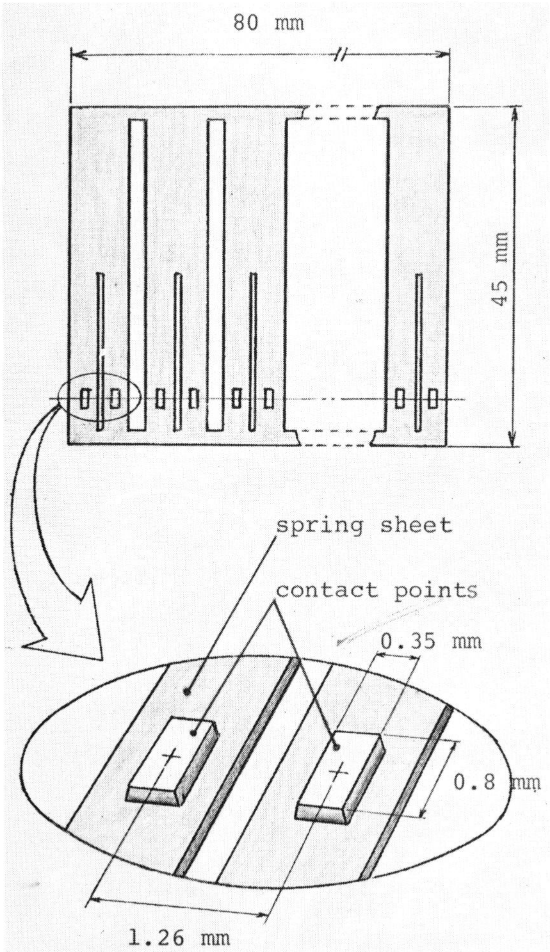

Fig. 1 Contacts and spring sheet using relay switch

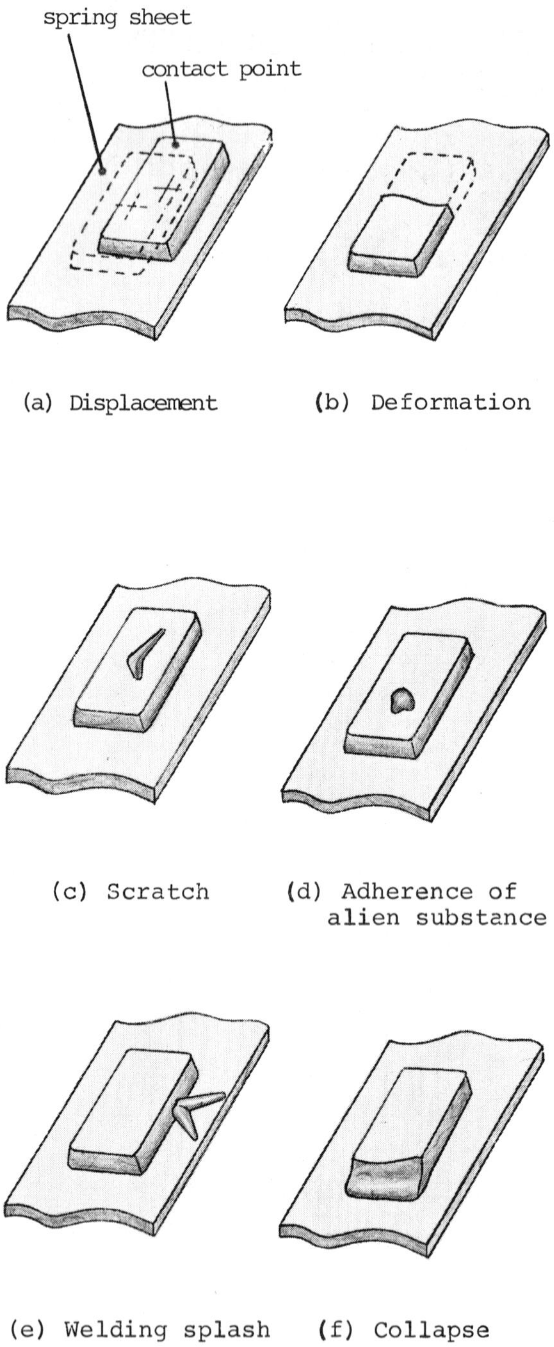

Fig. 2 Illustration of the contact point defects to be detected

Visual inspection criteria so far in connection with these defects has been as follows:

(a) Displacement from regular position

Displacement should be less than ± 0.1 mm to each direction along x and y axis.

(b) Deformation

The contact size should be larger than 0.32 x 0.8 mm.

(c) Scratch

A scratch should be less than 10 μm in width as well as less than 50 μm in length.

(d) Adherence of alien substance

Adherence of alien sybstance should be less than 50 μmø.

(e) Welding splash

A welding splash should be less than 20 μm in width at 0.2 mm apart from the side of contact points.

(f) Collapse

A collapse should be less than 0.2 mm in length from the side of contact points.

Formation of Inspection Device

Optical system of detection and its characteristics. Fig. 3 shows the optical system and its formation.

After several times of investigation, we have decided to adopt TV camera with 1/2 inches vidicon tube for detecting defects. In so far as the resolution of the camera is 650 lines / image frame width, it is appropriate to reflect two contact points in one image frame, judging from the size of the defects to be detected.

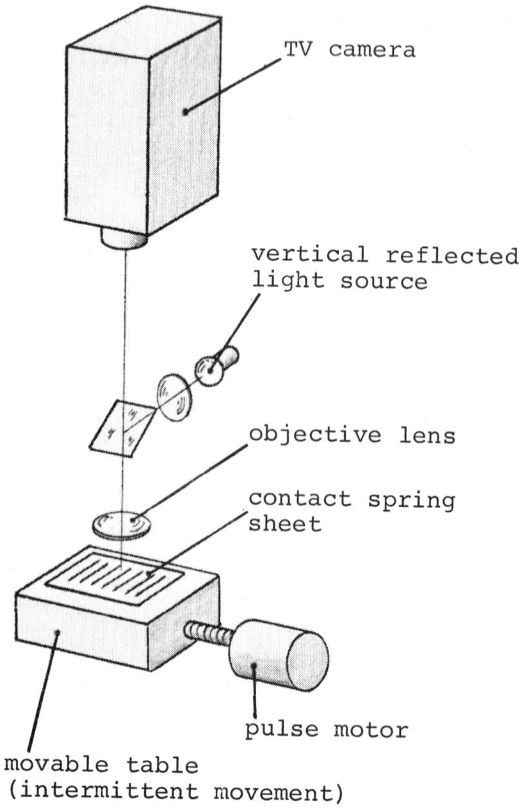

Fig. 3 Optical system for detecting the defects of the contact points

An objective lens of 5 times magnification was used in order to reflect the images of these two contact points on the effective surface of image tube.

Vertical reflected illumination method was adopted. When light is given from the above, as shown in Fig. 4, the surface of contact points is the brightest and the spring surface is second brightest; on the other hand, the outline of contact point is dark, and scratch, welding splash, etc. which should be detected as defects are also dark. Therefore we can discriminate them with sufficient contrast.

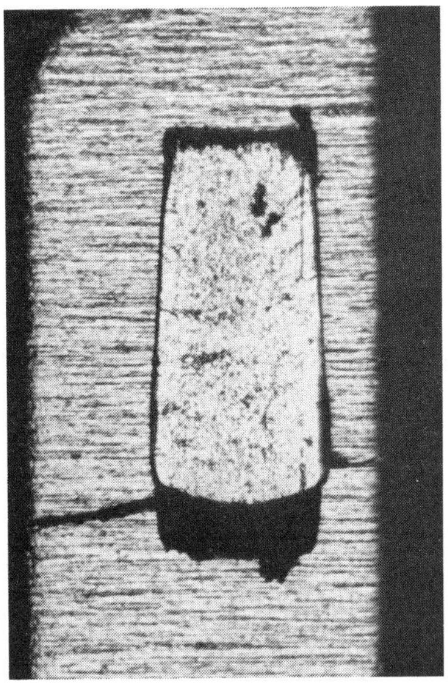

Fig. 4 Image of the contact point under vertical reflected illumination

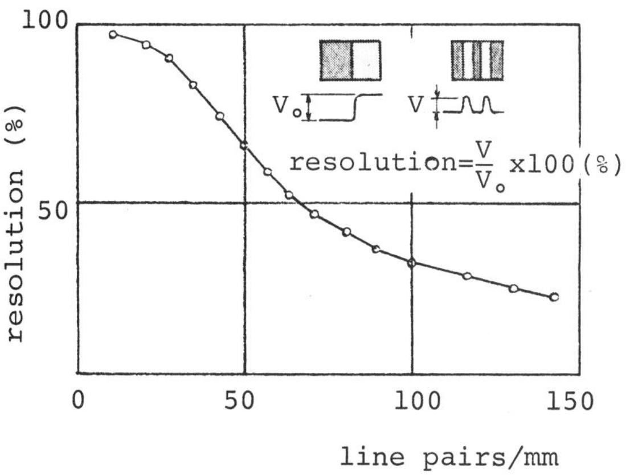

Fig. 5 Resolution of the optical system

Fig. 5 shows the result of the resolution test of this optical system. In spite of the fact that the width of the scratch to be detected is 10 mm, as clearly shown in Fig. 5, 50 % of the resolution was attained for the 8 μm width scratch. This is admitted to be the satisfactory outcome.

Pulse Motor shifts intermittently a movable plate on which contact spring is put. In order to simplify the shifting mechanism and to save the shifting time, a pair of TV cameras are used.

In this way, two different pairs of contact points are reflected on each TV screen simultaneously. Each TV camera is equipped with shading correction and linearity correction. The shading errors are less than 5 % and the linearity errors are less than 1 %.

Image input range. Taking into consideration that the tolerance of the shift from the regular position of contact points is ± 0.1 mm and the length of welding splash is 0.2 mm, the range including two contact points which should be inspected with their surrounding is determined approximately 2.3 x 1.5 mm in the direction of x and y axis respectively.

On sampling out the video signal with 6 Mhz, the picture of the image can be divided into 320 x 240 picture elements in the direction of x and y axis respectively. Out of which, we delete the outer side and we adopt the range including picture elements of 290 x 190. More over, the intermediate part of the two contact points doesn't need to be inspected. Thus, the image input range is limited in the area of 109 x 190 for each contact point as shown in Fig. 6 and the dimension of one picture element is 7.73 μm.

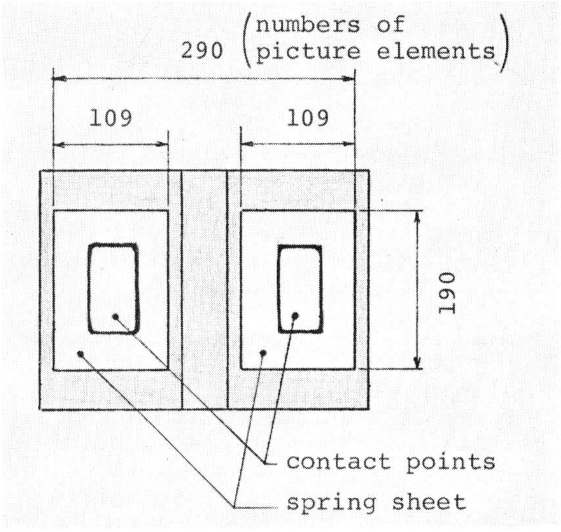

Fig. 6 Image input range

Defects Detection Algorithm

Defects detection algorithm should be made up in such a way that it is as simple as possible, easy to make hardware circuit and time required for inspection is as short as possible, on the premiss that bad articles should not be taken for good ones and vice versa.

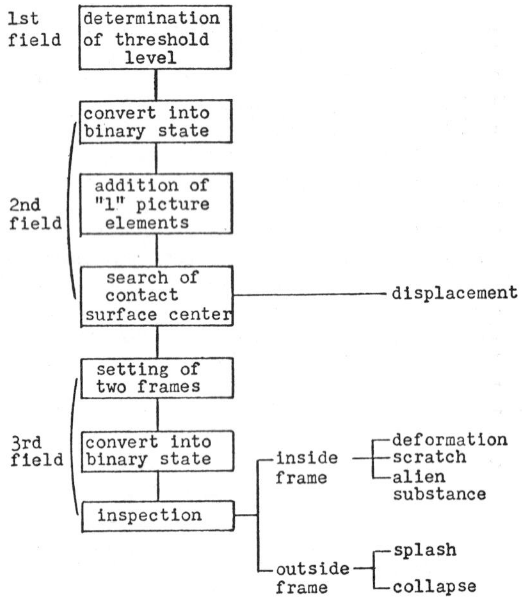

Fig. 7 Formation of defects detecting algorithm

Fig. 7 shows the whole formation of defects detection algorithm introduced after several repetition of tests and investigations.

First field. The first field is for the determination of threshold level to convert video signal into binary symbol of "1" or "0".

Zero-drift of video signal of the TV camera installed in this device is very big; and, moreover, output of video signal changes in accordance with changes of brightness of light itself and/or brightness of surroundings. Accordingly, threshold level has to follow these changes; and in the first field, we detect the maximum and minimum value in video signal — the brightest part and the darkest part — with peak-holder, and we set the threshold level for a given proportion which is specified in advance between maximum and minimum value. The darkest part exists somewhere on the outline of contact points of such defects as scratch, collapse and so on, and the brightest part exists somewhere on the surface of contact points. Maximum and minimum value of video signal changes according to the above mentioned drift etc., but the image prepared by using binary symbol of "0" or "1" (which is set with theshold level in a given proportion) does never change. Also, we recognize through tests the maximum and minimum brightness are almost the same with different contact points.

Second field. By converting video signal into binary value of "1" or "0" based on a pertinent threshold level which is decided in the first field, we search the location of the center of contact point from its outline and inspect the displacement. Fig. 8 shows the way of finding out the location of the center point.

Out of the image in binary state with outline of contact point, we add the number of picture element corresponding to "1" in the direction of x and y axis respectively, and we can get the histogram as shown in Fig. 8. As the histogram has two maximum values, we can easily get the coordinate of the center point. If it is out of the pre-determind $\pm$ 0.1 mm range, "no-good" signal is generated to show the displacement. As the accuracy of the stopping position of intermittent shifting device is less than 0.01 mm, the range for inspection of displacement is practically considered to be fixed on the picture.

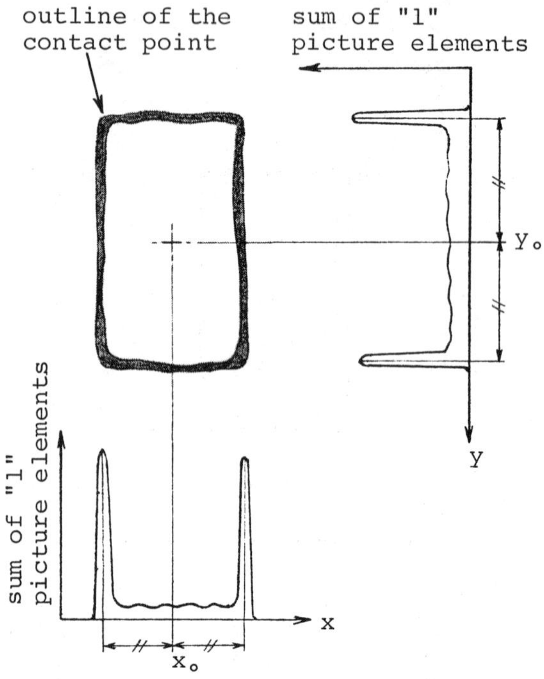

Fig. 8 Search of contact surface center

Third field. We limit the inspection range by setting the frames and set a different new threshold level in order to detect the other defects than displacement.

In the first place, we set two frames as shown in Fig. 9 center of which is the contact point center determined in the second field. The size of inside frame is 0.32 x 0.8 mm and that of outside frame is 0.72 x 1.2 mm.

The size of inside frame is allowable minimum size of contact points, in other words, contact point whose size is larger than the size of inside frame is considered good ones. By enlarging the idea, if defects such as deformation, scratch and adherence of alien substance on the surface of contact point don't exist within the inside frame, we consider there are no defects. According to this idea, we can limit the inspection range within the inside frame. Taking the size of defects which should be detected into consideration, as shown in Fig. 10, we make scanning all over the inside frame with 7 x 7 picture element matrix (54 x 54 square μm). And when there exist a continuous "1" picture element succession across the matrix, we decide the contact as bad one.

The outside frame is the border line, beyond which welding splash and collapse are not allowed to go, even if they run out of the allowable minimum size contact point. To simplify the algorithm, we have inspected all kinds of defects around contact point along the outside frame. Taking the inspection criteria into consideration, we make scanning with 3 x 3 picture element matrix (23 x 23 square μm) along the perimeter of the outside frame, as shown in Fig. 10. In case all of the 9 picture elements indicate the symbol of "1", the contact is considered bad one.

The frames serve for limiting inspection range but they are also used as border lines in case of introducing two threshold levels for getting two kinds of images in binary state. As mentioned before, the surface of spring looks darker than the surface of contact points. When there are fine scratches on the surface of contact point and at the same time fine welding splashes on the surface of spring, the difference of brightness is the cause of

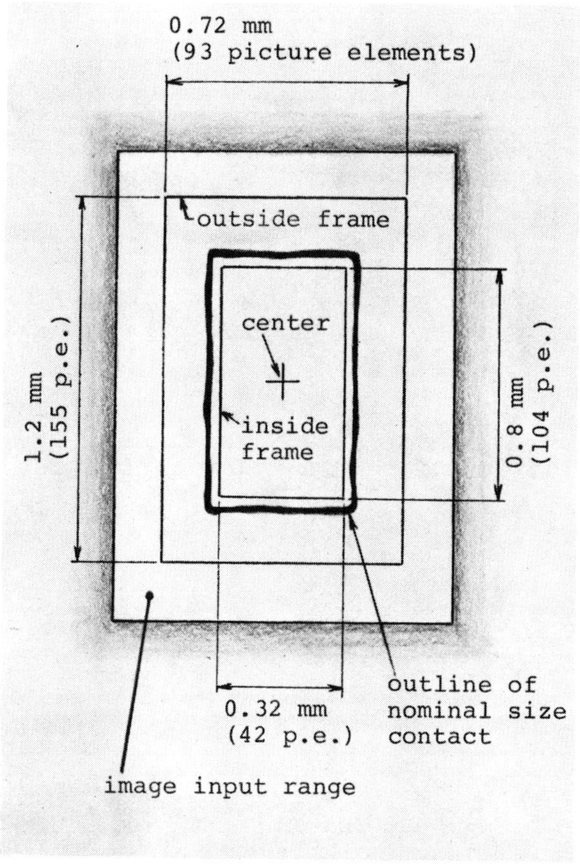

Fig. 9 Inside and outside frames

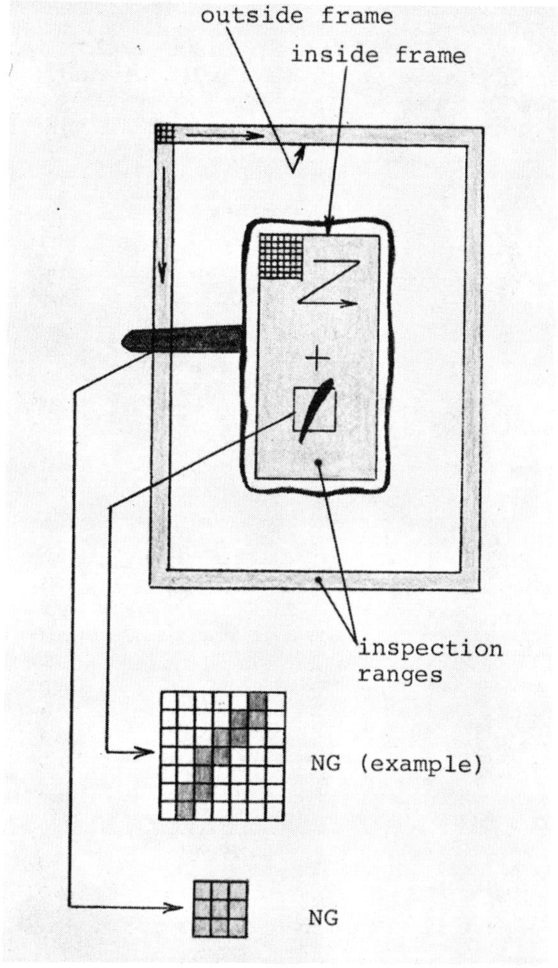

Fig. 10 Inspection range and scanning matrixes

difficulty for converting the images into binary state on the basis of the same threshold level. When we select the threshold level so as to get a clear image of welding sprash in binary state, the image of scratch in binary state become blurred; and on the other hand when we set the threshold level so as to get a clear image of scratch in binary state, the image of welding splash in binary state become thick, and in some cases dark part of the spring surface looks "black" ("1"). Because of the reasons mentioned above, it is necessary for us to set different threshold level for the contact points and for its surroundings to get each clear image in binary state. (In this way, we can get the most appropriate images in binary state.)

In case of adopting the above mentioned algorithm, the time required for the inspection of a contact is three fields or 50 ms.

The Experimental Results

The results of the simulation test through computer are described in this paragraph.

The result of the inspection with eyes through a microscope and the outcome by the above mentioned algorithm in relation to detecting the position of the center of contact point are shown in Fig. 11.

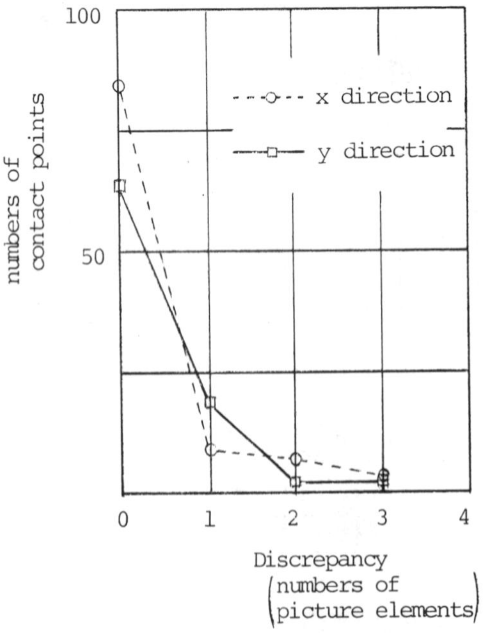

Fig. 11 Discrepancy between eyes and automatic inspection about the center position of contact point surface

They show good agreement. The discrepancy between them is not more than ± 3 picture elements which is caused by the difference in case of picking out the edge of contact point and practically there is no problem at all.

The result of the test concerning the images within and without the outside frame in binary state with different threshold level is shown in Fig. 12. In order to get an appropriate contact point surface image in binary state, high threshold level is used. In this case "black" ("1") parts are seen on the spring surface, but they give no bad effects because the inspection is carried out in the inner side of the inside frame. On the other hand, in the outer side of the outside frame, the spring surface looks "white" ("0") and welding splash looks "black" ("1").

We carried out the test of 200 pieces of samples with various kind of defects, the results were completely satisfactory.

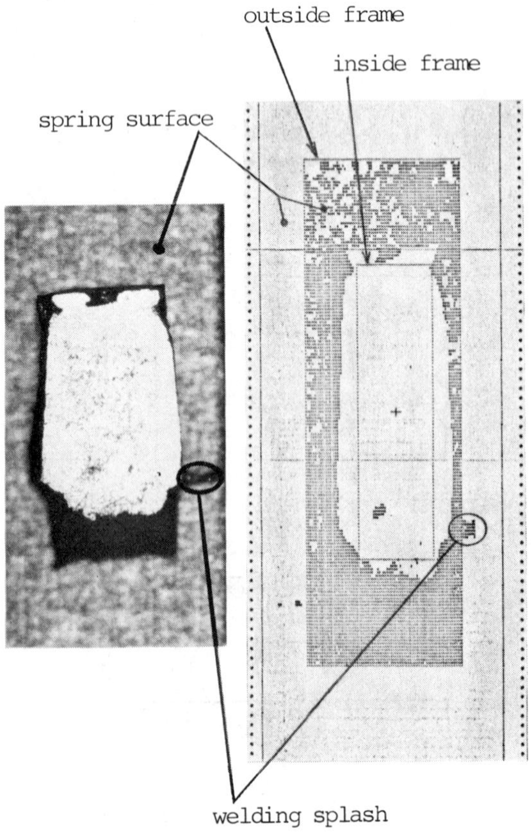

Fig. 12 Image to be inspected in 3rd field

The Device

Fig. 13 shows the appearance of the device installed in the production line for practical use. As mentioned before, there is two set of TV cameras, but the signal processing circuit is single and processes the signals coming from two TV cameras. The time necessary for the inspection for 32 contact points is 5.4 seconds and its breakdown is as follows.

Fig. 13 Device installed in production line

For inspection and judgment (32 contact points)----------------2.1 s
For shifting (10 times of intermittent motions)----------------2.9 s
For elimination of after-image and time lag for recieving signal--------0.4 s
Total time----------------5.4 s

Conclusion

We developed an automatic appearance inspection device with TV camera for detecting defects of contact points of relay switch. Algorithm for the detection of defects has the following characteristics and the outcome was satisfactory when compared with the result of eye-inspection through microscope.

1. We use a threshold level of floating type so as to get rid of the bad effect of drift of video signal.
2. Displacement can be inspected by setting the center from histogram of picture elements of "1" which compose of the outline of contact point.
3. Two frames are prepared on the basis of the position of the center and inspection is carried out within the limited range so as to avoid mis-judgment as much as possible.
4. As we introduce the two kinds of binary states within each range limited in the one of the frames, we can recognize the defects clearly and appropriately.

References

(1) C. A. Harlow et al, "Automated Inspection of Electronic Assemblies," IEEE Computer, Vol.8, 36 (April 1975).

(2) S. Kashioka et al, "A Transistor Wire-Bonding System Utilizing Multiple Local Pattern Matching Techniques," IEEE System, Vol. SMC.6, 562 (August 1976).

(3) G. Agin, "An Experimental Vision System for Industrial Application," Proc. 5th Int. Symp. on Industrial robots, 135 (1975).

(4) C. K. Chow and T. Kaneko, "Boundary Detection of Radio Graphic Images by a Threshold Method," S. Watanabe (Ed.), Frontires of Pattern Recognition, Academic Press, New York 61 (1972).

(5) M. W. Smith and W. A. Davis, "A New Algorithm for Edge Detection," 2nd Int, Joint Conf. on Pattern Recognition, Copenhagen, Denmark, (August 1974).

A REITERATIVE OPTIMIZATION TECHNIQUE FOR PIECEWISE LINEAR ALGEBRAIC FUNCTIONS AND ITS APPLICATION TO HARDWOOD FURNITURE MANUFACTURING

A.E. Fahim and R.M.H. Cheng

Concordia University, Montreal, H3G 1MG, Canada

ABSTRACT

One great concern of the hardwood furniture manufacturing industry is the availability of wood supply, and the conversion of the maximum amount of wood into useful products.

The authors have been engaged in developing a computer-aided rough-cut system with a view towards replacing human operators. The system consists of an optical scanning unit with a data link inter-connection to a mini-computer, which examines the surface data of the pieces of wood to determine the best cutting pattern according to a cutting bill.

The paper is primarily concerned with the processing of geometrical data in order to determine the effective width of the pieces of wood. This step for finding the effective width is required, since each individual piece of wood has a different size and shape and irregularities on the sides. The procedure described defines two parallel longitudinal lines on the surface of the wood such that the useful area between them is the maximum possible, subject to the provision that any irregularities between the two lines are considered as defective and useless areas.

Two methods have been developed. The first one is a straight forward trial and error method, which provides good results at the expense of time and computer space. A second and improved method relies on the mathematical optimization of a piecewise linear function. This latter technique is a fast converging one, thus requiring a comparatively short time and computer space. Both methods are described in the paper together with numerical illustrations and comparisons.

INTRODUCTION

The dwindling supply of wood as well as increasing demand and cost have forced Furniture manufacturing industries to become more aware of the necessity of improving the efficiency of wood utilization. The first step of production in the furniture making industry is to cut wood boards into smaller pieces according to a cutting bill. The cutting bill specifies the dimensions and number of pieces to be cut for a given production batch. A high degree of wastage normally results since the boards surfaces contain randomly distributed defect areas (knots, cracks, etc), and little time is available for optimal redistribution of the cutting bill items during production.

Almost all furniture manufacturing plants currently utilize human operators to perform the above production step, resulting in a wastage factor of about 35% during this step alone. Several automatic systems have been developed over the last few years to deal with the above mentioned problem. Among these systems are: -the "Auto Mark III" by Industrial Development and Design Inc. (Ref. 1),which uses ultra sonic defect detection with a simple logic circuit to control the cutting saw; -a system which simply markes the boards has been built by the School of Forest Resources at the North Carolina State University (Ref. 2), it uses individual photocell detectors and a mini-computer for decision making; -two machines built by Oliver Machinery Co., namely "Computerized Cut Off Saw No. 694" and "Mark III" (Ref. 3), the 'No. 694' uses a light beam cursor to aid the operator in entering the defect data locations into the computer and the 'Mark III' uses photoelectric diode sensors to collect data.

Both machines use a mini-computer for decision making.

Among the above systems, only the two machines built by Oliver Co. are of practical interest from the point of view of automated optimized wood cutting systems. The two machines use a "one dimensional" detection and optimization scheme along the board length. The authors, however, have built and tested a bench-top model (Ref. 4), shown in Fig. 1, which uses a two dimensional detection and optimization scheme.

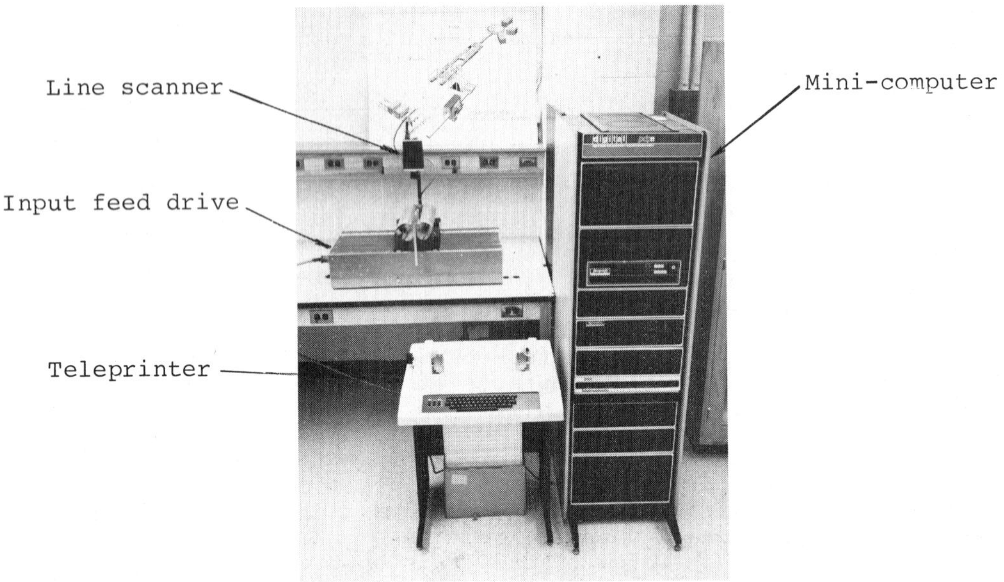

Fig. 1. Photograph of Bench Top Model

Tests on the model showed that a substantial reduction in wastage could be achieved, without adding too many system complications.

As the boards have rough edges, sometimes with loose knots and cracks, the problem of establishing two edge-defining parallel lines within the boundaries of a given board, is a major one. An optimization routine of some kind is hence required for proper allocation of these lines. This paper describes two such optimization methods. In both methods the two parallel longitudinal lines are defined such that the useful area between them is the maximum possible.

A description of the method of aquiring the edge data and the processing of this data into a suitable format for optimization is given first, followed by two methods for determining the effective width of the board. The first is a straight forward trial and error technique which yields good results at the expense of computer time and memory space. The other is based on a mathematical optimization of a piecewise linear function which approximates the geometry of the board edge. This latter method is fast, very accurate, and requires very little computer memory. The paper concludes with a comparison of these two algorithms, with the aid of a numerical example.

EDGE OPTIMIZATION METHODS

The data for the board edges and for the defects on the board surface are acquired using the combination of the electronic line scanner and the input feed drive shown in Fig. 1 (see Ref. 4 for details). The scanner detects the different light intensities on the board surface, using photodiodes, and converts them into binary signals. The edges and the defects are dark in colour and are represented by a logic "1", while the good wood is light in colour and is represented by a logic "0". Figure 2 shows a photograph of a wood board against a dark background, with the defects marked with a black marker.

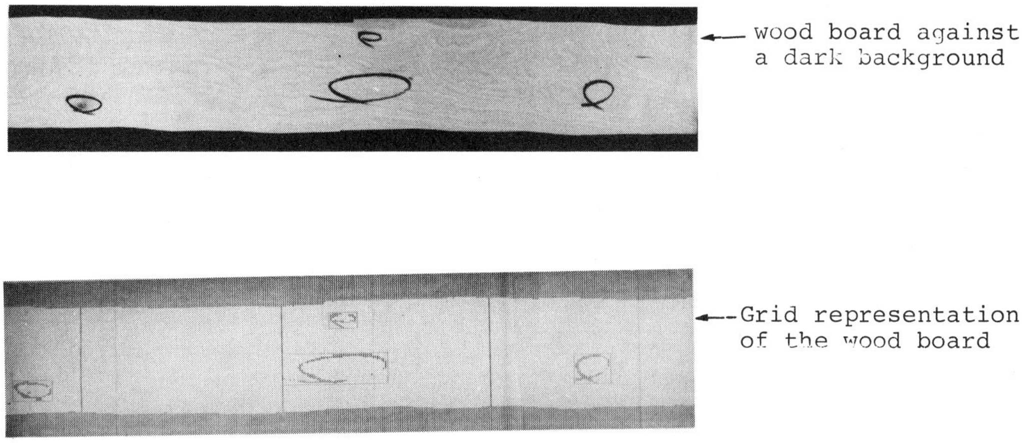

Fig. 2. Photograph of a wood board and its grid representation

The photograph also shows an image of the board formed through a grid of the binary data collected by the scanner.

The information about the edge irregularities of the board is contained in the outer boarder of the grid as can be seen in Fig. 2. In order to obtain a more suitable format for optimization, the wavy edges of the board are approximated using piecewise linear curves by joining the maximum and minimum points of each edge by straight line segments. Figure 3 shows a natural edge of a board (solid line) and the corresponding piecewise linear approximation (dashed lines).

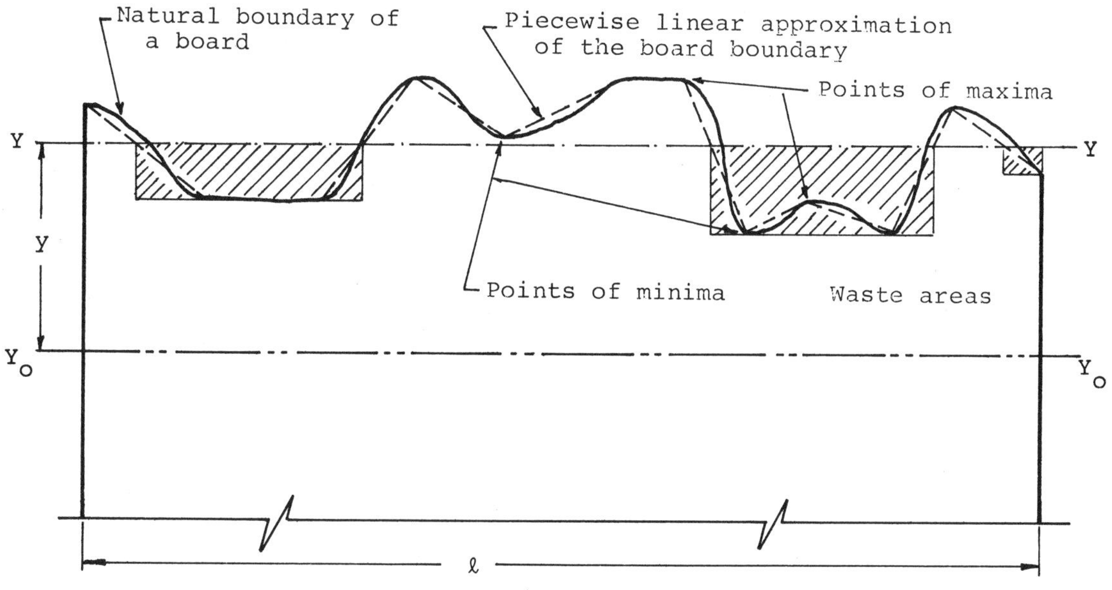

Fig. 3. Schematic of a wood board natural edge and its approximation

In the figure, the second segment which is shown to be flat (no maximum, or minimum) represents a "valley" in the board edge whose bottom is parallel to the longitudinal axis of the board. For a proposed straight line edge, which cuts the piecewise curve, such as Y Y in Fig. 3, irregularities lying below the proposed line are considered as defects. Rectangles are then drawn around these defects, and the total area of the rectangles (hatched area) is considered as waste.

In the two optimization methods described in this paper, the wood board is divided longitudinally into two parts by a straight line and each part treated separately. In Figure 3 one of these parts is defined by the dividing line Y_o Y_o and the approximated board edge. Referring to the figure, for a proposed straight edge Y Y, the useful area is given by,

useful area = total area (ℓxy) - sum of the waste areas

where ℓ is the length of the board, and y is the distance between Y_o Y_o and the proposed straight edge. The relation between the useful area of the board and y is a curve, whose maximum is the optimal location for the straight edge. The effective width of the board is the distance between the optimal locations for the straight edges of the two parts of the board.

Trial-and-Error Method

In this method, the position of the straight line Y Y is indexed from its maximum location (farthest distance from Y_o Y_o) inward towards Y_o Y_o by fixed increments. For each indexed location the useful area is calculated, and compared with the previous one. The position of Y Y which results in the maximum useful area is the optimal position for the required straight edge.

Mathematical Optimization of the Piecewise Linear Function

In this method, each of the parts of the board is subdivided into sections as shown in Fig. 4.

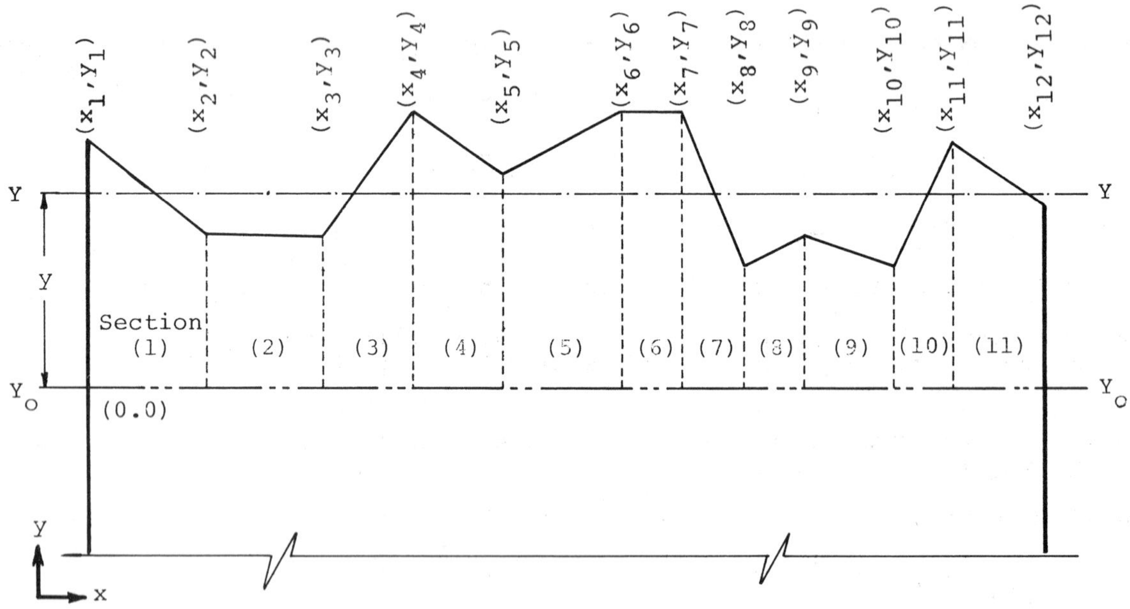

Fig. 4. Schematic of part of a board subdivided into sections

This is done by drawing perpendicular lines to Y_o Y_o passing through the maxima and minima points. For any straight edge Y Y, as shown in the figure, the subdivisions of the board can be grouped into three different categories, depending on whether the line segments joining the successful maximum and minimum points are,

a) above Y Y (e.g. Section 6, Fig. 4)

b) below Y Y (e.g. Section 2, Fig. 4)

c) intersecting Y Y (e.g. Section 1, Fig. 4)

Each of these categories can be labelled for convenience in further computations by two logic variables a_n and b_n.

Thus,

for those above Y Y;	$a_n = 0, b_n = 0$	when $y_{n+1} - y > 0$ AND $y_n - y > 0$
for those below Y Y;	$a_n = 0, b_n = 1$	when $y_{n+1} - y \leqslant 0$ AND $y_n - y \leqslant 0$
for those intersecting Y Y;	$a_n = 1, b_n = 0$	when $[y_{n+1} - y > 0$ AND $y_n - y < 0]$
		OR $[y_{n+1} - y < 0$ AND $y_n - y > 0]$

where n is an integer denoting the section.

Furthermore, depending upon the slopes of the line segments joining the maximum and minimum points, three more categories can be defined depending on whether they are

a) negative (as in Section 1)
b) positive (as in Section 3)
or c) zero (as in Section 2)

These categories are also represented by logic variables. Three variables are used in this case to simplify the subsequent formulation of the mathematical analysis. They are represented as follows:

For negative slopes	$c_n = 1, d_n = 0, e_n = 0$	when $y_{n+1} - y_n < 0$
For positive slopes	$c_n = 0, d_n = 1, e_n = 0$	when $y_{n+1} - y_n > 0$
For zero slopes	$c_n = 0, d_n = 0, e_n = 1$	when $y_{n+1} - y_n = 0$

where n is an integer denoting the section.

A general equation representing the area of each section can now be formulated:

$$A_n = (x_{n+1} - x_n)y - a_n d_n (y - y_n)^2 \cot\theta_n + a_n c_n (y - y_{n+1})^2 \cot\theta_n$$
$$- b_n d_n (x_{n+1} - x_n)(y - y_n) - b_n c_n (x_{n+1} - x_n)(y - y_{n+1}) -$$
$$b_n e_n (x_{n+1} - x_n)(y - y_n) \qquad (1)$$

where A_n is the useful area of the section n and $\cot\theta_n = (x_{n+1}-x_n)/(y_{n+1}-y_n)$

As an illustration of the use of the logical functions a_n, b_n, c_n, d_n, and e_n in the above equation, the area of section 3 in Fig. 4 is calculated as follows.

From the categories above the values of the logical functions are: $a_3 = 1$, $b_3 = 0$, $c_3 = 0$, $d_3 = 1$, and $e_3 = 0$.

When these values are substituted in Eqn (1), A_n is reduced to:

$$A_3 = (x_4 - x_3)y - 1 . 1 . (y - y_3)^2 \cot\theta_3 + 0 - 0 - 0 - 0$$
$$= (x_4 - x_3)y - (y - y_3)^2 \cot\theta_3$$

Since the total area of the part of the board shown in Fig. 4, is the sum of the areas of the constituent sections,

$$A = \sum_{n=1}^{n=m-1} A_n \qquad (2)$$

where m is the number of maximum and minimum points and A is the total useful area. The maximum area A is obtained by integrating Eqn (2) with respect to the variable y, and setting the result to zero; (in the integration the logical variables remain unaltered). Thus,

$$\frac{dA}{dy} = 0 = \frac{d}{dy}\left\{\sum_{n=1}^{n=m-1} A_n\right\}$$

$$= \sum_{n=1}^{n=m-1} \frac{d}{dy}[A_n]$$

$$= \sum_{n=1}^{n=m-1} [(x_{n+1} - x) - a_n d_n 2(y - y_n) \cot\theta_n + a_n c_n 2(y - y_{n+1}) \cot\theta_n -$$

$$b_n d_n (x_{n+1} - x_n) - b_n c_n (x_{n+1} - x_n) - b_n e_n (x_{n+1} - x_n)] \quad (3)$$

Rearranging Eqn (3), the optimal location of the edge of the board is given by

$$y = \frac{2\sum_{n=1}^{n=m-1} [a_n(d_n y_n - c_n y_{n+1})\cot\theta_n] + \sum_{n=1}^{n=m-1} [(x_{n+1}-x_n)(1-b_n d_n - b_n c_n - b_n e_n)]}{2\sum_{n=1}^{n=m-1} [a_n(d_n - c_n) \cot\theta_n]} \quad (4)$$

Equation(4), giving the optimal location of the edge of the board, is an implicit one, which can be solved by an iterative procedure. A first estimate of the location of the edge (say, the average of the maxima and minima points) is required to evaluate the initial values of the logic variables a_n and b_n. Utilizing these values, the location of a new edge is calculated using Eqn (4). The logical variables are then reevaluated, and a new value of y calculated. The iterative procedure is continued until a recalculated value of y does not bring any further changes in the value of a_n and b_n for all sections. The same values of a_n and b_n result in the same y.

TEST RESULTS AND COMPARISON BETWEEN THE TWO OPTIMIZATION METHODS

The part of the board shown in Fig. 4 will now be used as an example for comparative evaluation. The location of the optimal edge of the board in the figure is first calculated using the straight forward trial and error method, and later by the mathematical optimization method. The coordinates of the maxima and minima points of the schematic of Fig. 4 are listed in Appendix A. Figure 5 shows a plot of the useful area versus the position of the edge.

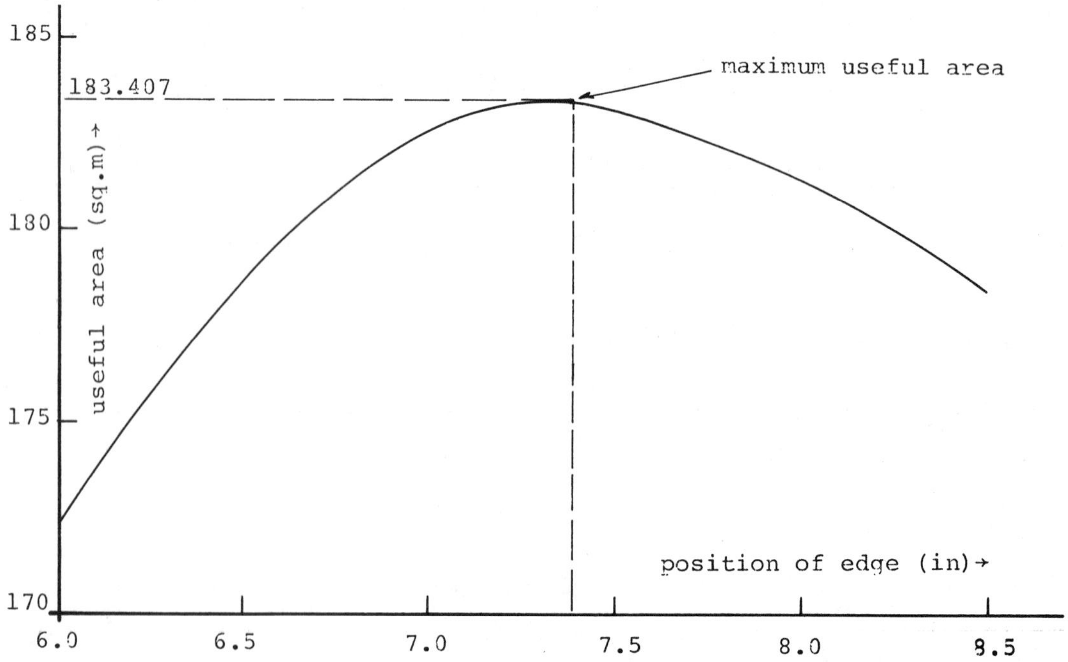

Fig. 5. Useful area of part of the board vs. the position of the straight edge

Using the trial and error method, the optimal edge position is found to be y = 7.5", after four attempts using increments of 0.5". A more accurate solution, however, may be obtained, using smaller increments and a larger number of attempts. In contrast, the mathematical optimization method (calculations given in Appendix A) locates the optimal edge for maximum useful area at y = 7.39" in only two iterations.

Fortran programs were written to carry out the two optimization methods. The algorithm using the trial and error method required 3K words of computer memory, for the software and the storage space, as compared to 2K words required by the mathematical optimization method. Thus a savings of 30% is realized using the latter method. Furthermore, the mathematical optimization method arrived at the optimal edge in 400 msec of computer time, which is about 27% less time than that required by the trial and error method. (The trial and error method requires an average of 550 msec to run). However, the deviation between the results from the two methods is within production tolerances.

CONCLUSION

This paper presents two methods for locating two parallel straight lines, on the surface of a board with irregular edges, such that the useful area between the lines is a maximum. Any irregularities between the two lines are bound by rectangles which areas are considered as waste. The method based on a mathematical optimization of a piecewise linear function derived in this paper has proven to be superior to the trial and error method. When implemented on a computer, the mathematical method required less memory space and executing time, as well as provided more accurate results.

The mathematical optimization of a piecewise linear function can be generalized to serve numerous other applications.

Acknowlegement

The authors wish to acknowledge the facilities provided by the Fluid Control Centre of Concordia University, including funding from the National Research Council of Canada (Negotiated Grant D-30).

They also wish to acknowledge Mr. Ronald DiMichele's assistance in the development of the software.

References

(1) Industrial Development and Design Inc., Auto-Mark III, Technical Literature, Salt Lake City, Utah

(2) A.G. Mullin, Computerized lumber, Furniture Design and Manufacturing, Sept. (1972).

(3) Oliver Machinery Co., 694 Computerized Cut-off Saw, Mark III, and Mark IV, Product Manual, Grand Rapids, Michigan

(4) R.M.H. Cheng, A.E. Fahim, & R. DiMichele, A Computer-aided wood cutting system for maximum utilization of material, submitted to ISA/77.

APPENDIX A

Referring to Fig. 4, the coordinates of the points of maxima and minima are as follows: (dimensions are in inches)

(x_1, y_1)	=	0,8	(x_7, y_7)	=	19,9
(x_2, y_2)	=	4,5	(x_8, y_8)	=	21,4
(x_3, y_3)	=	8,5	(x_9, y_9)	=	23,5
(x_4, y_4)	=	11,9	(x_{10}, y_{10})	=	26,4
(x_5, y_5)	=	13,7	(x_{11}, y_{11})	=	28,8
(x_6, y_6)	=	17,9	(x_{12}, y_{12})	=	32,6

The inverse of the slopes of the lines joining each two successive points are as follows:

$\cot\theta_1 = -1.33$		$\cot\theta_7 = -0.40$	
$\cot\theta_2 = 0.00$		$\cot\theta_8 = 2.00$	
$\cot\theta_3 = 0.75$		$\cot\theta_9 = -3.00$	
$\cot\theta_4 = -1.00$		$\cot\theta_{10} = 0.50$	
$\cot\theta_5 = 2.00$		$\cot\theta_{11} = -2.00$	
$\cot\theta_6 = 0.00$			

The starting location for y y is taken as the average of the maxima and minima points y_0, thus:

$$y_0 = \frac{\sum_{n=1}^{n=m} y_n}{m} \qquad \text{where m is the number of points (12 in Fig. 4)}$$

$$= 6.583$$

The logic variables for the slopes a_n, b_n, and e_n, are as follows:

n	1	2	3	4	5	6	7	8	9	10	11
a_n	1	0	0	1	0	0	1	0	1	0	1
b_n	0	0	1	0	1	0	0	1	0	1	0
e_n	0	1	0	0	0	1	0	0	0	0	0

For the edge location at y_0, the logic functionc c_n and d_n are as follows:

n	1	2	3	4	5	6	7	8	9	10	11
c_n	1	0	1	0	0	0	1	0	0	1	1
d_n	0	1	0	0	0	0	0	1	1	0	0

Substituting the valves of the logic variables and the coordinates of the points in Eqn (4), the position of the edge after the first iteration y_1 is calculated to be $y_1 = 7.6338$. Based on this value of y, the logic functions c_n and d_n for the edge location at y_1 are as follows:

n	1	2	3	4	5	6	7	8	9	10	11
c_n	1	0	1	1	1	0	1	0	0	1	1
d_n	0	1	0	0	0	0	0	1	1	0	0

Resubstituting in Eqn (4) and solving, the position of the edge after the second iteration y_2 is $y_2 = 7.39$". A reevaluation of the logic variables for the new edge show that they stay unchanged. Thus the valve $y_2 = 7.39$"is the optimal position for the edge for the maximum useful area. This value conforms with the value of y for the maximum useful area obtained from Fig. 5.

CLASSIFICATION OF GRASPED OBJECT'S SHAPE BY AN ARTIFICIAL HAND WITH MULTI-ELEMENT TACTILE SENSORS

G.-I. Kinoshita

Department of Electrical Engineering, Faculty of Science & Engineering, Chuo University, 1-13-27 Kasuga Bunkyo-ku, Tokyo, Japan

ABSTRACT

This paper describes a simple tactile sensor model for extracting the features of an object's surface and an experiment for classifying the shape of grasped object.

The proposed model of a tactile sensor consists of the two layers, a surface layer and sensor layer. The surface layer consists of an elastic material whose the mechanical properties are determined by the object's surface. These properties of the surface layer are expressed theoretically as the blurring function. The sensor layer derives information from the sensor arrays of a multi-element sensor.

An experiment on object classification by one-time grasping was performed by using an artificial hand with tactile sensors and a linear learning machine (nonparametric). After the training procedure, the machine gave 100 percent successful classification for columns, 55.6 percent for square pillars and 58.3 percent for prisms.

1. INTRODUCTION

A computer control artificial hand or manipulator system has been oriented toward active use rather than passive use such as numerical calculations of a computer. In early works, H.A.Ernst(Ref. 1) developed a manipulator system(MH-1 system) equipped with sensory feedback. The MH-1 system was able to learn about its environment with information gained from touch sensors. The present research emphasis in the field is towards the investigation of systems which attempt to solve a complex job in industrial handling situations. The extent and scope of works in computer controlled artificial hands or manipulator systems is clearly shown in the proceedings of the IJCAI in 1969, 1971, 1973, 1975 (Ref. 2) and the CISM-IFToMM SYMPOSIUM in 1973, 1976(Ref. 3) etc.

Advances in manipulators for handling individual solid materials are becoming increasingly dependent on the skillful perceiving of the information about the material's own state and surroundings. The main problems in this regard are considered to be the measurement of forces acting on the manipulator that measurement is made in the sensor systems. These systems can be regarded as the following three types of sensors :

1) Force sensors
2) Inertial sensors
3) Tactile sensors

Force sensors measure the three mutually orthogonal forces and three orthogonal torque components at the finger tip (Ref. 4). But, in general these forces are sensed respectively as different components by using the some sensors.

Inertial sensors feel the gravity and acceleration-generated reaction torques or forces versus inertia torques or forces.

Moreover, the tactile sensors make it possible to detect contact, pressure and slippadge at the contact points of the finger with the object. These sensors are defined as the contact sensor, pressure sensor and slippage sensor respectively.

Studies of the tactile sensors have resulted in many conclusions, some of which can be used for the development of manipulators(Ref. 5). A set of contact sensors mounted on the finger tip is used to determine the successive steps of active searching for the object and its position by lightly touching(Ref. 6). Also, the outputs from pressure sensors are fed back to the system analog inputs, so that they are available to the software system for the strategic control of motors (Ref. 7). Moreover, large sensor arrays of contact or pressure sensors with relatively high spacial resolution function to identify the local type of shape at the point of contact (Ref. 8,9).

The approches to the study of sensory system are important for developing computer controlled manipulators. The intent of this paper is to elucidate a model of a tactile sensor for providing shape resolution and its properties based mainly on the sensory information system of living systems.

2. A MODEL OF TACTILE SENSOR

2.1 The anatomical structure of skin tissue

Skin tissue has two principal layers : the epidermis and the dermis ; the subcutaneous tissue is under these layers as shown in Fig. 1. The epidermis varies in thickness from 0.07 to 0.12 mm. The dermis, elastic fibrous connective tissues, varies in thickness from 1 to 2 mm. The epidermis and the subcutaneous tissue represent the elastic properties under pressure, but in general the subcutaneous tissue is viscous.

Moreover the dermis has a visco-elastic property. An analytical model for tissue behaviour under pressure is proposed by using springs and dashpots (Ref. 10).

In the epidermis and dermis of volar surface of fingers, free nerve endings, Merkel's discs, Ruffini endings and Meissner's corpuscles are found (Ref. 11) as shown in Fig. 1. These nerve endings perceive stimulus of deformation in compressed skin. Thus, it is considered that deformation in compressed skin and its elastic behaviour play an important role in extracting a feature of object's surface at the contact point of finger.

2.2 A tactile sensor model

An one-dimensional tactile sensor model is proposed as shown in Fig. 2.

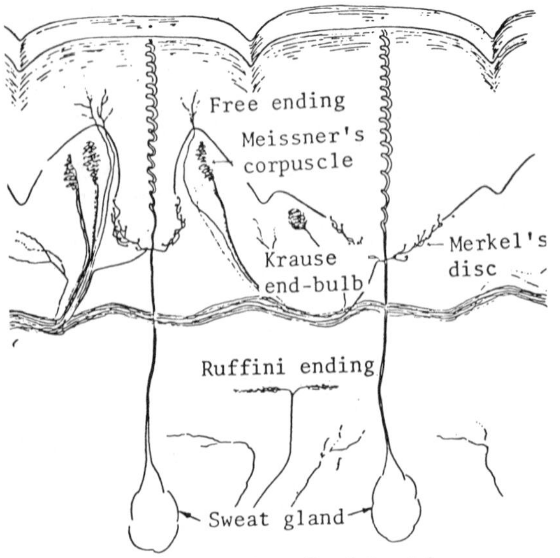

Fig. 1 Anatomy of skin tissue [N.R.Miller et al (1960)(Ref. 11)]

It is assumed that the elastic material layer covered on the elements of tactile sensors is considered as a semi-infinite elastic continuum, and the elements of tactile sensor are arranged at intervals of Δx uniformly on the basis of this assumption. Let p(x) be a pressure distribution applied to the model. Also, let g(x) be the characterlistic of elastic materials.

For the pressure $p(\xi)\Delta\xi$ at axis ξ, the displacement $\omega(x)$ at axis x is described by $p(\xi)\Delta\xi\, g(x-\xi)$. Then the response caused by a distributed pressure can be obtained integrating over the axis ξ as shown in Fig. 2.

$$\omega(x) = \int_{-\infty}^{+\infty} p(\xi)\, g(x-\xi)\, d\xi \qquad (2.1)$$

Suppose the sensor outputs depending on the displacement $\omega(x)$ and a characteristic of sensor θ are as follows.

$$a(x) = h[\omega(x), \theta, x] \qquad (2.2)$$

From Eq. (2.1), it is of interest to note that $\omega(x)$ results in the low-pass filtering characteristic g(x) of blurring operation. The outputs of the tactile sensors depend upon the blurring operation based on the elastic materials covered on the elements of tactile sensor. Let g(x) be the normal distribution of Eq. (2.3), then the characteristic of covered elastic materials can be considered as a variance σ_1.

$$g(x) = \frac{1}{\sqrt{2\pi}\,\sigma_1} \exp\left(-\frac{x^2}{2\sigma_1^2}\right) \qquad (2.3)$$

Assuming that there are three types

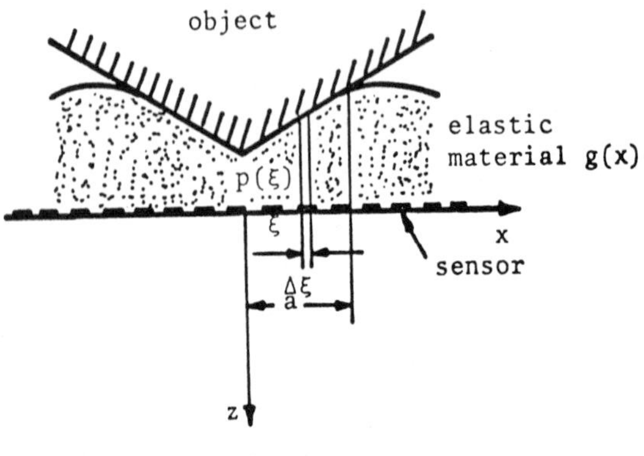

Fig. 2 A model of tactile sensor

of an object's shape : types of (a) wedge type, (b) rectangular type and (c) round type as shown in Fig. 3, the object's shape is considered as a cross-sectional shape of three dimensions. For the three types of object's shape, the displacement $\omega(x)$ are calculated as follows.

(a) Wedge type

$$\omega(x) = \frac{1}{2}(x+1)\,\mathrm{erf}\left(\frac{x+1}{\sqrt{2}\sigma_1}\right) + \frac{1}{2}(x-1)\,\mathrm{erf}\left(\frac{x-1}{\sqrt{2}\sigma_1}\right) - x\cdot\mathrm{erf}\left(\frac{x}{\sqrt{2}\sigma_1}\right) + \frac{\sigma_1}{\sqrt{2\pi}}\left\{\exp\left(-\frac{(x+1)^2}{2\sigma_1^2}\right) + \exp\left(-\frac{(x-1)^2}{2\sigma_1^2}\right) - 2\cdot\exp\left(-\frac{x^2}{2\sigma_1^2}\right)\right\} \quad (2.4)$$

(b) Rectangular type

$$\omega(x) = \frac{1}{2}\left\{\mathrm{erf}\left(\frac{x+1}{\sqrt{2}\sigma_1}\right) - \mathrm{erf}\left(\frac{x-1}{\sqrt{2}\sigma_1}\right)\right\} \quad (2.5)$$

(c) Round type

$$\omega(x) = \frac{1}{\sqrt{2\pi}\,\sigma}\exp\left(-\frac{x^2}{2\sigma^2}\right) \quad (2.6)$$

where $$\mathrm{erf}(x) = \frac{2}{\pi}\int_0^x \exp(-t^2)\,dt \quad (2.7)$$

$$\sigma^2 = \sigma_1^2 + \sigma_2^2 \quad (2.8)$$

Eqs. (2.4), (2.5) and (2.6) are normalized as follows.

$$\omega^*(x) = \omega(x)/\omega(0) \quad (2.9)$$

By normalization of $\omega(x)$, its shape is able to compare with the others. As shown in Fig. 4, a normalied value $\omega^*(x)$ is calculated and a dotted line shows the value of $p(x)$. It is clear that in the model, $\omega^*(x)$ represents the effect of blurring operation as shown in Fig. 4. The tactile sensors are sufficient to determine the shape of the surface at the point of contact. Suppose a set of contact sensors are arranged on the base at intervals of Δx along axis x.

From Eq. (2.2), the sensor output is

$$a_j(x) = \begin{cases} k & \omega_j^*(x) \geq \theta \\ 0 & \omega_j^*(x) < \theta \end{cases} \quad (2.10)$$

where a suffix j indicates a number of sensors and k indicates a constant. Thus, from Eq. (2.10), it is clear that the tactile sensor model provides the shape resolution by the function of large sensor arrays (Ref. 12). Substituting $\sigma_1 = 0.8$ into Eq. (2.3) and $\theta = \omega^*(x)/2$ (or $=0.5$) into Eq. (2.10), sensor outputs are obtained. As shown Fig. 5, different objects can be classified into the corresponding shape type from the width of the output along axis x.

3. A DESCRIPTION OF ARTIFICIAL HAND AND TACTILE SENSORS

3.1 An experimental system

A photograph of the artificial hand (CHUO HAND X1, X2) is shown in Fig. 6. The artificial hand consists of 5 degrees of freedom and five fingers. Each finger has three joints : CM (the first), MP (the second), and IP (the third) joints for thumb, and MP (the first), PIP (the second) and DIP (the third) joints for others.

The MP joint of the index finger is driven by an AC motor. The CM, MP (except thumb), IP and PIP joints are controlled independently by pneumatic cylinders (pressure, 4.5 kg/cm^2) which activate either full on or full off. Each DIP joint is bent in proportion to PIP joint motion. The artificial hand described above is controlled by minicomputer (PDP 8/e), which is 12-bit word length machine. The configuration used here has 16k words of memory and dual disks with 1.6M words of storage.

3.2 A control of finger joints

The finger joints except the MP joint of the index finger are controlled by pneumatic cylinders. The connections between the joint and a bit of the accumulator are one to one. If the bit of the accumulator is set a 1, the cylinder in the corresponding finger joint activates. The modes of prehension are decomposed to a sequence of finger actions. Therefore, the actions of fingers are carried on the sequence of stored words at regular intervals.

The finger control program can be given by the subroutine "FMANUL". This routine trains a sequence of finger actions and is able to reproduce these actions.

3.3 The tactile sensors

It is considered that the tactile sensors are to provide shape resolution by multi-element or large sensor arrays with relatively high spatial resolution. The tactile sensors described in this paper

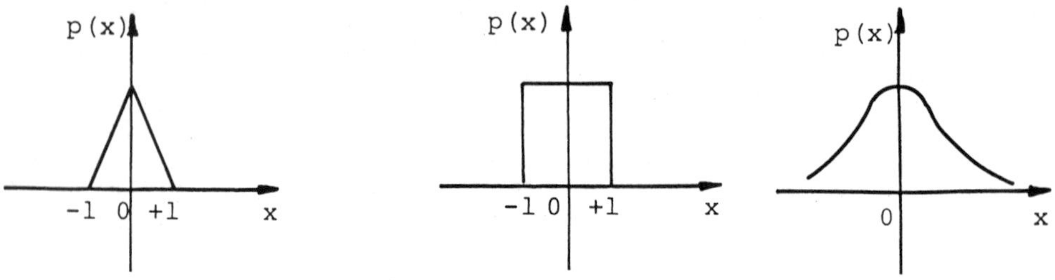

$$p(x) = \begin{cases} 1-|x| & |x| \le 1 \\ 0 & |x| > 0 \end{cases} \qquad p(x) = \begin{cases} 1 & |x| \le 1 \\ 0 & |x| > 1 \end{cases} \qquad p(x) = \frac{1}{\sqrt{2\pi}\,\sigma_2} \exp(-\frac{x^2}{2\sigma_2^2})$$

(a) Wedge type (b) Rectangular type (c) Round type

Fig. 3 Object's shape

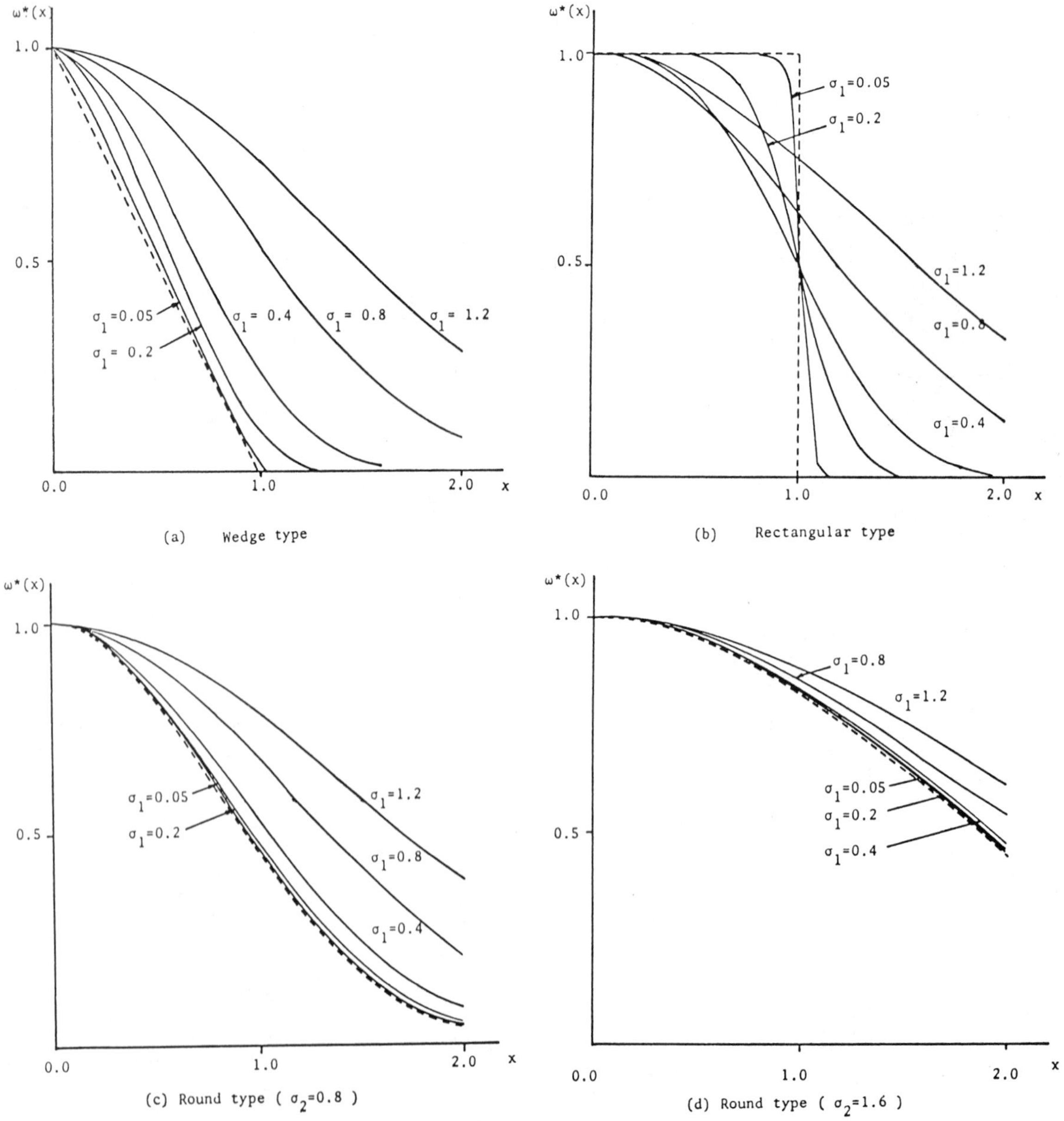

Fig. 4 Plot of Eq. (2.9) for different shapes

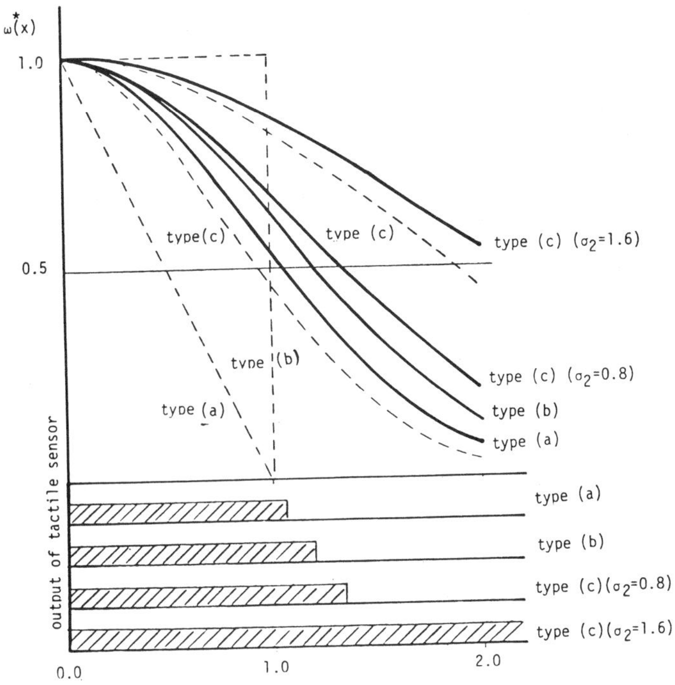

Fig. 5 The output of tactile sensors

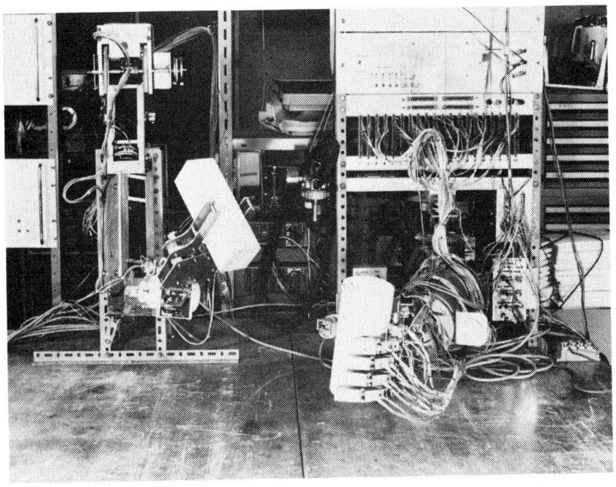

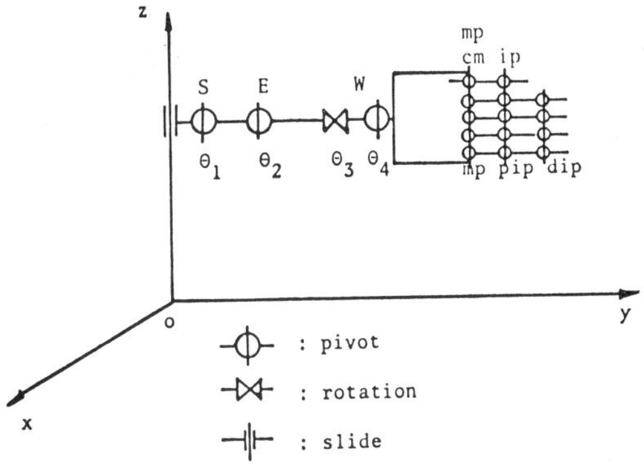

Fig. 6 Artificial hand system

consist of elastic and conductive sheets arched over a uniformly crossed array of binary sensors (on-off type) studded with micro-eyelets. The sensors close the contact points between the eyelets and conductive sheet by applied pressure. The shape of the pressure pattern due to the surface of object can be extracted by the pattern of the contact points. The tactile sensors are provided the tip and joint or both joints on the fingers as shown in Fig. 7. All of the tactile sensors installed on the finger consist of 384 individual contacts.

A contact pattern of the tactile sensors is acquired from the grasped object by the artificial hand. Subroutine "SENSOR" is able to select a routine of the contact pattern of the tactile sensor for either individual fingers or all fingers. The contact pattern of the tactile sensors is typed out on a keyboad and can be represented on a CRT display.

3.4 The contact pattern of the tactile sensors

Suppose that the objects used in this paper consist of three types : column, prism and square pillar. These objects are respectively grasped by the artificial hand and the contact pattern of tactile sensor is given as shown in Fig. 8. The pattern in Fig. 8(a) represents the contact pattern of a column (70 mmϕ).

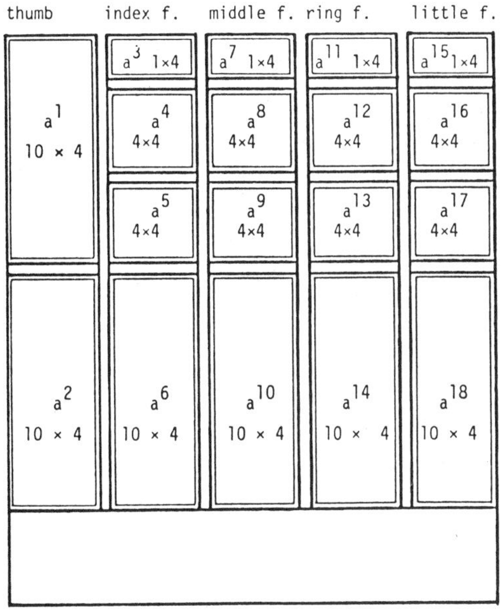

Fig. 7 The arrangement of sensors

```
A PATTERN OF TACTILE SENSORS

THUMB F    INDEX F    MIDDLE F   RING F     LITTLE F
+ + + +    + + + +    + + + +    + + + $    + + + +
+ + + +
+ + + +    + + $ $    + $ + +    + $ + $    + + + $
+ + + +    + + + $    + + + +    + + $ $    + $ $ $
+ + + +    + + + $    + + $ $    + $ $ $    $ $ $ $
+ + + +    + + + $    + + $ +    + + $ +    $ $ $ $
+ $ $ $
+ $ $ $    $ $ + +    + + + +    $ $ + +    + + + +
+ $ $ $    $ $ + +    $ $ + +    $ + + +    + + + +
+ $ $ $    $ + + +    + + + +    $ + + +    $ + + +
           + + + +    $ + + +    + $ + +    + + $ $

+ + + +    + + + +    + + + +    + + + +    + + + +
+ + + +    + + + +    + + + +    + + + +    + + + +
+ + + +    + + + +    + + + +    + + + +    + + + +
+ + + +    + + + +    + + + +    + + + +    + + + +
+ + + +    + + + +    + + + +    + + + +    + + + +
+ + + +    + + + +    + + + +    + + + +    + + + +
+ + + +    + + + +    + + + +    + + + +    + + + +
+ + + +    + + + +    + + + +    + + $ +    + + + +
$ + + +    + + + +    + + + $    + + + +    + + + +
+ + + +    + + + +    + + + +    + + + +    + + + +
```

(a) Column 70 mm ϕ (sensor output)

```
A PATTERN OF TACTILE SENSORS

THUMB F    INDEX F    MIDDLE F   RING F     LITTLE F
+ + + +    + + + +    + + + +    $ $ $ $    + + + +
+ + + +
+ + + +    $ $ $ $    $ $ $ $    $ $ $ $    $ $ $ $
+ + + +    $ $ $ $    + + + +    $ $ $ $    $ $ $ $
+ + + +    $ $ $ $    $ $ $ $    $ $ $ $    $ $ $ $
+ + + +    $ $ $ $    $ $ $ $    $ $ $ $    $ $ $ $
$ $ $ $
$ $ $ $    $ $ $ $    + + + +    $ $ $ $    + + + +
$ $ $ $    $ $ $ $    $ $ $ $    $ $ $ $    + + + +
$ $ $ $    $ $ $ $    + + + +    $ $ $ $    $ $ $ $
           + + + +    $ $ $ $    $ $ $ $    $ $ $ $

+ + + +    + + + +    + + + +    + + + +    + + + +
+ + + +    + + + +    + + + +    + + + +    + + + +
+ + + +    + + + +    + + + +    + + + +    + + + +
+ + + +    + + + +    + + + +    + + + +    + + + +
+ + + +    + + + +    + + + +    + + + +    + + + +
+ + + +    + + + +    + + + +    + + + +    + + + +
+ + + +    + + + +    + + + +    + + + +    + + + +
+ + + +    + + + +    + + + +    $ $ $ $    + + + +
$ $ $ $    + + + +    $ $ $ $    + + + +    + + + +
+ + + +    + + + +    + + + +    + + + +    + + + +
```

(b) contact pattern (Column 70mm ϕ)

```
A PATTERN OF TACTILE SENSORS

THUMB F    INDEX F    MIDDLE F   RING F     LITTLE F
+ + + +    $ $ $ $    + + + +    $ $ $ $    $ $ $ $
+ + + +
+ + + +    + + + +    + + + +    $ $ $ $    + + + +
+ + + +    + + + +    + + + +    $ $ $ $    $ $ $ $
+ + + +    + + + +    $ $ $ $    $ $ $ $    + + + +
$ $ $ $    + + + +    + + + +    $ $ $ $    + + + +
$ $ $ $
+ + + +    + + + +    + + + +    + + + +    + + + +
$ $ $ $    + + + +    + + + +    + + + +    + + + +
$ $ $ $    + + + +    + + + +    + + + +    + + + +
           + + + +    + + + +    + + + +    + + + +

$ $ $ $    + + + +    + + + +    + + + +    + + + +
$ $ $ $    + + + +    + + + +    + + + +    + + + +
$ $ $ $    + + + +    + + + +    $ $ $ $    + + + +
$ $ $ $    $ $ $ $    + + + +    $ $ $ $    $ $ $ $
+ + + +    $ $ $ $    $ $ $ $    $ $ $ $    + + + +
+ + + +    + + + +    $ $ $ $    + + + +    + + + +
+ + + +    + + + +    + + + +    + + + +    + + + +
+ + + +    + + + +    + + + +    + + + +    + + + +
$ $ $ $    + + + +    + + + +    + + + +    + + + +
+ + + +    + + + +    + + + +    + + + +    + + + +
```

(c) Contact pattern (Pris m, 70mm on a side)

```
A PATTERN OF TACTILE SENSORS

THUMB F    INDEX F    MIDDLE F   RING F     LITTLE F
+ + + +    + + + +    + + + +    + + + +    + + + +
+ + + +
+ + + +    + + + +    + + + +    $ $ $ $    $ $ $ $
+ + + +    + + + +    + + + +    $ $ $ $    $ $ $ $
+ + + +    + + + +    $ $ $ $    $ $ $ $    $ $ $ $
+ + + +    $ $ $ $    $ $ $ $    $ $ $ $    $ $ $ $
$ $ $ $
$ $ $ $    + + + +    + + + +    + + + +    + + + +
$ $ $ $    + + + +    + + + +    + + + +    + + + +
$ $ $ $    + + + +    + + + +    + + + +    + + + +
           + + + +    + + + +    + + + +    + + + +

+ + + +    + + + +    + + + +    + + + +    + + + +
+ + + +    + + + +    + + + +    + + + +    + + + +
+ + + +    + + + +    + + + +    + + + +    + + + +
+ + + +    + + + +    + + + +    + + + +    + + + +
$ $ $ $    $ $ $ $    + + + +    $ $ $ $    + + + +
$ $ $ $    + + + +    $ $ $ $    + + + +    + + + +
+ + + +    + + + +    + + + +    + + + +    + + + +
+ + + +    + + + +    + + + +    + + + +    + + + +
$ $ $ $    + + + +    + + + +    + + + +    + + + +
+ + + +    + + + +    + + + +    + + + +    + + + +
```

(d) Contact pattern (Square pillar, 60mm on a side)

Fig. 8 Contact pattern

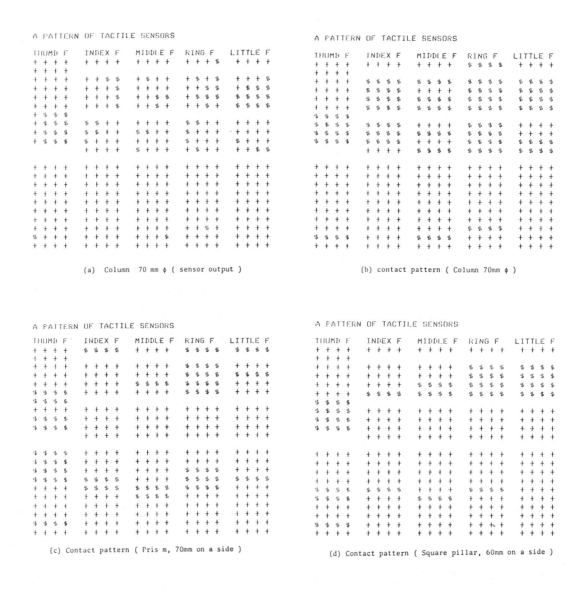

(a) Column (b) Prism (c) Square pillar

Fig. 9 The postures of grasped object

A symbol "\$" denotes the sensor of a closed contact point. A few closed contact points are missing. Then the contact pattern is arranged for its row pattern, namely for any row and $1 \leq q \leq 4$,

$$\text{if } \sum_{1\leq q\leq 4} a^i_{pq} > \hat{\theta}, \quad a^i_{pq} = 1 \qquad (3.1)$$

$$\text{if } \sum_{1\leq q\leq 4} a^i_{pq} < \hat{\theta}, \quad a^i_{pq} = 0 \qquad (3.2)$$

where $a^i_{pq} = 1$ denotes an element a_{pq} of sensor a^i and the closed contact point. Then the contact pattern in Fig. 8(a) is arranged in the pattern represented by Fig. 8(b). Examples of other arranged contact patterns are shown in Fig. 8(c),(d).

A feature of an object's surface is regarded as an edge type for satisfying the following equation.

$$\sum_{1\leq p\leq \hat{p}} a^i_{pq} \leq 2 \qquad (3.3)$$

where $\hat{p}$ denotes the maximum number of row for the tactile sensor i. Moreover, the feature is regarded as a round type for satisfying the following equation.

$$\sum_{1\leq p\leq \hat{p}} a^i_{pq} \geq 4 \qquad (3.4)$$

In case of $\Sigma a^i_{pq}=3$, the feature of object is regarded as an edge type or a round type.

4 EXPERIMENT ON CLASSIFICATION OF OBJECTS

As mentioned in Sec. 3,a feature of object's surface are obtained from the local type of shape at contact point by the tactile sensors. Then, classification of object's shape is performed by using some features of its surface. The different type objects considered in this paper are a column (70,80,90 and 100 mmϕ), prism (70,80,90 and 100 mm on a side), and square pillar (60,70 and 80 mm on a side). The postures of the grasped object are shown in Fig. 9. As mentioned in Sec. 3.4, the feature pattern is obtained as a feature of the contact pattern for the tactile sensor a^i , i = 1,2, ... ,18, respectively. Moreover, the type of the feature pattern is experimentally selected as follows. A feature pattern is regarded as the round type in the case of 9 contact patterns having more than 4 patterns of 4 rows for a^i, i = 1,2, ...,18.

The edge type is considered as the pattern having 6 open contacts or the case where the thumb makes contact with a flat portion of the object (6 rows or more for a^i) as shown in Fig. 9(c).

Experiments on classification of objects are performed by a simple non-parametric linear learning machine. The objects for different sizes are used and these feature patterns are regarded as input data of the learning machine.

Learning was performed by 4 iterative steps. Therefore, classification of the 66 samples of object (24, 24 and 18 respectively) resulted in the correct ansewer, 100 %, 58.3 % and 55.6 % respectively. It is clarified that low reliability for the prism and square pillar is caused by missing of the feature of object's surface on the joints. Also, the feature pattern is considered as the round type as an edge of an object contacts slantingly with the surface of the sensors. It appears that these problems are always occured in case of using the multi-joints type of finger.

5 CONCLUSION

This paper has described a 2-dimensional model of a tactile sensor and its blurring effect. A model provides the shape resolution of the object's surface by the large sensor arrays.

The artificial hand with tactile sensor based on the model grasps the object. Classification of the shape of the object is performed by the linear learning machine. Its data become a feature pattern which is extracted from the contact pattern. Reliability of classification for different objects has been experimentally demonstrated.

ACKNOWLEDGEMENTS

The author would like to thank professor M.Mori, Y.Umetani of Tokyo Institute of Technology and S.Aida of University of Electro-communications for their helps in the course of work reported here.

REFERENCES

(1) H. A. Ernst, MH-1, a computer operated mechanical hand, Proc. 1962 Spring Joint Computer Conference, National Press, 39(1963)

(2) Proc. First Int. Joint Conf. Artificial Intelligence, Washington, D.C. (1969); also in Proc. Second Int. Joint Conf. Artificial Intelligence, London (1971); also in Proc. Third Int. Joint Conf. Artificial Intelligence, Stanford (1973); also in Proc. Fourth Int.

Joint Conf. Artificial Intelligence, Tbilisi, Georgia USSR (1975)

(3) Proc. First CISM-IFToMM Symposium Udine (1973); also in Proc. Second CISM-IFToMM Symposium, Warsaw, Poland (1976)

(4) J.L.Nevins and D.E.Whitney, The force vector assembler concept, Proc. First CISM-IFToMM Symposium, Udine(1973)

(5) J.W.Hill and J.C.Bliss, Tactile perception studies related to teleoperator systems, Final report on NASA Contact NASA 2-5409, Stanford Research Institute Menlo Park, California (1971)

(6) T.Goto, K. Takeyasu, T. Inoyama and R. Shimomura, Compact packaging by robot with tactile sensor, Proc. of the Second Int. Symp. on Industrial Robots, Chicago, Illinois(1972)

(7) P.M.Will and D.D. Grossman, An experimental system for computer controlled mechanical assembly, IEEE Trans. on Computer, C-24, 9, 879(1975)

(8) G.Kinoshita,S.Aida and M.Mori, Pattern classification of the grasped object by the artificial hand, Proc. Third Int. Joint Conf. Artificial Intelligence, 665, Stanford (1973)

(9) V.S.Gurfinkel, A.Yu.Shneyder, Ye. M.Kanayev and Ye.V.Gurfinkel, Tactile sensitizing of manipulators, Engrg. Cybernetics, 12, 6, 47(1974)

(10) U.Dinnar, A note on the theory of deformation in compressed skin tissues, Mathematical Biosciences, 8, 71(1970)

(11) M.R.Miller, H.J. Ralston III and M. Kasahara, The pattern of cutaneous innervation of human hand, food and breast, Advances in Biology of Skin, Pergamon Press (1960)

(12) G. Kinoshita and M.Mori, Design method for spacing the receptor elements on an artificial tactile sense with multi-elements, Trans. of the Society of Instrument and Control Engineers, 8,5, 545(1972)

ON FORCE SENSING INFORMATION AND ITS USE IN CONTROLLING MANIPULATORS

B. Shimano and B. Roth

Mechanical Engineering Department, Stanford University, Stanford, Calif. 94305, USA

ABSTRACT

This paper treats the problem of force sensing as associated with mechanical manipulators under computer control. First it reviews the various methods of force sensing currently in use. Then it reviews the design requirements for a force sensing system. A novel method for the automatic calibration of a force sensing system is presented. This method has several advantages over present methods. It has been implemented on the Stanford Arm system; test results are presented which verify the expected efficiencies of this method.

1. INTRODUCTION

Until recently, most industrial mechanical manipulators have been employed as simple pick and place tools in material handling tasks and as such have operated quite successfully without the use of sophisticated sensor feedback. However, as more manipulators are applied to tasks involving parts assembly, the need for sensory feedback will become more crucial. This is because assembly tasks often require a high degree of positioning accuracy between mating parts.

One approach to solving this problem is to increase the accuracy of both the manipulator and the positions of the work pieces to a level where the task can be successfully completed. However, this approach could be very expensive for some applications. For instance, there are some types of castings for which high precision fabrication is cost prohibitive. Furthermore, as manipulators are applied to increasingly complex assemblies, there is a growing need for simple, economical means of performing error detection at each stage of the assembly.

Sensing the forces that develop between the manipulator and its environment is a very important source of feedback in many situations. Force sensing can be used to guarantee positive contact between two mating parts or alternately, it can be used to monitor the forces of interaction to insure that they do not exceed a safe limit. When force sensing is added to the manipulator's servo loop, active force compliance can be used to correct errors in the position of the manipulator to allow it to accommodate to the physical constraints within which it must work. This is the case when manipulators are used for inserting pins in holes or opening hinged lids. Finally, force sensing can be used to verify that assembled parts exhibit the proper motion capabilities without excessive binding.

In this paper, we describe the force sensing devices which are currently being used in conjunction with manipulators, and discuss in detail a new force sensing wrist that has been designed for use with the Stanford Arm.

2. FORCE SENSING TECHNIQUES

Existing force sensing devices generally can be classified into one of three categories according to their placement relative to the manipulator with which they are used. Force sensing devices are normally mounted: 1) on the joints of the manipulator, 2) on or close to the manipulator hand, or 3) on the support platform for the object to be handled. Within each of these categories, individual mechanical implementations vary a great deal. Some of the more common devices are described below:

2.1 Joint Torque Sensing

Sensing the torques that are produced at each of the manipulator's joints is perhaps the oldest of the three techniques and has been used very successfully for many years in master-slave manipulator systems. Typically, in this type of operation, the joint torques of the slave manipulator are sensed and then proportionally reflected back to the master. Normally, the slave's joint torques are determined either directly by monitoring the motor currents (in electrically driven arms) or the back pressures (in hydraulically powered arms) or by reading special joint torque sensors. If the master and slave manipulators have a similar configuration, this technique works quite well and the operator is able to distinguish the type of resistance that the slave is encountering.

Since the sensing devices are distributed throughout the manipulator, joint torque sensing has the added advantage of not only detecting forces and moments applied at the hand, but also those applied at other points on the manipulator. This is very useful in providing feedback information if, for instance, some portion of the manipulator were to unexpectedly encounter an obstacle.

Similar torque sensing systems have often been used with manipulators under computer control. Nakano [1] described a computer controlled system that employed joint torque sensors to detect the forces of interaction produced when two manipulators were used to simultaneously lift and move a large box. At the Stanford Artificial Intelligence Laboratory, the force sensing technique that has been employed for several years utilizes information relating to the currents in the driving motors. Since the force sensing is executed in conjunction with a software servo, this method has the advantage of requiring no additional hardware because the joint motor currents could be directly specified by the computer. Also, it is easy to use computer programs to determine, for each configuration of the manipulator, the gravity loading due to the mass of the links, the link inertia, and the apparent friction of each joint. This information can then be used to modify the actual currents so as to realize the desired force and moment applied by the manipulator's hand.

The single greatest draw back in sensing joint torques is that the accuracy with which the hand force and moment can be determined is restricted by the degree to which the dynamic coefficients of the manipulator can be accurately predicted. For many manipulators, the uncertainty in predicting the friction and joint damping is sufficient to preclude the possibility of accurately detecting small hand forces. Experiments have shown that for the Stanford Arm, forces as small as approximately four newtons can be reliably detected in almost any configuration. This is sensitive enough to make joint force sensing a very useful tool, but many important tasks require much greater accuracy.

One further disadvantage in using the joint force technique is that it is time consuming to convert from joint torques to an equivalent force and moment at the hand. In order to accomplish this conversion, for a six degree of freedom manipulator, one must perform an operation which is equivalent to solving a set of 6 linear equations in 6 variables. Often, this involves inverting a 6 by 6 matrix and the execution time can be many milli-seconds. Furthermore, since the coupling between joints of the manipulator is a function of the its geometry, it is generally not possible to simplify this computation without changing the design of the manipulator.

2.2 Force Sensing Wrists and Fingers

One approach to reducing the uncertainty in measuring and controlling hand forces is to isolate them from those produced by the links and joints. One means of accomplishing this is to mount a force sensing device close to the hand and below the last powered joint of the manipulator. This eliminates the motor torques and link dynamic affects from the measurement of the external forces at the hand. At most, compensation for the inertia and gravity loading of the hand has to be taken into account.

Force sensing devices of this type vary in complexity from the simple two degree of freedom sensing system used with the Olivetti SIGMA System [2] to the six degree of freedom sensing laser system developed at Draper Laboratories [3]. However, all of these devices share in common the potential to sense small hand forces and moments on the order of a few hundredths of a newton. Furthermore, since the conversion from sensor readings to hand forces and moments is a function of only the construction and geometry of the sensing device, most of these sensors have been designed to require extremely simple conversion routines, as opposed to that required by joint force sensing. In fact, a force sensing wrist that was develop at the Stanford Research Institute mechanically decoupled the affects of the various force components so that forces and moments could be detected separately [4].

While most force sensors of this type have been designed for mounting just above the hand of the manipulator at its "wrist", there have been several devices which have been mounted on the fingers of the hand. Mounting the sensors on the finger tips puts the reading elements as close to the work piece as possible where they are subjected to a minimum of interference from the structure of the manipulator. Furthermore, finger sensors are able to function not only as force sensors but also as touch sensors. However, because of the high gripping pressure required by most hands, these devices often experience noise problems when force sensing is attempted while an object is being held.

2.3 Force Pedestal

Since most automated assembly systems are intended for use in tasks that require that thousands of parts be handled, it would be financially prohibitive to mount force sensing devices on each of the parts. A feasible alternative to this idea is to instrument the structure on which each of the work pieces is placed. Devices of this type have been used for many years in parts fabrication operations to monitor the forces of interaction between mill tools and work pieces. Draper Laboratories has develop a Force Sensing Pedestal [5] based upon this idea which has high structural stiffness and good sensitivity.

3. DESIGN OF A FORCE SENSING WRIST

In designing a force sensor to be mounted on the wrist of a manipulator, there are several desirable properties that must be kept in mind. These properties not only relate to the ease, speed, and accuracy with which forces and moments can be detected but also to how the sensing device affects the positioning performance of the manipulator. Since most force sensing wrists function as transducers for transforming forces and moments exerted at the hand into measurable displacements at the wrist, it is important that the wrist motions generated by the force sensor not diminish the positioning accuracy of the manipulator. The required design specifications can be summarized as follows:

(1) *High Stiffness*: This has two advantages. First, since the natural frequency of a beam is directly related to its stiffness, high stiffness ensures that the frequency response of the wrist is such that disturbing forcing are quickly damped. This permits accurate readings to be taken quickly. Second, high stiffness reduces the magnitude of the deflections for an applied force or moment. Such deflections add to the positioning error of the hand, and if the deflections are large, an added variable correction must be used in determining the position of the manipulator.

(2) *Compact Design*: By placing the force wrist as close to the end effector as possible, the position error that results when the hand is rotated through small angles due to rotations in the force sensor can be minimized. Also, since it is desirable to measure as large a hand force as possible, minimizing the distance between the hand and the force wrist reduces the lever arm for forces applied at the hand. Finally, keeping the overall dimensions of the wrist small ensures that this device will not restrict the movement of the manipulator in tight quarters.

(3) *Good Linearity*: Ensuring that the response of force sensing elements is linear, with respect to applied forces and moments, permits the resolution of sensor readings using simple matrix operations. Furthermore, this simplifies the calibration of the force sensor since only linear equations are involved.

(4) *Low Hysteresis and Internal Friction*: Internal friction reduces the sensitivity of the force sensing elements since forces must first overcome friction before a measurable displacement can be produced. Also, internal friction produces a hysteresis effect so that the operation of applying and subsequently removing the same force does not restore the position measuring devices to their original readings.

Victor Scheinman has designed a force sensing wrist for use with the Stanford Arm which satisfies the stated requirements (fig. 1). The basic design of the force sensor is a modified six degree of freedom device of the 'Maltese Cross' configuration described by Flatau [6]. The wrist motions are measured by a series of semi-conductor strain gages mounted on the cross webbings. There is one gage on each side of the each of the four webbings, hence a total of 16 strain gages. The gages are wired in eight voltage divider pairs. Each provides a single reading that gives the differences in strain levels on opposite sides of a web. This arrangement reduces the problem of thermal drift since all sides of a given web will expand or contract by approximately the same amount for a given change in temperature. By machining the entire force sensor from

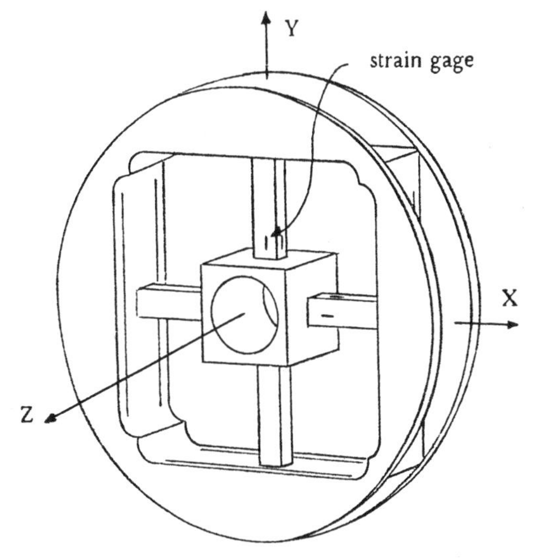

Figure 1: Scheinman Force Sensing Wrist

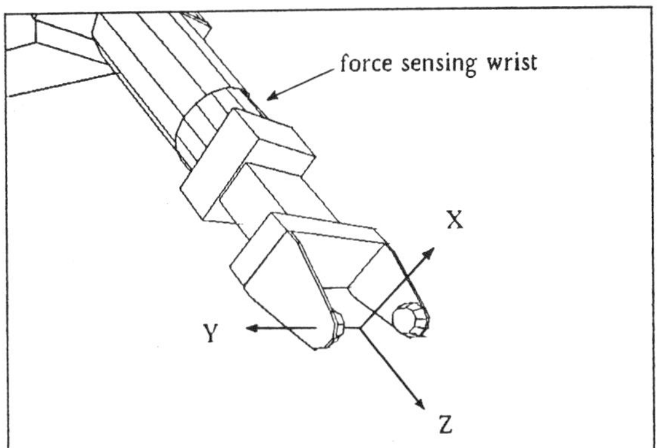

Figure 2: Hand Coordinate System

one piece of aluminum, the hysteresis which can arise from friction at the boundaries between the webs and the surrounding support structure has been avoided. The interface between the webs and the outer hub is a thin flexure which is machined into the support structure. Initial testing indicates that this design exhibits practically no hysteresis in the elastic range of the force wrist's material.

The force wrist is approximately 5.3 cm. in diameter and about 2.5 cm. thick. It is mounted between the last rotary joint of the manipulator and the housing for the hand motor (fig. 2). The wrist is aligned so that the Z axis of its coordinate system is collinear with the Z axis (the approach vector) of the hand and its X and Y axes are parallel to the X and Y axes of the hand coordinate system.

3.1 Resolving Forces and Moments

In predicting the response of the force sensing wrist to the application of a force and moment applied at its geometric center, we will make the following assumptions:

(1) The force wrist is operated within the elastic range of its material and the strain gages produce readings which vary linearly with respect to changes in their elongation. Hence, the principal of superposition can be applied.

(2) There is no coupling between the affects of applying orthogonal components of forces and moments.

Then from the Theory of Elasticity it can be shown that for the configuration and dimensions of the Scheinman Force Wrist, the components of a force vector, F, which act at the center of the cross webs can be computed from the ϵ vector, which contains the eight sensor readings $(\epsilon_1,\ldots,\epsilon_8)$, by performing the following matrix multiplication.

$$\begin{bmatrix} F_x \\ F_y \\ F_z \\ M_x \\ M_y \\ M_z \end{bmatrix} = \begin{bmatrix} 0 & 0 & c_{13} & 0 & 0 & 0 & c_{17} & 0 \\ c_{21} & 0 & 0 & 0 & c_{25} & 0 & 0 & 0 \\ 0 & c_{32} & 0 & c_{34} & 0 & c_{36} & 0 & c_{38} \\ 0 & c_{42} & 0 & 0 & 0 & c_{46} & 0 & 0 \\ 0 & 0 & 0 & c_{54} & 0 & 0 & 0 & c_{58} \\ c_{61} & 0 & c_{63} & 0 & c_{65} & 0 & c_{67} & 0 \end{bmatrix} * \begin{bmatrix} \epsilon_1 \\ \epsilon_2 \\ \epsilon_3 \\ \epsilon_4 \\ \epsilon_5 \\ \epsilon_6 \\ \epsilon_7 \\ \epsilon_8 \end{bmatrix} \qquad (1)$$

where the subscripts following each of the six components of the force vector, $(F_x,\ldots,M_z)$, indicate the axis in the wrist coordinate system along which each component is resolved. "F" is used to signify a force component and "M" signifies a moment component.

This last equation is valid so long as the coupling between the affects of applying different components of force and moment on the wrist is negligible. However, we have found that some coupling does exist and that it can produce an error of as much as 5 percent in the force resolution calculation. This error is the result of both mechanical coupling transmitted through the force sensor structure and inaccurate placement of the strain gages on the center line of the webs. Based upon our previous assumptions, equation (1) indicates that each component of the force vector should be a function of only two or possibly four of the sensor readings. In fact, it is necessary to consider each component of force to be a linear function of all eight sensors in order to correct for the coupling. Therefore, in practice it is necessary to replace the theortical, sparse 6 by 8 matrix with a matrix which contains 48 non-zero elements. This full matrix will be called the calibration matrix, C, and its determination will be discussed later in this paper. The corrected equation for converting from sensor readings to a force vector is as follows:

$$F = C * \epsilon \qquad (2)$$

where

$$C = \begin{bmatrix} c_{11} & \cdot & \cdot & \cdot & \cdot & c_{18} \\ c_{21} & \cdot & \cdot & \cdot & \cdot & c_{28} \\ \vdots & & & & & \vdots \\ c_{61} & \cdot & \cdot & \cdot & \cdot & c_{68} \end{bmatrix} \qquad (3)$$

In general, we are interested in resolving the sensor readings into a force vector that acts at a point other then the center of the wrist. For example, the force and moment at the manipulator's finger tips can be used to sense when the manipulator first comes in contact with another object or the force vector at the end of a tool being held by the manipulator many be used to maintain a steady pressure between the tool and a work piece. In all such cases, the problem is to determine the force vector at a point located at a distance $\{d_x,d_y,d_z\}$ from the force sensing wrist. For this linear translation, the new force vector, $\{F_x',F_y',F_z',M_x',M_y',M_z'\}$ is related to the force vector at the center of the wrist, $\{F_x,F_y,F_z,M_x,M_y,M_z\}$, by the following matrix equation.

$$\begin{bmatrix} F_x' \\ F_y' \\ F_z' \\ M_x' \\ M_y' \\ M_z' \end{bmatrix} = \begin{bmatrix} 1 & 0 & 0 & 0 & 0 & 0 \\ 0 & 1 & 0 & 0 & 0 & 0 \\ 0 & 0 & 1 & 0 & 0 & 0 \\ 0 & -d_z & d_y & 1 & 0 & 0 \\ d_z & 0 & -d_x & 0 & 1 & 0 \\ -d_y & d_x & 0 & 0 & 0 & 1 \end{bmatrix} * \begin{bmatrix} F_x \\ F_y \\ F_z \\ M_x \\ M_y \\ M_z \end{bmatrix} \qquad (4)$$

We now label the 6x6 matrix on the right "D". Then in order to directly resolve the strain gage readings into an equivalent force and moment at a point located at $\{d_x,d_y,d_z\}$ relative to the wrist, we combine equations (2) and (4) to obtain:

$$F' = D * C * \epsilon$$

Finally, it is at times desirable to resolve the force components relative to a set of axes which are rotated with respect to the wrist coordinate system. For example, we may want to determine the force vector resolved along the axes of the manipulator base coordinate system. Assuming that R is a 3 by 3 matrix which defines the rotation from the wrist coordinate system to the new coordinate system, the desired transformation can be performed as follows:

$$F' = R' * D * C * \epsilon \qquad (5)$$

where

$$R' = \begin{bmatrix} R & 0 \\ 0 & R \end{bmatrix}$$

Equation (5) is the total transformation that must be performed to convert the wrist force sensor readings into an equivalent force and moment applied at a specified distance from the wrist and resolved into components rotated with respect to the wrist coordinate system.

4. AUTOMATIC FORCE WRIST CALIBRATION

In our first tests, the elements of the matrix for converting from sensor readings to a force vector (3) were calculated using a calibration method that required that three orthogonally oriented forces and three orthogonally oriented moments be applied to the geometric center of the wrist. To accomplish this, an elaborate system of pulleys and weights was devised. While this type of procedure is acceptable for testing purposes, it is too time consuming to employ when the wrist is in daily use and has to be occasionally re-calibrated. Indeed, once the force wrist is mounted on the manipulator, applying pure forces and moments to the force sensing wrist may be impossible without either detaching the hand or attaching special collars. A more acceptable technique than either of these two alternatives is to use a method of calibration that can deal with arbitrary combinations of forces and moments. Also, in order to minimize the set-up time, it would be advantageous to employ a calibration method that requires the minimum number of special purpose attachments to the manipulator. With this in mind, the following calibration procedure was devised.

4.1 The Calibration Matrices

The objective of calibrating the force sensing wrist is to compute all 48 elements of the calibration matrix, C, based upon experimental information. In order to accomplish this task, we will first compute the elements of the pseudo inverse calibration matrix, CI, and then perform an operation which is analogous to matrix inversion to obtain C. The pseudo inverse, whose elements we will label ci_{ij} ($i=1,..,8$; $j = 1,...,6$), is the linear least squares approximation to the inverse of the non-square calibration matrix. To a first order approximation, multiplying the calibration matrix by its pseudo inverse yields the identity matrix, I, as follows:

$$I \sim CI * C \tag{6}$$

The pseudo inverse matrix can be used to relate the response of the wrist sensor elements to the application of a force vector. We will therefore compute this matrix by requiring that it exactly satisfy the equation:

$$\epsilon = CI * F \tag{7}$$

Once the pseudo inverse has been determined, the following approximate relationship, which was first presented by Watson [5], can be used for determining the desired calibration matrix.

$$C \sim (CI^T * CI)^{-1} * CI^T \tag{8}$$

You will note that if the force sensing wrist had only 6 sensors then the calibration matrix and its pseudo inverse would be square and all of the equations presented above would still apply and would yield exact answers. This is true, because equation (8) reduces to computing the exact inverse of the matrix CI if CI is square.

4.2 Computing the Pseudo Inverse Calibration Matrix

To compute the elements of the pseudo inverse matrix, six independent, known force vectors must be applied to the force sensor. These force vectors need not be orthogonal nor do they have to be pure forces or moments; however, we will require that their values be resolved at a single point whose position is known relative to the center of the force wrist. We will define the values of the force vectors and their corresponding strain gage readings as follows:

ϵ_{ij} = the reading of the jth strain gage due to the application of the ith force vector ($i=1,...,6$; $j=1,...,8$).

f_{ik} = the kth component of the ith independent force vector ($i=1,...,6$; $k=1,...,6$).

For each of the six independent force vectors, equation (7) must apply, therefore the relationship between the applied force vector and the resulting strain gage readings can be written as follows:

$$\epsilon_{ij} = ci_{j1} f_{i1} + \ldots\ldots + ci_{j6} f_{i6}$$

This last expression is valid for all permutations of $i = 1,2,..,6$; $j = 1,2,..,8$ and represents a total of 48 equations. If we now group together all of the equations relating to the response of a single strain gage, these 48 equations can be represented in matrix form as follows:

$$\begin{bmatrix} \epsilon_{1j} \\ \epsilon_{2j} \\ \epsilon_{3j} \\ \epsilon_{4j} \\ \epsilon_{5j} \\ \epsilon_{6j} \end{bmatrix} = \begin{bmatrix} f_{11} & f_{12} & f_{13} & f_{14} & f_{15} & f_{16} \\ f_{21} & f_{22} & f_{23} & f_{24} & f_{25} & f_{26} \\ f_{31} & f_{32} & f_{33} & f_{34} & f_{35} & f_{36} \\ f_{41} & f_{42} & f_{43} & f_{44} & f_{45} & f_{46} \\ f_{51} & f_{52} & f_{53} & f_{54} & f_{55} & f_{56} \\ f_{61} & f_{62} & f_{63} & f_{64} & f_{65} & f_{66} \end{bmatrix} * \begin{bmatrix} ci_{j1} \\ ci_{j2} \\ ci_{j3} \\ ci_{j4} \\ ci_{j5} \\ ci_{j6} \end{bmatrix} \tag{9}$$

This formula represents eight independent matrix equations each of which contains only 6 unknowns (ci_{jk}, $k = 1,...,6$) because the force components and strain gage readings can all been determined experimentally. As long as the six force vectors are independent, the 6x6 matrix in equation (9) will be non-singular. Therefore, by applying a standard routine that solves sets of linear equations, we can solve equation (9) for the values of the elements of one row of the inverse calibration matrix, ci_{jk} ($k = 1,...,6$). By repeating this procedure for each of the eight matrix equations, all of the elements of the pseudo inverse calibration matrix can be determined . With CI computed, equation (8) can be applied to compute the desired calibration matrix, C.

It should be noted that this basic method of calculating the pseudo inverse calibration matrix is applicable if the information from more than six force vectors is utilized. If n samples are taken (n≥6), the matrices in equation (9) can be replaced with n by m matrices and an approximate solution for the rows of the inverse calibration matrix can be found by the method of least squares. Furthermore, since no information has been used which relates to the mechanical construction of the force sensing wrist, other than the number of sensors which are read, this calibration method can be applied to any force sensing wrist which can sense all six components of applied forces and moments.

4.3 Calibration Procedure

As we are no longer restricted to applying pure forces and moments, we can calibrate the force wrist while it is mounted on a manipulator. In fact, we can utilize the positioning and orientational degrees of freedom of the manipulator together with the weight of its hand to aid in the calibration procedure.

Since the force wrist is mounted between the last active rotary joint and the hand of the manipulator, the known weight of the hand will be used as the reference weight. While the hand is not the optimum reference, due to its light weight compared to the maximum load that the force wrist can measure, it does have the advantage of being constant and ever present. Also, since the weight of the hand must be subtracted from readings that are taken with the force wrist, using it as a reference will reduce the absolute error when small forces are to be measured. Furthermore, since this calibration procedure only requires that static forces be read, many readings can be taken for each force vector and digital filtering can be applied to increase their precision.

We now present the outline of a simple program which can be used to calibrate the force sensing wrist automatically, i.e., without the intervention of a human operator. For our measurements, we will define HW to be the weight of the hand, DCM to be the distance from the center of mass of the hand to the center of the force wrist, and DH to be the distance from the center of the hand fingers to the center of the force wrist. We will resolve all forces and moments at the geometric center of the force wrist.

1. To obtain the first set of strain gages readings, the manipulator is moved to a position with the hand pointing directly down and a series of readings are taken (fig. 3). Then the manipulator is re-positioned so that the hand is pointing upward and a second set of readings are taken (fig. 4). The difference between the two sets of readings are saved as our ϵ_{1j} and the corresponding force vector will be {0,0,2HW,0,0,0}.

2. Next the wrist of the manipulator is rotated until the hand is horizontal and the X axis of the force balance is vertical (fig. 5). The readings taken in this position and with the hand rotated 180 degrees about its central axis correspond to the force vector {2HW,0,0,0,2HW*DCM,0}.

3. The third set of readings are to be taken in exactly the same manner as the second set except that the hand is first rotated about its central axis 90 degrees to align the Y axis of the force sensor with the vertical (fig. 6). The force vector associated with this set of readings is {0,2HW,0,-2HW*DCM,0,0}.

4. In order to obtain two more independent readings that combine forces and moments along the X and Y axes, the manipulator is now directed to locate and pick up any convenient object in the work area. After the object has been grasped, all that we need to know is the position of center of mass of the object relative to the center of the force wrist. For this purpose, it is convenient to work with a fairly symmetric object that can be grasped such that its center of mass coincides with the geometric center of the finger tips. If this is true, then the weight of the object can be determined by repeating step 1 with the object in hand. The new readings can be scaled against the old and the weight of the object can be determined in terms of the known weight of the hand (fig. 7). We will call the weight of the object WT. We can now repeat step 2 with the object in hand (fig. 8). The force vector corresponding to these readings will be {2HW+2WT,0,0,0,2HW*DCM+2WT*DH,0}.

5. We now duplicate step 3 with the weight in hand to obtain a new set of readings (fig. 9). The force vector produced by the combined weight of the hand and object will be {0,2HW+2WT,0,-2HW*DCM-2WT*DH,0,0}.

6. For the final force vector, the manipulator must grasp an object fixed in place. This can be a vise, another manipulator, or even a willing and strong human volunteer. After ensuring that no net forces or moments exist along any of the axes, the motor of the last rotary joint of the manipulator is driven with a constant and known torque, T (fig. 10). Readings are taken for the torque directed in both directions and the corresponding force vector is given by {0,0,0,0,0,2T}.

Once the strain gage readings for the six independent force vectors have been taken, the procedure discussed in the previous section can be used to compute the calibration matrix for the force sensing wrist.

4.4 Force Resolution Range and Accuracy

The method that has been described in the preceding sections has been used to determine the calibration matrix for a force sensing wrist with an attached hand that was not as yet mounted on a manipulator. Based upon these

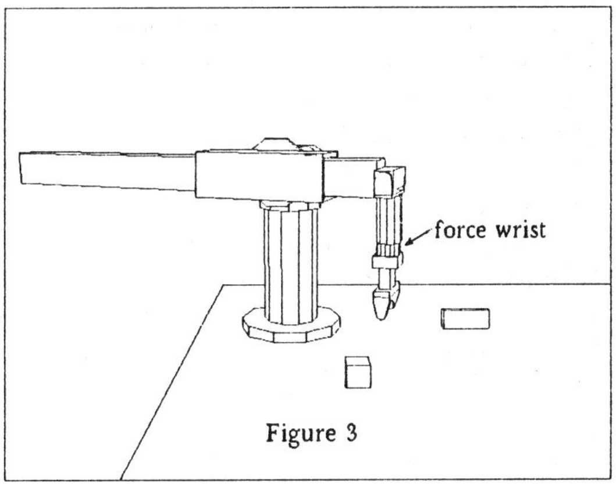

Figure 3

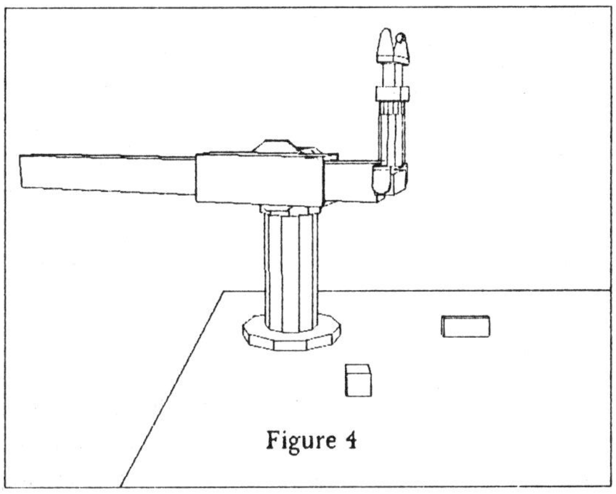

Figure 4

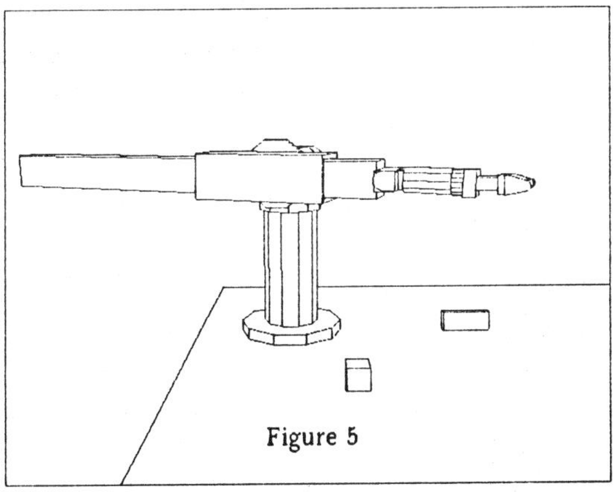

Figure 5

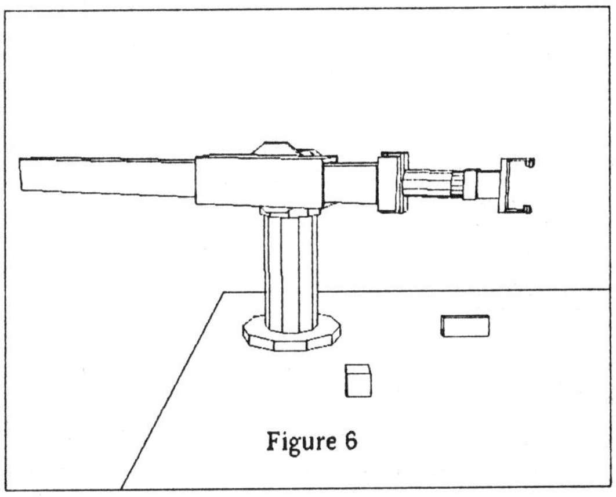

Figure 6

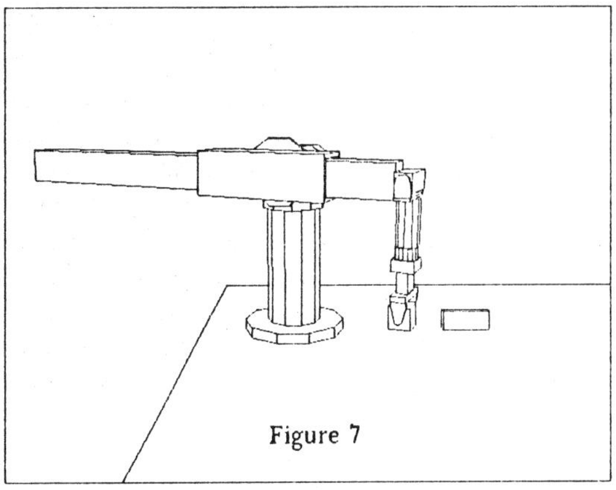

Figure 7

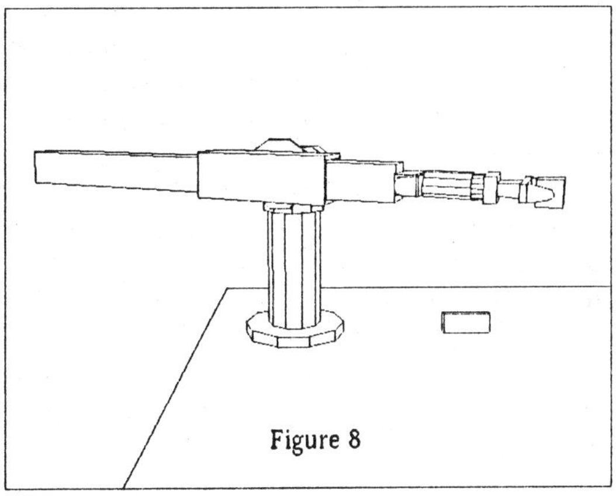

Figure 8

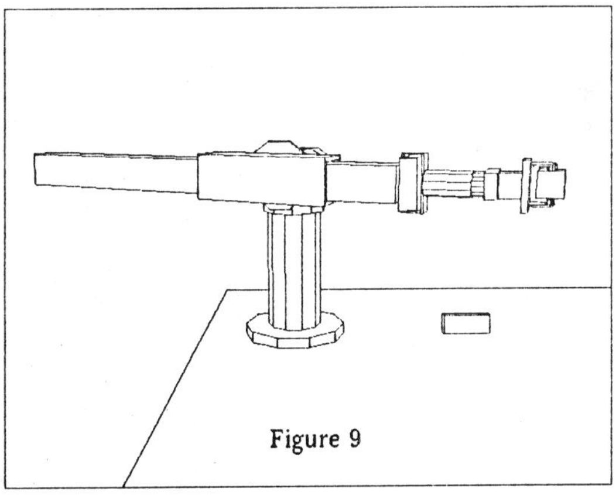

Figure 9

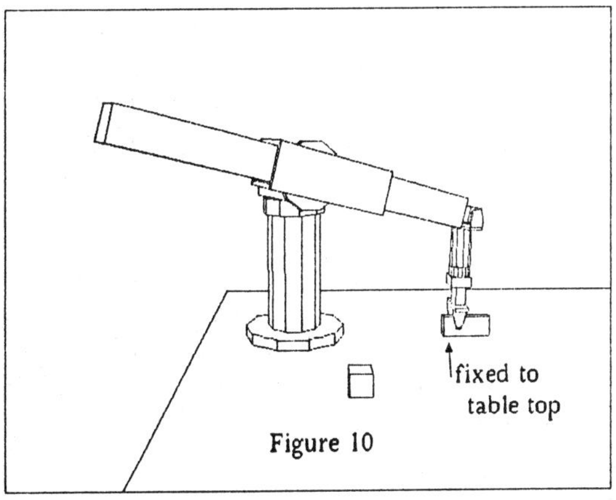

Figure 10

results, the full range of the forces and moments that can be detected by the Scheinman Force Sensing Wrist are presented in Table 1.

Table 1: Force Wrist Operating Range

Direction	Force (Nt.)		Torque (Nt.-cm.)	
	Min.	Max.	Min.	Max.
X	0.056	106	0.071	162
Y	0.056	106	0.071	162
Z	0.083	167	0.141	300

From our initial tests, it appears that the calibration method works quite well. We were able to compute a calibration matrix that could accurately resolve subsequent forces and moments to within 1% of their true values.

ACKNOWLEDGEMENTS

The financial assistance of the National Science Foundation through grants NSF-ENG-75-21710 and NSF-APR-74-01390-A04 is very much appreciated. We wish to express our special thanks to Victor Scheinman who designed, constructed, and maintained both the force sensing wrist and the manipulator we have been discussing. We would also like to acknowledge Bruce Baumgart whose program, GEOMED, was used to generate the illustrations for this paper.

BIBLIOGRAPHY

[1] E. Nakano, et al, *Cooperational Control of the Anthropomorphous Manipulator "MELARM"*, Proceedings of the 4th International Symposium on Industrial Robots, November 1974, pp. 251-260.

[2] A. d'Auria, M. Salmon, *Sigma - An Integreated General Purpose System for Automatic Manipulation,* Proceeding of the 5th International Symposium on Industrial Robots, September 1975, pp. 185-202.

[3] J. L. Nevins, et al, Exploratory Research in Industrial Modular Assembly R-800, Charles Stark Draper Laboratory, Inc., March 1974, pp. 149-160.

[4] C. Rosen, et al, Exploratory Research in Advanced Automation, Stanford Research Institute Report covering Oct. 1, 1973 to June 30, 1974, pp. 65-73.

[5] P. C. Watson, S. H. Drake, *Pedestal and Wrist Force Sensors for Automatic Assembly,* Proceeding of the 5th International Symposium on Industrial Robots, September 1975, pp. 501-511.

[6] C. Flatau, *Design Outline For Mini-Arms Based on Manipulator Technology,* Massachusetts Institute of Technology Artificial Intelligence Laboratory, Memo No 300, May 1973.

A ROBOT HAND WITH ELASTIC FINGERS AND ITS APPLICATION TO ASSEMBLY PROCESS

H. Hanafusa and H. Asada

Automation Research Laboratory, Kyoto University, Uji, Kyoto 611, Japan

ABSTRACT

We propose a versatile robot hand such that the handling force and the rigidity of the prehension system are adjustable with fingers control. The hand has three fingers which are driven by three individual motors through coil springs. Arbitrary prehension characteristics are obtained by synchronizing the motor movements with the finger movements. Static and dynamic prehension characteristics are formulated and the synthesis problems are discussed in order to obtain desirable prehension characteristics. Further control scheme is shown for some applications to assembly tasks of mechanical parts. Those theoretical results are verified by experiments and the versatility of such a robot hand is confirmed.

1. INTRODUCTION

As industrial robots are applied to various manufacturing fields, flexible structure and fine operation of robot hands come in necessery. For example, in mechanical assembly, relative position of a hand-held workpiece and a fixed workpiece has to be fitted into a specified state with keeping contact situations of the two workpieces. In such a case, flexible hands so as to keep contacts of the two workpieces and adaptive controllers which proceed the tasks according to various contact situations are required to the robots.

There have been several papers on flexible robot hands which control mutual position of hand-held objects and fixtures with force informations derived from deformations of elastic materials equipped at arms or wrists. Among such studies, precise insertion of a peg into a hole was realized and put into practical use [1,2], and the others reported about the cooperational control of a pair of arms [3,4].

In these reports elastic materials were used in order to detect contact forces and to absorb impact forces, and the hand-held objects are removed by movements of arms or wrists.

In this paper we propose a versatile robot hand such that the rigidity of prehension system is adjustable. The hand has three fingers which are driven by independent three fingers which are driven by independent three motors through coil springs. The motor movements are syncronized with finger positions and spring deformations. Such a robot hand is useful paticularly in the tasks where relative positioning of workpieces with various shapes are required, because the hand has the advantages that fine operations of workpieces are possible by the finger control and that prehension rigidities are properly adjustable according to the contents of tasks. Furthermore, the robot hand is suitable to grasp various workpieces with complicated shapes at proper states [5].

2. CONSTRUCTION OF A ROBOT HAND AND ITS CONTROL SCHEME

We propose a robot hand which can handle two-dimensional objects dexterously by controlling finger forces. Fig. 1 shows the schematic construction of the robot hand with elastic fingers. There are three fingers which open or close along proper guides in three directions. Each finger is driven by an individual motor through a transmition mechanism, such as links or reduction gears. Finger tips which contact with a peripheral surface of a gripped object consist of contact rollers in order to reduce friction in the tangential direction. So the finger tips slide on the object periphery smoothly according to the movement of the object.

Springs are inserted between the finger tips and the motors, hence the finger forces are in proportion with the deformation of springs.

$$f_i = k_i \nu_i, \quad i = 1,2,3 \tag{1}$$

where f_i is the finger force of the i-th finger, k_i the spring constant and ν_i the deformation of the spring. The spring deformation is dependent on the motor displacement d_i and the finger displacement σ_i as shown in Fig. 1. Setting the origin of a motor displacement proper, they have the follwing relation;

$$\nu_i = d_i + \sigma_i . \quad i = 1,2,3 \qquad (2)$$

When the motors are fixed, the finger force f_i varies only corresponding to σ_i, and the rigidity of prehension is determined by the physical spring constants k_i's. On the other hand, if the motors are driven by being synchronized with the finger tip movements, apparent spring constants are actively adjusted. For example, if the motors are driven so that $d_i = \sigma_i$, the apparent spring constants becomes twice of physical ones.

Moreover, each finger force can be related to the other two figer tip displacements under computer control in order to derive the more versatile function. Namely the motor displacement is controlled so that the spring deformation has the following relation.

$$\nu_i = \sum_{j=1}^{3} b_{ij}\sigma_j + c_i , \quad i = 1,2,3 \qquad (3)$$

where b_{ij} and c_i are arbitral constants which are to be adjusted to derive desirable prehension characteristics. Substituting Eq. (3) into Eq. (1),

$$f_i = k_i \left(\sum_{j=1}^{3} b_{ij}\sigma_j + c_i \right). \quad i = 1,2,3 \qquad (4)$$

Eq. (4) represents fundamental principles of the control scheme which constructs active elastic fingers system.

Now we describe a total prehension system at prehension state of an object. As shown in Fig. 2, two kinds of coodinate systems are employed, one is $\mathbf{x}$= column (x,y) fixed to the robot hand with an origin at its representative point and the other is $\boldsymbol{\xi}$=column (ξ,η) fixed to the gripped object with an origin at its sectional center. The position of the gripped object is represented by the coordinate of its sectional center, that is $\mathbf{x}_a$=column (x_a, y_a), and the attitude by the angular difference θ_a between x and ξ axes as shown in the figure. The i-th finger tip position $\mathbf{x}_i$=column (x_i, y_i) is on the locus of its movement, namely;

$$\mathbf{x}_i = \sigma_i \mathbf{u}_i + \mathbf{v}_i , \quad i = 1,2,3 \qquad (5)$$

where $\mathbf{u}_i$ is an unit vector which denotes the direction of the locus, and $\mathbf{v}_i$ is the coodinate of its origin as shown in Fig. 2. Each finger force f_i acts on the object periphery at the position $\mathbf{x}_i$ in the direction of $\mathbf{u}_i$, then the resultant force F_x, F_y and the resultant moment M with respect to the sectional center are generated. We denote F_x, F_y and M as $\mathbf{F}$=column (F_x, F_y, M) in the vector form and call it handling force.

Similarly position and attitude of the gripped object is denoted as $\mathbf{z}_a$=column (x_a, y_a, θ_a).

Fig. 3 shows a block diagram of the prehension system where the inputs are x_a, y_a and θ_a and the outputs are F_x, F_y and M. Block 1 means that the displacement of finger tip σ_i is determined as the function of object shape $h_i(\mathbf{z}_a)$, while Block 3 means that the handling force $\mathbf{F}$ is determined as a resultant of the finger forces f_i's.

Block 2 shows the finger force control system described in Eq. (4). Firstly the fingertip displacements, σ_i's, are detected, and desirable spring deformations ν_{ri}'s are calculated from Eq. (3). Subsequently motor drive signals are determined so as to reduce the difference between the reference spring deformations and their measured values. Finally the sum of σ_i and motor displacement d_i in Eq. (2) coinsides with the reference spring deformation and the finger forces described in Eq. (4) are generated.

3. ANALYSIS OF PREHENSION SYSTEM

3.1 Static Characteristics

We derive the relation of the handling force $\mathbf{F}$ with respect to the position and attitude of a gripped object $\mathbf{z}_a$.

When the friction due to rolling contacts between the finger tips and the object surface are ignored, the handling force is described as follows,

$$\begin{bmatrix} F_x \\ F_y \end{bmatrix} = - \sum_{i=1}^{3} \frac{f_i}{\cos \omega_i} \mathbf{n}_i ,$$
$$M = - \sum_{i=1}^{3} \frac{f_i}{\cos \omega_i} (\mathbf{x}_i - \mathbf{x}_a) \times \mathbf{n}_i , \qquad (6)$$

where $\mathbf{n}_i$ is an unit normal vector of the peripheral surface, ω_i is angular difference between $\mathbf{n}_i$ and $\mathbf{u}_i$ as shown in Fig. 2, and X means a vector product. $\mathbf{n}_i$ and ω_i depend on the object shape as well as its position and attitude.

Now we derive the explicit expression of $\mathbf{F}$ with respect to $\mathbf{z}_a$, taking account of the object shape. The first step is to rewrite Eq. (6) with use of the finger tip displacements. The peripheral curve of the object is assumed to be described by the following function with the coordinate $\boldsymbol{\xi}$.

$$H_a^*[\boldsymbol{\xi}] = 0 \qquad (7)$$

$H_a^*[\boldsymbol{\xi}]$ is (N+1)-times continuously differentiable with respect to $\boldsymbol{\xi}$ piecewisely. Further $\mathbf{x}$ and $\boldsymbol{\xi}$ coordinate systems have the following transformation.

$$x = x_a + A(\theta_a)\xi \ , \qquad (8)$$

where $A(\theta_a)$ is a 2×2 rotation matrix,

$$A(\theta_a) = \begin{pmatrix} \cos\theta_a \ , & -\sin\theta_a \\ \sin\theta_a \ , & \cos\theta_a \end{pmatrix}$$

Application of Eq. (8) to Eq. (7) leads to the following in x-y coordinate system,

$$H_a(x) \triangleq H_a{}^*[A'(\theta_a)\{x - x_a\}] = 0 \ , \qquad (9)$$

where $A^{-1}=A'$ is used.

Each finger tip contacts with the peripheral surface of the gripped object in the prehension state, then

$$H_a[x_i] = 0 . \quad i = 1,2,3 \qquad (10)$$

Differentiate the left hand side of Eq. (10) with respect to x_a, then the following is obtained.

$$\frac{\partial H_a(x_i)}{\partial x_a} = \frac{\partial H_a}{\partial x_i}\frac{\partial x_i}{\partial x_a} = \left\|\frac{\partial H_a}{\partial x_i}\right\| n_i' \ ,$$

$$i = 1,2,3 \qquad (11)$$

where $\partial H/\partial x_a$ is a 1×2 row vector, $\|a\|$ is the vector norm of a vector a and ' means the transpose of a vector or a matrix. On the other hand, the following form of the same differentiation is obtained from Eq. (5).

$$\frac{\partial H_a(x_i)}{\partial x_a} = \frac{\partial H_a}{\partial x_i}\frac{dx_i}{d\sigma_i}\frac{\partial \sigma_i}{\partial x_a}$$

$$= \left\|\frac{\partial H_a}{\partial x_i}\right\| n_i' u_i \frac{\partial \sigma_i}{\partial x_a}$$

$$= \left\|\frac{\partial H_a}{\partial x_i}\right\| \cos\omega_i \frac{\partial \sigma_i}{\partial x_a} . \quad i = 1,2,3 \qquad (12)$$

Equating Eqs. (11) and (12),

$$\frac{\partial \sigma_i}{\partial x_a} = \frac{n_i'}{\cos\omega_i} \qquad i = 1,2,3 \qquad (13)$$

Similarly differentiation of $H_a(x_i)$ with respect to θ_a leads to the following result

$$\frac{\partial \sigma_i}{\partial \theta_a} = \frac{1}{\cos\omega_i}(x_i - x_a) \times n_i . \quad i = 1,2,3 \qquad (14)$$

Substituting Eqs. (13) and (14) into Eq. (6), the following is obtained.

$$\begin{bmatrix} F_x \\ F_y \end{bmatrix} = -\sum_{i=1}^{3} k_i\left(\sum_{j=1}^{3} b_{ij}\sigma_j + c_i\right)\left(\frac{\partial \sigma_i}{\partial x_a}\right)' \ ,$$

$$M = -\sum_{i=1}^{3} k_i\left(\sum_{j=1}^{3} b_{ij}\sigma_j + c_i\right)\frac{\partial \sigma_i}{\partial \theta_a} \ . \qquad (15)$$

The second step is to derive the relation between σ_i and z_a. From Eqs. (5),(9) and (10),

$$H_a{}^*[A'(\theta_a)(\sigma_i u_i + v_i - x_a)] = 0 \qquad (16)$$

In the vicinity where $\partial H^*_a/\partial\sigma_i \neq 0$, σ_i can be described by an explicit function of x_a, y_a and θ_a.

$$\sigma_i = h_i(z_a) . \qquad i = 1,2,3 \qquad (17)$$

Here we introduce the referece position $\bar{z}_a$, and expand $h_i(z_a)$ to power series in the vicinity of $\bar{z}_a$, where $\bar{z}_a$ is the average position to be considered, and for the convenience of description, the following replacements are used.

$$(z_{a1}, z_{a2}, z_{a3})' = (x_a, y_a, \theta_a)'$$

Then the N-th order approximation of $h_i(z_a)$ is as follows,

$$\sigma_i \cong \overline{\sigma_i} + \sum_{n=1}^{N} \frac{1}{n!}\left(\sum_{m=1}^{3} \Delta z_{am}\frac{\partial}{\partial z_{am}}\right)^n h_i(z_a)\Bigg|_{z_a = \bar{z}_a} ,$$

$$\Delta z_{am} = z_{am} - \bar{z}_{am} \qquad (18)$$

where $\overline{\sigma_i}$ is the valve of σ_i at $z_a = \bar{z}_a$, and we use the symbol - as the same meaning from now.

Denote $\partial\sigma_i/\partial h_\ell$ with $h_{i\ell}$ then the approximation of $h_{i\ell}$ is as follows similarly.

$$h_{i\ell} \cong \overline{h_{i\ell}} + \sum \frac{1}{n!}\left(\sum_{m=1}^{3} \Delta z_{am}\frac{\partial}{\partial z_{am}}\right)^n h_{i\ell}(z_a)\Bigg|_{z_a = \bar{z}_a} ,$$

$$i, \ell = 1,2,3 \qquad (19)$$

Final step is to subsitute Eqs. (18) and (19) into Eq. (15) and derive the explicit expression of handling force with respect to z_a.

$$F_\ell = \bar{F}_\ell - \sum_i k_i h_{i\ell} \sum_m \Delta Z_{am} \frac{\partial}{\partial Z_{am}} (\sum_j b_{ij} h_j) \Big|_{Z_a = \bar{Z}_a}$$

$$- \sum_i k_i (\sum_j b_{ij}\sigma_j + c_i) \sum_m \Delta Z_{am} \frac{\partial h_{i\ell}}{\partial Z_{am}} \Big|_{Z_a = \bar{Z}_a},$$

$$- \sum_{n=2}^{N} \sum_i \frac{k_i}{n!} [(\sum_j b_{ij}\sigma_j + c_i)(\sum_m \Delta Z_{am} \frac{\partial}{\partial Z_{am}})^n h_{i\ell}$$

$$+ h_{i\ell} (\sum_m \Delta Z_{am} \frac{\partial}{\partial Z_{am}})^n (\sum_j b_{ij} h_j)] \Big|_{Z_a = \bar{Z}_a},$$

$$\ell = 1,2,3 \tag{20}$$

where infinitesimal more than (N+1)-order is ignored, and for the convenience of description the replacement of $(F_1, F_2, F_3)' = (F_x, F_y, M)$ is used.

In Eq.(20) the first and the second terms mean the lincar approximation of handling force. These are arranged in the following vector form.

$$F = -\bar{R}'\bar{f} - [\bar{R}'K B\bar{R} + \sum_{i=1}^{3} e_i' \bar{f} \cdot \bar{S}_i] \Delta Z_a, \tag{21}$$

$$f = K(B\sigma + C), \tag{22}$$

where B, K, R and S_i are 3×3 matrixes and C, σ, f and e_i 3×1 vectors as follows.

$$B = (b_{ij}), \quad C = (c_i), \quad \sigma = (\sigma_i)$$

$$f = (f_i), \quad e_i = \text{column}[0,.\underset{\wedge}{1}.0]$$

$$K = \text{diag.}(k_i).$$

$$R(Z_a) = \begin{bmatrix} \frac{\partial h_1}{\partial Z_a} \\ \frac{\partial h_2}{\partial Z_a} \\ \frac{\partial h_3}{\partial Z_a} \end{bmatrix} \tag{23}$$

$$S_i(Z_a) = \begin{bmatrix} \frac{\partial^2 h_i}{\partial Z_{a1}^2}, & \frac{\partial^2 h_i}{\partial Z_{a1}\partial Z_{a2}}, & \frac{\partial^2 h_i}{\partial Z_{a1}\partial Z_{a3}} \\ \frac{\partial^2 h_i}{\partial Z_{a1}\partial Z_{a2}}, & \frac{\partial^2 h_i}{\partial Z_{a2}^2}, & \frac{\partial^2 h_i}{\partial Z_{a2}\partial Z_{a3}} \\ \frac{\partial^2 h_i}{\partial Z_{a1}\partial Z_{a3}}, & \frac{\partial^2 h_i}{\partial Z_{a2}\partial Z_{a3}}, & \frac{\partial^2 h_i}{\partial Z_{a3}^2} \end{bmatrix}$$

The coefficients of Eq. (21) are denoted as follows.

$$P = -\bar{R}'\bar{f}, \tag{24}$$

$$Q = -[\bar{R}'K B\bar{R} + \sum_{i=1}^{3} e_i' \bar{f} \cdot \bar{S}_i] \tag{25}$$

Then P gives the handling force at the reference position, while Q gives the change of the handling force by a small deviation ΔZ_a.

Therefore Q means a kind of rigidity and is called as a rigidity matrix of the prehension system. The prehension system is characterized by P and Q as the first approximation.

3.2 Dynamic Characteristics

Dynamic characteristics of the prehension system is investigated through derivation of the transfer function based on the linear approximation of its static characteristics. In Eq. (21) the deviation of handling force F from the handling force at $Z_a = \bar{Z}_a$ is described as follows,

$$\Delta F = -\bar{R}'K B\bar{R}\Delta Z_a - \sum_{i=1}^{3} f_i \bar{S}_i \Delta Z_a \tag{26}$$

Similar deviation is obtained from differentiation of the exact handling force in Eq. (15) as follows.

$$dF = -\bar{R}df - dR \cdot \bar{f} \tag{27}$$

Comparision of the right hand sides of Eqs. (26) and (27) leads to that the both first terms mean the effect of the change of **f** on the handling force, and that the second terms mean the effect of the deviation of due to the change of contact positions of the fingers. The first terms relate with dynamics of motor control systems, while the second terms depend on the geometrical condition and have no delay time. Hence the problem is to derive the transfer function corresponding to the first terms.

Firstly the dynamics of Block 2 in Fig. 3 is investigated, where the inputs and outputs are σ_i's and f_i's. Laplace trnsformation of each signal has the following relations, as shown in the Finger

$$\nu_{ri}(s) = \sum_{j=1}^{3} b_{ij}\sigma_j(s) + c_i/s,$$

$$\mu_i(s) = G_{mi}(s)[\nu_{ri}(s) - \nu_i(s)], \tag{28}$$

$$\nu_i(s) = \mu_i(s) + \sigma_i(s),$$

$$f_i(s) = k_i \nu_i(s).$$

Pay attention to the deviation from $\bar{Z}_a$, Eq. (28) is arranged as follows in the vector form,

$$\Delta f(s) = K[I + G_m(s)]^{-1}[I + G_m(s)B]\Delta\sigma(s). \tag{29}$$

where I is a 3×3 unit matrix, and $G_m(s)$ 3×3 diagonal matrix of $G_{mi}(s)$. Addition of the geometric factors in the prehension system leads to the following transfer function $G(s)$,

$$G(s) = -\bar{R}'K[I+G_m(s)]^{-1}[I+G_m(s)B]\bar{R} - \sum_i e_i'\bar{f}\cdot S_i . \quad (30)$$

where $G(s)$ satisfies the relation of $\Delta F(s) = G(s)\Delta z_a(s)$, Using a 3×3 matrix B^* such that $B^* = B - I$, the above transfer function is divided as follows,

$$G(s) = -[\bar{R}'K\bar{R} + \sum_i e_i' f \bar{s}_i] - \bar{R}K[I + G_m(s)]^{-1}[I + G_m(s)B^*]\bar{R}. \quad (31)$$

When $B^* = 0$, $G(s)$ is equivalent to prehension rigidity matrix Q in Eq. (25), and has no dynamic delay. The first term of Eq. (31) corresponds to the original prehension rigidity depending on the physical springs, while the second term corresponds to virtual rigidity due to the active control of the finger forces.

3.3 Physical Meaning of Handling Force

The robot hand mentioned in previous sections has a paticular advantage that it can construct the prehension rigidity which conventional passive springs are impossible to realize. Now we investigate physical meanings of the handling force. Firstly the parameter matrix B is divided into two parts: a symmetric matrix B_c and a skew symmetric matrix B_v

$$B_c = (B + B')/2$$
$$B_v = (B - B')/2 \quad (32)$$

Note that the matrix $\bar{s}_i$ in Eq. (23) is symmetric, the prehension rigidity matrix Q is divided into the following symmetric and skew symmetric matrixes Q_c and Q_v.

$$Q_c = -[\bar{R}'KB_c\bar{R} + \sum_i e_i' f \bar{s}_i]$$
$$Q_v = -\bar{R}'KB_v\bar{R} \quad (33)$$

The symmetric matrix Q_c is transformed to a diagonal matrix D by a proper orthogonal matrix T.

$$T'Q_cT = D , \quad (34)$$

where diagonal components of D are the eigen values of Q_c , λ_i's .

On the other hand Q_v is divided into the following three elements.

$$Q_v = \gamma_1\Gamma_1 + \gamma_2\Gamma_2 + \gamma_3\Gamma_3 \quad (35)$$

$$\gamma_1 = \frac{q_{23}-q_{32}}{2}, \quad \gamma_2 = \frac{q_{13}-q_{31}}{2}, \quad \gamma_3 = \frac{q_{12}-q_{21}}{2}$$

$$\Gamma_1 = \begin{bmatrix} 0 & 0 & 0 \\ 0 & 0 & 1 \\ 0 & -1 & 0 \end{bmatrix}, \quad \Gamma_2 = \begin{bmatrix} 0 & 0 & 1 \\ 0 & 0 & 0 \\ -1 & 0 & 0 \end{bmatrix}, \quad \Gamma_3 = \begin{bmatrix} 0 & 1 & 0 \\ -1 & 0 & 0 \\ 0 & 0 & 0 \end{bmatrix} \quad (36)$$

According to the division of Q in Eq. (33), the handling force is divided into F_c and F_v. From Eqs. (21),(24) and (25),

$$F = F_c + F_v$$
$$F_c = P + Q_c\Delta z_a \quad (37)$$
$$F_v = Q_v\Delta z_a$$

Fig. 4 illustrates F_c and F_v, which are shown in Z_1- Z_2 plane, for the convenience of description. The vectors t_1 and t_2 show the principal axes which are obtained by the transformation T. The force F_c indicated by arrow ➡ is the resultant force generated by physical springs in the directions of t_1 and t_2 with virtual spring constants λ_1 and λ_2 respectively.

On the contrary the force F_v does not have such a physical meanings. The element $\gamma_3\Gamma_3$ of F_v in Z_1- Z_2 plane, is indicated by arrow ⇨ in Fig. 4. It draws a swirl counterclockwise where γ_3 represents its magnitude. When the object deviates in the direction of Z_1 , F_v acts in the direction of Z_2. Similarly for a deviation in the direction of Z_2, the object receives the force in the direction of Z_1. Thus the force F_v acts in the different direction from the object deviation.

Finally we shall show another description of the handling force by introducing a concept of potential, in order to make the above mentioned features more clear.

The force F_c is derived from the aspect of energy theory. Then we obtain a potential which represents total energy stored in the prehension system. It provides mathematical tractability in the analysis of prehension system. The necessery and sufficient condition that F has a potential function is as follows.

$$\mathrm{rot}F = 0 , \quad (38)$$

where rot denotes rotation of a vecter. If and only if $B_v = 0$, the above condition is satisfied, namely, from Eqs. (33) and (37)

$$\mathrm{rot}\, F = \mathrm{rot}F_c = \mathrm{rot}Q_c\Delta z_a$$

$$=[q_{32}-q_{23}, q_{31}-q_{13}, q_{21}-q_{12}]' = 0$$

We introduce the following scalar function U as a potential.

$$U = \frac{1}{2}\sigma' KB_c\sigma + c'K\sigma \quad (39)$$

In practice, the scalar function satisfies the following definition of a potential.

$$F = -\left(\frac{\partial U}{\partial z_a}\right)' \quad (40)$$

From Eqs. (17),(23) and (39), Eq. (40) is proved as follows.

$$-\left(\frac{\partial U}{\partial z_a}\right)' = -\left(\frac{d\sigma}{dz}\right)'[KB_c\sigma + K\sigma]$$

$$= -R'f = F \quad (41)$$

The derivation of Eq.(41) corresponds with the analysis of static characteristics mentioned in section 3.1, as far as $B_v = 0$. It is very simple in comparison with the previous method. The ellipses illustrated in Fig. 4 mean the iso-potential lines of U. Magnitude of F_c is large at a part where iso-potential lines are dense, and vice versa.

On the other hand, when $B_c = 0$, the force F_v is related with a vector potential V. The necessery and sufficient condition of the existence of a vector potential is as follows.

$$\mathrm{div}\, F = 0, \quad (42)$$

where div denotes divergence of a vector. Eq. (42) is proved directly by the fact that all the diagonal components of F are zero, as fae as $B_c = 0$. In the similar way, introduce the following vector function V, then it satisfies the definition of a vector potential as described in Eq. (44).

$$V = \begin{bmatrix} -\gamma_3 z_1 z_3 + \gamma_1 z_3^2 \\ -\gamma_2 z_1^2/2 - \gamma_1 z_1 z_2 \\ \gamma_3 z_2^2/2 + \gamma_2 z_2 z_3 \end{bmatrix} \quad (43)$$

$$F = \mathrm{rot}\, V \quad (44)$$

According to the above consideration, we call F_c and F_v as conservative force and vortical force respectively.

4. DESIGN OF HAND CONTROL SYSTEM

4.1 Parameters Adjustment of Hand Control System

When a robot hand with elastic fingers is applied to some tasks, it is useful that the hand provides prehension characteristics suitable to excute the tasks. In this section we discuss how the parameters of the hand control system, B and C, should be adjusted in order to construct the desirable prehension characteristics.

In order to simplify the syntheis, we deal with the linear approximation of static prehension characteristics, that is, P and Q. Then the problem is regarded as an inverse problem of Eqs. (22),(24) and (25).

The solution of those equations in the case that det $\bar{R} \neq 0$ is derived at the beginning. From Eq. (24) the following is obtained,

$$\bar{f} = -(\bar{R}')^{-1}P \quad (45)$$

Substituting Eq. (45) into Eqs. (25),

$$B = K^{-1}(\bar{R}')^{-1}[\Sigma e_i' (\bar{R})^{-1}P\cdot\bar{S}_i - Q](\bar{R})^{-1} \quad (46)$$

C is obtained by the substitution of Eq. (46) into Eq. (22) as follows,

$$C = -K^{-1}(\bar{R}')^{-1}P \quad (47)$$
$$-K^{-1}(\bar{R}')^{-1}[\Sigma_i e_i'(\bar{R}')^{-1}P\cdot\bar{S}_i - Q]\bar{R}^{-1}\bar{\sigma}$$

Here we consider the condition that det $R = 0$. From Eqs. (13),(14),(17) and (23),

$$\det\bar{R} = \prod_i \frac{1}{\cos\bar{\omega}_i} \det\begin{bmatrix} \bar{n}_1, & \cdots\cdots & \bar{n}_3, \\ (\bar{x}_1 - x_a)\times\bar{n}_1 & \cdots & (\bar{x}_3 - x_a)\times\bar{n}_3 \end{bmatrix}$$

Expansion of the right hand side determinant with respect to the third row leads to the following expression.

$$(\bar{x}_1 - x_a)\times\bar{n}_1\cdot\bar{n}_2\times\bar{n}_3 + (\bar{x}_2 - x_a)\times\bar{n}_2\cdot\bar{n}_3\times\bar{n}_1$$
$$+ (\bar{x}_3 - x_a)\times n_3\cdot\bar{n}_1\times\bar{n}_2 \neq 0 \quad (48)$$

Eq. (48) gives the condition of det $\bar{R} \neq 0$ which depends on the reference position $\bar{z}_a$, and the nomal vectors of object preiphery, while it is independence on the finger forces and their directions. As far as the reference position is chosen so as to satisfy Eq. (48), Eqs. (46) and (47) provide the parameters which construct the desirable handling force and rigidity. Eq. (48) does not hold far any $\bar{z}_a$, in case of a paticular object shape, for example a rectangular with considerablly long sides. We shall show general solution of synthesis problem including such a case.

In order to obtain the joint linear equations of Eqs. (24) and (25), the following

12x1 vectors and a 12x12 matrix are defined.

$$b^* = \text{column}[\bar{f}_1, \bar{f}_2, \bar{f}_3\ k_1 b_{11}, k_1 b_{21}, \cdots k_3 b_{33}]$$

$$q^* = \text{column}[-p_1, -p_2, -p_3, -q_{11}, -q_{21}, \cdots -q_{33}], \tag{49}$$

where p_i and q_{ij} are components of P and Q . Further the following matrix is introduced.

$$J = \begin{bmatrix} \bar{R}' & 0 \\ S^* & \bar{R}' \otimes \bar{R}' \end{bmatrix}, \tag{50}$$

where ⊗ means Kronecker's product and S* is a 9x3 matrix which is constructed from 3x1 column vectors S_{ji} of $\bar{S}_i$ (i,j=1,2,3) such as S*=(Sji). With use of Eqs.(49) and (50) the joint linear equations is as follows,

$$Jb^* = q^* . \tag{51}$$

The general solusion of Eq.(51) is derived through an ordinary method.

Here we consider the conditions that Eq. (51) has a solution, that is, the conditions of possibility to realize given prehension characteristics. If and only if the following expression is satisfied, the solution of the joint linear equations exists.

$$\text{rank}(J) = \text{rank}(J, q^*) = j_r \tag{52}$$

Eq.52 requires that q* is linearly dependent on column vectors of matrix J, hence only j_r components among twelve ones included in P and Q are possible to be assigned arbtrarily . On the contrary, as far as the P and Q which satisfy Eq.(52), the solution of Eq. (51) contains $(12-j_r)$ arbitral constants, namely, there are $(12-j_r)$ degrees of freedum in the parameters adjustment.

In addition, we prepared 12 parameters of b_{ij} and c_i in Eq. (3), that is the necessery and sufficient number of parameters in order to realize arbitrary prehension characteristics, P and Q, at a reference position $\bar{z}_a$ where det $\bar{R} \neq 0$.

A robot hand with three fingers has the simplest construction to handle two-dimensional objects with various prehension rigidities. However the condition of $f_i > 0$, that is, each finger can generate only pushing force against an object periphery, is not guaranteed to generate arbitral handling force by this construction. If a hand has m fingers more than three, though (m- 3) fingers are redundant for prehension, it has the advantage that all the finger forces are set to be positive by the redundancy.

4.2 Estimation of Position and Attitude of Gripped Objects and External Forces

When a robot handles gripped objects adaptively according to enviromental situations, it is necesserly that position and attitude of gripped objects and / or external forces due to contacts with other objects can be estimated. We shall show how they can be observed by this hand construction. From Eqs. (18) and (23), linear approximation of finger tip displacement in the vicinity of $\bar{z}_a$ is described as follows,

$$\sigma = \bar{\sigma}(\bar{z}_a) + \bar{R}'\Delta z_a \tag{53}$$

If det $\bar{R} \neq 0$, z_a is calculated with use of measured finger tip displacement,

$$\hat{z}_a = \bar{z}_a + (\bar{R}')^{-1}(\sigma - \bar{\sigma}(\bar{z}_a)) \tag{54}$$

where $\hat{z}_a$ is used to represent the estimation of z_a. When the more accurate position and attitude are required, iterate the calculation of Eq.(54) a few times, updating the reference position $\bar{z}_a$ with the solution $\hat{z}_a$ at the last calculation.

External force F_e acting on a gripped object is estimated using $\hat{z}_a$ in Eq.(54). Assume that the gripped object is in a state of equilibrium, then $F_e = -F$ is held. Hence F_e is calculated by substituting $\hat{z}_a$ into Eq.(21), or exactly into Eq.(20).

5. APPLICATION TO ASSEMBLY PROCESSES

The above mentioned robot hand with actively controlled prehension characteristics is applied to assembly processes. The robot hand is transferred along pre-determined passes by conventional sequence of point-to-point controls. When the relative position of a gripped object against a fixture becomes the pre-determined situation, the prehension forces and rigidities are adjusted to perform the successive task smoothly even if the hand is not situated at the specified position exactly.

Now we discuss how the handling force P and the prehension rigidity matrix Q at the reference position should be determined in order to carry out given tasks. For the convenience of description, another coordinate system X- Y is used, whose origin is at the same position as x- y coordinate, while the axis is parallel to a representative line of the fixture. Then the handling force is transformed as follows,

$$F^* = P^* + Q^* \Delta z^*_a , \tag{55}$$

where the components of F* are the handling force in the X and Y directions and the moment with respect to the sectional center of the hand-held workpiece.

Application 1.

To let a hand-held workpiece contact with a surface of a fixture, while the arm is moved in the X direction as shown in Fig. 5.

A proper constant force and soft compliance in Y direction is to be generated in order to follow the uneveness of the fixture surface. The prehension rigidities in the X direction as well as the rotary direction must be high enough in order to keep a constant attitude. Then the following prehension characteristices are adopted.

Prehension characteristics 1.

$$P^* = \begin{bmatrix} 0 \\ -p_Y \\ 0 \end{bmatrix} \qquad Q^* = \begin{bmatrix} q_{XX} & * & * \\ * & * & * \\ * & * & q_{\theta\theta} \end{bmatrix},$$

where p_Y is a proper positive, and q_{XX} and $q_{\theta\theta}$ are comparatively large positives. The marks * means arbitrary but small quantities.

Application 2.

To orientate a hand-held workpiece to a fixture line, while the arm approaches to a fixture as shown in Fig. 6.

If the prehension rigidity with respect to rotation is low in comparison with the rigidity in the X or Y directions, in the case of Fig. 6-(a), the peripheral surface AB is automatically put in parallel to the fixture. But in the case of (b), the hand-held workpiece may be rotated in the opposite direction of the moment caused by the contact force. In this case a crockwise moment is required to be generated according to a deviation in the Y direction. The component q^*_{32} of rigidity matrix Q^* means the ratio of moment to a deviation in the Y direction as follows.

$$q^*_{32} = \frac{\partial M}{\partial Y}\bigg|_{Z_a^* = \bar{Z}_a^*}$$

Hence assign a proper negative $-q_{\theta Y}$ as q^*_{32}, then clockwise active moment is generated. The component $-q_{\theta Y}$ corresponds to a vortical force mentioned in section 3.3.

Prehension characteristics 2

Case (a)

$$P^* = \begin{bmatrix} 0 \\ -p_Y \\ 0 \end{bmatrix} \qquad Q^* = \begin{bmatrix} q_{XX} & * & * \\ * & * & * \\ * & * & q_{\theta\theta} \end{bmatrix}$$

Case (b)

$$P^* = \begin{bmatrix} 0 \\ -p_Y \\ 0 \end{bmatrix} \qquad Q^* = \begin{bmatrix} q_{XX} & * & * \\ * & * & * \\ * & -q_{\theta Y} & * \end{bmatrix}$$

Case (a) and (b) are discriminated by using the estimation scheme mentioned in section 4.2.

Application 3.

To insert a hand-held workpiece to a gap of a fixture, while the arm is transfered to the -X direction as shown in Fig. 7.

When a hand-held workpiece is pressed to a vertex of a fixture as shown in Fig. 7 (a), it deviates relatively to the hand in the X direction and the crockwise direction. In this case if handling force in the -Y direction is generated, the hand-held workpiece slides in the same direction (b), and the insertion is established (c). The handling force in the Y direction is written componentwise as follows.

$$F^*_Y = p^*_Y + q^*_{21}\Delta X + q^*_{22}\Delta Y + q^*_{23}\Delta\theta_a$$
$$= p^*_Y + \frac{\partial F_Y}{\partial X}\Delta X + \frac{\partial F_Y}{\partial Y}\Delta Y + \frac{\partial F_Y}{\partial \theta_a}\Delta\theta_a$$

Hence assign proper negative $-q_{YX}$ and positive $q_{Y\theta}$ to q^*_{21} and q^*_{23} respectively, F^*_y is generated according to the deviations ΔX, $\Delta\theta_a$.

Prehension characteristics 3.

$$P^* = \begin{bmatrix} -p_X \\ 0 \\ 0 \end{bmatrix} \qquad Q^* = \begin{bmatrix} * & * & * \\ -q_{YX} & * & q_{Y\theta} \\ * & * & * \end{bmatrix}$$

Employing the estimation scheme of object position, whether a hand-held workpiece is inserted or not can be confirmed. The sequence of the arm movement goes to the next step after this confirmation.

6. EXPERIMENT

The developed robot hand with variable prehension rigidity is shown in Photo 1, where fingers open in the directions at intervals 120 degrees, namely, in Eq.(5),

$$u_1 = \begin{bmatrix} 1 \\ 0 \end{bmatrix}, \quad u_2 = \begin{bmatrix} -1/2 \\ \sqrt{3}/2 \end{bmatrix}, \quad u_3 = \begin{bmatrix} -1/2 \\ -\sqrt{3}/2 \end{bmatrix}, \quad v_i = 0 \quad i=1,2,3$$

Each finger is driven by a step motor through a twisting coil spring. The displacement of finger tip is measured by a potentiometer $P\sigma$ equipped at the rotary axsis of each finger. On the other hand, the finger force is measured by a small potentiometer $P\nu$ which is inserted inside the coil spring. A mini-computer aquirs data of these six potentiometers through A/D converter, and provides step motor driving signals. The maximum finger force generated by a step motor is 20N, and the spring constant defined by the ratio of the finger force and the tip displacement is 2.09 N/cm.

Fig. 8 shows experimental results of handling forces in the x and y directions, Fx and Fy, keeping the object attitude constant. The object is a triangular as shown in the figure (Object 1), and its displacement in the direction of β as shown in the figure is used as the abscissa d. The reference position is $\bar{z}_a = 0$, which corresponds to the finger arrangement illustlated by the marks • in Fig. 8. Parameters of hand control system, B and C, are as follows.

$$B = \begin{bmatrix} 2, & 0, & 0 \\ 0, & 0.5, & 0 \\ 0, & 0, & 0.5 \end{bmatrix} \qquad C = \begin{bmatrix} -3.65 \\ 0.85 \\ 0.85 \end{bmatrix} \text{ cm} \qquad (56)$$

The apparent spring constant of the first finger is twice of the physical one and those for the second and third fingers are 1/2. The mark ∮ illustrates amount of scatter. This is due to hysteresis caused by frictions between the finger tips and the object periphery.

The solid lines in the figure show the theory, which is obtained from Eqs.(24) and (25) as follows,

$$P = 0$$
$$Q = \begin{bmatrix} -4.70\text{N/cm}, & 0\text{N/cm}, & 0\text{N/rad} \\ 0\text{N/cm}, & -1.57\text{N/cm}, & 0\text{N/rad} \\ 0\text{N/rad}, & 0\text{N/rad}, & -44.1\text{Ncm/rad} \end{bmatrix}. \qquad (57)$$

According to displacements in the directions of β=0,45,90 degrees respectively, the following handling forces are generated.

$$Fx_0 = -4.70d, \quad Fy_0 = 0$$
$$Fx_{45} = -3.32d, \quad Fy_{45} = -1.11d \quad (N)$$
$$Fx_{90} = 0, \quad Fy_{90} = -1.57d.$$

The solid lines show Fx_0, Fx_{45}, Fy_{45} and Fy_{90} respectively. In the case of polygon, linear approximation of handling force provides the exact solution, because $(\partial/\partial x_a+\partial/\partial y_a)^n h_i=0$ for $n \geq 2$, as far as the attitude θ_a is constant.

The relation of the moment M v.s. the attitude θ_a is shown in Fig. 9, where the solid line shows the linear approximation,

$$M=-44.1\ \theta_a \quad (Ncm),$$

and the chain line the exact solution. Over the region of $|\theta_a|<15$ degrees, both the experiment and the linear approximation agree well with the exact one.

Now we consider synthesis problems. From Eq.(48), $\det \bar{R}=0$ at the reference position $\bar{z}_a=0$. In practice, moment M is zero regardless of finger forces at the finger arrangement illustrated in Fig. 8. From Eq.(50), the rank of J is 7, then c_i is determined uniquly, but b_{ij} is not. The b_{ij}'s that satisfy the following relations give the same prehension characteristics equivalent to Eq.(57), and Eq.(56) is one of the solutions.

$$b_{11}= b_{12}+b_{13}-b_{32}+2$$
$$b_{21}= b_{12}-b_{13}+b_{23}+b_{31}-b_{32}$$
$$b_{22}= b_{12}-b_{13}+b_{23}+0.5$$
$$b_{33}=-b_{12}+b_{13}+b_{32}+0.5$$

For an object illustrated in Fig. 10, the average handling force Fx, Fy shown by dots are observed, where the parameters are as follows,

$$\bar{z}_a=0$$

$$B = \begin{bmatrix} 1, & 0, -0.5 \\ 0, & 1, -0.5 \\ -0.5, -0.5, & 1.5 \end{bmatrix} \quad C = \begin{bmatrix} 1.00 \\ 0.45 \\ 0.69 \end{bmatrix} cm, \quad (58)$$

Prehension characteristics are,

$$P = \text{column}[-2.11N, -2.76N, 12.31Ncm]$$

$$Q = \begin{bmatrix} -4.39\ N/cm, -3.34\ N/cm, -42.1\ N/rad \\ -3.34\ N/cm, -6.75\ N/cm, 39.9\ N/rad \\ -42.1N/rad, 39.9N/rad, -74.6Ncm/rad \end{bmatrix}, \quad (59)$$

The solid lines show the theoretical linear approximations Fx_0, Fy_0 and Fy_{90} respectively, while the broken lines are the second order approximations.

Similarly the relation of M v.s. θ_a is shown in Fig. 9 by the mark ǫ, and the theoretical linear and second ordor approximations are shown by the solid and broken lines respectively.

Eq.(48) holds for the reference position $\bar{z}_a=0$, then the synthesis with use of Eqs.(46) and (47) is possible, and the derivation of Eq.(58) from Eq.(59) was confirmed.

Fig. 11 shows a step response of handling force, where the object is Object 1 in Fig. 8, $b_{ii}=2$, $b_{ij}=0$ $(i\neq j)$, $c_i=-3.65$ cm $(i,j=1,2,3)$ and the parameter is a motor drive gain k_m. Represent the characteristics of the step motors with $G_{mi}(s)=k_m/s$ $(i=1,2,3)$, the response of Fx for a step input $\Delta x/s$ is calculated from Eq.(31) as follows,

$$\Delta Fx(s) = -3.15\frac{\Delta x}{s} - 3.15\frac{k_m}{s+k_m}\frac{\Delta x}{s} \quad (60)$$

The theoretical response of Eq.(60) is illustrated by chain line. As mentioned in section 3.2, physical springs generate a half of the force at the steady state at the beginning. When $k_m=0.84$ and 1.68, the responses are not so steep as the theoretical ones. This is because the input frequency of the step motor is limited under 400 Hz in order to avoid irreguralty for excessive load.

7. CONCLUSION

A robot hand with three elastic fingers which are independenly driven by three individual motors was developed. The hand can grip objects with various shapes at various prehension rigidities by the finger force control.

Firstly, the construction of the robot hand and its control scheme was proposed. Secondly the handling force of the robot hand was analyzed, the static and dynamic characteristics were derived and the physical meanings of the handling force was investigated. Thirdly, the parameter adjustment in order to construct desirable prehension characteristics was proposed, and the estimation scheme of object position and external force was shown. Furthermore some applications to assembly tasks were discussed. Finaly, experiments were carried out for verifying the theoretical results and confirming the versatility of the robot hand.

REFERENCES

(1) J. L. Nevins, D. E. Whitney, Adaptable-programmable assembly systems: an information and control problem, Proc. 5th International Symposium on Industrial Robots, 387-406 (1975).

(2) K. Takeyasu, T. Goto, et.al., Precision insertion control robot and its application, ASME, J. Engg.Ind. B98-4, 1313 (1976)

(3) K. Takase, H. Inoue, et.al., The design of an articulated manipulator with torque control ability, Proc. 4th International Symposium on Industrial Robots, 261-270 (1974).

(4) E. Nakano, S. Ozaki, Cooperational control of the anthropomorphous manipulator "MELARM", ditto, 251-260 (1974).

(5) H. Hanafusa, H. Asada, Stable prehension of objects by the robot hand with elastic fingers, Trans. Society of instrument and control engineers, 13-4 (1977).

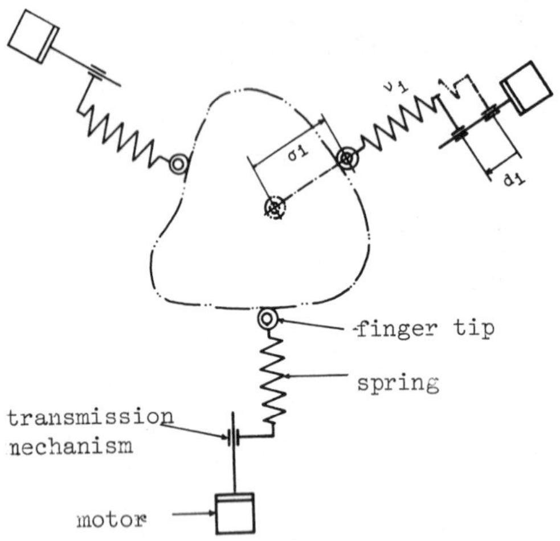

Fig.1 Schematic diagram of a robot hand

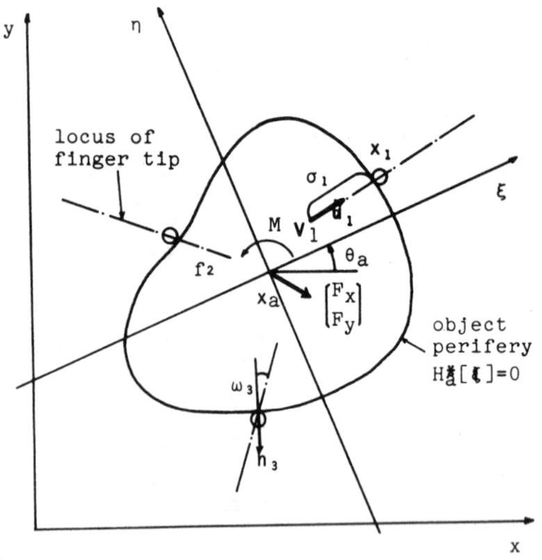

Fig.2 Description of prehension state

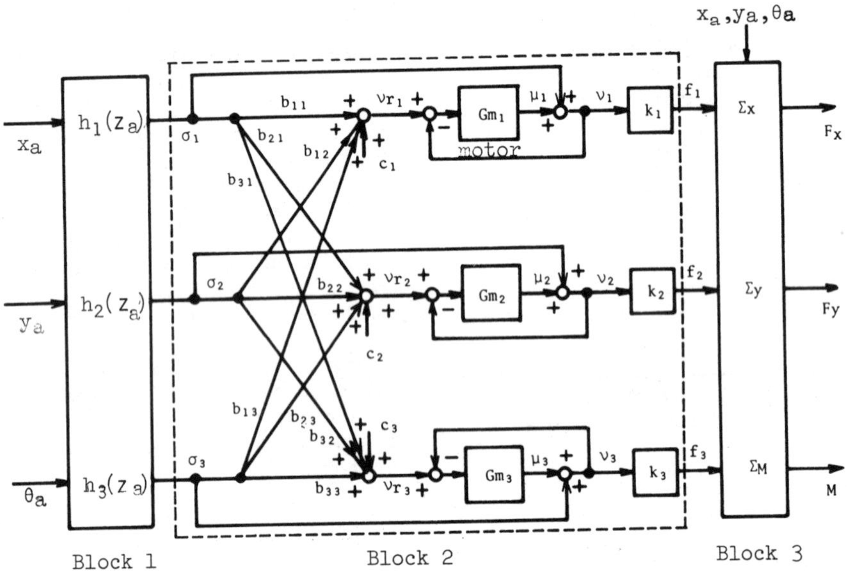

Fig. 3 Block diagram of prehension system

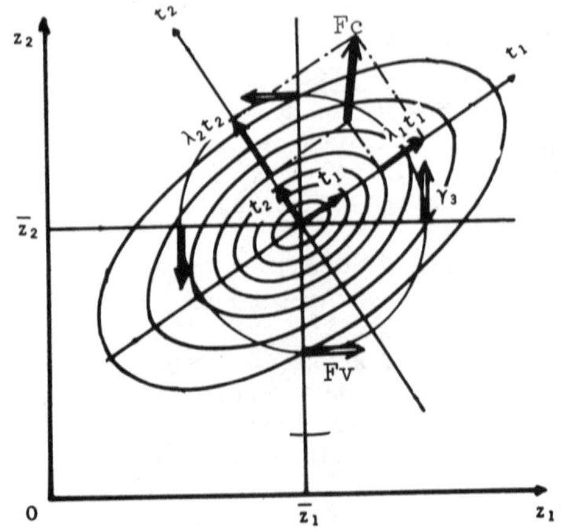

Fig. 4 Illustration of Fc and Fv

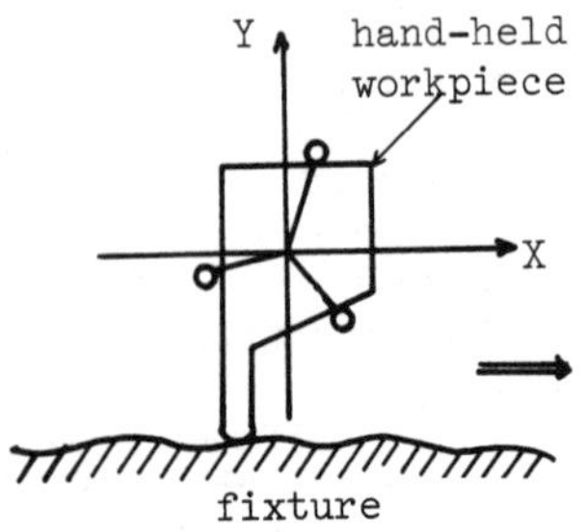

Fig. 5 Application 1 ; compliance

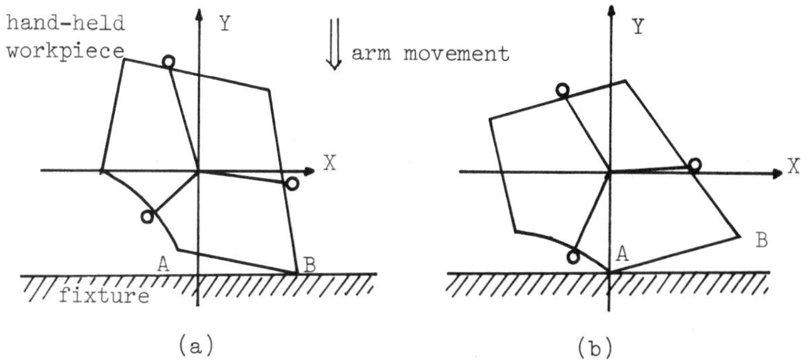

Fig. 6 Application 2 ; orientation

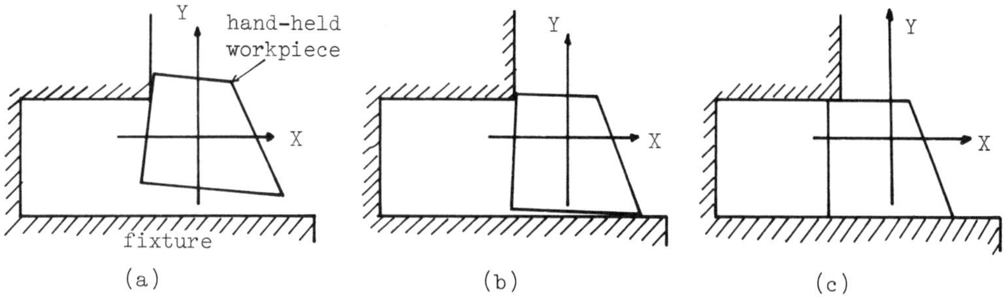

Fig. 7 Application 3 ; insertion

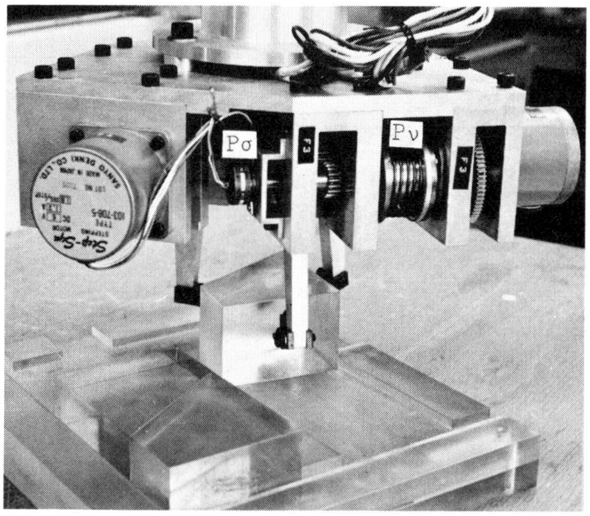

Photo 1 Developed robot hand with elastic fingers

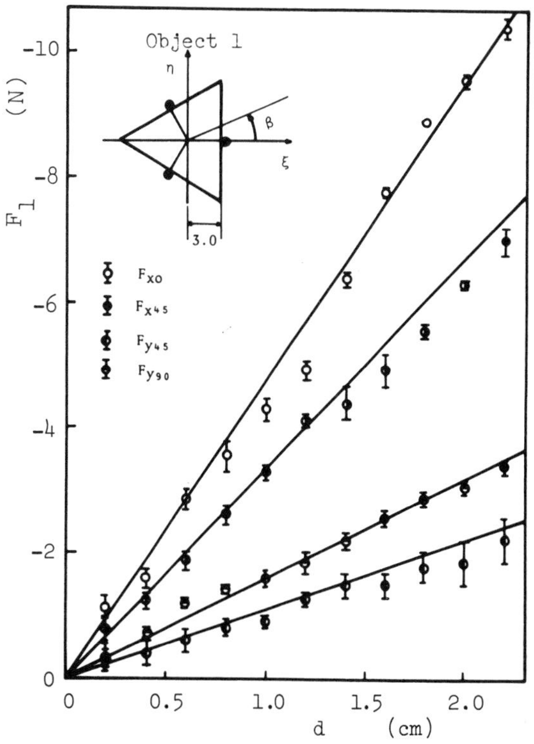

Fig. 8 Experiment of handling force F_1

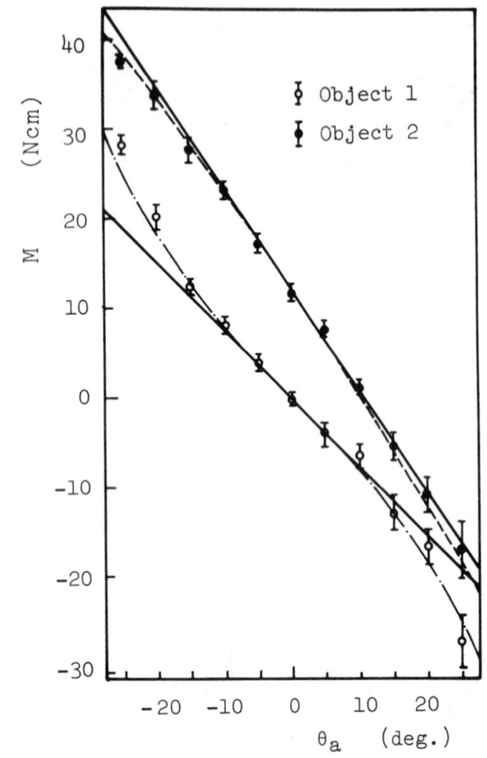

Fig. 9 Moment M v.s. θ_a

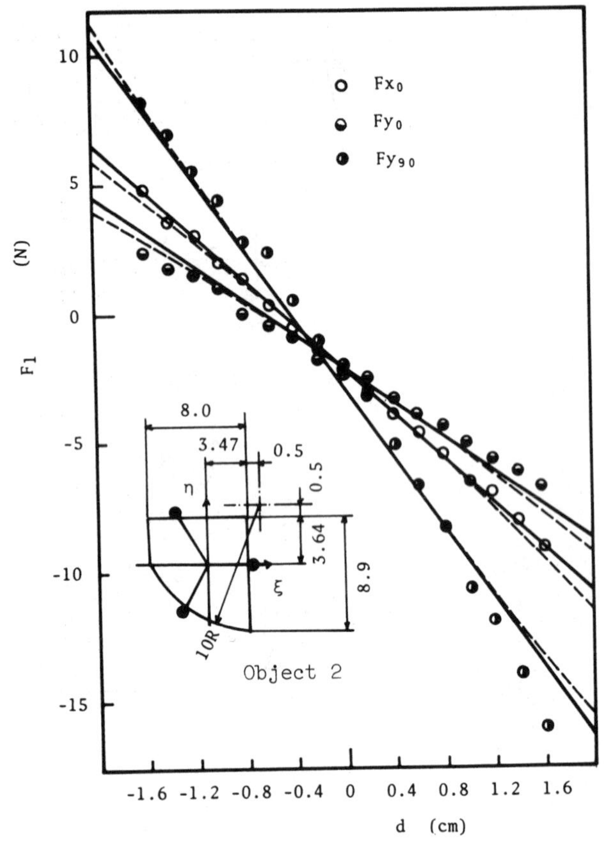

Fig.10 Handling force F_1 for Object 2

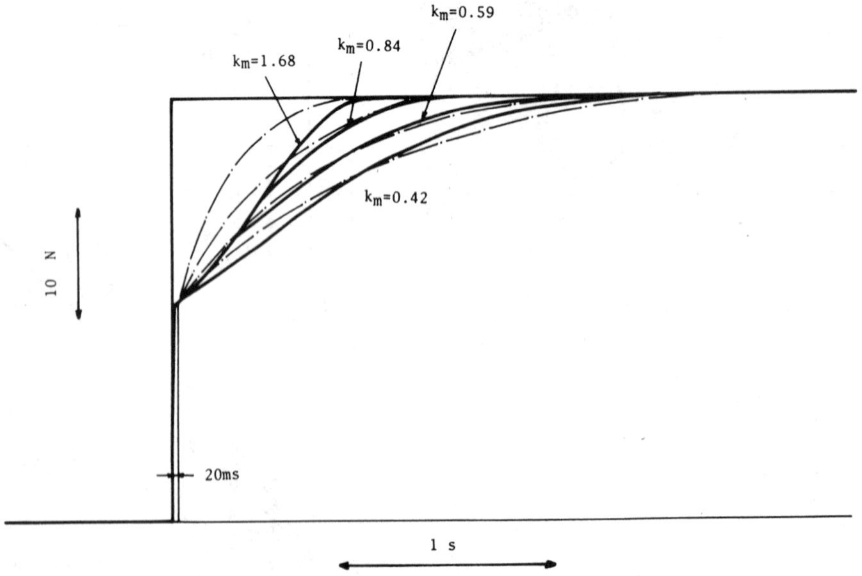

Fig. 11 Step response of handling force F_x

TASK-ORIENTED VARIABLE CONTROL OF MANIPULATOR AND ITS SOFTWARE SERVOING SYSTEM

K. Takase

Automatic Control Division, Electrotechnical Laboratory, 2-6-1, Nagato-cho, Chiyoda-ku, Tokyo, Japan

ABSTRACT

This paper describes the mathematical model of a manipulator and the software servo that controls the manipulator in a task-oriented coordinate system. A motion of the manipulator is decomposed into the six components of task-oriented coordinates, each of which is independently controlled as virtual manipulator freedom. The servoing method frees us from the physical manipulator mechanism and enables us to control the manipulator in any task-oriented coordinate system. It reduces the complexity of description of manipulations, especially in the case where motion is partially constrained.

1. INTRODUCTION

The first computer controlled arm was developed by Ernst.(Ref. 1) In the system he developed a computer calculated joint positions and outputted reference signals to a position-controlled mechanical arm. Force feedback was added to a computer controlled manipulator by Inoue and it became possible to carry out force-related tasks such as assembly.(Ref. 5) Paul developed a software servoing system for an arm in which position, velocity and force information were read into the computer and motor drive level was output by the computer. (Ref. 6) He combined this system with trajectory calculation and developed an arm which moved very smoothly and accurately. At ETL an articulated manipulator with torque control ability was developed.(Ref. 7) The joints of the manipulator were driven by magnetic powder clutches and joint torques were directly controlled by the computer.

In performing complex manipulatory tasks such as tool-handling, motion is described in terms of interactions of position, velocity and force of all joints. Description of motion, however, should be so organized that one can specify position, velocity, force or stiffness of each degree of freedom in the task-oriented coordinate system. The motion specified in this manner can not be controlled by a conventional servomechanism which closes the servo loop within one joint. It requires a servomechanism that controls task-oriented variables directly.

The equation of motion of the manipulator is represented by multivariable, nonlinear, differential equations with configuration-dependent coefficients. Those equations, however, are reduced to the nomalized form: $f_i = \ddot{h}_i$ (i=1-n), by compensating for the nonlinear terms such as gravity loading or coliolis force, and adjusting configuration-dependent coefficients in real-time. In this equation, h_i is a task-oriented variable and f_i is a generalized force which is a linear combination of joint torques. Consequently each variable h_i is controlled by f_i independently of other variables.

Task-oriented variable control can be easily realized by a software servoing system if it is implemented on a computer with sufficiently fast computing ability. But in order to constitute the control system in a conventional small computer, we must divide the system into two parts: a planning part and a real-time part. The planning part calculates motion trajectories and servo gain matrices preceding motion. The real-time part consists of a prediction part and a drive part. The prediction part computes configuration-dependent coefficients, gravity torques and force exerting torques. The drive part measures joint positions and velocities, calculates servo torques, determines total torques and then drives joints.

2. MATHEMATICAL MODEL OF A MANIPULATOR

2.1 Geometry

We will study an articulated manipulator with six degrees of freedom, shown in Fig. 1. The manipulator is made up of six links, each connected to the next by a rotary joint: let θ_i denote the i-th joint angular position. $\mathbf{p}_i$ is a unit vector which represents the direction of the i-th joint axis. C_i is an orthogonal coordinate system fixed on the center of mass of the i-th link. The three orthogonal axes of C_i will coincide with those of the absolute coordinate system C_0 when:θ_1= --- = θ_6 =0. Let unit vectors $\mathbf{e}_{i1}, \mathbf{e}_{i2}, \mathbf{e}_{i3}$ represent the direction of the three orthogonal axes of C_i. In the case of the manipulator we are considering, the direction of a line connecting the i-th joint and the i+1-th joint coincides with that of $\mathbf{e}_{i3}$.

2.2 Kinematics

2.2.1 Orientation

The orientations of the links of the manipulator are expressed by matrices $(\mathbf{e}_{i1}, \mathbf{e}_{i2}, \mathbf{e}_{i3})$ (i=1-6). Between two adjacent coordinate systems there is the following relationship:

$$(\mathbf{e}_{i1},\mathbf{e}_{i2},\mathbf{e}_{i3})=(\mathbf{e}_{i-1,1},\mathbf{e}_{i-1,2},\mathbf{e}_{i-1,3})\cdot A_i \quad (1)$$

where:

$$A_i=\begin{pmatrix}\cos\theta_i & -\sin\theta_i & 0\\ \sin\theta_i & \cos\theta_i & 0\\ 0 & 0 & 1\end{pmatrix} \quad (i=1,4)$$

$$=\begin{pmatrix}\cos\theta_i & 0 & \sin\theta_i\\ 0 & 1 & 0\\ -\sin\theta_i & 0 & \cos\theta_i\end{pmatrix} \quad (i=2,3,5)$$

$$=\begin{pmatrix}1 & 0 & 0\\ 0 & \cos\theta_i & -\sin\theta_i\\ 0 & \sin\theta_i & \cos\theta_i\end{pmatrix} \quad (i=6)$$

Therefore the orientation of the i-th link can be obtained by:

$$(\mathbf{e}_{i1},\mathbf{e}_{i2},\mathbf{e}_{i3})=A_1\cdot A_2\cdots A_i \quad (1)$$

2.2.2 Position

The distance vector from the j-th joint to the center of mass of the i-th link is given by:

$$\mathbf{r}_{ji}=-\sum_{k=j}^{i-1}\mathbf{l}_k\cdot\mathbf{e}_{k3}-\sum_{p=1}^{3}l_{ip}\cdot\mathbf{e}_{ip} \quad (2)$$

where l_k is the length of the k-th link; (l_{i1}, l_{i2}, l_{i3}) are coordinates of the i-th joint in the coordinate system C_i.
In general, the position of a point on the i-th link is given by:

$$\mathbf{r}=\mathbf{r}_{1i}+\sum_{p=1}^{3}x_{ip}\cdot\mathbf{e}_{ip} \quad (3)$$

where (x_{i1},x_{i2},x_{i3}) are the coordinates of the point in the coordinate system C_i.

2.2.3 Velocity

By differentiating the position we can obtain the velocity of the point:

$$\mathbf{v}=\frac{d}{dt}(\mathbf{r}_{1j}+\sum_{p=1}^{3}x_{ip}\cdot\mathbf{e}_{ip})$$
$$=\sum_{j=1}^{i}\frac{\partial}{\partial\theta_j}(\mathbf{r}_{1i}+\sum_{p=1}^{3}x_{ip}\cdot\mathbf{e}_{ip})\dot\theta_j \quad (4)$$

As:

$$\frac{\partial}{\partial\theta_j}(\mathbf{e}_{ip})=\mathbf{p}_j\times\mathbf{e}_{ip} \quad (j\le i)$$
$$=0 \quad (j>i)$$

Eq. 4 becomes:

$$\mathbf{v}=\sum_{j=1}^{i}[\mathbf{p}_j\times(\mathbf{r}_{ji}+\sum_{p=1}^{3}x_{ip}\cdot\mathbf{e}_{ip})]\dot\theta_j \quad (5)$$

2.2.4 Acceleration

Differentiating the velocity, we obtain:

$$\boldsymbol{\alpha}=\frac{d\mathbf{v}}{dt}=\sum_{k=1}^{i}(\frac{\partial\mathbf{v}}{\partial\dot\theta_k}\ddot\theta_k+\frac{\partial\mathbf{v}}{\partial\theta_k}\dot\theta_k)$$
$$=\sum_{k=1}^{i}[\mathbf{p}_k\times(\mathbf{r}_{ki}+\sum_{p=1}^{3}x_{ip}\cdot\mathbf{e}_{ip})]\ddot\theta_k$$
$$+\sum_{k=1}^{i}\sum_{j=1}^{i}\mathbf{u}_{kj}\dot\theta_k\dot\theta_j \quad (6)$$

where:

$$\mathbf{u}_{kj}=\mathbf{p}_j\times[\mathbf{p}_k\times(\mathbf{r}_{ki}+\sum_{p=1}^{3}x_{ip}\cdot\mathbf{e}_{ip})] \quad (k\ge j)$$
$$=\mathbf{u}_{jk} \quad (k<j)$$

2.3 Dynamics

A moment M_n that acts at the n-th joint can be obtained by:

$$M_n=\sum_{i=n}^{6}[\int(\mathbf{r}_{ni}+\sum_{q=1}^{3}x_{iq}\cdot\mathbf{e}_{iq})\times(\mathbf{g}-\boldsymbol{\alpha})dm]$$
$$+\mathbf{r}_n\times\mathbf{F}_c+M_c$$

where the first term is the integration of the moment due to inertia($-\boldsymbol{\alpha}$) and gravity($\mathbf{g}$) over the mass of links from the n-th to the sixth; the second term is the moment due to a force acting through a reference point; the third term is an external moment acting at the reference point.

The inner product of the moment M_n and the unit vector $\mathbf{p}_n$ coincides with the driving torque of the n-th joint, therefore we obtain the following equation:

$$T_n=-M_n\cdot\mathbf{p}_n=-\sum_{i=n}^{6}[\int(\mathbf{p}_n\times\mathbf{r}_{ni}+\sum_{q=1}^{3}x_{iq}(\mathbf{p}_n\times\mathbf{e}_{iq}))$$
$$\cdot(\mathbf{g}-\boldsymbol{\alpha})dm]-(\mathbf{r}_n\times\mathbf{F}_c)\cdot\mathbf{p}_n-M_c\cdot\mathbf{p}_n \quad (7)$$

Substituting for $\boldsymbol{\alpha}$ from Eq. 6 into Eq. 7, we obtain:

$$T_n=\sum_{k=1}^{6}a_{nk}\ddot\theta_k+\sum_{k=1}^{6}\sum_{j=1}^{6}b_{njk}\dot\theta_j\dot\theta_k$$
$$+T_{gn}+T_{Fn}+T_{Mn} \quad (n=1\text{-}6) \quad (8)$$

where:

$$a_{nk}=\sum_{i=r}^{6}[m_i(\mathbf{p}_n\times\mathbf{r}_{ni})\cdot(\mathbf{p}_k\times\mathbf{r}_{ki})$$
$$+\sum_{p=1}^{3}\sum_{q=1}^{3}I_{ipq}(\mathbf{p}_n\times\mathbf{e}_{iq})\cdot(\mathbf{p}_k\times\mathbf{e}_{ip})]$$
$$b_{njk}=\sum_{i=r}^{6}[m_i(\mathbf{p}_n\times\mathbf{r}_{ni})\cdot(\mathbf{p}_j\times(\mathbf{p}_k\times\mathbf{r}_{ki}))$$
$$+\sum_{p=1}^{3}\sum_{q=1}^{3}I_{ipq}(\mathbf{p}_n\times\mathbf{e}_{iq})\cdot(\mathbf{p}_j\times(\mathbf{p}_k\times\mathbf{e}_{ip}))]$$
$$(k\ge j)$$

$$=b_{nkj} \quad (k<j)$$

$$T_{gn}=-[(\sum_{i=n}^{6}m_i\mathbf{r}_{ni})\times\mathbf{g}]\cdot\mathbf{p}_n$$

$$T_{Fn}=-(\mathbf{r}_n\times\mathbf{F}_c)\cdot\mathbf{p}_n \qquad T_{Mn}=-M_c\cdot\mathbf{p}_n$$

and m_i is the mass of the i-th link; $I_{ipq}=\int x_{ip}x_{iq}dm$; $\mathbf{g}$ denotes the gravity vector $(0,0,-g)^T$ and $\mathbf{r}$ stands for max(n,k).

In vector notation Eq. 8 becomes:

$$\mathbf{T}=A\ddot{\boldsymbol\theta}+\dot{\boldsymbol\theta}^T B\dot{\boldsymbol\theta}+\mathbf{T}_c \quad (9)$$

where vector $\mathbf{T}$ and $\boldsymbol\theta$ denote joint torques $(T_1,---,T_6)^T$ and joint angular positions $(\theta_1,---,\theta_6)^T$, respectively; A is a 6x6 matrix $[a_{nk}]$; B is a 6x6 matrix $[\mathbf{b}_{jk}]$ whose components are vectors $(b_{1jk},---b_{6jk})^T$; $\mathbf{T}_c=(T_{g1}+T_{F1}+T_{M1},---,T_{g6}+T_{F6}+T_{M6})^T$.

3. DECOMPOSITION OF MOTION AND CONTROLLED VARIABLES

In normal operation, the manipulator handles an object after grasping it with the end link which is usually referred to as the hand. It is therefore important to consider motions of the hand. We now decompose a motion of the manipulator into a translation and a rotation of the hand each of which is further resolved into three components. Controlled variables corresponding to the components will be called H-variables(that is task-oriented variables) and expressed with the sign $H:H=(h_1,---,h_6)^T$. Where h_1,h_2,h_3 are controlled variables for the translation and h_4,h_5,h_6 for the rotation.

3.1 Controlled Variables for Translation

For the controlled variables of the translation, we choose orthogonal coordinates of the reference point on the hand. Other coordinates such as cylindrical coordinates are also necessary to execute manipulatory tasks, but are not described here in order to simplify the description.

Let coordinates (x,y,z) of the reference point be the H-variables (h_1,h_2,h_3) as shown in Fig. 2. The relationship between the absolute coordinates (X,Y,Z) and the coordinates (x,y,z) is expressed by:

$$(X,Y,Z)^T=(\mathbf{l},\mathbf{m},\mathbf{n})(x,y,z)^T+\mathbf{d}$$

where $\mathbf{l},\mathbf{m},\mathbf{n}$ are unit vectors which represent the direction of three orthogonal axes of C_{xyz} and $\mathbf{d}$ is a distance vector from the origin of the absolute coordinate system C_{XYZ} to the origin of C_{xyz}.

By solving this equation with respect to $(x,y,z)^T$, we obtain:

$$(h_1,h_2,h_3)^T=(x,y,z)^T=M[(X,Y,Z)^T-\mathbf{d})] \qquad (10)$$

where M is a 3x3 matrix: $M=(\mathbf{l},\mathbf{m},\mathbf{n})^{-1}$.

We now determine the relationship between H-variables and joint positions $\boldsymbol{\theta}$. The distance vector from the i-th joint to the reference point is given by:

$$\mathbf{r}_i=\mathbf{r}_{i6}+\sum_{p=1}^{3}\alpha_p\cdot\mathbf{e}_{6p}$$

where $\alpha_1,\alpha_2,\alpha_3$ are the coordinates of the reference point in the coordinate system C_6. As: $\mathbf{r}_1=(X,Y,Z)^T$, Eq. 10 becomes:

$$(h_1,h_2,h_3)^T=M(\mathbf{r}_1-\mathbf{d}) \qquad (11)$$

Differentiating Eq. 11, we obtain:

$$(\dot{h}_1,\dot{h}_2,\dot{h}_3)^T=M[\sum_{j=1}^{6}(\mathbf{p}_j\times\mathbf{r}_j)\dot{\theta}_j]=J_1\dot{\boldsymbol{\theta}} \qquad (12)$$

where :

$$J_1=[M(\mathbf{p}_1\times\mathbf{r}_1,---,M(\mathbf{p}_6\times\mathbf{r}_6)]$$

Again differentiating Eq. 12, we have:

$$(\ddot{h}_1,\ddot{h}_2,\ddot{h}_3)^T=J_1\ddot{\boldsymbol{\theta}}+\dot{\boldsymbol{\theta}}^T C_1\dot{\boldsymbol{\theta}} \qquad (13)$$

where C_1 is a symmetric 6x6 matrix $[\mathbf{c}_{1ij}]$ whose components are vectors:

$$\mathbf{c}_{1ij}=M[\mathbf{p}_i\times(\mathbf{p}_j\times\mathbf{r}_j)] \quad (i\leq j)$$

3.2 Controlled Variables for Rotation

A rotation of the hand can be represented by a change of a direction of an axis fixed on the hand and a revolution about the axis. The following rotations, important for manipulatory tasks, are considered here.

1) Little changes in both the direction and the angular position about the axis. (within 90 degrees)
2) Arbitrary revolution about an absolutely fixed axis. (within the physical limits of the manipulator)

We introduce unit vectors $\mathbf{o}_p$ and $\mathbf{o}_s$ fixed on the hand as illustrated in Fig. 3 to represent the orientation of the hand. They are calculated by:

$$\mathbf{o}_p=\sum_{q=1}^{3}\beta_q\cdot\mathbf{e}_{6q} \qquad \mathbf{o}_s=\sum_{q=1}^{3}\gamma_q\cdot\mathbf{e}_{6q}$$

where β_1,β_2,β_3 and $\gamma_1,\gamma_2,\gamma_3$ are components of $\mathbf{o}_p$ and $\mathbf{o}_s$ in the coordinate system C_6, respectively.

In case of 1), H-variables are defined as follows:

$$h_4=\mathbf{o}_p\cdot\mathbf{a} \quad h_5=\mathbf{o}_p\cdot\mathbf{b} \quad h_6=\mathbf{o}_s\cdot\mathbf{c} \qquad (14)$$

where $\mathbf{a},\mathbf{b},\mathbf{c}$ are unit vectors which are set up appropriately to express the rotation.

These H-variables are geometrically shown in Fig. 4. The direction of $\mathbf{o}_p$ is controlled by h_4 and h_5, the revolution about $\mathbf{o}_p$ is controlled by h_6.

Differentiating Eq. 14, we obtain:

$$(\dot{h}_4,\dot{h}_5,\dot{h}_6)^T=J_2\dot{\boldsymbol{\theta}} \qquad (15)$$

where :

$$J_2=\begin{pmatrix}(\mathbf{p}_1\times\mathbf{o}_p)\cdot\mathbf{a},---,(\mathbf{p}_6\times\mathbf{o}_p)\cdot\mathbf{a}\\(\mathbf{p}_1\times\mathbf{o}_p)\cdot\mathbf{b},---,(\mathbf{p}_6\times\mathbf{o}_p)\cdot\mathbf{b}\\(\mathbf{p}_1\times\mathbf{o}_s)\cdot\mathbf{c},---,(\mathbf{p}_6\times\mathbf{o}_s)\cdot\mathbf{c}\end{pmatrix}$$

Again differentiating Eq. 15, we obtain:

$$(\ddot{h}_4,\ddot{h}_5,\ddot{h}_6)^T=J_2\ddot{\boldsymbol{\theta}}+\dot{\boldsymbol{\theta}}^T C_2\dot{\boldsymbol{\theta}} \qquad (16)$$

where C_2 is a symmetric 6x6 matrix $[\mathbf{c}_{2ij}]$ whose components are vectors:

$$\mathbf{c}_{2ij}=\begin{pmatrix}(\mathbf{p}_i\times(\mathbf{p}_j\times\mathbf{o}_p))\cdot\mathbf{a}\\(\mathbf{p}_i\times(\mathbf{p}_j\times\mathbf{o}_p))\cdot\mathbf{b}\\(\mathbf{p}_i\times(\mathbf{p}_j\times\mathbf{o}_s))\cdot\mathbf{c}\end{pmatrix} \quad (i\leq j)$$

In case of 2), H-variables are defined as follows:

$$h_4=\mathbf{o}_p\cdot\mathbf{a} \quad h_5=\mathbf{o}_p\cdot\mathbf{b} \quad h_6=\tan^{-1}\left(\frac{\mathbf{o}_s\cdot\mathbf{b}}{\mathbf{o}_s\cdot\mathbf{a}}\right) \qquad (17)$$

Variables h_4 and h_5 would be set to zero by feedback control.

4. SERVO

In this section a servo system that controls the H-variables of the manipulator is considered. The equation of motion of the manipulator is represented by multivariable, nonlinear, differential equations with configuration-dependent coefficients. The characteristics of the manipulator are first improved by compensations and then the H-variables are controlled.

4.1 Equation of Motion with respect to H-variables

Combining Eq. 13 and Eq. 16, we have:

$$\ddot{H}=(\ddot{h}_1,---,\ddot{h}_6)^T=J\ddot{\theta}+\dot{\theta}^T\mathbf{C}\dot{\theta} \tag{18}$$

where J is a 6x6 matrix that is a combination of two matrices J_1 and J_2:

$$J=\begin{pmatrix} J_1 \\ -- \\ J_2 \end{pmatrix}$$

and $\mathbf{C}$ is a 6x6 matrix $[\mathbf{c}_{ij}]$ whose component is a combination of two vectors $\mathbf{c}_{1ij}$ and $\mathbf{c}_{2ij}$:

$$\mathbf{c}_{ij}=\begin{pmatrix} \mathbf{c}_{1ij} \\ ---- \\ \mathbf{c}_{2ij} \end{pmatrix}$$

Assuming that J^{-1} exists, and substituting for $\ddot{\theta}$ from Eq. 18 into Eq. 9, we obtain:

$$\mathbf{T}=AJ^{-1}\ddot{H}+\dot{\theta}^T D\dot{\theta}+\mathbf{T}_c \tag{19}$$

where D is a 6x6 matrix $[\mathbf{d}_{ij}]$ whose component is:

$$\mathbf{d}_{ij}=-AJ^{-1}\mathbf{c}_{ij}+\mathbf{b}_{ij}$$

4.2 Feedback Loop for Compensation

4.2.1 Compensation for $\dot{\theta}^T D\dot{\theta}$

In order to cancel the effect of the nonlinear term $\dot{\theta}^T D\dot{\theta}$, a feedback loop that measures joint positions and velocities is introduced. It calculates $\dot{\theta}^T D\dot{\theta}$ and adds it to the input torques of the manipulator in real-time. Fig. 5 illustrates this compensation feedback loop. Consequently, the equation of motion becomes:

$$\mathbf{T}_1=AJ^{-1}\ddot{H}+\mathbf{T}_c \tag{20}$$

where $\mathbf{T}_1$ are input torques of the system which includes the compensation feedback loop.

4.2.2 Gravity, External Force and Moment

The servo is required to compensate for gravity loading and to exert force and moment at the reference point of the hand. For this purpose gravity torques and force and moment exerting torques are calculated according to Eq. 8 and added to the input in real-time. The equation of motion then becomes:

$$\mathbf{T}_2=AJ^{-1}\ddot{H} \tag{21}$$

where: $\mathbf{T}_2=\mathbf{T}_1-\mathbf{T}_c$

4.3 Generalized Force

We introduce generalized forces defined by Eq. 22 so that the system response might be independent of the manipulator configuration.

$$\mathbf{T}_2=AJ^{-1}F \tag{22}$$

Substituting T_2 into Eq. 21, we have:

$$AJ^{-1}F=AJ^{-1}\ddot{H} \rightarrow F=\ddot{H} \tag{23}$$

Expressed in components, this becomes:

$$f_i=\ddot{h}_i \quad (i=1-6) \tag{24}$$

Eq. 24 shows that h_i is controlled by f_i independently of the manipulator configuration and other H-variables. Fig. 5 shows the servo system, simplified block diagram of the servo is shown in Fig. 6.

4.4 Control of H-variables

We will consider the feedback control of H-variables. In order to set the H-variables h_i at the stationary position, we apply the generalized force:

$$f_i=-k_v\dot{h}_i-k_e(h_i-h_{ic}) \tag{25}$$

where k_v and k_e are velocity and position feedback gain, respectively; h_{ic} denotes the stationary reference input.
Substituting the f_i into Eq. 24, we obtain the system response with respect to the H-variable:

$$\ddot{h}_i+k_v\dot{h}_i+k_e(h_i-h_{ic})=0 \tag{26}$$

The servo constrains one generalized degree of freedom of the manipulator. For example, if orthogonal coordinates are chosen for H-variables and one of these are thus controlled, the reference point of the hand will be constrained within a plane that is defined by: $h_i(X,Y,Z)=h_{ic}$.
In the case where two H-variables are controlled, the reference point will be constrained on the intersection of two planes. The structure of the servo system is suited for the control of partially constrained motions in the real world.

Trajectory planning for motion is easily performed in H-variable space. In this case the motion of the manipulator is specified in terms of the time histories of the H-variables. In order to make the H-variables h_i comply strictly with the planned time histories, we apply:

$$f_i=\ddot{h}_{ir}(t)-k_v[\dot{h}_i-\dot{h}_{ir}(t)]-k_e[h_i-h_{ir}(t)] \tag{27}$$

where $h_{ir}(t)$ is a function of time that express the time history of the H-variable; $\dot{h}_{ir}(t)$ and $\ddot{h}_{ir}(t)$ are the first and second derivatives of $h_{ir}(t)$, respectively.
The system response with respect to the H-variable becomes:

$$[\ddot{h}_i-\ddot{h}_{ir}(t)]+k_v[\dot{h}_i-\dot{h}_{ir}(t)]+k_e[h_i-h_{ir}(t)]=0 \tag{28}$$

This ensures that the physical motion of the manipulator will follow the planned motion without velocity and acceleration error.

5. SIMPLIFIED SOFTWARE SERVOING SYSTEM

The above-mentioned servo could be easily realized by servo programs which are implemented on a real-time computer with sufficiently fast computing ability. But as a preliminary to the research we have developed a simplified system which is implemented on a small real-time computer (PDP-12). In designing the servo system, the following approximations are introduced.

1) Precalculation of the time-comsuming computations.
2) Linearization of the real-time equation for determing the servo torques.

Fig. 7 shows the servo system which controls the planned trajectory motions. Assuming that we can compensate for the velocity-dependent nonlinear term by using $\dot{h}_{ir}(t)$ instead of $\dot{h}_i$, we have the modified system shown in Fig. 8, where the motion planning part prepares the time histories of the joint torques $\mathbf{T}_t$ for the real-time control.

In order to reduce the amount of real-time calculation, the H-variables are strictly computed only for the sampled positions and between two successive sampling instants they are linearly interpolated. Fig. 9 shows the modified real-time control part.

In the actual manipulator control system, the motion planning part sets up time histories of H-variables, calculates torques $\mathbf{T}_t$ and then computes servo gain matrices $AJ^{-1}K_vJ$, $AJ^{-1}K_eJ$ and the inverse of Jacobian matrix J^{-1} for several manipulator configurations during motion. These data are stored in tables. The real-time control part consists of a prediction part and a drive part. The former runs every 50 m sec. and the later every 10 m sec.. The prediction part computes H-coordinates, gravity torques and force exerting torques strictly and adjusts configuration-dependent servo gain matrices and the inverse of Jacobian matrix. The drive part measures the joint positions and velocities, calculates the servo torques using servo gain matrices, determines total torques and then drives joints.

6. CONCLUSIONS

A theory of task-oriented variable control has been established. In this control method motion of the manipulator is decomposed into the components of task-oriented coordinates, each of which is independently controlled as virtual manipulator freedom. The servoing method frees us from the physical manipulator mechanisms and enables us to make up virtual mechanical structures with which manipulatory tasks are carried out. The scheme of this control is suited for the advanced use of the manipulator.

A simplified servo system for task-oriented variable control has been implemented on a small computer. The system is able to perform complex tasks such as tool-handling. It has shown the feasibility and the usefulness of task-oriented variable control.

ACKNOWLEDGEMENTS

The author wishes to thank Dr. H. Inoue for having suggested the philosophy of software servoing and for the useful discussions during the cource of the work. He also wishes to thank the members of the robotics group at ETL for the many helpful discussions.

REFERENCES

(1) H. A. Ernst, MH-1 A Computer-Operated Mechanical Hand, Sc. D. Thesis, Massachusetts Institute of Technology, (1961).

(2) J. J. Uicker, JR., Dynamic Force Analysis of Spatial Linkage, Trans. of the ASME 418(1967).

(3) D. L. Pieper, The Kinematics of Manipulators Under Computer Control, Stanford Artificial Intelligence Project, Memo No. 72, (1968).

(4) D. E. Whitney, Resolved Motion Rate Control of Manipulators and Human Prosthesis, IEEE Trans. on Man-Machine Systems MMS-10-2, 47(1969).

(5) H. Inoue, Computer Controlled Bilateral Manipulator, Bulletin of the JSME 14-69, 199(1971).

(6) R. P. Paul, Modelling, Trajectry Calculation and Servoing of a Computer Controlled Arm, Ph. D. Thesis, Stanford University, (1972).

(7) K. Takase, H. Inoue, K. Sato, S. Hagiwara, The Design of an Articulated Manipulator with Torque Control Ability, Proceedings of the 4th ISIR, 261(1974).

(8) R. Finkel, R. Taylor, R. Bolles, R. Paul, J. Feldman, AL, A Programming System for Automation, Stanford Artificial Intelligence Project, Memo No. AIM-243, (1974).

(9) A. K. Bejczy, Robot Arm Dynamics and Control, Jet Propulsion Laboratory, Technical Memorandom 33-669, (1974).

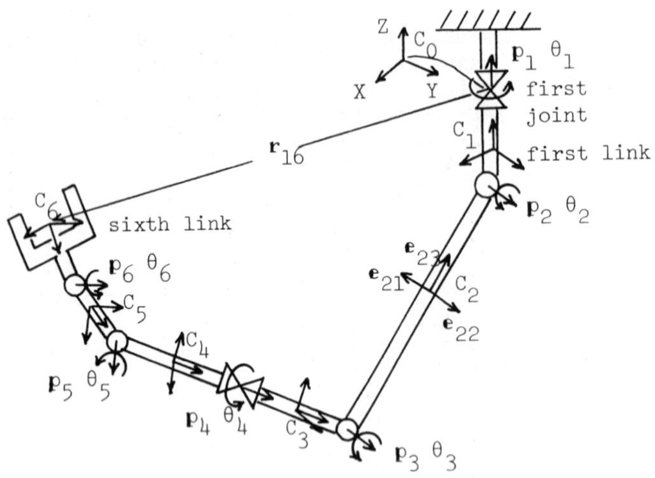

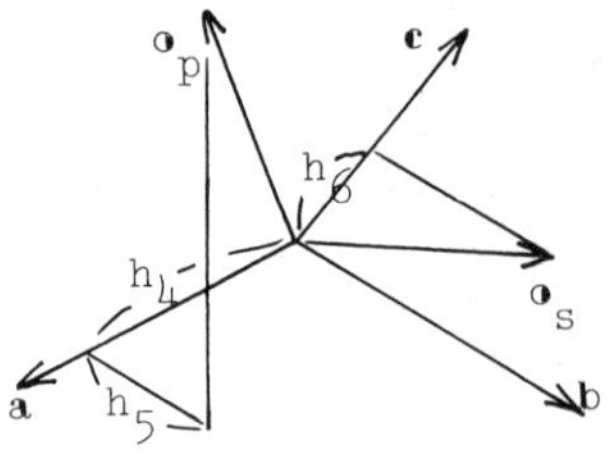

Fig. 4 H-variables
h_4, h_5, h_6

Fig. 1 Manipulator and its coordinate system

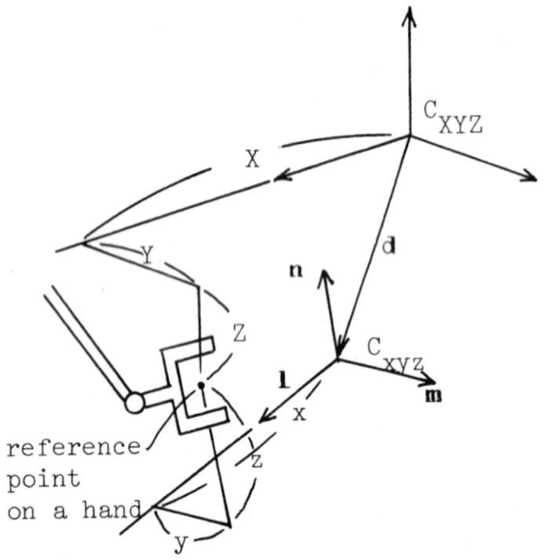

Fig. 2 Orthogonal H-variables

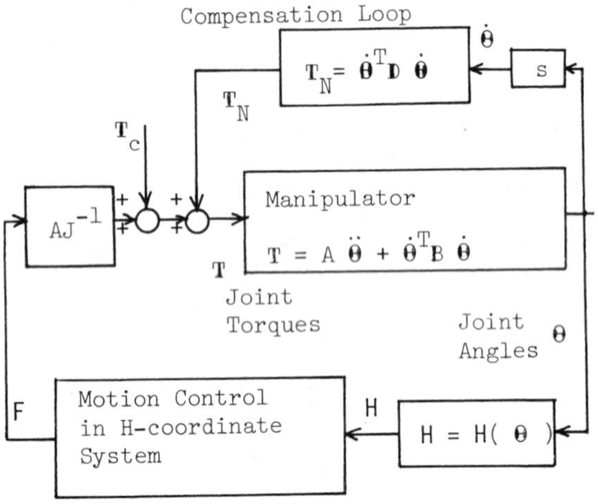

Fig. 5 Servo loop of manipulator

$$\mathbf{r}_h = \sum_{q=1}^{3} \alpha_q \cdot \mathbf{e}_{6q}$$

$$\mathbf{o}_p = \sum_{q=1}^{3} \beta_q \cdot \mathbf{e}_{6q}$$

$$\mathbf{o}_s = \sum_{q=1}^{3} \gamma_q \cdot \mathbf{e}_{6q}$$

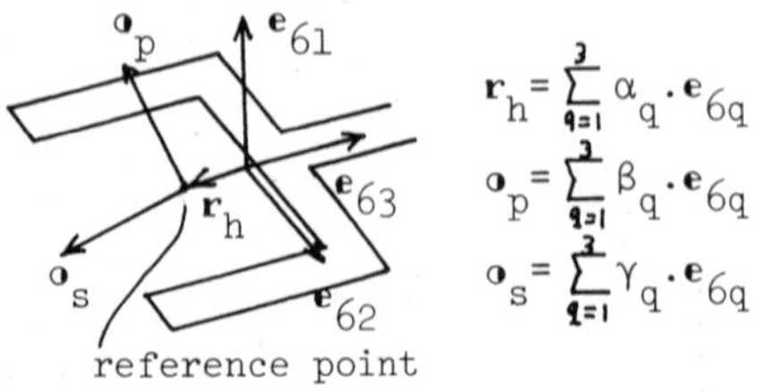

Fig. 3 Hand coordinates

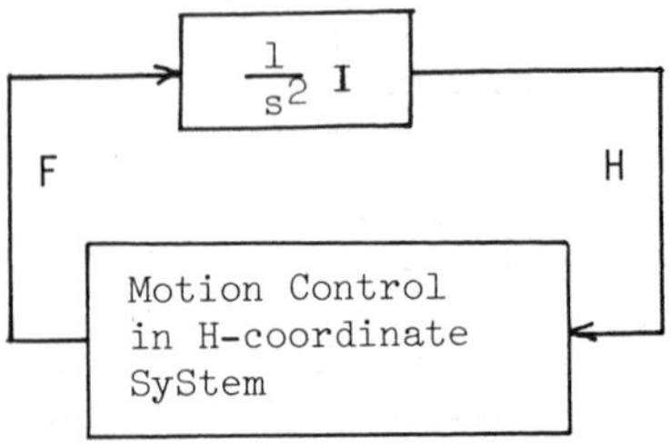

Fig. 6 Simplified block diagram
of the servo loop

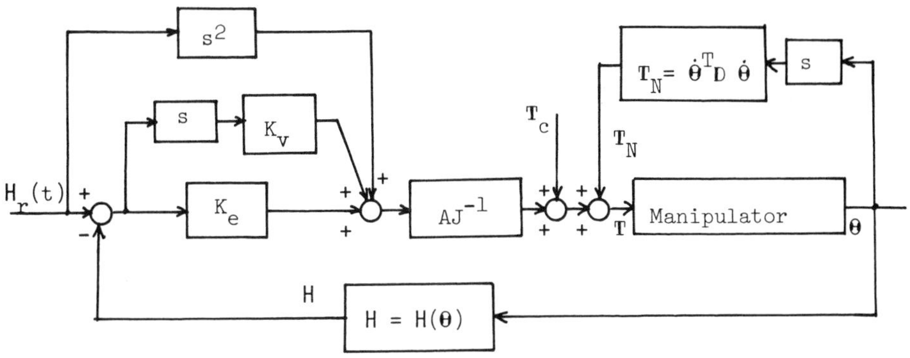

Fig. 7 Control system for trajectory motion

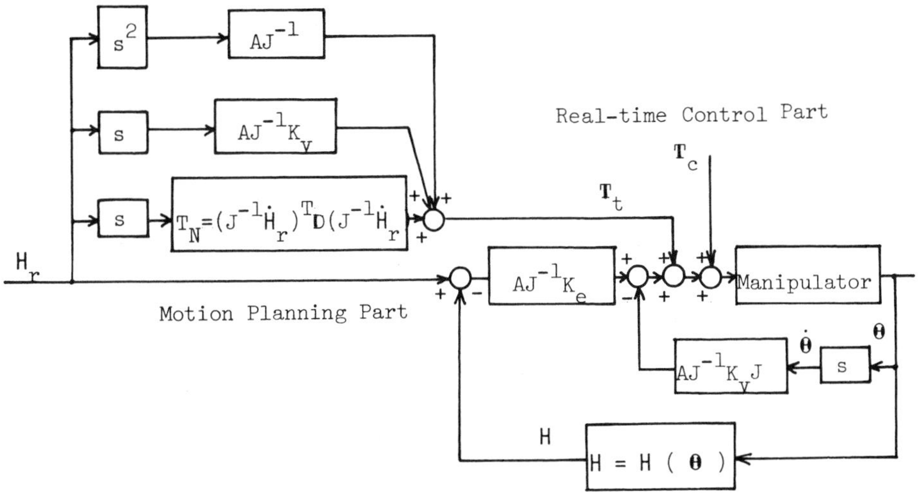

Fig. 8 Simplified control system for trajectory motion

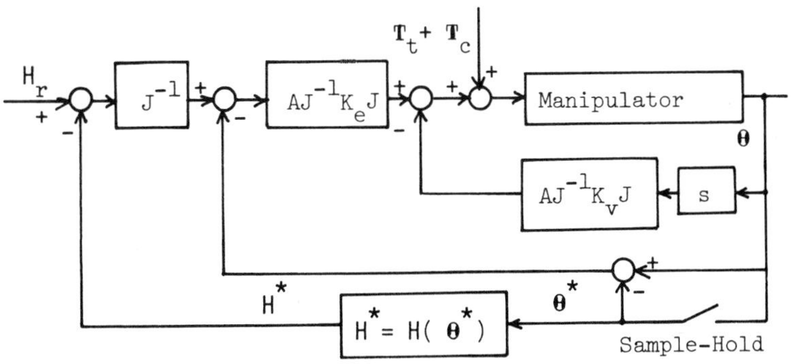

Fig. 9 Linearly approximated real-time control part

MATERIAL–HANDLING ROBOTS FOR PROGRAMMABLE AUTOMATION

C.A. Rosen

SRI International, 333 Ravenswood Avenue, Menlo Park, California 94025

ABSTRACT

This paper deals with the requirements, present development, and research issues concerning advanced material-handling systems based on programmable manipulators that are commonly called industrial robots.

Industrial robots are becoming increasingly important as part of programmable automation systems being developed for the production of batch-produced discrete part goods. As contrasted with hard or fixed automation, programmable systems are designed for flexibility, that is, for ease of set-up for new or changing products in small or variable lot sizes, and adaptively responsive to a variable environment.

Material handling entails the controlled manipulation of raw materials, workpieces, assemblies and finished products. Together with inspection and assembly, these functions represent essential parts of the total manufacturing process that are still highly labor-intensive.

The great majority of present industrial robots (first generation) are performing relatively simple repetitive material handling tasks in highly constrained or structured environments. They are also increasingly used in spot-welding and paint-spraying operations. Second generation robots which incorporate computer processors or minicomputers have begun to appear in factories, considerably extending rudimentary pick-and-place operations. More advanced robots are being developed which incorporate visual and tactile sensing, all under computer control. These integrated systems begin to emulate human capabilities in coping with relatively unstructured environments.

There are two major requirements for advanced material handling systems. The first requirement is for a programmed robot to be able to acquire randomly-positioned and unoriented workpieces, subassemblies or assemblies from stationery bins or from moving conveyors, in a predetermined manner, and to convey them via a predetermined path, safely, to some desired position and orientation.

The second requirement is for the robots to be able to place the acquired workpiece or assembly with a desired orientation in a position with a specified precision.

These two requirements share the need for sensor-controlled manipulation to varying degrees. Tactile sensing may be sufficient for a simple task in which the workpieces are already oriented and require crude end-positioning at the destination such as in a palletizing operation. Visual sensing may be required when the workpieces are unoriented originally, are in motion, or when the final position is not precisely determined. In some instances, both tactile and visual sensing would be the most effective method, as when packing an unoriented container with workpieces in a desired order. Finally, in automated assembly processes, visual and/or tactile sensing may be required to bring parts together in fitting operations, or for insertions of shafts or bolts in holes. In the latter cases, the precision requirements for a passive accomodation system, together with the completeness of jigging or fixturing would govern how much sensor control was necessary.

The major issues thus are the relative costs of orienting parts, of fixturing to preserve position and orientation, of high-performance robots (speed and precision) and on the trade-off attainable by the use of sensor control to reduce the cost of the other alternatives.

INTRODUCTION

This paper deals with the requirements, the present developments, and the research issues of advanced material-handling systems based on programmable manipulators, commonly designated industrial robots. The domain of interest is the fabrication of batch-produced discrete part goods for which programmable systems appear to be best matched, although programmable material-handling methods may also prove useful or sometimes superior to fixed or hard automation methods for high-volume mass-production applications.

As contrasted with hard automation, advanced programmable automation is characterized by flexibility and adaptability, that is, by the ease with which one can set-up for new or changing product mix in small or variable lot sizes, and by the capability of adaptively responding to variations in workpieces, assemblies, and associated machines.

Material handling entails the controlled manipulation of raw materials, workpieces, assemblies, and finished products. It is also an essential part of the inspection and the assembly processes; together, these are the three major elements of the total batch-production process that are still highly labor-intensive (1)(2).

For the purpose of this paper, programmable material-handling applications can be crudely divided into two classes that have important requirements in common. For convenience, these classes are tentatively labelled "predictable sequence material-handling" and "adaptive sensor-controlled material-handling"; they are described in the following sections.

Predictable Sequence Material-Handling Systems

In this class, raw materials, workpieces, assemblies, and finished goods are acquired, transported, repositioned, and oriented from one fixed location to another. The acquisition positions, the trajectory, and the deposition positions are known beforehand and variations in these parameters are sufficiently small so that no "fine tuning" is necessary. Typical examples include:

- The feeding of raw stock from a fixtured position to a stamping-machine, or to a press.
- The loading and unloading of parts to and from machine tools and furnaces, in which the accurate part position and orientation is effected using fixtures or mechanical stops.
- The stacking of cartons on pallets, in which position and orientation of the acquired cartons and of the pallet to be loaded are predetermined and fixed.

The majority of presently-used limited-sequence pick-and-place robots and many 5 and 6 degree-of-freedom robots equipped with more sophisticated internal sensors and control systems are successfully performing this class of operations. Occasionally, external photoelectric or electro-mechanical binary switches are incorporated into the handling systems as safety devices for interlocking multiple machines, and to select one of several stored programs. To a mild degree, these systems are adaptive, but they do not have provisions for altering the programmed orientations of the end-effector (hand) nor the trajectories of the arm during execution of a previously programmed sequence.

It is expected that robots for this class of operation will be gradually improved, and their utility extended by increasing performance factors such as speed and accuracy, and developing better end-effectors. There is little doubt that these relatively expensive robots will be increasingly used in large numbers for simple repetitive jobs which do not require adaptability. As it becomes more expensive to constrain the associated environmental conditions, one must turn to a more sophisticated class of robot--an adaptive sensor-controlled robot--which is discussed next.

Adaptive Sensor-Controlled Material-Handling Systems

The second class of material-handling systems provides for the acquisition, the safe transport, and the positioning or presentation of raw materials, workpieces, assemblies, and finished goods under variable and generally not fully predictable conditions. Examples include:

- The acquisition of randomly-oriented parts or assemblies, from a fixed or moving conveyor belt, their transport and deposition with a predetermined orientation and position into a tote box (buffer storage bin).
- The acquisition of randomly-oriented parts, one at a time, from a storage bin, their repositioning and reorienting in a predetermined manner for presentation to some other manufacturing process, such as inspection, machining, or assembly.
- The acquisition of workpieces (or assemblies), one at a time, from an overhead moving conveyor and the transporting and positioning of each workpiece on a rack, into a plating bath, a furnace or a similar processing machine.

These tasks require that the present capabilities of robots be extended so that they perceive and interact with the surrounding environment. In particular, it appears desirable to develop sensor-mediated computer-controlled robots which emulate human capabilities in identifying and locating parts, and in controlling the manipulation and presentation of these parts in a predetermined manner with a specified precision.

Human workers make use of both contact (force, torque, and touch) sensing and noncontact (visual) sensing. Similarly, sensors for programmable automation may be classified into contact sensors (force, torque, and touch sensors) and noncontact sensors (television cameras, diode arrays, optical proximity sensors, and range-imaging sensors).

A review of the use of sensors in programmable automation is given elsewhere (3). A potential strategy for control of manipulation is to make use of noncontact sensors for coarse resolution requirements and contact sensors for fine resolution. Thus, randomly-oriented workpieces can be located crudely using a television camera, and acquisition of the workpiece can be effected using touch sensors which can control the forces applied by fingers to within safe limits. A number of researchers have made use of electro-optical imaging sensors and force/torque/touch sensors to identify, locate, and manipulate workpieces. A few examples follow:

- Goto (4) built a hand with two fingers, each having 14 outer contact sensors and 4 inner, pressure-sensitive, conductive-rubber sensors. He used the touch information to acquire blocks randomly located on a table and packed them tightly on a pallet.
- Bolles and Paul (5) describe a binary touch sensor consisting of two microswitches, one on either side of each

finger. They used it to determine whether a part was present or absent and to center the hand during automated assembly of a water pump.

- Hill and Sword (6) describe a hand-incorporating force with touch and proximity sensors, attached to a Unimate robot for material-handling applications. The sensors include a wrist force sensor, using compliant elements and potentiometers to sense the relative displacement of the hand, as well as touch and proximity sensors. This hand was used for the orderly packing of water pumps into a tote box: The Unimate moves rapidly to a previously programmed starting position, then successfully moves along three orthogonal axes, stopping when threshold forces along these axes are reached, finally releasing the pump in a tightly packed configuration in the tote box.
- Takeda (7) built a touch-sensing device for object recognition. The device consists of two parallel fingers, each with an array of 8-by-10 needles that are free to move in a direction normal to each finger and a potentiometer that measures the distance between the fingers. As the fingers close, the needles contact the object's contour in a sequence that depends on the shape of the object. Software was developed to use the sensed touch points to recognize simple objects, such as a cone.
- Johnston (8) describes the use of multiple photoelectric proximity sensors used to control the positioning of a manipulator. Lateral positioning of a hand was controlled by signals from two sensors to center the hand over the highest point of the object.
- Heginbotham, et al. (9) describes the use of a visual sensor to determine the identity, position, and orientation of flat workpieces, from a top-view image obtained by a television camera. The camera and a manipulator were mounted on a turret in the same fashion as lens objectives are mounted on a common turret of a microscope. After the identity, position, and orientation of each workpiece had been determined, the manipulator rotated into a position coaxial with the original optical axis of the camera lens and acquired the workpiece.
- At Hitachi Central Research Laboratory (10), prismatic blocks moving on a conveyor belt were viewed, one at a time, using a Vidicon television camera. A low-resolution image (64-by-64 pixels) was processed to obtain the outline of each block. A number of radius vectors from the center of area of the image to the outline were measured and processed by a minicomputer to determine the identity, position, and orientation of each block. The block was then picked up, transported, and stacked in an orderly fashion by means of a simple suction-cup hand whose motion was controlled by the minicomputer.
- Olsztyn, et al. (11) describes an experimental system which was devised to mount wheels on an automobile. The location of the studs on the hubs and the stud holes on the wheels were determined using a television camera coupled to a computer, and then a special manipulator mounted the wheel on the hub and engaged the studs in the appropriate holes. Although this experiment demonstrated the feasibility of a useful task, further development is needed to make this system cost-effective.
- Yachida and Tsuji (12) describe a machine-vision system, including a television camera coupled to a minicomputer, which was developed to recognize a variety of industrial parts, such as gasoline-engine parts, when they were viewed one at a time on a conveyor. Resolution of 128-by-128 elements digitized into 64 levels of gray scale were used. In lieu of the usual sequence of picture processing, extraction of relevant features, and recognition, the system uses predetermined part models that guide the comparison of the unknown part with stored models, suggesting the features to be examined in sequence and where each feature is located. This procedure reduced the amount of computation required. Further, by showing sample parts and indicating important features via an interactive display, an operator can quickly train the system for new objects; the system generates the new models automatically from the cues given by the operator. The system is said to recognize 20 to 30 complex parts of a gasoline engine. Recognition time and training time were 30 seconds and 7 minutes, respectively.
- Agin and Duda (13) describe a hardware/software system under minicomputer control developed to determine the identity, position, and orientation of each workpiece placed randomly on a table or on a moving conveyor belt. This system, using a Unimate industrial robot, acquires that workpiece and moves it to its destination. The electro-optical sensors employed include a solid-state 100-by-100 area-array camera and a solid-state 128-by-1 linear array camera. A workpiece is recognized by using either a method based on measuring the entire library of features ("nearest-reference" classification) or a method based on sequential measurement of the minimum number of features that can best distinguish one workpiece from the others ("decision-tree" classification). Selection of the distinguishing features for the second method is done automatically by simply showing a prototype to the viewing station of the system. The decision-tree classification method was applied to recognition of different workpieces, such as foundry bastings, water-pump parts, and covers of electrical boxes. The time required for the

system to build a new sequential tree after showing examples of objects, and the time for recognition of a given object is less than a fraction of a second on a small minicomputer. (Digital Equipment Corporation PDP 11/40.)

There still has not been widespread use of these new techniques in industry. However, solid-state television cameras and micro-computers have been rapidly descreasing in price and it appears possible at present to provide a useful visual sensing subsystem for approximately $5,000; the remaining hurdle is the cost of generating appropriate picture processing software and integrating the visual system with existing industrial manipulators.

RESEARCH ISSUES

There are numerous research issues that require serious study and attention in nascent robot technology. The basic issue is to develop a theory and understanding of manipulation sufficiently broad to encompass a wide variety of applications to material handling, assembly, and prosthesis. This is a complex area and has been very slow to develop. More current issues involve applied research aimed at the near term goals of implementing economically-viable manipulators for industrial use. These latter issues include the choice of alternatives for open loop or closed loop control of manipulation, safety considerations, and ease of programming. These issues are discussed in the following sections.

MODELS AND THEORY OF MANIPULATION

Material handling research and development using industrial robots has been conducted almost entirely by empirical and experimental means. Hardware configurations for robot manipulators and end-effectors crudely emulate simplified versions of the human arm, wrist, and hand with far fewer degrees of freedom and far less manipulative capability. It is true that engineering concepts in kinematics, dynamics, servomechanisms, sensors, electronic control, pneumatic, hydraulic and electrical activators, and so on, have been cleverly utilized in producing relatively high performance industrial robots and teleoperators. These machines can exceed the performance of the human arm and hand for some applications. They cannot, however, match the human in dexterity and in adaptability for a wide range of application. The development of a theory of manipulation is required that can lead to descriptive and analytic models of arm, wrist, and hand that are valid for both human and machine manipulation. With such models, designers can develop robots that are either adapted for more general purpose use or optimized for peak performance for a restricted class of tasks.

It should be noted that important work on subsets of the general problem has been proceeding, primarily in large universities and research laboratories, often directed at the goal of providing a scientific base for developing good prosthetic limbs. In a recent symposium held in Warsaw (14), a number of papers were presented, reporting on the results of research in dynamic and kinematic modeling of manipulators (15)(16), effects of strength and stiffness constraints on the control of manipulators (17), optimization of manipulator motions (18), and others.

Of particular importance is the need to develop some insight into the design of general purpose end-effectors. How many mechanical fingers do we need? How many degrees of freedom? What kind of sensors? How many are needed? Where placed? Should we add a microprocessor to make a "smart end-effector? Shall we dispense with mechanical fingers altogether and rely on easily-changeable specialized tools? At the very least, there is required a canonical classification of dexterous manipulative operations based on classes of tasks.

OPEN LOOP AND CLOSED LOOP CONTROL

As previously noted, the majority of present material-handling robots are used in an open loop control mode in well-structured environments. Objects to be manipulated must generally be carefully positioned and oriented by fixtures or other means. This is often too expensive to implement or causes intolerable delays.

The trend in manipulator design has been to continually improve performance by increasing both precision and speed of response as new requirements for manipulation arise, such as required for assembly processes. This trend follows the history of numerically controlled (NC) machines. Unfortunately, increasing the precision and speed of response is very costly. This trend has led to the following requirements: More rigid structures, thus requiring more powerful drives to accelerate the increased masses; position sensors with increased resolution (12 to 15 bits); faster-acting valves to improve stopping characteristics; more complex servo mechanisms (position, velocity, and pressure feedback) to ensure stability, and so on. This expensive approach is characteristic of all open-loop, feed-forward control systems. With the advent of economic visual and tactile servoing it has become timely to explore an alternative approach, namely a closed-loop feedback robot system in which manipulator trajectories are mediated by real-time contact and noncontact sensory feedback to achieve comparable speed and precision of performance with far less expensive manipulators.

There are thus two contending methods of approach for achieving desired performance: open-loop internally-controlled precision manipulation operating on highly-constrained (in position and orientation) objects, and closed-loop externally-controlled manipulation with far less constraints on positions and orientations of objects.

Research is required to determine the

applicability of each of these methods to the various classes of tasks.

SAFETY

The size and power of large robots make it mandatory to develop equipment, software, and procedures to ensure that human workers are not hurt and expensive machinery and workpieces are not damaged by any link of the fast-moving manipulator and its load.

It is not yet feasible to have constant surveillance by one or more television cameras (with associated computers) to ensure safety in all possible configurations and trajectories. The processing of pictures by scene analysis techniques is still in its infancy. At present, safety for humans can be partially assured by the use of fences, warning signs, pressure mats, proximity detectors and so on. For the next generation of adaptively-controlled manipulators, the trajectories of each link and of the load will not be precisely known a priori. It may be possible to predetermine volumes in space which define the outer limits of possible paths for each link and load for any given task during training, and thus by monitoring these volumes continuously with suitable sensors, avoid collisions (19)(20). This may require a separate microcomputer system, devoted to this purpose, independent of the other computer(s) controlling the main functions of the manipulator. Novel new approaches would be welcome.

TRAINING AND PROGRAMMING

The training and/or programming of a robot for a new task must be acceptably simple and rapid for the user to ensure acceptance in the factory. Training aids have been explored that include special input devices such as speech input (6), joystick controls that invoke coordinated simultaneous actions by all the manipulation links (6), and special software which automatically generates visual identification programs in a "training by showing" mode (12)(13).

A number of robot software programs and languages have been and are being developed (21) that are designed to simplify the training procedure and provide some editing facilities to reduce the time for modifications and debugging.

All of these programs are in a developmental state, and as yet there is no dominant program which more than one organization has adopted. Clearly it would be highly advantageous for all to arrive at some degree of standardization (similarly to the use of APT in NC machines) such that the various programs for manipulation being generated could be shared.

One inviting option for a good programming/training system is to provide a trained but nonprofessional user with a high-level interactive language with the capability of training a sensor-controlled manipulator system using high-level commands, such as "Pick up the box from the moving conveyor and transfer it to the platform". Obviously this implies a highly-advanced "intelligent" master program, able to understand the command, then able to interrogate the trainer to determine, unambiguously, the details implied in the command, and finally to assemble stored subprograms in an appropriate sequence to carry out the task.

A more conventional and far simpler option is to develop a high-level language and procedure (with good editing facilities) that will enable a professional programmer to assemble the required program for the task, with an interface designed to permit minor modifications and fine tuning by an unsophisticated user.

The latter option will most certainly be the first to be implemented by many. It is quite possible that a mixed strategy employing elements of both options will be attempted and the programming system will become more "intelligent" with time, as experience is gained in constructing intelligent programs.

REFERENCES

(1) R. H. Anderson, Programmable automation: The future of computers in manufacturing, Datamation, 18, 46 (1972).

(2) D. Nitzan and C. A. Rosen, Programmable automation, IEEE Transactions on Computers, C-25, 1259 (1976).

(3) C. A. Rosen and D. Nitzan, Use of sensors in programmable automation, to be published in Computer (1977).

(4) T. Goto, Compact packaging by robot with tactile sensors, Proc. 2nd. Int. Symp. on Industrial Robots, IIT Research Institute, Chicago, Illinois (1972).

(5) R. C. Bolles and R. Paul, The use of sensory feedback in a programmable assembly system, Stanford Artificial Intelligence Project, Memo. No. 220, Stanford University, Stanford, California (1973).

(6) C. A. Rosen, et al., Exploratory research in advanced automation, Rpts. 1 through 6, prepared by Stanford Research Institute under National Science Foundation Grant G138100X (December 1973 to December 1976).

(7) S. Takeda, Study of artificial tactile sensors for shape recognition--algorithm for tactile data input, Proc. 4th Int. Symp. on Industrial Robots, 199-208, Tokyo, Japan (1974).

(8) A. R. Johnston, Proximity sensor technology for manipulator end-effectors, Proc. 2nd. Conf. on Remotely Manned Systems, California Institute of Technology, Pasadena, California (1975).

(9) W. B. Heginbotham, et al., Visual feedback applied to programmable assembly machines, Proc. 2nd. Int. Symp. Industrial Robots, IIT Research Institute, Chicago, Illinois, 77-88 (May 1972).

(10) Hitachi Hand-Eye System, Hitachi Review, 22, No. 9, 362-365.

(11) J. T. Olsztyn, et al., An application of computer vision to a simulated assembly task, Proc. 1st. Int. Joint Conf. on Pattern Recognition, 505-513 (1973).

(12) M. Yachida and G. Tsuji, A machine vision for complex industrial parts with learning capacity, Proc. 4th Int. Joint Conf. on Artificial Intelligence, 819-826 (1975).

(13) G. J. Agin and R. O. Duda, SRI vision research for advanced industrial automation, Proc. 2nd. USA-Japan Computer Conf., 113-117 (1975).

(14) A. Morecki and K. Kedzior, editors, On the Theory and Practice of Robots and Manipulators, 2nd. CISM-IFT.MM Symp., WN-Polish Scientific Publishers, Warsaw, Poland (1976).

(15) A. Liegois, et al., Mathematical models of interconnected mechanical systems, presented at symp. ref. 14 (1976).

(16) B. Shimano and B. Roth, Ranges of motion of manipulators, presented in symp. ref. 14 (1976).

(17) W. J. Book, Characterization of strength and stiffness constraints on manipulator control, presented at symp. ref. 14 (1976).

(18) M. K. Ozgoren, Optimization of manipulator motions, presented at symp. ref. 14 (1976).

(19) T. Lozano-Perez, The design of a mechanical assembly system, Artificial Intelligence Laboratory, M.I.T., Cambridge, Massachusetts, Report AI-TR-397 (1976).

(20) B. Dobrotin and R. Lewis, A practical manipulator system, to be published in IJCAI (1977).

AUTOMATIC ASSEMBLY IN BATCH PRODUCTION

A. d'Auria

OSAI — Olivetti Sistemi per l'Automazione Industriale — Ivrea

ABSTRACT

In light manufacturing industries, assembly operations play an important economic role.
The development of advanced technologies and the automation of manufacturing processes has led to ever decreasing prices for components while assembly operations continue to be carried out manually.
It may thus happen that it is cheaper to manufacture a part than it is to assemble it. The traditional methodes of mechanising assembly operations consist in rotating table or transfer machines of very high cost and suitable for high volume productions. The main obstacle to the wide diffusion of the traditional automation equipment is its rigidity; this makes it unsuitable in the presence of varying production rates, product modifications or product diversification for different markets. Further in real industrial environments, one often finds small and medium sized production volumes which require a job-lot organization rather than a continuous-flow one. To solve these problems one needs flexible automation ecuipment which may be readily and easily re-tooled to pass from one product to another.
Modern second generation computerised industrial robot technology enables this important problem area to be faced. However, to develop a new technology one must not only design and manufacture new equipment; but one must also study the problems connected with the introduction of such equipment in the production process. In the following pages we will therefore attempt to analise the peculiar characteristics of the assembly process to determine conditions which must be respected during the design of the products and the organizational implications which drive from the introduction of such equipment.
Finally we will examine the information flows which interest the assembly process.

2. Assembly from a technical point of view

Let us suppose that the input to the assembly process be n piles of random bulk parts and that the output be m assembled units.
The transformation process, passing from input to output, requires the orientation of each component in a suitable way and placing it in a time-ordered sequence with respect to the others, according to well-defined trajectories which are a function of the geometry of the parts and of the structure of the unit being assembled. In an automatic process it is convenient that the trajectories be as simple as possible; in particular, it is useful if each component can be assembled independently and the assembly direction is unique.
In this way it is possible to define an assembly cycle in terms of successive overlays, reducing to a minimum the number of degrees of freedom of the parts manipulator.
A particular case of assembly is found in selective fitting; in this case, we must first measure a geometric dimension of the component and then fit it to a second one picked from amongst several classes of pre-selected parts. It is thus necessary that the output of the measuring instrument be fed to the system so as to determine the successive steps.

3. Assembly from a organizational point of view

The organization of an assembly line implies a flow of materials which guarantees the arrival of the right components at the right moment and in the right place so as to ensure the required output of products both in type and in quantity.

The assembly organization may be either serial or parallel. It is called serial when in one station or work-place all the components required to form the unit are assembled. The organization is said to be parallel when in each of the m stations of the line one and only one component is added.
A serial organization is suitable to small and medium volume productions, while parallel systems are suitable for high volume productions. A significant parameter of an assembly process is the number of components to be handled. With a parallel organization, if the number of components and therefore of stations is high, the overall reliability of the system, which corresponds to the product of the reliability of each station, is low. On the other hand, if a system is capable of handling only a limited number of components it is necessary to break down the product to be assembled into a certain number of sub-assemblies. Such sub-assemblies must be connected in such a way ad to avoid them falling apart during the successive unloading operations. This also is a consideration to bear in mind during the design phase.

4. Considerations on the quality of the components used in the assembly process

Modern assembly processes are bases on Fordism, that is, on the principle, applied for the first time by Henry Ford in the production of automobiles, of the interchangeability of component parts by means of the appropriate use of tolerances.
Further, mass production processes guarantee that the parts be on average of sufficient quality but the statistical control methods which are normally applied result in the acceptance of lots which contain a percentage, be it a small one, of faulty parts. While this fact is perfectly acceptable in manual assembly, since it is the assembly line worker which carries out a final selection when the part is not suitable, it causes a series of problems and of stops in processes based on automatic systems of the deterministic type. This fact is particularly serious in parallel systems; in these, each reject in one of the m stations may prejudice the correct functioning of all the succeeding ones. Attempts have been made to eliminate this problem by placing, after each assembly station, a station which controls the assembly operations; this station blocks the completion of the sub-assembly in the successive stations of the assembly line.
Even with this solution, there is the risk of drastically reducing the overall productivity of the system.
Modern computerized systems for serial assembly work tend to resolve this problem by applying to the grippers suitable general-purpose force and position sensors; these enable the system to check that each phase of the assembly process has been carried out successfully. Further, should this not happen, it is possible to activate suitable emergency procedures (eventually of an interactive nature) to enable the system to terminate the operation successfully.
Naturally these sensors and the relative procedures work only when the fault in the part makes it impossible to assemble it.
Whenever the defect is of a nature which has no bearing on the assembly process (eg esthetic type of defects) it will be necessary to carry out controls on the output of the system.

5. Parts feeding

Normally, in a production process, the parts are produced in lots and stored in a random bulk manner. Only in a few cases are the components supplied ordered, in special containers, e.g. integrated circuits or reeled components.
Normally however, the storing of parts in an ordered manner may be discarded for the following reasons:

a) the final operations of the production cycle randomize the components (heat treatments, surface treatments etc)

b) the high number and cost of special purpose containers

c) the difficulty of handling the circulation of a high number of specific containers.

In manual assembly processes the work-stations are therefore fed from piles of random bulk parts; the worker, coordinating his movements under the control of his sight and touch organs, pre-orients each part before assembling it.
The elementary steps of the process consist of separating one and only one piece from the pile and successively orienting it in space during the closing-in phase so as to have it in the most suitable position to facilitate the final "placing" trajectory.
If one attempts to design an anthropomorphic type of system, one is faced with technological and, more importantly, economic difficulties. Some interesting attempts have been made in important research institutes, but these were aimed

at relatively simple cases of manipulation of prismatic objects.
On the other hand however, the real industrial environment requires equipment capable of repeating thousands of times the same cycle and with adeguate performance.
We feel therefore that the solution must entail the design of general-purpose orientation devices capable of operating off line at high speed and feeding to the assembly system proper, the parts in an ordered manner and in specially designed containers.
The possibility of rapidly converting the orientation device from the handling of one component to another, would enable this work to be carried out at the input to the assembly machine; this could reduce to a minimum the number of specific containers required.

6. Information flow in assembly processes

From what stated in the preceeding paragraphs, it may be seen that in each of the steps in which we have subdivided the automatic assembly process, it is necessary to add to the components being assembled a certain amount of information.
This concept may be summarized in the following way:

- Random parts + information on required orientation = ordered parts
- Ordered parts + information on the trajectories = set of elementary assembly operations
- Set of elementary operations + information on their sequence = assembly cycle
- Assembly cycle + operating conditions information fed back from the system = historical date.

For a serial system fed from a general purpose orientation device,the various steps of the process may be represented by the following block diagrams.

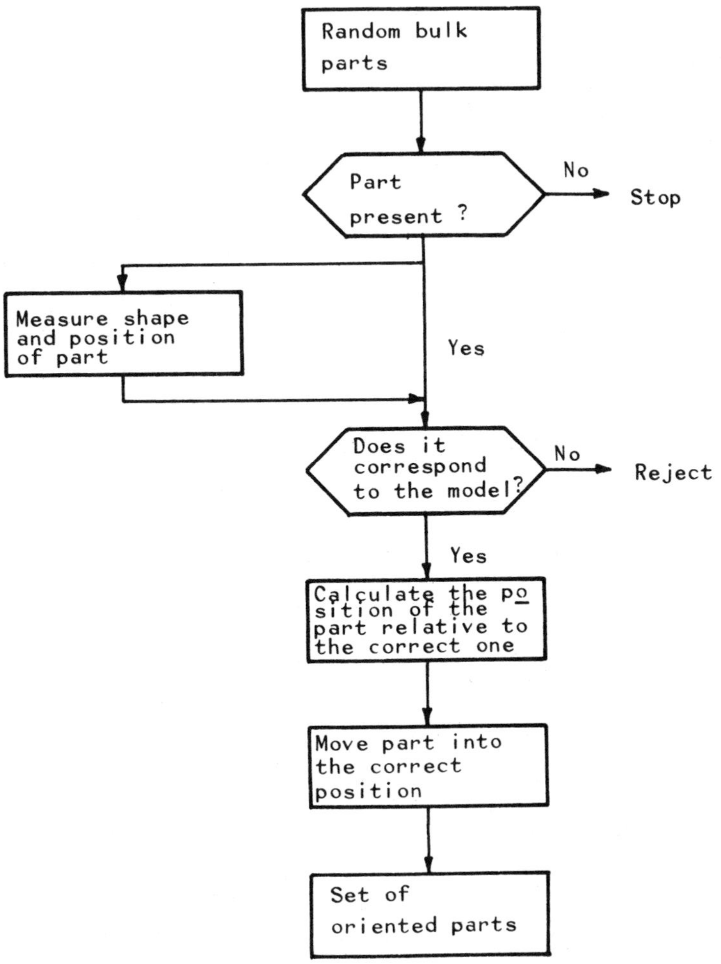

Fig. 1 Orientation device

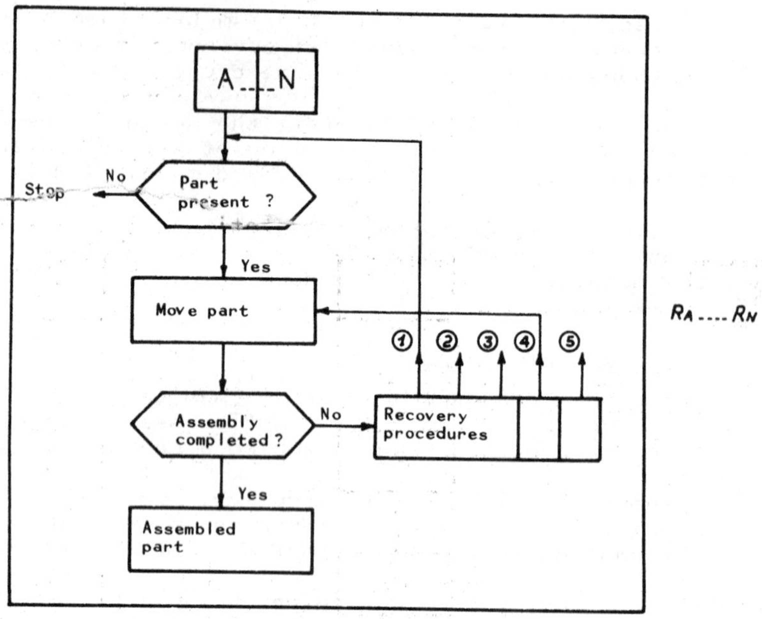

Fig. 2 Set of the elementary assembly operations

A, B .., N = Parts feeding (preoriented)

Ra, .., Rn = Elementary assembly routines for each part (controlled by the sensors).

We may have several recovery procedures:

(1) = Reject part A and try again

(2) = The system goes in stop

(3) = Unload partly assembled unit and start new cycle from the beginning

(4) = Shift a certain distane in a certain direction and try again.

(n) =

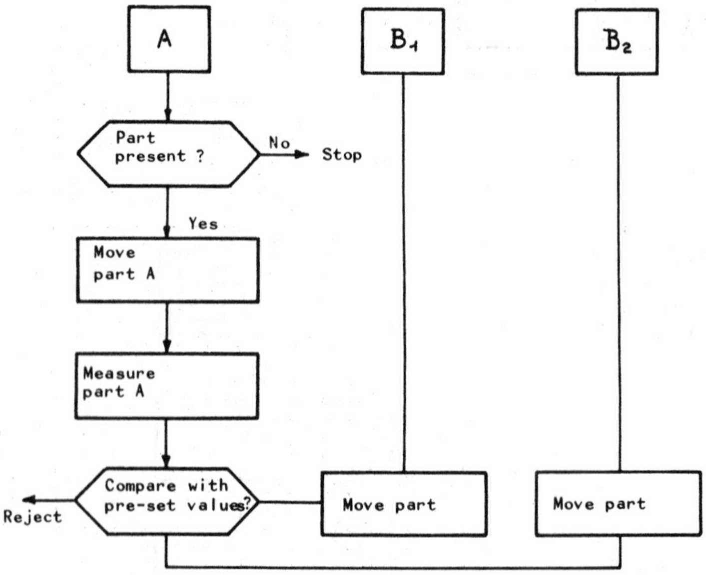

Fig. 3 Selective fitting cycle

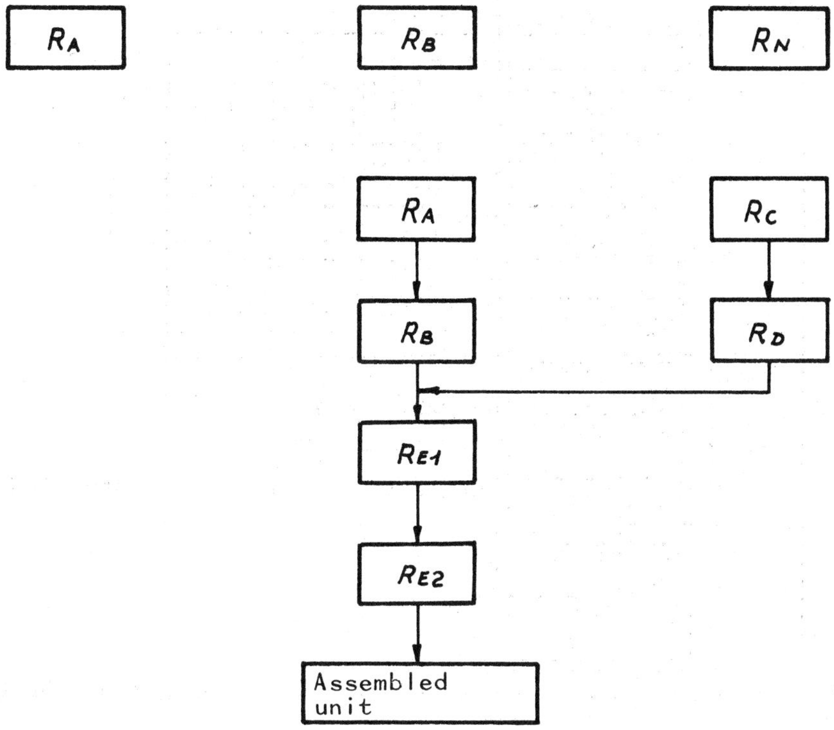

Fig. 4 Assembly cycle

The set of elementary assembly operations integrated with informations about the secuence of operation yeld the right assembly cycle. Such sequence is not univocable determinated because the branch of each recovery procedures (fig.2) can produce different path and then different cycle. The artificial intelligence techniques may help in solving the problem of finding the optimal strategy.

Finally, at the running time it is possible to log historical data about the system behaviour

Number of assembled units
Number of rejected units
Number and type of faulty parts
Number of recovery calls
Stops of the system (No feeded parts)

A SYSTEM RECOVERING METHOD FROM TRACKING CONFUSIONS IN CONVEYOR SYSTEM

H. Takenouchi*, S. Miyamoto*, S. Seki* A. ShimizuM. Sasaki**, and S. Ishikawa****

**Systems Development Laboratory, Hitachi, Ltd., 1-280 Higashi-koigakubo, Kokubunji, Tokyo, Japan*
***Taga Works, Hitachi, Ltd., 1-1-1 Higashitago, Hitachi, Ibaragi, Japan*

ABSTRACT

The most serious problem of a conveyor system which includes a variety of material handling machines is confusion of tracking. In the present paper, a method to recover the system from the confused status, which makes the tracking function recover with the minimal downtime, is described.

INTRODUCTION

In manufacturing factories, the modernization of material handling facilities seems to be left behind those of assembling equipments and testing systems. Lately the modernization of material handling systems has become of major interest.

A variety of material handling machines have been developed, and moreover many studies are continued to control all the machines included in the system systematically and effectively. Each material handling machine, in general, treats many objects of various types, and its handling process varies depending on the type of object. Therefore it is needed to track all the objects to be processed.

The most serious problem of those systems is confusion of tracking. Once a certain fault which disturbs the tracking function occur, its influence will cover wide range of the system, that is, many objects will be processed inadequately.

In order to solve the problem a method to recover the system from the confused status has been developed, which makes the tracking function recover with the minimal downtime. This method identifies the fault which has caused on the confusion, seizes the actual status of the system being based on the identified fault, then corrects tracking information so that it agrees with the actual status.

The fault identification algorithm and the procedure of the system recovering are described with an example of conveyor system. The method developed is expected to contribute to the complete automatization of conveyor systems.

STRUCTURE OF CONVEYOR SYSTEM AND ITS PROBLEM

Conveyor systems consist of some material handling machines, and each of the machines is connected to some of the others through conveyor. Generally they include many confluence and branching points. Computers in the systems recognize the type of object to be processed through tracking and send each of the material handling machines the control directive. A model of conveyor system is shown in Fig. 1.

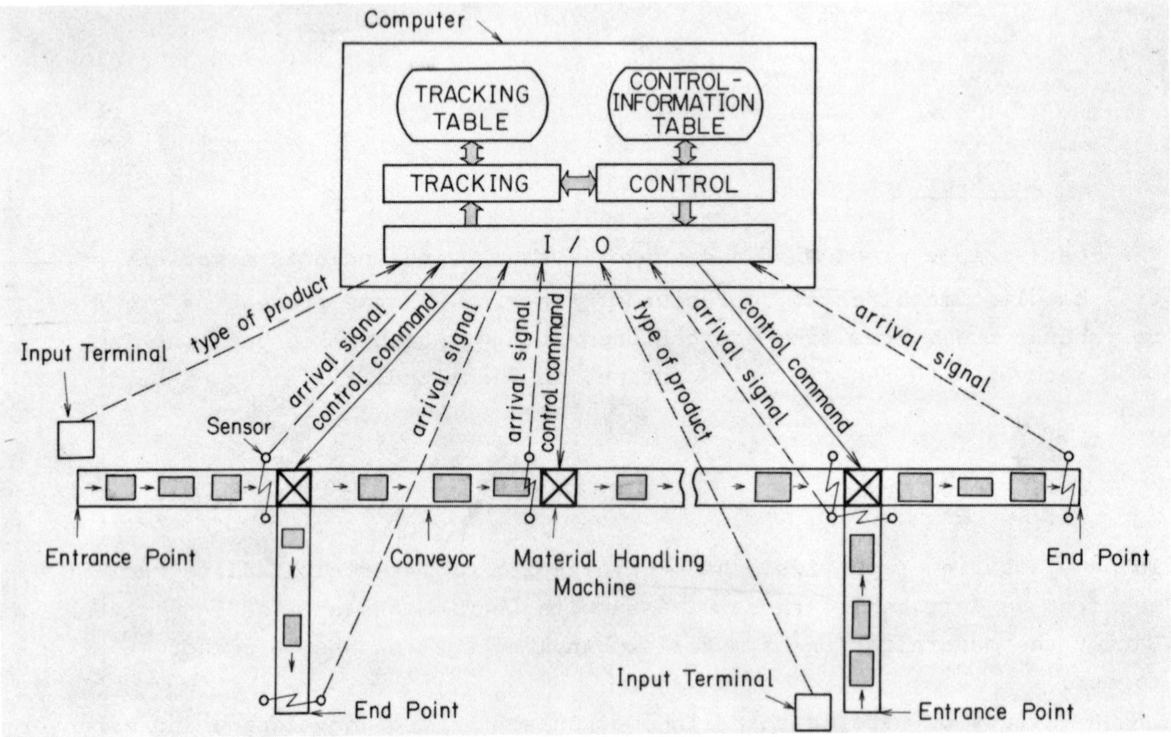

Fig. 1. A model of conveyor system

At each carrying-in points there is an input terminal, e.g., a key board or an industrial eye, which sends the computer the type of object when it is carried in. As the type of object is sent from an input terminal, the computer resisters it in tracking table, which is the file to memorize the order of objects at each section of conveyor. At each control point of material handling machines there is a sensor which senses arrival of object and sends the computer an arrival signal. Then the computer picks out the corresponding type of object from the tracking table, decides the control directive being based on the recognized type of object and the situation of the system, sends the control directive to the material handling machine, and renews the tracking table. The material handling machine processes the object according to the control directive sent from the computer.

Because the identification of object is based on tracking, once the tracking function is disturbed by a certain cause, incorrect data will be picked up and the tracking table will be renewed incorrectly. Consequently even a trivial fault may affect on the wide range of the system, then the system must be forced to be down. This is one of the most serious problems involved in the conveyor system. In order to maximize the availability of those systems a new method for recovering the systems has been developed. In the following the details of the method is shown.

FAULT IDENTIFICATION ALGORITHM

Strategy for Fault Identification

In order to minimize the system's downtime the fault must be identified while the system is in operation. According to this way the fault identification is completed by inputting only the type of object at some fixed points, so automatization of the fault identification may be accomplished easily.

In the model investigated the input terminals are placed only at the carrying-out points, however, the number of the input terminals is the more the time needed for the fault identification may become the shorter.

Classification of Faults

The faults in the conveyor system which cause on the confusion of tracking are as follows:

A. fault of sensor
 (1) excess of sensing
 (2) missing of sensing

B. fault about transit of objects
 (3) falling out of object
 (4) exchanging of order between two objects

C. faults of material handling machine
 (5) fault of confluence direction
 (6) fault of branching direction

D. faults about input
 (7) mistake of recognition of object
 (8) missing of input
 (9) input error

E. faults of data transmission

Formulation of Tracking Confusion

The phenomenon of tracking confusion brought about by each fault is expressed with the relation between tracking information and actual order of the objects. Now let's consider the conveyor system model shown in Fig. 2. The route of conveyor is divided into 5 sections (A - E) by every confluence point and branching point.

Notations are defined as follows:

T(S,k) : type of object picked up from tracking table for the k th arrival signal at the end point of section S.

$R(S,k)$: actual type of object for the k th arrival signal at the end point of section S.

$I(S_1,S_2,k)$: this denotes the tracking data for the k th arrival signal of section S_1 correspond those for the $I(S_1,S_2,k)$ th arrival signal of section S_2.

$P(T(S,k))$: set of the sections which the object corresponding to $T(S,k)$ has passed.

The event that tracking is normal is expressed as follows:

$$\forall S\in\{A,B,C,D,E\}\forall k \quad R(S,k)=T(S,k) \qquad (1)$$

Conversely

$$\exists S\in\{A,B,C,D,E\}\exists k \quad R(S,k)\neq T(S,k) \qquad (2)$$

means tracking is confusing.

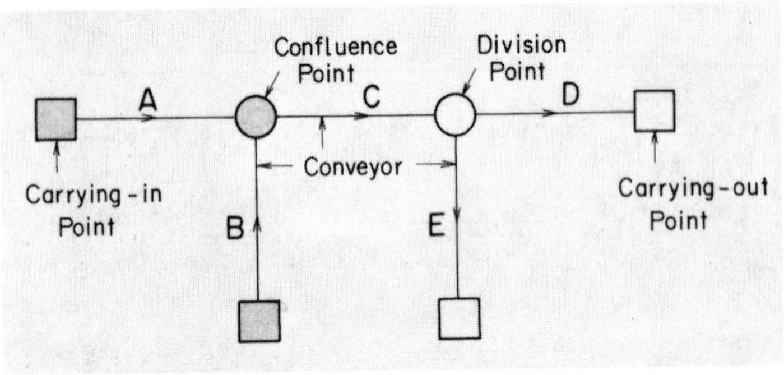

Fig. 2. the example of conveyor layout

Now let's consider what phenomenon is occurred by the preceding faults. Following example is about the case that an excess of sensing has happened at the end point of section A. Let the arrival signal corresponding to the fault was the m th one.

The phenomenon at section A is denoted by next expressions.

$$R(A,m)=\emptyset \qquad (3)$$
$$\forall k>m \quad R(A,k)=T(A,k-1) \qquad (4)$$
$$\forall k<m \quad R(A,k)=T(A,k) \qquad (5)$$

At section C it is denoted as follows:

$$\forall k\geq I(A,C,m) \quad B\in P(T(C,k+1))\rightarrow R(C,k)=T(C,k+1) \qquad (6)$$
$$\forall k\geq I(A,C,m) \quad B\in P(T(C,k))\cap A\in P(T(C,k+1))\rightarrow R(C,k)=T(A,I(C,A,k+1)-1) \qquad (7)$$
$$\forall k\geq I(A,C,m) \quad A\in P(T(C,k))\cap A\in P(T(C,k))\rightarrow R(C,k)=T(C,k) \qquad (8)$$
$$\forall k<I(A,C,m) \quad R(C,k)=T(C,k) \qquad (9)$$

At section D and section E, they are approximately as same as about section C. In section B tracking has been kept normal.

Similarly, all the tracking confusions of the conveyor systems can be formulated.

Fault Identification Algorithm

In order to execute the fault identification effectively the method was adopted that gradually deletes the faults conflicting with the actual phenomenon. In the following the fault identification algorithm is described. Let P_k show the phenomenon brought about by fault C_k.

Preparation 1 : Make $\overline{P_k}$, negation of P_k, for every k.
Preparation 2 : Clarify all the inclusion relations between each P .

STEP 1 : $X \leftarrow \{C_1, C_2, \cdots, C_n\}$
$Y \leftarrow \{P_1, P_2, \cdots, P_m\}$

STEP 2 : Discriminate whether $\overline{P_k} \in Y$ is included in the actual phenomenon. If not go to STEP 6.

STEP 3 : For all $\overline{P_l} \in \overline{P_k}$, if there is $C_i \in X$ for which $C_i \rightarrow P_l$, delete C_i from X.

STEP 4 : Delete all $\overline{P_l} \in \overline{P_k}$ from Y.

STEP 5 : If there is $\overline{P_i} \in Y$ for which $\forall C_k \in X\ C_k \rightarrow P_i$ or $\forall C_k \in X\ C_k \rightarrow \overline{P_i}$, delete $\overline{P_i}$ from Y.

STEP 6 : Repeat from STEP 2. to STEP 6. for all $\overline{P_k} \in Y$.

STEP 7 : Repeat from STEP 2. to STEP 6. for every input untill the number of the remaining items of X reduces to 1. At last the fault is identified.

SYSTEM RECOVERING METHOD

The system recovering method developed ammends tracking table so that it agrees with the actual phenomenon. This method is executed by following steps.

STEP 1 : Switch over the operation mode of the system from normal one to abnormal one.
STEP 2 : Identify the fault which caused on the confusion by the preceding fault identification algorithm.
STEP 3 : Correct tracking table so that it agrees with the actual order of the objects.
STEP 4 : Return the operation mode to normal.

In the above steps the abnormal operation mode means the mode in which the type of object is input at each carrying-out point while the system is in operation. After identifying the fault, the tracking table is corrected, at STEP 3 , by means of simulation based upon the identified fault and the present tracking table. The system recovering is completed at STEP 4 .

APPLICATION

The system recovering method developed has been applied on a certain mass production factory of household electric appliances. The conveyor system of this factory is shown in Fig. 3. Confluence of products is controlled by the local controller without identifying the type of product. So tracking is done from the industrial eye to each carrying-out point. The material handling machines are controlled so that every product is carried in one of the warehouses which is settled in advance corresponding to the type of product and they are palletized according to the corresponding palletizing pattern.

In this system the detection of tracking confusion is performed by human inspectors. They detect it through the event that one assortment storage line, in which the products of same type must be stored, includes plural types of products or that the product which must be carried in another warehouses is carried in. Input of the type of product when tracking is confused is done at the point of A,B,and C.

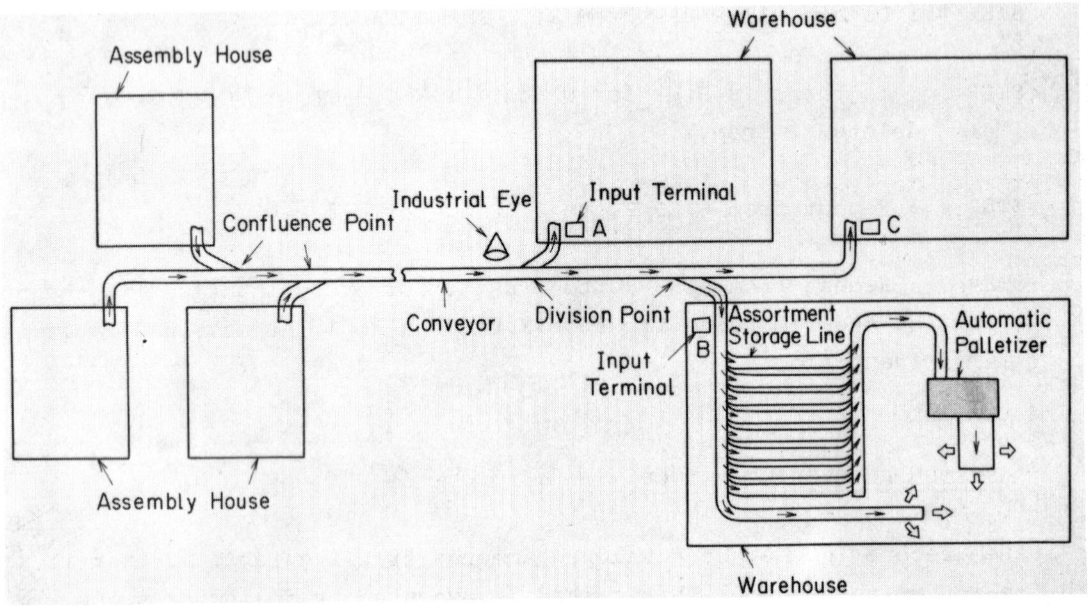

Fig. 3. Layout of the application system

The average downtime of the coveyor system was about 84 minutes a day. According to the use of the developed method it has reduced to about 19 minutes a day. The method developed has successfully contributed to the increase of the system's availability from 82 % to 96 %.

CONCLUSION

The system recovering method of conveyor system based on fault identification has been developed and applied on a certain mass production factory. The characteristic of the method is that only inputting at some fixed points is needed for the system recovering. According to this characteristic, even in the case the input is left to operators, the decrease of the availability of the conveyor systems can be minimized, moreover, if the input can be performed automatically it will become nearly equal to 0. In the preceding factory, the system's availability has increased by 14 %.

The method is expected to be utilized for the purpose of the realization of completely automated conveyor system.

ADVANTAGES AND CONDITIONS FOR A DIRECT MEASUREMENT OF THE WORKPIECE-GEOMETRY ON NC-MACHINE TOOLS

T. Pfeifer and A. Fürst

Werkzeugmaschinenlabor, TH Aachen, Germany

SUMMARY

The present development stage of NC-machine tools and progress made in the field of 3-D-measurement techniques apparently permit a measurement of the manufactured product-geometry directly on the machine tool itself. This is not only technically possible but also economically feasible. Based on the measurement of the operating accuracy of machine tools and the developments made in the field of 3-D-measurement techniques, CNC techniques and more recent measurement methods, this paper deals with the direct measurement on machine tools itself.

INTRODUCTION

The functional safety and suitability of the products manufactured on machine tools is governed primarily by the geometry of the finished work-piece. For years, it has been the common aim of all manufacturing industry to have quality control as close as possible to or integrated within the manufacturing process. Then, only by a direct feed-back of measured quality parameters, the time and economical disadvantages of the classical "quality control after processing" in manufacturing processes can be avoided (Ref. 1, 2). In medium and small lot manufacturing process - this is the range being handled here - production control during the process is aimed at or has already been rea-lised with the help of the following strategies:

1. Workpieces with simple geometries, for example rotatory-symmetrical parts, are checked for their per-manence in dimensions with special process intermittent or on-line devides. The measurement values are processed in an automatic control system in such a way that the deviations of the workpiece dimen-sions are minimized.
2. In geometrically oriented AC-systems (ACG) the static and kinematic parameters of the production machines are monitored with suit-able sensors and high precision distance measurement systems, - e.g. the laser interferometer - and fed into an automatic control system that corrects the machine parameter influencing the geometry. (Ref. 3)
3. In flexible interlinked manufac-turing systems measurement stations are built in the material flow between the separate processing stations. In order to guarantee a fast measurement and information feed back the use of automatic 3-D-measurement machines operating on an NC-basis as measurement station is now being experimented upon. A wellknown example is the Prisma II-processing link, which was developed in the DDR (Ref. 1).

Among these strategies, the first mentioned one is closest to the integrated quality control. It may, however, be considered to be an economical solution for only certain machine types - those with a restric-ted production spectrum, as for example grinding and turning machines. The measurement and control devices normally employed are expensive and are meant for determining specific, simple and mostly one dimensional characteristic quantities of work-pieces - such as the diameter.
Today geometrically oriented AC-Systems can only be employed where precision of the workpiece geometry is given the highest priority. Only in such cases can the software efforts for the setting up process models to describe relationship between the measured process parameters and their effects on the nominal geometry be justified. The integration of general purpose measurement machines or 3-D-measurement machines in flexible manufacturing systems is preferred to the other strategies because of the versitality of parts to be examined. Arguements speaking against the realisation of the third

strategy are the high investment costs for 3-D-measurement machines on the one side and the error influence resulting from reclamping of the workpiece between the separate measurement and machining stations on the other.

In the following chapter a model for a process intermittent workpiece measurement conducted on a combined NC-machine-tool and measuring machine will be discussed. With this configuration most disadvantages of the three above mentioned strategies can be avoided.

CONDITIONS FOR A DIRECT WORKPIECE MEASUREMENT

Concept for the Realisation of a combined NC-Machine-Tool and Measuring Machine

The computer controlled 3-D-measurement machines, that are available in the market have much similarity with the NC or CNC machine tools with regard to their mechanical set-up, their motion axes and also their control systems. They differ essentially in the precision of their slideways and measuring systems and also that in place of a tool, 1-D, 2-D or 3-D measuring probes are used. The positioning of these probes in the operating area of the measuring machine resembles the positioning of tools. The positioning is mostly computer-aided and in accordance with a programme oriented to the nominal geometry. The similarity in technologies leads to the suggestion of attaching the probe in the place of a tool in the revolver system of a NC machine and conducting a process-intermittent workpiece measurement directly on the machine tool. The geometrical data so obtained can be processed in a control loop and used for workpiece correction.

Figure 1 shows an example of a NC-machining and measuring-center already realized. The machine is used in the automobile industry for reworking of chassis models. However, it is to be observed, that this is not a conventional milling-machine but a high precision one that is only employed for operations that require a low machine load.

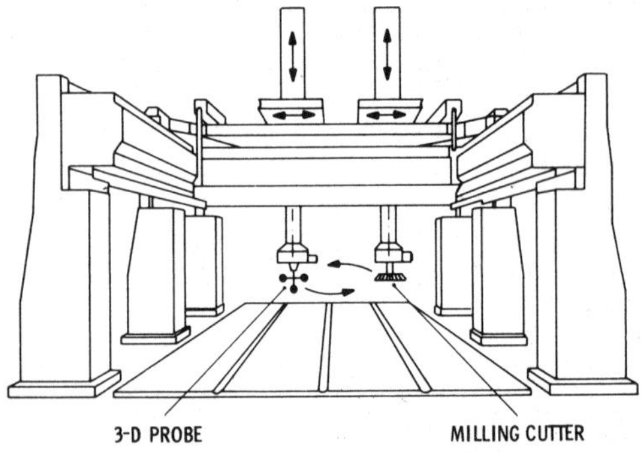

Fig. 1. Structure of a combined NC-machining and measuring-center

In order to conduct process intermittent measurement of prismatic workpieces such as casings with conventional NC-machine-tools, two basic requirements are to be fulfilled:

- availability of suitable 3-D-measuring probes that can be used under normal operating conditions of machine-tools
- existence of a sufficiently accurate measurement reference to determine the probe position in space.

While the first requirement is widely catered to by the measuring probes available in the market (see chapter 4) the second requirement is to be fulfilled by special algorithms that can be coupled to the CNC of the machine tool by means of software.

One possibility to solve this problem, as being currently worked upon at the Werkzeugmaschinenlabor, TH Aachen, is sketched in Fig. 2.

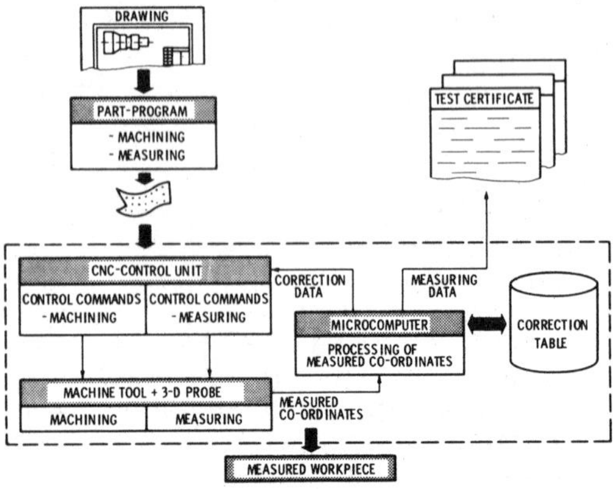

Fig. 2. Model of on-line integration of quality control

The basis of this model is the orientation of the probe motion to the machine measurement systems on the one hand and the correction of erroneous coordinate values of the machine measurement systems with the help of a correction matrix on the other. The correction matrix can - for example - be stored in a ROM (Read Only Memory) of a microcomputer. The correction matrix is a mathematical simulation of the systematic components of the volumetric positioning error of the unloaded machine-tool that have determined with the aid of external measurement systems. Random errors, - arising for example through the invluence of friction in the slideways -, can also be described by mathematical statistics, due to their nature however, they cannot be considered in a strategy for error compensation.

With the concept to compensate the systematic, positioning error in space that for example, consist of errors in the machine measurement systems, straightness errors and errors in orthogonality of the slideways, it is possible to realise a measurement-reference basis by means of the machine measurement system itself. This enables a process-intermittent measurement of complex workpiece geometries directly on the machine-tool. According to the measurement strategy used, process intermittent measurement of workpiece geometry may be understood as measurement between different operations on the same workpiece - e.g. between rough and fine machining - or as control of single workpieces chosen at random from a product series. The workpiece is measured directly on the unloaded machine without reclamping it.

If the actual measured values of the workpiece geometry are fed into a correction loop in the CNC, it will be possible to recognise many process specific errors of the system. "Workpiece-Machine-Tool" at their source and correct them during finishing. Examples of such errors are wear and presetting errors of tool as well as statical and dynamical deformations of the whole system (Fig. 3). In this manner the operation uncertainty of numerically controlled machines is considerably improved.

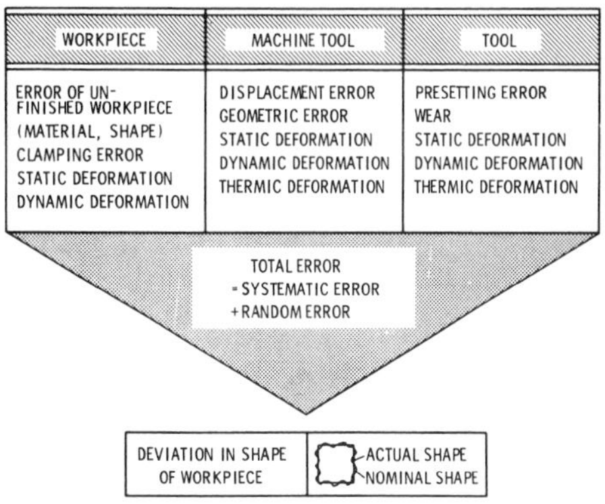

Fig. 3. Geometric error of workpiece resulting from the total error of Workpiece-Machine Tool-Tool

A model description of the combination NC-machine-tool and measuring-machine is thus provided. Available reference measurement systems for determining volumetric positioning errors of machine tool, the mathematical illustration in matrix form of these errors and the prerequisites of suitable probes and measurement strategies will be explained next.

Formulation of solutions to realise the model

As already mentioned, it is necessary to have external reference measurement systems or length standards for determining the volumetric positioning error of a machine-tool in order to set up the correction matrix. The reference measurement systems must be able to distinguish between random and systematic errors. Due to wear the mechanical errors of machine components (slideways, bearings) undergo changes with time so that the correction matrix must be set up and updated with the 3-D positioning error regularly and not just once. This may be done either by self-calibrating the measuring and operating machine or a repeated measurement of the machine tool.

In order to obtain an economical solution, the reference measurement systems must on the one hand, be characterised by a high degree of automation. On the other hand suitable probes and measuring strategies for workpiece measurement on the operating machine must be available.

Measurement of systematic volumetric positioning error

According to the present developments in measurement techniques, a length standard based on laser technology to determine the volumetric positioning error of a machine tool may be utilized. It would be ideal if a 3-D comparison apparatus were available. However, due to the lack of such a system, it is necessary to determine the individual components of the systematic positioning error in space and then combine these values with mathematical methods to obtain the total positioning error.

For this purpose, the positioning error in each numerically controlled axis will be determined separately using a laser measurement system. This is a double-frequency laser interferometer, that serves as a suitable length standard because of its known advantages. The impulses from the electronic evaluation unit of the laser interferometer (actual values) are coupled together with the impulses from the machine measuring system or NC-control unit (nominal values) by means of an electronic unit and then fed into a small scale computer (Fig. 4). With these input signals the computer is able to calculate the actual positioning error.

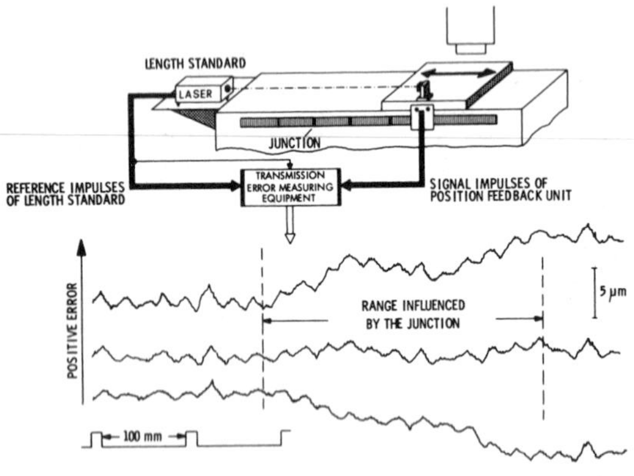

Fig. 4. Measurement of an incremental position feedback unit

Furthermore with the aid of the small scale computer, it is possible to distinguish between systematic and random error components by applying statistical methods (Ref. 4). The systematic error components can be intermediately stored and further examined with a Fourier-Analyzer so as to enable a mathematical illustration of the results.

The error components of the measurement systems and controls can be accurately determined using the method described above. However, the influence of the geometrical error of the machine still remains uncertain. The total positioning error in space can be determined by additionally measuring the straightness parallel and orthogonality errors of the slideways. With these additional measurements the error component can be assigned to their causes and thus the total error can be calculated. The example shown in Fig. 5 describes the effect of errors in the slideways on the volumetric error of a particular motion. The components $\Delta x, \Delta y, \Delta z, \Delta\alpha, \Delta\beta, \Delta\gamma$ are due to the straightness and orthogonality errors as well as the yaw of the machine elements (tool-holder, workpiece-table) about their respective axes. An addition of these components results in a volumetric error vector given by:

$$F = P_B(x,y,z,\alpha,\beta,\gamma) - P'_B(x+\Delta x,\ y+\Delta y,\ z+\Delta z,\ \alpha+\Delta\alpha,\ \beta+\Delta\beta,\ \gamma+\Delta\gamma).$$

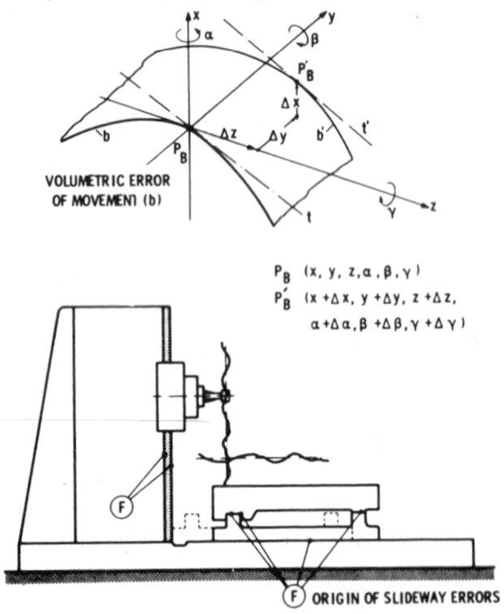

Fig. 5. Effects of slideway errors on the motion of a 3-D-machining and measuring center

There are two laser measurement systems available for determining the geometrical errors of a motion. Both systems fulfill the requirements made on a reference measurement system with respect to measuring accuracy, automation of measurement data acquisition and measurement data processing. The systems are listed below:

- A straightness laser measurement system (Tooling-Laser), that uses the laser beam as the reference line for measuring the straightness according to the height method (Ref. 5). A position sensitive photo-diode is fixed to the movable machine part (Tool clamp workpiece table) and converts the relative displacement between movable part and reference beam to signals proportional to this displacement. Measurements of orthogonality can be made by bending the beam by 90° using a calibrated Penta-prism.

- The double frequency laser interferometer together with a special straightness optic (Wollaston-prism and double plane mirror reflector) is also used for straightness measurement according to the height method. Measurements of orthogonality may also be conducted with this equipment (Ref. 6)

We preferably use the Tooling-Laser instead of the double frequency laser interferometer because of the following advantages that characterise it:

- simultaneous measurement in two axes orthogonal to the laser beam
- measuring length upto 15 m are possible
- not very sensitive to vibration
- insensitive to beam interrupt
- simple allignment
- easy handling, particularly during squareness measurements. The squareness in 3 orthogonal axes in space can be determined, simultaneous to the straightness measurement, by just 2 positions of the laser head (Fig. 6).

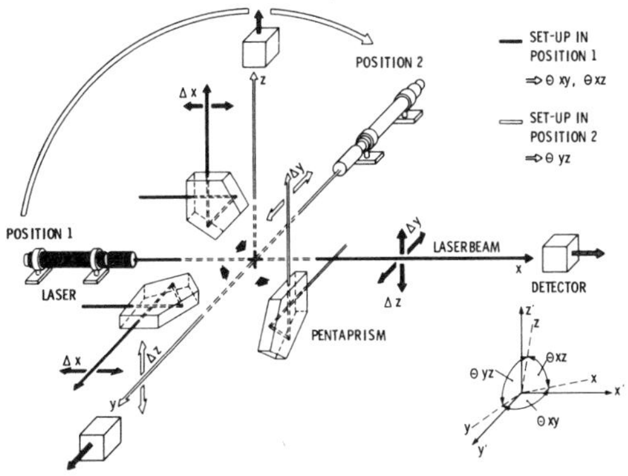

Fig. 6. Evaluation of out-of-straightness in 3 orthogonal axes

The further development of the electronic evaluation unit and improvements in the optical components of the system have contributed to improving this well-known measurement apparatus, so that currently straightness measurements can be conducted with an accuracy of 1,5 μm/m (Ref.7).

The evaluation unit of the measurement system delivers computer compatible output signals that are processed and documented by the small-scale computer in the on-line mode.

The results of the squareness and straightness measurements obtained by using this system on the operating and measuring machine described in chapter 2 are shown in Fig. 7.

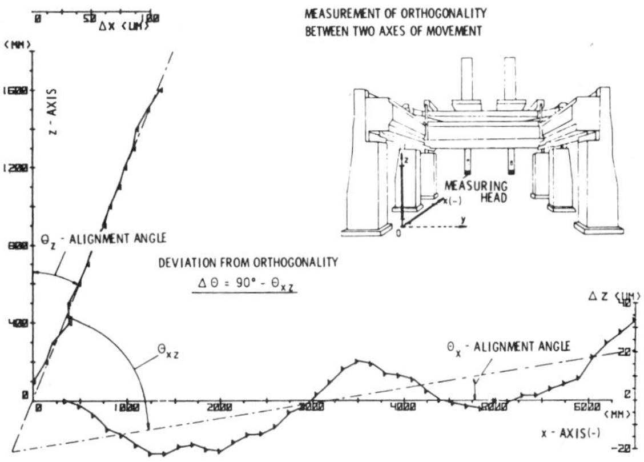

Fig. 7. Measurement of the orthogonal error between two axes of movement (measuring system: Tooling Laser)

The positioning errors determined with the system described are specific to the machine. Beside these errors there are other error influences noticeable in NC-machine tools that are caused by the control system (interpolation errors) or by the interaction between machine components (trailing errors). The recently introduced Laser Transducer measurement (Ref. 8) system is a valuable aid to determine such errors. The splitting of the emission beam of a single laser head and the use of individual receiver elements permit an interferometric measurement in six axes simultaneously.

The application of this measurement system to determine the typical errors of a NC-lathe with continuous path control is shown in Fig. 8. The results of measurements along a circular curve are reproduced on the right-hand side of the figure. The trailing errors at the reverse points of each machine axis are particularly noticeable. The interpolation error of the continuous path control can also be determined with the existing software. This is not possible with the single-axis measurement described earlier.

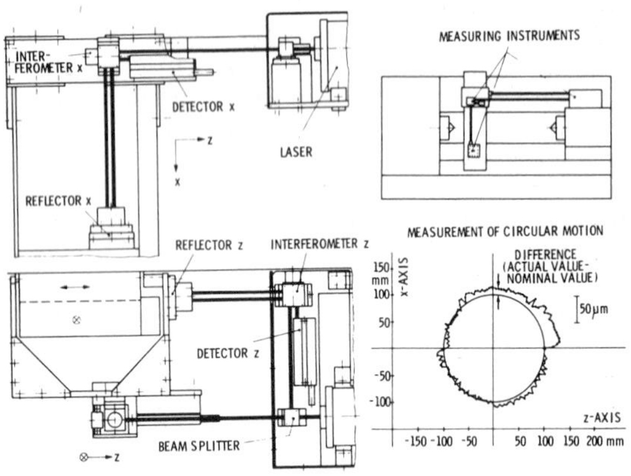

Fig. 8. Mechanical and optical assembly for simultaneous measurement of two axes of motion of a lathe

Mathematical description of the systematic volumetric positioning error

The external reference measurement system described - Double Frequency Laser Interferometer, Tooling-Laser and Laser Transducer - provide the components for measuring the systematic positioning error in space. However, detailed examinations are to be conducted regarding the mathematical combination of the individual error components as well as their illustration and storage.

Basically, the problem can be solved by a vectorial addition of the individual error components. The examinations carried out at the Cranfield Institute of Technology (Ref. 9) serve as a good fundament for further work. The work contains very detailed theoretical descriptions of vectorial calculation of the 3 D-accuracy of multi axis machines.

Another paper (Ref. 10) gives a solution for the mathematical representation of a 3 D-error vector field. This solution is characterised by the fact that it can be integrated in a CNC-concept. Experience gathered from the measurement of several NC-machine tools shows that every motion error can be described by a linear component and a series of phase-shifted sinus-oscillations having different amplitudes and phases. Therefore, it seems actual to apply the Fourier-analysis to process the measurement signals of the reference measurement systems mentioned. The error in space can be mathematically represented in the form of a 3-D vector field shown in Fig. 9. The diagram contains the graphical illustration of such a vector field in one plane for a turning machine. All the coefficients of the given equation system with the exception of a_o, b_o, c_o can be determined with the aid of transmission error measurements in 3 orthogonal axes in space. The coefficients a_o, b_o and c_o characterise the axis displacement of the machine slideways. These error components can - as already described - be determined with the Tooling-Laser.

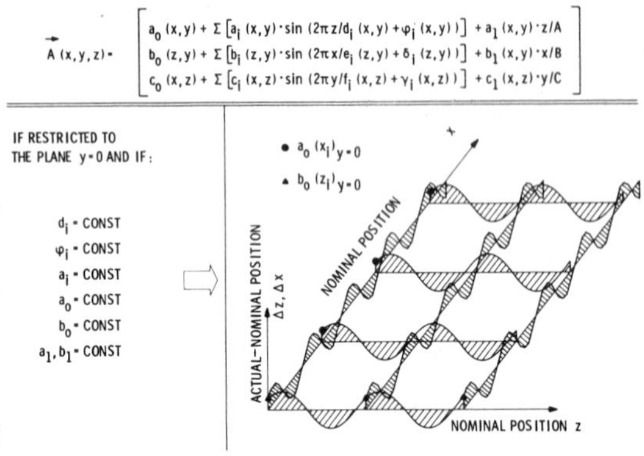

Fig. 9. Example of a mathematical description of positioning error in the operating plane of a turning machine

This mathematical method of transformation in the frequency range results in a considerable condensation of information which is very convenient for the storage of the error matrix. Instead of describing the positioning error in space with several pairs of values a mathematical description with a few parameters will suffice.

Suitable measurement-strategy for measurement of the workpiece

As mentioned in the introduction, the knowledge acquired in 3-D-measurement techniques can be exploited for measuring the workpiece geometry. The strategy for workpiece sampling (scanning), programming the points of measurement and processing the sampling coordinates to geometrical characteristic values of the workpiece can be adapted from the 3-D-measurement technique to a wide extent.

Suitable 3-D probe heads are necessary for sampling the workpiece and issuing impulses to signal the take-over of the coordinate values by the machine measurement systems. The most important sampling principles available today are shown in Fig. 10. In the case of both probes on the left, the displacement of the probe tip caused by contact with the workpiece is converted to proportional signals via plate spring parallelograms and inductive pick-ups. By turning the CARY-Probe 90° about its z-axis a 3-D-sampling can be carried out. Both probe systems can be clamped in their respective axes, thus enabling a defined sampling in one of 3 orthogonal axes in space (x,y,z). Both probe systems on the left cannot be clamped in the axis so that it is not possible to sample the workpiece in a privileged direction (e.g. normal to the workpiece). Besides, the measuring force alters with the sampling direction.

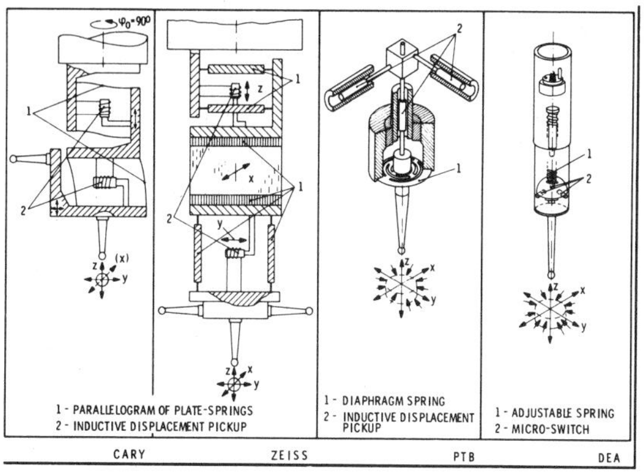

Fig. 10. Principles and variations in dimensions of 3-D-probes

In case of the switching probes, the zero-point constancy of the micro-contacts is the decisive accuracy criterium. A shift in the zero point due to wear is, in general, very difficult to correct. This is relatively easily done with probes having displacement pick-ups by conducting a post calibration. With the switching probes a continuous sampling of the object is not possible.

Inspite of its disadvantages, the switching probe should be used on machine tools since its comparatively small dimensions (see Fig. 10) permit it to be fixed to the tool holder or revolving head of a working machine. Beside, its small mass makes the probe insensitive to machine vibrations that can never be completely eliminated under rough operating conditions. The fairly low costprice also speaks for the application of this 3-D measuring probe.

Regarding the sampling strategy it is suggested to apply the point-wise work-piece sampling used today on most 3-D-measurement machines. According to this method the workpiece is sampled per programme oriented to its nominal geometry. Besides the relatively simple and easy to handle software this strategy is characterised by the quick sampling that is very essential for a process intermittent workpiece measurement. An economical 3-D workpiece measurement on a NC-machine tools demands on the one hand an automatic measurement data acquisition and processing that can be achieved by extending the CNC-system. On the other hand, it demands a uniform generally valid and easy to learn programming language that permits external programming for the machining and control data as well as evaluation of the measurement data. Based on the similarity between workpiece machining and measurement, a programming language for 3-D measurement techniques is being currently developed at the Werkzeugmaschinenlabor, TH Aachen and other research institutes in Germany. It is aimed to directly implement the experience of NC-manufacturing in this programming language by trying to build this analogous to the already known languages for NC-lathes (APT, EXAPT, etc.) (Ref. 11). The input programme of the system developed under the name NCMES (Numerical Controlled Measuring and Evaluation System) is a part programme (Fig. 11). The geometrical description of the workpiece to be measured, the description of the measurement tasks and the description of the drawing dimensions (nominal geometry) are contained in this programme that has a syntax similar to APT/EXAPT.

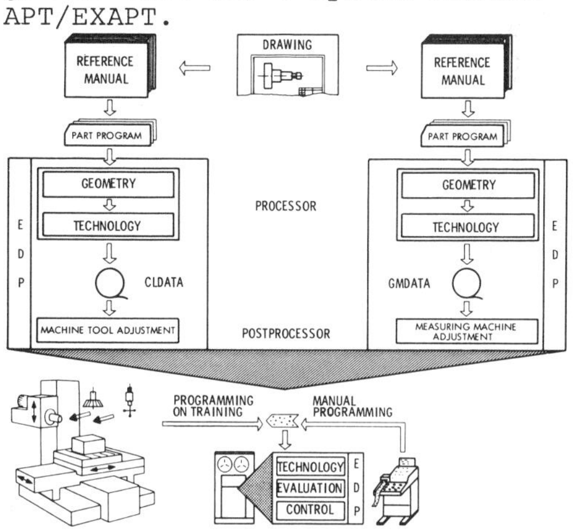

Fig. 11. Programming of a combined NC-machining and measuring center

From this input programme, the computer for part programmes will punch a paper-tape that contains information according to the normed CLDATA-format. The programme splits complicated measuring tasks in single tasks, determines sampling points, sampling sequence and sampling paths. These tasks will be conducted by the so-called geometrical and technological processor. By virtue of the parallel programme preparation for workpiece machining and measurement it is possible to produce a single paper-tape for both operations (machining and measurement). In the manner is it not only possible to achieve a complete integration of machining and measuring in the manufacturing process but also integrate the input of information concerning the machining and measuring sequence.

REFERENCES

(1) J. Peters, Metrology in Design and Manufacturing, Facts and Trends, Draft of the CIRP Keynote Paper to the STC ME (Jan. 1977)

(2) J.M. Evans, Keynote Address at Symposium on Automated Inspection and Product Control, Proceedings of the 2nd Conference on Automated Inspection and Product Control (Oct., 1976)

(3) T. Pfeifer, H. Golüke, Geometrische Überwachung von Werkzeugmaschinen und Produkten mit Prozeßrechnern Proceedings of 7th IMEKO Conference London (1976)

(4) VDI/DGQ Richtlinie 3441, Statistische Prüfung der Arbeits- und Positioniergenauigkeit von Werkzeugmaschinen, (1977), Beuth Verlag GmbH, Berlin

(5) T. Pfeifer u.a., Verfahren und Methoden zur Beurteilung der Arbeitsgenauigkeit von Werkzeugmaschinen, (1975), Seminarunterlagen WZL, TH Aachen

(6) Laser Measurement System, (1973), Manual, Hewlett-Packard

(7) T. Pfeifer, M. Bambach, C.A. Schneider, Geometrische Prüfungen mit dem Laser-Geradheits-Meßsystem, Industrie-Anzeiger 6, p. 92-94, (1977)

(8) Laser-Transducer System,(1976) Manual, Hewlett-Packard

(9) W.J. Love; A.J. Scarr, The Determination of the Volumetric Accuracy of Multi Axes Machines, Proceedings of 14th MTDR Conference, Manchester, (1973)

(10) H. Golüke, Ein Beitrag zur meßtechnischen Ermittlung und analytischen Beschreibung systematischer Anteile der Arbeitsunsicherheit von Fertigungseinrichtungen,(1976) Dissertation WZL, TH Aachen

(11) W. Eversheim; D. Koerth, G. Stute; A. Berner, Programming of NC-Measuring-Machines, Proceedings of Prolamat Conference, Glasgow, (1976)

A PROPOSAL OF THE MULTILAYERED CONTROL OF MACHINE TOOLS FOR FULLY AUTOMATED MACHINING OPERATIONS

T. Sata and K. Matsushima

University of Tokyo, Hongo, 7-3-1, Bunkyo-ku, Tokyo

ABSTRACT

To realize the fully automated machining system, a control system for turning operation has been built based on the concept of multilayered hierarchical system. On the first layer, the cutting torque, the vibration of tool and workpiece, and the power consumption are monitored in-process. The pattern of tool wear is also examined with a TV camera post-process. Cutting variables, such as feed rate and cutting speed are controlled for getting the minimum machining cost under predetermined constraints. On the second layer the parameters involved in the machining economy are modified with the results gathered in the turning operations. When any unfavorable cutting state is observed on the third layer, the tool material or tool geometry is changed according to the rules which are obtained by self-organizing process from the cutting data gathered in previous cutting.

INTRODUCTION

As machine tools become more and more automated, the human being is moved away from them. This will demand that the machine assumes the functions previously required for the man such as monitoring the cutting state, and running condition of the machine tool. The functions required are: 1) to select the most economical cutting variables, such as feed rate and cutting speed which ensure the required surface finish of the workpiece, and 2) to store the knowledge and experience possessed by the operator previously, to process, and to refer, if necessary. In recent years, marked progress has been made in the field of electronics, resulting in the increasing computational speed and decreasing cost of the digital computer, which allows computer control applicable in metal cutting. In this study, by using the concept of multilayeared hierarchy system (Ref.1), a computer control system for turning operation has been developed to provide the NC lathe with the functions such as monitoring the cutting situation optimizing the cutting variables, modifying the cutting parameters, recognizing, the tool wear pattern and displaying the instruction to be taken.

STRUCTURE OF THE CONTROL SYSTEM

The general structure of the system proposed in this study is shown in Fig.1. The system consists of three control layers. On the first layer, numerical control of the machining operation and optimization of cutting variables, such as feed rate and cutting speed are performed. On the second layer, the results of the tool wear are observed and the parameters in the objective function for optimization are modified by the results observed. Then, on the third layer the tool wear pattern is recognized, and a decision is made whether another tool material is used or the tool geometry is changed when an undesiable tool wear pattern is found. By utilizing the learning process, the decision table for tool selection is prepared in advance, and then, modified later at a certain interval based on the machining experiences obtained.

The control on all layers is basically on-line, but there is a difference in times of response. Control on the first layer acts on continuous basis. The second and third layer respond at the interval of every tool changing. Only on the first layer, the control variables are the actual physical variables while the second and third layers send the instrucions to the lower layer. The details on the functions of each layer are described in the following.

a) First Layer

The optimization of cutting process is performed with respect to the production cost under the several constraints to assure the stable cutting situations. The constraints involved in the control are:

the maximum machine tool power available,
the maximum spindle torque available,
the maximum and minimum feed rate available,
and the maximum and minimum cutting speeds available.

The cost of machining a workpiece may be separated into the costs associated with the operating time of th machine tool and that associated with the cutting tool. The cost for machining on a lathe can be written as follows:

$$H = M_c(t_m + t_p + \frac{t_m}{T} t_c) + \frac{t_m}{T} C_c \quad (1)$$

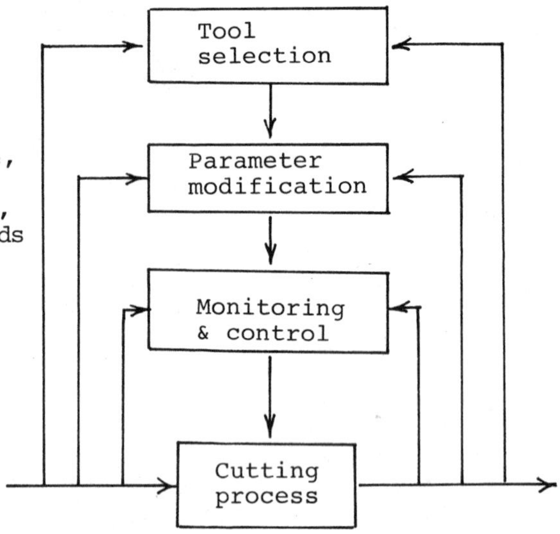

Fig.1 Block diagram of hierarchical control system

where,

H:	cost	(yen)
tm:	cutting time	(min)
tp:	set-up time	(min)
T:	Tool Life	(min)
tc:	tool change time	(min)
C_c	cost of cutting tool	(yen)
Mc:	over head cost	(yen/min)

and,

$$tm = \frac{A}{f \cdot v} \quad (2)$$

where,

f:	feed rate	(mm/rev)
v:	cutting speed	(m/min)
A:	area to be removed	(for trunings)

The tool life is related to the cutting speed and the feed rate by the tool equation as follows;

$$V f^m T^n = c \quad (3)$$

where,

m,n:	expornents determined experimentally	
T:	tool life	(min)
c:	constant determined experimentally	

After substitution, the cost equation (1) becomes;

$$H = K_0 + \frac{K_1}{fV} + K_2 f^{\frac{m}{n}-1} V^{\frac{1}{n}-1} \quad (4)$$

where

$K_0 = M_c t_p$
$K_1 = M_c A$
$K_2 = A(t_c \ M_c + Cc)/c^{\frac{1}{n}}$

It is known that in a numerically controlled lathe, the variables V and f are controllable at each time, The problem to determine the optimal feed rate(fopt) and cutting speed (Vopt) can be considered as a non-linear optimization problem under the constraints. However, the problem can not be solved analytically, because some constraints in machining operation are not formulated in the explicit form but only measured during the operation. In metal cutting, the values of the parameters, m and n, in equation (4) are

$$0 < m < n < 1 \quad (5)$$

therefore the cost decreases with increasing the feed rate though it is limited by one of the constraints above mentioned. Then, the optimal cutting speed (Vopt) at the given feed rate is determined as follows.

$$\frac{\partial H}{\partial V} = 0 \quad (6)$$

thus,

$$Vopt = k\ f^{-m} \qquad (7)$$

where,

$$k = \left(\frac{K_1}{K_2}\right)^n \left(\frac{1}{n} - 1\right)^n \qquad (8)$$

Then, by substituting equations (7) and (8) into equation (3), the optimal tool life Topt, to give the minimum cost is obtained as

$$Topt = \left(\frac{1}{n} - 1\right)\frac{K1}{K2}$$

Here, the tool life is defined the total cutting time until the tool wear reaches to a predetermined value.

Based on the analysis above mentioned, the physical values related to the constraints are monitored at a certain interval and the feed rate and the cutting speed are controlled along the optimal locus given by equation (7) when the most critical constraint is found varied. (See Fig. 2)

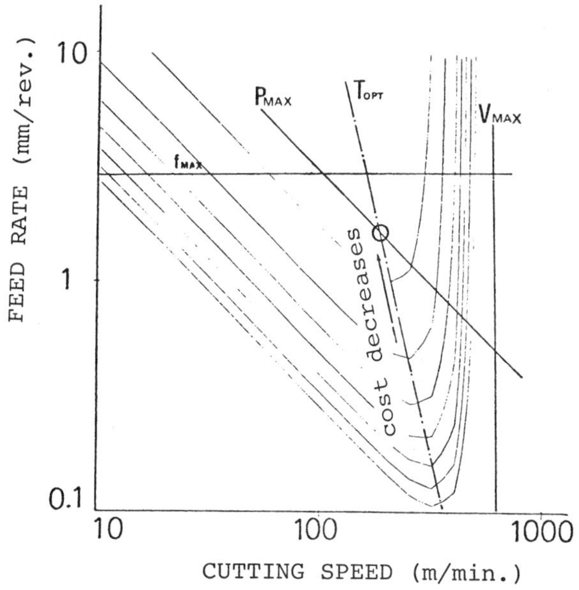

Fig.2 Illustration of the economical cutting condition

b) Second Layer

At the end of a pre-set cutting time corresponding to the optimum tool life, the tool is changed when the tool wear can be measured. The measured value is usually not to coincide with that expected due to variate of the properties of the workpiece and the tool. Then, the parameters involved in the tool life equation have to be modified to adapt to the change of the circumstance.

If the growth of the tool wear with the cutting time is expressed by the following empirical equation

$$V_b = V_{b0} + e^{-C}\ V^N\ f^M\ t^P \qquad (9)$$

where

V_b	: width of tool flank wear	(mm)
V_{b0}	: a constant	($\simeq$ 0.05)
V	: cutting speed	(m/min)
f	: feed rate	(mm/rev)
t	: cutting time	(min)
C,M,N,P:	exponents	

we can have a more convenient form by taking the logarithm of the equation(9), as.

$$\log(V_b - V_{b0}) = -C + N\log V + M\log f + P\log t \qquad (10)$$

When the p sets of the data, or the data vector Yp, are obtained for the tool wear variable $\log(V_b - V_{b0})$ against the different cutting conditions, Ap, equation(10) is written in the matrix expression as

$$Yp = ApX \qquad (11)$$

where X is the q-parameter vector. Here q is the number of the variables, thus, also Ap is a pxg matrix. By use of the least square method, the solution vector X is dtermined as

$$X = ({}^tAp\ Ap)^{-1}\ {}^tAp\ Yp \qquad (12)$$

Now suppose a new measurements is obtained; the parameter vector, X_{p+1}, becomes

$$X_{p+1} = ({}^tA_{p+1}A_{p+1})^{-1}\ {}^tA_{p+1}Y_{p+1} \qquad (13)$$

$$A_{p+1} \simeq \begin{bmatrix} A_p \\ {}^ta \end{bmatrix},\ Y_{p+1} \simeq \begin{bmatrix} Y_p \\ y \end{bmatrix}$$

where

a: the new variable vector
y: the new data

Looking at the expression (13), one can notice that the inverse of the matrix ($^tAp\ Ap$) must be computed at every measurement. To simplify the computation with a new data, the recursive formula is derived from equation (13) using the matrix inversion lemma.
Denoting Pp as

$$P_p = ({}^tA_p\ A_p\ )^{-1} \quad (14)$$

then we have

$$P_{p+1}^{-1} = {}^tA_{p+1}\ A_{p+1} = {}^tA_pA_p \quad (15)$$

The matrix inversive lemma give

$$P_{p+1} = P_p - P_p\ a\ (\ a\ P_p\ +1\ )^{-1}\ {}^ta\ P_p \quad (16)$$

Substituting (16) into (13), the recursive equation is obtained:

$$X_{p+1} = X_p + P_p\ a\ ({}^ta\ P_p\ a + 1)^{-1}(y-{}^ta\ X_p) \quad (17)$$

The second term in the right side of equation(17) corresponds ot the modification by the new data. In this procedure, only the inverse of a scalar value ($^taPpa+1$) is computed instead of computing the inverse of a (p+1) x (q+1) matrix in equation (13)

In practice, there exists a case when the circumstance changes very suddenly. The method for modification of the parameters descrived above, can not follow such a change in short time, because the diagonal elements in the covariance matrix Pp, contributing mostly to parameter modification become less and less when the circumstance is stable, being insensitive to a sudden change of the circumstance. To be able to follow such a sudden change, the new method called the variance perterbation method has been proposed (Ref.3). In the method the diagonal elements in the covariance matrix in equation(17) is increased intentionally by a certain great amount if a sudden change of the circumstance is detected. The control system is so designed that the mode of parameter modification is switched from the former to the latter when change of a parameter by modificaiton is detected to exceed a set value four times in succession.

3) Third Layer

The third layer is burdened the decision task of the high level concerning preparatation of the operation such as choise of the machine tool, determination of the cutting sequence, and selection of the tool and fixture. From the results obtained, the cutting situation is assigned to one or another class, and the optimal control action to the class is taken according to the rules prepared in advance. In the study, the worn tool is examined at every tool changing, and the morphology of the tool wear is classified by using the pattern recognition techniques. When an undesirable morphlogy of the worn tool is found, the tool material or tool geometry is changed according to the decision table. As known well, the morphology of the tool wear, shown in Fig.3 for example, depends on a number of factors such as tool materials, workpiece materials tool geometries or cutting conditions. Since, mechanism of growth of the tool wear is not well known at present, the machining operation is usually prepared by the experiences of production engineers in a machine shop. To improve such a situation, here a training algorithm is applied to construct the decision table

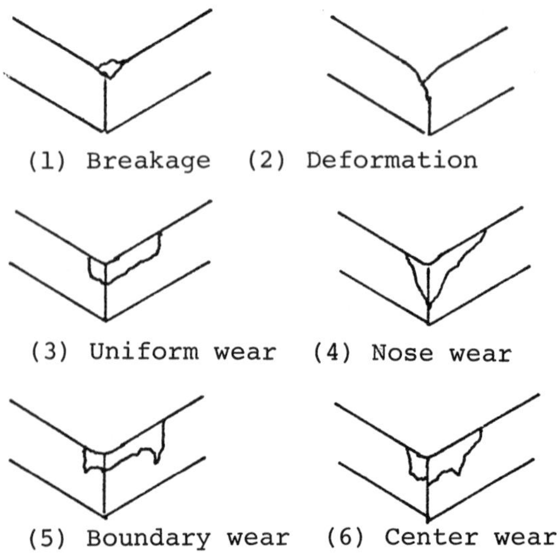

Fig.3 Morphology of tool failure

to select the optimal tool. The schematic diagram of the learning control system for the tool selection is shown in Fig.4. Learning is automatically carried out in the following ways, (1) to recognize the morphology of the tool wear, and (2) to modify the control law, so that the previous control-choices reflect the evaluation. In this system, the modification of the control law is accomplished by a reinforcement learning algorighm (Ref.4)

Let Pif (n) be the probability that the control action Ui is the best one for the class Sj at instant n when the observation is made. By assuming, no apriori knowledge on the problem, initially all Pij is set as

$$P_{ij}(0) = 1/m \qquad (18)$$

Where m is number of the control actions available. Then Pij will be modified according to the following algorithm.

$$P_{ij}(n+1) = \alpha\, P_{ij}(n) + (1-\alpha)\, \lambda(n) \qquad (19)$$

where λ (n) is taken 1 or 0 depending upon whether the performance of the system at the instant n, due to the i-th control action is satisfactory or not, and α is called the learning parameter. The larger the learning parameter α is the slower the probabilities Pij converge, and this results in a slower learning rate. As learning progresses, most of the probabilities Pij will approach either 1 or0 (100% or 0%). In this system the following five control actions are assumed :

1. to take no action,
2. to change the tool material for a harder one,
3. to change the tool material for a more tough and softer one,
4. to round off the cutting edge, and
5. not to round off the cutting edge.

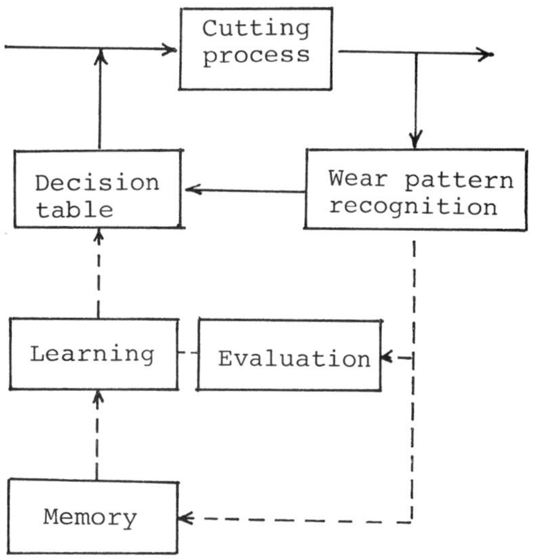

Fig.4 Control system of tool selection

EXPERIMENTAL METHOD

Cutting experiments were carried out by turning several kinds of steel with different grades of carbide tool. The experimental set-up of the control system is shown in Fig.5.

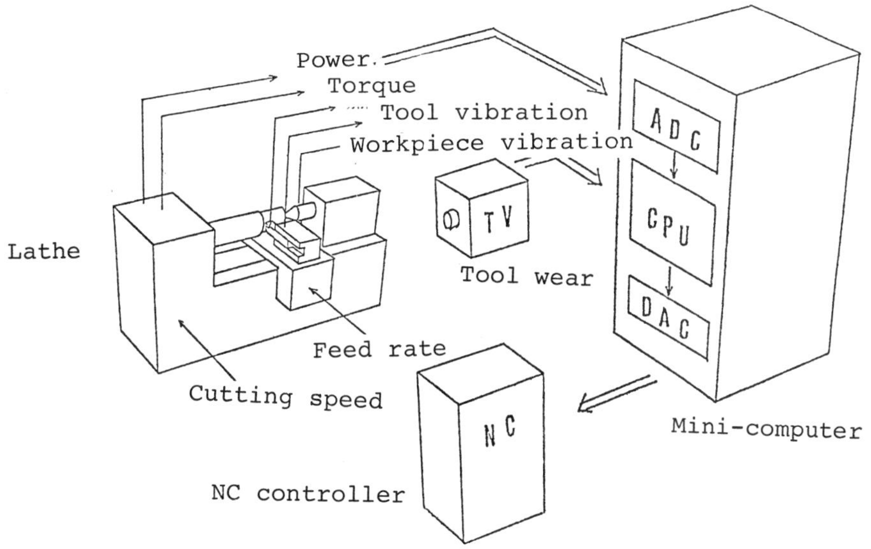

Fig. 5 Schematic of experimental set-up

The set up consist of the NC lathe, mini-computer, TV camera and several in-process sensors. The signals from the sensors associated with the constraints are converted into the digital sampled values by use of the analog-to-digital converter (ADC). The power consumption of the spindle motor is measured by the wattmeter and the torque for cutting is estimated by measureing the current of the motor. Tool and workpiece vibration is measured by the accelerometers mounted on the tool post and the center of the lathe, respectively.

At every 500 msec during the cutting operation, the signals from the sensors are sampled and compared with the set value for each constraint. Depending on whether any constraint is violated or not, the cutting condition of the feed rate and the cutting speed is brought lighter or heavier along the optimal locus derived from the formula (7). When marked vibration is found to take palce, the system sends the signal to stop the machine tool. After a tool is changed at the predetermined cutting time, the tool tip is observed by the TV camera for measuring the tool flank wear and examining the morphology of the wear pattern. The instructions for the feed rate and the cutting speed are sent from the computer to each driving device, through the digital-to-analog converter (DAC). The signals from the TV camera are sampled by means of the high speed analog-to-digital converter with the buffering memory unit, then, the data are transmitted to the computer through the direct-memory-access (DMA) channel. The measured values of the flank wear are utilized to modify the parameters of the tool wear equation as mentioned berore.

To classify the wear patterns as easily as possible, it is desirable to extract small number of the significant features from the image of the tool wear observed by the TV camera. After many trials it is found that the following two fearures, the maximum width of the flank wear, and the position of the maximum flank wear are suitable for the pattern recognition. To normalize these two data, they are divided by the average value of the flank wear and the width of cut respectively. (See Fig.6) Here, the wear pattern are classified into the following four classes: 1) breakage, 2) uniform or nose wear, 3) boundary wear, and 4) center wear as seen Fig.3. (1),(3) and (4),(5), and (6) respectively. The each class is further divided into two, the acceptable one and the unacceptable one, depending on the extent of the tool failure. The decision tree to classify the tool failure is shown in Fig.7. The probabilities associated with the control actions in the decision table is up dated according to the rule shown in formula (19)

EXPERIMENTAL RESULTS

Experiments of turning carbon steel bars (C = 0.45%) and cast steel (C =0.2%) were carried out to examine the effectiveness of the control system proposed in the study. The results on each control layer are described in the following.

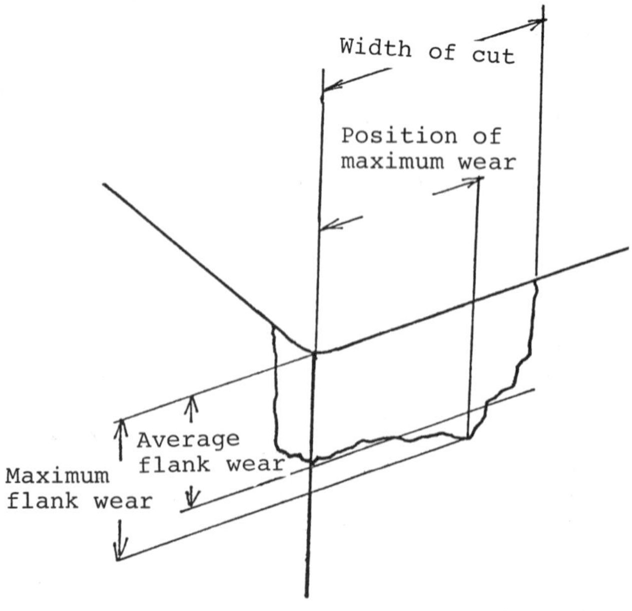

Fig.6 Feature extraction of tool wear

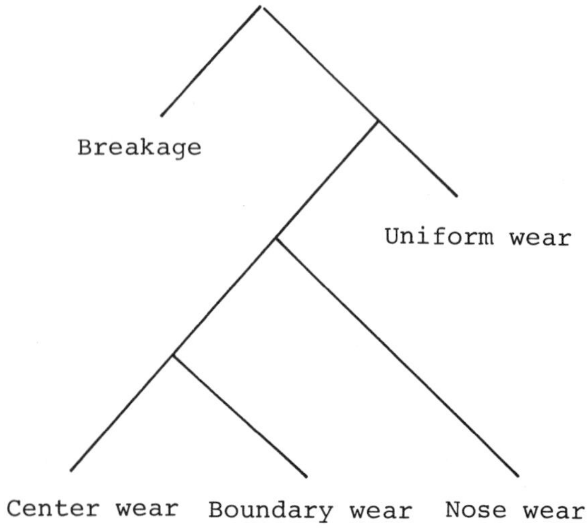

Fig.7 Decision tree for classification of tool wear

1) Economical machining under the constraints

Control on the first layer of the system was tested first. The optimal locus for the cutting variables with carbon steel and the critical value for each constraint, power consumption, torque and vibration, were set in advance. Cutting with a constant depth of cut 1.5mm started at the feed rate 0.05mm/rev which is apparently allowable against all the constraints. The controlled results on the feed rate and cutting speed after start of cutting are plotted in Fig. 8.

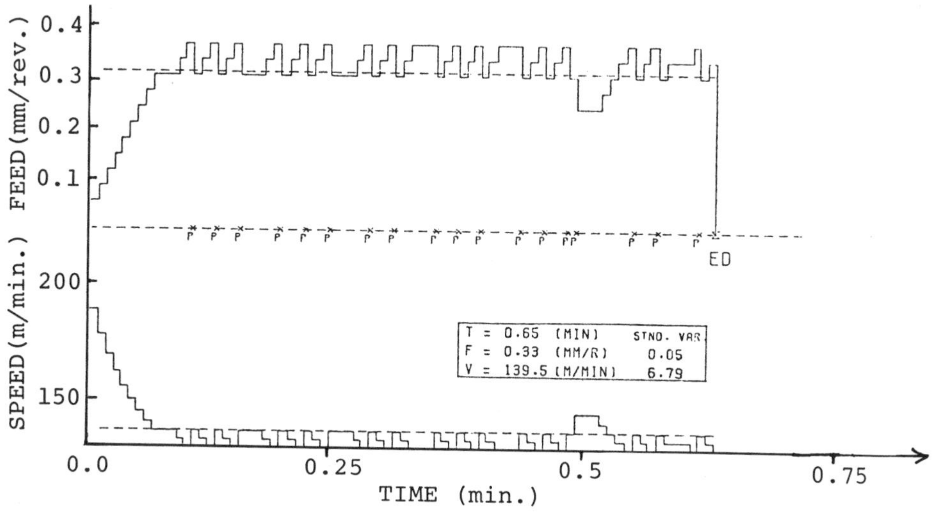

Fig. 8 Results of control of cutting variables (on the first layer)

As seen in the figure, the feed rate is increased by a certain set value 0.05/rev at each sampling time untill one of the constraints, that is, the power consumption in the case, is violated. It is also seen that the cutting speed is lowered with increasing the feed rate along the optimal locus. After reaching the critical condition for one of the constraints, the feed rate and cutting speed are kept nearly constant, when the most economical machining situation under the constraints is realized. These results shown in Fig. 8, prove the satisfactory function of the control on the first layer.

2) Modification of the parameters

To investigate the performance of the parameter modification on the second layer in the control system, carbon steel was turned first for considerably long time, and then the work material was changed to cast steel without giving notice the computer. Change of the parameters by the modification algorithm is shown in Fig. 9. where the solid lines correspond to the average value of each parameter for both materials. It is seen in the figure that during machining same material each parameter remains roughly constant and that after change of the work material the parameters can follow the change in very short time, converging to those with the new material respectively.

3) Learning of tool selection rules

Cutting experiments were carried out about thirty times with various combination of three kinds of carbide grade (P10, P20, and P40) and two kinds of tool finishing, and the tool wear pattern obtained in each experiment was classified. By utilizing these results, the decision table for tool selection is constructed by the reinforecement learning algorithm. The results are shown in Table 1, where the probabilities to select one of the control actions are tabulated for each wear pattern. Here the high value of a probability means that the control action is advisable. Since the iterations of learning are not enough, the greatest value of the probabilities for the control actions goes to 40 - 50% at most, still the results coincide well with the industrial experiences. In case of tool breackage, for example, use of carbide tool of lower grade is most recommended.

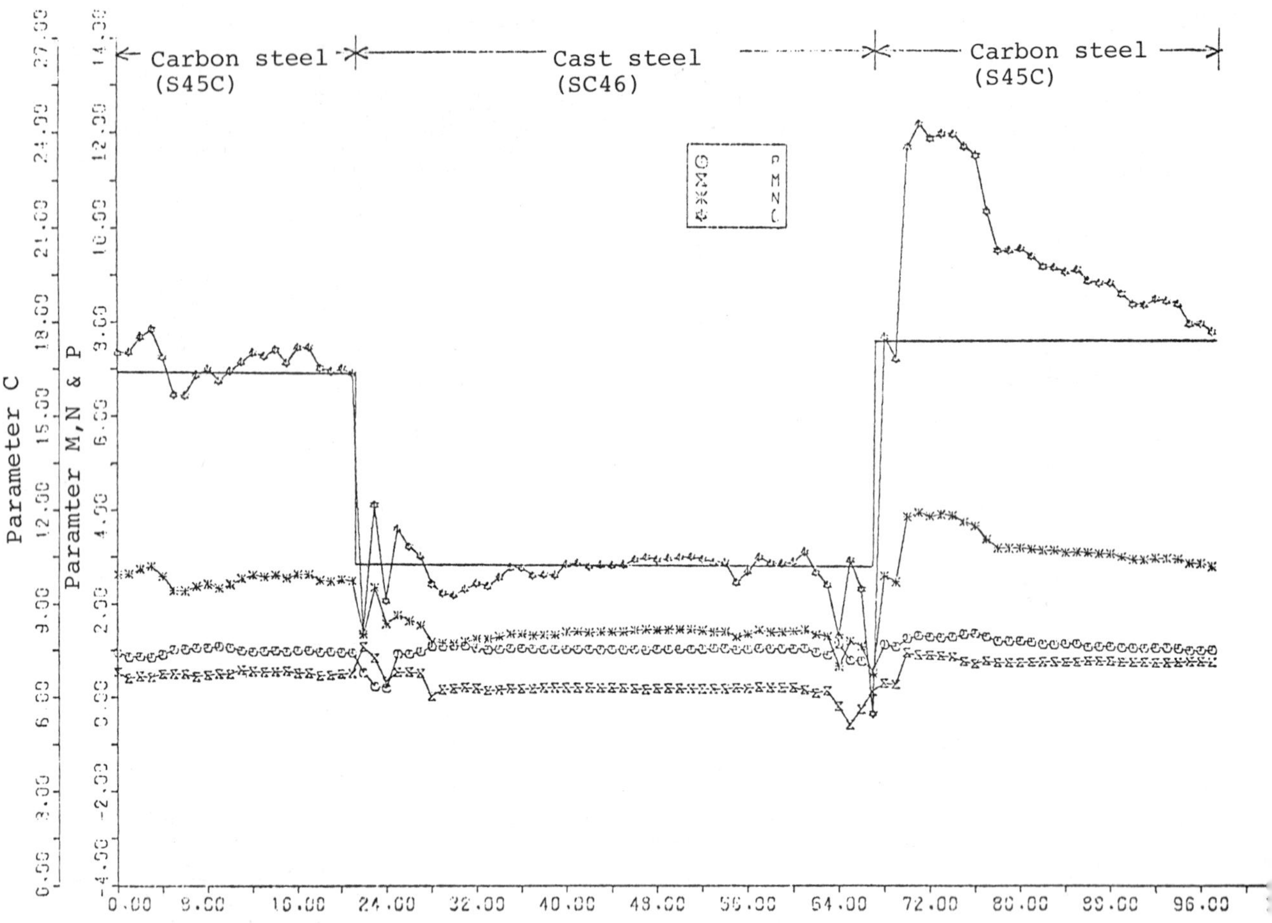

Fig.9 Modification of cutting parameters

Table 1 Decision table for tool selection

Action / Tool failure	NO action	More tough & Softer grade	Harder grade	Rounding tool edge	Not rounding
Breakage	14.46	45.32	8.58	23.07	8.58
Uniform & nose wear	30.06	5.00	39.58	10.45	14.90
Boundary wear	13.23	38.73	21.92	18.76	7.35
Center wear	6.81	18.73	17.48	50.17	6.81

Figure 10 shows a picture displayed from the computer. Here, we see that the wear pattern shown in Fig.10(1) is classified in D class and that the control action to be recommended is to round off the tool edge.

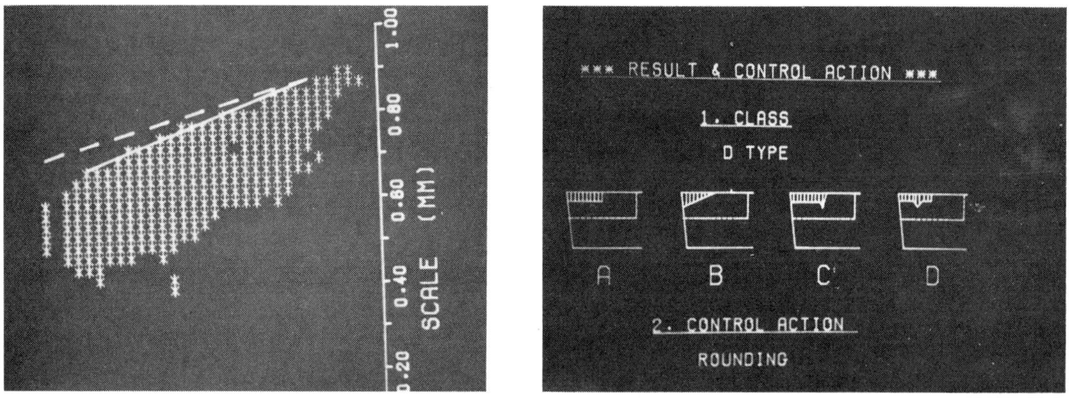

(1) wear pattern (2) result of classification and instruction

Fig.10 A picture displayed on recognition of wear pattern and instruction

CONCLUSION

A hierarchical control system for machining has been developed for fully automated operation of a machine tool. The system consists of three layers. On the first layer, the cutting variables such as the feed rate and cutting speed are controlled to get the economical cutting condition by monitoring the power consumption, torque, and vibration. After every tool changing the tool is observed by the TV camera. On the second layer of control, the cutting parameters used for controlling the cutting variables are modified by the observed results of tool wear. Then on the third layer, the tool wear pattern is recognized, the instrucion to be taken is displayed according to the decision table which has been constructed by the learning process. The experimental results has proved the effectiveness of the control system proposed in the study.

ACKNOWLEDGEMENT

The authors wish to thank Mr. S. Kawabe and Mr. T. Kawabata for their assistance in the experiments. The study was supported by the scientific research fund supplies by the Ministry of Eduction. Japan.

REFERENCES

1. M.D.Mesarovic, D.Macko, and Y.Takahara, (1970), Theory of Hierarchical Multilevel Systems, Academic Press, New York.

2. R.C.K.Lee, (1964), Optimal Estimation, Identification and Control M.I.T. Press, Mass. U.S.A.

3. H.Tamura, Stream Quality Modeling by Distributed-Lag Model and Recursive Estimation of Lag Coefficients, System and Control, Japan 20, 253 (1976)

4. J.M.Mendel and K.S.Fu, (1970), Adaptive, Learning and Pattern Recognition Systems, Academic Press, New York.

A METHOD OF TOOL PATH DISTRIBUTION ON A CNC

M. Kiyokawa

Computer Works, Mitsubishi Electric Corporation, Kamakura, Japan

1. Introduction

One problem encountered when using Numerical Control (NC) machine tools is the great amount of time required in the preparation of NC command punched tape. With the appearance of the CNC, sophisticated functions have been extended, and since it processes on on-line real time, the time required for tape preparation may be reduced and the tape length shortened. With these advantages in mind, the tool path distribution function for rough cutting on a lathe has been developed on the CNC thus increasing the utility of the CNC.

This paper describes a method for tool path distribution where the distribution sub-program is previously stored in the memory and repeatedly called out after the necessary data for the sub-program has been calculated according to the stored command punched tape for the workpiece's finishing shape and the tool path distribution information, then the sub-program is used to distribute the tool path automatically for rough cutting on on-line real time.

2. The Function

The tool path for rough cutting of the workpiece is shown in Figure 1.

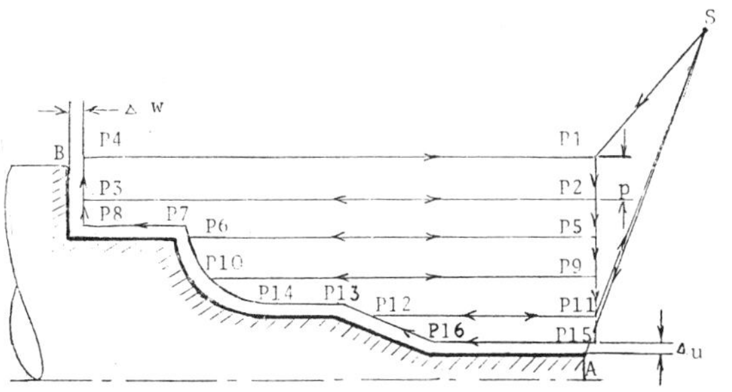

Fig. 1 Tool paths for rough cutting

For cutting the finishing shape of the workpiece as shown by the thick line, the motion of the tool starts at S and continues through the cutting cycles as follows:

(1) $P_1 - P_2 - P_3 - P_4 - P_1$
(2) $P_1 - P_2 - P_5 - P_6 - P_7 - P_8 - P_3 - P_2$
(3) $P_2 - P_5 - P_9 - P_{10} - P_6 - P_5$
(4) $P_5 - P_9 - P_{11} - P_{12} - P_{13} - P_{14} - P_{10} - P_9$
(5) $P_9 - P_{11} - P_{15} - P_{16} - P_{12} - P_{11}$
(6) Return to starting point S

The rough cutting of the workpiece ends here and only the finishing allowance of the workpiece remains.

Usually the rough cutting mentioned above is commanded sequentially by a command punched tape, ie. each tool path is commanded by the punched tape, so the tape is very long and consequently requires much time for calculating the coordinates of each tool path. The time required to calculate the coordinates and the excessive length of the tape are significant problems in the operation of NC machine tools so the tool path distribution function has been developed on the CNC to remove these obstacles.

The function of the tool path distribution is like the command punched tape shown below and is read by the tape reader from G 21 EOB to G 20 EOB. The command punched tape for the finishing shape of the workpiece between G 21 EOB and G 20 EOB is stored in the memory and when G 71 H (n) U (2Δu) W (Δw) P (p) F (fr) EOB of the path distribution command is read by the tape reader, the tool path for rough cutting will distributed automatically in the sequence as shown in Figure 1.

The Command Punched Tape

G 21 EOB	Memory write start
N (n) GO U (2u1) W (w_1) EOB G1 U (2u2) W (w_2) F (f_f) EOB ⋮ G 23 EOB	command punched tape for finishing shape of the workpiece (S-A-B), hereafter each motion command will be called "block"
G 20 EOB	memory write stop
G 71 H (n) U (2Δu) W (Δw) P (p) F (fr) EOB	distribution command
G 22 H (n) EOB	call out command

A key for the numerals used in block G 71 is as follows:

H: sequence number of stored punched tape (n)
U: allowance of X-axis (2 Δu) diameter destination
W: allowance of Z-axis (Δw)
P: cutting pitch (p)
F: rough cutting feedrate (fr)

As the calling out command G 22 H (n) EOB is read by the tape reader, the stored punched tape of the workpiece finishing shape will be cut. This function is the option of the CNC MELDAS 5100C, and an external view of it is shown in Figure 2.

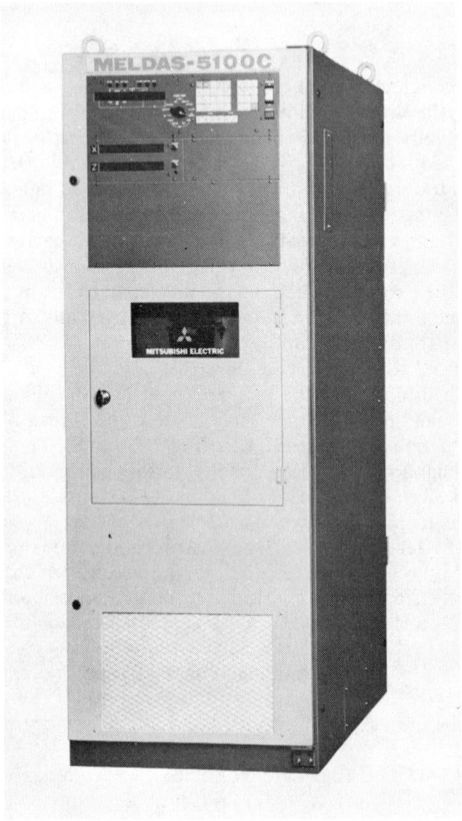

Fig. 2 External view of CNC MELDAS 5100C

3. The Method

For simple tool path distribution, a sub-program can be utilized repeatedly from data calculated by the equation derived below.

3.1 The basic concept of tool path distribution

The basic concept of distribution is shown in Figure 3, and the procedure is as follows:

(1) The sub-program (later described) must be previously be stored at the time of system generation.

(2) The command punched tape for the finishing shape of the workpiece is pre-stored in the memory by utilizing the memory write function.

(3) The pre-stored command punched tape is called out block by block in reverse, ie. in the order: B– A– S, leaving the finishing allowance of the workpiece, the data necessary for the sub-program is calculated by the equation derived hereafter.

(4) The tool paths are distributed according to the data by executing the sub-program as shown in Figure 3 and follows the order: a– b– c– d.

(5) The stored command punched tape is called out and executed to cut the finishing allowance of the workpiece subsequent to the rough cutting mentioned above. The arrow shows the direction of the cutting.

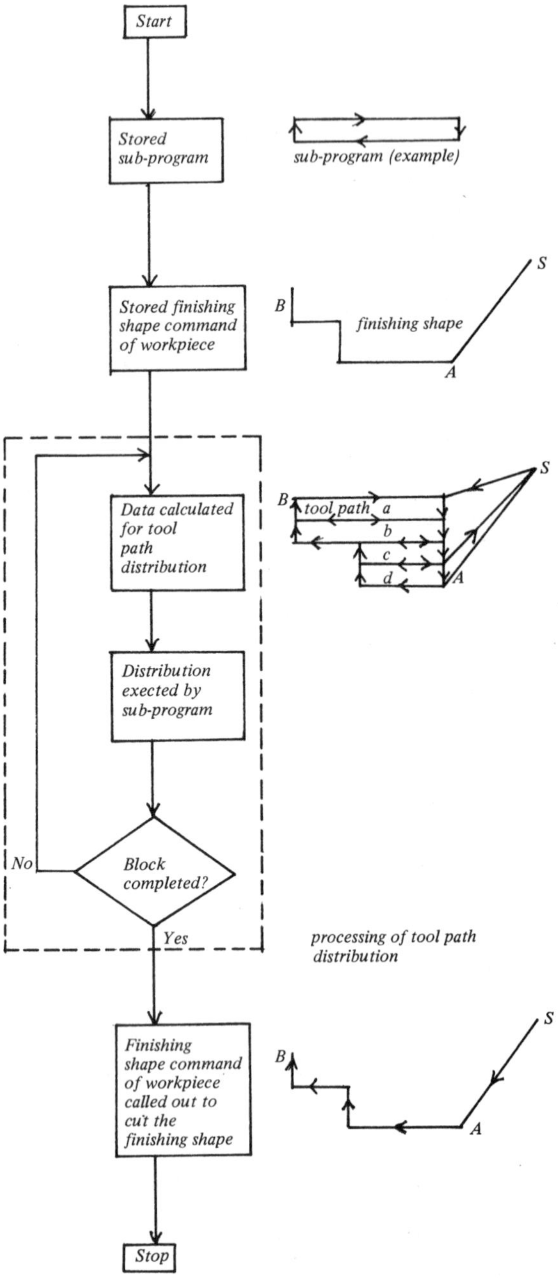

Fig. 3 Basic concept of tool path distribution

3.2 The sub-program
As shown below in NC language, the tool path is generated by the sub-program. According to the data computed with the equation below, different types of tool paths shown in Table 1 are easily generated by the sub-program.

(1) GOU (u1) EOB
(2) G 1 W (w2) EOB
(3) G (g3) U (u3) W (w3) I (i3) K (k3) EOB
(4) G 1 W (w4) EOB
(5) G (g5) U (u5) W (w5) I (i5) K (k5) EOB
(6) G O W - (w2 + w3 + w4 + w5)

The tool paths necessary for cutting a finishing shape such as Figure 1 are selected from Table 1.

Figure 4 shows the representative shape of the tool path generated by the sub-program. The data of p, Σ_l, γ, and q are easy to obtain with the tool path distribution command and the stored punched tape for the workpiece's finishing shape, so the data is omitted here. But the data of δ_1, δ_n, δ_l, α_1, α_n, α_l, and β_1, β_n, β_l must be calculated by the equation explained below. The equivalent meanings for the symbols used in **Table 1** are as follows:

p: cutting pitch
δ_1: difference of Z direction of first distribution of present block
α_1, β_1: circular arc central reference coordinates of starting point for circular arc of first distribution of present block
Σ_l: sum of incremental command of Z direction from starting block to present block
δ_n: Z direction differences of each distribution except first and last one
α_n, β_n: circular arc center reference coordinates to starting point of circular arc of each distribution except first and last one
γ: cutting remaining in X direction of previous block
δ_l: cutting remaining in Z direction of previous block
α_l, β_l: coordinates of circular arc center reference to starting point of circular arc of remaining part of previous block
q: Z direction increments of horizontal block
a: $\Sigma_l - \delta_n$
b: $\Sigma_l - \delta_1$
c: $p - \gamma$

Table 1 Tool path types and corresponding data

Type	Tool Path Shape	Data												
		u1	w2	g3	u3	w3	i3	k3	w4	g5	u5	w5	i5	k5
A		p	Σ_l	1	p	0	0	0	0	1	0	0	0	0
B1	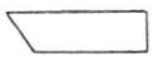	"	a	"	"	δ_n	"	"	"	"	"	"	"	"
B2		"	"	2	"	"	δ_n	β_n	"	"	"	"	"	"
B3		"	"	3	"	"	"	"	"	"	"	"	"	"
C1	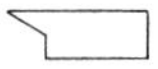	"	Σ_l	1	C	"	0	0	"	"	r	δ_l	"	"
C2		"	"	"	"	"	"	"	"	2	"	"	α_l	β_l
C3	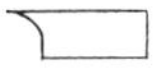	"	"	"	"	"	"	"	"	3	"	"	"	"
D1		"	b	1	"	"	"	"	"	1	"	0	0	0
D2	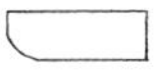	"	"	2	"	"	α_1	β_1	"	"	"	"	"	"
D3		"	"	3	"	"	"	"	"	"	"	"	"	"
E1	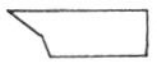	"	"	1	"	"	0	0	"	"	"	δ_l	"	"
E2		"	"	2	"	"	α	β	"	"	"	"	"	"
E3	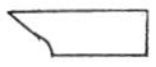	"	"	3	"	"	"	"	"	"	"	"	"	"
E4		"	"	1	"	"	0	0	"	2	"	"	α_l	β_l
E5		"	"	2	"	"	α_1	β_1	"	"	"	"	"	"
E6		"	"	3	"	"	"	"	"	"	"	"	"	"
E7		"	"	1	"	"	0	0	"	3	"	"	"	"
E8	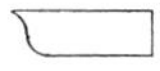	p	b	2	C	δ_1	α_1	β_1	0	3	r	δ_l	α_l	β_l
E9		"	"	3	"	"	"	"	"	"	"	"	"	"

F1	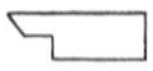	"	Σ_ℓ	1	"	"	0	0	q	1	"	δ_ℓ	0	0
F2		"	"	"	"	"	"	"	"	2	"	"	α_ℓ	β_ℓ
F3	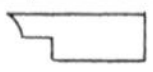	"	"	"	"	"	"	"	"	3	"	"	"	"
G	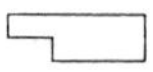	"	"	"	"	"	"	"	"	1	"	0	0	0
H1		"	b	"	"	"	"	"	"	"	"	"	"	"
H2	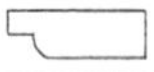	"	"	2	"	"	α_1	β_1	"	"	"	"	"	"
H3		"	"	3	"	"	"	"	"	"	"	"	"	"
I1		"	"	1	"	"	0	0	"	"	"	δ_ℓ	"	"
I2		"	"	2	"	"	α_1	β_1	"	"	"	"	"	"
I3		"	"	3	"	"	"	"	"	"	"	"	"	"
I4		"	"	1	"	"	0	0	"	2	"	"	α_ℓ	β_ℓ
I5		"	"	2	"	"	α_1	β_1	"	"	"	"	"	"
I6		"	"	3	"	"	"	"	"	"	"	"	"	"
I7		"	"	1	"	"	0	0	"	3	"	"	"	"
I8		"	"	2	"	"	α_1	β_1	"	"	"	"	"	"
I9		"	"	3	"	"	"	"	"	"	"	"	"	"

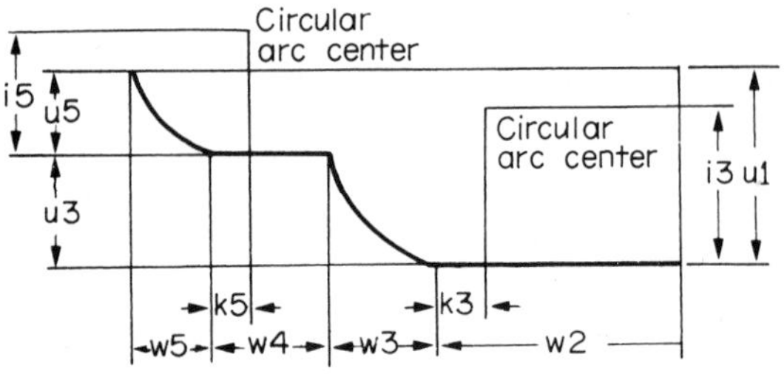

Fig. 4 Representative shape of tool path

3.3 The data equation

The data equation of a distributed tool path may be classified as linear or circular arc. Each equation is derived from a geometrical relationship.

(1) The data equation of linear (G1) - - - for δ is illustrated below. The difference for Z direction δ as shown in Figure 5 may be obtained by the equation as follows:

$$\delta_1 = \left| \frac{w}{u} x (p - \gamma) \right| \tag{1}$$

$$\delta_n = \left| \frac{w}{u} x\, p \right| \qquad (n = 2 \sim \iota - 1) \tag{2}$$

$$\delta_\iota = \left| \frac{w}{u} x\, \gamma' \right| \tag{3}$$

The data for u and w in equations (1) --- (3) is given in the present distributed block (hereafter called the present block). The value of p is given in the tool path distribution command, and γ or γ' is the cutting remaining from the previous or present block; therefore, δ_1, δ_n and δ_ι can be calculated by the equation. Now the sign of the data is the same as w of the present block.

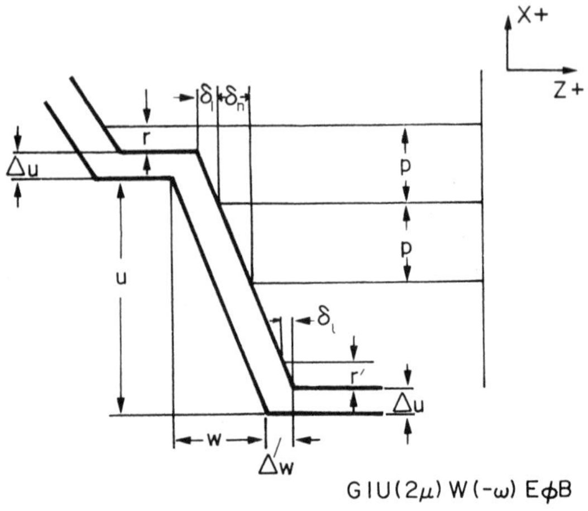

Fig. 5 Geometric relationship of the linear

(2) The data equation for the circular arc (G2 and G3) for δ, α and β are illustrated below. For the concave circular arc, the Z direction difference δ and coordinates α, and β of the circular arc as shown in Figure 6 can be obtained with the equations as follows:

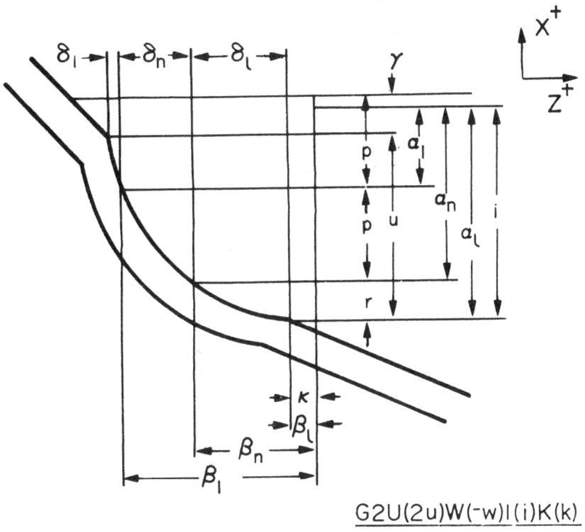

Fig. 6 Geometric relationship of the concave circular arc

$$\delta_1 = \left\| \sqrt{i^2 + k^2 - (|i| - |u|)^2} \right| - \left| \sqrt{i^2 + k^2 - [|i| - (\gamma + |u| - p)]^2} \right\| \quad (4)$$

$$\alpha_1 = \left| |i| - (\gamma + |u| - p) \right| \quad (5)$$

$$\beta_1 = \left| \sqrt{i^2 + k^2 - [|i| - (\gamma + |u| - p)]^2} \right| \quad (6)$$

$$\delta_n = \left\| \sqrt{i^2 + k^2 - [|i| - [\gamma + |u| - (n-1)p]]^2} \right| - \left| \sqrt{i^2 + k^2 - [|i| - [\gamma + |u| - np]]^2} \right\| \quad (7)$$

$$\alpha_n = \left\| i| - (\gamma + |u| - np) \right| \quad (8)$$

$$\beta_n = \left| \sqrt{i^2 + k^2 - [|i| - [\gamma + |u| - np]]^2} \right| \quad (9)$$

$$\delta_\iota = \left\| \sqrt{i^2 + k^2 - (|i| - \gamma')^2} \right| - |k| \Big| \quad (n = 2 \sim \iota - 1) \quad (10)$$

$$\alpha_\iota = |i| \quad (11)$$

$$\beta_\iota = |k| \quad (12)$$

For the convex circular arc, the difference of Z direction δ and coordinates α and β of the circular arc center reference to the starting point of the circular arc as shown in Figure 7, can be obtained with the equations as follows:

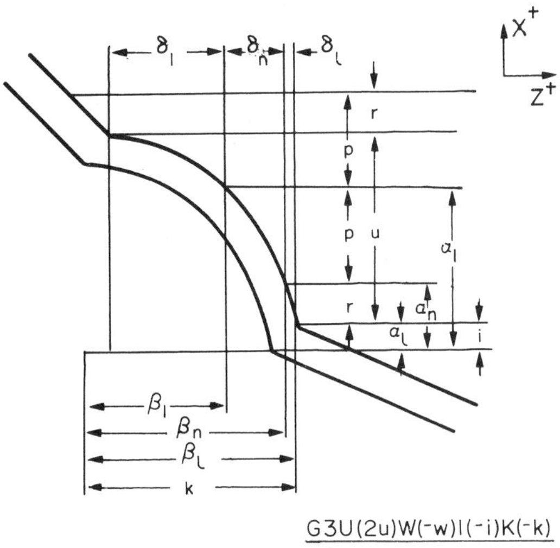

Fig 7 Geometric relationship of the convex circular arc

$$\delta_1 = \left\| \sqrt{i^2 + k^2 - [|i| + (\gamma + |u| - p)]^2} \right| - \left| \sqrt{i^2 + k^2 - (|i| + |u|)^2} \right\| \quad (13)$$

$$\alpha_1 = \left\| i| + |u| + \gamma - p \right| \quad (14)$$

$$\beta_1 = \left| \sqrt{i^2 + k^2 - (|i| + |u| + \gamma - p)^2} \right| \quad (15)$$

$$\delta_n = \left\| \sqrt{i^2 + k^2 - [|i| + |u| + \gamma - np]^2} \right| - \left| \sqrt{i^2 + k^2 - [|i| + |u| + (n-1)p]^2} \right\| \quad (16)$$

$$\alpha_n = \left\| i| + |u| + \gamma - np \right| \quad (17)$$

$$\beta_n = \left| \sqrt{i^2 + k^2 - (|i| + (|u| + \gamma - np))^2} \right| \quad (n = 2 \sim \iota - 1) \quad (18)$$

$$\delta_\iota = \left\| k| - \left| \sqrt{i^2 + k^2 - (|i| + \gamma')^2} \right\| \right. \quad (19)$$

$$\alpha_\iota = |i| \quad (20)$$

$$\beta_\iota = |k| \quad (21)$$

If the equations (4) —— (12) for the concave circular arc are compared with equations (13) —— (21) for the convex circular arc, the equation are the same if i is calculated with sign (not absolute), thus the data equations for the circular arc are as follows:

$$\delta_1 = \left\| \sqrt{i^2 + k^2 - (i - |u|)^2} \right| - \left| \sqrt{i^2 + k^2 - [i - (\gamma + |u| - p)]^2} \right\| \quad (22)$$

$$\alpha_1 = |i - (\gamma + |u| - p)| \quad (23)$$

$$\beta_1 = \left| \sqrt{i^2 + k^2 - [i - (\gamma + |u| - p)]^2} \right| \quad (24)$$

$$\delta_n = \left\| \sqrt{i^2 + k^2 - [i - [\gamma + |u| - (n-1)p]]^2} \right| - \left| \sqrt{i^2 + k^2 - [i - [\gamma + |u| - np]]^2} \right\| \quad (25)$$

$$\alpha_n = |i - (\gamma + |u| - np)| \quad (n = 2 \sim \iota - 1) \quad (26)$$

$$\beta_n = \left| \sqrt{i^2 + k^2 - [i - [\gamma + |u| - np]]^2} \right| \quad (27)$$

$$\delta_\iota = \left\| \sqrt{i^2 + k^2 - (i - \gamma')^2} \right| - |k| \Big| \quad (28)$$

$$\alpha_\iota = |i| \quad (29)$$

$$\beta_\iota = |k| \quad (30)$$

The data for i, k and u of equations (22) – (30) is obtained from the present block, p is acquired from the tool path distribution command, and γ or γ' is the remaining cutting from the previous or present block. Consequently, δ_1, α_1, β_1, δ_n, β_n as well as δ_ι, α_ι, β_ι can be calculated with the equation and the following relationships can be observed:

(1) The data signs of δ_1, δ_n, and δ_ι are the same as w of the present block.

(2) For the concave circular arc (G2) the signs of α_1, α_n and α_ι are the same as u of the present block.

The data signs of β_1, β_n, and β_ι are not the same as w of the present block.

(3) For the convex circular arc (G3) data signs β_1, β_n and β_ι are the same as w of the present block.

The data signs of α_1, α_n, α_ι are not the same as u, of the present block.

3.4 Algorithm for deciding type of tool path

The algorithm in Figure 8 illustrates a classification system for tool path types. Tool paths which are not of the first distribution are classified as either A or B type. If there is no cutting remaining or if it is the last processing, even though the tool path is not of the first distribution, it is classified as either A or B. Type A and B can be further classified by whether or not the present block is vertical: if the present block is vertical then it is type A, if not vertical then type B.

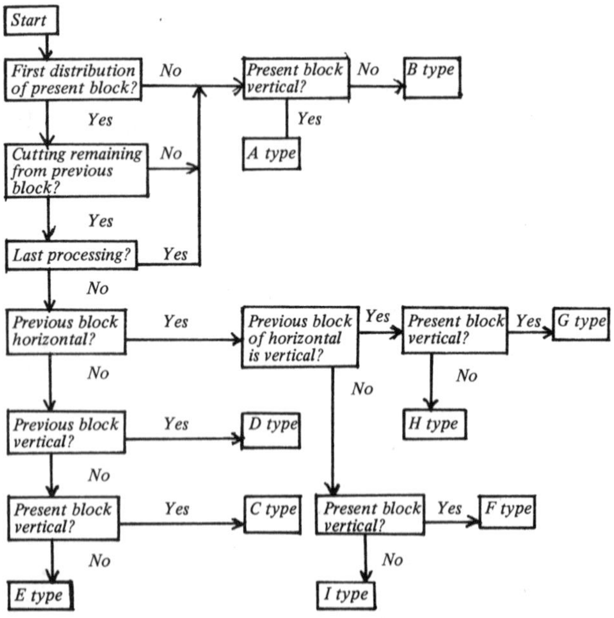

Fig 8 Algorithm for deciding type of tool path

If the tool path is classified as neither A nor B, it can be assigned a classification based on the configuration of the previous block. If the previous block is horizontal then it is classified as F, G, H, or I.

Further reclassification of C, D, and E types where the previous block is not horizontal is based on the following:

(1.)If the previous block is vertical then it is type D.

(2.)If the previous block is not vertical and the present block is vertical then it is type C.

(3.)If the previous and present blocks are not vertical then it is type E.

With type F, G, H, and I where the previous block is a horizontal, further classification of these types is based on the following:

(1.)If the previous block of the horizontal is vertical and the present block is vertical then it is type G.

(2.)If the previous block of the horizontal is vertical but the present block is not vertical then it is type H.

(3.)If the previous block of the horizontal is not vertical but the present block is vertical then it is type F.

(4.)If neither the previous block of the horizontal is vertical nor the present block is vertical then it is type I.

All categories excluding A and G may be reclassified according to the G1, G2, or G3 of the previous and present blocks.

4. Conclusion

A method for tool path distribution for rough cutting on a lathe has been described and this method allows reduction of the time required to prepare punched tape and permits shortening of the tape length. It has been illustrated how a tool path sub-program for generating the finished shape of the workpiece can be used repeatedly according to data calculated from derived equations and easily realized in practice on the CNC.

There is no constraint on finishing shape as long as the shape is increasing or decreasing constantly in one direction, but if the shape is concave or convex then this method cannot be applied.

The shape of the tool path discussed here is only two stage, but this method can be extended to multi-stage for adapting workpiece finishing shapes which are formed by small stages. Regarding this method practically, if the cutting that remains is smaller than the allowable value, eg. 0.1 mm, it is left for finishing cutting rather than wasting time with additional rough cutting.

MULTIMICROPROCESSOR CONTROL SYSTEM FOR SPECIAL PURPOSE MACHINE TOOLS

A. Kuisma*, K. Mäkelä* and E. Rasi**

**Control Engineering Laboratory, Tampere University of Technology, Finland*
***Valmet Oy, Linnavuori Works, Finland*

ABSTRACT

Special purpose machine tools are used when the selection of parts is limited. Control problems in these machines differ from machining centers and other widely used NC and CNC machines. There can be many tools working on the same work piece from different directions and each tool must be controlled independently. Special machines are not produced in large quantities, but are mostly specially tailored for each application. In this paper a control system for them is introduced. It is a hierarchical system with microprocessors. It consist of a lower level position and speed controller for slide units and a higher level controller for work cycle control, display, programming and interface between the user and machine.

INTRODUCTION

There are exceptional features in the programming of special purpose machine tools, which in this case are mainly multi-way multispindle machines. Traditional NC-systems do not suit well for them, as there are many units, which must be controlled. In the first part of this article the requirements for programming are collected and two different programming systems are considered. The first one is more versatile but more tedious when writing programs. The latter is a modified version of normal NC-programming code so it is easier to use, more familiar to the user but not as versatile as the first one.

The latter part describes the control system hardware and software. The system is built with 8-bit microprosessors. It consists of a unit controller, that takes care of the position and speed control of thee slide units and a main controller, that takes care of work cycle control, display, user interface, spindle drives, auxiliary devices and data transfer to and from unit controllers. Microprocessors are used, because the control system must be modular and easy to tailor for each application.

SPECIAL PURPOSE MACHINE TOOLS

Machining centers are widely used nowadays. Most of them are equipped with NC-systems with paper tape as program memory. CNC is also coming very strongly with programming facilities beside the machine. When the lots of parts are medium or large, but not large enough for transfer machines, it would often be economical to consider special purpose machine tools.

These machines are designed to produce a limited selection of parts. An example of such a unit-built machine is in Fig. 1. This machine consists of transfer table, two multispindle drilling units, and two milling units. This kind of machine is very suitable for machining of part families in which parallel surfaces are to be milled and holes drilled from two opposite directions.

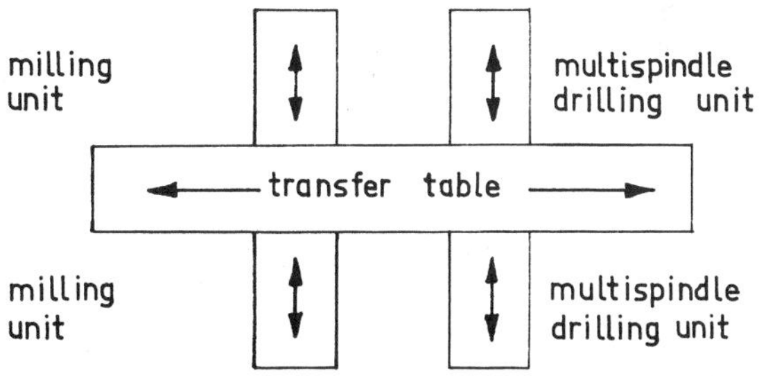

Fig. 1. A unit-built special purpose machine.

REQUIREMENTS OF CONTROL AND PROGRAMMING SYSTEM

There are some special features in the programming of special purpose machine tools, which are mainly multi-way multispindle machines.

The number of units can be high. In Fig. 1 it is five. The motions are straight and in a direction of a measurable axis, so no curve interpolation is necessary. To make work cycles efficient the units of machine should work independent from each other. The transfer table can take the work piece to the next position while milling units are going to their home positions and drilling units start to more towards the work piece.

The number of different programs is not very

high. However the change from one program to another must be easy and quick. This will not put great demand only on programming and control system, but also on drive systems, which must be easy to control with a wide dynamic range.

New programs are not needed often and some machines can even be equipped with fixed programs, where certain parameters like spindle speeds, feed rates and slide position command values can be altered. However there are machines where the user must be able to do the programming easily beside the machine.

Because special purpose machine tools are not produced in quantities, but are mainly designed individually for each user, the control and programming system must be modular to be easily tailored for each application.

PROGRAMMING

In the programming of special purpose machine tools following requirements must be considered.

Every unit must work independently from each other. A unit can do drilling through two walls with rapid traverse between the walls while another unit performs an ordinary drilling cycle. However there must be possibility to tie the movements of units. For example while drilling the same hole from two opposite directions.

Once the programming is done the position commands and spindle and slide speeds must be easy to alter to optimize the machining. It can also be necessary to alter, change, or add the statements in the programs easily.

If programming is to be done with pushbuttons on the control unit, it must be simple, easy to learn, check, and correct.

Special made fixed subprograms in the machine make programming easier.

Work piece handling systems such as robots must be easy to interface with the control system. For simple manipulators a sequence control is needed.

Two different types of programming system were considered.

Condition programming

While the first requirement of independent movements between the units is the most important to make the programs efficient, the condition programming was developed.

In Fig. 2 there is a block diagram of a work cycle, where there is first milling and then drilling. The machine could be for instance the same type as in Fig. 1 and work cycles for both milling units and both drilling units are alike.

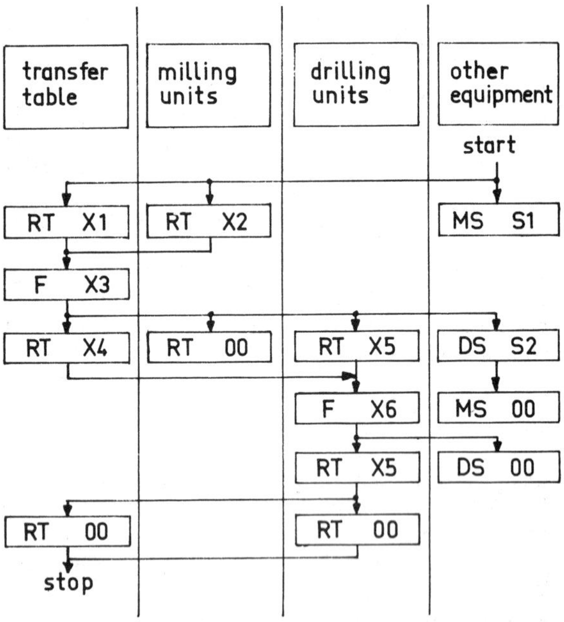

RT X1 ≙ rapid traverse to position X1
F1 X3 ≙ slide goes to position X3 with feed rate F1
MS S1 ≙ milling spindle start with speed S1
DS S2 ≙ drilling spindle start with speed S2
00 ≙ home position or zero speed

Fig. 2. A sample work sycle.

First transfer table takes the work piece to start position for milling. At the same time the milling units move to the milling position and milling spindles are started. Once all these tasks are completed the milling can be started and work piece goes between the milling units. After that transfer table takes the work piece to the drilling position, milling units more to their home positions, drilling units start to move towards the work piece, and drilling spindles are started and milling spindles stopped. After the drilling is done the drills are taken out by moving the unit to the same position where the drilling started. Finally the drilling unit and transfer table are taken to their home positions.

To write the block diagram in Fig. 2 into program you must collect all the conditions (previous tasks) that must be completed, before a certain block can be started. In a block you can do one elementary operation like move slide unit or start and stop spindle motors with certain speeds etc. With this kind of programming method you can split the work cycle into small pieces and state the condition code that has to be filled before the block can be started. A unit can work independently or be tied to another with the condition code. The system can be made modular, so it would be easy to add or take away units.

The programs would however be rather lengthy and difficult to handle by the user. Subprograms would also be difficult to use. These were the main reasons why the following approach became more appealing.

Block programming

This programming system is an application of the normal machine tool programming code that is widely used. It cannot be utilized as it is,while it is designed mainly for only 2 or 3 axles, which are dependent of each other (curve interpolation, etc).

If we split a block into subblocks, which consist of small programs for one unit, we can get a programming system which suits for our application.

The program for block diagram in the Fig. 2 is in the Fig. 3.

block	unit	G	X	F	S	D	M	
1	1	00	X1					block
	2	00	X2		S1		03	
2	1	01	X3	F1				
3	1	00	X4					subblock
	2	00	00				05	
4	3	81	X5 X6	F2	S2		03	
5	1	00	00				02	
	3	00	00				05	

Unit 1 transfer table
2 milling units
3 drilling units

X slide position
F feed rate
S spindle speed
D delay

G 00 rapid traverse
G 01 feed
G 81 drilling

M 02 end of program
M 03 spindle start (clockwise)
M 05 spindle stop

Fig. 3. A sample program.

With this kind of programming system units cannot be made independent, while a block has to be completed before the next are can start to be executed. This makes programs a little slower, but that can be compensated with efficient G-codes for each unit so that every simple task doesn't need a block of its own. The number of G- and M-codes can be increased as needed and it is possible to make a special code for a robot or some other auxiliary device. This programming method is also easy to learn if you already know the code that is used in NC-systems. Programs will also be much shorter than with the condition code method.

CONTROL SYSTEM

In realizing the control many approaches are available. Limit switches for position indication and programmable logic for sequence control could be used. In this case limit switches were not suitable as they are unconvenient to tune and the dynamics of the slide control system cannot be made fast with them.

The remaining systems were hardwired or microprocessor based numerical control.

Because of versatility, modularity, and lowering prices of microprosessor components the latter system was chosen. While medium speed low cost 8 bit processors were wanted to use, one processor has not time enough to control the whole machine. So the control system is hierarchical with many processors as is seen in Fig. 4.

The higher level main controller controls the whole machine. For thee units there is one unit controller, that gets information from the higher level and takes care of slide motions.

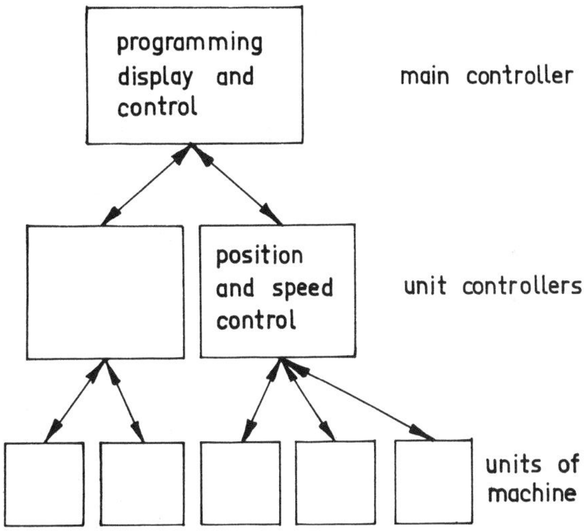

Fig. 4. Control system structure.

Unit controller

The block diagram of the unit controller with one slide system is in Fig. 5.

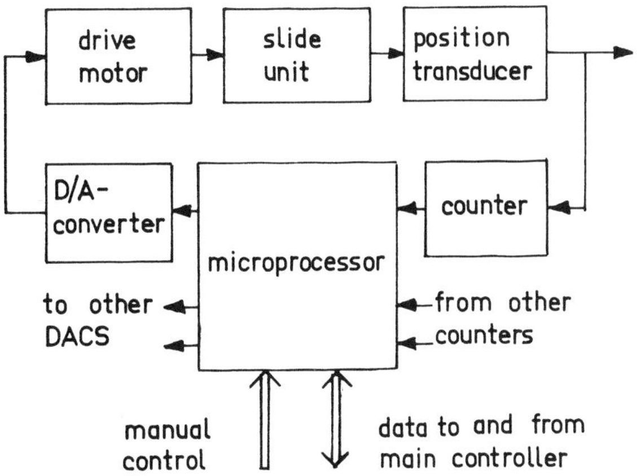

Fig. 5. Unit controller block diagram.

There are many ways how to measure slide position. The most popular are rotating or linear incremental transducers like resolvers and different magnetic or optical systems. In our experiments linear and rotating incremental pulse transducers were used. The rotating transducer was assembled to the ball screw. Better absolute accuracy was achiened with linear transducer, but if distances are long they are too expensive. If rotating transducers are reseted often enough the accuracy is acceptable.

The pulses from transducers are fed to 21-bit binary counter. Every slide unit has a counter of its own. The counter is read by processor and slide position is compared with the command value and the output signal to D/A-converter is calculated with this error signal. Each slide unit has a D/A-converter of its own and it acts also as a buffer memory.

If the controller is in automatic mode, it gets new position and speed values from main controller. According to the speed value a position increment is calculated and every time the control program is executed the position command value is increased or decreased with this increment until the wanted position is reached. At that moment unit controller also sends a ready pulse to main controller. After that controller keeps the slide on the wanted position until the next position and speed values are got.

Feedrate override control is achieved by changing the interrupt frequency, which tells how often the control program is executed.

With manual control the position command value can be increased of decreased with one pulse or continuously at a selectable rate.

Controller contains also feed hold control, which prevents the change of the position command, and zero point search to reset the counter.

Processor also performs some tests. For instance the control programs checks that the error signal is within acceptable limits.

The block diagram of unit controller software is in Fig. 6.

The most popular drive motor nowadays is electric DC-motor with solid state control. Their dynamic performance is very good. Variable speed AC-motor drives are also developing strongly, but they are so far too expensive.

Main controller

Main controller takes care of the whole machine. Below are mentioned its tasks.

- work cycle control
- traffic to and from unit controllers
- programming
- program editing and parameter changing
- display
- spindle drive and auxiliary device control

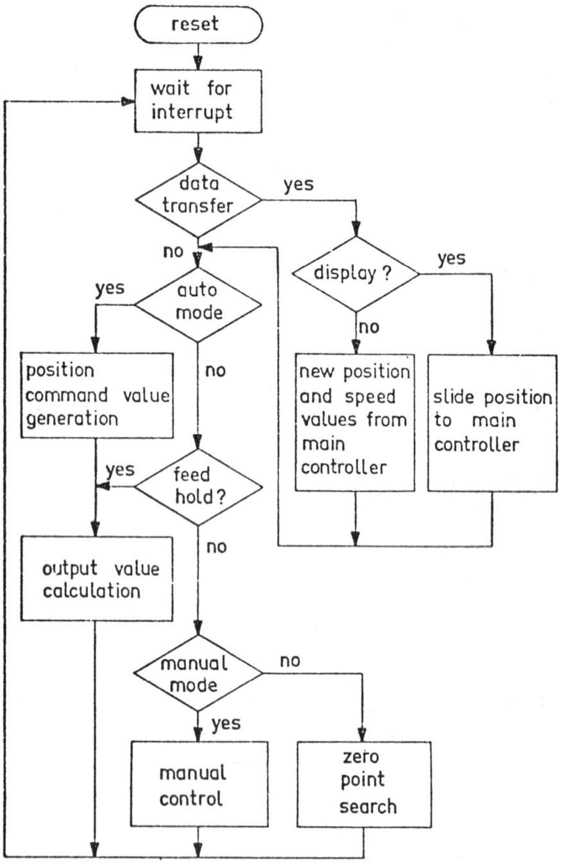

Fig. 6. Unit controller software blockdiagram.

- error diagnostics

Different memories for machining programs are used today. Besides the classical paper tape there are magnetic tape cassettes, floppy discs, and many kinds of semiconductor memories. The latter ones are more promising in our application. Their main disadvantage is that with random access memory (RAM) the data is lost with power failure. In read only memories (ROM) data is not lost but the user programmable ROMs can be programmed either once, if they are so called fusable ROMs, or many times, if they are erasable. The data in erasable ROMs (EROM) is erased with ultra violet light and all the data must be reprogrammed. With MNOS-technology RAMs can be produced where data is not lost with power failure. However they are rather slow memories, but as they are strongly developing they can give a good possibility in the near future.

In machines where machining programs are fixed, fusable ROMs can be used. The parameters that must be alterable can have basic values also in ROMs, but during machining these values are read from RAM with battery back-up, where the user can change them.

If machining programs are written by the user, main controller contains a number of EROMs. The program, that is being used, is in backed-up RAM. Then it can be corrected or altered and new programs are also written into that memory. The contents of RAM can be programmed to an erased EROM. By selecting EROM the user can choose different programs.

The program in EROMs is in source form. The statements are easy to read for display and user access. For efficient machining control one block at a time is compiled and work cycle control programs reads the compiled cycle from small buffer. In work cycle control program there must be a library for G- and M-codes.

In the user programmable machine the display and keyboard play an important part. CRT-displays are becoming widely used and a lot of information can be shown or them. In this application 7-segment numerical displays are considered efficient enough. A numeric keyboard and a number of special push buttons are also needed.

The control of spindle drives and auxiliary devices is also left to main controller.

While distances between controllers are short 8-bit parallel data transfer is used. The parallel interface ports in micro-processor systems are easily programmed either for input or output, so the same 8-bits can be used for both directions.

A small monitor program takes care of executing other programs.

The parts of main controller software system are in Fig. 7.

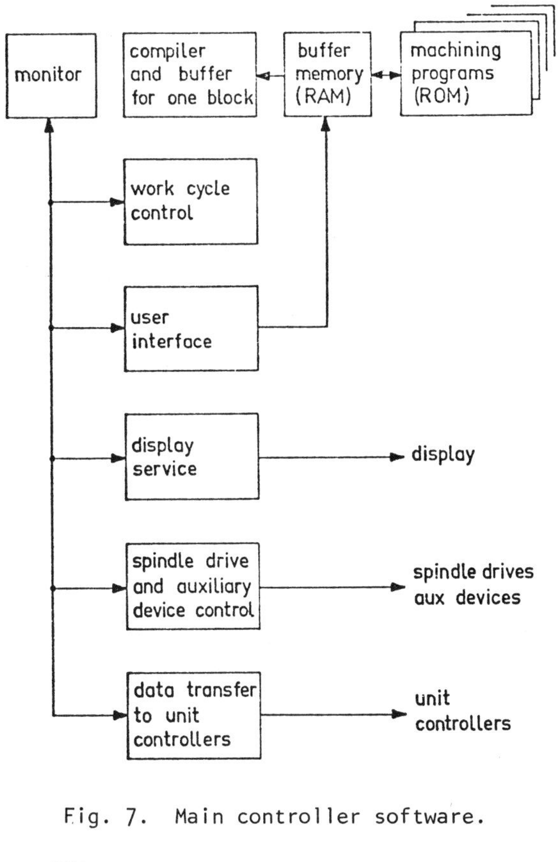

Fig. 7. Main controller software.

CONCLUSIONS

In this paper described special purpose machine tool control system has been partly tested with a one real slide system with DC-motor drive. Other units were simulated. The unit controller is built with M6800 microprocessor and it meets the specifications that were fixed at the start of the design. The main controller is at this moment realized with Motorola Exorciser development system, but separate hardware is being developed.

ACKNOWLEDGEMENTS

This system is developed in the co-operation project between Control Engineering Laboratory in Tampere University of Technology and Valmet Oy, Linnavuori Works. The authors would like to express their gratitude to the head of the Laboratory prof. Pauli Karttunen and the personal of the machine tool development department in Valmet.

REFERENCE

[1] Rasi, E., *The design and realization of motor drives and position control in the machine tool slide unit.* Thesis for the degree of diploma engineer in Tampere University of Technology, 1977, (in Finnish).

AN ADAPTIVE CNC SYSTEM OF A MILLING MACHINE TOOL

T. Watanabe*, S. Iwai* and Y. Nawata**

**Department of Precision Engineering, Faculty of Engineering, Kyoto University, Kyoto, Japan*
***Nippon Steel Co., Kimizu, Japan*

ABSTRACT

An adaptive CNC(computer numerical control) system of a milling machine tool using a precise tool wear rate model is presented. In the system, the bending moments on the spindle are sensed and used for computing the fundamental parameters of cutting conditions such as work material hardness, cutter sharpness, and others. The flank wear land temperature of the tool tip is computed from these parameters. Then, the tool wear rate is expressed as a function of these parameters and the flank wear land temperature, which is essential information to compute the performance index representing productivity or efficiency of the system.

Results of preliminary off line cutting experiments verify that the above mentioned methods to compute the parameters, the temperature, and the tool wear rate are correct.

An adaptive control cutting test adjusting the feedrate to keep the tool wear rate at constant value shows that this system can successfully reply to the variations of the tool wear phenomena.

A method to identify the other important cutting condition parameters such as width and depth of cut is also studied.

INTRODUCTION

In an adaptive control system of a machine tool, feedrate and spindle speed are altered in response to such conditions as varying width and depth of cut, changing work material hardness, varying tool wear and others with respect to a performance index. As the performance index, profit rate, production rate, accuracy of surface, and others are used.

When the purpose of an adaptive control is to improve the profit rate or the production rate, tool wear rate must be measured on line to calculate the profit rate or the production rate.

But, the direct measurement of the tool wear rate is difficult. Therefore, some other phisical values which depend on the tool wear rate must be measured. For example, R.M. Centner measured the tool tip temperature θ_p using tool-work thermocouple and the differential value of spindle torque, then, he calculated the tool wear rate da_f/dt by the following tool wear rate model (from his pioneer work Ref. 1):

$$\frac{da_f}{dt} = C_1 snwh_d + C_2\theta_p + C_3\frac{du}{dt} \qquad (1)$$

where

- a_f: flank wear land length on clearance face of tool
- s: feedrate
- n: spindle speed
- w, h_d: width and depth of cut
- θ_p: tool tip temperature
- u: spindle torque
- C_1, C_2, C_3: constants.

The defects of Centner's method are as follows.
(1) The tool tip temperature θ_p does not directly correlate with the flank wear rate da_f/dt as illustrated in Fig. 1, and One of the causes is that

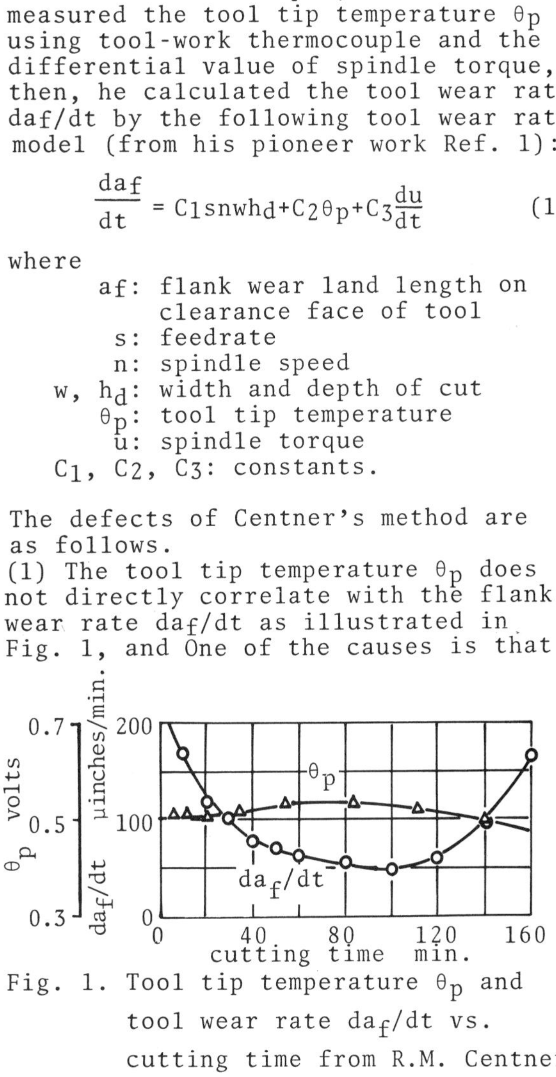

Fig. 1. Tool tip temperature θ_p and tool wear rate da_f/dt vs. cutting time from R.M. Centner (Ref. 2).

θ_p indicates the mean value of temperatures over all tool work interface.

(2) The measurement of θ_p is not so easy (Ref. 3).

(3) The third term in Eq.(1), the rate of change of spindle torque du/dt, was introduced to compensate the defect of (1). But,the measurement of du/dt is not feasible due to noise. Consequently, this term was eliminated from the on line tool wear calculation by Centner.

(4) The relation between the tool tip temperature, and the feedrate and spindle speed is not clear. Therefore, the optimum feedrate and spindle speed can not be calculated arithmatically. The actual response of the tool tip temperature corresponding to the change of feedrate and spindle speed to seek the optimum must be investigated in process.

(5) In Centner's system, the values of the width and the depth of cut must be given by an operator.

Other systems developed after Centner's system have used similar methods in basic princple or eliminated the function to adapt to the tool wear rate change due to the variations of the cutting conditions.

In this paper, an adaptive CNC system of a milling machine tool is presented, in which information of the cutting conditions is introduced by a different method. Fig. 2 shows the system, and the features of the system are as follows.

(I) Bending moments acting on the spindle are measured using semiconductor gages attached to the spindle, measuring of which is easier than that of tool tip temperature.

(II) The fundamental parameters such as hardness of work material, sharpness of tool, and others are calculated using values of the above mentioned bending moments.

(III) Using a theoretical temperature model, the tool tip temperature at the flank wear land is calculated from the feedrate, the spindle speed, and the parameters introduced in (II). Therefore, the optimum feedrate and spindle speed can be calculated arithmatically.

(IV) By modification of R.Holm's theory, the tool wear rate at the clearance fase is represented as the function of the parameters introduced in (II) and the tool tip temperature in (III).

(V) The values of the width and the depth of cut are calculated by sensing and analyzing the spindle torque and the bending moments as occasion demands.

IDENTIFICATION OF CUTTING CONDITIONS

Fundamental Parameters of Cutting Conditions

The fundamental parameters to represent the cutting conditions are as follows (See Fig. 3).

- β: angle between total force acting on rake face and its component f_h in direction of tool tip motion
- ϕ: angle of shear plane
- τ_s: shear stress of work material at shear plane
- τ_w: shear stress of work material before getting strain hardening effect
- τ_r: shear stress of chip at rake face
- H_w: hardness of work material corresponding to τ_w

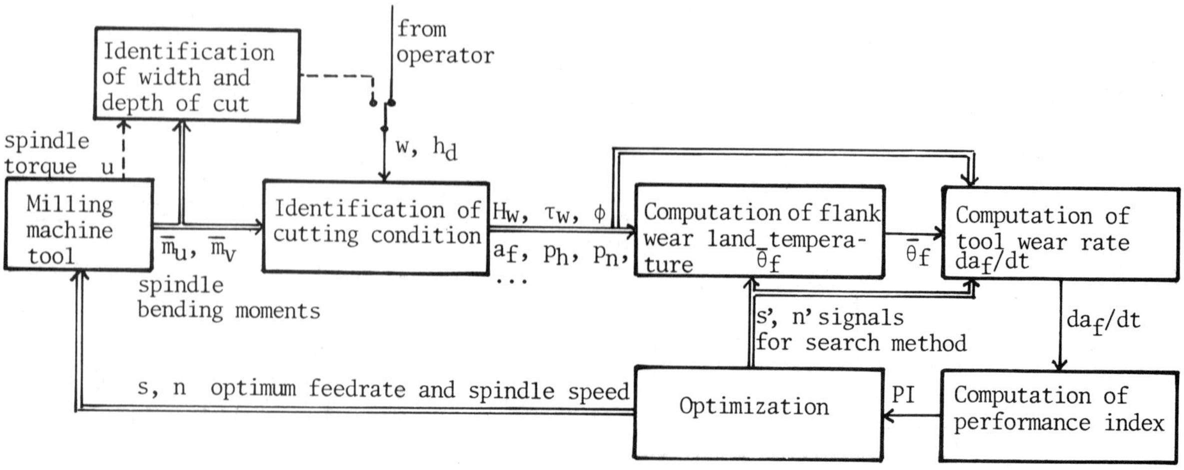

Fig. 2. Block diagram of the adaptive control system presented in this paper.

p_h: force per unit depth of cut acting on flank wear land in direction of tool tip motion
p_n: force per unit depth of cut acting on flank wear land normal to direction of tool tip motion
a_f: length of flank wear land
a_{ft}: length of real contact of tool with work at flank wear land

All these parameters are independent of the variations of the feedrate s and the spindle speed n. Shear plane length a_s, tool chip contact length a_r, and "uncut" chip thickness t_w shown in Fig. 3 are variables determined by using s, n, and the above mentioned parameters. These variables are used to calculate the temperature of the tool tip.

Measurement of Bending Moments

The bending moments m_1, m_2 are sensed by a set of semi-conductor gages attached to the spindle and applied for a co-ordinate transformer and a low pass filter. Through these processes, mean bending moments $\bar{m}_u$ and $\bar{m}_v$ are obtained; $\bar{m}_u$ is a moment of total cutting force in the direction of feed about the center of the gages and $\bar{m}_v$ is a moment of total cutting force normal to the direction of feed about the center of the gages as illustrated in Fig. 4.

The bending moments $\bar{m}_u$ and $\bar{m}_v$ are functions of the above mentioned parameters, the feedrate s, and the spindle speed n as follows.

$$\bar{m}_u = \bar{m}_{us} + \bar{m}_{uo}$$
$$\bar{m}_v = \bar{m}_{vs} + \bar{m}_{vo}$$

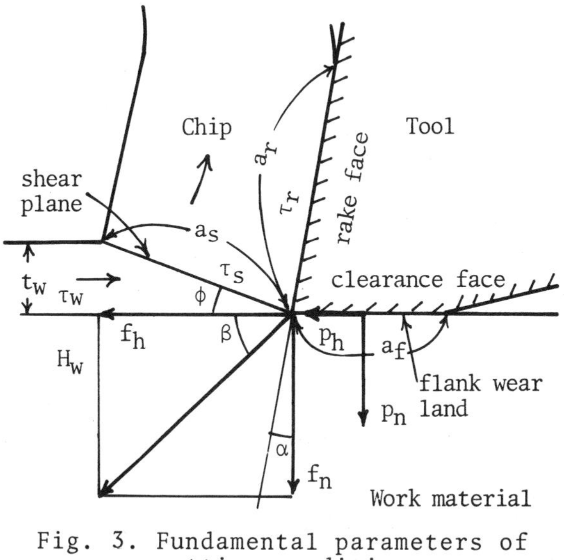

Fig. 3. Fundamental parameters of cutting conditions.

$$\bar{m}_{us} = \frac{h_d}{8\pi}\left(L - \frac{h_d}{2}\right)\frac{s\tau_s\cos\beta}{n\sin\phi\cos(\phi+\beta)} \times \left\{1 - \cos 2\psi_w - \tan\beta(2\psi_w - \sin 2\psi_w)\right\}$$

$$\bar{m}_{uo} = \frac{h_d}{2\pi}\left(L - \frac{h_d}{2}\right)Z_T\left\{p_h\sin\psi_w - p_n(1-\cos\psi_w)\right\}$$

$$\bar{m}_{vs} = \frac{h_d}{2\pi}\left(L - \frac{h_d}{2}\right)\frac{s\tau_s\cos\beta}{n\sin\phi\cos(\phi+\beta)} \times \left\{2\psi_w - \sin 2\psi_w + \tan\beta(1 - \cos 2\psi_w)\right\} \quad (2)$$

$$\bar{m}_{vo} = \frac{h_d}{2\pi}\left(L - \frac{h_d}{2}\right)Z_T\left\{p_h(1-\cos\psi_w) + p_n\sin\psi_w\right\}$$

where

$\psi_w = \cos^{-1}\left(1 - \frac{2w}{D}\right)$: angle corresponding to width of cut
$\bar{m}_{us}, \bar{m}_{vs}$: bending moments generated by cutting forces acting on rake face of tool
$\bar{m}_{uo}, \bar{m}_{vo}$: bending moments generated by cutting forces acting on flank wear land of tool tip
L: length between tool tip and bending moments sensor
D: diameter of tool
Z_T: number of tool teeth.

The method to separate $\bar{m}_{uo}$ and $\bar{m}_{vo}$ from $\bar{m}_{us}$ and $\bar{m}_{vs}$ respectively is as follows. The feedrate s is set at two low constant values s_1 and s_2 with an

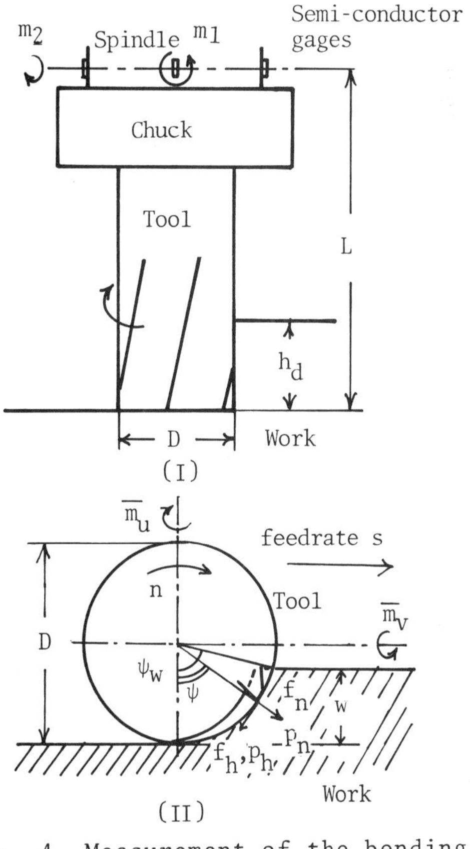

Fig. 4. Measurement of the bending moments.

adequate time interval, and the values of bending moments corresponding to s_1 and s_2 are measured. From these measured values, the values of moments at feedrate(s=0) are extrapolated, which represent the moments $\overline{m}_{uo}$ and $\overline{m}_{vo}$ generated by cutting forces acting on the flank wear land.

Identification of Cutting Condition Parameters

The process to determine the fundamental parameters($\beta, \phi, \tau_s, \tau_w, \tau_r, H_w, p_h, p_n, a_f, a_{ft}$) using cutting dynamics theories is illustrated in Fig. 5.

Fig. 6 shows examples of idetified β, $\phi, \tau_s, \tau_r, \tau_w, p_h, p_n, a_f$ and microscopically observed a_f vs.cutting time. These data were got during cutting experiment using Mo alloy high speed steel tool with S45C steel work material.

The facts that τ_w is kept at constant value 45kg/mm^2 and p_h, p_n, a_f increase with cutting time verify the correctness of the identification.

Fig. 7 shows τ_w and ϕ vs. feedrate s. The increase of τ_w against the decrease of s is due to strain hardening effect of work material which occures by the previous tool tip cutting.

COMPUTATION OF TOOL TIP TEMPERATURE

In this system, the temperature of the flank wear land of the tool tip is computed from the fundamental parameters of the cutting conditions stated in the previous chapter, which is an indispensable component to form a

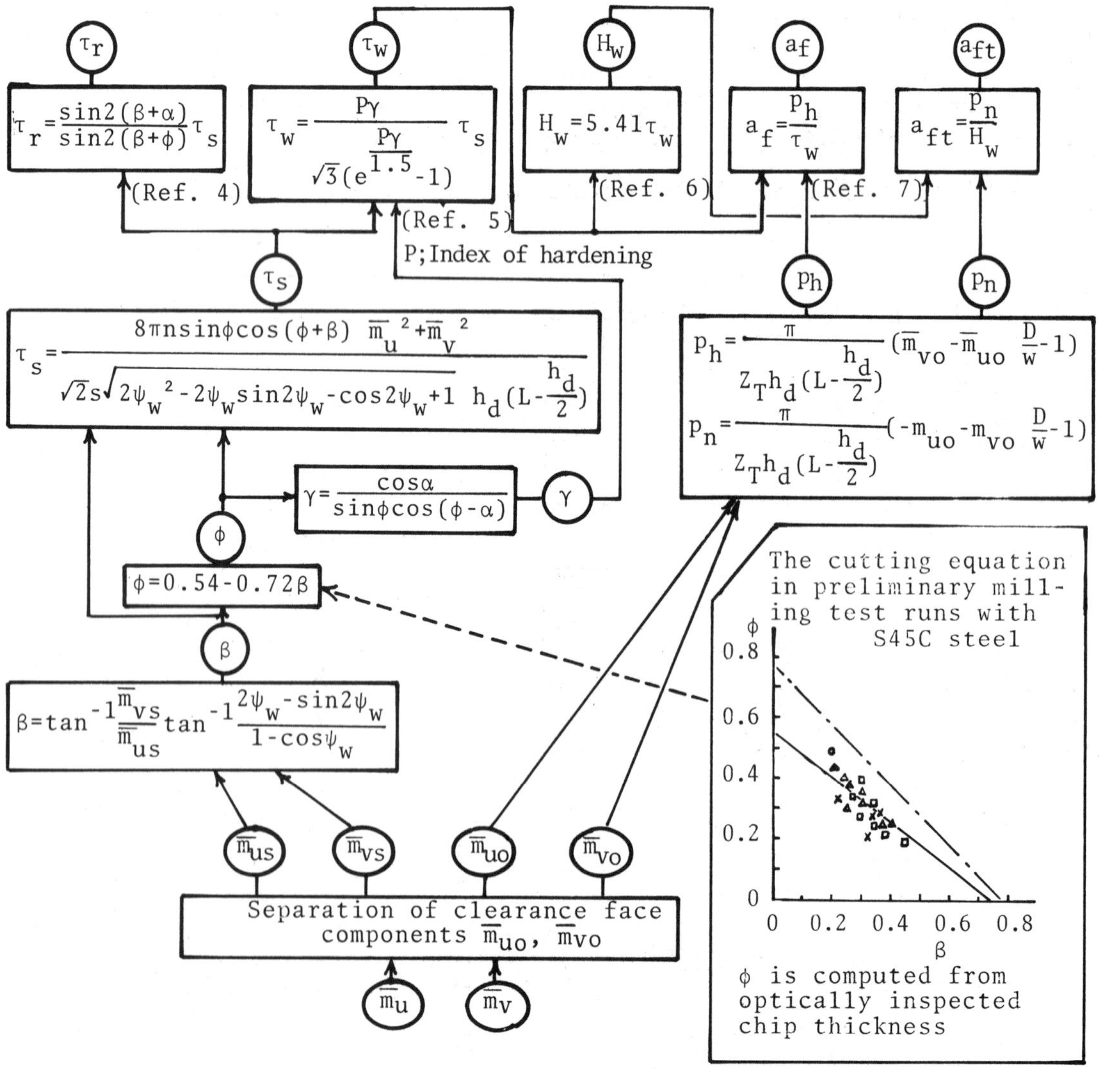

Fig. 5. Process to identify the fundamental parameters of cutting conditions.

tool wear model at the clearance face.

Few researches theoretically analyzed the temperature of the flank wear land of the tool tip in milling. Our temperature model is introduced by modification of M.C. Shaw's temperature model for lathe machine (Ref. 8) and by simplification of milling cut model as follows.

(1) The actual "uncut" chip thickness t_w is varied corresponding to the tool rotation, but here, it is assumed that the "uncut" chip thickness is constant:

$$\bar{t}_w = \frac{1}{\psi_w}\int_0^{\psi_w} t_w d\psi = \frac{s}{nZ_T}\ \frac{1-\cos\psi_w}{\psi_w} \qquad (3)$$

where

$\bar{t}_w$: mean "uncut" chip thickness.

(2) Instantaneous heat generated at the tool tip varies corresponding to the tool rotation, but here, it is assumed that time delay of the tool tip temperature rises to a steady state value corresponding to $\bar{t}_w$ as soon as the tool tip contact with the work.

On the other hand, our model contains detailed consideration about phenomena which are neglected in Shaw's analysis related to lathe machine, that is,

(1) Bidirectional heat conduction through the tool material between the rake face and the clearance face. (See Fig. 8).

(2) Heat conduction through the work material from the shear plane to the

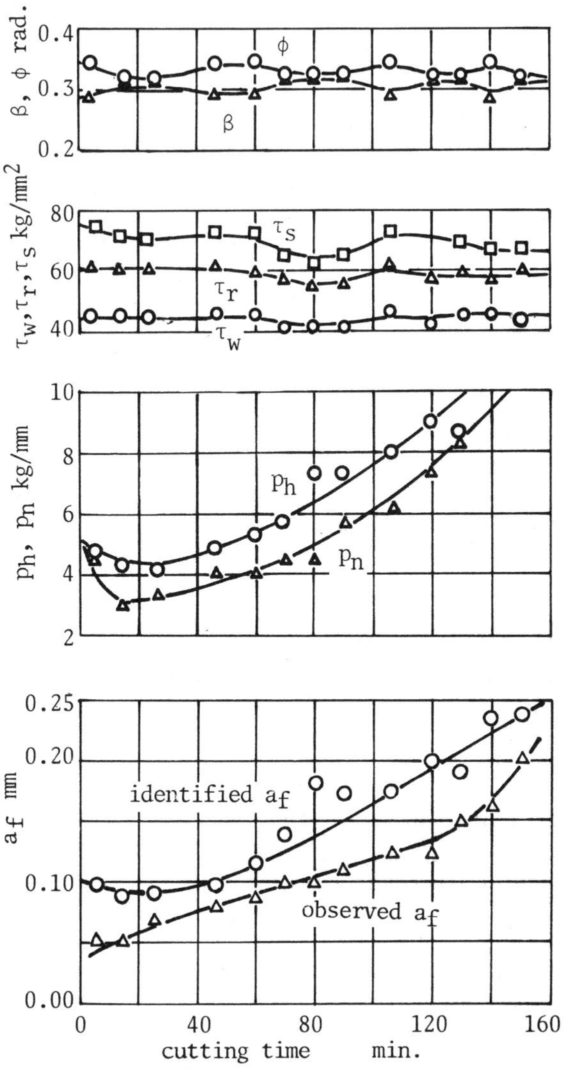

w=9mm, h_d=4.5mm, down cut, s=7.5cm/min, n=319rpm

Fig. 6. Identified parameters of cutting condition for 2 teeth endmill with S45C steel

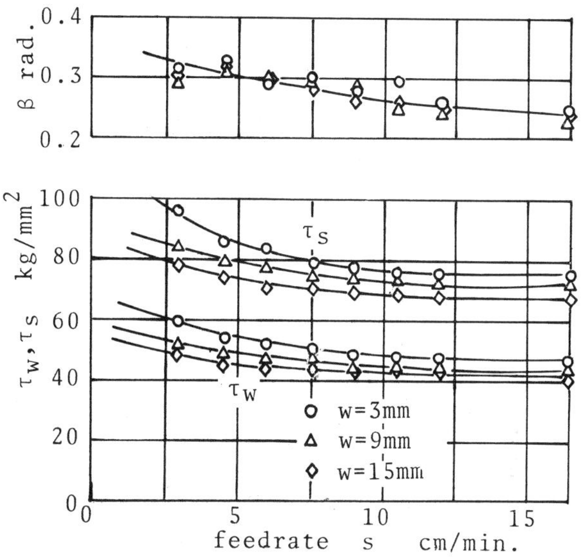

n=319rpm, h_d=4.5mm, D=20mm, Z_T=2

Fig. 7. β, τ_s, τ_w vs. feedrate

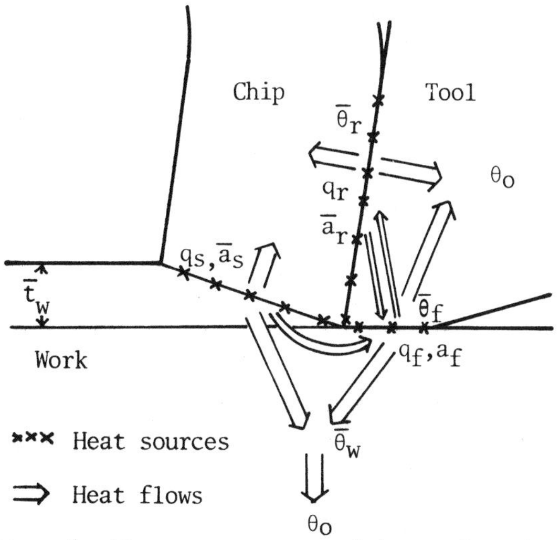

Fig. 8. Heat sources and heat flows at tool tip.

flank wear land on the clearance face.
(3) Temperature rise at cutting face of the work due to the heat generated by the previous tool tip cuttings.

To compute the tool tip temperature, the variables of cutting conditions which are dependent on the feedrate s and the spindle speed n must be calculated as follows.

$$\begin{aligned}
\bar{a}_s &= \frac{t_w}{\sin\phi} \\
\bar{a}_r &= \frac{\sin(\beta+\phi)}{\sin\phi\cos(\beta+\alpha)} t_w \\
v &= \pi D n \\
v_s &= \gamma \sin\phi \; v \\
v_c &= r_c v \\
q_s &= \frac{\tau_s v_s}{J} \\
q_r &= \frac{\tau_r v_c}{J} \\
q_f &= \frac{\tau_w v}{J}
\end{aligned} \tag{4}$$

where

$\bar{a}_s$: mean length of shear plane
$\bar{a}_r$: mean length of tool chip contact
v: cutting speed of tool tip
v_s: shear speed at shear plane
v_c: speed of chip
q_s, q_r, q_f: heat generations per unit time per unit area on shear plane, rake face and flank wear land
$\gamma = \frac{\cos\alpha}{\sin\phi\cos(\phi-\alpha)}$: shear ratio
$r_c = \frac{\sin\phi}{\cos(\phi-\alpha)}$: cut ratio
α: rake angle
J: mechanical equivalent of heat.

By the analysis based on thermo dynamics theories, the mean temperature of the flank wear land on the clearance face $\bar{\theta}_f$ is computed as follows.

$$\begin{aligned}
\bar{\theta}_f = {} & C_b(R_{ft} - R_{fr}C_{rf})a_f q_f \\
& + C_b(R_{rf} - R_{rt}C_{rf})\bar{a}_r q_r \\
& + \left\{C_b C_{rf}\left(1+\frac{R'}{R_{sw}}\right) + C_a C_{sf}\right. \\
& \left. + C_a \frac{R'}{R_{sw}}\right\} R_s \bar{a}_s q_s + \theta_o
\end{aligned} \tag{5}$$

$$C_a = \frac{R_{ft} - C_{rf}(R_{fr}+R')}{R_{ft} - C_{rf}(R_{fr}+R') + R_{fw} + R'}$$

$$C_b = \frac{R_{fw}+R'}{R_{ft} - C_{rf}(R_{fr}+R') + R_{fw} + R'}$$

$$C_{rf} = \frac{R_{rf}}{R_{rc}+R_{rt}}$$

$$R_s = \frac{R_{sw}R_{sc}}{R_{sw}+R_{sc}}$$

$$R_{sc} = \frac{1}{C_w \rho_w t_w}$$

$$R' = \frac{R_o R_{sc}}{1+R_{sc}} \; \frac{Z_T \psi_w}{2\pi}$$

$$R_{sw} = \frac{0.752\sqrt{K_w}}{\lambda_w\sqrt{\bar{a}_s v_s}}$$

$$R_{rc} = \frac{0.752\sqrt{K_w}}{\lambda_w\sqrt{\bar{a}_r v_r}}$$

$$R_{fw} = \frac{0.752\sqrt{K_w}}{\lambda_w\sqrt{a_f v}}$$

$$R_o = \frac{1}{2\lambda_w} A\left(\frac{2h_d}{\psi_w D}\right)$$

$$R_{rt} = \frac{1}{\lambda_t} A\left(\frac{h_d}{\bar{a}_r}\right)$$

$$R_{fr} = \frac{1}{\lambda_t}\left\{B_\psi\left(\frac{h_d}{a_f}\right) + B_\chi\left(\frac{\bar{a}_r}{a_f}\right)\right\}$$

$$R_{rf} = \frac{1}{\lambda_t}\left\{B_\psi\left(\frac{h_d}{\bar{a}_r}\right) + B_\chi\left(\frac{a_f}{\bar{a}_r}\right)\right\}$$

$$C_{sf} = \frac{\bar{a}_s'}{a_f}\left\{\left(\frac{a_f}{\bar{a}_s'}+1\right)^{1.5} - \left(\frac{a_f}{\bar{a}_s'}\right)^{1.5} - 1\right\} \times \frac{\cos\alpha}{\cos\phi\cos(\phi-\alpha)}$$

$$a_s' = a_s \cos\phi$$

$$\begin{aligned}
A(\Psi) &= \frac{2}{\pi}(\ln 2\Psi + 0.5) + \frac{2}{3\pi}\frac{1}{\Psi} && ;\ \Psi \geq 21 \\
&= \frac{2}{\pi}(1 + 0.387\sqrt{\Psi}) && ;\ 21 > \Psi > 1 \\
&= \frac{1}{\Psi} A\left(\frac{1}{\Psi}\right) && ;\ 1 \geq \Psi \geq 0
\end{aligned}$$

$$B_\psi(\Psi) = \frac{2}{\pi}(\ln 2\Psi + 0.5)$$

$$B_\chi(\chi) = \frac{2}{\pi}\left\{\ln 2 - \frac{1}{2}\ln(1+\chi^2) - \frac{1}{\chi}\arctan\chi - \frac{1}{2\chi}\left(\operatorname{arccot}\chi - \frac{\pi}{2}\right) - \frac{\chi}{2}\operatorname{arccot}\chi\right\}$$

$C_w, \rho_w, \lambda_w, K_w$: specific heat, density, heat conductivity, and thermal diffusivity of work material
heat conductivity, and thermal diffusivity of work material

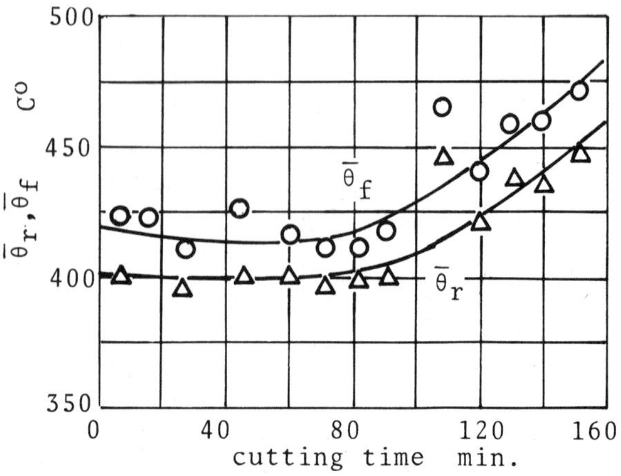

s=7.5cm/min., n=319rpm., w=9mm, h_d=4.5mm, down cut.

Fig. 9. Flank wear land temperature $\bar{\theta}_f$ and rake face temperature $\bar{\theta}_r$ vs. cutting time.

λ_t, K_t: heat conductivity and thermal diffusivity of tool
θ_o: room temperature

The temperature of the rake face $\overline{\theta}_r$ is also computed by a similar method. Fig. 9 shows the temperature plots of the rake face and the flank wear land versus cutting time. The temperature rise in accordance with the tool wear are clearly indicated.

TOOL WEAR RATE EQUATION

Trigger and Chao(Ref. 9) modified Holm's theory(Ref. 10), and expressed the adhesion wear at the tool-chip interface on rake face as follows.

$$\frac{w_v}{l_v} = e^{-\frac{E+E'}{R\,\theta_r}}\,\frac{p_r}{H} \tag{6}$$

where
w_v: worn volume on rake face per unit depth of cut
l_v: sliding distance of chip
p_r: force per unit depth normal to rake face
R: universal gas constant
E: energy activation
E': heat activation of chip material
H: hardness of work material

By applying Eq. (6) for the clearance face and by taking mechanical wear caused by scrach and shock wear caused by impact of the tool tip with the workpiece into consideration, the tool wear rate(flank wear land length rate) in milling is expressed as follows.

$$\frac{da_f}{dt} = C_m\frac{D}{2}\,\frac{n\psi w\ a_{ft}}{a_f} + C_t\frac{D}{2}\,e^{-\frac{C_t'}{\overline{\theta}_f}}\,\frac{n\psi w a_{ft}}{a_f} + C_s\frac{n}{a_f} \tag{7}$$

where
C_m, C_t, C_s: weighting factors to mechanical wear, adhesive thermal wear, and shock wear.

For application of the least squares method to decide the undetermined weighting factors(C_m, C_t, C_s), the exponential characteristics of Eq. (7) is approximated as summation of linear segments.

$$\frac{da_f}{dt} = \sum_{i=1}^{M} C_i x_i \tag{8}$$

where

$C_1 = C_m$, $\quad x_1 = \frac{D}{2}\,\frac{n\psi w a_{ft}}{a_f}$

$C_2 = C_{t1}$, $\quad x_2 = x_1 F(\overline{\theta}_f, \theta_1)$

$\vdots \qquad \vdots$

$C_{M-1} = C_{tM-2}$, $\quad x_{M-1} = x_1 F(\overline{\theta}_f, \theta_{M-2})$

$C_M = C_s$, $\quad x_M = \frac{n}{a_f}$

$F(\overline{\theta}_f, \theta_i) = \overline{\theta}_f - \theta_i \quad ; \overline{\theta}_f \geqq \theta_i$
$\qquad = 0 \quad ; \overline{\theta}_f < \theta_i$

$C_{t1}, \cdots, C_{tM-2}$; weighting factors to depend on C_t, C_t'

The integral form of Eq. (7) is as follows.

$$a_f = \sum_{i=1}^{M} C_i \int_0^T x_i\,dt \tag{8}$$

T: cutting time.

A series of preliminary metal cutting experiments to determine the tool wear rate weighting factors C_i were done under the various combinations of values of the width of cut and those of the feedrate. During each experiment, the width of cut and the feedrate were maintained constant throughout the life of tool. The depth of cut and the spindle speed were maintained constant throughout all the experiments. All cutting experiments were performed using two teeth Mo alloy high speed steel helical endmill with S45C steel workpiece.

A total of fifteen sharp tools were installed, and each one was worn to the end of life in each test run. During each test, the bending moments were measured, the integrals in Eq. (8) were computed , and the length of flank wear land a_f was measured by optical inspection. But, in the case of using high speed steel tool, the generation of tool wear on the rake face is greater. Therefore, the observed flank wear land length a_f can not represent the true tool wear at the clearance face as illustrated in Fig. 10. Then, an assumed flank wear

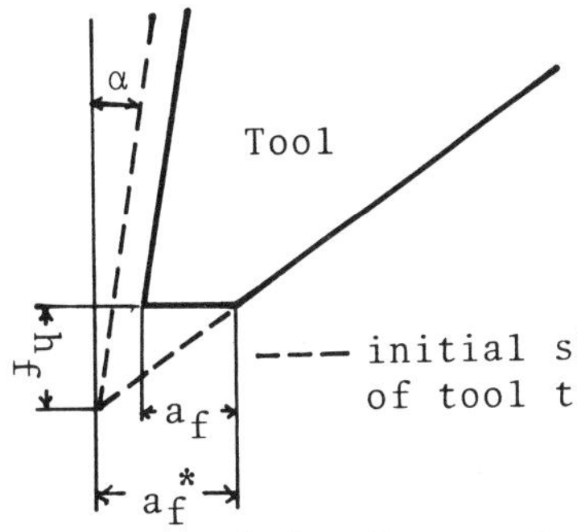

Fig. 10. Assumed flank wear land length a_f^*, observed flank wear land length a_f, and flank wear depth h_f.

land length a_f^* illustrated in Fig. 10 is applied for the left hand of Eq. (8) in stead of a_f.

The equations of TABLE 1 are tool wear rate equations with the weighting factors $C_1 \sim C_M$ determined by using the least squares method. Column A indicates Eq. (8). Column B~D indicate the modifications of Eq. (8). In column B, a_{ft}/a_f is omitted. In column C, the term of wear rate by shock contains the work material hardness H_w. In column D, the shock wear volume by each impact is propotional to a_f. TABLE 1 also shows the curves showing the relation between the tool wear rate and the flank wear land temperature for the equations, and the mean error percentages of the assumed flank wear land length a_f^* calculated for the test results by the equations. By comparison of these tool wear rate equations, it is clear that the error percentage of Eq. (8) is the least and the relation between the tool wear rate

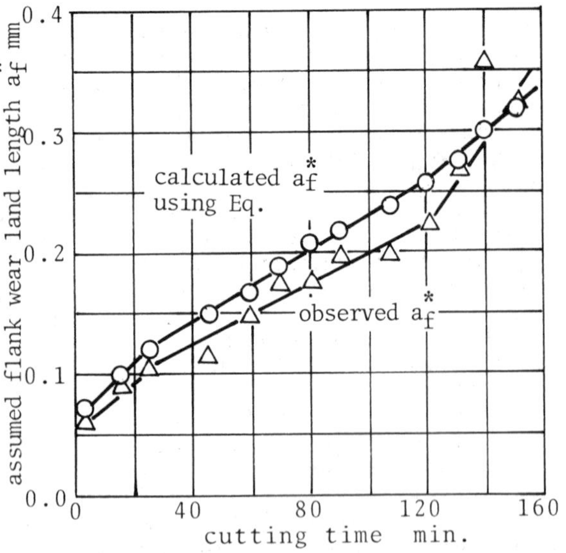

Fig. 11. Comparison of assumed flank wear land length a_f^* calculated by the tool wear rate equation with assumed flank wear land length a_f^* observed by microscope.

TABLE 1 Tool Wear Rate Equations Determined by Adopting the Least Squares Method for Preliminary Cutting Test Results, Curves Showing the Relation between Tool Wear Rate and Flank Wear Land Temperature $\bar{\theta}_f$ for the Equations, and Mean Error Percetages of Assumed Flank Wear Land Length Calculated by the Equations Respectively

A	B	C	D
$\frac{da_f^*}{dt} = \frac{nD\psi_w}{2}\frac{a_{ft}}{a_f}\{5.0\cdot10^{-7} +3.7\cdot10^{-9}F(\bar{\theta}_f,300) +4.8\cdot10^{-9}F(\bar{\theta}_f,400) +1.9\cdot10^{-8}F(\bar{\theta}_f,500)\} +3.9\cdot10^{-6}\frac{n}{a_f}$	$\frac{da_f^*}{dt} = \frac{nD\psi_w}{2}\{7.3\cdot10^{-8} +8.4\cdot10^{-10}F(\bar{\theta}_f,300) +1.8\cdot10^{-10}F(\bar{\theta}_f,400) +2.9\cdot10^{-9}F(\bar{\theta}_f,500)\} +3.9\cdot10^{-7}\frac{n}{a_f}$	$\frac{da_f^*}{dt} = \frac{nD\psi_w}{2}\frac{a_{ft}}{a_f}\{-8.1\cdot10^{-7} +2.0\cdot10^{-8}F(\bar{\theta}_f,300) -1.4\cdot10^{-8}F(\bar{\theta}_f,400) +2.2\cdot10^{-8}F(\bar{\theta}_f,500)\} +1.3\cdot10^{-9}\frac{nH_w}{a_f}$	$\frac{da_f^*}{dt} = \frac{nD\psi_w}{2}\frac{a_{ft}}{a_f}\{-1.0\cdot10^{-7} +1.3\cdot10^{-9}F(\bar{\theta}_f,300) +8.4\cdot10^{-11}F(\bar{\theta}_f,400) +2.1\cdot10^{-9}F(\bar{\theta}_f,500)\} +4.6\cdot10^{-6}n$
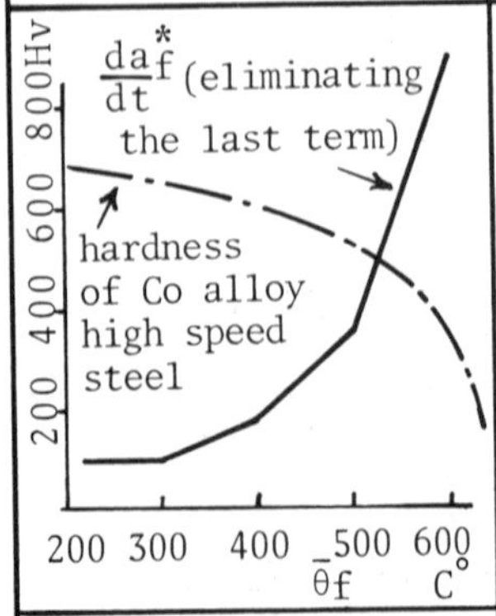	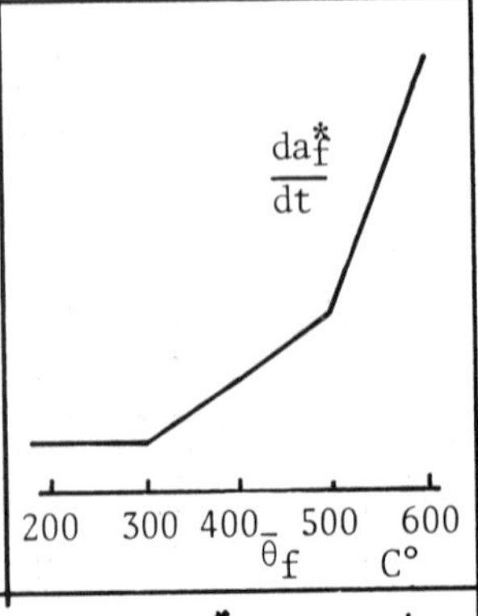	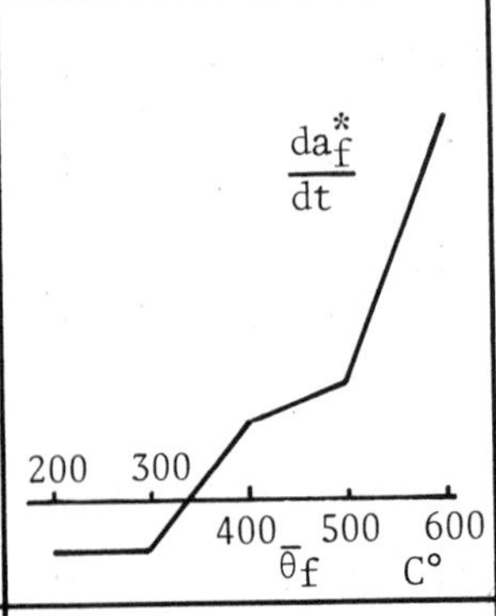	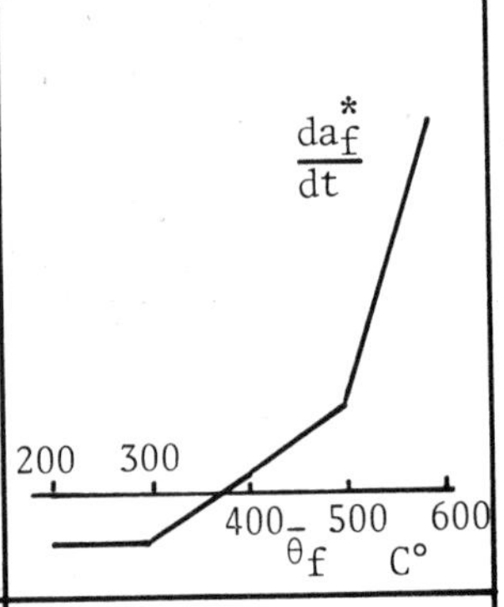
$\frac{100}{N}\cdot\sum_{j=1}^{N}\frac{\lvert a_f^*\rvert_{calculated} - a_f^*\rvert_{measured}\rvert}{a_f^*\rvert_{measured}}$ =8.26 %	9.25 %	10.55 %	10.59 %

and the tool tip temperature of Eq. (8) is the fittest to the exponential characteristics in Eq. (7) and to the hardness characteristics of Mo alloy high speed steel in high temperature.

Fig. 11 shows plots of a_f^* computed by the equation of column A and observed a_f^* vs. cutting time. The computed a_f^* curve is obviously characterized by a period of initial rapid wear, followed by a period of reduced almost constant wear rate for the bulk of the remaining tool life, and followed by a period of increasing wear rate near the end of the tool life as same as the observed a_f^* curve.

CONSTITUTION OF ADAPTIVE CNC SYSTEM AND ON LINE CUTTING EXPERIMENT

An adaptive control program using the above mentioned methods is organized in conjunction with numerical and servo control programs on a complex computer control system(Ref. 11)# as illustrated in Fig. 12. To make clear the distinctive features of the tool wear rate equation, the adopted algorism to decide the optimum feedrate is one which maintains the tool wear rate at the directed constant value during cutting time.

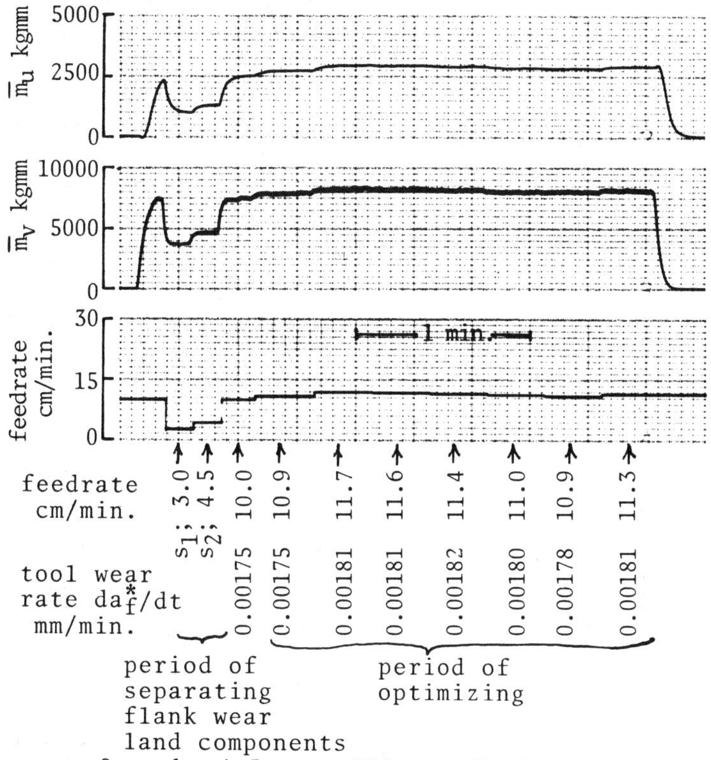

w=9mm, h_d=4.5mm, n=319rpm, Z_T=2, D=20mm
Mo alloy high speed steel endmill with S45C steel work material ,down cut.

Fig. 13. An example of adaptive control cutting test run in which the tool wear rate is expected to hold the constant value 0.0018mm/min.

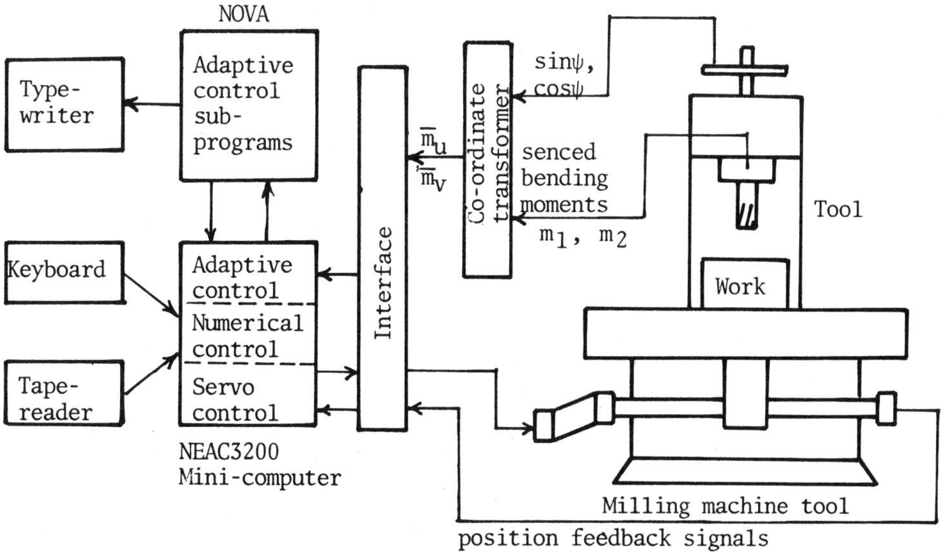

Fig. 12. Adaptive CNC system of milling machine tool organized for on line cutting test.

About 4Kword memories in NEAC and about 10Kword memories in NOVA are used for the software of this system (containing programs to identify w and h_d in the following chapter).

Fig. 13 shows an adaptive control action. Setting of the feedrate at s_1, s_2 to separate the flank wear land components $\bar{m}_{uo}$, $\bar{m}_{vo}$ from the measured moments is repeatedly done with an adequate cutting time interval. During the interval after setting the feedrate at s_1, s_2, the measurement of $\bar{m}_u$, $\bar{m}_v$, the computation of parameters $\beta, \phi, \tau_s, \tau_w, \cdots$, and resetting of the feedrate to maintain the tool wear rate constant are repeated. It takes about 1.5 sec. to search the optimum feedrate, which is rather short, because the tool tip temperature is calculated mathematically in this system. A little modification of the optimum feedrate after the adjustment of the feedrate at the optimum value is caused by the variations of the parameters $\beta, \phi, \tau_s, \tau_w, \cdots$ with the change of the feedrate(See Fig. 7).

Fig. 14 shows the optimum feedrate and the assumed flank wear land length a_f^* vs. cutting time from the start to the end of the tool life during an adaptive cutting test run. The optimum feedrate increases in the first period, gradually decreases in the middle, and rapidly decreases in the period near to the end of the tool life. This verifies that the adaptive control of the system functions well in response to the variations of the tool wear characteristics indicated in Fig. 1 and Fig. 11.

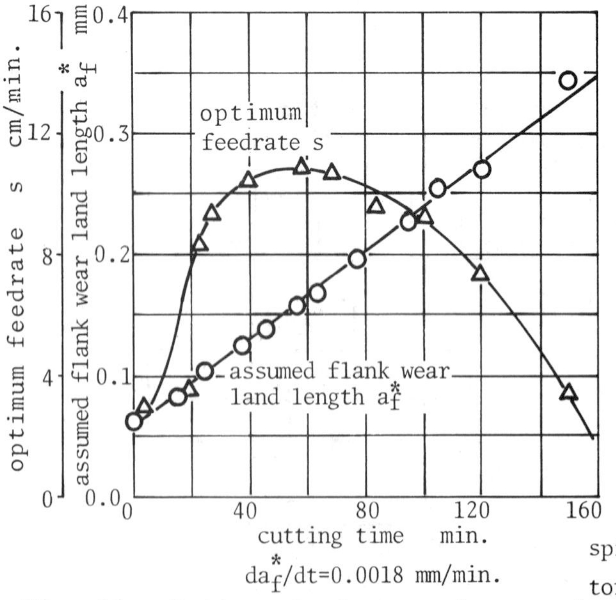

Fig. 14. Optimum feedrate and assumed flank wear land length vs. time over all tool life in adaptive control cutting test under the same condition as in Fig.13.

IDENTIFICATION OF WIDTH AND DEPTH OF CUT

In the above mentioned on line experiment, information about the width of cut and the depth of cut are given by an operater.

In the above mentioned on line experiment, information about the width of cut w and the depth of cut h_d are given by an operator. In case that w and h_d vary frequently during cutting, inputs of w and h_d by an operator decreases the covenience of using adaptive control. Therefore, a method to identify w and h_d from the measured spindle torque and bending moments is investigated.

Identification of Depth of Cut

If a helical angle cutter tool is used, the time interval t_h during which the spindle torque is increasing is proportional to h_d as follows.

$$t_h = \frac{2\tan\delta}{\pi D n} h_d \tag{9}$$

for

$h_d < \pi D/(Z_T \tan\delta)$ and

$w < D/2$

where

δ: helical angle of cutter.

Fig. 15 illustrates the circuit obtaining the signal proportional to t_h, and its output plot vs. h_d.

Identification of Width of Cut

The ratio of absolute value $\sqrt{\bar{m}_{us}^2 + \bar{m}_{vs}^2}$

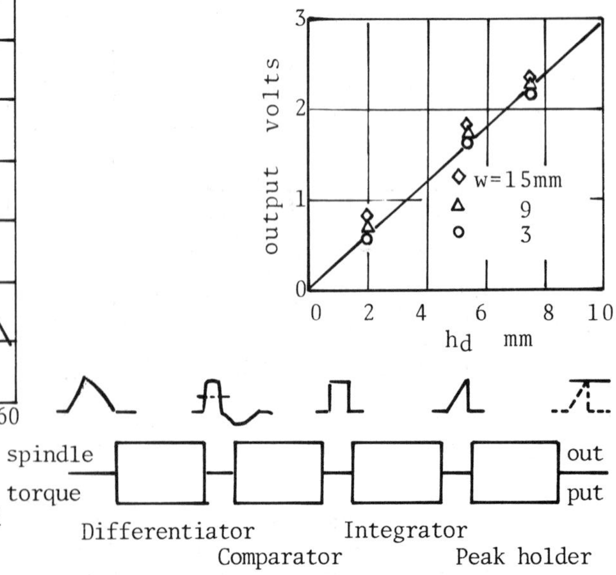

Fig. 15. Method to identify depth of cut.

of the bending moments to the spindle torque $\bar{u}_s$, both of which are generated by the cutting forces acting on the rake face, is expressed as a function of w and h_d as follows.

$$\frac{\sqrt{\bar{m}_{us}^2+\bar{m}_{vs}^2}}{\bar{u}_s} = \frac{(L-h_d/2)\sqrt{1-\cos 2\psi_w+2\psi_w(\psi_w-\sin 2\psi_w)}}{\sqrt{2}\cos\beta(1-\cos\psi_w)D} \qquad (10)$$

Then, the width of cut w is decided by searching the condition that the value given by Eq. (10) is identical with the measured ratio $\sqrt{\bar{m}_{us}^2+\bar{m}_{vs}^2}/\bar{u}_s$. In this search method, the following performance index $PI'(w,h_d)$:

$$PI'(w,h_d) = G\left(\frac{\sqrt{\bar{m}_{us}^2+\bar{m}_{vs}^2}\Big|_{\text{observed}}}{\sqrt{\bar{m}_{us}^2+\bar{m}_{vs}^2}\Big|_{\text{calculated by Eq. (10)}}}\right) \qquad (11)$$

where

$$G(y) = y \quad ; \quad y \le 1$$
$$= 1/y \quad ; \quad y > 1$$

is used. Fig. 16 shows the values of the performance index.

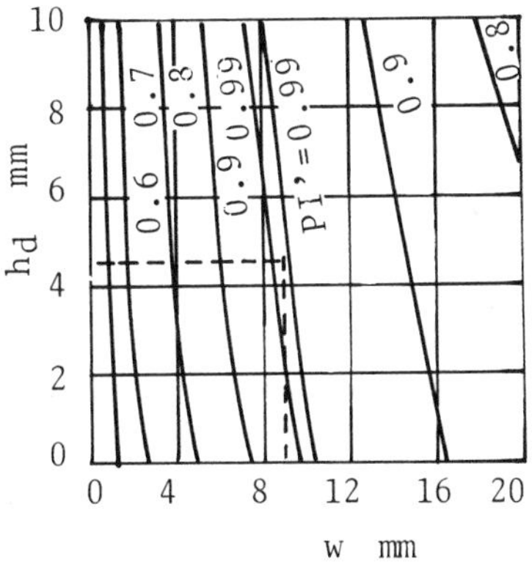

true width w=9mm
true depth h_d=4.5mm

Fig. 16. Performance index to search for width of cut.

CONCLUSIONS

An adaptive control system of a milling machine tool has been presented. The following methods, which are used in this system, have been studied in detail.

(1) The method to obtain the fundamental parameters related to cutting conditions such as work material hardness, sharpness of tool, and others from the spindle bending moments.

(2) The method to compute the flank wear land temperature separately from the rake face temperature.

(3) The method to compose a detailed tool wear rate model using the above mentioned parameters and flank wear land temperature.

Preliminary cutting experiments have verified the correctness of these methods.

A computerized adaptive and numerical control system of the milling machine tool has been constructed, in which the tool wear rate has been adjusted at a constant value. An adaptive cutting test run using this system has verified that this system has more adaptability to the variations of tool wear phenomena than ordinary systems.

ACKNOWLEDGMENTS

This work was supported by the Science Foundations of the Ministry of Education:Test-II 985021 and General-C 95507, and by Howa Sangyo Co.

REFERENCES

(1) R.M. Centner, Development of adaptive control techniques for numerically controlled milling machines, Report No.ML-TDR-64-277 of USAF, 33 (1964).

(2) " ,109 ".

(3) K.J. Trigger, R.K. Campbell, and B.T. Chao, A tool work thermo couple compensating circuit, Trans. of ASME. 80I, 302, (1958).

(4) Toshio Sata, Friction process of cutting mechanism, Trans. of JSPE. 21, 417 (1955).

(5) translated by Ichro Hasegawa,(1965) Metal cutting theory,Tokyo-Tosho, Tokyo, p.121 (Original:А.М. Розенберг and А.Н. Еремин, ЭЛЕМЕНТЫ ТЕОРИИ ПРОЦЕССА РЕЗАНИЯ МЕТАЛЛОВ).

(6) ", p.153.

(7) E.G.Thomsen, A.G. Macdonald, and S. Kobayashi, Flank friction studies with carbide tool reveal sublayer plastic flow, Trans. of ASME. 84B, 53 (1962).

(8) E.G. Loewen and M.C. Shaw, On the analysis of cutting tool temperatures, Trans. of ASME. 76, 217 (1954).

(9) K.J. Trigger and B.T. Chao, The mechanism of crater wear of cemented carbide tools, Trans. of ASME. 76, 217 (1954).

(10) R. Holm, Electric contacts, Hugo Gebers Förloig, Stockholm, 214 (1946).

(11) Toru Watanabe, Mini-computer interface for DDC of machine tool, Materials of JAACE. B-75-10-1, 131 (1975).

CNC APPLICATIONS

R. Nozawa, H. Kawamura and M. Kawamata

Fujitsu FANUC Ltd, Hino Tokyo, Japan

1. Introduction

The demands to increase productivity of numelically controlled machine tools have stimulated CNCs to have more sophisticated softwares. Therefore CNCs are increasing more capabilities with the development of softwares and are contributing to raise productivity in various areas of metal working industries. FANUC 200 abbriviated to F200, which is one of the CNC, has contributed to increasing productivity also.

Though F200 has been applied to various machines, only some applications in machining center field are presented here.

2. Coordinate rotation for easy handling of heavy work

One of the problems to machine big and heavy work pieces is to load the work piece on the right position to be machined. It takes many hours to place the work on the position it should be. The problem has been solved by using CNC F200.

In this case the work piece can be set on the proper place where an operater can easily set, though there will be a deviation from the position where part program is expecting that the work piece is placed. In conventional ways, it will take many hours to inspect the deviation of actual work position from programmed position and to reproduce new NC command tape. In the way using F200, in order to avoid the loss of hours, some points are measured using inspecting probe attached instead of cutting tool and the measured data are stored into F200 memory. Then, F200 machines the work piece by transforming the partprogram coordinate into the the actual work coordinate by calculating the deviation using the measured data. The Fig. 1. shows an example of a work which is placed with some angle to machine coordinate axes.

X, Y are partprogram coordinate axes which are usually parallel to machine coordinate axes, x, y are

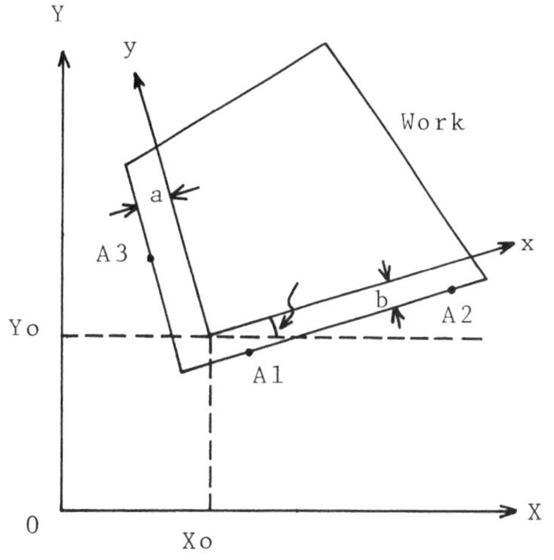

Fig. 1. A work placed with some angle to machine coordinate axes

work coordinate axes, A1 and A2 are points on the line parallel to x axis A3 is a point on the line parallel to y axis, and a,b are given by operater as the amount of shift value of x,y axes from the lines thru A1,A2 or A3 which are usually the work edge lines. Measuring these points A1,A2 and A3, Xo,Yo and θ are calculated, and partprogram coordinates are converted into work coordinate using Xo,Yo and θ. This conversion is done simulteneously with machine control without interrupting any normal NC processing.

3. Inductosyn scale error compensation for increasing accuracy

The accuracy of machine motion is depends on the accuracy of Inductosyn scale. But Inductosyn scale itself has some errors though the machines for precise control are using Inductosyn scale. To machine a work more precisely, the errors of Inductosyn scale should be removed. For the purpose of this compensation, the errors are measured using a measuring device such as laser measuring device and the measured errors are stored in memory of F200 beforehand. F200 compensates the errors according to the position of machine using stored data. The data of scale srror at each increment, 10mm increment in this case, are measured from zero point of machine coordinate system. F200 has a table of compensation values of scale errors according to the each increment in machine coordinate as shown in Fig. 2. Machine coordinate system is set up in F200 when the machine returned to fixed reference point. F200 updates the position in machine coordinate system with the motion of each axis, pick up the error compensation values according to the position and compensates the motion of each axis. Fig. 3. and Fig. 4. shows an example of positioning accuracy compensated by Inductosyn scale error compensation method.

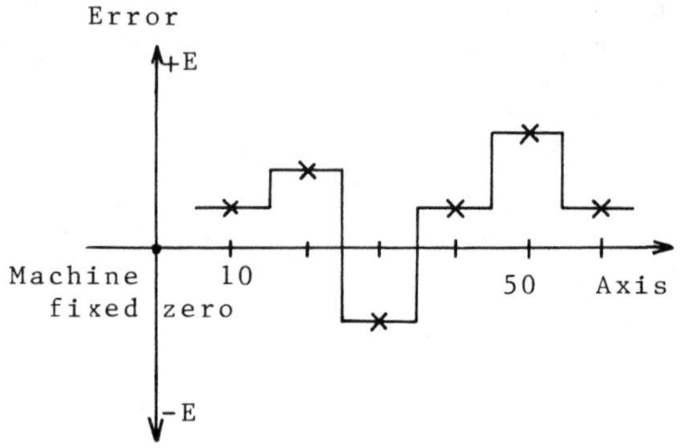

Fig. 2. The scale error data stored in F200

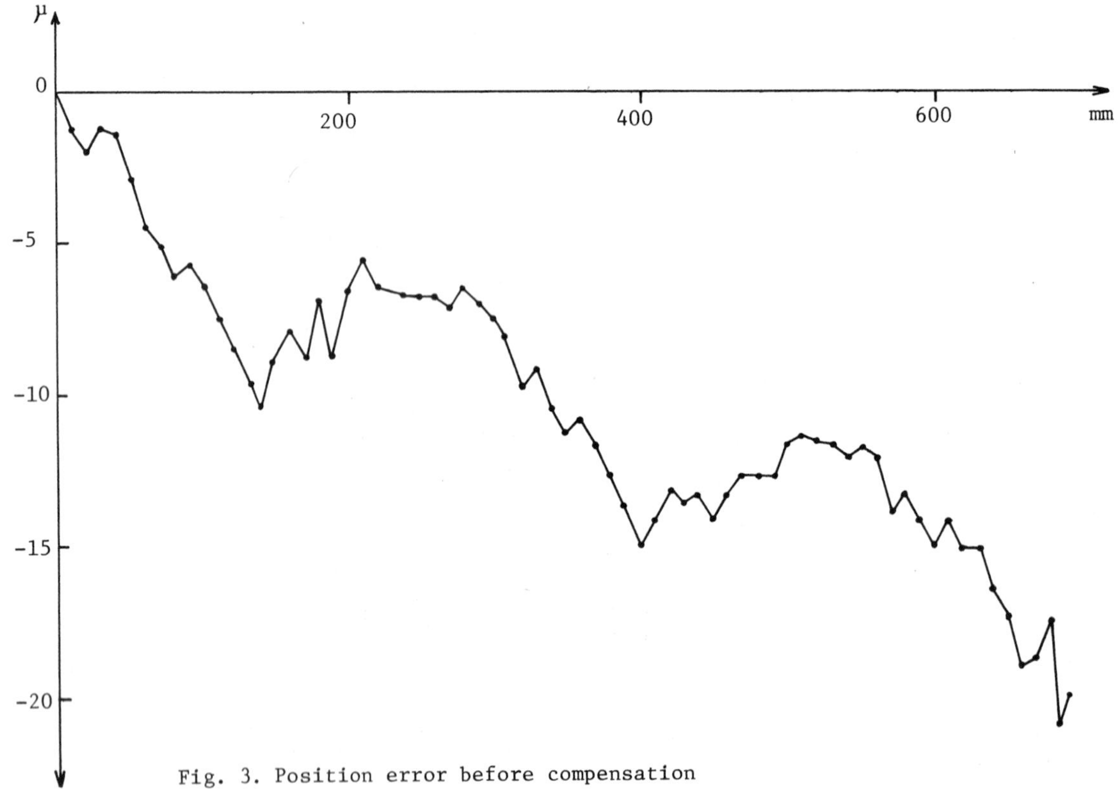

Fig. 3. Position error before compensation

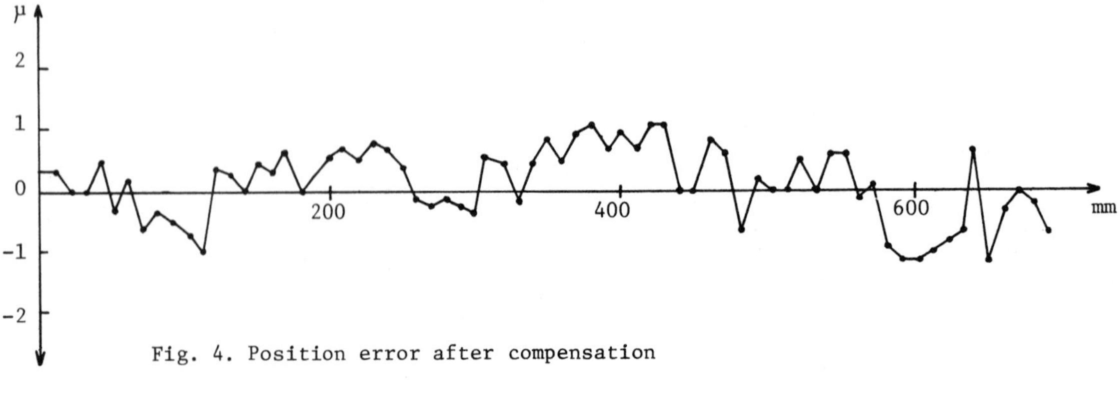

Fig. 4. Position error after compensation

4. Double check system for expensive work

Expensive work does not allow to be gouged even at malfunction of NC. NC should stop as fast as possible when a malfunction is found. This demands are asked specially from airplane manufacturer who uses titan-alloy, a manufacturer who builts big heat exchangers for atomic power station, etc. Fig. 5. shows the diagram of double check system.

Thre are two tape reader which inputs are compared and checked. Pulse distribution control distributes pulses to two Acc & dec circuits, which conrol acceleration and deceleration of feedrate, per axis. The output pulses of two Acc & dec circuits are compared and checked. Simulater simulates servo control, motor, and machine behavior as primaly lag function. Position counter finds the machine position receiving feedback signals from Inductosyn scale. The outputs of simulater and position counter are compared, and the defference is added to servo control. If the defference is greater than a set value, alam signal is generated. Position counter has capability to check unusual feedback signal level also. In the case of positioning command, position check circuit checks if machine has reached in the commanded position. In this way, double checks are made, and if alarm signal is generated at each checking circuit, the machine motion is stopped at once.

5. Combined system with numerical control and tracer control

There are the cases that it is difficult to partprogram complicated work or the work designed by artists like die model for automobile. For those works, the NC combined with tracer control can be used. The feed axes, X,Y axes, are controlled by CNC and can be moved as programmed. Other axis, Z axis, is controlled by tracer control. Furthermore feedrates of X,Y axes are controlled adaptively to decrease cutting errors and to increase cutting speed. In order to achieve the above purpose, CNC receives the deflection value of stylus from tracer control and controls the feedrate of feed

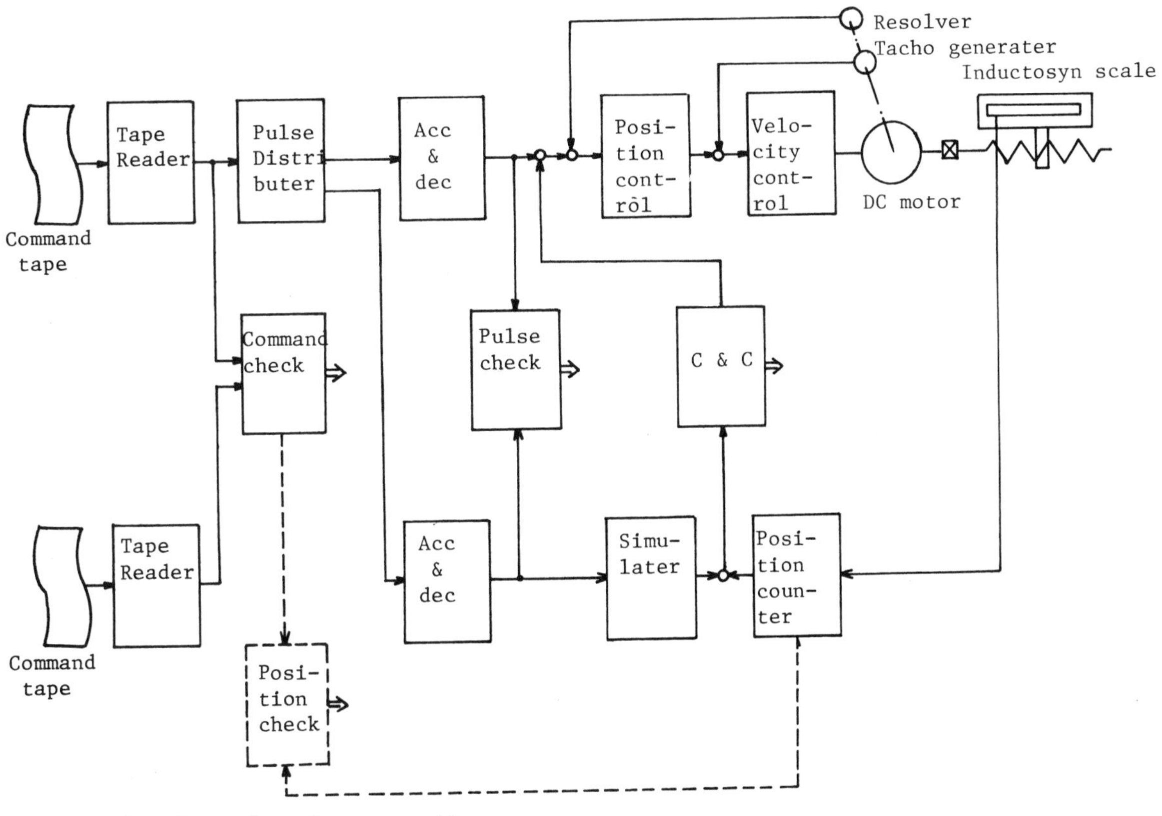

C & C : Comparison & compensation

Fig. 5. Double check system

axes. The relation between the feedrate of feed axes and the deflection of stylus is shown in Fig. 6.

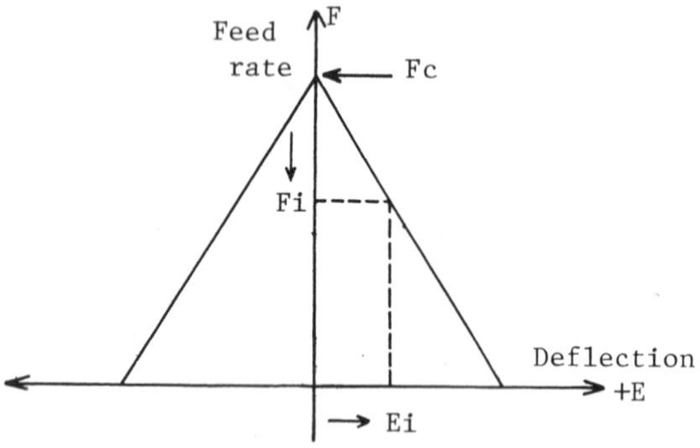

Fig. 6. Relation between feedrate and deflection value

Where the deflection of stylus is equal to zero, the feedrate becomes Fc which is specified value by partprogram. The feedrate decreases in proportion to the increase of deflection.

Such control is realised by CNC. The result has decreased cutting time 20% in our experience.

6. For more flexible programming

Though CNC is "softwired", it is still difficult for user to add its own capability by itself. "Users macro" is the function to satisfy user's wish to make his own capability in CNC. User can store of CNC instructions as macro body in memory of F200 which can be called by G code in normal NC command sequence. In addition to the ordinary NC instructions, operations such as addition, subtraction,etc. can be used in the macro body with variables which actual values can be given with call instructions or calculated in macro body. Therefore flexible macro instructions peculiar to each user, such as fixed cycles, pattern functions and so on, can be prepared in F200, and used as if they were parts of CNC functions.

Macro body takes following format;

ER CR G93 CR
Un Dummy arguments CR Macro body n CR
Um Dummy arguments CR Macro body m CR

G94 CR ER

whre;

Un: Macro number n
Um: Macro number m
G93: indicates the followings are macro bodies to be stored in memory.
G94: indicates the end of macro bodies to be stored.
Dummy arguments: variables which values are decided when the macro is called.
Macro body: series of normal NC commands including dummy arguments and variables.

Macro body can have the following instructions in addition to the normal NC commands;

Instructions	Meanings
G101AaBb	a=b
G102AaBbCc	a=b+c
G103AaBbCc	a=b-c
G104AaBbCc	a=bxc
G105AaBbCc	a=b/c
G106AaBb	$a=\sqrt{b}$
G107AaBb	a=bxsin(c)
G108AaBbCc	a=bxcos(c)
G200An	jump to a block of sequence number n unconditionally
G201AnBb	if b=0, jump to a block of sequence number n
G202AnBb	if b<0, jump to a block of sequence number n

where;
a: variables
b,c: variables or constants
n: sequence number

The macro body stored in memory can be called by the following macro instruction.

G95 Un Actual arguments CR

where;

G95: indicates to call macro number n
Un: macro number
Actual arguments: parameters to give the actual value to the dummy argument.

Example of macro and macro body are shown below;

Macro body

U1V1V2	Macro number,arguments
G101AV3B-361	V3=-361
N101G102AV3BV3C1	V3=V3+1
G108AV4BV2CV3	x=V2 cosV3
G107AV5BV1CV3	y=V1 sinV3
G90G01XV4YV5	Move to point (x,y)
G202A101BV3	If V3 0,go to N101

Macro call

G95U1H50000I80000 CR

7. Conclusion

The applications described here are only a small part of many applications achieved by CNC. There is no doubt for CNC to contribute to increase productivity more and more in various field. The problem left is how to increase the productivity of software development for CNC.

ON THE AUTOMATION OF CAM PROFILE CONTROL

M. Krawczyński* A. Oledzki*, I. Siwicki* and F. Zrudelny**

**Institute for Aeronautical Engrg. and Applied Mechanics, 00-665 Warsaw. ul. Nowowiejska 22/24, Poland*

***Institute for Nuclear Research, Warsaw, Poland*

ABSTRACT

Real cam-profile differs from the theoretical one due to the unavoided manufacturing errors. Those errors can be a source of dynamical troubles, especially in high-speed cam mechanisms like those of automotive engines.

Very common, and rather insufficient cam-profile-control in factories is such that camshafts are controlled only occasionally and only on statical way. During such a control, a real cam-follower's displacement is measured and compared with data of a theoretical one.

Usualy a crude rule "of thumb" is responsible for the answer to the basic question:"good or bad is the cam". That procedure can be supplemented by numerical calculation of real acceleration of the follower, and from the coincidence of acceleration curves the quality of the cam will be judged.

All those measurements are very time consuming, while performed by human operator. Two or three people are usualy involved in that activity and their tiredness is an other source of errors.

Circumumstances of that kind were a stimulus for the authors of this paper to create an automatic system of cam profile control.

A special transducer was built first, which enables very accurate measurements of the cam-follower's displacement. Electric signals from that transducer pass by typical A/D convertor (interface) to the memory of a desk calculator (TEKTRONIX) and are stored there for small increments of a camshaft's angle.

In a first version of the system the camshaft was driven by a hand. After completing records for all the profiles of a comshaft a special program was used, numerical calculations using a finite-difference proceder and their results plotted. It was possible to obtain 1 diagram in less than half of an hour (which was about 10 percent of the previously used time.).

In the second version of the system a step-motor was adapted and a special programing device built which enables an automatic performance of all the operations for one profile in less than 20 minutes.

Data of the theoretical acceleration curve are stored in the memory of the calculator too. So the final set of real curves are plotted against a theoretical with a tolerance area. Thus a quick decission can be made concerning the acceptance or no-acceptance of the product.

1. INTRODUCTION

Accuracy of the cam mechanism necessary for obtaining its proper operation under dynamic conditions depends mainly upon accuracy of machining the kinematic pair: cam-follower.

Usually discrepancies between dimensions of real and theoretical profiles are not as critical for the dynamic behaviour of the mechanism as the discrepancies between corresponding acceleration curves. Therefore the only resonable basis for quality control of the cam mechanism should be acceleration curve of the cam-follower, or better, of the last link in kinematic chain measured at the operation speed of the mechanism. Acceleration signal after integrations gives remaining kinematic quantities - velocity and displacement. Information obtained in such a way is sufficient enough and valuable for designers and quality-control laboratories but not adequate in the negative cases for the purposes of the master - cam correction, or in the case of n.c. machines-for the correction of punch or magnetic tapes. Thus, in industrial praxis, an approximate acceleration curve based upon data obtained from very accurate mesurements of a real profile is, usually, a substitute for a real dynamic properaties ies of the system.

2. METHODS FOR THE EVALUATION OF CORRECTNESS OF THE REAL CAM MANUFACTURING

Measurements of a real follower displacements and their comparison with a theoretical ones, are most commonly used method in factory praxis. For those measurements an optical dividing head and Abbe's displacement -meter usually have been used (Ref.1, 2,4) A serious disadvantage of this method is due to the lack of information concerning remaining kinematic quantities of the follower motion. This is a reason for the designers to tighten tolerances of the cam-follower's displacement as a remedy for an elimination from exploitation a faulty cams, cams for which a suspicion may arise that their real acceleration curves differ from the theoretical ones.

This is a rather expensive procedure, since it leads to the sorting out of the whole camshafts which, although machined apart from permissible displacement-tolerances, are completely correct from dynamic point of view. This is a reason that in the other methods, the displacement data obtained from the mesurements are only input data for the calculation of the anticipated accelerations.For those purpose mostly interpolation formulas of Stirling (Ref. 3,6,7) are used.

It is worth mentioning here that a condition for an appropriateness of those formulas is an existence of adequate number of the derivatives of a motion-function. (In case of the acceleration it is necessary to have first four derivatives with respect to angle of rotation, of the displacement - function.).

Anticipated accelerations obtained in such a way are compared with theoretical ones, and it is expected that errors between limits of about ± 10 percent will cause no problems under dynamic conditions of the mechanism operation. Nobody, however, pays attention to the character of the acceleration curve alterations inside of a tolerance-zone, and here lays a serious insufficiency of this method.

All the methods mentioned above are very time consuming As a rule, a 30′ increments of cam angular-displacement (automotive engines) are used during measurements. Thus the number of obtained data can be as large, as 3 ÷ 7 thousands. Measurements, usually taken manualy cause a quick fatigue of operators, because of their monotony. In many cases this is an additional source of errors. All these circumstances call for automation of cam-profile control. Such an automation is a subject of the further part of this paper.

3. AUTOMATION OF THE CAM PROFILE CONTROL

3.1 THEORETICAL BASIS

The method of the cam-profile control presented here is based upon the concept of movable mean, to be used in the investigation of so called time-series (Ref.3).

It is assumed that the function of the follower displacement $h(\varphi)$ is a function of a real variable φ, continuous and differentiable and that a sequence 2m+1 number values of the variable φ with an increment $\Delta\varphi$ is given

$$-m,\ m+1,\ \ldots,\ 0,\ldots,m-1,\ m \qquad (1)$$

It is assumed as well, that in some way a sequence of according number values of the function $h(\varphi)$ was found. Number values of h were obtained with unknown random errors.

The only assumptions made here, is that these errors are independent, and have a normal distribution with an expected value equal to zero and a constant value of mean deviation δ.

The function h can be approximated by a following polinomial:

$$a_\varphi = \sum_{j=0}^{j=p} a_j \varphi^j \qquad (2)$$

where p - degree of movable parabola.

Coefficients a_j should be such, that for all the values $\varphi = k$, the condition

$$\sum_{k=-m}^{k=m} \left[h(k) - a(k)\right]^2 = \min \qquad (3)$$

is satisfied.

These coefficients will then fulfill a system of linear equations

$$a_o \sum_{k=-m}^{m} k^j + a_1 \sum_{k=-m}^{m} k^{j+1} + \ldots$$
$$\ldots + a_p \sum_{k=-m}^{m} k^{j+p} = \sum_{k=-m}^{m} h(k).k^j \qquad (4)$$

where j=0,1,2..., p.

Left hand terms of eq.(4)do not depend upon h(k), and right hand sums are linear combinations of h(k). Thus roots a_o, a_1,...,a_p can be obtained as linear combinations of h(k) with constant coefficients.

Now only the value a_o is significant as being a value of polinomial at φ=k=0, and thus being the best (in the given meaning) approximation of h(0). Similar procedure can be taken for the functions h(φ) value in optimal point under the condition, however, that the sequence of the h(φ) values in 2m+1 points: φ-m, φ-m+1,...,φ , φ+1,..., φ+m is known.

Function h(φ) value of which for any given φ is equal to the coefficient a_o calculated for the very same point φ^o is called a "movable mean".

Let $\{h\}$ denotes a measured sequence of a follower-displacements obtained for equally ($\Delta\varphi$ = const) spaced values of φ . The substitution of that sequency by a sequence: $\{\hat{h}\}$ values of a movable mean gives the best approximation in the sense of the condition (3), of the primary coordinates by "smoothed" coordinates.

There are two parameters m and p in Equations (1) and (2). Numerical value of p should be as small as possible in order to ensure a good "smoothing" of the function, and at the same time large enough for a good approximation of inflexion points. Number of points m should exceed p by 2 (at least) in order to obtain more effective smoothing of the curve. However, number 2m + 1 should be not too large in comparison with the number of terms in sequence $\{h\}$, since it is rather difficult to obtain a good approximation for a long segment to be smoothed.

According to these hints p=3 and m=5 was assumed here (comp.Ref.6.)

Approximate values of accelerations were found from interpolation formulas. For that purpose a smoothed sequence of displacement values $\{\hat{h}\}$ was substituted by interpolation polinomial of Stirling, and approximate value of the displacements second derrivative was found.

A choice of Stirlings formulas but not Lagrange's or Newton's was based upon following reasons:

- there exists a sufficient number of derrivatives of the displacement's-function;
- interpolation nodes are equally spaced;
- interpolation polinomial is a mean interpolation node.

The first condition is fullfiled easily in case of cam mechanisms since even for theoretical follower's displacement-curves with slight discontinuity (the third derrivative equal to infinity), their practical realization will assure a large, but finite valuea of those derrivatives, thus with no discontinuity.

The last condition derives from the fact that all the measurements of the cam profile have been performed for an angle-range not exceeding 2π , and so the interpolation polinomial was a mean interpolation node.

It is worth mentioning here that one of the authors of this paper plans to use other interpolation formulas (like those of Bessel) in the future, and to compare results of statical measurements with those obtained directly from measurements taken by means of accelerometers.

3.2 AUTOMATIC CONTROL RIG

Automatic rig for the control of cam profiles, designed and built by the authors of this paper, consists of two systems (Fig.1).

The first one provided for the automatic measurements of the follower displacement includes a specialy built capacitance-transducer-2,3 for measurements of the cam-profile-1 (Ref.8), TEKTRONIX 31/53 measuring system (instruments DM 501 and DC 503 interface-4, calculator TK31-5, and plotter X-Y, -6). The second system realizes automated angular division of the cam motion. It consists of a step motor-7, a controling device-8, reducing gear-box-9, and electronic system for the programming of the cam angular movement and its control -10.

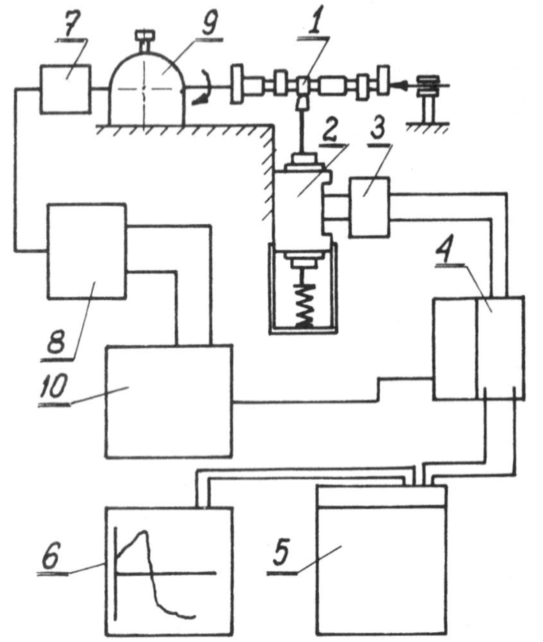

Fig.1 Automatic control rig

The value of an electric tension signal proportional to the follower displacement is measured at the output of the transducer, by means of a digital voltmeter DM501, and transferred through an interface to the memory of the calculator. /Equally spaced values (step $=\Delta\varphi$) of displacement can be printed or recorded on a magnetic type./

After a single data is fed into computer's memory a calculator gives a command to the device - 10 (Fig.1), and cam is rotated through the next step. The device-10 can be programmed for any desired value of $\Delta\varphi$.

After completing all the measurements for the given range of angular displacement of the cam the measuring procedure is stopped, and a special program is started. This program computes (Ref.5):

- first differences Δ h between results of adjacent measurements;
- second differences of displacements $\Delta(\Delta h)$ (value of Δ h minus a previous value);
- rough accelerations $a_n = \dfrac{\Delta(\Delta h)}{(\Delta\varphi)^2}$
- smoothed acceleration

$$\hat{a}_n = \frac{1}{1000} \sum_{i=-5}^{5} W_i\, a_{n+1}$$

This subroutine is universal and allows usage of different steps and different coefficients w_i. In above described case values of w_i were constant, and calculated (Ref.6) for previously chosen numerical values p=3 and m=5. All the data, including theoretical values of accelerations and admissible tolerances (a separate subroutine) stored in the memory of the computer can be printed on paper tape or plotted in the form of diagrams. The final result - plotted together curves of theoretical and real accelerations with admissible tolerances is a basis for evaluation of a cam profile correctness.

4.TESTNG OF A NEW SYSTEM

There were special tests performed simultaneously on a new system (Fig.1), and a traditional one where an Abbe's longitudal-meter was used. These tests were carried out without a step motor,but included a new transducer connected to the shäft of Abbe's-meter.

One example of obtained results is presented in Fig.2. It concerns an exhaust cam of an engine WOLA H6A (License Henschel). A diagram presented there shows discrepancies between measured values and theoretical ones versus angle of cam rotation.

As an evaluation criterion here were taken a deviations between values of smoothed accelerations a_n and theoretical ones. Fig.3 shows the results obtained from these, parallel tests plotted against area of admissible tolerances ($\pm$ 10% of the theoretical values - according to the requirements of the license-owner). It is clear from comparisson of the curves in Fig. 3 that results obtained there are similar in two ways.

Worth mentioning here is fact, that symmetrical interpolation formulas used in the above described procedure are a source of certain distortions in the shape of acceleration curves, when a sudden change of the function sign takes place (comp. Fig.3).

5.FURTHER DEVELOPMENT OF THE SYSTEM,AND CONCLUSIONS

System presented in this work was developed for a single cam profile. However, it can be used, for the shafts with many profiles too,

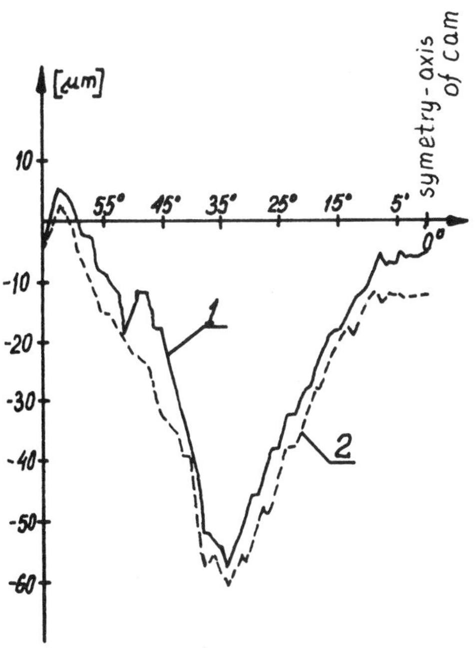

Fig.2 Accuracy test of a new system;
1-results obtained by traditional way;
2-results from automatic system.

but it will require manual changes of the transducer positions along the shaft axis. In further development of the system it is assumed that 6 to 12 parallel transducers will be used, and measurements of all the shafts will be taken at the same time and simultaneously marked in the memory of the computer.
It will enable to shorten the whole procedure to the great degree, and to give complete quality - information of the camshaft in a realy short time.

It is not necessary to underline here how valuable is information of that type for designers, in factory praxis, and in workshops for maintenance and repairs purposes.

Still not answerd, however, reminds the question how good are accepted criteria of the cam-quality evaluation; the proper choice of parameters p and m in Eqs. (1) and (2), and correctness of the used interpolation formulas.

Evaluation of the correctness of described here methods will be possible in the future after performing planned investigations with sufficient number of cams, suplemented with direct measurements of real accelerations.

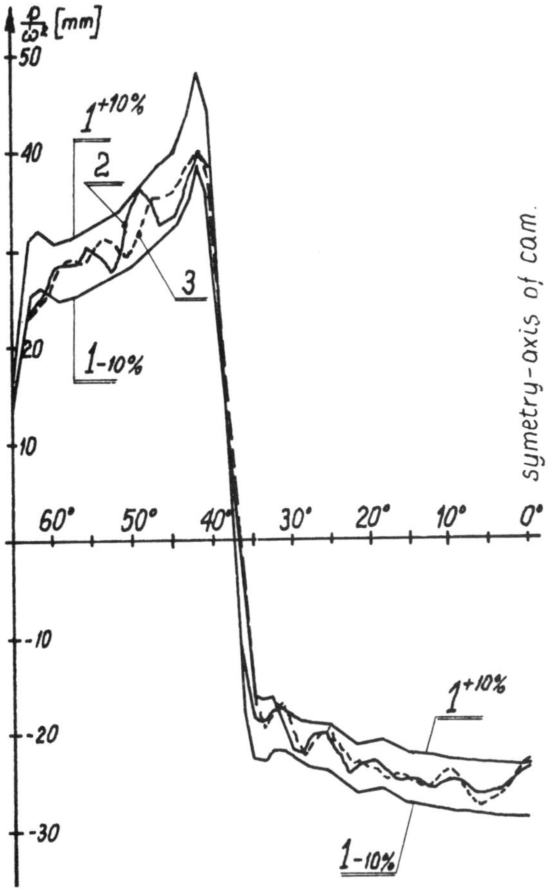

Fig.3. Fragment of acceleration diagrams
1-theoretical curve, 2-curve obtained from measurements with Abbe's displacement mater,3-curve obtained from automatic system.

References

1. Engel S., Müller J: Messeinrichtungen für Kurvengetriebe. Maschinenbautechnik, 1974, Heft 12.
2. Hommelwerke GmbH: Fertingungsprogram.Kurven-und Nockenform-Messmaschine". Ausgabe 9-73.
3. Kendall M.P.:Advanced Theory of Statistics London 1947.
4. Krawczyński M., Żrudelny F.: O statycznej metodzie oceny poprawności wykonania profilów krzywek. Silniki Spalinowe 1976, Nr 4.
5. Krawczyński M., Olędzki A., Siwicki I., Żrudelny F.: O możliwości automatyzacji kontroli zarysu krzywek. Pomiary,Automatyka, kontrola 1976 Nr 11.

6. Oderfeld J.: O pewnym zastosowa - niu rachunku wyrównawczego do kine kinematyki mechanizmów. Zastosowania Matematyki IV 2/1958.
7. Sarsten A., Valland H.: Computer assistance in valve design; a university approach. Design Technology Transfer ASME 1974.
8. Żrudelny F., Iwiński I.: Układ do pomiaru małych zmian pojemności zwłaszcza w pomiarach wielkości nieelektrycznych. Patent PRL nr 68205.

This project was assisted by U.S. National Science Foundation under Grant OIP 73-002266 A01.

CONTROL SYSTEM OF NC MACHINE TOOL FOR HIGH WORKING ACCURACY

N. Nishiwaki*, N. Hashiba and M. Masuko*****

**Tokyo University of Agriculture & Technology, Nakamachi 2-24-16, Koganei Tokyo 184, Japan*

***Tokyo Institute of Technology, O-okayama 2-12-1, Meguro-ku, Tokyo 152, Japan*

****Mushashi Institute of Technology, Tamazutsumi 1-28-1, Setagaya-ku, Tokyo 158, Japan*

ABSTRACT

This study deals with the development of a new system which is used to control the position of the cutting tool of a numerical control machine tool, to obtain high working accuracy and fine finished surface. So far, high accuracy in-process sensors have been only used for controlling the cutting tool, but the method followed in this new system is quite different from previous processes.

In this system, after the rough cut the mark indicating the position of the finished size is put on the cutting surface of the workpiece by ultrasonic or vibration cutting. The cutting is then continued until the mark just disappears, this position being observed by the use of a simple in-process sensor. In this investigation the optical fiber installed inside the shank of the cutting tool is used as the in-process sensor. This in-process sensor can be used to detect not only the mark but also the finished surface roughness, tool wear, chattering or faulty material, because the finished surface is always optically scanned by this in-process sensor.

It is expected that by the use of this system a dimensional accuracy can be obtained up to the order of the surface roughness and the finishing can be always carried out with a good surface condition.

INTRODUCTION

In the engineering industry there is an ever-growing demand for both increased machining precision and fewer skilled workers. Therefore, machine tool control have been developing more and more towards an automatic control system, namely, a numerical control system. But these demands are not sufficiently met by numerical control system alone, because there are several errors which arise from tool wear, workpiece deflection, thermal distortion in the amchine tool, thermal expansion in the workpiece, etc. and a finished surface can not be constantly watched during machining process. So, in the past few years an adaptive control system for the finished accuracy and finished surface, which is a kind of advanced automatic control system, has been designed and at the same time an in-process sensor has been developed for establishing the adaptive control system.

Many kinds of in-process sensors (Ref. 1) have been developed for controlling the cutting tool of the NC machine tool during the machining process, for changing the cutting condition, or for changing the cutting tool because of the tool wear. And measurement of the absolute finishing size or the finished surface roughness during the working process has, in the past, been tried by using the in-process sensor. But it seems that the in-process sensor developed so far has only one function of measuring the size or the surface roughness. But the measuring method of this type has a few weak points; for example, the measuring value from this type of in-process sensor is affected by the thermal expansion of the workpiece, the workpiece deflection, the vibration of the machine tool, the cutting atmosphere or the finished surface roughness. Therefore, in general its size is large, its design is complex and its cost is expensive.

It is expected as an in-process sensor that its size is small and it is set up inside the cutting tool, and that both finishing accuracy and finished surface condition can be measured by using it.

Therefore, this study deals with the development of a new control system of NC machine tool for high working accuracy and at the same time for obtaining a good surface condition, the method of which is quite different from the previous process of so-called in-process sensor. In this study, the optical fiber installed inside the shank of the cutting tool (Ref. 2) is used as the in-process sensor of this system.

In the case of using this system, it is expected that by using only one in-process sensor not only a dimensional accuracy can be obtained up to the order of the surface roughness but also the finishing surface condition can be always scanned, that is, the tool wear or the chattering can be detectted.

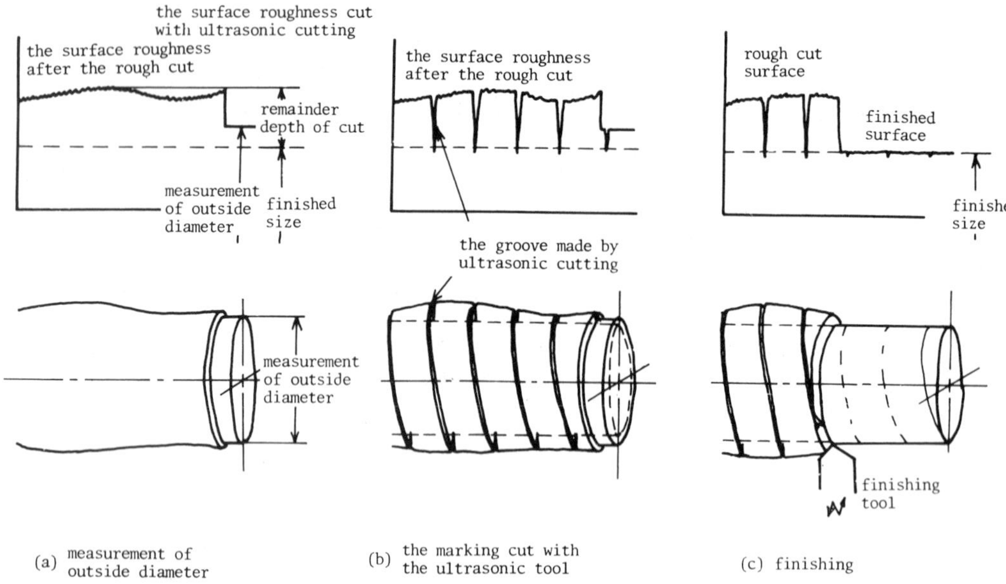

Fig. 1. The principle of this system.

CONCEPTION OF THIS SYSTEM

Control System for High Working Accuracy

The method of this control system of NC machine tool for high working accuracy is quite different from the previous process of the so-called in-process sensors, and authors have already published a part of the conception of this system (Ref. 3). But the conception of this system is a bit different from previous conception. Figure 1 shows a schematic diagram of this method for cutting an outside diameter. This system consists of three operation steps as follows.

At the first step (Fig. 1a), after rough cut a part of the workpiece is cut with ultrasonic cutting (Ref. 4), the cutting depth of which is very small. And its size is measured on the chuck-held, no cut and static condition by the conventional static measuring method. Therefore, it is possible to measure the workpiece size to a very high accuracy, because the errors mentioned above are absent when there is no cutting and the workpiece is also in static condition.

At the second step (Fig. 1b), the mark (for example, of the shape of the spiral groove) indicating the position of the finished size (the depth of this mark is determined from the first step) is put on the cutting surface by ultrasonic cutting. The characteristic of this ultrasonic cutting method is that the cutting force is very small and a built-up edge does not occur on the cutting edge. Therefore, it is possible to cut to the intended depth. The weak points of ultrasonic cutting, however, are that cutting speed is low and a heavy cut can not be carried out.

At the third step (Fig. 1c), the cutting is continued up to the position where the mark just disappears, this position observed by the use of a simple in-process sensor. This in-process sensor is used only to detect the existence or disappearance of the mark. In this investigation the optical fiber installed inside the shank of the cutting tool is used as the in-process sensor. A block diagram of the operation, showing all three steps, is given in Fig. 2.

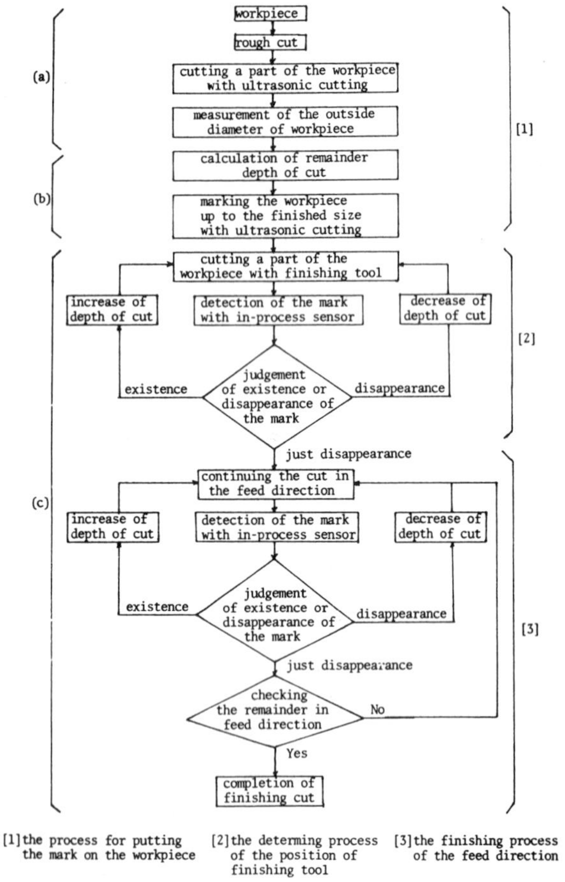

Fig. 2. Block diagram of this system.

Machinery Accuracy of the Mark Cut with Ultrasonic Cutting

The machining accuracy of the mark cut with ultrasonic cutting is very important in this system. However, the marking accuracy de-

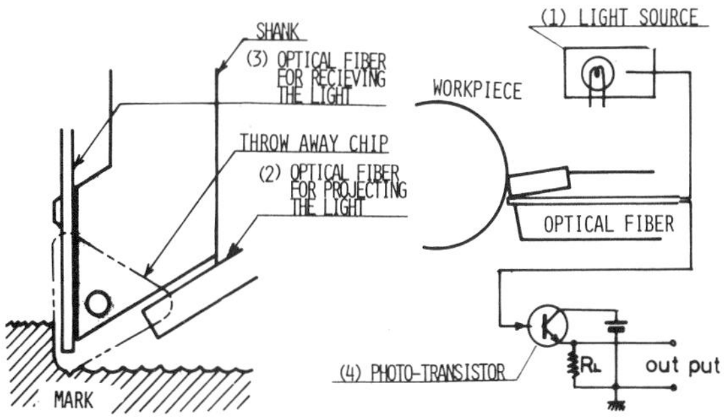

Fig. 3. Setup of this in-process sensor.

manded in this system is not always met by NC machine tool. Then, when the mark is machined with NC machine tool, it is necessary to investigate the misaligment of the machine by using ultrasonic cutting and then to machine the mark considering the compensation of the error of misaligment. If the above method is tried, marking accuracy does not depend on the working accuracy of the NC machine tool used in case of putting the mark on the surface.

Measurement of the Mark

It is necessary to study the feasibility of the in-process sensor, which can easily detect the existence or disappearance of the mark, because the performance of this sensor is a key point in this system. The in-process sensor used in this investigation is schematically shown in Fig. 3. It is made with two bundles of optical fibers, one (2) for projecting the light from the light source (1) to the finished surface and the other (3) for receiving the reflected light from the finished surface and then guiding to the photo-transistor (4). There is an extra photo-transister for guaranteeing the surrounding temperature. Conception of measuring the mark with this sensor is shown in Fig. 4. When there is no mark on the finished surface, a bundle of light projected from the optical fiber on the finished surface reflects and is hardly detected by the receiving optical fiber (Fig. 4a), but when there is the mark, that is the groove of the V-shape on the finished surface, a part of the bundle of projected light from the optical fibers reflects on the surface of the groove and is detected by the receiving optical fibers and is detected by the phototransistor (Fig. 4b).

As mentioned above, the mark can be easily detected by the light reflected from the mark. Therefore, it seems that the mark can be detected with this sensor because of the existence of the reflected light from the mark even if a part of the mark is already cut with the edge of the cutting tool, The actual finished surface as shown in Fig. 6a is not a flat surface as shown in Fig. 4, so a part of the scattering light on the finished surface is always detected by the photo-transistor as the noise signal which is shown in Fig. 6b. Therefore, it is expected that the surface condition, that is, the surface roughness or the chattering, can

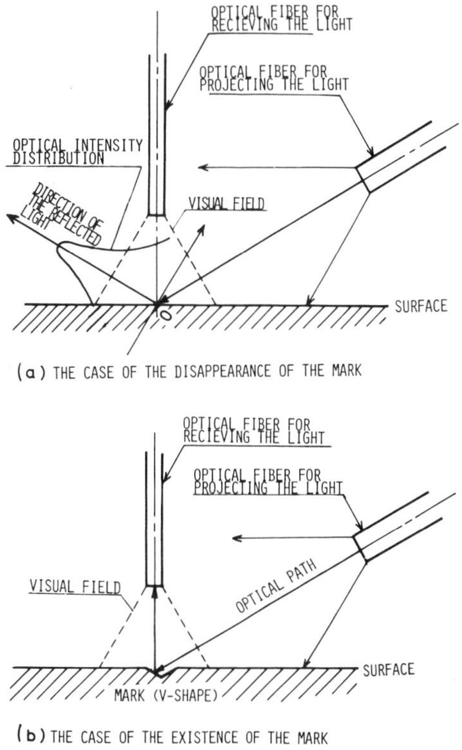

Fig. 4. The principle of measuring the mark with this sensor.

be detected by this sensor.

Here, the optical fibers of the same diameter are bundled up to a diameter of 2mm and are used for lighting the finished surface, twenty five pieces of a single thread optical fiber (the diameter of which is 50μm) are disposed in a line and are used as

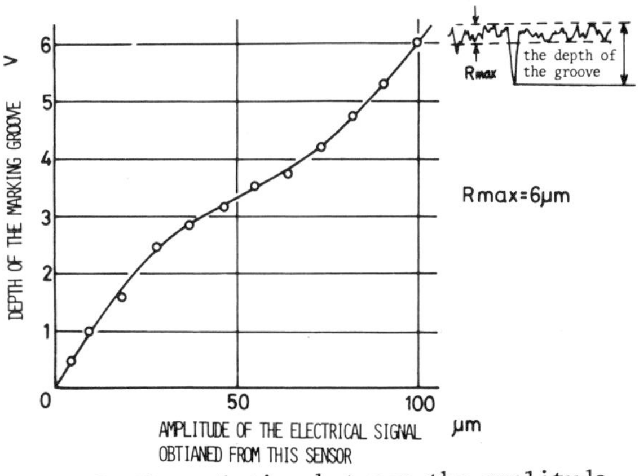

Fig. 5. The relation between the amplitude of the electrical output signal of this sensor and the depth of the marking groove.

the optical fibers for receiving the reflected light. Moreover the direction of receiving optical fibers are the same as that of the spiral groove marking.

Next, grooves of different depths are cut with ultrasonic tool and the actual output of the electrical signal obtained by using this in-process sensor from these grooves are compared as shown in Fig. 5. The relationship between the output obtained from this sensor and the depth of the marking groove is not exactly linear, but in this system the linear

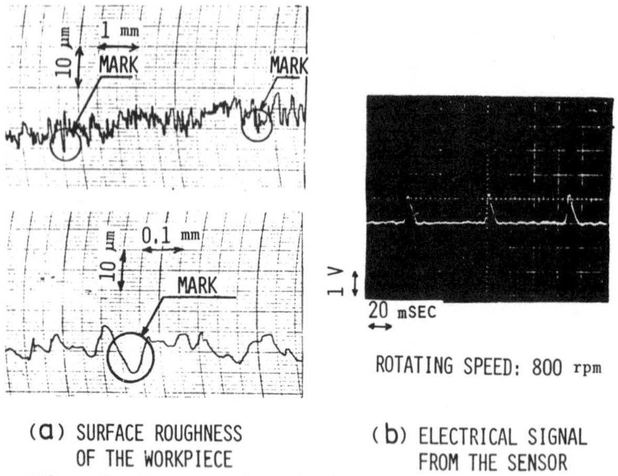

Fig. 6. An example of the measurement of the mark by sing this sensor

relationship is not needed. The example of the detection of the mark is shown in Fig. 6.

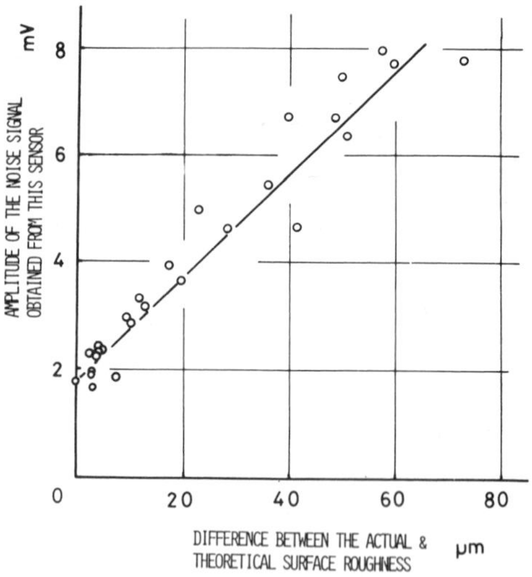

Fig. 7. The relation between the surface condition and the amplitude of the noise signal from this sensor.

INVESTIGATION OF FINISHED SURFACE CONDITION

Surface Roughness

In general, the roughness finished surface is measured along the feed direction perpendicular to the machined surface. But by the use of in-process sensor it is easy to measure the surface condition along the direction of rotation rather than along the feed direction. While, the actual roughness of finished surface is generally different from the theoretical surface roughness which is obtained from feed rate and shape of cutting tool, because over-cut or under-cut is caused by the existence of built-up edge or the vibration of the machine tool. Therefore, it is expected that the amplitude of the electrical signal of the sensor obtained from the finished surface along the direction of rotarion, that is the amplitude of the electrical noise signal as shown in Fig. 6b, is related to the difference between the actual (Rmax) and theoretical surface roughness. In the experiment, the relationship between the difference and the amplitude of electrical signal which is passed through the high pass filter of 500 Hz is studied for many kinds of surface conditions cut with carbide tool, as shown in Fig. 7. By the use of this sensor, the actual roughness of finished surface can be calculated from the results of Fig. 7, if the feed rate and sharp of the cutting tool is known.

Detection of Tool Wear

The machining accuracy of the roughness of finished surface is generally affected by the tool wear. But in case of using this system it is expected to be possible to know the roughness of finished surface along the direction of rotation. Therefore, the period of exchanging the used cutting tool for a new one can be estimated with the same sensor as mentioned above. As a reason for this, it can be mentioned that wear condition of the tool can be determined from the roughness of the surface, because the dimensional accuracy is always guaranteed by using the mark. Therefore, the electrical signals obtained from the finished surface cut with carbide tools of several degrees of wear are passed through the frequency analyzer and the result are shown in Fig. 8. The characteristic of the tool wear can be found from this figure at the frequency range from 500 Hz to 2 KHz. So it can be concluded that if a suitable electrical bandpass filter is used, the condition of the tool wear can be detected.

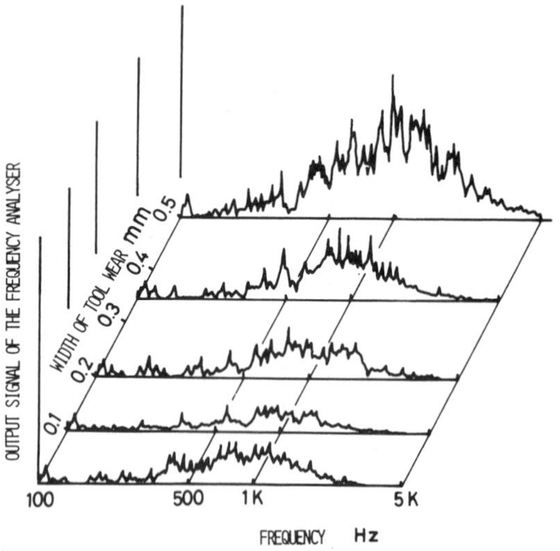

Fig. 8. The frequency analysis of the signal of this sensor from the finished surface cut with weared tools.

Detection of Chatter

It is considered that if the chattering can be detected by using the in-process sensor, the cutting condition can be changed for the chatter to be prevented. Considering that the surface of the chatter has some special characteristic, it was traced along the direction of rotation by this sensor and its electrical signal was passed through the

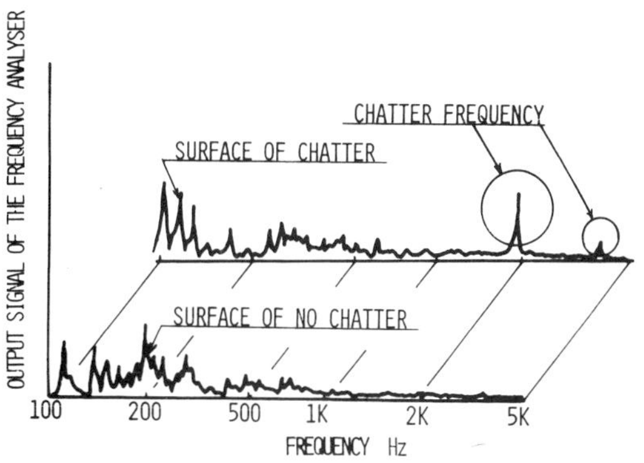

Fig. 9. The frequency analysis of the signal from the surface of the chatter.

frequency analyzer. The result obtained is as shown in Fig. 9. The characteristic of the chatter can be found this figure at the position near 2 KHz.

As mentioned above, as the characteristic of this sensor, it can be concluded that not only the existence or dissappearance of the mark can be detected but also the roughness of finished surface, the tool wear and the chatter can be measured by this sensor, that is the condition of finished surface can be sufficiently measured by this sensor.

MERITS AND DEMERITS OF THIS METHOD

The following matters about the merits and demerits of this method may be considered.

Merits

(1) It is seemed that this method can be applied even if the working errors (arise from tool wear, thermal deflection of the machine tool and workpiece, elastic deformation of the machine tool and etc.) existed. Because the mark indicating the position of the absolute finished size of the workpiece is already put on the surface of it before finishing.

(2) It is certainly expected that the dimensional accuracy can be obtained up to the micro-meter order, because a part of the workpiece size at rough cut condition with ultrasonic cutting is more accurately measured with the conventional static measuring method than with the previously developed in-process sensor. It is possible to put the mark of the exact depth on the workpiece with ultrasonic cutting and the in-process sensor is enough to detect the existence or disappearance of the mark of the surface roughness order. Therefore, it is expected that the dimensional accuracy can be obtained up to the order of surface roughness. And moreover the optical fiber installed inside the shank of the cutting tool, used here as in-process sensor, can be easily handled and its size is very small.

(3) As the finished surface is always scanned by this in-process sensor, the surface roughness the chipping of tool, the fault of material or the chattering can be instantly detected.

(4) The marking of the workpiece surface assists in the smooth removal of chip. The danger of damaging the work-piece due to wrap-round of the chip is absent, because the chip becomes discontinuous at the area of the marking groove. The frequency of this discontinuation depends on the number of grooves cut on the work-piece surface.

(5) The position of the measuring sensor is close to the cutting edge. So in this case, the cleaning area for measurement is very small and thereby the cleaning process also becomes very simple.

(6) It is theoretically seemed that the idea of this method can be used in the case of the workpiece of any shape.

Demerits

(1) The special vibration cutting equipment is invariably needed.

(2) There is slight possibility of the mark to remain on the finished surface. It is considered that the depth of the mark remained is up to 2μm but, in general, the mark on the finished surface is hardly noticeable.

TRIAL EXPERIMENT OF THIS SYSTEM

In this study, an engine lathe is used instead of NC lathe, and an equipment with pulse motor is used as shown in Fig. 10 for controlling the depth of cut. The pulse motor is controlled by an electrical driving circuit. And the electrical driving circuit is controlled by the control circuit of the electrical output signal obtained from the sensor which is installed inside the shank of the cutting tool.

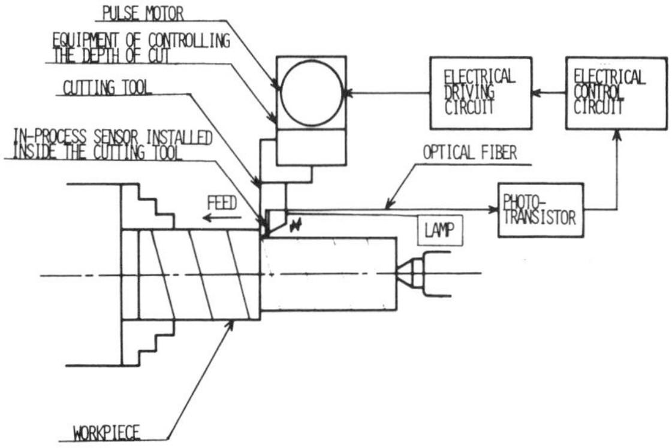

Fig. 10. The trial equipment of this system.

The Control Circuit of the Electrical Output Signal obtained from the Sensor

The block diagram of the control circuit is shown in Fig. 11 and its timing chart is shown in Fig. 12. Here, the working of the main block is explained as follows.

(1) Photo Tr.1 and Photo Tr.2: Photo transistor 1 is the one with which the light obtained from the optical fiber is transformed into electrical signal. Photo transistor 2

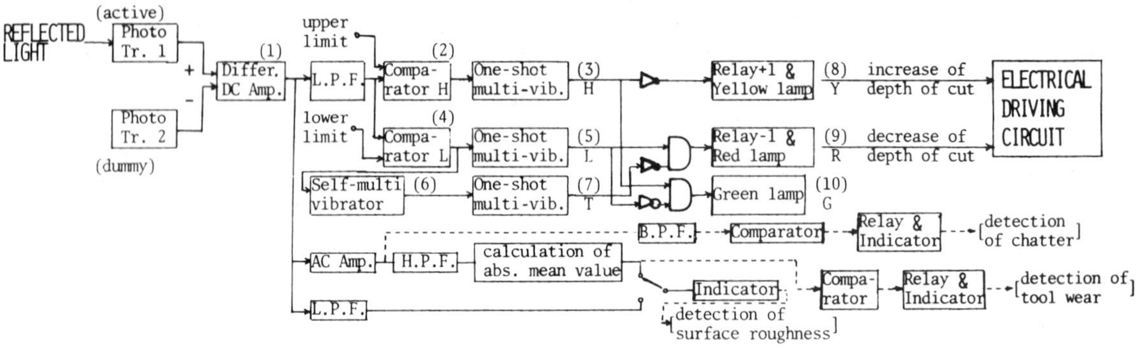

Fig. 11. Block diagram of the control circuit.

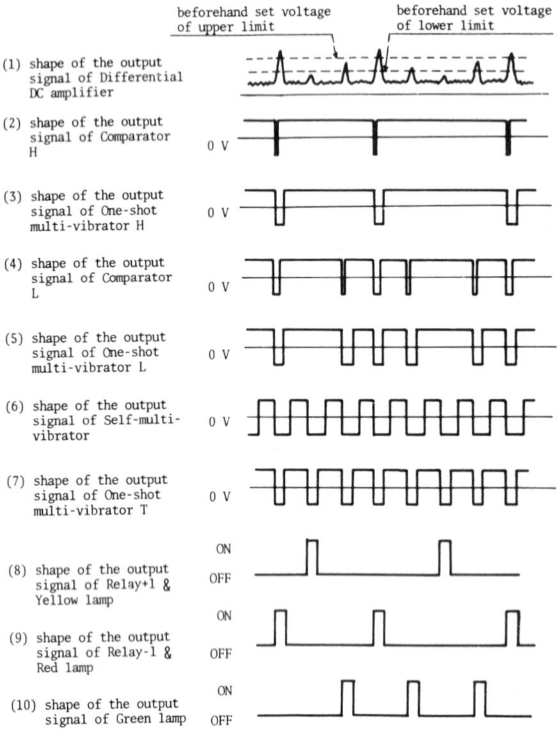

Fig. 12. Timing chart of the control circuit.

is used for the compensator of the electrical noise or surrounding temperature.

(2) Comparator H and Comparator L: The Comparator H and Comparator L respectively generate the unit pulse when the depth of the mark is larger than the beforehand set depth of upper limit and lower limit.

(3) Self-multi vibrator: The pulse of constant interval which is synchronized to the position of the mark by Comparator L is generated by this circuit.

(4) One-shot multi vibrator: The electrical pulse obtained from Comparator L, Comparator H, or Self-multi vibrator is transformed into the pulse of the constant width.

(5) Relay+1 and Yellow lamp: When depth of the mark is larger than its beforehand set upper limit, Yellow lamp is illuminant and the command of increasing the depth of cut is given to the electrical driving circuit of the pulse motor by this Relay+1. And the depth of cut is increased.

(6) Relay-1 and Red lamp: When the depth of the mark is smaller than its beforehand set lower limit, Red lamp is illuminant and the command of decreasing the depth of cut is given to the electrical driving circuit of the pulse motor by this Relay-1. And the depth of cut is decreased.

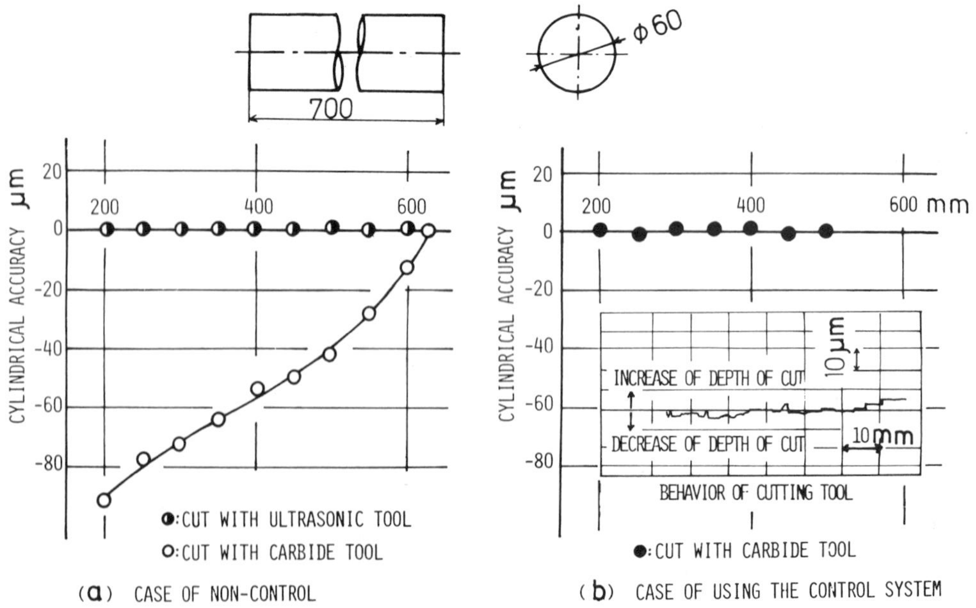

Fig. 13. An example of the maching by using this control system.

(7) Green lamp: When the depth of the mark exists within the limits of the intended depth, Green lamp is illuminant and the depth of cut is not changed.

AN EXAMPLE OF THE MACHINING BY USING THIS CONTROL SYSTEM

An example of the machining by using this control system is shown in Fig. 13. Fig. 13a shows the maching accuracy of the workpiece (diameter: 60mm, length: 700mm, feed rate: 0.05 rev./mm, cutting speed: 102m/min., depth of cut: 0.6MM) cut with carbide tool without applying any control. It is considered that the error of the cylindrical accuracy of this workpiece mainly arise from thermal expansion of the workpiece and cutting tool, elastic deflection occured in tool and workpiece, etc. While Figure 13b shows the machining accuracy of the workpiece of the same shape under the same cutting condition but machining was performed by using this control system. From these figures it is seen that the cylindrical accuracy of the workpiece is improved in case of using the control system in comparison with the case of non-control.

From the experiment it is seemed that it is possible to use this system in actual field if the ultrasonic cutting is used and the optical fiber installed the cutting tool is used as the in-process detector.

CONCLUSION

We developed control system, by which the conventional NC machine tool can be changed into the nearly perfect closed-loop system, by using a mark (as a template of a copy lathe) indicating the position of the finished size. This mark is made by ultrasonic cutting which is considered as the nearly ideal cutting.

The special characteristics of this system are as follows:

(1) This in-process sensor is used here not only to detect the existence or disappearance of the mark but also to measure the condition of finished surface.

(2) This system can be used for any workpiece shape as the workpiece itself is a kind of template of copy lathe and this in-process sensor installed inside the shank of the cutting tool.

(3) The roughness of finished surface can be constantly detected and moreover the chipping of tool, the fault of material or the chattering can be instantly detected.

(4) The marking made on the workpiece surface greatly helps in the smooth removal of chip as the chip is broken at the marking.

Investigating the working accuracy of this system, it is found that the total error of this system is up to some micrometers.

The investigations presented in this paper reveal that the use of this system in practical field is quite feasible. Moreover the troubles arise from the in-process sensors used so far can be easily avoided by using this system.

REFERENCES

(1) H. Tipton, In-process measurement and control of workpiece size. MTIRA 93, reprinted from Machine Tool Research October (1966).

(2) M.G. Jona, Contribution to the development of Geometical Adaptive Control in turning, 11th Int. MTDR Conf. 429 (1970)

(3) M. Masuko, N. Nishiwaki, Y. Kembo and B.S. Shing, New automatic control system of NC machine tool for high working accuracy. 16th Int. MTDR Conf. 125 (1975).

(4) Cutting to Get a Fine Surface at Low Speed (Sub-Zero, Reversal Finish, and Ultrasonic Cutting). Bull. Jap. Soc. Mech. Engrs. 2, 487 (1959).

ONE-TRACK m-n-p CODES AND CONJUGATE CLASS OF GROUP ELEMENTS

M. Shikata

Tokyo College of Economics, Kokubunji, Tokyo 185 Japan

ABSTRACT

One-track m-n-p codes can be obtained by considering conjugate class of the group elements, that originally produce one of the one-track m-n-p codes. The codes are good to digitize angular or linear analog quantity with small amounts of errors.

INTRODUCTION

The A-D converter in an angle-position encoder is a device to convert angular analog quantity into digital quantity. The digitized angular positions are indicated by code words. Transition from such a code word to another tends to produce angular position errors and hence errors in code words. The Gray code has been used traditionally together with V brushes to minimize such errors. To overcome the same difficulty, Kamoi(1966) devised a code, which has been developed to one-track m-n-p codes(for example, Shikata 1974a), that is found to be made by the use of the conjugate class of the group elements, where the group is of the cyclic permutations of symbols in code words. The one-track m-n-p code is a generalized SIB code(Singleton 1966).

CLASSIFICATION OF CODE WORDS

Let us suppose that n symbols of "1" or "0" are arranged in a horizontal row, where p symbols out of n are "1's" and n-p out of n are "0's." All the operations of permutation of symbols in this row form a symmetric group of degree n. We pick out an arbitrary element of this group G and write P_k for it, as it may be regarded as the k-th element of the group.
We also write a_1 for the row of symbols constructed above, which contains p of "1's" and n-p of "0's." After interchanging symbols of a_1 by permutation P_k, the resultant row of symbols will be written $P_k a_1$, which is also a code word.
If we write R for the cyclic permutation of n symbols, i.e. if

$$R=P(1234...n), \qquad (1)$$

then any set of code words, used for constructing track codes, for example, in Kamoi and Shikata(1966), includes code words such as

$$P_k a_1 (\text{or } R^n P_k a_1),\ RP_k a_1, ...$$
$$...R^{n-1} P_k a_1. \qquad (2)$$

By changing P_k, all the necessary sets of code words will be obtained, which were needed for construction of one-track m-n-p codes. Here, the permutation R is necessarily included in P_k, and naturally R appears in P_k when the product RP_k is constructed. This implies that R may appear both in R and P_k. However, since this does not cause any substantial difference in the following arguments, we leave the situation as it is above.
After writing out as many sets of code words as the number of different P_k, we take out non-degenerate(Kamoi and Shikata 1966) and mutually different sets of code words. For example, for n=3 and p=1, the set

100, 010, 001 (3)

is the only possible set. For n=5, p=2, the two sets,

11000, 01100, 00110, 00011, 10001

(4)

10100, 01010, 00101, 10010, 01001 (5)

are the only possible ones. Etc. Thus, the classification of code words with a given n into sets is carried out by means of R and P_k. Likewise, instead of expression (2), a set of code words can be constructed by P_1 as

$$P_k a_1 (\text{or } P_1^n P_k a_1),\ P_1 P_k a_1,\ P_1^2 P_k a_1, \ldots \ldots, P_1^{n-1} P_k a_1, \quad (6)$$

where P_1 is an arbitrary element of group G.
For example, for P_1 such as

$$P_1 = P(132), \quad (7)$$

the code words

100, 001, 010 (8)

form a set for n=3 and p=1. For n=5, p=2 and for

$$P_1 = P(14235), \quad (9)$$

the code words

11000, 00110, 01001, 10100, 00011 (10)

01100, 00101, 10001, 10010, 01010 (11)

form two sets.
Since P_1 is a permutation, it must be obtained from R through the operation of some permutation upon R. A permutation group is in general not an Abelean group, and therefore P_1 is obtained by multiplying some permutations x and y from the left and the right hand sides of R as

$$P_1 = xRy. \quad (12)$$

This relationship corresponds with the new numbering of brushes on coder plate of an angle-position encoder by P_1, while the brushes have been numbered formerly by R in Kamoi and Shikata(1966). This implies that, after the cyclic permutation of the set of brushes (with respect to the coder plate) by the angle described by R^2, the new numbering of brushes must correspond with the permutation P_1^2. Hence,

$$P_1^2 = xR^2y. \quad (13)$$

However, at the same time, the left hand side of this equation must be equal to

$$P_1^2 = xRyxRy. \quad (14)$$

From the above two equations, it is obtained that

$$y = x^{-1}. \quad (15)$$

Putting this relationship into equation(12), we obtain

$$P_1 = xRx^{-1}. \quad (16)$$

This group element P_1 is called the conjugate of R under conjugation by x^{-1}. Conversely, the group element R is the conjugate of P_1 under conjugation by x.

NAMING OF CODE WORDS BY MEANS OF GROUP

When code words were classified in the preceding section. they were expressed in the form $R^j P_k a_1$. Namely, naming of a code word is over, when j and k are decided for an arbitrarily given a_1. However, if R is included in P_k, R will be doubly multiplied giving two names(numbers) for certain code words. Hence, in order to avoid this inconvenience, R may be excluded from P_k. But, in any case, the code words, which appear in the sets of code words in the first half of the preceding section, can be named(numbered) in a unique manner. Likewise, in the generalization presented in the latter half of the preceding section, all the code words are named (numbered) by $P_1^j P_k a_1$.

ORDERING OF CODE WORDS

In the sets of code words obtained in

the first half of section "classification of code words," the code words are ordered according to the powers of R. Namely, since R^1, R^2, R^3,..... ..,R^n are multiplied in front of $P_k a_1$, the code words can be numbered by 1, 2, 3,..., n, the exponents of R. Likewise, in the second half of section "classification of code words" code words in a set are numbered by 1, 2, 3, ..., n, the exponents of P_1^1, P_1^2, P_1^3,..., P_1^n.

CONSTRUCTION OF BASIC MATRIX USING ORDERED CODE WORDS

In the construction procedures of basic matrix explained in Kamoi and Shikata(1966) and Shikata(1966a), symbols in the (i_1+1)st row(code word) were shifted by a single digit to the right. There, it was also shown that the track codes constructed by leftward shifts of symbols are included in the track codes obtained by rightward shifts.
In the following section, an observation will be made on the relationship between the construction of track codes by rightward shifts(R) of symbols and the construction of track codes by permutations(P_1) of symbols.

CONSTRUCTION METHOD OF SUFFICIENT TRACK CODE

Track codes constructed by P_1 are included in the track codes constructed by R. First, we are going to review briefly the construction procedure of track codes by R. In the first row of a basic matrix, a code word(this may be the first code word of a set) is written from a set (this may be the kl-th set) of code words. In the second row, a code word from some other set(this may be called the k2-th set) is written, etc., and finally in the (i_1+1)st row the second code word of the kl-th set is written. Namely, the constructed basic matrix will be as

$$\begin{array}{l} P_{k1}a_1 \\ R^{j2}\ P_{k2}a_1 \\ R^{j3}\ P_{k3}a_1 \\ \vdots \\ R^{ji1}P_{ki1}\ a_1 \\ R\ P_{k1}a_1 \end{array} \qquad (17)$$

The last row of the above matrix is not to be included in the basic matrix, but it is placed there in order to show that the symbols of the code word in the first row are shifted rightward by one digit when placed at the (i_1+1)st row. Here, j2, k2, j3, k3, etc. are some appropriate values of j and k for the second set, for the third set, etc.
Corresponding with the above procedure of constructing basic matrices, a basic matrix will be obtained by using permutation P_1 as

$$\begin{array}{l} P_{k1}a_1 \\ P_1^{j2}\ P_{k2}a_1 \\ P_1^{j3}\ P_{k3}a_1 \\ \vdots \\ P_1^{ji1}P_{ki1}a_1 \\ P_1^{ji}\ P_{k1}\ a_1 \end{array} \qquad (18)$$

Here, care must be taken that a pair of any adjoining code words have only two different digits(Kamoi and Shikata 1966).
Since each row of the basic matrix (18) is a code word, any row can be changed into some other row by some permutations of symbols. If z, an element of group G, is multiplied to (18) from the left hand side, the expression (18) will be changed into

$$\begin{array}{l} z\ P_{k1}\ a_1 \\ zP_1^{j3}P_{k2}a_1 \\ zP_1^{j3}P_{k3}a_1 \\ \vdots \\ zP_1^{ji1}P_{ki1}a_1 \\ z\ P_1\ P_{k1}\ a_1 \end{array} \qquad (19)$$

It is necessary for the above matrix (19) to be a basic matrix obtained through R (i.e. basic matrix (17)) that the first row becomes equal to the (i_1+1)st row by rightward shift of symbols by a single digit. I.e., it is required that

$$Rz=zP_1. \qquad (20)$$

This implies that

$$R = zP_1 z^{-1} \tag{21}$$

or that

$$P_1 = (z^{-1})R(z^{-1})^{-1}. \tag{22}$$

By comparing this with equation(16), we find that the condition (20) is satisfied, if we use such a z as

$$x = z^{-1}. \tag{23}$$

Since the same relation is required between the second and (i_1+2)nd row, between the third and (i_1+3)rd row, etc. of matrix (19), the matrix (19) can be rewritten as

$$\begin{matrix} x^{-1}P_{k1}a_1 \\ x^{-1}P_1^{j2}P_{k2}a_1 \\ x^{-1}P_1^{j3}P_{k3}a_1 \\ \vdots \\ x^{-1}P_1^{ji1}P_{ki1}a_1 \\ Rx^{-1}P_{k1}a_1 \end{matrix} \tag{24}$$

and the matrix, which follows the above matrix will be written as

$$\begin{matrix} Rx^{-1}P_1^{j2}P_{k2}a_1 \\ Rx^{-1}P_1^{j3}P_{k3}a_1 \\ \vdots \\ Rx^{-1}P_1^{ji1}P_{ki1}a_1 \\ R^2x^{-1}P_{k1}a_1 \\ \vdots \end{matrix} \tag{25}$$

Thus, it has been shown that the basic matrices constructed through permutation P_1 can necessarily be derived from the basic matrices constructed through R. As shown in Kamoi and Shikata(1966), track codes are obtained by reading the vertical columns of basic matrix. In the basic matrices constructed by R, columns are read from right to left, namely in the order reverse to R, and from top to bottom. Likewise, in the basic matrices constructed by P_1, the columns are read in the order reverse to the order of P_1, and from top to bottom in each column. Namely, for example, if P_1 is P(132), the second row is read first, the third row the next, and the first row is read at last. If the matrices such as matrix (25) is written below the basic matrix such as matrix (24), columns are interchanged by P_1 at the every (i_1+1)st row, and any column of the total matrix will be the same as any other column but the vertical rotations of symbols, which gives a single track code from a single basic matrix.

In reading the symbols, i.e. the track code, of a basic matrix constructed by P_1, it was noticed that columns are interchanged by P_1, at the every (i_1+1)st row. In reading the track code of a basic matrix constructed by rotation R, columns are interchanged(cyclically permuted) by R at the every (i_1+1)st row. This implies that the two track codes read out from the basic matrices constructed by P_1 and R are the same, if matrices (17) and (19) are equal. Since such an equality can always be obtained by using group element x of equation (16) as in equation (23), it is concluded that the track codes constructed by P_1 can always be constructed by R.

<u>Track codes constructed by R are included in the track codes constructed by P_1.</u> Suppose that we have constructed a basic matrix by R as expression (17) in the preceding section. We multiply some permutation z to every row of the matrix (17) as

$$\begin{matrix} zP_{k1}\,a_1 \\ zR^{j2}P_{k2}\,a_1 \\ zR^{j3}P_{k3}\,a_1 \\ \vdots \\ zR^{ji1}P_{ki1}\,a_1 \\ zRP_{k1}\,a_1 \end{matrix} \tag{26}$$

If this matrix is equal to some matrix constructed by P_1, the condition

$$P_1(zP_{k1}a_1) = zRP_{k1}a_1 \tag{27}$$

must be satisfied, which requires that

$$zR = P_1 z. \tag{27a}$$

This implies that

$$P_1 = zRz^{-1}. \quad (28)$$

Namely, it is required that P_1 and R are conjugate. This condition is satisfied by using x of equation(16) for z, i.e.,

$$z = x. \quad (29)$$

Thus we know that the basic matrices constructed by R are always derived from the basic matrices constructed by P_1.
Concerning track codes, we obtain a result similar to that of the preceding section, i.e., the track codes constructed by R are included in the track codes constructed by permutation P_1.

Track codes constructed by R and P_1 are equivalent. Combining the results in the preceding two sections, the following result is obtained: All of the track codes constructed by cyclic permutation R can be constructed by permutation P_1, and vice versa. In other words, the two construction procedures of track codes by R and P_1 give a same collection of track codes, which means that the construction procedure of track codes by either one of R and P_1 already yields sufficient track codes.

DISCUSSION

In one-track m-n-p codes, order of "reading out" code words must be assigned to a set of brushes. This order may be cyclic permutation R or some appropriate permutation P_1. In the (i_1+1)st row of a basic matrix, columns are interchanged by R or P_1, and each brush starts to read a new column after every i_1 rows. Correspondence between R or P_1 and the condition for a code to be one-track seems to need some more investigations.
In basic matrices constructed by R and P_1, code words are ordered from top to bottom in the same order as the order of the sets used for construction. This order of sets is indicated in matrices (17) or (18) by k1, k2,..., ki_1, which is repeated in the matrices following the basic matrices as is seen in matrix (25). Modes of classification of code words into sets are different according to different R and P_1. For example, the classification by R as in (4) and (5) are different from that by P_1 in (10) and (11). More precisely, the first code word in (4) is classified into (10), the second code word in (4) is classified into (11), etc. Therefore, when a basic matrix is constructed by R, code words 11000 and 01100 belong to a same set and necessarily do not appear at the same time in a basic matrix, while they may appear at the same time in a basic matrix, when the basic matrix is constructed by P_1, as they may belong to different sets.
If we take the example of Kamoi's Advanced Two Out of Five Code(Kamoi 1966),

```
00011
00101
01100
10100
10001        (30)
10010
00110
01010
11000
01001
```

and exchange the third and fourth olumns as

```
00101
00011
01010
10010
10001        (31)
10100
00110
01100
11000
01001
```

then we find the code words 01100 and 11000 in the eighth and ninth rows, respectively, while the matrix (31) still gives a one-track m-n-p code. Thus, although it seems to be a little difficult to see any regularity in the order of code words only. A regularity is always observed, when the order is considered from the side of the order of sets. This ordering of code words may have some significance in encoding and decoding of our codes into or from some other codes. Some related results are also given in Shikata(1966a&b, 1974a&b, & 1976).

REFERENCES

A. Kamoi (1966). Advanced two out of five code and its applications. IFAC 3rd Congress, Session 9, Paper9A, London(June).
A. Kamoi and M. Shikata (1966). An application of group theory to K-E

code. <u>RAAG Research Notes</u> Third Series No.102.

M. Shikata (1966a). Permutation of symbols in code words of a certain angle-position encoder. <u>RAAG Research Note</u> Third Series No.100.

M. Shikata (1966b). Construction of one-track m-n-p system by conjugate class of group elements. <u>RAAG Research Notes</u> Third Series No.106.

M. Shikata (1974a). Generation and error-correcting properties of 1-track K-E codes for angle-position encoders. <u>Electronics and Communications in Japan</u>, 57-A, 10-17.

M. Shikata (1974b). Code for a 1-track angle-position encoder with K-E conditions. <u>Electronics and Communications in Japan</u>, 57-A, 20-27.

M. Shikata (1976). An absolute angle-position encoder in degrees and seconds. <u>Journal of Humanities and Natural Sciences</u>(Tokyo College of Economics) 43, 11-48.

R. C. Singleton (1966). Generalized snake-in-the-box codes, <u>IEEE Trans.</u> EC-15, 4, 596.

EXTRA-CYCLIC PASSAGES OF GRAY CODES AND THEIR APPLICATIONS FOR NUMERICAL CONTROL DESIGN

H.J. Leśkiewicz

Warsaw Technical University, Chodkiewicza 8, 02-525 Warszawa, Poland

ABSTRACT

A procedure of finding a Gray code, which will prevent the occurence of hazard phenomena in the case when the sequence of coded states does not form a cycle, is presented. Those Gray codes do not exist for all cases of sequence of coded states. The procedure was limited up to sixteen coded states.

INTRODUCTION

In numerical control design there is a need to avoid hazard phenomena. One of the possible measures is a proper coding of states when their sequence of transition is known. If Gray codes are used for this purpose the transitions between the coded states should be cyclic. If they are not, there is still a probability to find a proper Gray code with suitable extra-cyclic passages. To answer the question whether such a code does exist or not, and how many of Gray codes could give a proper answer, a special computer programme was written. The number of cases to be considered is much too large to do it in any other way.
The paper presents the basic ideas and some results of this procedure.

DEFINITION OF EXTRA-CYCLIC PASSAGES

Let us consider an even number of states forming a cycle and coded with a Gray code. A passage will be called an extra-cyclic passage only when it connects two states which are situated not successively in a cycle, and, when it has the properties of Gray code in the sense that the transition changes only one letter in the coding expressions.

DEFINITION OF DOMINANT GRAY CODES

If there is a Gray code possessing the same extra-cyclic passages, for the same number of coded states, as some others have, then it will be called a dominant Gray code among those others. Shifting and reversing of any Gray code does not change its dominant code. A dominant Gray code may be also a dominant code for itself. For each even number of coded states there may be several dominant Gray codes.

SETS OF DOMINANT GRAY CODES

A computer programme was written to select dominant Gray codes for given even numbers of states. In this way the full description of the codes, including the extra-cyclic passages, was obtained. The procedure was limited to sixteen states due to the rapidly growing consumption of computer time. Table 1 presents quantities of dominant Gray codes found by this computer programme for even numbers of states up to sixteen.

Table 1 Quantities of Dominant Gray Codes for Even Numbers of Coded States

numbers of coded states	6	8	10	12	14	16
quantities of dominant Gray codes	1	2	5	15	21	9

For example, one of the found dominant Gray codes was,

4, 10 CG /1, 2, 3, 4, 3, 2, 3, 1, 3/ 0000

Figure four standing at the beginning of the expression denotes the number of positions in the code, and the following figure ten denotes the number of coded states. Four zeros after the parenthesis are the coded first state, and the figures in parentheses, indicate the position to be changed, in a coding expression, going from right to left. This concerns cyclic changes only.

The following expression written with the code

/2,7/ /3,6/ /5,8/ /7,10/

indicates all the extra-cyclic passages. In this expression each extra-cyclic passage is presented by two figures in parentheses, indicating these states in the cycle between which the extra-cyclic passages have been found.

GRAPHIC PRESENTATION OF EXTRA-CYCLIC PASSAGES IN A GRAY CODE

The dominant Gray code described in the previous paragraph is presented graphically in Fig. 1

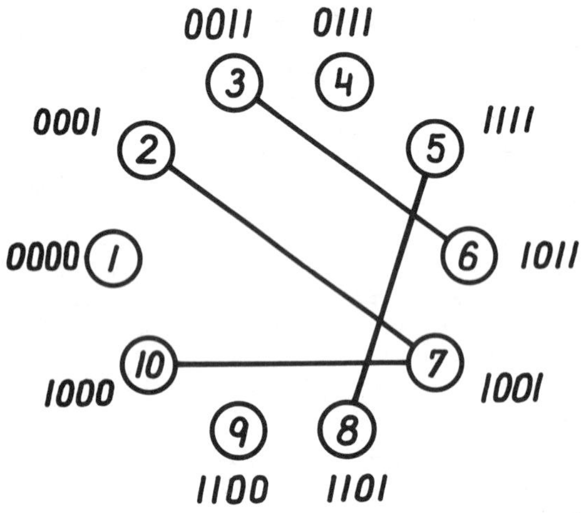

Fig. 1 The graphic presentation of a dominant Gray code.

This presentation consists of some lines representing extra-cyclic passages which form chords inside a round cycle of states. It is evident that the reverse picture formed by these chords may be obtained by changing the clockwise direction of state numeration into the anticlockwise one, or vice versa. This has been taken into consideration when writing the computer programme for finding the sets of dominant Gray codes, and consequently these sets have become smaller as compared to the sets obtained by clockwise numeration only. Apart from the change in a clockwise circulation there is a possibility of shifting the numeration by a certain number of coded states.

SEQUENCE OF STATES TO BE CODED FOR PRACTICAL PURPOSES

If some states are to be coded for practical purposes, an attempt is made to use Gray codes in order to avoid hazard phenomena. It can be done evidently when the number of coded states is even and when they form a cycle. If it is not so, the sequence of coded states is to be presented in the form of a quasi-cycle with some chords. This presentation should be made with regard to minimize the number of chords. Figure 2a and Fig.2b illustrate the procedure in a graphic form.

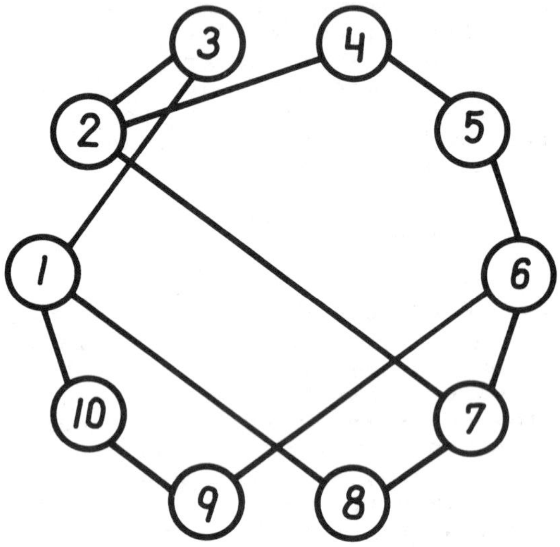

Fig. 2a The sequence of states before minimizing the number of chords.

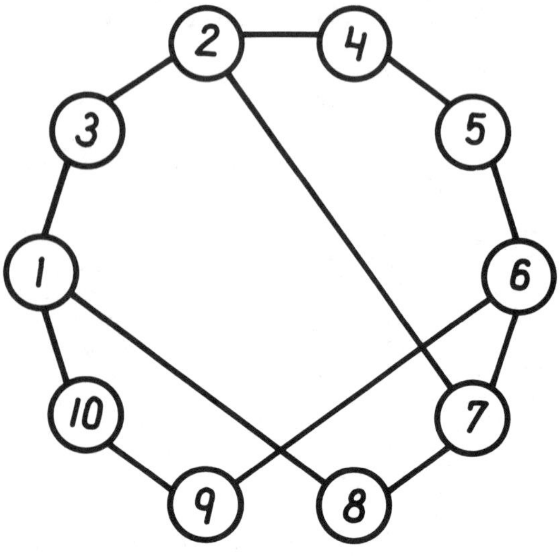

Fig. 2b The same sequence of states after minimizing the number of chords.

Once the problem is presented in a cyclic form with the minimum number of chords, such Gray code is searched in which extra-cyclic passages will cover those chords. Although it is not always feasible, but it provides an ideal anti-hazard protection.

ANTI-HAZARD CODING AIDED BY EXTRA-CYCLIC PASSAGES

The idea expressed in the previous paragraph provided the base for the computer programme. The programme uses the previously found, through another programme, sets of dominant Gray codes for each number of states. To use the programme, first the number of states to be coded /even number only/ must be known. If the number of states is odd, one additional state can be introduced. Then it is necessary to minimize the number of chords in a quasi-cyclic presentation of the passages between those states by means of a proper numeration. Using these data the programme will give three types of answers, and namely, the first which says there is no required Gray code, the second which names a proper code and tells how much it must be shifted, and the third which names a code and tells to reverse it, and then how much it must be shifted.
The two latter answers may occur simultaneously.

EXAMPLES OF APPLICARIONS

Example I:

Ten states with three chords

/1,8/ /3,7/ /6,9/

Answer:
a proper dominant Gray code cannot be found.

Example II:

Ten states with three chords

/1,8/ /4,7/ /6,9/

Answers:

1. take the dominant Gray code

   4,10 CG /1,2,3,4,3,2,3,1,3/0000;

   /2,7/ /3,6/ /5,8/ /7,10/

   and shift increasing the numeration of states by one. Then extra-cyclic passages of the code will be

   /3,8/ /4,7/ /6,9/ /8,1/,

   what solves the problem,

2. take the same code as in answer 1 reverse the state numeration and shift increasing by two. Then the extra-cyclic passages of the code will be

   /2,7/ /1,8/ /9,6/ /7,4/

   what solves the problem,

3. take the dominant Gray code

   4,10 CG /1,2,3,4,3,1,3,4,3/0000;

   /3,6/ /3,10/ /4,9/ /5,8/ /7,10/

   and shift increasing the numeration of states by one. Then the extra-cyclic passages of the code will be

   /4,7/ /4,1/ /5,10/ /6,9/ /8,1/

   what solves the problem,

4. take the same code as in answer 3 reverse the state numeration and shift increasing by two. The extra-cyclic passages of the code will be

   /1,8/ /1,4/ /10,5/ /9,6/ /7,4/

   what solves the problem.

Example III:

Ten states with four chords

/2,5/ /4,7/ /5,10/ /6,9/

Answer:
take the dominant Gray code

4,10 CG /1,2,3,4,3,2,3,1,3/0000;

/2,7/ /3,6/ /5,8/ /7,10/

reverse the state numeration and shift increasing by eight. Then the extra-cyclic passages of the code will be

/8,3/ /7,4/ /5,2/ /3,10/

what solves the problem.

This is the only one ansver.

LIMITATIONS OF THE PRESENTED PROCEDURE

The main limitation of the presented procedure is the maximum number of states fixed as sixteen for which the whole procedure has been develo-

ped.
In the majority of cases in numerical control design this maximum number of states is large enough. For a larger number of states which is sometimes needed, a special simplified procedure should be eventually developed in the future.

REFERENCES:

1. M.Cohn, S.Even, A Gray Code Counter, IEEE Trans.Computers 7, 662-664 /1969/.
2. C.N.Liu, A state variable assignment method for asynchronous sequential switching circuits, J. ACM 10, 209-216, /1963/.
3. G.K.Maki, J.H.Tracey, State assignment selection in asynchronous sequential circuits, IEEE Trans.Computers 7, 641-644 /1970/.
4. J.H.Tracey, Internal state asignments for asynchronous sequential machines, IEEE Trans. Electronic Computers 4, 551-560 /1966/.

AN ANALYSIS OF WATER SUPPLY AND STORAGE CAPACITY

T. Odanaka

Metropolitan College of Technology, Tokyo, 6-6, Asahigaoka, Hino-City, Tokyo, Japan

ABSTRACT

Lack of sufficient storage capacity in a water supply system led to frequent changes in the load on the filters and hence to poor quality. H.C. Hamaker carried out experimentally to decide how much the storage capacity should be enlarged and how the crude water supply can be controlled in order to obviate these troubles. In this case study, we give the theoretical background for his numerical analysis from the standpoint of the control processes with certain probability criterion.

INTRODUCTION

Lack of sufficient storage capacity in a water supply system led to frequent changes in the load on the filters and hence to poor quality. H.C. Hamaker carried out experimentally to decide how much the storage capacity should be enlarged and how the crude water supply can be controlled in order to obviate the troubles.[1]

In this case study, we give the theoretical background for his numerical analysis from the standpoint of the control processes with certain probability criterion. The Philips Factories in Eindhoven possess their own water supply system which operates according to the following principle.

Water Sources → Crude Supply Pumps → Filters

Storage Tanks → Delivery Pumps → Factories

A variable load on the filters lends to a deterioration in the chemical purity of the water and is for that reason undesirable. Hence the load on the filters should, as far as possible, be kept at a constant level and the inevitable random fluctuations in the consumption should be buffered by a sufficient storage capacity. Three factors determine the problem of errors in the estimated consumption and the size of the discrete steps by which the crude water supply can be controlled.

(1) To avoid the complications due the daily period we considered 24-hour intervals starting each day at 8 o'clock in the morning. Week-ends were excluded. As a first approach we assumed that the consumption for the next 24 hours would be the same as for the last 24 hours.

(2) In many cases, the level of supply can be changed only in steps of $100m^3$/hour by switching off a pump at one source and switching on a pump at the other, which causes fairly heavy fluctuations in the loads on the filters. But, on the basis experimental results it was decided that water supply systems adjustable in steps of $50m^3$/hour would suffice. These do not unduly increase the unavoidable errors in the prediction.

The full 24-hour weekdays are to be divided into a day period from 8 to 17=9 hours with high consumption, and a night period from 17 to 8=15 hours with a low consumption. For November and December of year 1955 we computed an average consumption of $1765m^3$/hour in the night period. The average weekday consumption was $\{9\times 1765+15\times 1330/2\}/24=1493m^3$/hour. The surplus consumption during the day period is $9\times(1765-1493)=2448m^3$ and there is an equal deficit consumption during the night period.

Once a day, say at 8 o'clock in the morning the position is checked and the supply required for the next 24 hours is decided on. At that moment the storage tank should contain half of its full capacity $+1250m^3$. Deviations from this level will be called the surplus, a deficit being counted as a negative surplus. The supply needed in the next 24 hours will thus be the consumption of the past 24 hours minus the surplus divided by 24. In doing so it has been assumed that the supply pumps have been changed so that the water supply can be altered in steps of $50m^3$/hour.

The numerical computations presented were performed for a total of 28 successive weeks. Figure 1 shows a histogram of the storage surpluses observed on these 140 days. Except for one extreme case these fluctuate between $-2100m^3$ and $+2700m^3$. In order fully to cope with these fluctuations a storage capacity of $4800m^3$ would be needed.

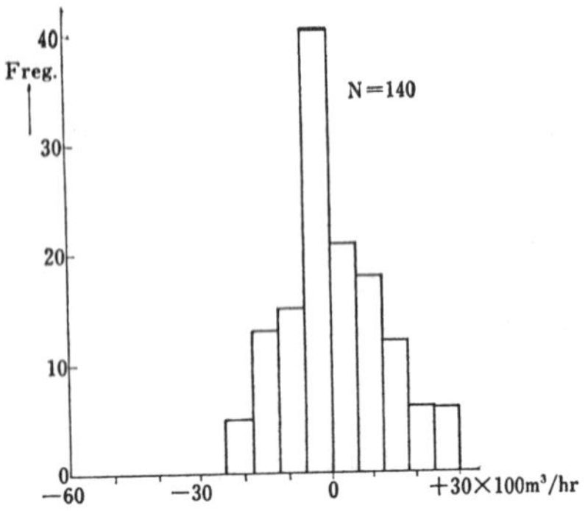

Fig. 1

(3) The error in the predicted consumption is the main source of the fluctuations. In the strategy of (2), this error accumulates over 24 hours because we check our stock only once per day. It is conceivable that a more frequent check may lead to a further reduction of the fluctuations and hence of the storage capacity required.

To see how much improvement can be achieved in this manner we investigated an alternative strategy with two checks in 24 hours, one at midday and the other at midnight. This seems particularly appropriate for at both these moments the storage tank should be half full.

Adopting this alternative strategy we again computed the variations in the storage level from hour for the two weeks beginning November 21 in which according to Figure 2 the variations are large and irregular. Figure 3 presents the results. We see that a double check per 24 hours leads to a pronounced improvement. While with a single check the $\pm 2000m^3$ line was transgressed three times in these two weeks, this occurs only once when we take stock of our position twice a day.

In this case, we have the following three problems.

(1) The criterion for decision is not evident.

(2) What is the fundamental theory of the optimal policies?

(3) There is not the economical consideration.

We have considered our problems as the inventory control problem. And we have used the method of inventory control with some probability criterion. So, we have given the theoretical background for (1) and (2) of our problems.

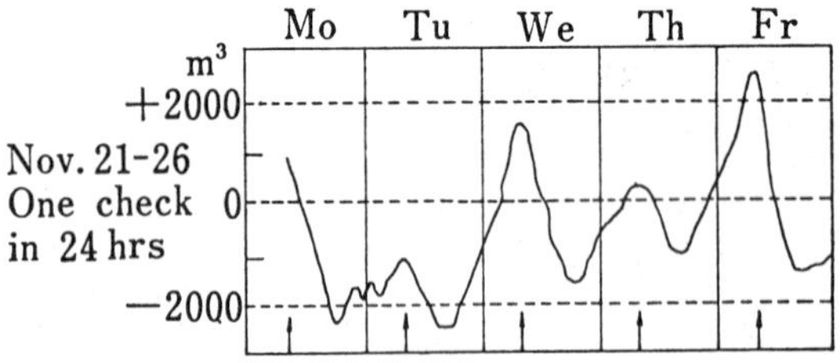

Fig. 2

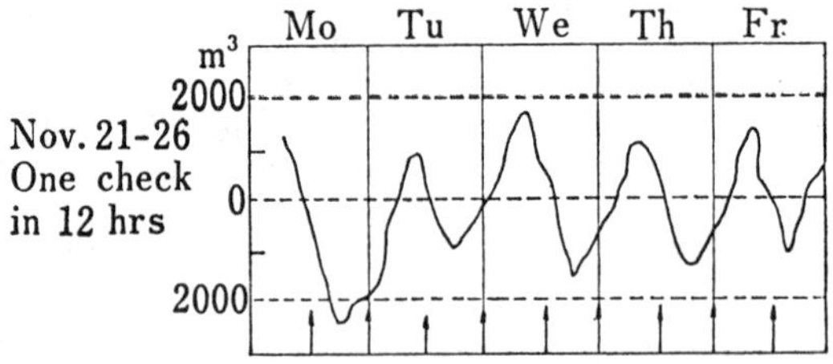

Fig. 3

<u>Inventory Control with Certain Probability Criterion</u>

1. Optimal capacity

Our problem is to research how to determine the size of the warehouse. In this case, we are faced the following two kinds of risk.[2) 3)]

(a) The case that flow over the warehouse capacity, increasing the inventory.

(b) The case that did not meet the demand, decreasing the inventory.

Let us be uniformed of the mean of the input and the output at each stage. But there is the variation of input and output.

Let us be σ_1 and σ_2 their variance. α is warehouse capacities and β is lower bound of control. $\sigma^2 = \sigma_1^2 + \sigma_2^2$

If the reliabilities over warehouses is the probability that does not exceed α and β, then its reliability is represented by

$$\phi(\alpha,\beta) = \frac{4}{\pi} \sum_{m=0}^{\infty} \frac{1}{2m+1} \left[\sin \frac{\alpha-\beta}{\alpha}(2m+1)\pi\right] e^{-\frac{\sigma^2 (2m+1)^2 \pi^2}{2\alpha^2}} \tag{1}$$

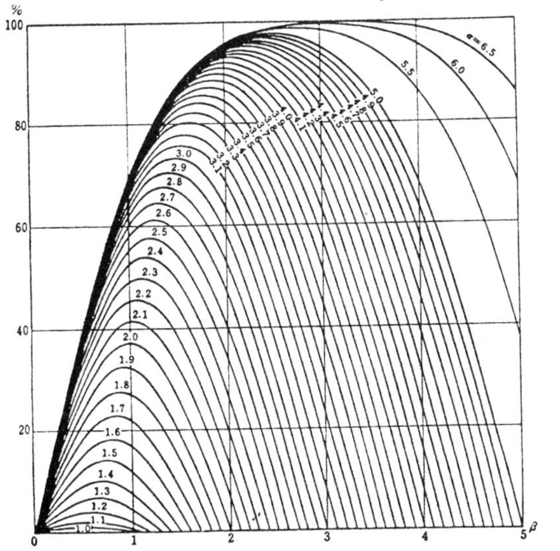

$$\sigma(\alpha,\beta)=\frac{4}{\pi}\sum_{m=0}^{\infty}\frac{1}{2m+1}\left\{\sin\frac{\alpha-\beta}{\alpha}(2m+1)\pi\right\}e^{-\frac{(2m+1)^2\pi^2}{\alpha^2}\frac{1}{2}}$$

Fig. 4

2. Optimal policy

In our process, we regard as the question of stocking a single items which is subject to stochastic demand at certain specified times which we denote by 0,1,...,N. The problem we set ourselves is that of determining the policy or policies which minimize the probability that stock level in each stage exceed the specified bound. In many cases, there is the purchase cost, the outage cost, but its estimations are very difficult. We shall assume that these cost is unknown in our discussions. Let us assume the distribution of demand at any stage only.

Let us define the following quantities:

(a) x_n =the stock level at the nth stage, prior to the delivery of the quantity ordered at the nth stage and the demand at the nth stage. $(n=k,k+1,\dots,N-1)$

(b) y_n =the quantity ordered at the nth stage. $(n=k,k+1,\dots,N-1)$

(c) z_n =the demand at the nth stage. $(n=k,k+1,\dots,N-1)$

The quantity y_n depends upon the observed stock level x_n and the quantities ordered proceeding stages y_{n-1}, $\dots,y_{n-d}$. It is assumed that y_n must be determined before z_n is observed and $y_n \geq 0$.

We have the following relations

$$x_{n+1}=x_n-z_n+y_n, \quad x_k=x. \tag{2}$$

$(n=k,k+1,\dots,N-1)$

Assumptions

(a) The demand z_n at nth stage is predicted by $\sum_{m=k}^{n-1} a_m z_m$, and practically.

It is assumed that observed z_n is equal to $z_n=\sum_{m=k}^{n-1} a_m z_m + w_n$, where w_n is observed error.

(b) $\{w_n\}$ are identically, independently distributed random variables and the density function is devoted by $\psi(w)$.

(c) The following conditions are imposed on the density function.

i) $\psi(z)>0$, for $z\geq 0$, $\int_0^{\infty}\psi(z)dz=1$,

$$\int_0^{\infty} z\psi(z)dz=0. \tag{3}$$

ii) $\int_y^{y+0}\psi(z)dz\leq a<1$, for $y\geq 0$, $\Delta=\alpha-\beta$.

iii) $\psi'(t)$ is continuous and unimodal in $[\alpha, \infty)$.

iv) $\psi''(z)<0$ for some interval of $2(\alpha-\beta)$ at least.

(d) $|y_n|<A$.

We now wish to determine the policy function $\{y_n\}$ which will minimize the J for stochastic functions of the $\{z_n\}$, where

$$J=\text{Prob.}\{(\max_{k\leq n\leq N} x_n>\alpha) \text{ or } (\min_{k\leq n\leq N} x_n<\beta)\},$$
$$x_k=x \tag{4}$$

This probability is taken over the random variables $\{z_n\}$. Let us the n for $n\geq k+d$, introduce the sequence of function defined by

$$f_n(x,z_k,z_{k+1},\dots,z_{n-1})=\min J \tag{5}$$

The notation min indicate that the minimization is over all policy functions.

We have $f_N(x,z_k,\dots,z_{n-1})=1$, $(x\geq\alpha,\ x\leq\beta)$

$$=0, \text{ (otherwise)} \tag{6}$$

More generally, we have for $N-1\geq n>k$

$$f_n(x,z_k,\dots,z_{n-1})=1, \quad (x\geq\alpha,\ x\leq\beta)$$

$$=\min_{|y|<A}\Big[\int_{x+y-\sum_{m=k}^{n-1}a_m z_m-\beta}^{\infty}\psi(z)dz+\int_{-\infty}^{x+y\sum_{m=k}^{n-1}a_m z_m-\alpha}\psi(z)dz + \int_{x+y-\sum_{m=k}^{n-1}a_m z_m-\alpha}^{x+y-\sum_{m=k}^{n-1}a_m z_m-\beta} f_{n+1}(x+y-\sum_{m=k}^{n-1}a_m z_m-z,z_k, \dots,z_{n-1})\psi(z)dz\Big], \text{ (otherwise)} \tag{7}$$

We have following results:4)

The optimal policy $y_n^*=y_n^*(x,z_k,\ldots,z_{n-1})$ is of the following form. There exists an $\bar{x}_n$ such that

$$y_n=\sum_{m=k}^{n-1} a_m z_m+\bar{x}_n-x, \quad (x\geq\bar{x}_n)$$
$$=\sum_{m=k}^{n-1} a_m z_m+x-\bar{x}_n, \quad (x<\bar{x}_n), \tag{8}$$

where $\bar{x}_n$ is determined satisfying

$$\int_{x+y-\Sigma a_m z_m-\alpha}^{x+y-\Sigma a_m z_m-\beta}(1-f_{n+1}(x+y-\sum_{m=k}^{n-1} a_m z_m-z,z_k,\ldots,$$
$$z_{n-1})\psi'(z)dz=0 \tag{9}$$

In our case, we have $a_k=\ldots=a_{n-2}=0$, $a_{n-1}=0$. So, $\sum_{m=k}^{n-1} a_m z_m=z_{n-1}$.

3. Double check

We observed at times 0,1,2,... and controlled. Following, we want to observe at time 0, 1/2, 2/2,... and control. The inventory period I_0, $I_{1/2}$, $I_{2/2}$,... are numbered from left to right. At the beginning of the period n/2 (n=0,1,...,N,...), we assume to be taken a regular order. Assuming that we are given the probability density $\psi_{1/2}(z)$ of demand at any stage n/2 and α,β, we wish to determine ordering policies which minimize the probability that the stock level exceed the specified bound through for infinite stage.

If x represents the current stock and $f_n(x)$ represents the minimum probability for 2n/2 period problem when an optimal policy is followed, then

$$f_n(x)=\min_{y,y_1}[L(x+y,\psi_{1/2})+L(x+y+y_1,\psi_{2/2})$$
$$+\int_{-\infty}^{\infty} f_{n+1}(x+y+y_1-z)\psi_{2/2}(z)dz], \tag{10}$$

where let us assume that current stock is x_i and orders y_i, (i=0,1/2,2/2,...)

Then $L(w,\psi)$ represents

$$L(w,\psi)=\int_{w-\beta}^{\infty}\psi(z)dz+\int_{-\infty}^{w-\alpha}\psi(z)dz \tag{11}$$

and the stock to be received in period $i_1,i+1,\ldots j$ is y.

The optional policy $w=x+y$ for the infinite period problem may be obtained directly by solving the equation.

$$L'(x+y,\psi_{1/2})+L'(x+y+y_1,\psi_{2/2})$$
$$+\int_{-\infty}^{\infty} f_{n+1}(x+y+y_1-z)\psi_{2/2}(z)dz=0 \tag{12}$$

Otherwise, we want to consider the case I_0, I_1, I_2... . It is possible to write a functional equation as before.

If $F_n(x)$ represents the minimum probabiliby for n period problem when an optimal policy is followed, then

$$F_n(x)=\min_y[L(x+y,\psi_{1/2})+L(x+y,\psi_{2/2})$$
$$+\int_{-\infty}^{\infty} F_{n+1}(x+y-z)\psi_{2/2}(z)dz] \tag{13}$$

The optimal policy for the infinite period problem may be obtained by solving the equation

$$L'(x+y,\psi_{1/2})+L'(x+y,\psi_{2/2})$$
$$+\int_{-\infty}^{\infty} F_{n+1}'(x+y-z)\psi_{2/2}(z)dz=0 \tag{14}$$

It is evident that

$$F_n(x)\geq f_n(x) \tag{15}$$

We are able to estimate $F_n(x)-f_n(x)$ using equations (10) and (13).

Discussion

1. Probability criterion and cost criterion

Some interesting subject matter arises in the decision problems related to establishing optimal inventory level. The published recommended decisions rules give probabilistic decisions criteria in the form. Establish capacity so the probability the demand exceeds it is held to some tolerably low level; i.e., where x is the random variable representing population. The k is capacity and α is the proportion of days one can subjectively accept shortage, choose k such that

$$\sum_{x=k}^{\infty} p(x)\leq\alpha_0 \tag{16}$$

where suggested α_0 is on the order 0.05, 0.01 or some other value or some other value venerated in applied statistics.

We may also use a classical economic basis for decisions; increasing capacity until the cost of addition of the kth unit of capacity is no longer recovered in the value of avoiding expected shortage. For each added unit of capacity there is an incremental decrease in the expected overflow of the system. When the product of incremental decrease in expected overflow and the unit cost of overflow would be for the first time for the (k+1)th unit less than cost of adding that unit, capacity is established at k. Since the incremental decrease in expected overflow for the kth unit is equal to the tail of the population distribution beyond k, the decision rule is; choose k such that

$$\sum_{x=k}^{x=\infty} p(x)\geq c_1/c_2, \quad \sum_{x=k+1}^{x=\infty} p(x)<c_1/c_2 \tag{17}$$

where c_1 is the daily cost of providing the k unit, and c_2 is the cost of each shortage on a given day, where also c_1 is assumed to be linearly related to k and c_2 is a constant.

A virtue of the infinite capacity model just described is that the intuitively felt relation between probability decision criterion and economic once are formally expressible an identities. This makes it plausible in an actional decision situation to reconcile subjective notions of utility with measure of tangible cost and intuitively acceptable operating conditions. The redundancy of using the several approaches to decision serves either to check the consistency of cost estimates or to input costs from revealed acceptability of frequency of shortage. (Table 1)

We want to express the relation between the probabilistic decision criterion and economic once more generally. In the previous section we introduced some concept for upper limit α, lower limit β and constant is stock level $\bar{x}$, with the purpose of developing inventory control systems when the profit functions or the loss function is unknown. Let us apply these concepts, order are delivered immediately and we propose to study on ordering rule which can be expressed by

$$y=\bar{x}-x, \quad \text{for} \quad \bar{x}\geq x$$
$$=0, \quad \text{for} \quad \bar{x}<x \tag{18}$$

where, $\bar{x}$ is the solution such that satisfy the x of Table 1.

Table 1

	probability criterion	cost criterion
one period	$\int_0^x \psi(z)\,dz=\alpha$	$\int_0^x \psi(z)\,dz=\frac{p-c}{p+k}$
infinite period	$\int_0^x \sqrt{\frac{\pi}{2}}\, e^{-\frac{S^2}{2}} dz=\alpha$	$\int_0^x \psi(z)\,dz=\frac{p-c}{p+h-ac}$
finite period	$\int_{x-\alpha}^{x-\beta} f_n'(x-z)\psi(z)\,dz =0$	$\int_0^x \{p+f_n'(x-z)\psi(z)\,dz =p-c$

The problem we propose now to solve is how to determine α and β such that the inventory control system becomes an optimum one. Let us use the method of simulation. Let $z_1, z_2, \ldots$ denote the past demand, and let x denote the inventory at beginning. If we use the inventory rule of the equation (17), we can compute the quantity that would have been ordered at each period in the past. We recognize here that for inventory level x_{n+1}, of the (n+1) period

$$x_{n+1}=x_n-z_n+y_n \tag{19}$$

We can now assume a pair of numerical values for α and β, and with the aid of equation (18) and (19) we can compute for each inventory period the quantity that would have been ordered and the inventory level that would have been realized. We can repeat this calculation for a number of combinations of α and β, and then we can ask which of these α, β values is the best. If we had all the costs available, including the cost of a shortage, we could compute from this simulation the cost associated with each pair of α and β, and we could select the values which give the lowest cost. Suppose, however, that we do not have all the cost available. What can we do in such a case?

2. Ordering cost with setup cost

Also, we shall analyze the dynamic model for the important practical case in which the ordering cost has the form

$$C(y)=C_y+K(y) \quad K(y)=\begin{cases} K, & y>0 \\ 0, & y=0 \end{cases} \tag{20}$$

and we wish to choose y, subject to the constraint $\sum_{m=k}^{N-1} C(y_n)\leq m$, so as to minimize the probability

$$\text{Prob.}\{(\max_{k\leq n\leq N-1} x_n\geq\alpha) \text{ or } (\min_{k\leq n\leq N-1} x_n<\beta)\} \tag{21}$$

We consider the new problem of minimizing the following expression using Legrange multiples λ

$$J=[\text{Prob.}\{(\max_{k\leq n\leq N-1} x_n\geq\alpha) \text{ or } (\min_{k\leq n\leq N-1} x_n\leq\beta)\}]e^{\lambda\Sigma C(y_n)} \tag{22}$$

Let us define min $J=f_k(x)$, then we have

$$f_k(x)=1, \quad (x\geq\alpha,\ x\leq\beta)$$
$$=\min_w [e^{\lambda C(w-x)}\{\int_{\alpha-w}^{\infty}\psi(z)\,dz+\int_{-\infty}^{\beta-w}\psi(z)\,dz + \int_{\beta-w}^{\alpha-w} f_{k+1}(w-z)\psi(z)\,dz\}], \tag{23}$$
$$(\text{otherwise})$$

with

$$f_{N-1}(x)=\min_{zN-1}(e^{\lambda C(w-x)})=1, \quad (x\geq\alpha,\ x\leq\beta)$$
$$=0, \quad (\text{otherwise})$$

We shall prove, under the previous assumptions upon $\psi(y)$. Let us put $C=0$, without of the generality, we have the result that the optimal policy is given by the rule

$$z_k=|S-x|, \quad \text{for } |x|\le s. \qquad (24)$$
$$=0, \quad \text{for } x>s.$$

where $0<s<S<\infty$.

A policy of this type is the "s-S policy."

Finally, if the cost exceed the specified bound, is known too, then the measure of effectiveness can be replaced by a single cost figure, and with the aid of retrospective analysis the values of α and β can be selected so that this cost becomes the lowest possible.

So far, we have assumed that both α and β are determined only once for all. A more elaborate procedure would involve a forecast demand for the next period, and then the value of α and β could be influenced by this forecast.

3. Conclusion

We can make some general remarks on control.

(1) When inventory exceed the specified bounds, α, β, a now value should not be substituted customatically. An attempt to find the cause of the change (i.e., the "assignable cause") should be made. If such a cause is found then it may be a cause that will not continue and hence the substitution should not be made.

(2) If no assignable cause can be found then the new value should be substitute for the old, but particular attention should be given to the value in the immediately succeeding periods to see if and how its value "settle down," and also to search for any dues to the cause for the change.

The control system was setup as follows.: The only time we place an order is when the inventory is below

$$y_n=z_n-x \quad (\bar{x}_n\ge x) \qquad (25)$$
$$=0 \quad (z_n<x)z,$$

where $\bar{x}_n$ is the optimal inventory level such that

$$\int_{-\infty}^{\infty} m(w-z)\psi'(z)dz=0, \qquad (26)$$
$$m(w-z)=1-f_{n+1}(w-z) \quad (\beta\le w-z\le\alpha)$$
$$=0, \quad (\text{otherwise})$$

The optimal order quantity specified that the order quantity is as long as initial stock x is less than $\bar{y}_n'$. This means, then that when we do order we are replenished up to the level $\bar{y}_n'$. A simple chart was prepared to assist the planners. It is shown in Figure 5.

The problem of establishing the measures of effectiveness is a very fundamental one. In inventory control we are faced with making decision under uncertainty. The criterion which minimize the probability that the inventory over all stage exceeds a fixed level is of probably greater importance. The theory we have developed in this paper has much relation for preceding inventory control theory, and it will be interesting to see how such theories influence.

warehouse capacity ————————
No ordering.
What is the assignable cause?

$\bar{x}_n$ ————————
Let us order $(\bar{x}_n-x)$
What is the assignable cause?

α ————————
Let us order $(\bar{x}_n-x)$ only

β ————————
Let us order $(\bar{x}_n-x)$
What is the assignable cause?

nul inventory ————————

Fig. 5

Often, demand variables z_n are modeled as being generated by a difference equation. Equation of this type are known as autoregressive moving average (ARMA) equations.[5] This is the future problem.

Reference

1) H.C. Hamaker and D. Alma: An analysis of water consumption and storage capacity for the Philips Factories in Eindhoven. (in Japanese), *Keiei-Kagaku*. vol. 4, no. 2. (1961).
2) K. Kunisawa: How to determine the size of a warehouse, *Operations Research as a Management Science*, vol. 3, no. 5. (1958).
3) R. Bellman, I. Glicksberg and O. Gross: On the optimal inventory equation, *Management Science*, vol. 2. (1955).
4) T. Odanaka: *Stochastic Control Process*, Morikita Pub. Co. (in Japanese), (1976).
5) G.E.P. Box & G.M. Jenkins: *Time Series Analysis forecasting and control*, Holden-Day, (1970).

CIRCULAR-POLAR CONFIGURATIONS OF DYNAMIC MULTIPLE-CONNECTED SUB-SYSTEMS

V.M. Levykin* and B.F. Womack**

**Kharkov Institute of Radio Electronics, Ukrainian Soviet Socialist Republic, Kharkov, USSR*
***Department of Electrical Engineering and Electronics Research Center, The University of Texas at Austin*

ABSTRACT

Frequently the information-control issues in manufacturing automation processes become very complex and cannot be separated from the economic and social issues of large complex systems. In many instances well-defined subsystems are a basic part of the overall system and interconnections and controllers for the total system become critically important. This research recognizes that multiple-connected systems play an important part in the theory of automatic control. One can achieve better results when controlling these systems if more exact and definitive mathematical models can be developed for these processes.

Formative methods for static multiple-connected systems have already been developed. However, static models are not effective in a dynamic operating mode. Therefore, the development of dynamic models for multiple-connected sub-systems is considered essential to the design of future systems. Mutual influence among parameters and signals is a typical attribute for such systems. If any parameter changes, this change may affect many signals and the total system itself. Only with the availability of an appropriate dynamic model of the system can one take into account how strong is the influence of a parameter variation or a signal perturbation.

INTRODUCTION

A typical interactive dynamic system is shown in Fig. 1. The two subsystems have been assumed to be described by linear differential equations of second order. From the many categories of multiple-connected subsystems, it is possible to identify three categories of interconnections. These types are:

a) Polar-circular (see Fig. 2)

b) Circular (see Fig. 3)

c) Polar (see Fig. 4)

Suppose there are n linear multiple-connected subsystems, each of which can be described by the differential equation of the second order. (Fig. 2). It is desired to determine the equation of the system state of the form $\dot{\underline{x}} = \underline{A}\underline{x} + \underline{B}\underline{r}$. There are connections between each of the subsystems, therefore by definition we have equation (1) for the polar-circular configuration system, where $\underline{x}$ is a mx1 partitioned vector; $\underline{A}$ is a mxm partitioned matrix with 2n rows and 2n columns; $\underline{B}$ is a mxn partitioned matrix, and $\underline{r}$ is a mx1 vector.

From this equation we can determine two other kinds of systems, namely circular and polar configuration systems, where:

$\underline{C}_{ij}$ - connections between subsystems,

n - the number of subsystems.

$$\begin{bmatrix} \dot{\underline{x}}_1 \\ \dot{\underline{x}}_2 \\ \dot{\underline{x}}_3 \\ \dot{\underline{x}}_4 \\ \vdots \\ \dot{\underline{x}}_{n-1} \\ \dot{\underline{x}}_n \end{bmatrix} = \begin{bmatrix} \underline{A}_1 & \underline{C}_{12} & 0 & 0 & \cdots & \underline{C}_{1n-1} & \underline{C}_{1n} \\ \underline{C}_{21} & \underline{A}_2 & \underline{C}_{23} & 0 & \cdots & 0 & \underline{C}_{2n} \\ 0 & \underline{C}_{32} & \underline{A}_3 & \underline{C}_{34} & \cdots & 0 & \underline{C}_{3n} \\ 0 & 0 & \underline{C}_{43} & \underline{A}_4 & \cdots & 0 & \underline{C}_{4n} \\ \vdots \\ \underline{C}_{n-1,1} & 0 & 0 & 0 & \cdots & \underline{A}_{n-1} & \underline{C}_{n-1,n} \\ \underline{C}_{n1} & \underline{C}_{n2} & \underline{C}_{n3} & \underline{C}_{n4} & \cdots & \underline{C}_{n,n-1} & \underline{A}_n \end{bmatrix} \begin{bmatrix} \underline{x}_1 \\ \underline{x}_2 \\ \underline{x}_3 \\ \underline{x}_4 \\ \vdots \\ \underline{x}_{n-1} \\ \underline{x}_n \end{bmatrix} + \begin{bmatrix} \underline{B}_1 & 0 & 0 & 0 \cdots 0 \\ 0 & \underline{B}_2 & 0 & 0 \cdots 0 \\ 0 & 0 & \underline{B}_3 & 0 \cdots 0 \\ 0 & 0 & 0 & \underline{B}_4 \cdots 0 \\ \vdots \\ 0 & 0 & 0 & 0 \cdots \underline{B}_n \end{bmatrix} \begin{bmatrix} r_1 \\ r_2 \\ r_3 \\ r_4 \\ \vdots \\ r_n \end{bmatrix}; \quad (1)$$

If we have $\underline{C}_{1,n-1} = \underline{C}_{n-1,1} = \underline{C}_{2n} = \underline{C}_{n2} = \underline{C}_{3n} = \underline{C}_{n3} = \ldots = \underline{C}_{n,n-2} = \underline{C}_{n,n-2} = 0$ we obtain the equation for the circular configuration system:

$$\begin{bmatrix} \dot{\underline{x}}_1 \\ \dot{\underline{x}}_2 \\ \dot{\underline{x}}_3 \\ \dot{\underline{x}}_4 \\ \vdots \\ \dot{\underline{x}}_{n-1} \\ \dot{\underline{x}}_n \end{bmatrix} = \begin{bmatrix} \underline{A}_1 & \underline{C}_{12} & 0 & 0 & \ldots 0 & \underline{C}_{1n} \\ \underline{C}_{21} & \underline{A}_2 & \underline{C}_{23} & 0 & 0 & 0 \\ 0 & \underline{C}_{32} & \underline{A}_3 & \underline{C}_{34} & 0 & 0 \\ 0 & 0 & \underline{C}_{43} & \underline{A}_4 & 0 & 0 \\ \vdots & & & & & \\ 0 & 0 & 0 & 0 & \underline{A}_{n-1} & \underline{C}_{n-1,n} \\ \underline{C}_{n1} & 0 & 0 & 0 & \underline{C}_{n,n-1} & \underline{A}_n \end{bmatrix} \begin{bmatrix} \underline{x}_1 \\ \underline{x}_2 \\ \underline{x}_3 \\ \underline{x}_4 \\ \vdots \\ \underline{x}_{n-1} \\ \underline{x}_n \end{bmatrix} + \begin{bmatrix} \underline{B}_1 & 0 & 0 & 0 & \ldots & 0 \\ 0 & \underline{B}_2 & 0 & 0 & & 0 \\ 0 & 0 & \underline{B}_3 & 0 & & 0 \\ 0 & 0 & 0 & \underline{B}_4 & & 0 \\ \vdots & & & & & \\ 0 & 0 & 0 & 0 & \ldots & \underline{B}_n \end{bmatrix} \begin{bmatrix} r_1 \\ r_2 \\ r_3 \\ r_4 \\ \vdots \\ r_n \end{bmatrix} \qquad (2)$$

If we have $\underline{C}_{12} = \underline{C}_{21} = \underline{C}_{23} = \underline{C}_{32} = \ldots = \underline{C}_{n-1,1} = 0$, we have the equation for the polar configuration system:

$$\begin{bmatrix} \dot{\underline{x}}_1 \\ \dot{\underline{x}}_2 \\ \dot{\underline{x}}_3 \\ \dot{\underline{x}}_4 \\ \vdots \\ \dot{\underline{x}}_{n-1} \\ \dot{\underline{x}}_n \end{bmatrix} = \begin{bmatrix} \underline{A}_1 & 0 & 0 & 0 & \ldots 0 & \underline{C}_{1n} \\ 0 & \underline{A}_2 & 0 & 0 & 0 & \underline{C}_{2n} \\ 0 & 0 & \underline{A}_3 & 0 & 0 & \underline{C}_{3n} \\ 0 & 0 & 0 & \underline{A}_4 & 0 & \underline{C}_{4n} \\ \vdots & & & & & \\ 0 & 0 & 0 & 0 & \underline{A}_{n-1} & \underline{C}_{n-1,n} \\ \underline{C}_{n1} & \underline{C}_{n2} & \underline{C}_{n3} & \underline{C}_{n4} & \underline{C}_{n,n-1} & \underline{A}_n \end{bmatrix} \begin{bmatrix} \underline{x}_1 \\ \underline{x}_2 \\ \underline{x}_3 \\ \underline{x}_4 \\ \vdots \\ \underline{x}_{n-1} \\ \underline{x}_n \end{bmatrix} + \begin{bmatrix} \underline{B}_1 & 0 & 0 & 0 & \ldots & 0 \\ 0 & \underline{B}_2 & 0 & 0 & & 0 \\ 0 & 0 & \underline{B}_3 & 0 & & 0 \\ 0 & 0 & 0 & \underline{B}_4 & & 0 \\ \vdots & & & & & \\ 0 & 0 & 0 & 0 & & \underline{B}_n \end{bmatrix} \begin{bmatrix} r_1 \\ r_2 \\ r_3 \\ r_4 \\ \vdots \\ r_n \end{bmatrix} \qquad (3)$$

It is possible to show this solution for four subsystems in all configuration;

a) For the polar-circular configuration:

$$\begin{bmatrix} \dot{\underline{x}}_1 \\ \dot{\underline{x}}_2 \\ \dot{\underline{x}}_3 \\ \dot{\underline{x}}_4 \end{bmatrix} = \begin{bmatrix} \underline{A}_1 & \underline{C}_{12} & \underline{C}_{13} & \underline{C}_{14} \\ \underline{C}_{21} & \underline{A}_2 & \underline{C}_{23} & \underline{C}_{24} \\ \underline{C}_{31} & \underline{C}_{32} & \underline{A}_3 & \underline{C}_{34} \\ \underline{C}_{41} & \underline{C}_{42} & \underline{C}_{43} & \underline{A}_4 \end{bmatrix} \begin{bmatrix} \underline{x}_1 \\ \underline{x}_2 \\ \underline{x}_3 \\ \underline{x}_4 \end{bmatrix} + \begin{bmatrix} \underline{B}_1 & 0 & 0 & 0 \\ 0 & \underline{B}_2 & 0 & 0 \\ 0 & 0 & \underline{B}_3 & 0 \\ 0 & 0 & 0 & \underline{B}_4 \end{bmatrix} \begin{bmatrix} r_1 \\ r_2 \\ r_3 \\ r_4 \end{bmatrix} ; \qquad (4)$$

b) For the circular configuration $\underline{C}_{13} = \underline{C}_{31} = \underline{C}_{24} = \underline{C}_{42} = 0$

$$\begin{bmatrix} \dot{\underline{x}}_1 \\ \dot{\underline{x}}_2 \\ \dot{\underline{x}}_3 \\ \dot{\underline{x}}_4 \end{bmatrix} = \begin{bmatrix} \underline{A}_1 & \underline{C}_{12} & 0 & \underline{C}_{14} \\ \underline{C}_{21} & \underline{A}_2 & \underline{C}_{23} & 0 \\ 0 & \underline{C}_{32} & \underline{A}_3 & \underline{C}_{34} \\ \underline{C}_{41} & 0 & \underline{C}_{43} & \underline{A}_4 \end{bmatrix} + \begin{bmatrix} \underline{B}_1 & 0 & 0 & 0 \\ 0 & \underline{B}_2 & 0 & 0 \\ 0 & 0 & \underline{B}_3 & 0 \\ 0 & 0 & 0 & \underline{B}_4 \end{bmatrix} \begin{bmatrix} r_1 \\ r_2 \\ r_3 \\ r_4 \end{bmatrix} ; \qquad (5)$$

c) For the polar-configuration $\underline{C}_{12} = \underline{C}_{21} = \underline{C}_{23} = \underline{C}_{32} = \underline{C}_{13} = \underline{C}_{31} = 0$

$$\begin{bmatrix} \dot{\underline{x}}_1 \\ \dot{\underline{x}}_2 \\ \dot{\underline{x}}_3 \\ \dot{\underline{x}}_4 \end{bmatrix} = \begin{bmatrix} \underline{A}_1 & 0 & 0 & \underline{C}_{14} \\ 0 & \underline{A}_2 & 0 & \underline{C}_{24} \\ 0 & 0 & \underline{A}_3 & \underline{C}_{34} \\ \underline{C}_{41} & \underline{C}_{42} & \underline{C}_{43} & \underline{A}_4 \end{bmatrix} \begin{bmatrix} \underline{x}_1 \\ \underline{x}_2 \\ \underline{x}_3 \\ \underline{X}_4 \end{bmatrix} + \begin{bmatrix} \underline{B}_1 & 0 & 0 & 0 \\ 0 & \underline{B}_2 & 0 & 0 \\ 0 & 0 & \underline{B}_3 & 0 \\ 0 & 0 & 0 & \underline{B}_4 \end{bmatrix} \begin{bmatrix} r_1 \\ r_2 \\ r_3 \\ r_4 \end{bmatrix} ; \quad (6)$$

SPECIFIC SUBSYSTEMS

The difficulty of solving equations (1-3) depends on the form of the subsystem transfer function. It is possible to show the solution for subsystems having transfer functions (see Fig. 5 for polar-circular configuration).

$$G_{ii} = \frac{g_2^j}{\lambda_o^j s^2 + \lambda_1^j s + \lambda_2^j} ;$$

$i=1,2,\dots,n$; $j=1,2,\dots,n-1$;
n=number of the subsystems.

If we divide the numerator and denominator of the equation by λ_o^j and let:

$$\frac{g_2^j}{\lambda_o^j} = a_2^j ; \quad \frac{\lambda_1^j}{\lambda_o^j} = b_1^j ; \quad \frac{\lambda_2^j}{\lambda_o^j} = b_2^j ,$$

then we have transfer functions in the following form:

$$G_{ii} = \frac{a_2^j}{s^2 + b_1^j s + b_2^j} ;$$

Then the state equation for four subsystems are:

$$\begin{aligned} &\dot{x}_1 = -b_1 x_1 + x_2, \quad \dot{x}_3 = -b_1' x_3 + x_4, \quad \dot{x}_5 = -b_1'' x_5 + x_6, \\ &\dot{x}_2 = b_2 x_1 - a_2 e_1, \quad \dot{x}_4 = b_2' x_3 - a_2' e_2, \quad \dot{x}_6 = b_2'' x_5 - a_2'' e_3 \\ &\dot{x}_7 = -b_1''' x_7 + x_8, \quad \dot{x}_8 = b_2''' x_7 - a_2''' e_4 . \end{aligned} \quad (7)$$

Let us determine a view of the feedback between the subsystems. Let us assume that the feedback has such form as

$$\alpha_{21} = (d_{21} s + d_{21}') \, C_2(s) ; \quad (8)$$

then

$$e_1 = r_1 - x_1 + \alpha_{21} + \alpha_{31} + \alpha_{41}$$

or

$$\begin{aligned} e_1 = r_1 - x_1 + d_{21}\dot{x}_3 + d_{21}' x_3 + d_{31}\dot{x}_5 + d_{31}' x_5 + \\ d_{41}\dot{x}_7 + d_{41}' x_7 = r_1 - x_1 + (d_{21}' - d_{21} b_1') x_3 + d_{21} x_4 + (d_{31}' - \\ d_{31} b_1'') x_5 + d_{31} x_6 + (d_{41}' - d_{41} b_1''') x_7 + d_{41} x_8 ; \end{aligned}$$

and for e_i:

$$\begin{bmatrix} e_1 \\ e_2 \\ e_3 \\ e_4 \end{bmatrix} = \begin{bmatrix} -1 & 0 & K_{21} & d_{21}' & K_{31} & d_{31} & K_{41} & d_{41} \\ K_{12} & d_{12} & -1 & 0 & K_{32} & d_{32} & K_{42} & d_{42} \\ K_{13} & d_{13} & K_{23} & d_{23} & -1 & 0 & K_{43} & d_{43} \\ K_{14} & d_{14} & K_{24} & d_{24} & K_{34} & d_{34} & -1 & 0 \end{bmatrix} \begin{bmatrix} x_1 \\ x_2 \\ x_3 \\ x_4 \end{bmatrix} + \begin{bmatrix} 1 & 0 & 0 & 0 \\ 0 & 1 & 0 & 0 \\ 0 & 0 & 1 & 0 \\ 0 & 0 & 0 & 1 \end{bmatrix} \begin{bmatrix} r_1 \\ r_2 \\ r_3 \\ r_4 \end{bmatrix} \quad (9)$$

Where:

$K_{12} = d_{12}' - d_{12} b_1$ $\quad K_{21} = d_{21}' - d_{21} b_1'$ $\quad K_{31} = d_{31}' - d_{31} b_1''$ $\quad K_{41} = d_{41}' - d_{41} b_1'''$

$K_{13} = d_{13}' - d_{13} b_1$ $\quad K_{23} = d_{23}' - d_{23} b_1'$ $\quad K_{32} = d_{32}' - d_{32} b_1''$ $\quad K_{42} = d_{42}' - d_{42} b_1'''$

$K_{14} = d_{14}' - d_{14} b_1$ $\quad K_{24} = d_{24}' - d_{24} b_1'$ $\quad K_{34} = d_{34}' - d_{34} b_1''$ $\quad K_{43} = d_{43}' - d_{43} b_1'''$

Hence, the state equation we can write in the form:

$$\begin{bmatrix} \dot{x}_1 \\ \dot{x}_2 \\ \dot{x}_3 \\ \dot{x}_4 \\ \dot{x}_5 \\ \dot{x}_6 \\ \dot{x}_7 \\ \dot{x}_8 \end{bmatrix} = \begin{bmatrix} -b_1 & 1 & 0 & 0 & 0 & 0 & 0 & 0 \\ b & 0 & -a_2K_{21} & -a_2d_{21} & -a_2K_{31} & -a_2d_{31} & -a_2K_{41} & -a_2d_{41} \\ 0 & 0 & -b_1' & 1 & 0 & 0 & 0 & 0 \\ -a_2'K_{12} & -a_2'd_{12} & b' & 0 & -a_2'K_{32} & -a_2'd_{32} & -a_2'K_{42} & -a_2'd_{42} \\ 0 & 0 & 0 & 0 & -b_1'' & 1 & 0 & 0 \\ -a_2''K_{13} & -a_2''d_{13} & -a_2''K_{23} & -a_2''d_{23} & b'' & 0 & -a_2''K_{43} & -a_2''d_{43} \\ 0 & 0 & 0 & 0 & 0 & 0 & -b_1''' & 1 \\ -a_2'''K_{14} & -a_2'''d_{14} & -a_2'''K_{24} & -a'''d_{24} & -a_2'''K_{34} & -a_2'''d_{34} & b''' & 0 \end{bmatrix} \begin{bmatrix} x_1 \\ x_2 \\ x_3 \\ x_4 \\ x_5 \\ x_6 \\ x_7 \\ x_8 \end{bmatrix} + \begin{bmatrix} 0&0&0&0 \\ 1&0&0&0 \\ 0&0&0&0 \\ 0&1&0&0 \\ 0&0&0&0 \\ 0&0&1&0 \\ 0&0&0&0 \\ 0&0&0&1 \end{bmatrix} \begin{bmatrix} r_1 \\ r_2 \\ r_3 \\ r_4 \end{bmatrix}; \qquad (10)$$

Where: $b=(b_2-a_2)$; $b'=(b_2'-a_2')$; $b''=(b_2''-a_2'')$; $b'''=(b_2'''-a_2''')$.

If we let $K_{13}=K_{31}=K_{24}=K_{42}=0$, we will have the circular configuration system.

$$\begin{bmatrix} \dot{x}_1 \\ \dot{x}_2 \\ \dot{x}_3 \\ \dot{x}_4 \\ \dot{x}_5 \\ \dot{x}_6 \\ \dot{x}_7 \\ \dot{x}_8 \end{bmatrix} = \begin{bmatrix} -b_1 & 0 & 0 & 0 & 0 & 0 & 0 & 0 \\ b & 0 & -a_2K_{21} & -a_2d_{21} & 0 & 0 & -a_2K_{41} & -a_2d_{41} \\ 0 & 0 & -b_1' & 1 & 0 & 0 & 0 & 0 \\ -a_2'K_{12} & -a_2'd_{12} & b' & 0 & -a_2'K_{32} & -a_2'd_{32} & 0 & 0 \\ 0 & 0 & 0 & 0 & -b_1'' & 1 & 0 & 0 \\ 0 & 0 & -a_2''K_{23} & -a_2''d_{23} & b'' & 0 & -a_2''K_{43} & -a_2''d_{43} \\ 0 & 0 & 0 & 0 & 0 & 0 & -b_1''' & 1 \\ -a_2'''K_{14} & -a_2'''d_{14} & 0 & 0 & -a_2'''K_{34} & -a_2'''d_{34} & b''' & 0 \end{bmatrix} \begin{bmatrix} x_1 \\ x_2 \\ x_3 \\ x_4 \\ x_5 \\ x_6 \\ x_7 \\ x_8 \end{bmatrix} + \begin{bmatrix} 0&0&0&0 \\ 1&0&0&0 \\ 0&0&0&0 \\ 0&1&0&0 \\ 0&0&0&0 \\ 0&0&1&0 \\ 0&0&0&0 \\ 0&0&0&1 \end{bmatrix} \begin{bmatrix} r_1 \\ r_2 \\ r_3 \\ r_4 \end{bmatrix}; \qquad (11)$$

If we let $K_{12}=K_{21}-K_{23}=K_{32}=K_{13}=K_{31}=0$ we will have the polar configuration system.

$$\begin{bmatrix} \dot{x}_1 \\ \dot{x}_2 \\ \dot{x}_3 \\ \dot{x}_4 \\ \dot{x}_5 \\ \dot{x}_6 \\ \dot{x}_7 \\ \dot{x}_8 \end{bmatrix} = \begin{bmatrix} -b_1 & 1 & 0 & 0 & 0 & 0 & 0 & 0 \\ b & 0 & 0 & 0 & 0 & 0 & -a_2K_{41} & -a_2d_{41} \\ 0 & 0 & -b_1' & 1 & 0 & 0 & 0 & 0 \\ 0 & 0 & b' & 0 & 0 & 0 & -a_2'K_{42} & -a_2'd_{42} \\ 0 & 0 & 0 & 0 & -b_1'' & 1 & 0 & 0 \\ 0 & 0 & 0 & 0 & b'' & 0 & -a_2''K_{43} & -a_2''d_{43} \\ 0 & 0 & 0 & 0 & 0 & 0 & -b_1''' & 1 \\ -a_2'''K_{14} & -a_2'''d_{14} & -a_2'''K_{24} & -a_2'''d_{24} & -a_2'''K_{34} & -a_2'''d_{34} & b''' & 0 \end{bmatrix} \begin{bmatrix} x_1 \\ x_2 \\ x_3 \\ x_4 \\ x_5 \\ x_6 \\ x_7 \\ x_8 \end{bmatrix} + \begin{bmatrix} 0&0&0&0 \\ 1&0&0&0 \\ 0&0&0&0 \\ 0&1&0&0 \\ 0&0&0&0 \\ 0&0&1&0 \\ 0&0&0&0 \\ 0&0&0&1 \end{bmatrix} \begin{bmatrix} r_1 \\ r_2 \\ r_3 \\ r_4 \end{bmatrix}; \qquad (12)$$

It is possible to show the solution for n subsystems (Fig. 2).

$$\begin{bmatrix} \dot{x}_1 \\ \dot{x}_2 \\ \dot{x}_3 \\ \dot{x}_4 \\ \dot{x}_5 \\ \dot{x}_6 \\ \vdots \\ \dot{x}_{m-1} \\ \dot{x}_m \end{bmatrix} = \begin{bmatrix} -b_1 & 1 & 0 & 0 & 0 & 0 & 0 & 0 \\ b & 0 & -a_2K_{21} & -a_2d_{21} & 0 & 0 & -a_2K_{n1} & -a_2d_{n1} \\ 0 & 0 & -b'_1 & 1 & 0 & 0 & 0 & 0 \\ -a'_2K_{12} & -a'_2d_{12} & b' & 0 & -a'_2K_{32} & -a'_2d_{32} & -a'_2K_{n2} & -a'_2d_{n2} \\ 0 & 0 & 0 & 0 & -b''_1 & 1 & 0 & 0 \\ 0 & 0 & -a''_2K_{23} & -a''_2d_{23} & b'' & 0 & -a''_2K_{n3} & -a''_2d_{n3} \\ \vdots & & & & & & & \\ 0 & 0 & 0 & 0 & 0 & 0 & -b_1^{n-1} & 1 \\ -a_2^{n-1}K_{1n} & -a_2^{n-1}d_{1n} & -a_2^{n-1}K_{2n} & -a_2^{n-1}d_{2n} & -a_2^{n-1}K_{3n} & -a_2^{n-1}d_{3n} & b^{n-1} & 0 \end{bmatrix} \begin{bmatrix} x_1 \\ x_2 \\ x_3 \\ x_4 \\ x_5 \\ x_6 \\ \vdots \\ x_{m-1} \\ x_m \end{bmatrix} +$$

$$\begin{bmatrix} 0 & 0 & 0 & \dots & 0 \\ 1 & 0 & 0 & \dots & 0 \\ 0 & 0 & 0 & \dots & 0 \\ 0 & 1 & 0 & \dots & 0 \\ 0 & 0 & 0 & \dots & 0 \\ 0 & 0 & 1 & \dots & 0 \\ \vdots & & & & \\ 0 & 0 & 0 & \dots & 1 \end{bmatrix} \begin{bmatrix} \\ r_1 \\ \\ r_2 \\ \\ r_3 \\ \\ r_n \end{bmatrix} \qquad (13)$$

We can determine the state equations for the circular and polar configuration of the systems. If we let $K_{1,n-1} = K_{n-1,1} = K_{2n} = K_{n2} = \dots = K_{n-2,n} = K_{n,n-2} = 0$ we have the equation for the circular system.

$$\begin{bmatrix} \dot{x}_1 \\ \dot{x}_2 \\ \dot{x}_3 \\ \dot{x}_4 \\ \dot{x}_5 \\ \dot{x}_6 \\ \vdots \\ \dot{x}_{m-1} \\ \dot{x}_m \end{bmatrix} = \begin{bmatrix} -b_1 & 1 & 0 & 0 & 0 & 0 & 0 & 0 \\ b & 0 & -a_2K_{21} & -a_2d_{21} & 0 & 0 & -a_2K_{n1} & -a_2d_{n1} \\ 0 & 0 & -b'_1 & 1 & 0 & 0 & 0 & 0 \\ -a'_2K_{12} & -a'_2d_{12} & b' & 0 & -a'_2K_{32} & -a'_2d_{32} & 0 & 0 \\ 0 & 0 & 0 & 0 & -b''_1 & 1 & 0 & 0 \\ 0 & 0 & -a''_2K_{23} & -a''_2d_{23} & b'' & 0 & 0 & 0 \\ \vdots & & & & & & & \\ 0 & 0 & 0 & 0 & 0 & 0 & -b^{n-1} & 1 \\ -a_2^{n-1}K_{1n} & -a_2^{n-1}d_{1n} & 0 & 0 & 0 & 0 & b^{n-1} & 0 \end{bmatrix} \begin{bmatrix} x_1 \\ x_2 \\ x_3 \\ x_4 \\ x_5 \\ x_6 \\ \vdots \\ x_{m-1} \\ x_m \end{bmatrix} +$$

$$\begin{bmatrix} 0 & 0 & 0 & \dots & 0 \\ 1 & 0 & 0 & \dots & 0 \\ 0 & 0 & 0 & \dots & 0 \\ 0 & 1 & 0 & \dots & 0 \\ 0 & 0 & 0 & \dots & 0 \\ 0 & 0 & 1 & \dots & 0 \\ \vdots & & & & \\ 0 & 0 & 0 & \dots & 1 \end{bmatrix} \begin{bmatrix} \\ r_1 \\ \\ r_2 \\ \\ r_3 \\ \vdots \\ r_n \end{bmatrix} \qquad (14)$$

If we let $K_{12}=K_{21}=K_{23}=K_{32}= \ldots =K_{n-1,1}=K_{1,n-1}=0$, we have the equation for the polar configuration system:

$$
\begin{bmatrix} \dot{x}_1 \\ \dot{x}_2 \\ \dot{x}_3 \\ \dot{x}_4 \\ \dot{x}_5 \\ \dot{x}_6 \\ \vdots \\ \dot{x}_{m-1} \\ \dot{x}_m \end{bmatrix} =
\begin{bmatrix}
-b_1 & 1 & 0 & 0 & 0 & 0 & 0 & 0 \\
b & 0 & 0 & 0 & 0 & 0 & -a_2K_{n1} & -a_2d_{n1} \\
0 & 0 & -b_1' & 1 & 0 & 0 & 0 & 0 \\
0 & 0 & b' & 0 & 0 & 0 & -a_2'K_{n2} & -a_2'd_{n2} \\
0 & 0 & 0 & 0 & -b_1'' & 1 & 0 & 0 \\
0 & 0 & 0 & 0 & b'' & 0 & -a_2''K_{n3} & -a_2''d_{n3} \\
\vdots & & & & & & & \\
0 & 0 & 0 & 0 & 0 & 0 & -b_1^{n-1} & 1 \\
-a_2^{n-1}K_{1n} & -a_2^{n-1}d_{1n} & -a_2^{n-1}K_{2n} & -a_2^{n-1}d_{2n} & -a_2^{n-1}K_{3n} & -a_2^{n-1}d_{3n} & b^{n-1} & 0
\end{bmatrix}
\begin{bmatrix} x_1 \\ x_2 \\ x_3 \\ x_4 \\ x_5 \\ x_6 \\ \vdots \\ x_{m-1} \\ x_m \end{bmatrix} +
$$

$$
\begin{bmatrix}
0 & 0 & 0 & \ldots & 0 \\
1 & 0 & 0 & \ldots & 0 \\
0 & 0 & 0 & \ldots & 0 \\
0 & 1 & 0 & \ldots & 0 \\
0 & 0 & 0 & \ldots & 0 \\
0 & 0 & 1 & \ldots & 0 \\
\vdots & & & & \\
0 & 0 & 0 & \ldots & 0 \\
0 & 0 & 0 & \ldots & 1
\end{bmatrix}
\begin{bmatrix} r_1 \\ r_2 \\ r_3 \\ \vdots \\ r_n \end{bmatrix} \qquad (15)
$$

Additional results for other types of subsystems have been developed by the authors but will be omitted here because of space limitations.

STABILITY ANALYSIS OF POLAR-CIRCULAR CONFIGURATION SYSTEMS

The polar-circular, circular and polar configuration systems are classes of large interconnected systems. The determination of the stability of such systems for many subsystems is a difficult task ; therefore let us determine stability of the polar configuration system with limited number of subsystems, for example four. This result is then generalized to the other two configurations.

Let us show two ways for the determination of the stability of such systems. Let us suppose that every subsystem is stable and all subsystems have the same order of transfer functions (see Eq. 7).

Take the Laplace transform (see Eq. 6) and solve for X(s) to obtain:

$$s\underline{X}(s)+\underline{X}(o)=\underline{A}\underline{X}(s)+\underline{B}r(s)$$

$$(SI-\underline{A})\underline{X}(s)=\underline{X}(0)+\underline{B}r(s) \qquad (16)$$

$$\underline{X}(s)=(SI-\underline{A})^{-1}[\underline{X}(0)+\underline{B}r(s)].$$

If we let $(SI-\underline{A})=\alpha_1$, then

$$\alpha^{-1}=\frac{\text{adjoint } \alpha}{|\alpha|}$$

We can get α^{-1} in the next form.

$$\alpha^{-1}=\frac{1}{|\alpha|}\begin{bmatrix} A_{11} & A_{12} & A_{13} & A_{14} \\ A_{21} & A_{22} & A_{23} & A_{24} \\ A_{31} & A_{32} & A_{33} & A_{34} \\ A_{41} & A_{42} & A_{43} & A_{44} \end{bmatrix}$$

where A_{ij} - cofactor of α. With zero initial conditions Eq. 16 becomes:

$$X(s)=\alpha^{-1} \cdot \begin{bmatrix} \underline{B}_1 & 0 & 0 & 0 \\ 0 & \underline{B}_2 & 0 & 0 \\ 0 & 0 & \underline{B}_3 & 0 \\ 0 & 0 & 0 & \underline{B}_4 \end{bmatrix} \begin{bmatrix} r_1 \\ r_2 \\ r_3 \\ r_4 \end{bmatrix} \qquad (17)$$

The solving of this equation is a difficult task, but this method can be used for a lower number of subsystems. Therefore it is more convenient to use the Routh Hurwitz criterion for the determination of the stability of this class of systems.

In order to use the criterion we must get the characteristic polynominal in the form

$$F(s)=a_0 s^n + a_1 s^{n-1} + a_2 s^{n-2} + \dots \qquad (18)$$
$$a_{n-1} s + a_n = 0.$$

First of all let us show the solution for two subsystems. For Eq. 7 we can write the state equation in the next form:

$$\begin{bmatrix}\dot{x}_1\\ \dot{x}_2\\ \dot{x}_3\\ \dot{x}_4\end{bmatrix} = \begin{bmatrix} a_1 & 1 & 0 & 0\\ a_{21} & 0 & e_{23} & e_{24}\\ 0 & 0 & a_3 & 1\\ e_{41} & e_{42} & a_{13} & 0\end{bmatrix}\begin{bmatrix}x_1\\ x_2\\ x_3\\ x_4\end{bmatrix} + \begin{bmatrix}0 & 0\\ 1 & 0\\ 0 & 0\\ 0 & 1\end{bmatrix}\begin{bmatrix}r_1\\ r_2\end{bmatrix} \qquad (19)$$

Where, e_{ij} - a connection between subsystems (Every subsystem will be stable, if

$$a_1<0;\ a_3<0;\ a_{21}<0;\ a_{43}<0;) \qquad (20)$$

For Eq. 19 we can write the characteristic polynominal in the form:

$$F(s)=s^4+s^3(-a_1-a_3)+s^2 a_1 a_3 + s^3[a_3(e_{24}e_{42}-e_{21}) + a_1(e_{43}-e_{24}e_{42}) - e_{24}e_{41} - e_{23}e_{42}] + s^4(a_1 e_{23} e_{42} + a_3 e_{24} e_{41} + e_{21} e_{43} - a_1 a_3 e_{24} e_{42} - e_{23} e_{41}) \qquad (21)$$

Let us define the coefficients of s_i accordingly as A_0, A_1, A_2, A_3, A_4; then we have:

$$F(s)=A_0 s^4 + A_1 s^3 + A_2 s^2 + A_3 s + A_4 .$$

According to the Routh-Hurwitz's criterion, the necessary and sufficient condition for stability of the system is satisfied if all roots of the polynomial F(s) lie in the left half of the s-plane. This condition will be satisfied, if all the elements of the first column have the same sign.

We can check this condition by the array

s^4	A_0	A_2	A_4
s^3	A_1	A_3	0
s^2	$\dfrac{A_1A_2-A_0A_3}{A_1}=A$	A_4	0
s	$\dfrac{AA_3-A_1A_4}{A}=B$	0	0
s^0	A_4		

If $A_1>0$, $A>0$, $B>0$, $A_4>0$ such system will be stable.

First condition. $A_1>0$, if $a_1<0$ $a_3<0$; (22)

Second condition. Let us determine the condition $A_4>0$, which appears with S^0 line because A_4 occurs in s^1 line. We have

$A_4=a_1e_{23}e_{42}+a_3e_{24}e_{41}+e_{21}e_{43}-a_1a_3e_{24}e_{42}-e_{23}e_{41}$; or $a_1e_{23}e_{42}+a_3e_{24}e_{41}+e_{21}e_{43} > a_1a_3e_{24}e_{42}+e_{23}e_{41}$.

The left part of this inequality will always be more than the right part, if the connections between subsystems will have different signs. For example,

$$e_{23}<0,\ e_{24}<0,\ e_{41}>0,\ e_{42}>0, \qquad (23)$$

then $A_4>0$.

Third condition. $A=\dfrac{A_1A_2-A_0A_3}{A_1}>0$, but $A_0=1$, $A_1>0$, $A_2>0$. We can determine the sign of A_3:

$A_3=a_3e_{24}e_{42}+a_3e_{21}+a_1e_{43}+a_1e_{24}e_{42}-e_{24}e_{41}-e_{23}e_{42}+e_{41}$ or $a_3e_{24}e_{42}+a_1e_{43}+a_3e_{21}+a_1e_{24}e_{42}+e_{41}>e_{24}e_{41}+e_{23}e_{42}$.

We can see that $A_3>0$, because the left part of the inequality always will be positive due (to the first and second conditions.) It is possible to see that

$A_1A_2>A_oA_3$, or $-a_1a_1a_3-a_1a_3a_3>a_1(e_{43}+e_{24}e_{42}) + a_3(e_{21}+e_{24}e_{42})+e_{41}-e_{24}e_{41}-e_{23}e_{42}$.

The left and right parts will be positive, therefore the left part will be greater than the right, if

$$a_ia_j>2e_{ij}e_{ji}\ , \qquad (24)$$

and then A>0.

Fourth condition. $B=\dfrac{AA_3-A_1A_4}{A}>0$. We have $A>0$, $A_3>0$, $A_1>0$, $A_4>0$, therefore if $AA_3>A_1A_4$, or $(A_1A_2-A_0A_3)A_3>A_1^2A_4$, then B>0. It is possible to see that this condition is satisfied also. These kind of systems will be stable if:

1. $a_i<0$ $i=1,2,\dots n$.
2. $a_ia_j>2e_{ij}e_{ji}$;
3. there are two connections between every subsystem;
4. the connections between two subsystems have different signs.

It is possible to develop similar information for four subsystems. We can write (from Eq. 10):

$$\begin{bmatrix} \dot{x}_1 \\ \dot{x}_2 \\ \dot{x}_3 \\ \dot{x}_4 \\ \dot{x}_5 \\ \dot{x}_6 \\ \dot{x}_7 \\ \dot{x}_8 \end{bmatrix} = \begin{bmatrix} a_1 & 1 & 0 & 0 & 0 & 0 & 0 & 0 \\ C_{21} & 0 & C_{23} & C_{24} & C_{25} & C_{26} & C_{27} & C_{28} \\ 0 & 0 & a_3 & 1 & 0 & 0 & 0 & 0 \\ C_{41} & C_{42} & C_{43} & 0 & C_{45} & C_{46} & C_{47} & C_{48} \\ 0 & 0 & 0 & 0 & a_5 & 1 & 0 & 0 \\ C_{61} & C_{62} & C_{63} & C_{64} & C_{65} & 0 & C_{67} & C_{68} \\ 0 & 0 & 0 & 0 & 0 & 0 & a_7 & 1 \\ C_{81} & C_{82} & C_{83} & C_{84} & C_{85} & C_{86} & C_{87} & 0 \end{bmatrix} \begin{bmatrix} x_1 \\ x_2 \\ x_3 \\ x_4 \\ x_5 \\ x_6 \\ x_7 \\ x_8 \end{bmatrix} + \begin{bmatrix} 0 & 0 & 0 & 0 \\ 1 & 0 & 0 & 0 \\ 0 & 0 & 0 & 0 \\ 0 & 1 & 0 & 0 \\ 0 & 0 & 0 & 0 \\ 0 & 0 & 1 & 0 \\ 0 & 0 & 0 & 0 \\ 0 & 0 & 0 & 1 \end{bmatrix} \begin{bmatrix} r_1 \\ r_2 \\ r_3 \\ r_4 \end{bmatrix} \qquad (25)$$

This system will be stable if we satisfy the conditions. The connections between every subsystem have such signs:

$\alpha_{12}<0,\ (C_{23}<0;\ C_{24}<0)$ $\quad \alpha_{24}>0,\ (C_{47}>0,\ C_{48}>0)$

$\alpha_{21}>0,\ (C_{41}>0,\ C_{42}>0)$ $\quad \alpha_{42}>0,\ (C_{83}>0,\ C_{84}>0)$

$\alpha_{23}<0,\ (C_{45}<0,\ C_{46}<0)$ $\quad \alpha_{34}>0,\ (C_{67}>0,\ C_{68}>0)$

$\alpha_{32}>0,\ (C_{63}>0,\ C_{64}>0)$ $\quad \alpha_{43}<0,\ (C_{85}<0,\ C_{28}<0)$

$\alpha_{13}<0,\ (C_{25}<0,\ C_{26}<0)$ $\quad \alpha_{14}<0,\ (C_{27}>0,\ C_{28}<0)$

$\alpha_{31}<0.\ (C_{61}<0,\ C_{62}<0)$ $\quad \alpha_{41}>0,\ (C_{81}<0,\ C_{82}>0)$

and also:

a) $C_{21}<0;\ C_{43}<0;\ C_{65}<0\ C_{87}<0$,

b) $a_i<0;\ a_i a_j>2C_{ij}C_{ji}$,

c) there are two connections between subsystems.

We can see that the stability depends on the configuration of the system.

If we let $\alpha_{12}=\alpha_{21}=\alpha_{23}=\alpha_{32}=\alpha_{31}=\alpha_{13}=0$, then we will get the polar configuration system and we must change the sign by α_{24} $(C_{47}<0;\ C_{48}<0)$. If we let (for example) $\alpha_{24}=\alpha_{42}=\alpha_{13}=\alpha_{31}=0$, then we will get the circular configuration system and we must change the sign by $\alpha_{41}<0,\ (C_{81}<0,\ C_{82}<0)$, because for such systems the connections between subsystems must be different except first and last subsystems.

For circular and polar configured systems the stability does not depend on the number of subsystems.

CONTROLLABILITY OF POLAR-CIRCULAR CONFIGURATION SYSTEMS

The controllability of the systems depends on the structure of the system. The system will not be structurally controllable if there is a pair (A, b) of the form

$$A = \begin{matrix} A_{11} & 0 \\ A_{21} & A_{22} \end{matrix} \ ; \ b \ \begin{matrix} 0 \\ b_2 \end{matrix}$$

where $A_{11}\varepsilon R^{kxk}$, $A_{21}\varepsilon R^{(m-k)xk}$,

$A_{22}\varepsilon R^{(m-k)x(n-k)}$, $b_2\varepsilon R^{(m-k)}$ $(1\leq k\leq m)$.

For polar-circular, circular and polar configuration systems there are several possible structures. They differ depending on the expression of the transfer function and the connections between the subsystems. (α_{ij}).

Let us examine the polar configuration system in (Eq. 12) for conditions of controllability. The system is completely state controllable if the matrix

$P=[B;\ A;\ B,\ \ldots\ A^{m-1}\ B]$ has rank equal m.

It is possible to check this condition. We have:

$$\underline{B} = \begin{bmatrix} 0 & 0 & 0 & 0 \\ 1 & 0 & 0 & 0 \\ 0 & 0 & 0 & 0 \\ 0 & 1 & 0 & 0 \\ 0 & 0 & 0 & 0 \\ 0 & 0 & 1 & 0 \\ 0 & 0 & 0 & 0 \\ 0 & 0 & 0 & 1 \end{bmatrix};$$

$$\underline{AB} = \begin{bmatrix} a_{12} & 0 & 0 & 0 \\ 0 & 0 & 0 & a_{28} \\ 0 & a_{34} & 0 & 0 \\ 0 & 0 & 0 & a_{48} \\ 0 & 0 & a_{56} & 0 \\ 0 & 0 & 0 & a_{68} \\ 0 & 0 & 0 & a_{78} \\ a_{82} & a_{84} & a_{86} & 0 \end{bmatrix};$$

$$\underline{A}^2\underline{B} = \begin{bmatrix} C_{11} & 0 & 0 & C_{14} \\ C_{21} & C_{22} & C_{23} & C_{24} \\ 0 & C_{32} & 0 & C_{34} \\ C_{41} & C_{42} & C_{43} & C_{44} \\ 0 & 0 & C_{53} & C_{54} \\ C_{61} & C_{62} & C_{63} & C_{64} \\ C_{71} & C_{72} & C_{73} & C_{74} \\ C_{81} & C_{82} & C_{83} & C_{84} \end{bmatrix}$$

From the matrix $\underline{A}^2\underline{B}$ we can see that there are many conditions, when the determinant does not equal zero. ($C_{71}-C_{82}-C_{81}C_{72}=0$, if $C_{71}C_{82}=C_{81}C_{72}$ or $C_{72}C_{84}-C_{74}C_{82}=0$, if $C_{72}C_{84}=C_{74}C_{82}$ and e.e.)

For circular and polar-circular configurations of the system there are similar conditions. So, for such configurations of the system we must assure these next conditions:

1. the rank of the matrix $\underline{B}$ is not less than n.

2. the matrix $\underline{P}$ does not have a determinant dimension from 2x2 to mxm equal 0.

If these conditions hold, the system will be controllable.

CONCLUSIONS

This paper has considered three different configurations of dynamic multiple-connected subsystems, namely circular, polar, circular-polar configurations. The general state variable equations for n subsystems are given for each configuration. For a specific class of subsystems and n=4, complete input-output relations are developed.

An investigation of stability is presented for the specific cases of two subsystems and four subsystems. Controllability conditions for four subsystems is presented for all three configurations.

Additional results have been omitted because of space limitations.

ACKNOWLEDGEMENTS

This research was supported in part by the DoD Joint Services Electronics Program through the Air Force Office of Scientific Research (AFSC) Contract #F49620-77-C-0101.

Other support was provided by the International Research and Exchanges Board.

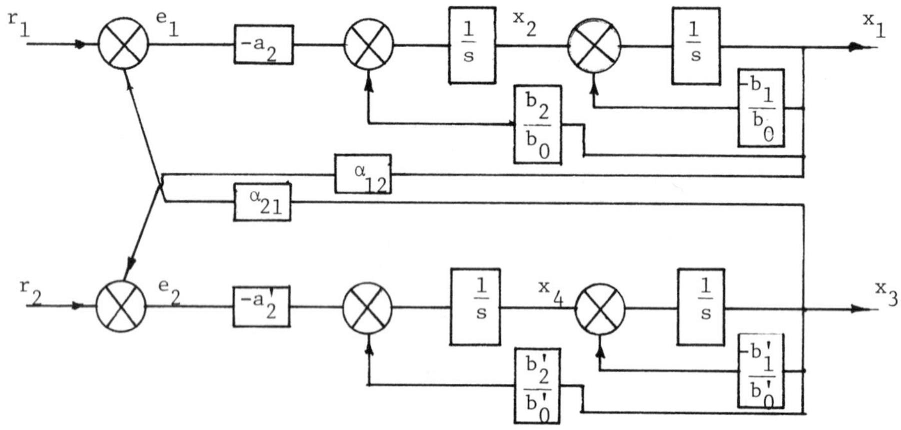

Figure 1

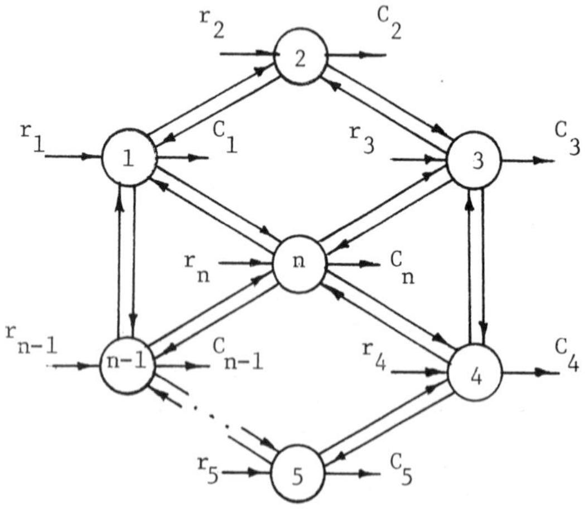

Figure 2

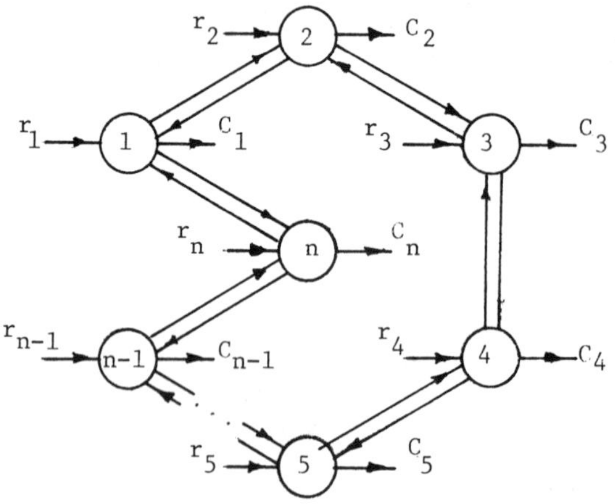

Figure 3

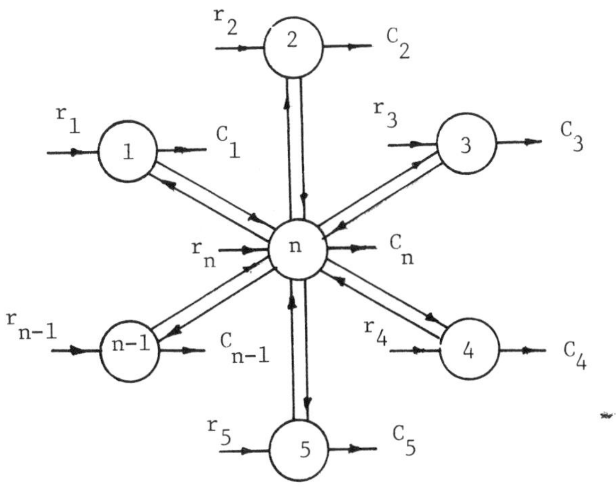

Figure 4

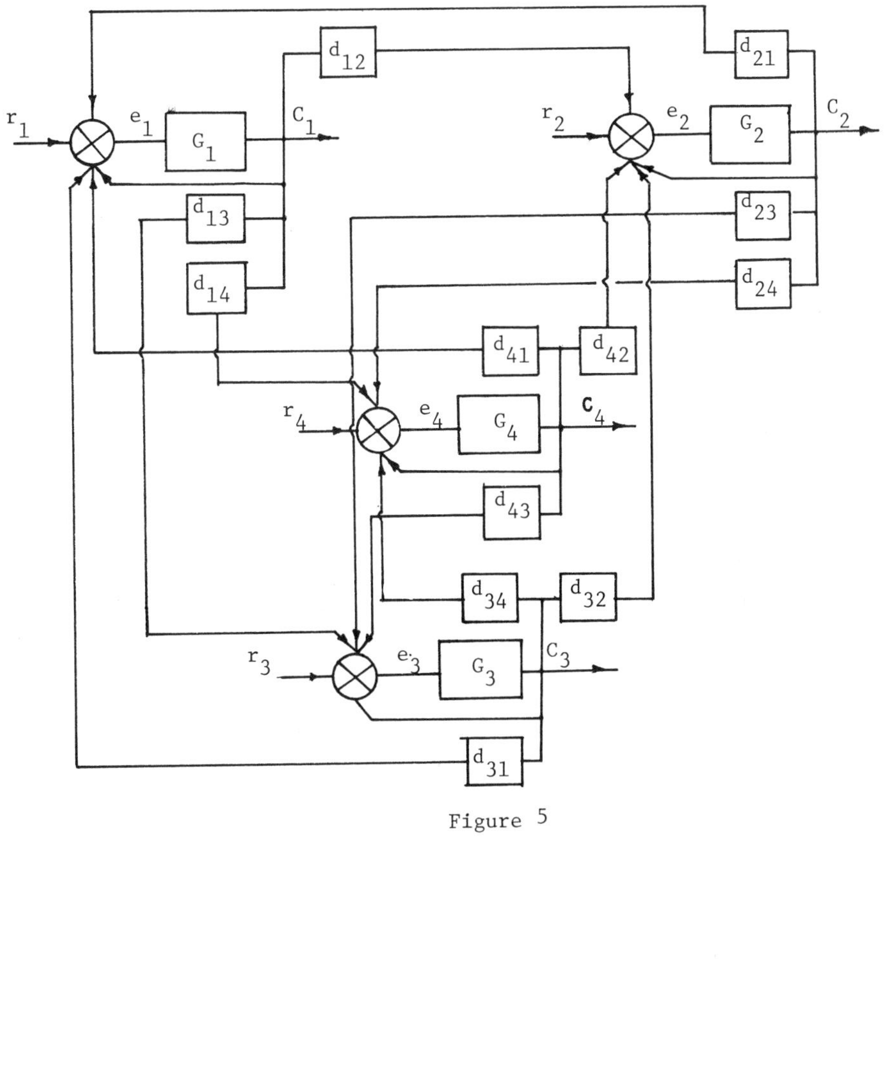

Figure 5

INFORMATION CONTROL IN MANUFACTURE

A.C. Chaturvedi

Irrigation Commission, U.P., Canal Colony, Lucknow-226001

ABSTRACT

Production has a very high priority in our national economic development plan and information control by computer aided devices plays a vital role in furthering manufacture by adaptive control of machine tools. We are using powerful and growing multi-access computer systems and relatively slender numbers of staff with modern bands with communication links to other computer systems in various parts of the state of Uttar Pradesh and elsewhere in our country. This ensures planning and decision making in order to produce information to ensure correct manufacture and construction. A whole series of basic tools are shaped, consolidated and improved as experience grows of industry by interaction with research. The widest possible exploitation of results was obtained by making suitable arrangements for marketing and the provision of service by other organisations. The constant feedback of the computer system provided a powerful control in the direction of computer system development, thus ensuring that the total system evolved on the right lines. We were very much concerned with command processing. When using the tektromix terminal device, the input was largely keyboard oriented. Fortran, Algol, MAD, BASIC were used and new manufacturing devices and new materials have given rise to less expensive and more powerful computing equipment. Vertical circular indexing was used where the work was circle indexed automatically in a vertical plane. The work pieces were automatically clamped in the interlocked trunion fixture and were indexed through the various operations of spot drilling, drilling spot facing reaming, and counter-boring. An automatic time delay mechanism was arranged in the machine when the tools reverse. An automatic coolant system for cooling the tools and automatic lubrication to the drill heads and machine ways were provided. Automated broaching operations were recommended where a large volume of identical pieces was used with a number of independent machine units through them aided by specially designed handling equipment. A typical inline indexing transfer machine for high production of automotive parts was designed. The parts produced on this machine were torque converter adaptor plates. The complete machine was arranged as a group of single production units with all necessary controls in a central position, enabling the operator to manipulate from the main console. Other individual remote push buttons were also strategically located in various positions, assuring additional instant control and safety.

Typically electronic phase-sensitive demodulators were also designed. The tubes acted as gating devices or switches that permitted the input signal to reach the output only during certain intervals. Both tubes were supplied with the same plate voltage which caused the anode potentials of both tubes to be positive with respect to cathode during a portion of each cycle and negative for the remainder of each.(1)

INTRODUCTION

Manufacture both for the promotion of exports as well as consumption in the domestic market has a very high priority in our national fifth five-year plan as well as the (20 point) economic development plan of Mrs. Indira Gandhi. The term computer aided design has gained respectability in the manufacturing world over the past five years. We have its wide application in the fields of manufacture as also in other disciplines which use the computer as a technique in which man and machine are blended in a problem-solving team intimately coupling the best characteristics of each, so that this team works better than either alone and offering the possibility for integrated teamwork using a multi-discipline approach. The paper deals with fundamental aspects of information manufacture as well as important areas of application.

During the last five years, the term information in manufacture has gained respectability in the technical world. Large discussion is needed in order to afford wide attention to computer aids in information. We have to go in for definition and analysis of CAD in order to identify those aspects of the design process and computer technology that continue to produce successful CAD applications. We need a look at software philosophy: system software, methodology of building, CAD system, CAD oriented data structures and the relation with more general data bases, transportability, evolutionary properties and lifetime of software.[2]

Information in manufacture is a process of planning and decision making in order to produce designs to ensure correct manufacture or construction. This applies to all design processes and thus computer systems are used to improve communication information flow and decision taking. The whole series of basic tools are shaped, consolidated and improved through the interaction and feedback that arises from the shared use of a linked computing system. Encouraging the use of the same system by research groups and by industry leads to more rapid acceptance, testing and adoption of new ideas and techniques. We are currently extending the computer system by establishing medium band width communication links to other computer systems in India. Our development potential is highly geared up by the policy of working through a large number of collaborative agreements with other organisations in industry, government and research. Finally the widest possible exploitation of results is achieved by making suitable arrangements for marketing and the provision of service by other organisations.

The computer system requirements depend upon considerations of the users' activities; we should try to identify factors which differentiate these activities in a way meaningful to the system designer. There is yet relatively little experience to fall back on in India. Our early work was based on the existing non-CAD system or on equipment (e.g. interaction graphic devices) developed for uses other than design. Thus although many of the technical problems were identified some years ago, the problem feedback has a considerable effect in producing a better specification of overall systems for CAD. This is largely because the problems are not only technical but also organisational. The forces of economics increasingly dictate the use of multi-access computers, interconnected computers, not only because of hardware costs (which in some cases are actually decreasing) but mainly through the effect of software costs which are wage-rate-dependent and increase as the sophistication of the user increases.

As the use of multi-access systems and network increases it becomes economically possible to provide progressively more flexible facilities in the form of software tools for special classes of users, more varieties of terminal and satellite equipment and access to several kinds of central processing equipment, according to the needs. Hence the support services necessary to exploit such flexible computing facilities must depend on these systems so that particular classes of users will be able to obtain selectively the equipment and services suited to their particular needs.

This evolutionary development involves organisational problems and it cannot be planned in detail, but must proceed within a broad strategy. It does not preclude the examination of detailed questions of the best way of using mind computers and large dedicated systems, but the answers need to be tested against various alternatives within the over-all context. The form of particular information in manufacture is determined essentially by the balance of effort put into these activities. Optimisation leads to a requirement for interaction and sometimes visualisation, hence there is strong need for interactive methods when the frequency of decision making is high and the compression is important. Information processing tends to lead to a requirement for larger computer systems, offline processing, special filing facilities and careful attention to overall system designs.[3]

Interactive graphics is not particularly difficult to obtain and use nowadays but the integration of design with design realisation, the information processing associated with design, has rarely been achieved in a major application. The costs incurred in the design and manufacture of a product increase generally from low at the design stage to high at the production stage. On the other hand, the relative importance of the decisions made at each stage is quite opposite. This is another reason for stressing the overall system approach. We have to think on these lines and make suitable provision in our budgets.

In our systems approach, the computer systems will be chosen and the software designed to deal with the total design to manufacture situation. If CAD is under consideration for use only at the design stage—the stage up to manufacturing instructions—then the importance of better and quicker design optimisation should be quantified in the costing. Information for manufacture is made available to a variety of users in research organisations and industrial companies under financial arrangements suitable to all parties. The major uses are in the development of pilot projects. The computer system provided can be more powerful and have more comprehensive facilities than could be justified by any single user. After applications have proven, the user can transfer to a more modest and by then definable computer system of his own or in the case of a major development to another multi-access system with suitable facilities which may be part of a network of a separate system. The constant feedback of user requirements provides a powerful control on the direction of computer system development, thus ensuring that total system evolves on the right lines. Application software may be developed as part of the system whilst also being made generally available. Wide range collaborative working provides identification, thus introducing a gearing effect, which reduces cost and time. Interdisciplinary groups may readily be formed around the focus of such a computer network which can then provide sufficiently versatile facilities for all persons. Equipment and software requirements can change over the course of a development project, either as the major emphasis shifts from research towards exploitation or as the essential requirements become clearer. The problems of changing from one computer system to another merely because new facilities are needed which can cause major delays or be costly are thus avoided. The main advantage in this approach lies in continuity and interdisciplinary collaboration which result.

Information processing fundamentals concern (1) machine organisation, (2) programming basics such as data structures, but microprogramming and executive system design and data communication basics such as codes, formats, data rates and types of transmission. The solutions to problems of information of manufacture are usually new ways of adapting our surroundings to our needs. Where these problem solutions come to function as physical contrivances, it means doing some design work or esoteric solutions. The problems are usually broad and complex and most specification of needs are not initially obvious and the solution is offered by system science which brings order to problem definitions and devises operations to match the functions that add to the solutions. We have to set criteria on the functions so that intelligent tradeoffs can be made, and operate from a point of view that recognises functional similarities. One of our major efforts has been in the synthesis of alternative methods of implementing an idea. This leads to trial solutions in attempts to make the system output meet the overall specifications of the problems. Another major effort has been in the analysis of these alternatives to fortify the decisions. [4]

As the interest in displays for scientific computing rises sharply, equipment manufacturers have to begin offering displays tailored to the new market that are less costly and easier to program than their military counterparts. We have to offer new displays and new graphic input devices have to be developed and demonstrated. As displays are put into more use, the need for unifying graphic languages and facilities for manufacturing data structures dynamically become more evident. Remote units are aimed at providing low cost consoles that communicate over standard telephone lines. Sophisticated consoles are being designed with versatile performance as their key feature. To provide power to the dynamic display with real time interaction, small general purpose computers have to be intimately coupled with displays. These units can then talk to a large time-sharing system or stand alone. Features such as pictures, subroutines, rotation, translations, scaling, light pen tracking, etc., have to be provided, sometimes with hardware and sometimes with software. Hardware is to be organised to make these functions easy to program and to require a minimal lead for the computer. The very latest display consoles have hardwared microprograms in them such that routine display supports are available essentially as macro-instructions. The force behind design optimisation by adaptive control is the minicomputer.

For a long time, our designers have sought better ways to express their ideas to perform analysis to fortify their decisions. Early drawings were of the layout type. In fact, they were carvings not drawings. As units of measure were agreed upon, the physical dimensions of drawing took on a new significance and became data. With development of principles of element design, calculations were made to substantiate the validity of a drawing's dimensions and one could then have the physical properties of the entities. Computers were then brought in for deposition and collection of stored facts. While using the information retrieval capabilities of a design system, the user knew that he was going to exercise discrimination on the data he was trying to retrieve, consequently a system was needed which allowed specification of attributes of the desired information and selectivity of retrieval sets. Information storage and retrieval meant the collection not of stored facts, but of parameters being picked up (transducer monitored) from physical models for the purpose of having real parameters in the mathematical model. The computer helped to observe the real models (or manufacturing operation) which designers used. Computer augmented design manifested itself in many ways. In the area of information storage and retrieval, because the growth of knowledge has increased almost experientially in recent years, being able to access the deposit in this large storage of knowledge had to be done automatically. [5]

GRAPHICS

With the advent of computer graphics it has become obvious to many people that engineers would like to convey trends, distribution, topologies, dimensions and concept or feelings for physical systems. It is possible to do this even in the batch mode when we talk about output from the computer, but with interactive graphics the designer can now convey or topology or some other graphic concept to the computer in a picture which is worth a thousand computer words. It is important that people who are to be creative in CAD appreciate the specialities involved. This serves as a guide to the literature and to other researchers. We have to be familiar with basic computer operation and organisation so that we can imagine new uses from computing besides interup handling, quaring, data structures, etc. In programming it is necessary to understand the basics of programming multiple state code, re-entrant code, various data structures, etc., so that one can be creative in developing new systems which synergistically interact with the engineering designer. It is extremely important, whether in the area of interactive computing or something that relates to data acquisition that communications either between devices and machines or between men and machines is understood by the builders of CAD systems. We must be able to develop software which will yield the most economical use of available computer power in whatever system is being designed.

INTERACTIVE GRAPHICS

We should have the ability to communicate graphically in either input or output mode formative analysis. The major considerations in interactive graphics have to be (1) the speed of tracking, which is important from the human factor standpoint, and (2) the graphic data structure which dictates the selectability of the components of any particular representation, and also the ability for the representation to be data for an analysis algorithm. Also extremely important, it seems natural for the user. This has become simplified considerably in current years to the extent that even light buttons are becoming extinct. Finally the analysis graphic software coupling is important if a system is to interpret correctness or curve shape as data for analysis algorithm. [6]

Interactive graphics is generally implemented on either a refresh type or a storage CRT. The refresh type can use either a light pen, a tablet, a mouse, a grafpen, a joystick or several other devices for input. In storage type CRT you cannot input through the CRT. It remains a simplex device. The software necessary to support a refresh type CRT is generally housed in a small mind computer which is an integral part of the graphics conode, whereas a storage type CRT is generally just a peripheral device to some central machine. Hence with the erase speed of the screen as an upper bound, the dynamics of a storage type CRT depends on the transmission rate from the central machine to the peripheral.

We have to convey the concept that depending on one's perspective, instructions to one man may be data to another. The whole process of understanding information processing is that one can be creative in the computer aided design field. Within the computing environment resides the individual whose responsibility is to maintain the Fortran computer. The computer algorithm takes the data as the entire program of the engineer, scientist, or businessman. The compiler is in fact the instructions and the user's entire Fortran statements and data are all data to him. The individual at the compiling facility who is responsible for the basic operating system, which can in fact manipulate more. The fundamental assembly language provides the interup handling and input/output programming for the computer system is essentially the code that is constant for various operating systems.

At the end of the spectrum, we have increasing higher level languages and more complex systems. It is quite possible that when taking the language MMIC for instance which is a dynamic simulation language generally implemented in Fortran, it is much easier to conceive of a dynamic analysis program stated in the MMIC than in Fortran. Consequently MMIC statements are taken in and Fortran statements are generated from them. If one were to put an interactive graphic front and on this analysis scheme the user would merely have to draw his physical system on the CRT and the graphic support software would interpret this in terms of MMIC statements which would in turn generate Fortran statements, etc.

DESIGN INFORMATION CONCEPTS

The structure of engineering design information has been developed from the general engineering design process. This has been done viewing the engineering designer as an information processor with capabilities such as intuition, experience, stored facts, judgement and creativity who communicates with the outside world through a working interface to solve design problems. Applications are tending more and more to employ mini-computers, either as devices integral in something that is being designed or as peripheral information processors to a large central CAD system. It is anticipated that there will be great strides in trying manufacturing facilities into CAD systems and the development of CAD systems that communicate with the designer by employing his other senses using such techniques as audio.

There is a major difference between programs to handle design and more conventional applications programs. The program is there to handle engineering problems. Where a program is to be used more than once, these engineering problems will always arise at the most inconvenient times and the program will require instant maintenance. All designers want instant access at peak periods. Clearly when resources are fully stretched, 90% of the load must be handled in a batchmode. Most files are permanently stored on the secure and cheap medium of magnetic tape. However, the system allows remote access for tentative modifications and interrogations from disc via TV and NDU devices. Any official issue operation then constitutes an extraction back into mag tape. EDS and DRUM has been used for some time for operation like error analysis or simulation where filed are selectively copied. Full graphical interaction is discouraged as there just are not the resources available. Computer output to micro film is essential as a means of outputting the vast numbers of drawings (say 10,000 in a realistic time). However, the advent of this medium accommodates more useful facts on less sheets of paper. Secondly, it permits output or far more type of production data such as detailed assembly drawings. Thirdly the absence of a paper master has brought control to a very high standard. No longer is it possible to quietly alter the master drawing to correct for some aberration of the program.

EDITING COMMANDS

The meaning of the series of editing commands and their options are obvious. They permit strings in the input buffer to be modified or replaced. The SCAN command initiates a series of questions which permit the user to look electively at a large amount of output data. The routing and saving commands are analogous to switches which direct output in the low speed terminal printer, card punch, paper tape punch, magnetic tape or a system save file (or disc). When the terminal is turned off through the term off command no output goes to the terminal, although questions continue to be asked.

The file manipulation commands are to be understood in the light of the library structure which is used by the system. Each user has an individual library in which files are named with alphameric names. A group of users may share a group library. The names of the files in this library are always preceded by a single asterisk. The installation may have a library in which all users may place files. Finally there may be a highly restricted library which may be constructed and modified only by a very limited number of system managers. Each library may be subdivided into shelves, files, sets, volumes, and pages. Specific information on a page may be referred to by column and row numbers. This kind of organisation is very analogous to the way printed material is stored and has therefore high mnemonic value.

The file manipulation commands permit great flexibility in the construction and manipulation of files. In response to a question a user may specify that a particular file be used through the CET command. That is instead of typing the necessary information the system will retrieve information from the file which is referenced. A question and answer sequence may be initiated to ensure that the proper data is retrieved. The store command similarly enables data which has been produced by a program to be inserted into a named file. The establish, destroy, reshelve, and rename commands have meanings which are straight forward and permit easy manipulation of the files. Data and program files may be protected against listing. This protection may be removed through the allow command. The pool and full commands permit programs to be posted in the group libraries removed from them. (10)

CONCLUSIONS

We have made a small beginning in the design of interactive computing systems which are truly user oriented. It is clear, however, that the development of such systems would have a major impact on computer-aided design. This tends to make computers much more accessible to engineers and designers without the necessity of a long and unproductive bearing period. A prototype system which embodies many of these concepts is operational in U.P. Additional features are in the process of being installed. The limited experience with this system has been very favourable. It permits early use of prepared programs without the need for very much additional documentation. The automatic handling of data files is perhaps the least developed of this system. In a design environment this may prove to be the most important part of a system.

REFERENCES

1. Chaturvedi, A.C. System science application to agricultural engineering. *Proceedings of National Symposium*, Ludhiana, Dec. 6, 7, 1976, Agricultural University.

2. Chaturvedi, A.C. System science in water management. *Proceedings of International Symposium* 9/76. Technical University, Wroclaw, Poland.

3. Chaturvedi, A.C. Water Resources Information, 28.6.77. Agricultural Research Centre, State University, Fort Collins, Colorado, U.S.A.

4. Chaturvedi, A.C. Optimisation in irrigation, 12.3.77. Papers of all India Seminar on Automatic Control. Institution of Engineers, Calcutta.

5. Chaturvedi, A.C. Planning environmental systems, 2.6.77. National Systems Conference, P.S.C. College of Technology, Coimbatore.

6. Chaturvedi, A.C. Thermal and hydel projects, 2.3.77. Papers of the All India Symposium on the Golden Jubilee of the Central Board of Irrigation and Power, New Delhi.

7. Chaturvedi, A.C. Alternate sources of energy, 9.4.77. All India Seminar on Technology for Agricultural Development, Institution of Engineers (I), Chandigarh.

8. Chaturvedi, A.C. Urban, regional and national planning in India. Papers of IFAC Workshop on UNRENAP Organising Committees.

9. Chaturvedi, A.C. Space electronics, Jadavpur University. All India Seminar on Space Electronics, 27.12.76.

10. Chaturvedi, A.C. Data processing optimisation, 26.5.77. Papers of 4th International Conference, Bulgarian Academy of Sciences, Verne, Sofia.

11. Chaturvedi, A.C. System modelling in India, 6.9.77. Papers of International Conference on System Science IV. Institute of Engineering Cybematics. Polish Committee of Measurement and Automation. Technical University, Wroclaw, Poland.

12. Chaturvedi, A.C. Water resources modelling India. IFIP Working Committee, 6.9.77. Ghent, Belgium.

A PROPOSED INFORMATION SYSTEM TO MASTER THE MAINTENANCE PROGRAM IN AN IRON & STEEL COMPLEX

S.A.K. El Sheshe*, A.G. Hamdy, and S.E. Aidarous*****

**Metallurgical Dept., The General Organization for Industrialization*
***Head of Instrumentation & Control Dept., The Egyptian Iron & Steel Co.*
****Computer & Control Section, Faculty of Engineering, Ain Shams University, Cairo*

ABSTRACT

There is a variety of units existing in the Egyptian Iron & Steel Complex In Helwan area that has been installed in several steps, during a period of two decades. Different suppliers and companies took part in the delivery, erection, and putting into operation of production and auxiliary components of the plant. This situation created difficulties in maintenance, spare parts availability, also some problems in the programming for preventive maintenance duties.

In this paper, an information system was developed and adapted to suit the local conditions with the aim to control maintenance work spare parts production in the local workshops, and to have an inventory control over spares and consumption materials.

Such a system was developed taking into consideration the relations between dependent shops, loading of adjacent shops, besides, looking after safe stock level of spares without overloading the economy of the plant. The success of such a system depends upon data collection, continuous information flow from different production shops, and is mainly dependent on people monitoring the system and the efficient computer center in the plant.

INTRODUCTION

Egyptian Iron and Steel Company is the first integrated steel plant, originally delivered by DEMAG A.G., West Germany. The plant was commissioned in stages starting from June 1958 and consists of 2 Blast Furnaces each 570 m^3 volume, 4 Thomas converters each 17 tons/heat, 2 electric steel making furnaces 12 tons/heat, a blooming mill, a heavy section mill and a plate mill, with an original ingot steel capacity of 265000 tons per year. With a loan from the USSR, an expansion of 1,2 million tons per year ingot steel capacity has been planned and executed.

The full expansion contains the following main shops:

a) Sintering shop contains 4 sintering machines, each has 75 m2 area with designed capacity of 8000 tons/day.

b) Blast furnace shop consists of 2 B.F. each 1033 m3 volume, with design capacity of 1915 tons/day.

c) Oxygen Converter Shop consists of 3 converters each with 80 tons/heat.

d) Continuous Casting Shop consisting of 3 two-strand slabing machines and 3 six-strand billeting machines.

The first stage, which is planned for 600,000 tons/year, has been completed and consists of two sintering machines, one B.F. two LD converters, and three continuous casting machines. The second stage is scheduled for commissioning during the second half of this year.

MAINTENANCE PROBLEMS

The efficiency of carrying out the maintenance program for the original plant delivered by Demag A.G. was rather appropriate. Reasonable loading of the workshops to manufacture urgent and simple spares was invisaged. Other intellicet and electric spare were imported in enough quantities to provide safe level of inventory.

The problem of maintenance programming and its effect on the efficiency of the units and the plant economy as a whole, began to arise with the completion of the complex project. The deversity and complexity of the spares needed for different production shops, either imported or locally made, either for preventive maintenance or planned capital repairs, created a situation that dictated the need for an adequate information system to help solving maintenance problems and make correct immediate decisions.

After a study on the administrative level of the plant, it was found necessary to have a regular field information system giving the following:

1- Update information about production equipments in different areas of the plant. (67 areas).

2- Spares inventory tabulated according to different areas, and different areas, and different materials ... etc.

3- Information about the production of spares inside shops, or during importation procedure.

The objective of such information system is to reduce the time of unplaned stopages and the amount of spares kept in stock.

With the help of the USSEC, the system was developed and adapted to the local conditions of Helwan plant to use local computer and microfilm equipment. The project is now in the course of implimentation, in few areas in the old part of the plant.

PREVENTIVE MAINTENANCE PROGRAM

One of the primary functions of the Maintenance Planning Office is to perform all the administrative aspects for planning, schedulling, manhour allocation, and preparation of the work-order information to assist performing the filed work efficiently. In this manner Central Maintenance Managers will be provided with updated information to perform the required tasks. The quality and quantity of information supplied to these managers will, to a great degree, permit them to obtain maximum efficiency from their work force and shop equipment. This will, consequenly improve the quality and quantity of actual work performed in the shortest time with the most economic methos. Therefore, it is important for all work order requests to be sent to the Maintenance Planning office so that this group can properly allocate manpower, plan, and schedule all field jobs to obtain the desired and results.

Preplanning and the quantity and quality of information supplied to the various crafts involved in a field repair job are essential to accomplish a job successfully in the shortest period of time. In addition to knowledge of the overall scope of the job the crews should know and have hand-on at the job site, all the materials required such as tools special equipment (mobile crane, forklift, air compressor etc.) and spare parts, crew size, the right craftsmen, and special instruction pertaining to the job.

This system will provide the type of information mentioned above and maximize the efficient utilization of manpower and increase equipment availability.

In the sequel, we will consider one of the important aspects in the preventive maintenance, that is the inventory control system.

The overall objective of this program is to have the right quantity & quality of spares availabel when needed to avoid costly production delays and to achieve this objective with a minimum investment in spare parts. Specific objectives are;

1- To carry in stock the minimum number of spares required to assure uninterrupted operation of Works production and support facilities.

2- To tage or otherwise mark spares for easy identification.

3- To stock spares in an orderly manner and adequately protected in a minimu number of areas having controlled access.

4- To locate the right spare promptly when needed.

5- To identify and dispose of obsolete and surplus spares.

6- To adopt and use a sound procedure for replenishing deplete stocks.

7- To adopt and use a practical system for maintening spares stock records.

A good spares program is vital for a maintenance program and thus it is an important factor in effecting the production department's primary responsibility.

In order to facilitate record keeping and to provide a basis for accumulating and summarizing various kinds of information and data a computer based program to maintain perpectual stock records has been developed and installed. It is the recommended method of maintaining stock records for spares control.

DATA ABOUT THE COMPUTER

I.B.M. Computer 360/20 CAPACITY: 12 K = 12288 storage Unit. DIVISIONS: 1 DIVISION. 2 DRIVES: each can carry one disc of model 12 with capacity of 2,700,000 character. 2 TAPES Model 2514 very slow, 2501 card reader model A_1. 1442 card PUNCH.

PROPOSED STEPS IN IMPLEMENTING SPARES PROGRAM WERE AS FOLLOWS:

1- Obtain support from the Works top management for initiating and maintaining the spare program.

2- Develop an organization:

   a. To perform the preliminary work of identifying and stocking spares.

   b. For maintaining the program once it has been established.

3- Develop and get works agreement on a procedure for maintaining perpetual stock records. Mechanical Spares Control System is to be used for this purpose.

4- Designate storage areas and buildings to set aside for stocking spares and establish a coding pattern for storage location identification.

5- Establish a coding pattern for spare parts in accordance with the available eleven digit commodity code.

6- Locate and identify existing spare parts and record the data necessary to maintain the spares program for those items which, in the judgement of works.

7- Assign a commodity code and a storage location code to each spare part.

8- Prepare traveling requisitions for all spares.

9- Tag or otherwise mark the spares for ready identification.

10-Move spares to assigned storage areas and arrange in accordance with established good house keeping practices.

SPARES INVENTORY CONTROL AND INFORMATION SYSTEM

The spares control program utilizes three basic computer output documents and the traveling requisition to provide Works personnel with the basic data needed to meet the objective of the Spares Program. In addition to these documents, there are a number of optional computer outputs, analytical reports, and catalogue listings that are available upon request. All required computer input data is recorded on one of two standard forms:

BASIC COMPUTER OUTPUT DOCUMENTS

1- Spares Stock Record

The Spares Stock Record is printed annually for all items in the master file and weekly for all items with activity (cumulative) since the last annual printing. The report will be printed in one of three sequences

(a) storage area by Commodity Code.
(b) storage area by Local Code, or
(c) Commodity Code by storage area.

Data are invesaged to be as follows:

a. Commodity Code.
b. Unit of Measure.
c. Local Code (Blueprint and mark or other code the Works desirable.
d. Description (30 digits - full order description can be found on the travelling requisition).
e. Storage area and location within storage area.
f. On-hand balances for usable and repairable spares by stock

location and total for commodity
g. Quantity on order includes new purchase requisitions and repairable items that have actually been sent to shops for repair.
h. Danger point.
i. Reorder data (order quantity, reorder point and code).
j. Year-to-date activity - quantities received, disbursed, scrapped, and inventory adjustments.
k. Last disbursement date.

2- Stock Reorder List

The Stock Reorder list is published weekly and is divided into two sections:

Section A:

Critical spares (Reorder Code 1) that have reached the reorder point and should be reordered immediately. Spares are considered at the reorder point when the quantity on hand plus the quantity on order is at or below the reorder point. These items will be repeated on the Stock Reorder List each week until ordered, until the reorder point is changed, or until the reorder code is changed from 1 (critical) to 2 (less critical). Before any item is reordered a review, based on actual experience, should be made to determine if the reorder quantity, reorder point, or quantity on hand should be changed to reflect actual usage.

Section B:

Less-critical spares (Reorder Code 2) that have reached the reorder point but are to be ordered only after review. Spares classifiedas Reorder Code 2 will appear on this report whenever a disbursement is reported for an item that is at or below the reorder point and/or at the review date in the master file (The review date serves as a reminder file enabling the manager to delay purchase decisions.) Items appearing in Section "B" of this report will not appear on subsequent reports until another disbursement is reported or until activated by an updated review date in the master file.

Stock Reorder Lists should be reviewed by department managers or other responsible personnel for the purpose of indicating whether items are to be reordered or not, and whether changes are to be made in order quantities, reorder points, reorder codes, and/or new review dates established. After this review the spares clerk will process traveling requisitions for items to be ordered and data changes for other items as noted.

Date furnished on the Stock Reorder List are:

a. Commodity Code.
b. Unit of Measure.
c. Local code.
d. Description - 30 digits (Full order description is found on the traveling requisition).
e. Storage Area.
f. Quantities on hand (Usable & Repairable).
g. Quantity on Order.
h. * for items that have reached the Danger Point.
i. The normal order quantity.
j. Consumption History for past 2 year period:

 (1) Current quarter
 (2) 1st prior quarter
 (3) 2nd prior quarter
 (4) 3rd prior quarter
 (5) Total of next 4 prior quarters

k. Last purchase order on which the item was bought.
l. The last unit cost reported.
m. Section A-The number of weeks Reorder Code 1 spares have appeared on the Stock Reorder list. Section B- an asterisk (*) for items which are listed because of a review date in the master file.

3- Monthly Spare Summary

The Monthly Spares Summary summarizes spares activity for the month to Egyptian Pounds, and can be used for management control and trend data analysis. Data furnished on the Monthly Spares Summary are:

a. Storage area and title.
b. L.E. Balance - this month and prior month. (L.E. bala-nce includes any usable items on hand. Repairable items are at no value until repaired, at which time they are transferred to usable category).
c. Current months values for receipts and disbursements.
d. Value of items scrapped and/or sold.
e. Value of adjusted items and number of occurrences for which inventory adjustment were processed.
f. Momorandum value of repairable items. (Value it items were in usable condition).
g. Value of items on order (New items plus repairable items actually sent to shops for repair, at new item unit costs.)
h. Surplus Stock values.(Surplus stock is usable stock on hand which exceeds the reorder point plus reorder quantity.)

i. Price adjustments - The amount of L.E. balance change that results from changes in unit cost.

4- Traveling Requisition

The recommended method of reordering spare parts is through use of the traveling requisition. The use of this form eleminates the necessity of writing or typing purchase requisitions each time an order is placed.

The traveling requisition file also serves as an order catalogue file since it contains the complete order description & reorder data and provides a historical record of purchases. Other information such as number of units in service, etc., can also be noted on this form.

5- Optional Computer Output Documents

The following analytical reports and special catalogue listings are available on a request basis. Requests are made on the appropriate report request form depending on the sequence selected for the (Spares Stock Record) and submitted with the Computer Input Documents.

1. Surplus Spares.
2. Spares Univentoried in Last (Specify) Months.
3. Spares Consumption History.
4; List of Spares with No Usage For (Specify) Months.
5. Spares Usage By Facility Trend Data.
6. Spares Inventory Adjustments (Monthly Detail).
7. Catalogue Listing.

   a. By Alphabetical Description.
   b. By Commodity Code.
   c. By Local Code.
   d. By Interim Class Code.
   e. By Storage area.
   f. By Equipment Code.

COMPUTER INPUT DOCUMENTS

Spares Input data are reported on two documents as indicated below. Each page submitted must indicate the Works code and the report date, and each line entry on all submittal forms must be completed for the following:

Commodity Code:

Eleven digits are required for all entries.

Unit of Measure:

2-digit code.

Storage Area and Stock Location:

The 2-digit storage area code is required on all entries.

The 4-digit stock location is required only when reporting physical stock movements (i.e. receipts, disbursements, physical inventories stock transfers, and on-hand quantities).

Note: The System provides for carrying a single commodity code in any number of storage areas and up to six (6) stock locations (within each storage area).

Control totals are to be entered on each page of both computer input forms. When the detail submitted to the computer does not balance with the control total. The detail data will be entered into the computer files and a listing of the out-of-balance data will be sent to the Stores Department for verification of the controls and corrections as required.

When activity is reported for items not in the master file (match on commodity code, unit of measure, storage area, and on Location for disbursements and repairable-hour) the item will be rejected and reported to Stores Department correction and resubmission.

1. Spares New Items and Data Changes

This form is used to enter new items into the master file, to record data changes, and to delet items from the master file. In addition to commodity code, unit of measure, and storage area & stock location, information is to be furnished as follows:

a. New Items - Enter a line, the transaction code column and complete all other columns as far as possible. The quantity on hand purchase order (P.O. or requisition) number and quantity on order can be entered at this time or entered later on the Spares Activity Reporting form.

b. Data Cahnges - Enter a 2 in the transaction code column and only the corrected data in other columns. All other information will remain in the master file.

c. Deletions of items from the Master File - Enter a 3 in the transaction column. This will delete the entire item from the master file providing the quantities on hand and on order are zero. If an item is to be deleted when the quantity on hand and/or on order is not at zero (obsolete item being scrapped or sold), write OBSOLETE in the description (Col. 35-42).

2. Spare Activity Input

This form is used for reporting on order data, receipts, disbursements physical inventory checks, and stock location transfers. In addition to commodity code, unit - of measure, and storage area & stock location, information is to be furnished as follows:

a. On order - Indicate purchase order number and date and the quantity.

b. Receipt - Indicate date of receipt quantity received, unit price, and whether the quantity received is a partial shipment or will complete the on order quantity. (The computer will deduct quantity received from the on order quantity when a "C" is indicated.)

c. Repairable Spares - Enter quantity of used spares returned for future repair in the Repairable - Received column. When these repairable items are actually sent to the shop for repair, enter them as on order and delete them from the repairable spares in the "Out" column. Also report repairable items that are scrapped rather than repaired in the out column to delete them from the repairable inventory.

d. Disbursements - Indicate the usable quantity used, usable quantity scrapped and/or sold, and the cost center and equipment code (when available), where the spare was used.

e. Physical Inventory - Indicate the quantity on hand and the date of inventory.

Note: Only one Inventory will be accepted for a single commodity in any one week. The quantity reported must be the quantity on hand after recording all transactions for that week. If two inventories are reported in the same week, only the last will be recorded.

f. Transfers to - Indicate the 4-digit stock location and quantity being transferred for all items that are relocated from one stock location to another.

(Transfers between storage areas must be reported as a delete from one area and a new item in the other) If the item is a repairable item, enter an "R" in that column. If it is a usable item, leave the "R" column blank.

FINAL REMARKS

In the above sections, the preventive maintenance program, of the Iron & Steel Complex, has been explained. The difficulties associated with the old system raise the urgent need for a computerized information system to overcome these difficulties. A general description of the system has been presented with emphasis on the data preparation for processing. The system is in the course of implementation for the time being, and it is early to have some indicators for the general evaluation. However, priliminary results of implementation in some areas of the plant give beter visualization for the operation and maintenance duties.

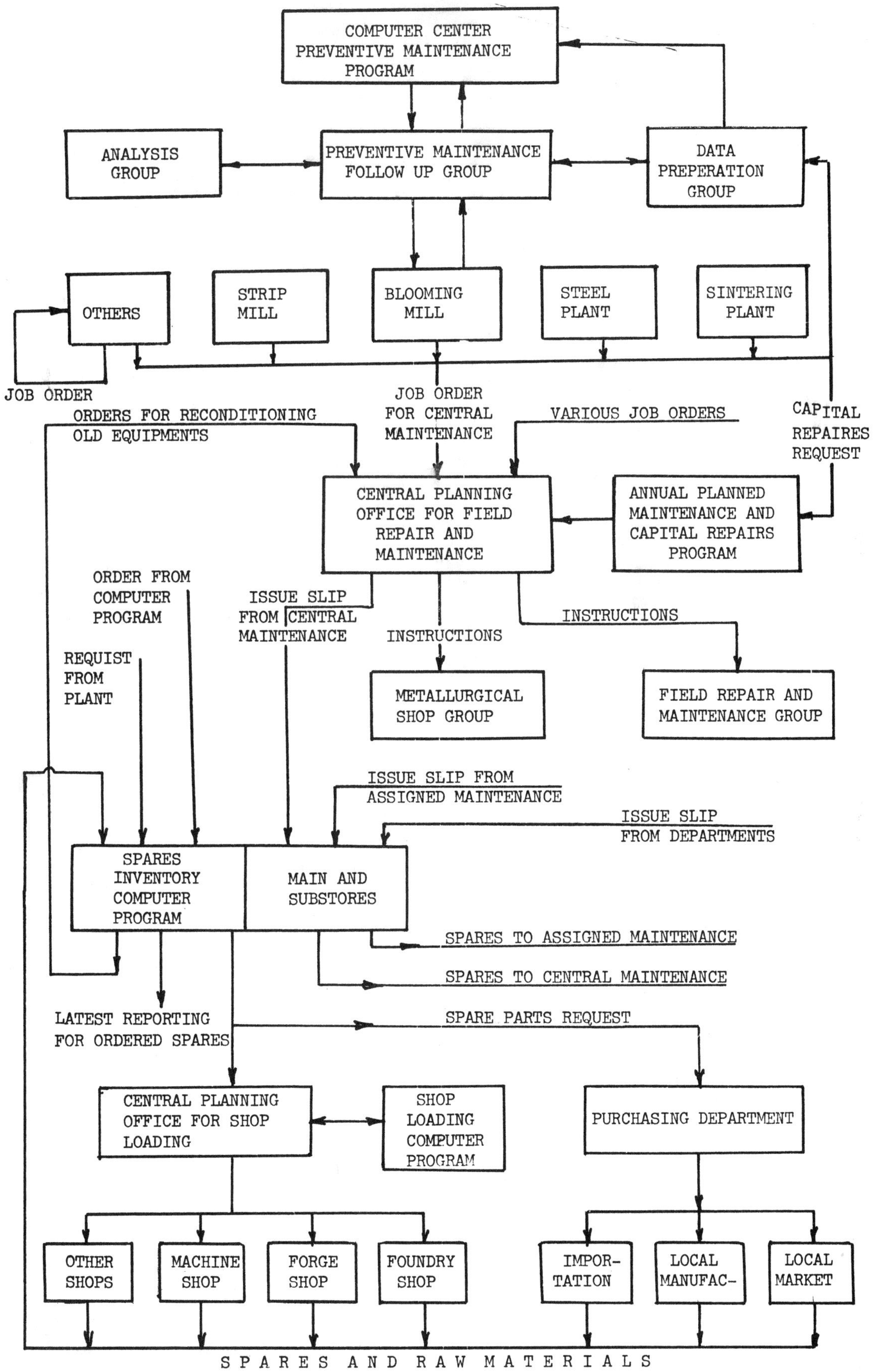

SCHEMATIC DIGRAM OF
PREVENTIVE MAINTENANCE IMPLEMENTATION

IMPLEMENTING AN INFORMATION CONTROL SYSTEM FOR MANUFACTURING

J.A. Aseltine

United Nuclear Corporation, Falls Church, Virginia, USA

ABSTRACT

An information control system for manufacturing -- a shop floor control system -- is described. The history of development of the system in a manufacturing plant is presented. During development, some approaches worked and others didn't, and from these experiences, steps for successful application of information control are suggested.

INTRODUCTION

> "The medium, or process, of our time -- electric technology -- is reshaping and restructuring patterns of social interdependence and every aspect of our personal life."*

The computer creates an environment in a manufacturing plant. It is much more than a report generator or an event counter and tabulator. It becomes not just a communication medium, but a shaper of the way communication takes place.

THE SYSTEM

The data base which is the heart of our system as it exists today is shown in Figure 1. The integrated data base accessed in real time by a variety of users.

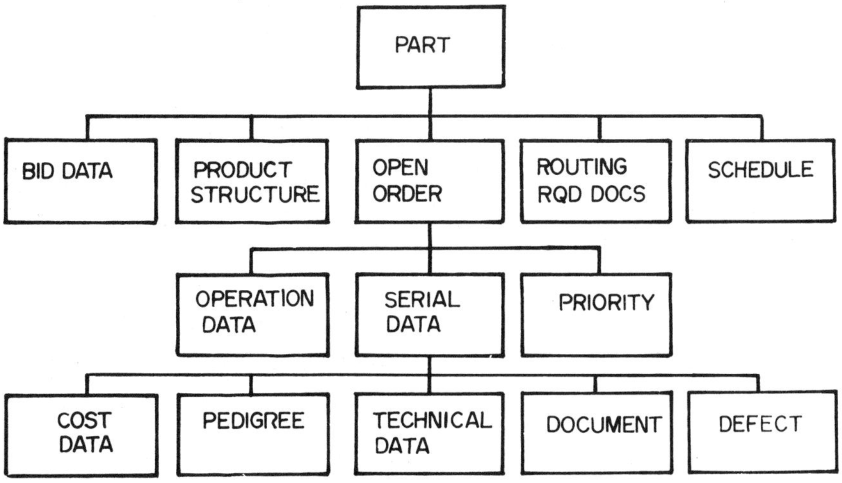

Fig. 1. Integrated Data Base

---

* Marshall McLuhan and Quentin Fiore, The Medium is the Massage, Bantam Books, New York, 1967.

A typical access subsystem is shown in Figure 2.

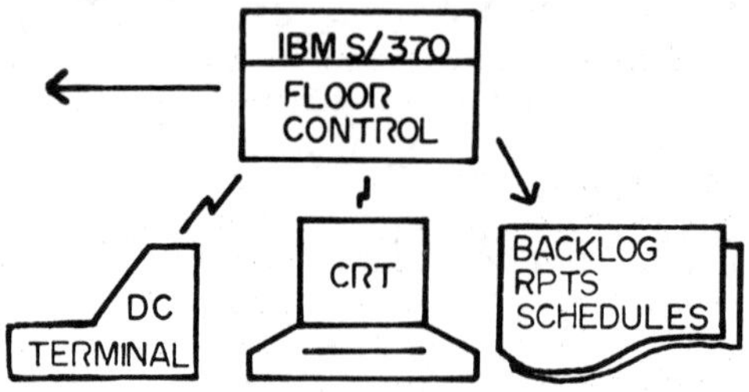

Fig. 2. Typical Real-time Access Subsystem

The floor control system enters by part or serial number, and uses data on routing, scheduling, priority and operations to produce work center queuing data. Similarly, access is made by subsystems for the following functions:

Subsystem	Functions
Planning	Shop Capacity Material Requirements Inventory Analysis
Engineering	Rework Planning Process Control
Inventory Control	Part Location Cyclic Inventory
Document Control	Forms Specifications Document Status
Finance	Bid Data Cost Data Labor Reporting
Production	Bill of Materials Parts Status

Each function is performed by access to the same integrated data base.

Currently, the data base and access software are installed on an IBM S/370 Model 145. Access is provided by 3270 cathode ray tube (CRT) terminals located throughout the shop floor. The plant employs about 1200 persons.

HISTORY

It took about three years to install the system and get sufficient floor support to make it work.

In the beginning our plant was being run by many individuals, each with much experience, but little or no sense of overall objectives. Let us name such a man Stanley. He is the man on the manufacturing floor with a notebook who knows what to do. Actually, there are lots of Stanleys. He is a foreman, or a superintendent, or sometimes just an old-timer on the floor. You can find him in production control, or in engineering, or in stores. We had dozens of Stanleys.

Stanley doesn't communicate much. He doesn't have to--he just knows what to do. He especially doesn't communicate with management. As he sees it, they represent a force against progress. "Those guys in the front office don't understand."

Of course, we needed Stanley. Three years ago, he really did run the place. In fact, he is still with us, but he is on management's side now. The difference is the computer-provided environment and is measurable as a 50% increase in productivity.

In other words, three years ago our plant was being run day-to-day by isolated individuals who viewed management as an impediment.

How did we get Stanley on management's side? We needed to start somewhere, so we picked an area which was barely under Stanley's control--where even he was in trouble. That place was product inventory which was being done manually every two months. It took two to three days, 50 people (mostly on overtime) and a 1-day plant shutdown. All of this was run by two Stanleys, each with a ledger full of inventory data. (Stanleys don't trust each other, so separate records are kept.)

Automation worked. The inventory is now a routine daily activity. The ledgers are gone because the records are in the computer file. In fact, the Stanleys help keep the data accurate.

The latter was a key step because it was the beginning of a shared data base, accessible to all from the factory floor.

We didn't fully appreciate what we had then, but we later found this to be true:

The absolute foundation of floor control is accurate information about product movement, because the data base is the means for floor communication.

Accuracy in the data base comes from interactive use by Stanley. He needs it to replace his personal files.

At that time we also tied our data base to our labor reporting system to capture movement of components from one work center to the next.

Since our approach was to win over the Stanleys, we needed access to data in real time. We began to place interactive terminals (3270's) liberally on the floor. Of course, some of these provided data that could have been obtained by batch report; but our strategy was to make data readily available. We had begun to understand that our data base was becoming a communication system among the people responsible for getting the work of the factory done.

We now began to see other results from our floor control system. For example, parts ready to move could do so. This is an essential ingredient in smoothing the flow of product. We found that available machines could be paired with available parts in a routine way.

Another result was to make it hard to hide a hard problem. "To scrap or not to scrap" is one such hard problem. Without the visibility that the on-line data base provides, such problems were often saved by Stanley "for later."

SOME LESSONS

During the development of the system, lessons were learned, sometimes at the expense of going back and starting over. Some of these are listed below.

1. Real-time Access Is Important

Much of the information provided by the system could be produced a day later by batch processing with little loss of currency. However, the accuracy of the data base depends in this system on interaction by users. The cost of CRT terminals on the floor is more than offset by resulting data base accuracy.

2. Don't Isolate Data Processing

System development requires cooperation between programmers and manufacturing users. Each must become familiar to some extent with the other's problems. Joint development is essential.

3. Users must benefit

An accurate data base comes from a user who derives benefit from access to it. The implicit feedback of such a system keeps the data base purged of errors and current. Assignment of a disinterested person to update the file almost always fails.

4. Avoid All-purpose Solutions

It is better to build a small, working control system than a large, elaborate one which is somehow never finished. Global solutions are almost sure to fail. Small systems which are compatible with one another will grow together to form the comprehensive system desired.

5. Build Around Success

Discard failures quickly. The modular approach in Number 4 above makes it easy to move on from a small failure to a small success.

6. Keep the software flexible

As the system matures, redefinition of fields, interconnections and the like will be necessary.

7. No Multiple Data Base

One set of data can be kept accurate.

8. Keep the Computer Up

As the dependence grows, so does the need to keep the computer running to keep the plant running.

CONCLUSIONS

The real-time system described has formed an environment for manufacturing that yields significantly improved productivity. The same software and systems techniques have been applied to such divergent applications as personnel information and mine production. The lessons learned in development continue to be valid as new systems are developed. The medium really does seem to be the message.

"PASS": AN INTERACTIVE ONLINE SIMULATOR FOR PREDICTIVE PRODUCTION CONTROL

K. Tabata*, K. Mori*, S. Mitsumori*, K. Ohshima, H. Ono** and K. Inoue*****

**Systems Development Laboratory, Hitachi, Ltd., Kokubunji, Tokyo 185, Japan*
***Ohmika Works, Hitachi, Ltd., Hitachi, Ibaraki 319-12, Japan*
****Industrial Processes Group, Hitachi, Ltd., Chiyoda-ku, Tokyo 100, Japan*

ABSTRACT

An interactive online simulator PASS (Predictive Adaptive Simulation System) has been developed as a packaged tool for predictive production control systems. PASS is a man-machine system to enhance the following functions: prediction of process status and evaluation of alternative precautionary measures. In this paper, the present version (a job shop model) is described in terms of the prediction and evaluation functions, the simulation model, and the software structure.

INTRODUCTION

Online computers have been taking the place of man's decision-making tasks for production control. A variety of dynamic scheduling systems illustrate examples (1)(2)(3). This approach has been successfully adopted in highly-automated production systems like automobile, iron and steel industries. In the average industries, however, full-computerized control is not always possible. This is due to the difficulties in manipulating complex factors in which man has to intervene. An alternative approach would be a man-machine system in which computers enhance prediction and evaluation functions. Prediction of process status and evaluation of alternative precautionary measures would improve adaptability to fluctuating environments. Aiming at such a production control scheme, the authors have developed an interactive online simulator "PASS"--Predictive Adaptive Simulation System.

In the past, numerous simulators were developed (4)(5). Most of them are for the offline use or analytical studies. The online simulator of Ferguson and Jones (6) is for experimental studies of computer aided decision systems rather than a production control system. In contrast to the conventional simulators, PASS has the following features: (a) an interactive online simulator for daily production control, (b) a packaged software incorporating man-machine communication functions.

The present version of PASS is for progress management in job shops. In this paper, the present version is described in terms of the prediction and evaluation functions, the simulation model, and the software structure.

FUNCTIONS

Conventional production control systems have improved two functions (Fig. 1): (a) to grasp the current process status, (b) to make up new production schedules in response to changing process status. Man has to intervene in some problems which computers can not cope with. Prediction of such problems and evaluation of precautionary measures are not sufficiently supported by conventional systems. These tasks are almost entirely left to man.

PASS has been developed to overcome these defects. The basic functions of PASS are: (a) prediction of future problems, (b) evaluation of alternative precautions. They are described as follows (Fig. 2).

Prediction of Future Problems

PASS predicts future problems such as delays from scheduled due dates, overload or underload, excessive in-process inventories and so on. These problems are detected and displayed on CRT terminals. Warnings are sent out, requesting precautionary measures. The prediction is carried out based on production schedules and current process status. These input data must be given by the user's system.

Evaluation of Alternative Precautions

Typical precautionary measures are to change production schedules in terms of due dates, job priorities, production capacity and job assignment among shops. To help man make a decision on the alternatives, PASS provides him with "what if" information. Thus, PASS simulates the process behavior under the conditions specified by the alternatives, and estimates quantitatively the impacts of the possible precautions.

These functions are realized by an online simulator and interactive display terminals.

OPERATION MODES

PASS is operated in one of the following three modes.

T Mode

Built-in timers can automatically start the operation of PASS. This mode is called the timer mode or "T mode" (Fig. 3-a). When PASS detects problems exceeding preset levels, warnings are sent out. Simulation horizon and shops to be studied must be specified in advance as the simulation condition data. Several sets of the condition data can be specified, and PASS simulates for each of them. Thus, the T mode is to watch automatically the process status. Since the outline of the problems is shown by a T mode operation, man is releaved from being tied down to CRT terminals.

P Mode

A user program can use PASS and have an access to the results. This mode is called the program mode or "P mode" (Fig. 3-b). PASS runs as a subroutine of the user program in this mode.

K Mode

PASS can be operated through CRT terminals. This mode is called the keyboard mode or "K mode" (Fig. 3-c). The objectives of this mode are: (a) to display on CRT terminals the results of the T or P mode, (b) to detect future problems and search for precautionary measures by repeating interactive simulations.

INPUT/OUTPUT DATA

Input Data

PASS needs four kinds of input data: (a) production schedules, (b) current process status, (c) simulation condition data, (d) control commands. Data (c) (d) are given through CRT terminals.

Production schedules. Since the present version is for job shops, production schedules are described in PERT diagrams. Thus, due dates, work amount, order relations of each product are assigned to a set of nodes and arcs. Priorities among the products and production capacity of each shop are also specified.

Current process status. Progress data on the scheduled products must be given to PASS.

Simulation condition data. Simulation can be repeated under different conditions which modifies the production schedules. The modifications of simulation models are specified by the simulation condition data. Specifically, due dates, job priorities, production capacity and job assignment among shops can be modified.

Control commands. Control commands for data input or output, simulation, CRT display, and other operations of PASS are put in through CRT terminals.

Output Data

Simulation results are displayed on CRT terminals. Figure 4-a is an example of the summary display. Each row, which corresponds to one shop, summarizes the predicted work load, progress balances among the operations and delays. Interactions among the shops are illustrated by the matrix on the left. Figure 4-b shows a predicted progress of a product whose activities 91 $\sim$ 97 are assigned to shops 101 $\sim$ 109. Delays are predicted for each node and the critical path is indicated. Figure 4-c shows the work load of shop 106 as compared with its production capacity. Unlike in Fig. 4-a, the data are given in time series with detailed numerical figures. Abnormal situations where the work load exceeds the capacity are emphasized by different colors.

Figure 4-d shows a list of the delayed products. These listed products will be watched carefully. Detailed information on each product or on related shops are obtained from Fig. 4-b or 4-c. These simulation results can be saved in user's data base.

SIMULATION MODEL AND ALGORITHM

Multi-Level PERT

The simulation model is developed from that of the PERT technique. The key issue here is how to realize online simulations under severe constraints on computation time and memory size. To solve this problem, the "multi-level PERT" method is adopted. This method is a hierarchical modelling of the production process, reflecting different levels of management such as departments, sections and groups. The idea of the multi-level PERT is illustrated in Fig. 5. Suppose, for example, the user is concerned with the overall behavior of the factory. Then the aggregate model on the first level in Fig. 5 will be used. If the user is in charge of the manufacturing department, the more detailed model on the second level will be used. Thus, the idea is similar to the "work breakdown structure" method of PERT diagrams.

PERT data for any level must be prepared in the user's data base. PASS determines an appropriate level of simulation based on the user's specifications. Only the related PERT data of the selected level are transferred into PASS. Since each level can be described by a small number of nodes and arcs, the multi-level PERT method decreases computation time and memory size.

Simulation Flow

The simulation of PASS is essentially to estimate the completion dates. Production lead time, i.e., the time interval between the starting and completion dates, is equal to the sum of the net production time and the waiting time. The net production time is assumed to be given. So the problem is how to estimate the waiting time.

Two factors make production operations wait: overload of the production facility, and the time differences between the completion dates of the related parts. These factors can be simulated by well-known queuing models such as GPSS and SIMSCRIPT. Their descriptions are, however, too detailed and time-consuming. A more macroscopic simulation method is required for online simulations. So the following procedures have been developed.

Figure 6 shows the simulation flow. First, the waiting time due to overload of the production facility is estimated. Secondly, the estimated waiting time is added to the net production time. This sum is regarded as the activity time of PERT diagrams. Lastly, completion dates are estimated, meeting the constraints on the precedence order among the activities. This approach is to solve a modified single-project PERT problem. So the calculation is simple.

Algorithm

Since the PERT model describes the production operations as arcs, the terms "arcs", "activities" and "operations" will be used interchangeably. PASS takes into account different priorities among the products. To facilitate the description of the algorithm, however, we assume no priorities exist among the products in this section.

Following notations will be used:

k = the index for the products,
A^k = the set of the arcs of product k,
i or j = the index for the nodes,
t_i^k = the scheduled due date for node i of product k,
$\hat{t}_i^k$ = the estimated completion date for node i of product k,
w_{ij}^k = the net production time of arc (i,j) of product k,
y_{ij}^k = the estimated waiting time (due to overload) of arc (i,j) of product k,
$z_{ij}^k = w_{ij}^k + y_{ij}^k$
d_{ij}^k = the shop to which arc (i,j) of product k is assigned,
m = the index for the shops,
$S_{mT} = \{(i,j,k): d_{ij}^k = m,\ t_i^k < T \leq t_j^k\}$, i.e., the set of the arcs which are assigned to shop m at time T where T = 1, 2, ...,
C_{mT} = the production capacity of shop m at time T,
L_{mT} = the scheduled work load of shop m at time T,
F_{mT} = the estimated work amount which shop m will complete at time T,
R_{mT} = the estimated work amount which shop m will leave over at time T.

Esimation of the work load. Assume the operation of arc (i,j) starts at $t_i^k + 1$, and continues at a constant rate until its due date t_j^k. Then the work amount per day for this arc is $w^k_{ij}/(t^k_j - t^k_i)$. Shop m is scheduled to process at time T all the arcs in S_{mT}. So the work load of shop m at time T is estimated as:

$$L_m(T) = \sum_{(i,j,k)\in S_{mT}} w^k_{ij}/(t^k_j - t^k_i). \qquad (1)$$

Estimation of the completed work amount. $R_m(T-1)$ denotes the work amount which is left over at time T - 1. The total load at time T is equal to $L_m(T) + R_m(T-1)$. Shop m will complete the loaded activities within the limit of its capacity by the following amount:

$$F_m(T) = \mathrm{Min}\{L_m(T) + R_m(T-1),\ C_m(T)\}. \qquad (2)$$

The remaining load $R_m(T)$ will be left over to the succeeding days, where:

$$R_m(T) = L_m(T) + R_m(T-1) - F_m(T), \qquad (3)$$

and $R_m(0) = 0$. Solve equations (2) and (3) for $F_m(T)$'s and $R_m(T)$'s.

Estimation of the waiting time due to overload. Work load exceeding the production capacity is left over as shown by equation (3). Let t' denote the time when the operation scheduled at time t will be actually processed. Then t' satisfies the following relation:

$$\sum_{T=1}^{t} L_m(T) = \sum_{T=1}^{t'} F_m(T). \qquad (4)$$

Let u(t) denote the mapping from t to t'. Also assume arc (i,j) of product k is given to shop m at time t^k_i where $m = d^k_{ij}$. Then this arc will be completed at time $u_m(t^k_j)$. The time interval between t^k_i and $u_m(t^k_j)$ is equal to the sum of w^k_{ij} (the net production time) and y^k_{ij} (the waiting time due to overload). Therefore,

$$z^k_{ij} \equiv w^k_{ij} + y^k_{ij} = u_m(t^k_j) - t^k_i. \qquad (5)$$

Estimation of the completion dates. The completion date for mode j is defined as the earliest time when all the precedent arcs of node j are completed. Regard z^k_{ij} as the activity time of arc (i,j) of product k. Then, the completion date for node j is estimated as:

$$\hat{t}^k_j = \max_{(i,j)\in A^k} (\hat{t}^k_i + z^k_{ij}). \qquad (6)$$

SOFTWARE STRUCTURE

Basic Components

The software structure of PASS is illustrated in Fig. 7. PASS will be installed in existing production control systems. So as to facilitate the installation, PASS is packaged, incorporating display functions for man-machine communication. Besides, the simulation model is generated or modified based on user's inputs. Only the following components are left to be developed by each user: (a) the data base to provide PASS with the production schedules and process status data (b) linkage programs for data input and output (c) a starting task for P mode (d) an afterwork task. Additional descriptions on these components will be given in the next section.

Users Linkages

PASS needs communications with the user's software system for the following purposes: (a) to accept the requests for simulations (b) to take in data and send out simulated results (c) to notify the completion of PASS. These communications are realized by the following methods.

Requests for simulations. Standard forms of T and K mode operations have been developed. PASS installs the starting tasks (i.e., programs) for these modes. On the other hand, P mode is to use PASS as a subroutine of user's programs. To satisfy user-oriented requirements, the starting task for P mode is to be developed by each user.

Data input and output. Data bases which store the production schedules and process status data may have different structures depending on users. Therefore, the data input and output tasks are to be developed by the user. It is important, however, to keep the consistency of data. So PASS provides the user with macro instructions to control the timing of these tasks.

Notification of the completion of PASS. PASS notifies the completion to the user's system by starting the user's task called the afterwork task.

APPLICATION

PASS is now being applied to progress management at an inspection department in a home appliance factory. This department deals with trial products and affects the manufacturing policy of new products. PASS is newly introduced because the existing scheduling system does not provide online simulation functions for man-machine communication.

The simulation horizon of this application is 12 months with a pitch of weeks. About 50 kinds of products are studied, each of which has 50 to 60 inspection operations. These operations are aggregated by the multi-level PERT technique, and each product is represented as a PERT diagram with less than 20 arcs. The program size is 40 kw (kilo-words), and an additional 25 kw is required for the data area. PASS is installed in a process computer HIDIC 80; Production schedules and process status data are fed from a business computer HITAC 8450 through the communication channel.

ACKNOWLEDGMENT

The authors would like to thank Takeo Miura, General Manager, of the Systems Development Laboratory, Hitachi, Ltd. and Yutaka Takuma, Manager, of Ohmika Works, Hitachi, Ltd. for their technical guidance and continued encouragement. The authors are also grateful to Tatsuo Koyama, Assistant Chief Engineer, of Process Computer and Control Department, Hitachi, Ltd. for suggesting this study.

REFERENCES

(1) A. Hosaka, Tsutomu Shibata, Akira Yoshida, Tadahiko Murakami and Masahiko Asada, Computers Control System of Production and Information, Hitachi Hyoron, 52, 696 (1970).

(2) M. Kisaka, Shuichi Watanabe, Isao Matsuo, Yasuaki Hashida and Osamu Chinone, Integrated Production Planning and Control System for Plate Manufacture in the Iron and Steel Industry, Hitachi Hyoron, 55, 1155 (1973).

(3) M. Takei, Moichi Murano, Keitaro Inoue and Akira Takemoto, Production Control System in Automobile Assembly Plants, Hitachi Hyoron, 55, 188 (1973).

(4) K. Mitome, Susumu Tsuhara and Susumu Seki, "MAFLOS"--A Generalized Manufacturing System Simulator, Hitachi Hyoron, 55, 799 (1973).

(5) E. S. Buffa (1968), Production Inventory Systems: Planning and Control, Richard D. Irwin, Homewood, Illinois.

(6) R. L. Ferguson and C. H. Jones, A Computer Aided Decision System, Management Science, 15, B-550 (1969).

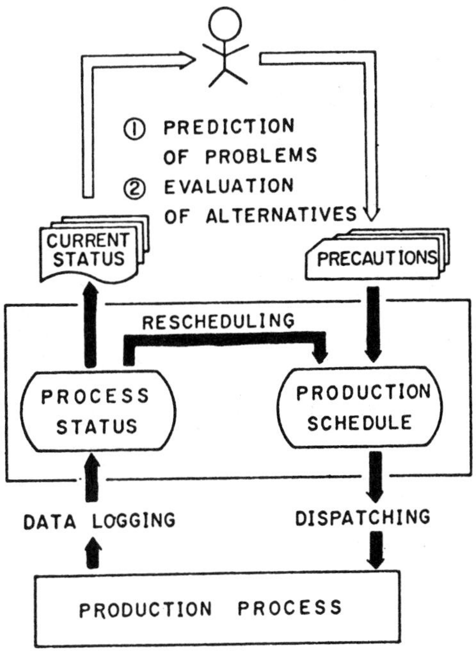

Fig. 1. A production control system without prediction and evaluation functions.

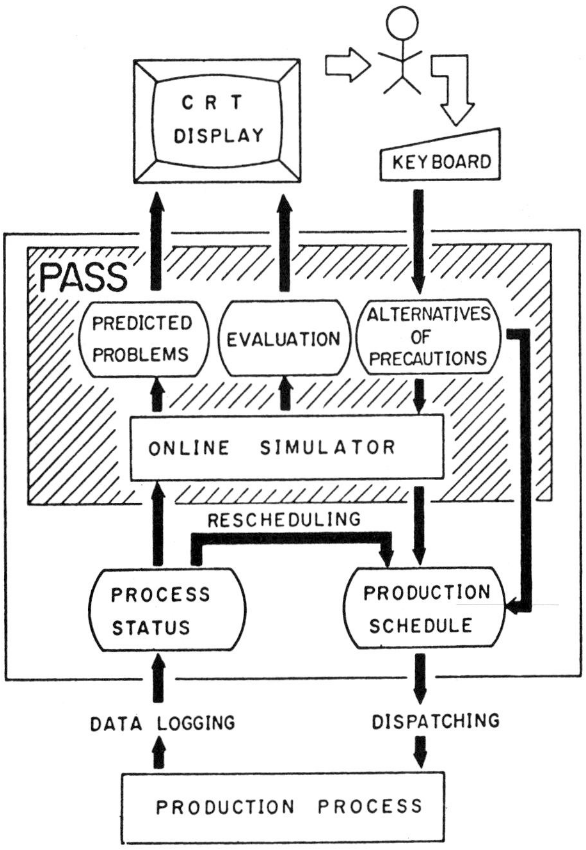

Fig. 2. Basic functions of PASS.

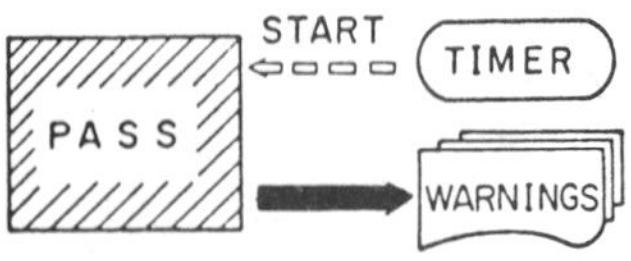

(a) T mode.

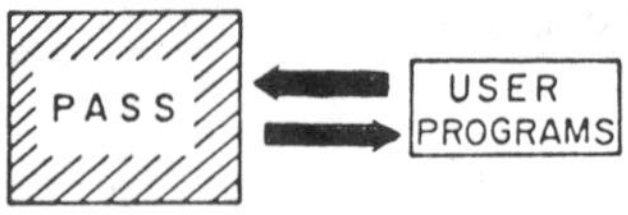

(b) P mode.

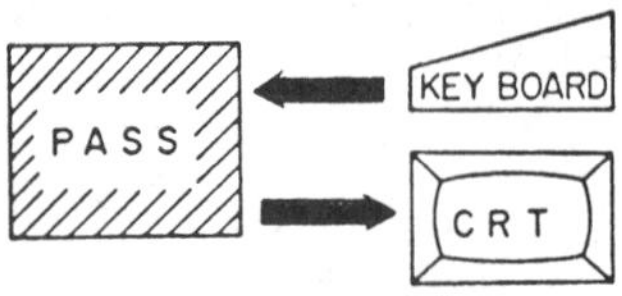

(c) K mode.

Fig. 3. Operation modes of PASS.

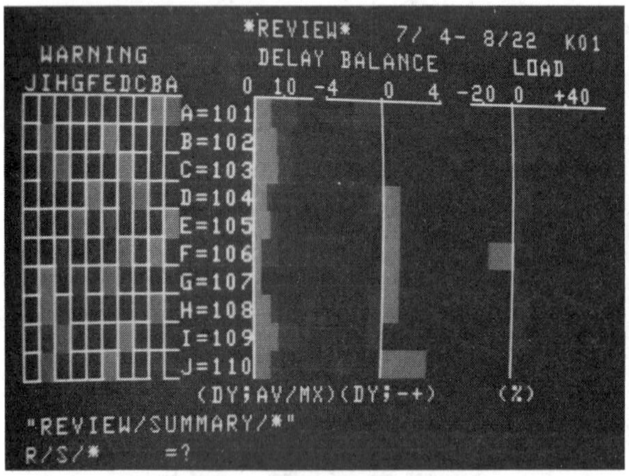

(a) A summary display.

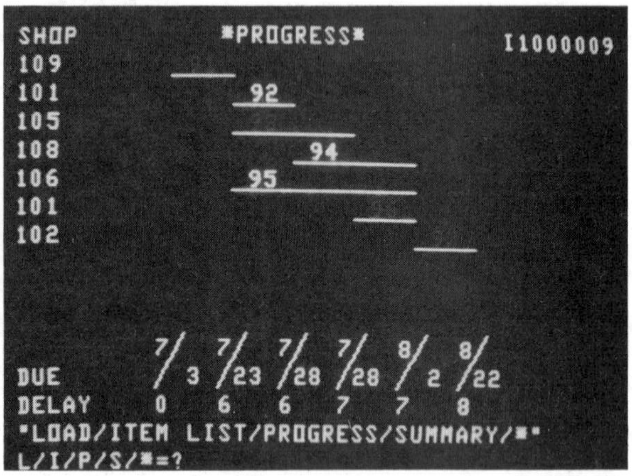

(b) A progress display.

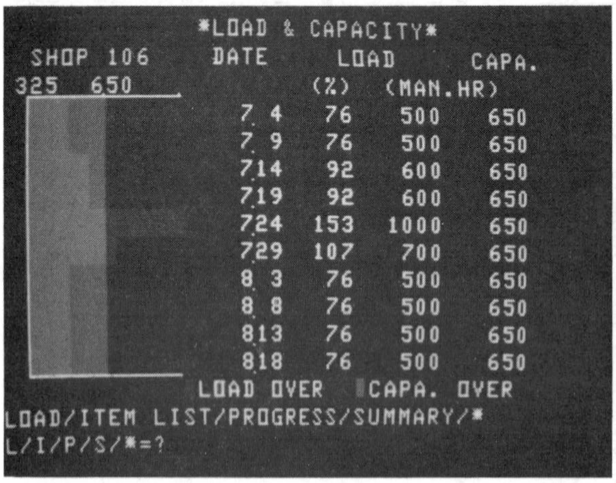

(c) A load display.

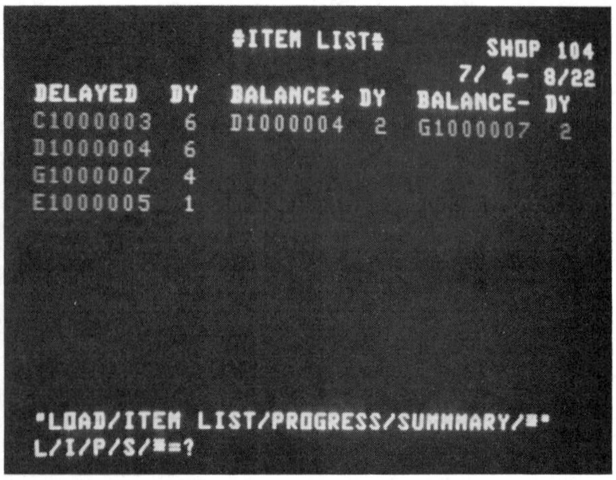

(d) An item-list display.

Fig. 4. Examples of the CRT displays of PASS.

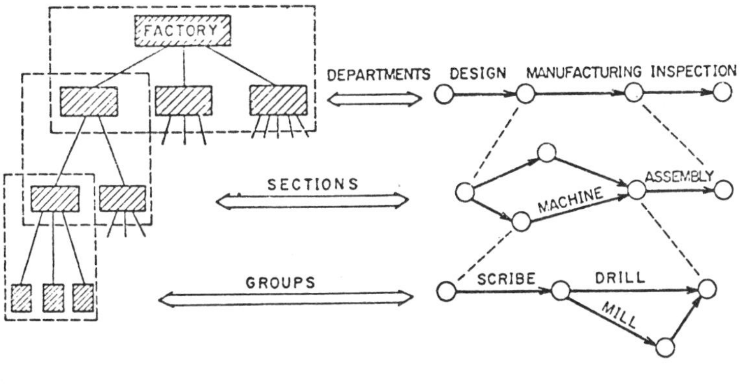

Fig. 5. The multi-level PERT model.

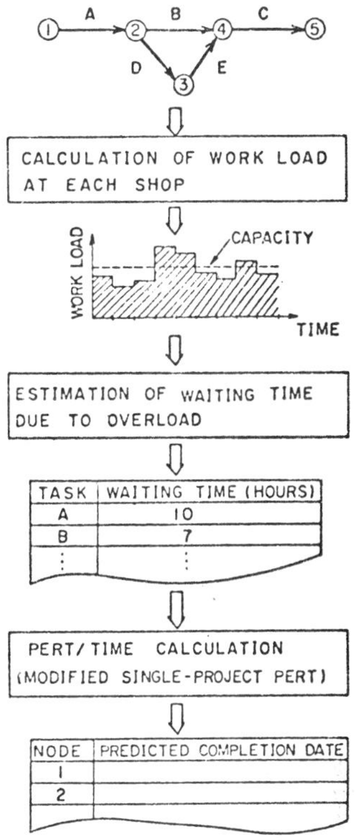

Fig. 6. The simulation flow of PASS.

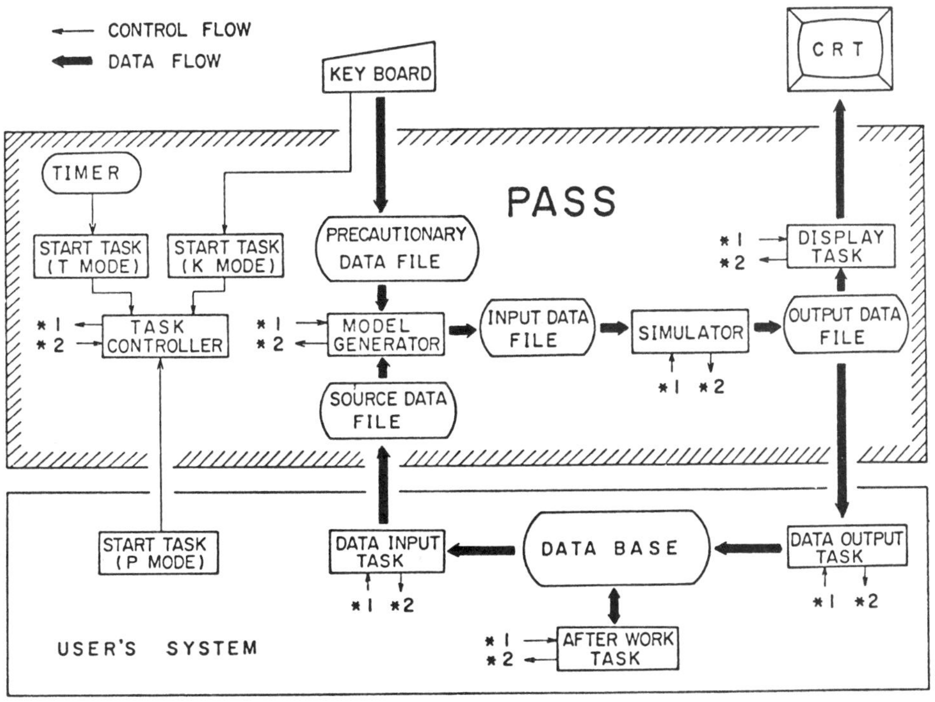

Fig. 7. The software structure of PASS.

INFORMATION AND CONTROL IN COMPUTERIZED MANUFACTURING SYSTEMS

J.J. Talavage and M.M. Barash

Purdue University, West Lafayette, Indiana, U.S.A.

ABSTRACT

Specifications are provided for a sufficient set of information which can be the basis for the design of a wide class of coordination and control policies for Computerized Manufacturing Systems.

INTRODUCTION

Computerized Manufacturing Systems (CMS) is the term used here to describe manufacturing facilities which also have been called "Flexible Manufacturing Systems," "Variable Mission Manufacturing Systems," "Computer-Managed Parts Manufacturing Systems," "Multiple Station Manufacturing Systems," etc. The components in such systems consists of four major types: machine tools with their tooling and fixturing, material handling system, auxiliary equipment, and control/computer configuration.

The development of CMS has been based on the perception that it is an ideal production system for products made in batches of less than fifty. Such products apparently comprise about 70 percent of all metalworking manufacturing.

Within the production environment, the attributes of a CMS that are important to company management include average production rate and long-term machine and system reliability. These measures are significant to control of CMS production within the context of a larger manufacturing organization. We will return to this viewpoint later. Other more detailed aspects of the system, such as the location of each part and tool, the number of operations performed on each part, and so forth, may be said to specify the current status of the system. Information concerning this current status obtained by observation or measurement can be employed for the relatively short term purpose of coordinating and controlling the flow of movable entities within the CMS. Such entities may include parts, carts, tools, spindles, as well as other components.

In general, it is not economical to provide material handling systems which provide a separate path of transport between every possible pair of destinations. Thus, it will usually be necessary to make choices when moving system entities regarding which ones are to be moved, when they are to be moved, and by what route. The complexity of the choice decision varies depending on the type of material handling system. For example, these decision are simple ones for "random access" systems such as circular conveyors, but may be quite complex for "addressable" delivery systems in which carts may be moved by various routes to assigned destinations. Whether these choices are made by a man or by use of computerized decision algorithms, the choices will be intelligent only if appropriate and accurate information on the current status of the system is available on which to base the decision.

Our NSF-sponsored project has, as one aspect of the project, resulted in the development of a simulation for an existing CMS at Caterpillar Tractor Company. This simulation incorporates decision rules for movement of both parts and carts. The development of such computerized algorithms provided us with the appreciation for the information requirements of such rules. We are now in the process of developing a general-purpose simulator called GCMS which can model any existing or proposed CMS. Such a simulator must allow for a wide variety of decision rules to be incorporated into the model by the user. To do this, it was necessary to specify and provide all the information in an appropriate form that such a user might need. The complete specifications are available and are summarized below. Such a list of information specifications is not only of interest to simulation modelers, but also to system designers who must provide for the collection and distribution of such information.

INFORMATION FOR DECISIONS

It should be clear that certain information is necessary in order to invoke a given system decision rule. However, two other aspects of the relationship between information and decision rules should not be overlooked. One of these aspects has to do with which information must be known in order to determine which, if any, of the decision rules should be invoked at a given time. That is, the state of the system must be identified to determine whether it is among that set of states in which one (or more) of the decision rules need be exercised. The other aspect of the relationship is more definitive and concerns the changes that need be made to the information structure as a result of some decision.

All three of the above aspects of the information/decision relationship are considered later for an example decision rule. The full set of decision rules for any CMS has at least six elements including decision rules for:

1. introducing raw castings into the system,
2. finding the next operation for a part,
3. selecting a station to perform an operation,
4. selecting a material handling entity,
5. scheduling movements of mateial handling entities,
6. selecting the next part to be machined from a queue of parts at a machine.

Each of these rules is incorporated into the GCMS simulator and, depending on the system structure, may be invoked to obtain efficient system operation.

As a result of our simulation efforts (and real world experience at Caterpillar), we believe that a minimal set of data for employing the above rules is contained in the "system description" and the "status vector" of GCMS.

The system description consist of five parts corresponding to the five major types of system components. These component-types are the material handling system (MHS) configuration, parts, stations, pallets, and MHS devices. Table 1 shows the system description in terms of arrays with a brief statement about the contents of each array element. From the standpoint of volume of information, it is especially important to note that each array may be duplicated as many times as there are members of a set of components. For example, our simulator allows a maximum of thirty stations, and so there may be up to thirty arrays of the type STATN.

The system status can also be described in terms of the five component-types. This is shown in the form of annotated arrays in Table 2.

The system status completely identifies the dynamic system state at any time, and the system description displays the important static system characteristics. It seems reasonable to take the union of these two sets of information as a sufficiently large information source on which to base initiation and execution of the six decision rules shown earlier.

Let us consider as an example the initiation and execution of the third decision rule in the previous list; namely, the rule for selecting a station to perform an operation. The decision rule is initiated by a change in the status of some part in the system. In particular, by the change in the assignment of a next operation as shown in array element 8 in the array PARST. Execution of the decision rule may assume the existence of a set of available stations. This question of existence is assessed by checking the first and the twenty-first element of each STAST array in the system status. In flexible systems, a number of stations might exist for performing the given operation. One version of this rule for those systems would be to select the highest priority station for this operation, whether it is available or not. That priority is available from array ROUTE in the system description, where stations performing the same operations are listed in order of their priority. In any case, the result of applying this decision rule will be to affect the system status. In particular, element number 9 of array PARST in the system status will be updated to its new value.

In summary, the design of short term coordination and control algorithms for a given CMS depends on the particular structure of the CMS. We believe that the relatively small set of data provided in Table 1 and 2 is a sufficient basis for the specification of such algorithms for any present or proposed CMS structure.

TABLE 1 System Description

Part Description

	1	2	3	4	5
PADIS part type	maximum number allowed in system	decision rule when finding next operation	decision rule when finding a cart	priority for part type	target production for each shift

	1 . . . 50	
ROUTE part type	sequence of operations	for each operation list of 9 stations to perform operation

Station Description

	1	2	3	4	5	6	7	8	9
STATN station no.	number of different operations performed	number of on-shuttle queue positions	number of off-shuttle queue positions	decision rule when picking part from shuttle	shuttle to track time [also track to machine time]	shuttle to machine time	track position on-shuttle	track position off-shuttle	station type for reliability distribution

	1	2 50	51
OPER operation no.	time	. . . . .	decision rule

	1	2	3
RESTA	(time) for parts to be removed	station number for operation	time left for operation on part at station

Pallet Description

	1	2-10	11
PALL pallet types	number that exist	part types it can be used for	number in system busy

Cart Description

	1	2	3	4	5
CART cart type	number that exist	number of pallet-holding positions	average speed over all portion of track	decision rule to use when moving	portions of track it can move across
RECAR cart number	cart number for all assignments in breakdown	0 - do not remove parts 1 - remove parts	decision point where cart moves for repair	decision point where cart returns	

Track Description

	1	2 - 5	6
TRACK decision points	station number if station exist	successors to this decision pt.	speed for conveyor

Track Description (continued)

DISTA node A	node B distance only for correcting decision points

TABLE 2 System Status

Part Status

	1	2	3	4	5	6	7
PARST part number	part type	priority	pallet number	cart no. when assigned	current station	current operation	next operation -1.0 when done

	8	9	10	11	12 - 43
NPART	next station	no. operations left to do	1.0 - on-shuttle 2.0 - off-shuttle 0 - neither	time entered system	list of operations completed

	1	2 - 6	7 - 11	12 - 20
STAST station number	+ - last starting time 0 - idle - - operation completed but part still in machine	designated on-shuttle queue (Part #)	designated off-shuttle queue	general queue

	21	22
	0 - active 1 - down	time available in case of breakdown

Cart Status

	1	2	3	4	5
CARST	current location	time of passing	current speed 0 - stopped	destination	cart type

	6	7	8	9	10
	0 - idle 1 - picking up part 2 - dropping off part 3 - waiting for part 4 - out of way of another cart	part number	part number	part number	0 - active 1 - down

	11	12 - 50
	time when available	current route

Pallet Status

	1	2	3
PALST pallet number	+ - part number if loaded 0 - empty	if empty station number at which it resides	type

Track Status

	1	2
TRAST decision point	0 - active 1 - down	time when available

Information gathering and processing, as described above, and actions taken upon it are functions of the CMS control subsystem; they ensure optimal execution of system's assignment. However, for the Computerized Manufacturing System to perform optimally as part of the total production process, two conditions must be met: the system must be provided with all its needs, and the assignment given to it must be one which best meets production process requirements at the given time. Thus, for example, raw materials, tools, etc., must be available as needed without maintaining excessive inventories, and the products of the system must be those most needed in, e.g., the assembly section, and again, without inventory buildup. Similar considerations apply to provision of software, fixtures, maintenance, etc. There is need for constant monitoring of all the variables throughout the entire production process from orders to shipments, on-line evaluation of status and preparation of forecasts for different time horizons, and for selection of best decisions for corrective action. These problems have always existed in manufacturing, and their severity has been continually increasing with the growing complexity and size of industrial enterprise.

The volume of information to be processed daily in an industrial enterprise is very large. A plant employing only 200 persons may execute 4,000 transactions a day [1]. There is reason to suspect that the number of transactions increase faster than the number of productive "units", or persons in this case. Theoretically this can be based on the fact that the number of links between all units, productive and controlling (management) increases faster than the number of units. Glushkov [2] shows that this indeed is the case. For example, if we assume that each transaction has ten arithmetic operations requiring 10 seconds each, an enterprise handling manually, i.e., without electronic computers, 4,000 transactions a day requires 14 "management" persons, or 7 percent of the total work force. For a large country, such as the USA or USSR, the number of arithmetic operations in national economy is according to Glushkov 10^{16} a year. To handle them manually, 10 billion persons are required, which is 50 times the population of the country, or 100 times its work force. One may draw the conclusion that to simplify management, enterprises should be kept small. However, economies of scale as a rule are against small enterprises. Moreover, while volume of information in the enterprise would decrease if each were small, number of potential links between enterprises would vastly increase.

The electronic computer has, of course, changed the situation drastically. Even at a speed of only 10^6 operations per second, a medium computer can easily handle all the management information in a sizeable enterprise. The problem now is not the computing ability of the hardware, but proper structuring of the information and control system.

In the last decade computers have gained increasing acceptance in the management environment and such concepts as "management information systems" have arisen. In most cases they have distinguished themselves by unexceptional performance and often outright failure. Without going into details, one can identify as the main cause of this state of affairs the absence, as yet, of a basic, theoretically underpinned methodology for the construction of such management information and control systems. Recently, however, some progress has been made. A fairly detailed conceptual (but not theoretical) presentation of computerized production information and control system has been offered to the public [3,4]. Theoretical work is also beginning to take form, such as, for example by Doumeingts [1].

It is not the purpose of this paper to discuss the features of such management tools which can be found in the original sources. We shall, however, show that only if effective and reliable production information and control systems are available can Computerized Manufacturing Systems offer their full potential.

Existing production management systems, including those based on computers, are applied to the conventional mode of manufacturing, because it is still by far the dominant mode. A conventional machine tool employed in batch manufacturing "acts" upon the product about 5 percent of the total time the product spends in the shop. Thus, if the entire machining cycle requires 2 hours, the product will "be around" for 40 hours.

In a CMS, with a utilization factor of only 50 percent (which is not difficult to achieve and can be greatly exceeded), the part leaves after 4 hours. The system's internal control can respond instantaneously to any changes in the original schedule, but to be truly effective, the instruction for such change must reach the system without delay, otherwise numerous "wrong" products will be made, and there will be a shortage of "correct" ones. Not only instruction for the CMS has to be issued, but also for all supporting activities, such as delivery of the correct raw materials, tools, fixtures and possibly even software. If CMS is to become the main mode of manufacture (for batch production), the ability to issue such instructions at practically a moment's notice (from higher management, sales, etc.) must be the standard operating procedure, and not just an emergency feature. Without this ability, the enterprise would have to maintain vast inventories, economically prohibitive, and in many cases may be unable to meet customer demand even with them.

To be fully effective, the system must be all-encompassing. Manufacturing interacts with all other activities of the enterprise, such as design, research, quality assurance, sales, finance, and personnel, with a definite permissible maximum "signal delay time" in each link, which is vastly shorter in automated than in conventional manufacturing. Inside the manufacturing domain, the activity of the CMS is closely linked with other activities, such as overall plant monitoring and control, maintenance, purchasing, stores control, master production schedule planning, etc., etc. The complexity of the algorithmic structure (not to mention the actual programs) required to create a reliable and foolproof cybernetic system meeting the above demands is staggering. It is almost axiomatic that such system will be hierarchial, and possibly distributed at lower levels. The fundamental problem is how to ensure that each hierarchy level passes on the critical information, which poses the question as to what is "critical." Lack of imagination (or intuition) on the part of human subordinates and superiors has been the downfall of many organizations. How does one build an "imaginative" computer system? Clearly, the limits to flexible automation lie on our ability to create its total controls.

It is planned that the NSF-sponsored project into CMS, ongoing at Purdue University, will in its later phases include the management information and control aspects of the operation of a group of systems, and their interaction with the production environment. We hope that with completion of the project we shall be able to present a version of the management information and control system philosophy suited for the CMS mode of manufacturing.

References

1. Doumeingts, Guy. "Hierarchal Production Control System Using Decision Making Procedures." Proceedings of the 14th Annual Meeting and Technical Conference of the Numerical Control Society, March 13-16, 1977, Pittsburgh, Pennsylvania, pp. 239-266.

2. Glushkov, V. M. "Introduction into Automated Production Management Control Systems." (Vvedeniye v ASU), Tekhnika, Kiev, 1972 (Russian).

3. Orlicky, Joseph. *Material Requirements Planning*, McGraw-Hill, New York, 1975.

4. IBM Corporation. "COPICS - Communications Oriented Production Information and Control System." Vols. I-VIII. White Plains, New York, 1972.

THE CONTROL OF FLEXIBLE MANUFACTURING SYSTEMS: REQUIRED INFORMATION AND ALGORITHM STRUCTURES

G.K. Hutchinson

University of Wisconsin-Milwaukee

ABSTRACT

A class of manufacturing systems known as the Flexible Manufacturing System (FMS) shows promise of a substantial reduction in manufacturing costs for mid-volume, discrete manufacturing in which parts following different routings are simultaneously processed. These systems consist of machine tools and a material handling system in which normal operation is under computer control. This paper considers the issues and problems associated with FMS's and the information/algorithms that are necessary for their control and efficient operation. The control mechanisms are viewed in the context of the general problem of allocating scarce resources to achieve multiple, conflicting objectives simultaneously. The objectives of FMS's are described in relation to management's goals. The operational decisions necessary to achieve these goals are derived and the information required for decision making outlined.

Typically, the control of FMS is achieved through computer-implemented algorithms which make the second-by-second operational decisions. These algorithms are organized in a hierarchical structure for efficiency and flexibility, i.e., the ability to modify the decision-making process to adapt easily to different environments such as work station configurations, workload, and mission. The algorithms are supported by corresponding information structures. These structures and the man-machine interfaces necessary for control are described.

FMS's are complex, dynamic systems. Although much was known about their components at the time of their design, there were no firm data on the operation of their components as a unified entity. A generalized simulation of these systems was developed and used as a basis for control concept checkout, uncertainty reduction, and design verification. The use of the model is discussed together with the implications for actual systems. Finally, it is suggested that the strategy used in the design and parameterization of the FMS control mechanisms may be of general use in the control of dynamic, complex systems.

INTRODUCTION

The rate of productivity increase in the United States over the period 1960-1973 has been the lowest of any industrialized Western nation (Reference 1). A class of manufacturing systems called the Flexible Manufacturing System (FMS) shows promise of great productivity improvements in the mid-volume (batch) part production range. Cook (Reference 2) estimates that cost reductions of up to 90% are possible when FMS systems are compared with traditional job shop methods. The mid-volume range is generally considered to run from approximately 100 to 15,000 parts per year, an area that encompasses a high percentage of American manufacturing (estimates run as high as 80%). There is little doubt that these systems have the potential to substantially change traditional manufacturing, lower production costs, and lead eventually to an improved standard of living.

FMS's are essentially automated job shops and have all of the traditional problems associated with the control of job shops, including dispatching, work station assignment, load leveling, capital utilization, task sequencing, and due date performance. The major differences between job shops and FMS's are that human functions are automated, including decision making, and that jobs pass through FMS's in a time span measured in hours rather than weeks or days. The purpose of this paper is to describe the control mechanisms used in implementing these systems, by discussing the algorithms used to determine resource allocation, and to indicate their hierarchical nature. The mechanism described is not necessarily identical to any actually implemented in FMS's, but it has served as the basis for several and provided the structure used in modeling FMS's.

The following sections describe manufacturing system functions, FMS overview, FMS decisions required, control philosophy, and the hierarchical control structure. The use of simulation as a tool in the development of the control algorithms and hierarchy is stressed. The control structure appears to have the capability of controlling a large domain of FMS type systems, and the control approach appears to be generally appropriate for complex, dynamic systems.

MANUFACTURING SYSTEM FUNCTIONS

To explain the operation of a modern machine shop doing mid-volume part production, a brief outline of the steps necessary to process one operation on a single machine follows:

1. The part is assigned to a particular machine and machinist.

2. The machinist checks the part routing (the series of operations necessary to produce the part) to insure that a) the proper fixture to hold the part is available, b) the tools necessary to machine the part are on hand, and c) the part program to drive the machine tool is present.

3. The machinist moves the part onto the machine and completes the proper positioning--the set-up process.

4. The part program is loaded and controls the processing of the part on the machine.

5. Upon completion of part processing, the machinist removes the part from the machine, arranges for its movement to the next operation on its routing, and disposes of the part program, tools, and fixtures.

The only step in the entire operation where the machine itself is necessary is step 4. During the remaining steps, the expensive machine sits idle waiting for the other necessary functions to be performed. In some job shops, the average machine tool is idle over 85% of the time, representing an inefficient use of capital and contributing to the high cost of manufacturing.

Essentially, FMS's automate the above process through direct numeric control (DNC) of the machines, an automated material handling subsystem (MHS), and computer algorithms which control both the DNC and MHS functions. DNC stores part programs and uses them to drive the machine tools. MHS moves the parts about the FMS on pallets. The computer algorithms control the MHS and the DNC systems as well as providing for all management functions. Under normal operation there are many different types of parts being processed simultaneously. In the next section the basic elements of the FMS are discussed, followed by a description of the computer algorithms and data structures which provide the required information.

FMS SYSTEM OVERVIEW

FMS's are designed for the production of individual workpieces, or parts, each mounted on a pallet which serves as a physical interface between the MHS and the work area, or station, usually a machine tool. Figure 1 shows the basic elements, and Figure 2 shows an actual system. The stations generally have shuttles that move the parts to and from the MHS and serve as a buffer for both the machine (in) and the MHS (out).

The processing of the parts is determined by a routing, an ordered list of operations that must be performed. The operations identify the stations that can perform an operation, the part program, the necessary tools, and the time required by each potential station for an operation. Further complicating the situation, the operations are grouped into sequences, which are logically independent routings that are linked by physical requirements such as part reorientation on the pallet or part placement on a different pallet. The routing of a part defines a part-kind, a class of parts. Associated with each part-kind is the type(s) of pallet(s) for each sequence (a pallet may serve more than one part-kind sequence combination).

The MHS moves the parts about the FMS on individual carriers called carts, which travel predetermined paths defined by stops. Carts move only in one direction between any pair of stops; hence, the topology of the MHS can be defined by giving, for each stop, its successor(s). When a stop has multiple successors, it is a branch; if it has multiple predecessors, it is a join. To reduce the possibility of accidents, only one cart is allowed at a stop. All major decisions on cart travel are made at branches.

Associated with each part-kind is a set of parameters used to control production and to specify physical limitations. For each sequence, these parameters are the following: the production rate required, given in parts per day; the number of sequences; the number of castings (for first sequence) or semifinished parts available per sequence (PAS); maximum PAS allowed per sequence, due to physical limitations; maximum number of parts in process per sequence; and a list of pallet types which can hold the part-kind. Associated with each pallet-type are the number available and their current disposition. For each station, the shuttle(s) and pallet positions are given.

FMS DECISIONS REQUIRED

The control of a FMS, as an automated job shop, includes all of the decisions typically associated with the job shop. These decisions have as their goal the maximum utilization of FMS resources under the constraint of meeting management's production requirements. Often this goal is threatened, for a decision which maximizes machine utilization may cause excessive MHS activity or delay completion of a high priority part. The management problem is to use FMS resources--MHS carts and stops, pallets, stations and parts--to meet production requirements as defined above.

The management decision process begins with the original decision to acquire the FMS. The set of machine tools considered necessary to produce the planned production, the supporting MHS, and the computer control mechanisms are specified and acquired. Once it is in operation, a continuous series of decisions is necessary to control the FMS and manufacture the parts for which it was acquired.

These decisions take place under two essentially different operating modes, management involvement and automated operation. The management involvement mode consists of two different types of interaction with the system. Management interacts with the FMS to improve its operation by modifying the control parameters used in internal decision making; the computer gives utilization and production information as a basis for such changes. Management is also given assistance by the operating system in coping with operating environment changes and in resolving unplanned events and situations, such as a MHS failure. The software to handle error detection and correction constituted approximately 40% of the total code for the FMS installed by Kearney and Trecker at Allis-Chalmers (Reference 3), a significant part of the total software effort.

During normal FMS automated operation (the second mode), a hierarchical decision structure controls the system based on current system status and management's operating strategy. At the top of this structure are the process control decisions on the parts to be produced (the dispatching function). At the next lower level are the decisions on the assignment of system resources. The lowest level decisions involve the MHS choices of cart movements and the order of workpiece processing at stations. The details of these decisions are given in Reference 4.

The above describes the day-to-day control system. In the longer run, management may wish to modify the overall FMS capacity by changing the set of work stations in the system, i.e., modifying the FMS components. This modification would have capital implications, and the time frame for implementation would be measured in months. Furthermore, it is doubtful that such a decision would be made strictly as a manufacturing one, that is, without consideration of alternative uses of capital, internal interest rates, and capital availability.

CONTROL PHILOSOPHY

Ashby (Reference 5) has provided the Law of Requisite Variety, which permits one to make precise statements about the inability of a control mechanism to provide the desired control over a specific system. Unfortunately, there are problems in measuring variety in actual systems, and there is no indication as to how one should actually go about implementing this control. Tocher (Reference 6) lists the "necessary conditions for a precise control problem to exist:

1. There must be a specified set of times at which a choice of action is possible.

2. At each such time, there must be a specified set of actions from which to choose.

3. A model must exist which can predict the future history of the system under every possible choice.

4. There must be a criterion or objective on which the choice of action is based by a comparison of predicted behavior of the system with the objective."

The real issue, then, is determining a method for choosing the appropriate action at each action time for every system state. Tocher points out that automatic control really consists of choosing an algorithm and then implementing it. "This prompts the unfamiliar view that automatic control is not the example par excellance of on-line control: on the contrary, it is off-line control automatically implemented." The large number of possibilities for system status and the requirements imposed by multiple, possibly non-linear objectives make mathematically precise solutions difficult, if not impossible.

The method adopted was to consider, at each action time, each of the several objectives independently. For each objective, an algorithm was devised that calculated a value for each choice of action based on that single objective. This calculated value could then be used to rank the actions if there were only one objective. Since there were multiple objectives, a weighting parameter was assigned to each and used in conjunction with the action value for that objective to calculate the utility of choosing that action. The actions were then ranked by utility and the best one chosen.

As previously noted, one must have a model which can predict the consequences of the particular action chosen. This model is necessary for both the development of the algorithms, calculating action values, and the choice of the weighting parameters. In complex, dynamic systems it is often very difficult to isolate the impact of a particular decision as it may influence many future decisions and the operating environment. It was quickly determined that individual models of the separate decisions would be of little or no value. Consequently, the approach adopted was the development of a generalized, dynamic model of FMS's (Reference 7) which included all instances of decision-making requirements and the ability to display the resulting system operation. Using this model, various algorithms and weighting parameters were tested and evaluated. Actually, the model proved to be of great value in the development of FMS concepts, the configuration design of actual systems, and the fine tuning of systems (Reference 8).

HIERARCHICAL CONTROL STRUCTURE

The control structure includes both automatic and adaptive control mechanisms in a five-level hierarchy as shown in Figure 3. At the lowest level are automatic control algorithms which make the second-by-second operating decisions, with the adaptive control loops making decisions over increasingly longer time horizons. Automatic control algorithms which are most frequently invoked are labeled Operating Tactics; they make the MHS and work station decisions. These decisions are based upon current system status and the current Operating Strategy. The algorithms are structured as outlined in a previous section. The consequences of these decisions change the status of the system and influence subsequent decisions. In general, these algorithms are themselves parameterized as are the methods used to measure the values upon which they operate. For instance, the backlog of work at a station may be measured either by hours of work or by number of assigned tasks, or a linear combination of the two.

At the next higher level, Operating Strategy, the decisions related to the dispatching of parts into the FMS are controlled. These decisions are invoked by such events as the completion of a workpiece, the arrival of work at the system, or the availability of a pallet and are part of the ongoing operation. Their frequency of occurrence is much less than that of the Operating Tactics. The Dispatching Decisions depend upon the production rate of the system, which is the integration of system activity over time and involves an inherent delay in the information flow. Considerable effort was devoted to determining how best to measure the actual production rate. Basically, the algorithms determine the set of feasible actions and, if there is more than one in the set, rank them according to the current Operating Strategy. Together with the Operating Tactics, the Dispatching Decisions constitute the basic elements for on-line control of the FMS.

The current Operating Strategy uses the management-determined Weighting Parameters and System Operating Objectives as the basis of control. The System Operating Objectives include the set of resources available and the Management Production Plan, which is the desired production rate for each part-kind, i.e., the total work to be done by the FMS. The Weighting Parameters are used to determine the trade-offs between conflicting objectives of resource utilization. Actually, these resource utilization objectives are at a lower level than is the prime objective of production. The resolution between these levels of objectives is achieved through adaptive control, as described later. The Operating Strategy, the error detection-correction software, and human interface software constitute the basic online functions which drive the FMS without human control functions for normal operation. In fact, most FMS systems require a high degree of human intervention because of failures in both hardware and software, human error, maintenance, and changes in operating environment.

The algorithms and Weighting Parameters were developed using the previously mentioned FMS model. All models are imperfect, and the one used was no exception. Thus it was necessary to provide management with a higher level control mechanism which could be easily understood and could correct short-run deficiencies in system operation. Note that in a longer time horizon, the decision algorithms could be replaced. In the short run, management can quickly influence system operation by changing the Weighting Parameters. For example, a fluctuation in work load might result in a temporary heavy load on work stations and a reduction in MHS requirements, as would occur if the average station cycle time were increased. If this situation were recognized, i.e. from Resource Utilization, management might increase the emphasis given the now relatively scarce work stations (with respect to the MHS) by increasing their Weighting Parameter. From the point of change on, decisions would reflect this modification and the tendency would be toward optimal work station utilization. In fact, management could choose weights such that all decisions reflected only work station optimization (or any other objective).

It is important to note that this and higher level adaptive control depends upon human intervention. Conditions requiring correction must be detected, appropriate modifications determined, and decisions implemented.

At the next higher level of control, management may change its Management Production Plan. One can easily conceive of a situation in which the requirements of a production plan, even one under optimal control, could not be met or the system resources were poorly utilized. At this level, management might wish to modify its plan, for instance, by introducing a new part that makes heavy use of a work station with low utilization. These decisions usually take place over a longer time horizon, perhaps weeks.

At the highest level, management can change the FMS components. The situation commonly considered is one needing additional capacity. In FMS's, a work station that is no longer required can be removed from the system. These decisions, however, are obviously of a longer time horizon, say months, and usually involve corporate considerations.

Perhaps the most interesting aspect of this control structure is that it has been used with success, as the basis for the control of FMS's of widely varying designs and operating environments. For instance, the FMS installed at Allis-Chalmers has 13 work stations and a complex MHS (Figure 2) while the North American Rockwell system (Figure 4) has 9 stations and a basic loop with loading siding MHS. The complexity of the control problem and the relative success of implementations suggest that this approach may be of wider general use.

SUMMARY

FMS's are complex, dynamic systems whose control poses a difficult task. The FMS components have been described and the decisions necessary for their operation outlined. The basic philosophy of control has been considered and its implementation in a hierarchical structure illustrated, using both automatic and adaptive controls. Basic control algorithms and control parameters were developed using a generalized, dynamic FMS model. It is suggested that this general approach to the control of complex systems may be applicable to many situations and operating environments.

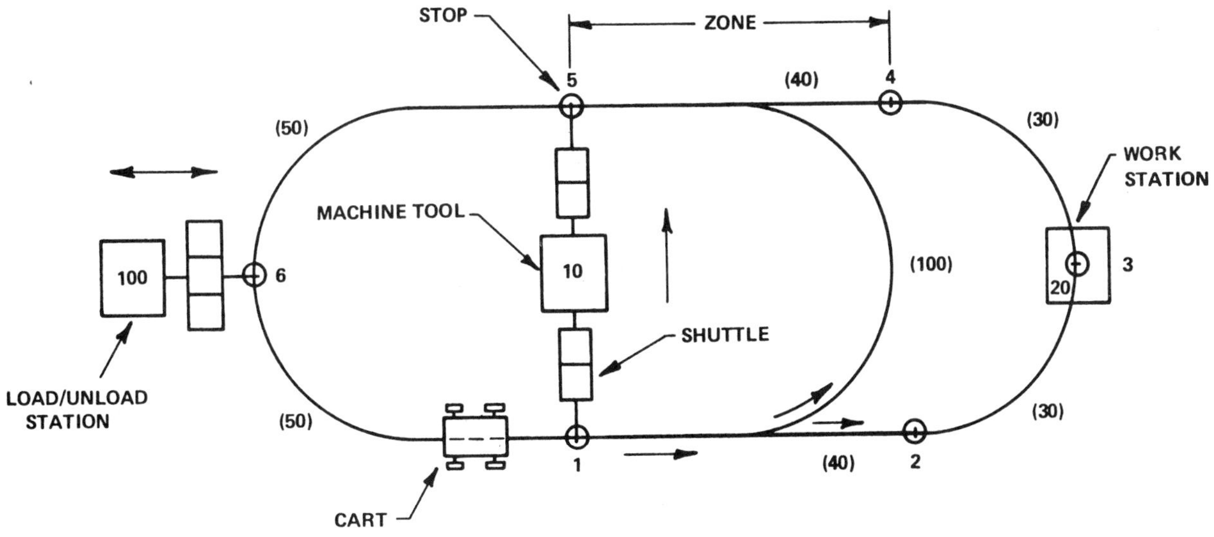

SIMPLE FMS EXAMPLE

(SHOWING BASIC SYSTEM ELEMENTS)

Figure 1

ALLIS-CHALMERS FLEXIBLE MANUFACTURING SYSTEM
PLANT LAYOUT
PRODUCTION: 25 TRACTORS PER DAY

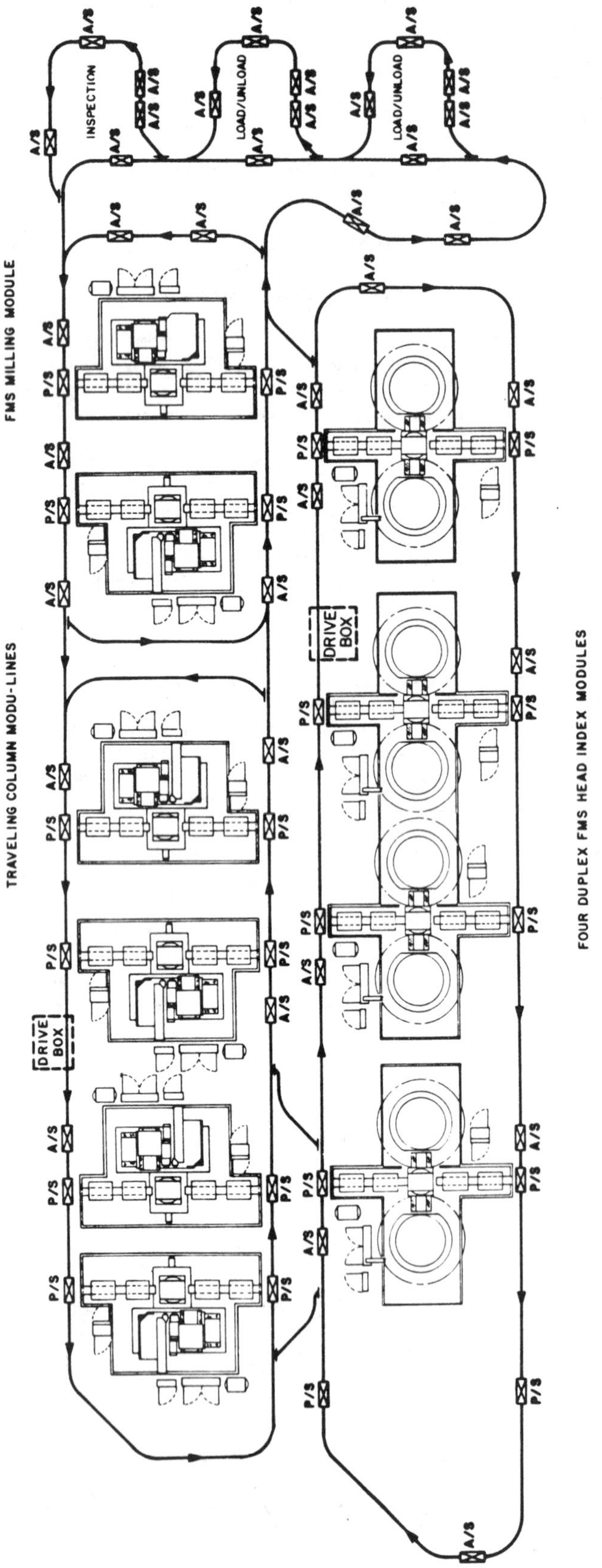

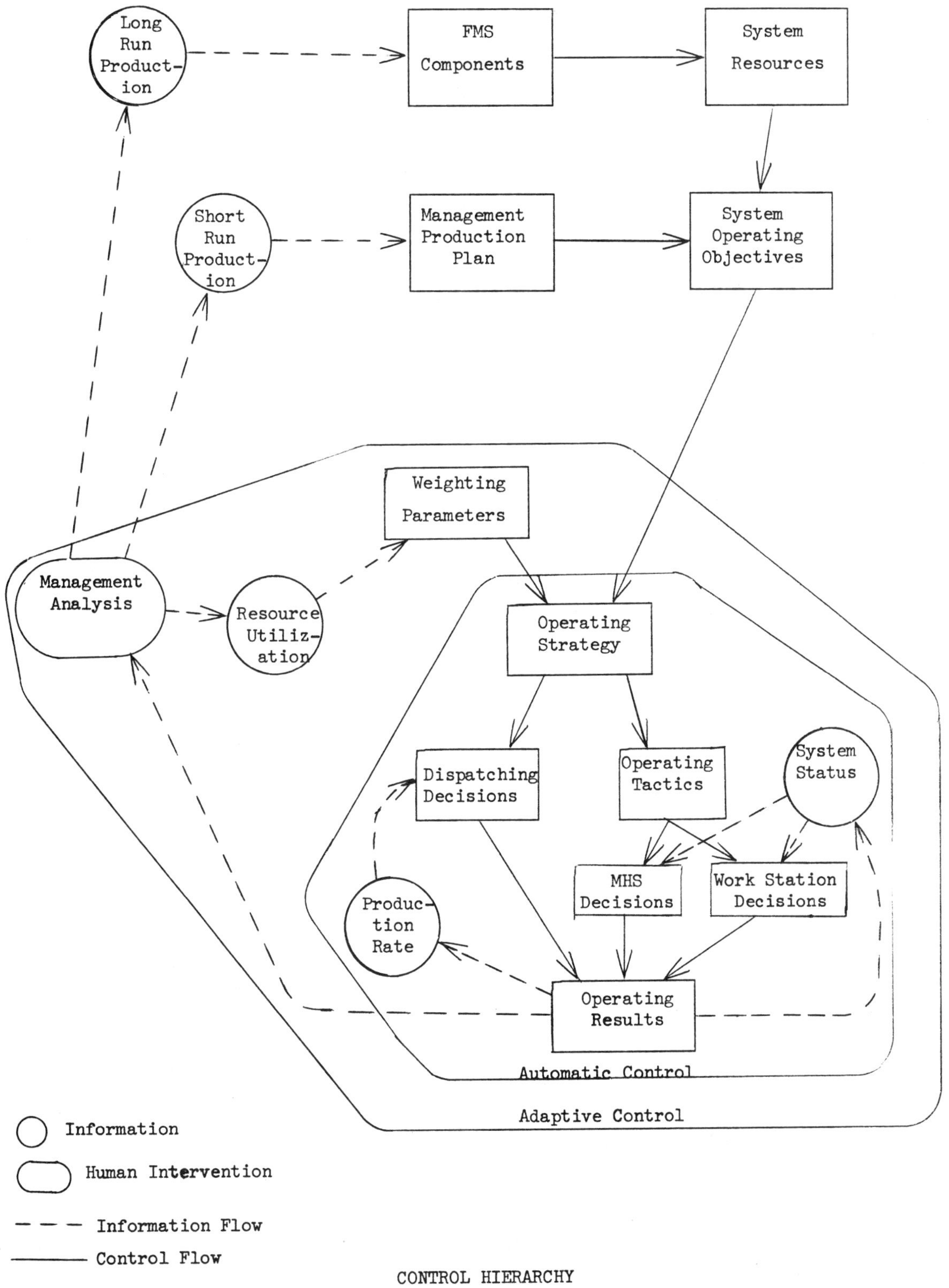

CONTROL HIERARCHY

Figure 3

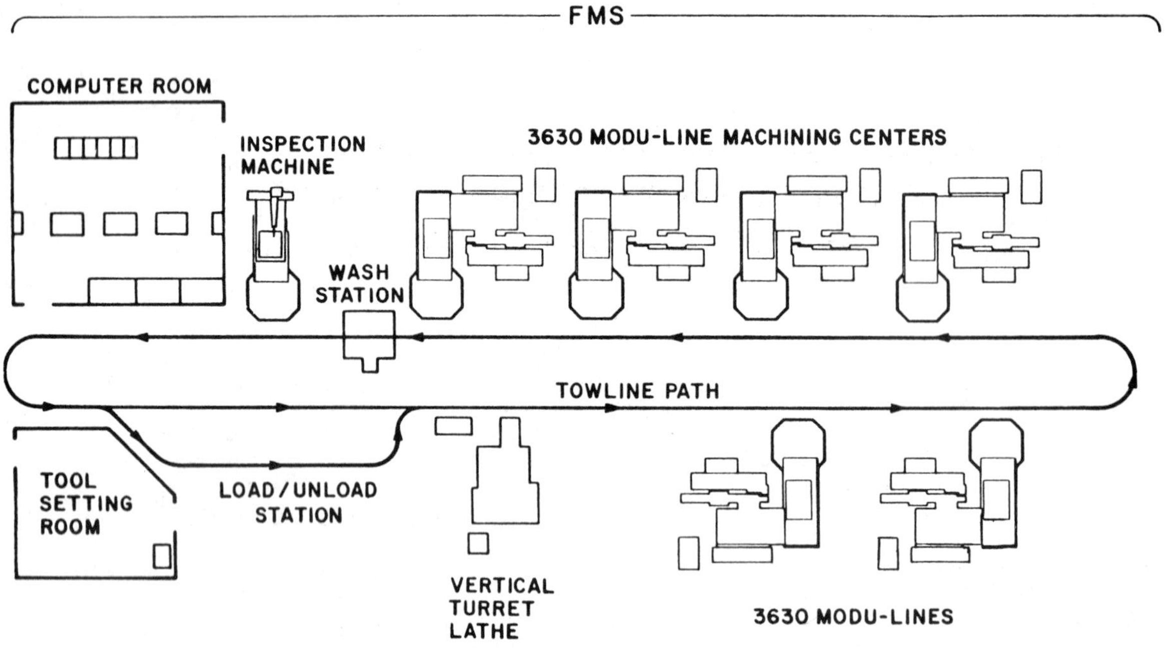

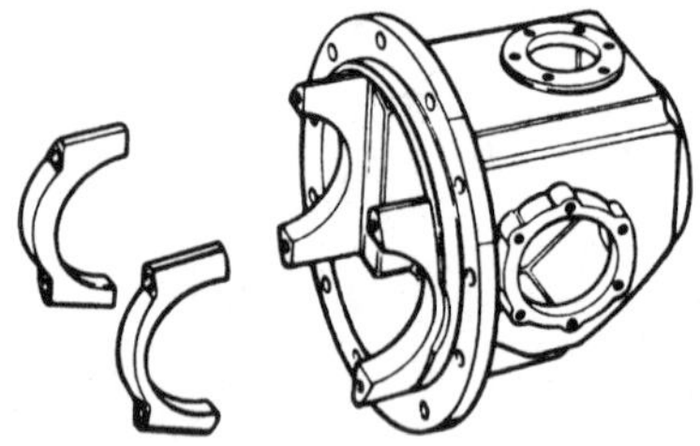

DIFFERENTIAL CARRIER PRODUCTION

THE PRODUCTION MIX:

31 Different Differential Carriers
31 Part Numbers totaling an annual output of 24,000, ranging in volume of from 4 to 2100 pieces per part number.

PROCESSING METHOD: Random.

8 Part Numbers can be processed randomly at one time.

Figure 4

REFERENCES

(1) Manufacturing technology--a changing challenge to improved productivity, Report to the Congress by the Comptroller General of the United States, LCD-75-426, 3 June 1976.

(2) N. H. Cook, Computer-managed parts manufacturing, Scientific American 21-29 (February 1975).

(3) Robert M. Olker, Application of the mini-computer to control a large scale flexible machining system, Society of Manufacturing Engineers Technical Paper MS75-441, Dearborn, Michigan.

(4) G. K. Hutchinson, The control of flexible manufacturing systems via DSS, University of Wisconsin School of Business Working Paper (1976).

(5) Ashby, W. Ross (1956), An Introduction to Cybernetics, Chapman Hall, New York.

(6) K. D. Tocher, Control, Operational Research Quarterly 21, 2.

(7) G. K. Hutchinson and J. J. Hughes, A generalized model of flexible manufacturing systems, Proceedings-Workshop on Multi-Station, Digitally Controlled Manufacturing Systems, University of Wisconsin-Milwaukee (1977).

(8) J. J. Hughes, G. K. Hutchinson, and K. E. Gross, Flexible manufacturing systems for improved mid-volume productivity, Proceedings of the Third Annual AIIE Systems Engineering Conference, November 1975. Reprinted in Understanding Manufacturing Systems: Volume I, Kearney and Trecker Corporation, Milwaukee (1976).

REMOVING BARRIERS TO THE APPLICATION OF AUTOMATION IN DISCRETE PART BATCH MANUFACTURING*

J.M. Evans

Office of Developmental Automation and Control Technology, Institute for Computer Sciences and Technology, National Bureau of Standards

INTRODUCTION

The National Bureau of Standards program in automation technology focuses NBS resources on developing a basic understanding of the technology of computer based automation and then develops those standards and guidelines that will stimulate the diffusion of this technology to enhance productivity in both Government and industry.

Specifically this program attempts:

1) to provide standards for the interfaces between modular components of computer-aided manufacturing systems,

2) to provide standards for the computer control languages used to program automation systems.

3) to provide performance measures for specification and procurement of robots and numerically controlled machine tools, and

4) to carry out research in dynamic measurement and computer control for computer based automation systems.

The primary barrier to the use of computer based automation technology to increase productivity is the high cost of that technology. This barrier has been identified by the U.S. General Accounting Office and confirmed by U.S. industry. This paper will explore the strategy of the NBS program in encouraging the use of information control technologies and standards concerning these technologies to reduce costs in automatic systems for discrete part batch manufacturing operations.

AUTOMATION AND PRODUCTIVITY

There are three different types of manufacturing industries, each with a distinct and identifiable process technology, that is, a distinctly different way of manufacturing their products. Continuous process industries such as petroleum, chemicals, and steel account for 47% of the value added in the manufacturing sector of the US economy. These industries operate on a continuous flow of material and are already highly automated. Mass production techniques for discrete part manufacturing pioneered by US industry are also highly automated. These two segments of manufacturing industry account for approximately 60% of the total value added.

The remaining 40% of manufacturing is in the batch industries. In batch production, goods are made in small lots or batches on general purpose machine tools with labor intensive techniques. It is this segment of the manufacturing industry which contains the potential for major gains in productivity through the use of computer control technology.

About 25 years ago a new technology appeared for discrete part batch manufacturing, based on the application of a computer to control the motions of a general purpose machine tool. This new machine tool was called a numerically controlled machine tool, or NC machine tool, because the motions of the tool are controlled by numbers on a paper tape or in the memory of a control computer. One can change the part being manufactured by simply changing the part program, that is, the numbers on the tape or in the computer memory. NC machine tools typically increase productivity by a factor of 3 or more, that is 300%.

This experience of increasing productivity is borne out by our experience in our own instruments shops at NBS, where we have four NC machine tools and one NC inspection machine in operation. For example, we manufacture metric weights that are used as references by state government weights and measures authorities. A full set of these weights made with NC machine tools costs $700, one third the cost of a set made with conventional tools. Again, a mirror mount is a typical low volume product made in our shops. When made with NC, a mirror mount costs $62. When made manually, it used to cost over $200. These figures are typical of industry experience with numerical control.

INFORMATION CONTROL IN NC MACHINE TOOLS

The reason for this increase in productivity is the speed with which a computer can process the information concerned with the control of the machine tool.

The computer can provide bandwidths of hundreds of cycles per second on each tool axis and can coordinate the motion of up to six axes in simultaneous motion. In contrast, a machinist can control only one axis at a time. This speed of operation and multiaxis control explain the increased productivity of NC machines.

Hence, NC machines are using speed of information processing in machine control to increase productivity. However, the full potential of this concept has not been fully explored. Specifically, NC tools still use mechanical precision of the ways and leads screws to achieve positioning accuracy. The actual position of the cutting tool is not sensed and controlled by the computer. Instead, the angular position of each lead screw is controlled. This requires unnecessarily expensive precision mechanical systems. In fact, we believe that new concepts of machine design based on on-line dynamic measurement rather than on mechanical precision can result in a new generation of automated manufacturing machines that will cost 1/2 to 1/4 as much as equivalent conventional NC tools.

When using a conventional manual machine tool, the machinist uses the dials on the ends of the lead screws to measure the position of the tool. He knows that the readings on these dials are truly accurate only over relatively short distances and so he resorts to in-process gaging with an instrument, such as a micrometer, to measure the dimensions of the part. Accuracy is achieved by successive approximation, and a skilled machinist can product a part to the accuracy to which he can measure that part.

An NC tool control also gets feedback on the position of the tool from the angular position of the lead screw. However, there is no in-process gaging of the part. Therefore, an NC tool must operate precisely throughout its entire working volume. Hence, NC tool designs require high precision ways and precision ball screws, which of course makes them more expensive.

High precision machine tools, such as jig borers and inspection machines, are truly hand built. Surfaces and ways are hand scraped with diamond tipped chisels, resulting in very expensive tools.

NBS TECHNICAL PROJECTS RELATED TO NC TOOLS

We are investigating the replacement of this expensive mechanical precision with dynamic measurement and calibration techniques to allow better use of the capabilities of real time computer control. We believe that this strategy offers opportunities for both increased precision and reduced costs.

The Three Dimensional Metrology work at NBS has proved that error maps can be made for machine tools and that these maps can be used for calibration. This work has been done with a conventional inspection machine used for calibration services at NBS. Our work has shown that machine errors can be measured and that these errors are repeatable and hence can be calibrated out with a computer. Using computer calibrations, the absolute positioning accuracy of our inspection machine is being improved by a factor of 100, down to 1/4 micron. Machine tool calibration to 3 to 5 microns should be routinely possible.

Such calibration techniques can remove static inaccuracies of the tool such as non-orthogonality of the axes, straightness errors in the ways, and internal static load deformations.

Dynamic errors of a machine tool include thermal distortion and dynamic load (cutting force) distortion. By measuring the temperature of the tool frame at several points, the thermal state of the tool can be measured and dimensional distortions can be calculated for control purposes.

Data developed at the Lawrence Livermore Laboratories in the United States has shown that simple lumped parameter models of frame expansion can match observed thermal distortion behavior of a large machine tool to within 5 microns, the static accuracy of the tool, during expansions of up to 25 microns or more. More sophisticated models should do even better.

Dynamic load distortions can be calibrated and removed from the machine if the dynamic cutting forces can be measured. This is possible once the sensors for an adaptive control system are installed. Current adaptive control systems control feeds or speeds to maintain constant cutting forces or torques, but the same sensory data could be used by the control computer to calculate and correct for frame distortions caused by those forces or torques.

Thus the effective measurement of process variables in real time and the use of this information by the control system can improve the performance of machine tools and inspection machines. In fact, significant improvements in performance and reductions in cost are possible through the effective use of information control. In turn, this will result in removing the barrier of high costs and help industries use this technology to improve productivity.

ROBOT SYSTEMS

Exactly the same technologies of dynamic measurement and computer control can be applied to robot systems for materials handling and assembly operations. Of particular interest to NBS is the use of robots to load and unload parts from an NC machine tool. NBS feels that general purpose, programmable robots should be dedicated to materials handling in conjunction with NC tools as the basic unit of automated factory of the future. Experiments in Japan, Germany, Norway, and the United States have explored this concept. There are two basic problems here. The first is an effective off-line programming capability for small lot manufacturing. The other problem is the development of sensors to detect the slight misalignment of parts that are uneconomical to control in a batch manufacturing environment.

Effective off-line programming for a robot should be similar to that for an NC machine tool. This is essential for coping with small lots or batches of parts in a job shop environment.

The computer control system needs information on part location if the robot is to successfully grasp the part. To do this the location of the part must be accurately determined by mechanical systems such as jigs, fixtures, pallets or feeding devices, or it must be measured with a sensor system. NBS has successfully investigated proximity and touch sensing as means to detect small offsets or misalignments of parts that might be encountered in a factory. The scale of these errors is in the centimeter or few degree range. General vision systems will probably find use in the near future in automated inspection systems rather than in part location applications.

NBS projects in robot systems have encompassed this sensor work, developing performance data on the efficiency of various levels of computer control, developing techniques for faster off-line programming of robots, and encouraging robot manufacturers to adopt the same standard communications interface as an NC machine tool (an EIA RS-232-C interface) to expedite integration of robots into total computer aided manufacturing systems.

THE NEED FOR STANDARDS

The use of individual computer controlled machine tools, robots, and automated inspection systems can cause increases in productivity of several hundred percent. When these technologies are combined in integrated computer aided manufacturing systems, with hierarchies of computers used in the control of individual machines up to the overall management functions, the resulting productivity increases can reach 1000 to 2000 per cent or even more.

The key to achieving these revolutionary increases in productivity will be the development of a common basic architecture of computer aided manufacturing and the use of interface standards to implement that system architecture. In this way various modular components of computer aided manufacturing systems can be obtained from different competitive manufacturers and integrated into a total system with a minimum of special engineering and software development. The use of effective interface standards in no way impedes or limits the creativity of engineers and computer programmers in the creation of individual application modules, but it does require the control of the information flow between modules to insure compatibility.

We can now create systems where a man can sit at a graphics terminal, and design a part. The data base that is created in the computer describing that part can then be used to produce drawings on computer controlled drafting boards and to produce the computer programs or punched tapes for operating the machine tools. Eventually, design, process planning, and scheduling and control will all be integrated together with machine tool control systems in an overall integrated system.

Recently, concepts of CAM have been based around the idea of a centralized data base, with its own data base manager, maintaining all of the data files for the various applications programs in an application independent format. This allows maximum flexibility in writing and integrating various CAM applications programs into an integrated system, However, fourth generation computer systems are likely to be highly distributed, with both distributed processors and distributed data bases. The question of interface standards that are required to integrate various modular components of CAM systems, both hardware and software, now becomes a crucial issue in the development and widespread implementation of CAM systems. It is this area that is of fundamental interest to our program at the National Bureau of Standards.

The use of effective interface standards to control the creation of integrated systems can reduce total system costs by at least a factor of two, according to informal industry estimates. More importantly, the marginal economics of developing additional modules will be easier to justify in a systems context. No country can afford to reinvent the same technology over and over within each individual company when the development cost for a total integrated CAM system can run into the tens of millions of dollars.

There are many NBS projects that address this interface area. Specifically, the Institute for Computer Sciences and Technology of NBS is authorized by Congress to develop standards for the Federal procurement and use of computer systems. This includes many standards relevant to the interfaces of computer aided manufacturing systems. In particular, standards on higher level programming languages, including FORTRAN and COBOL, standards on Data Base Management Systems, standards on the interfaces between computers and peripheral equipment, and the standards on communications interfaces and communications codes and protocols are all necessary to creating integrated computer aided manufacturing systems with components procured from different suppliers.

SUMMARY

The use of information in dynamic control systems can improve productivity in individual machine tools and in integrated computer aided manufacturing systems by hundreds or even thousands of percents. NBS is carrying out research in the technologies of dynamic measurement and computer control and is developing effective standards that will reduce cost barriers and thus help Government and industry achieve those potential increases in productivity.

AUTOMATION RESERCH IN GERMANY AND ITS ROLE REGARDING NATIONAL PRODUCTIVITY

Ulrich Rembold* and Ingward Bey**

**Institut für Informatik III, Universität Karlsruhe, Zirkel 2, D-7500 Karlsruhe, Federal Republic of Germany*
***Gesellschaft für Kernforschung mbH, Projekt PDV, Postfach 3640, D-7500 Karlsruhe - 1, Federal Republic of Germany*

1. Introduction

The Federal Republic of Germany has a population of 61.7 million people. The nation has to import most of its raw materials and a large portion of its food supply. To pay for these imports the economy depends heavily on manufacturing. Approximately 60 % of the GNP is being produced by technical processes. The manufacturing sector employs a total of 13.215.000 people. The mechanical engineering and electrotechnical industries are the two largest industrial groups in the manufacturing sector, they have an estimated total of 2.3 million employees.

In order to be able to maintain and increase its present standard of living the country must export goods with high technological contents. This means that raw materials and energy has to be imported and converted by technological know-how into products which can compete favorably on the international market. Such a goal can only be achieved by employing the most modern technologies and by training a workforce which is able to apply these technologies in an efficient manner.
The country can not afford to depend in Key-technologies on other nations, otherwise it will have no competitive advantage. This very critical aspect has been viewed by the German Government with great concern for many years. Several significant research programs were started in areas which appeared to be vital to increase the productivity of the German industry and to improve the working environment of the workforce. Most of the projects were joint endeavors, with universities, research institutes and German industry. There are presently three major programs in which work is performed on automation research. These are:

- Data Processing
- Production Technology
- Huminization of the Working
- Environment

The first 2 programs are almost entirely devoted to automation, whereas in the last program only a smaller part concerns itself with this subject. This paper will give an overview of the programs, their present goals and achievements.

2. HISTORICAL DEVELOPMENT AND DESCRIPTION OF PROGRAMS

2.1 DATA PROCESSING

The Federal Government of Germany started in 1967 a series of a program to advance the data processing technology for business, industrial and medical applications. This program was considered to be of great national importance in order to improve the productivity of industry and to help the country to be more competetive on the world market. The data processing program consists of 3 phases.

Phase	1	2	3
Year	1967-1970	1971-1975	1976-1979
Funding in Mill. of Germ. Marks	353	1.811	1.75

2.1.1 PHASE 1

The largest portion of the fund for this phase was used to develop data processing systems and to perform research work on data processing technology, computer structures and on programming languages.

2.1.2 PHASE 2

This phase greatly extended the scope of the first phase. It was considered necessary to set up good training facilities for data processing personnel, to further data processing applications and to do industrial research and development.
The fund was distributed as follows:

Supported Activity	% of Total Fund
Universities and DP Training	21
DP Applications	31
Industrial Research & Development	40
Special Programs	8
Total	100

PROGRAM GOALS

The following goals were to be achieved under the second phase:

- Improve and broaden applications of data processing in business and science as an instrument of automation and increased productivity.

- Automate and improve the productivity of the service of the public offices with the help of data processing equipment.

- Build up DP know-how in order to be able to master it as a key-technology.

- Obtain a balanced competetive situation on the expanding DP market.

Research and development work of new applications was to be supported to enhance the system and application know-how. Thus data processing would serve the public and private institutions as a planning, decision making and automation tool. Support was to be given in the following areas:

- Computer supported information processing, planning and decision making.

- Data processing in education.

- Data processing in medicine.

- Computer aided design and development.

- Application of process control computers.

Pilote projects were to be realized in the public domain in areas of particular interest to the administration.

German industry was to be supported to be able to build and market own computers. Pre-financing of rental equipment was to be facilitated by considering the financial participation of the Federal Government in the rental business. Particular interest was to be given to standardize software and hardware. The development of large computers was to be considered of national interest. Therefore it was necessary to support on-going work to build general purpose and process control computers.

PROGRAM RESULTS

The intermediate results of the programs can be summarized as follows:

- A line of large Siemens 7700 series computers was developed.

- Lines of Siemens 300 and AEG 80 process control computers were developed.

- The large scientific computer TR 440 was developed. However, it was economically not justifiable.

- Successful projects were started in the medical field.

- Several pilote installations were installed in public offices as computer aided planning, decision making and automation tool.

- Educational facilities were advanced to a point where they were selfsufficient.

2.1.3 PHASE 3

In the third phase the support of the development of data processing applications and data processing equipment will be continued until the end of 1979. More emphasis will be given on small computers and peripheral equipment. The budgetted funds will be applied as follows:

Supported Activity of computer applications	% of Total Fund
Information Systems	29.4
Health	25.1
Computer Aided Design	11.7
Process Computer Control	18.8
Total	100

PROGRAM GOALS

For the support of computer applications the following general goals have been set:

- Support directly the work of individual job functions by utilizing new possibilities of decentralized and application oriented data processing methods.
- Create better communication between people in their work areas and between their supporting data processing systems.
- Facilitate and improve software development systems.
- Facilitate and improve software development aids.

The main points can be further detailed:

- Development of software for data banks, including data protection, data security, distributed datafiles and investigate problems of compatability.
- Development of integrated information systems to support planning, scheduling and decision making activities in business and public administration. This also includes aids to facilitate access and communication with such systems.
- To develop and prove out DP applications for diagnostic, therapeutic and managerial tasks in health care.
- Development of new soft and hardware to apply DP in education.
- Development of methods, procedures programs and equipment for computer aided design.
- Development of procedures, programs and equipment for process control by computers.
- Development of communication equipment and programs to facilitate computer to computer communication and remote programming. This includes concepts of data security and data protection in distributed computer networks.
- Development of programming aids for computers and methods for program portability.
- Development of programs and equipment to process optical, acoustical and graphical pattern.

In the area of computer development the main goal is to create a healthy and competetive industry which is able to:

- Compete on the markets with a broad product line of computers, except for very large units.
- Be self-sufficient to produce and market for business and the public domain all necessary computer hardware.
- Avail highly qualified jobs.
- Obtain knowledge and capabilities to interconnect data processing with communication technology and other techniques to process information.
- Be active as an influential partner on the world market and on international cooperation.

Strong emphasis is given to the following development tasks:

- Computers, peripheral equipment & system software.
- Software for data communication.
- Subsystems for the connection of terminals and peripheral equipment.
- Language translators.
- Obtain system compatibility.
- Test and maintenance software.
- Supporting software.

2.1.4 MODERNIZATION OF MANUFACTURING TECHNOLOGY

Of particular interest is the part of phase 3 which concerns itself with the modernization of manufacturing technology. Here an effort is made to improve the entire manufacturing process form the design stage to the assembly. The program covers two parts. These are computer aided development and manufacturing (CAD/CAM) and process control by computer. Both of these programs will be covered in more detail:

COMPUTER-AIDED DEVELOPMENT, DESIGN AND MANUFACTURING

- Development of automated planning, design and calculation methods for the designer in order to reduce duplicating routine work. This effort includes customer order processing, bill of material processing, production scheduling and accounting.
- Design of modular programs for all phases of the production of a series of selected products.
- Production testing of presently available software systems for technical applications and development of additional programming modules for selected purposes.
- Development of different sizes of CAD/CAM computer systems for different applications and different sizes of manufacturing organizations.

PROCESS CONTROL BY COMPUTER

- Development of general aids for computer controlled manufacturing processes.
- Development of new concepts of improved control panels and control systems to aid personnel to control processes.
- Development of process control computer compatible processors, measuring instruments, controllers and signal transmission systems, which are capable of doing a limited amount of signal processing.
- Development of network structures and decentralized processors, memory and data processing peripherals, including data transmission procedures and standard interfaces.
- Development of hierarchical programming systems, programming aids and program testing aids, including a standardized programming language for technical processes. Also to find methods for the implementation of the languages on different types of computers and decentralized computer networks.
- Development of methods and procedures to find algorithms to optimize technical processes.
- Development of simulation methods for entire installations, processes and subprocesses.
- Development of general methods to design completely functional and economical computer controlled processes, including the construction and testing of actual installation for selected processes. (Trafic control, electrical utilities, steel making, chemical processes, manufacturing installations)

All developments have to be done in close cooperation with computer manufacturers, computer users, manufacturers of processing equipment, software houses and research institutes.

2.2 PRODCUTION TECHNOLOGY

Presently a major national program is being devised to support research work on new production technologies. It is aimed at the discrete manufacturing processes in particular at equipment for capital investment. Latter equipment contributes largely to the gross national product of Germany.

The goal of this project is to improve the manufacturing technology, whereby new fields such as information processing are to be included. Also a search has to be made for alternate processes. To increase the overall efficiency of the manufacturing organization, a total system approach will be taken, where material flow, material handling, information flow etc. will be included.

This program is the youngest one to be considered here. It is in preparation since 1975 and will start officially at 1.1.1978 with a funding budget of about 10 million DM. Funds will reach 25 million DM in 1980.

The Production Technology Program can be considered as a "child" of the Humanization Program, which will be discussed later. Several projects which are presently being funded will be separated next year and put into the PTP. Some of these projects, which are being funded in 1977 are as follows:

- Flexible Manufacturing System for gear parts batch production.
- Material handling aids for parts separation, selection, classification, tagging and sorting.
- Powder metallurgy process to replace normal castings and forgings.

- A search for alternate methods to remove oxides from metals by grinding. New milling methods are investigated which generate less dust and noise.

- Investigation of substitution materials for metal, such as plastics.

Although the definition phase of the program is not yet completed it is possible to give some ideas of its scope:

- The program will concentrate on discrete parts manufacturing and parts handling, especially on processes related to capital goods production. This is because of their impact on German gross national product and German export figures.

- The funding of projects in this area will give an opportunity for small and medium companies to develop better and marketable products.

- Within the program efforts will be made to develop new manufacturing methods whereby new technologies such as information control will be applied.

- Projects to be funded must consider aspects related to working environment and their influences on man, i.e. qualification problems, salary, working time, working conditions, man-machine-interrelationship.

A full description of the program will be available at the end of 1977.

2.3 HUMANIZATION OF THE WORKING ENVIRONMENT

2.3.1 HISTORICAL DEVELOPMENT

In 1972 a law was enacted in which on-going efforts to humanize the working environment were to be supplemented by research and development work. Presently known methods to improve the working environment had to be developed further and ways and means had to be found to disseminate the scientific know-how in the administration and management of business organizations. Furthermore, new humane manufacturing technologies had to be developed and pilot operations were to be set up to demonstrate good examples of business organizations and pleasant work areas. To accomplish this task it was required that scientific know-how, employers and employees had to be brought together. Funds were to be provided by the Government and were to be used on joint application oriented projects. The funding was planned as follows:

Year	1974	1975	1976	1977-	--1980
Funding in Million German Marks	9	30	45	70	150 estimated

2.3.2 GOAL OF THE PROGRAM

The protection of the worker in his working environment has been of great concern to the government and private organizations for a long time. However, the great number of accidents and the amount of health damage caused by manufacturing equipment, unproperly designed work areas and manufacturing processes make further improvements necessary. In highly developed industrial and service organizations man is subjected to additional hazards of physical and psychological nature.

Humanization efforts should not only try to reduce stresses but they should also render opportunities for people to be selfconfident and creative. It clearly can be noticed that boring jobs with little creativity and responsibility are in declining demand. The major goal of this program is to adapt the working environment to the needs of the worker. To find practical solutions to this problem should be the target of this research and development effort.

Not all individual goals of this program will lead to additional automation. However, most of the projects will try to create a working environment which will enhance the productivity of manufacturing and business organizations.

2.3.3 STRUCTURE OF THE PROGRAM

The Program can be divided into the following four areas.

a. COLLECTION OF DATA ON SAFETY ASPECTS

To provide information to increase the safety of machines, manufacturing equipment and work areas, including the establishment of minimum safety tolerances and guide rules for safety measures. There are more fundamental data needed to improve the working conditions, and to establish well thought-of governmental and private rules and regulations. It is necessary to establish new laws, administrative regulations and preventative procedures which will be enforced by safety commissions and trade associations. The hereby gained knowledge may also serve as important information to assist negotiations for wage agreements.

The following additional subjects are to be investigated

- Which of the present criteria to establish maximum physical stresses of workers are outdated?
- In what areas are these criteria uncertain?
- Is there a necessity to establish new measuring techniques and new measuring scales?
- How can physical stresses be quantified?

b. DEVELOPMENT OF NEW MAN ORIENTED TECHNOLOGIES

The introduction of new man oriented technologies is necessary to improve intolerable working conditions. First it is necessary to study the manufacturing processes and tools for which new technologies are needed. This may require the design of new machines, robotic devices, controls and means of transportation. It is also necessary to determine how the innovation time for these technolgies can be shortened. Particular emphasis has to be given to the possibility of eliminating intolerable work places and to find a substitution for these.

Investigations have to be made to find out how new manufacturing processes and products may adversely affect employers. For every new technology it must be determined what contribution it offers to improve the working conditions.

The development of new technologies will make it necessary to introduce new measuring techniques and instruments to determine physical stresses imposed on man.

c. DEVELOPMENT OF MODEL ORGANIZATIONS AND DESIGN OF NEW WORK PLACES

Carefully thought-of models should be devised which demonstrate properly designed work areas. Thereby it is intended to show feasible technical as well as organizational solutions. This means that new management techniques should also be devised.

d. DISSEMINATION AND APPLICATION OF NEW SCIENTIFIC ACHIEVEMENTS

The dissemination and application of new scientific achievements is of particular importance to the practitioners. Here the following questions have to be clarified.

- How can scientific results be effectively disseminated?
- How can already known information be easily found and retrieved.
- What are the barriers of introducing new scientific results, and how can they be easily overcome?

2.3.4 PRESENT PROJECTS

Presently a total of 275 projects have been funded. Grants were given to industry, universities and research institutes. These projects are subdivided as follows:

Group 1: Organizational Measures (58 Projects)

- Improvement of the quality of work of piece rate production, mass production, service, administration and others.

Group 2: Ergometric Measures (157 projects)

- Reduction of physical stresses caused by noise and vibrations, hazardous materials (dust etc.), climate and combined stresses.
- Design of new tools, provisions for medical aid and new means for information processing (light signals etc.).
- Safety improvements for handling of hazardous materials.

Group 3 Technological Measures (44 projects)

- Reduction of physical stresses by providing new technical aids and manufacturing processes and equipment.
- Safety improvements by design of new technical aids and manufacturing processes and equipment

Group 4 Disseminating Measures (16 projects)

Avail handbooks, manuals seminars and professional meeting to reduce hazardous working conditions.

3. PROJECT MANAGEMENT

Since 1971 the Federal Ministry of Research and Technology (BMFT) has established several administrative bodies for the projects within its broad field of research and development activities. These Project Administrations are located in general at well known scientific research centres.

Within the Data Processing Program there are four project administrations:

GENERAL DP APPLICATIONS AND SYSTEM DEVELOPMENT

Gesellschaft für Mathematik und
Datenverarbeitung mbH
Postfach 1240
5205 St. Augustin-Birlinghoven
Telefon: (02241) 14-1

HEALTH CARE

Gesellschaft für Strahlen- und
Umweltforschung mbH
Ingoldstädter Landstr. 1
8042 Neuherberg
Telefon: (089) 3 87 41

EDUCATION

Forschungs- und Entwicklungszentrum für objektivierte Lehr- und Lernverfahren GmbH
Postfach 467
4790 Paderborn
Telefon: (05251) 2 65 69

COMPUTER AIDED DESIGN AND PROCESS COMPUTER CONTROL

Gesellschaft für Kernforschung mbH
Postfach 3640
7500 Karlsruhe
Telefon: (07247) 821

The Humanization Program and the Production Technology Program are administrated by the German Aeronautics and Space Laboratories (DFVLR).

Deutsche Forschungs- und Versuchsanstalt für Luft- und Raumfahrt e.V. (DFVLR)
Projektträger "Humanisierung des Arbeitslebens"
Kölner Straße 64
5300 Bonn-Bad Godesberg
Telefon: (02221) 37 66 61

The main tasks of the project administrations are the definition of program goals, the coordination of funded projects, distribution of funds, organization of expert meetings and dissemination of results. Thus it is intended to increase the efficiency of the funding process and to relieve the Ministry's work. The executive staff of a project administration requires about 3 % of the total funds available for distribution. There has been good experiences with this new kind of program administration.

By using these administrative procedures a good cooperation between universities, industrial companies, manufacturing associations of different disciplines and the federal government has been achieved and this despite of the fact that the staff of the project management often experts a strong influence on selecting and directing the supported projects towards national goals.

Projects may be started generally from unsolicited proposals (in this case being modified in discussion before approval), but also by direct solicitation from the executive staff. Because funds are not sufficient there is a need to select only the most promising and rewarding projects. For industrial companies, the government support level is in general only 50 % of the total project cost.

Project results are shared throughout industry via the report system. In addition, there are special seminars, workshops, conferences or exhibitions. Although in many cases there is a satisfying dissemination of results and application know-how, the need for an even better technology transfer is being recognized by all participants. User associations will play an increasing role to fulfill this need. In cooperation with the project executive staff they could exert in the future a considerable influence on standardization, even in an early stage of product development.

4. FUTURE TRENDS

It is apparent that many programs showed good results. There is a line of well designed business computers and process control computers. The manufacturers of large business computers probably will obtain no further supporting funds after 1978. No firm decision on continuing the support of the development of small business computers and process control computers has been made as yet.

Germany has one of the highest number of computer installations in the world. The different programs helped to contribute to this success. However, most of the installations are at larger companies. There still is a need to support the small and medium sized companies who do not have the means and the personnel to successfully apply computer technology. If the present philosophy on supporting automation efforts of small business will continue it is expected that further funds will be made available after 1979. There will be an endeavor to standardize software and hardware modules for selected applications which are common to a large number of users.

It is felt that the educational institutes are well staffed and equipped to train the rising number of specialists needed within the near future who are able to apply computer technology in industry and business.

There is a trend to coordinate data processing efforts between different European countries. The European Community has drafted a program to support computer and peripheral equipment manufacturers as well as the development of electronic components. This effort will include standardization of software and measures to increase software portability. The starting date of the 5 year program is planned for 1977. About 100 million Dollars will be spent.

Literature:

"Zweites Datenverarbeitungsprogramm der Bundesregierung"
Der Bundesminister für Bildung und Wissenschaft, Printed: Bonner Universitäts-Buchdruckerei, Bonn 1971

"Drittes Datenverarbeitungsprogramm der Bundesregierung,1976-1979",
Der Bundesminister für Forschung und Technologie, Printed: Bonner Universitäts-Buchdruckerei, ISBN 3-88135-007-1, 1976.

Statusbericht "Humanisierung des Arbeitslebens" DFVLR, 31.12.1976, 5300 Bonn-Bad Godesberg, Kölnerstr. 64

INTRODUCTION TO SOME INFORMATION CONTROL TECHNIQUES IN MANUFACTURING TECHNOLOGY

Toshimasa Mitsui* and Masao Itoh**

Managing Director, General Manager, Technical Headquarters, Mitsubishi Heavy Industries, Ltd., Marunouchi, Chiyoda-ku, Tokyo, Japan
***Vice Manager, Technical Administration Department, Technical Headquarters, Mitsubishi Heavy Industries, Ltd., Marunouchi, Chiyoda-ku, Tokyo, Japan*

1. FOREWORD

We feel greatly honored to present a special lecture at the IFAC Symposium on Information-Control Problems in Manufacturing Technology, in compliance with the request of our respected Chairman, Mr. Y. Oshima. We are concerned that we will not be able to talk to the purpose of this symposium, because we are not very specialized in this field. We will, however, explain some techniques used in Mitsubishi Heavy Industries, Ltd. (M.H.I.) in connection with the subjects of the symposium.

Mitsubishi has twelve works throughout Japan. Its products are varied, including ships, steel structures, power supply plants, aircraft, chemical plants, iron and steel manufacturing machinery, industrial machinery, rolling stock, physical distribution equipment, special vehicles, refrigerators, air conditioners, machine tools, and construction machinery. Most of its products except for air conditioners, machine tools and construction machinery, are order-made products, and most are designed for small-to-medium manufacturing.

Of Mitsubishi's businesses, we will today mainly talk about the area of shipbuilding — the information-control techniques used in their construction; concerning the other product areas, we will explain only a few instances as supplementary information.

2. INFORMATION–CONTROL TECHNIQUES IN OUR SHIPBUILDING AREA OF PRODUCTION

2.1 GENERAL

It has already been over a decade since Japan's shipbuilding industry emerged as the world's leader in this field. Through all these years, Mitsubishi Heavy Industries in particular has played an important role.

Today, ships built by us range in size from some 1,000 to 400,000 deadweight tons, coming in an impressive array of such different types as cargo ships, bulk carriers, LPG and LNG carriers, container carriers, and ULCCs.

We believe that what has enabled us to build any type of ships within a very short period, at a lower cost, and with high quality is our continued efforts for improvement in such fields as administration and production control, as well as in design and construction.

Among the new shipbuilding techniques which we have developed, the technique for the block construction of large ships is probably the most significant. Although originally intended for the consecuitive construction of large ships of the same type, this technique has greatly contributed to the construction of different types of small vessels as well.

In the following sections, some new shipbuilding techniques which we have developed and put into practical use, will be described.

2.2 COMPUTER PROGRAMS FOR SHIP DESIGN AND PRODUCTION

We are pleased to present an outline of the representative programs and systems widely used in the shipbuilding department of our company. By fully utilizing these programs and systems, we have accomplished the optimum in planning, manpower-saving, speedy management, and improvement in the quality and accuracy of our products.

(1) PRELIMINARY DESIGN

We have various kinds of programs for preliminary design involving the hull form, the arrangement of hull and machinery, power estimation, etc. At this design stage, the following programs are useful and powerful tools for designers in getting the best design by making it possible to carry out much design analysis within a limited time. An integrated preliminary design system, in either a batch or interactive mode, can also be used to increase the efficiency of the design work much more.

These programs are as follows.

1) Hull form and its hydrodynamic characteristics.
   Determination of the hull form and analyses of propulsion, resistance, sea-keeping and maneuvering characteristics about the hull form.
2) Propeller design and power estimation.
3) Hydrostatic calculation on a hull form.
   Displacement, capacity, trim and stability, flooding, launching, and other calculations.
4) Longitudinal-strength calculation.
5) Estimation of hull net steel weight.
   Estimating hull net steel weight of various types of hulls based on the accumulated data of the weight of ships already completed.
6) Others.
   Profitability of ship operation, analysis of such trial-run data as speed and maneuvability, analysis of actual navigation data, automatic drawing of the arrangement plan of a ship's compartments.

(2) HULL DESIGN

We have programs for analyzing the structural characteristics of the hull, programs, which are helpful in determining the shapes, scantling and arrangement of the structural members of the midship part and the fore-and-aft part.

These programs are prepared for both general use and exclusive use. In the case of a tanker, bulk carrier, or ore carrier, an exclusive to each is used.

Furthermore, an integrated system with a data base is used for determining the shapes and arrangement of the hull structural members.

These programs are as follows.

1) Wave-induced external force calculation
   Calculation of wave-induced ship motion and load (shearing force, bending and torsional moment), as well as wave-induced external pressure distribution on the hull surface.
2) Hull strength analysis
   Three-dimensional strength analysis, with regard to the finite element or frame work, analyzing the longitudinal, transverse, and torsional strength.
3) Hull-vibration analysis
   Calculation of the natural frequency of the main hull for horizontal, vertical, and torsional vibrations.
   Calculation of the natural frequency of local structures, such as the superstructure, funnel, and double bottom.
4) Design of midship structure
   Calculation of the scantling of the midship structural members required by the rules of classification societies.
   Calculation of section modulus of the hull girder and hull net steel weight of the midship part:
   Drawing of the determined midship structure plan.

(3) OUTFITTING DESIGN

Outfitting design includes various functions, for instance, a consideration of the many kinds of equipment involved and the characters of each of three categories, i.e., the hull part, the machinery part and the electric part. Therefore, the programs are prepared over a wide range of scale.

The following are some typical examples.

1) Performance calculation of piping system
   Pressure drop, thermal stress, etc. are analyzed for piping systems. For a tanker, the optimum configurations of the cargo oil pumping system can be obtained through a simulation with this kind of pumping system.
2) Heat-balance calcualtion for ship turbine plant
3) Wiring design
   Automatic layout of each wire along the main passage, and derivation of such production data as wire-cutting length.
4) Lighting design for accommodation space
   Automatic selection of electric equipment in accordance with the grade of each room while checking the electric power consumption, level of illumination, etc., and derivation of equipment lists and diagrams of the whole system.
5) Electric power design
   Checking of various aspects of performance such as the power consumption throughout the electric system, with the power demand of all the equipment, and making drawings of the diagrams and power table.
6) Others
   There are many other programs for performance analysis and the determining the particulars of various types of functional outfitting equipment and system, for example, the ventilation system, the cargo-handling system, and the refrigeration system.

(4) N/C LOFTING

(4.1) SHIP SYSTEM (Fig. 1, Fig. 2, and Fig. 3)

The SHIP (Systematic Hull Information Processing) system shown in Fig. 1 is an integrated system for carrying out efficiently the lofting work, such as lines-fairing, definition of internal members, and nesting. In this system, all the data concerning the arrangement and form of hull-structural members are processed numerically.

This system is made up of the following subsystems.

1) Body-plan subsystem (Fig. 2)
Fairing of hull lines, formation of main hull structures (bulkhead, etc.).
2) Landing subsystem
Arrangement of seam lines and longitudinal frames on the shell.
3) Expansion subsystem
Expansion of shell plates and frame members.
4) Internal-member-definition subsystem
Definition of location and shapes of structural member pieces, and preparing for EPM (Electro Print Marking) templates.
5) Nesting subsystem (Fig. 3)
Preparing N/C cutting tapes.
6) Others
Preparing offset data for curved block supporting jig., etc.

Feartures:

1) Increase of accuracy in fabrication and assembly work.
2) Time-saving of lofting work.
3) Reliable results, even by unskilled workers.
4) Accumulation of know-how on defining internal members in the form of a convenient macro library, which reduces input load.
5) Easy expansion and modification of system by means of its modular configuration.
6) Low-cost data processing with many application programs and data bases, which are founded on actual hull-design and production practices.

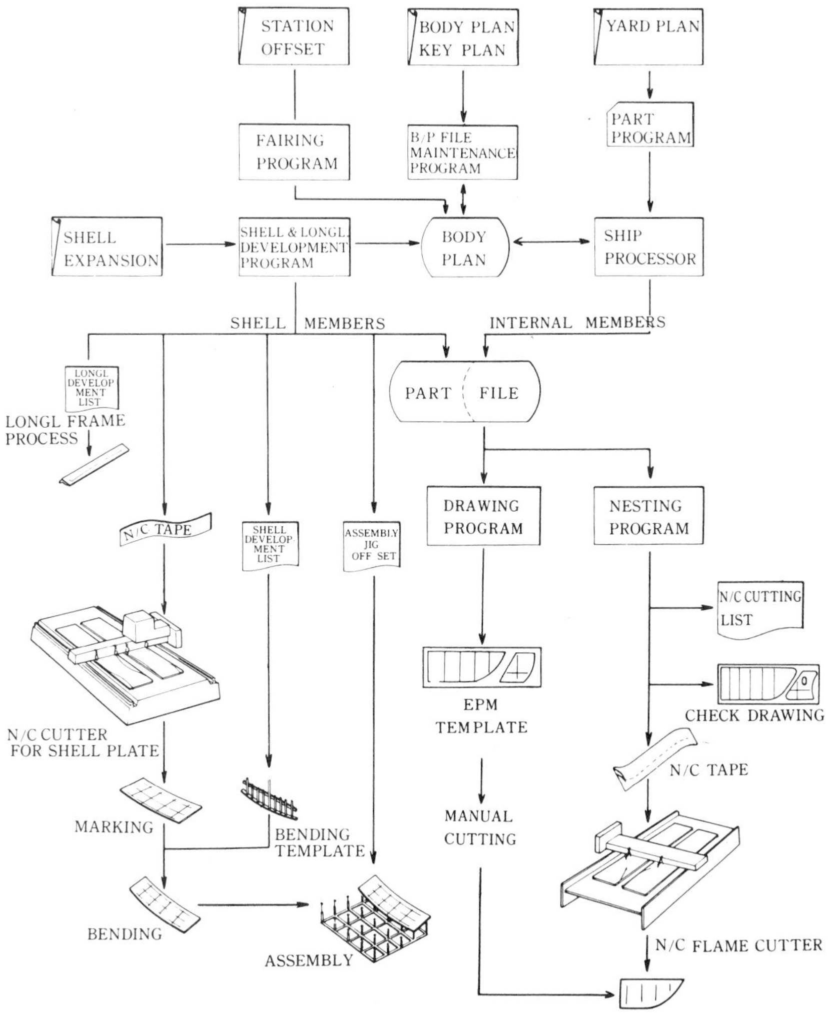

Fig. 1 Flow diagram of the SHIP system

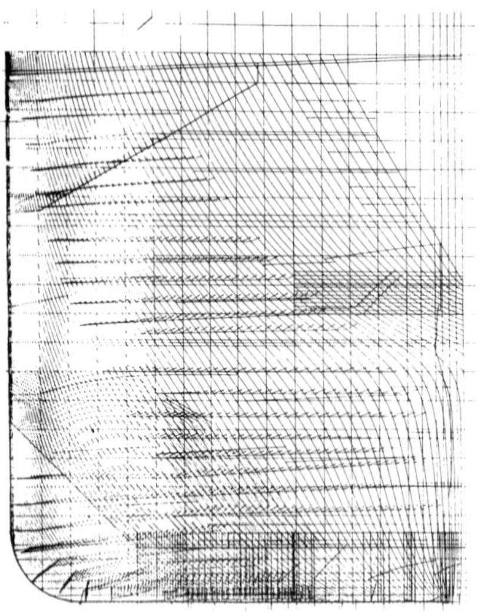

Fig. 2 Body Plan

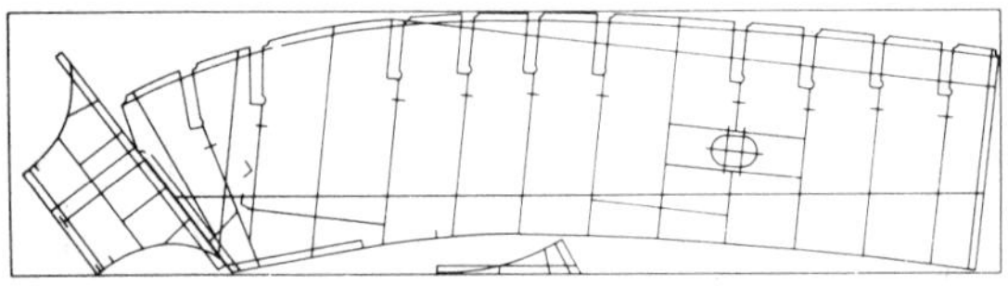

Fig. 3 Cutting Arrangement

(4.2) PIPE SYSTEM (Fig. 4, Fig. 5, and Fig. 6)

The PIPE system is an integrated system extending from the design to the production stages for pipe outfitting; it is an important tool for the rationalization of outfitting work. In this system appropriate pipes and valves are selected by feeding in piping data picked up from a detailed pipe arrangement plan; the piping data are checked and corrected with reference to the fabrication criteria, and then a piece drawing of the pipe is obtained.

This system can be easily connected with other systems, such as the production control and N/C lofting systems, through the data base.

The system configuration is as follows.

1) Language processor
   Translating input piping data coded with PIPE language, and breaking-down into a series of pipe piece data (to be stored in the data base).
2) Standard file maintenance program
   Storing fabrication practice, particulars and patterns of pipes, valves, etc.
3) Drawing program
   Drawing pipe lines in various forms such as projection, profile and bird's-eye views. (Fig. 4 and Fig. 5).
4) Pipe-piece drawing program
   Output of pipe lists and piece drawings. (Fig. 6)

Features:

1) Increase in accuracy and efficiency of fabrication and assembly work.
2) Saving of man-power and time in piping design.
3) Reliable results, even by unskilled workers.
4) Capable of connection with production-control system for outfitting work, as well as with the N/C pipe-fabrication system.
5) Easy input by means of designer-oriented PIPE language.
6) Easy expansion and modification of the system by means of its modular configuration.
7) Reduction of the input load by a number of standard files.

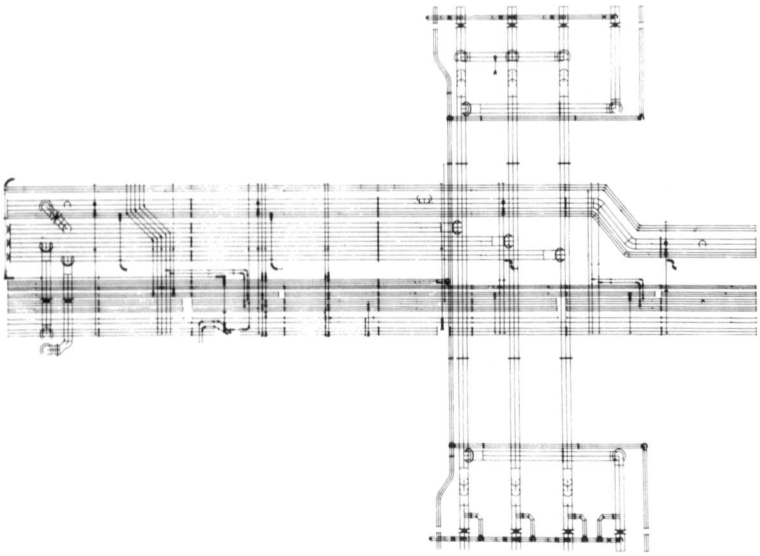

Fig. 4 A piping arrangement plan

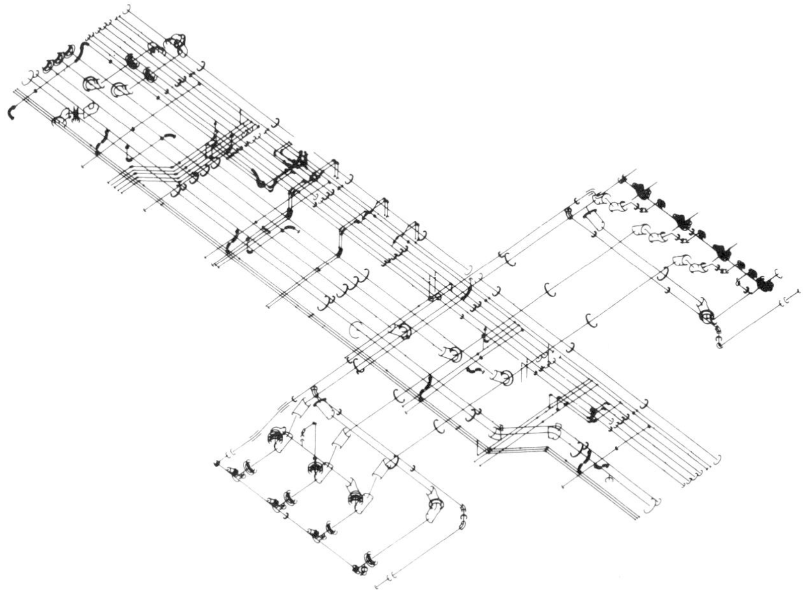

Fig. 5 Projection

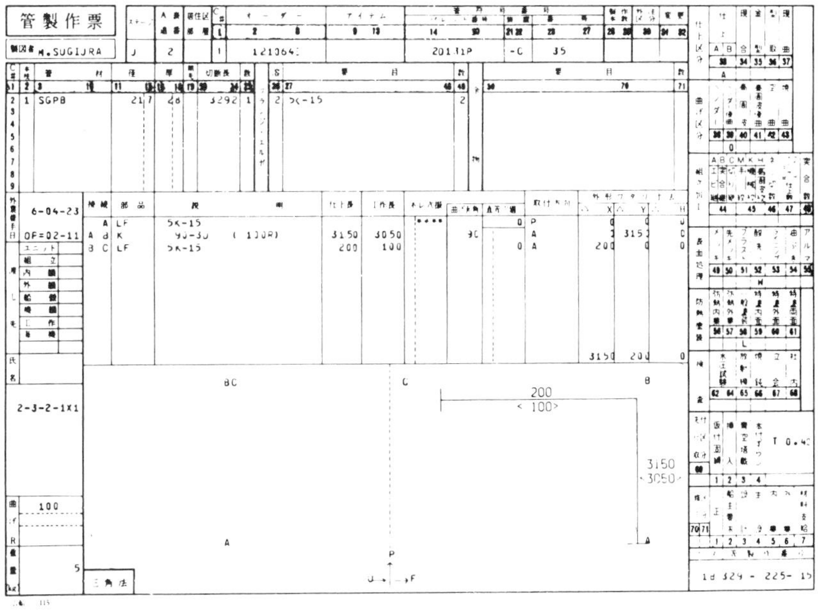

Fig. 6 Pipe piece drawing

(5) PRODUCTION PLANNING AND CONTROL

(5.1) MATERIAL MANAGEMENT SYSTEM (Fig. 7)

An integrated management system shown in Fig. 7 covers all phases of ship-outfitting-materials flow, such as budgeting, designing, scheduling, purchasing, storing, issuing, cost-accounting, and other related stages. This system has been developed for the smooth supply of the necessary kinds and amounts of outfitting materials at the right time and to the right place, while minimizing the stock cost.

Features:

1) Availability of the same data by means of the data-base technique on material status for all the stages concerned — design, purchasing, and production.
2) Recognizing material status in real time through on-line inquiry terminals, resulting in timely correcting action in case alteration is required.
3) Consistency of material management, well-coordinated between all the stages concerned.
4) Manpower-saving in making up orders, and correctness in the follow-up of material receiving.

5) Quick supplying of materials and manpower-saving for inventory control by utilizing an auto-warehouse.

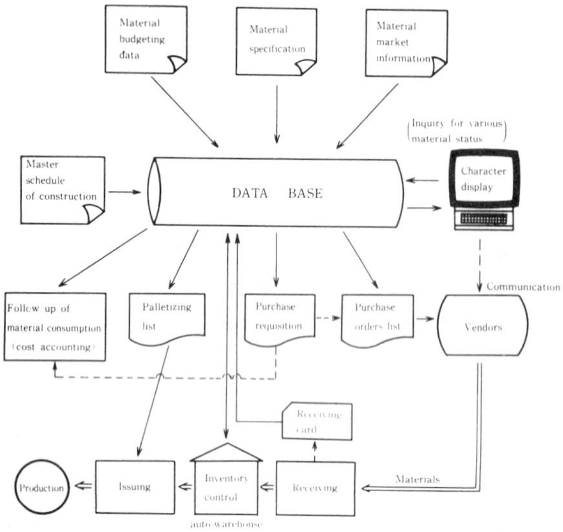

Fig. 7 System configuration of the MATERIAL MANAGEMENT SYSTEM

(5.2) OTHERS

There are many other systems covering all the planning and control actions in the process of ship production, as will be shown bellow;

1) Production planning and control
   (a) Initial scheduling
   Determination of the date of keel laying, launching and delivery.
   (b) Detailed scheduling
   Detailed scheduling for the design stage, the erection stage, the hull-construction stage, and the outfitting stage by means of the network technique, the job-shop scheduling method, etc.
   (c) Control of issuing of drawings
   (d) Production control
   Progress and efficiency control, follow-up of cost accounting, etc.
2) Ship-materials management system (for steel plate)
   A ship-materials management system covering budgeting, material planning, ordering, and follow-up of materials, cost-accounting, inventory control and material handling, etc.

2.3 SHIPBUILDING EQUIPMENT AND APPARATUS

(1) N/C PLATE MARKING AND CUTTING MACHINE (Fig. 8)

Controlled with a paper tape prepared by the N/C lofting system (SHIP System), this machine cuts steel plates with flame or a plasma jet. It can also be used for plate marking.

Features:

1) Compared to cutting by hand, plates can be cut with greater precision.
2) All control instructions are given by N/C tape. Manual operation is required only for starting and stopping.
3) Automatic bevelling is also possible.
4) Plates can be plasma-cut at great speed. This improves cutting accuracy, because heat deformation is less than in flame cutting.
5) Having a co-ordinate converting function, the machine is capable of simultaneously cutting symmetric members for both the port and starboard sides, following N/C tape instructions for the port-side members alone.

Fig. 8 N/C plate marking and cutting machines

(2) N/C PROFILE MARKING AND CUTTING MACHINE (Fig. 9)

This highly efficient and accurate machine marks and gas-cuts the profile, including the angle steel, by means of numerical control. It has now been made fully automatic, the first instance in this kind of machine. The machine can process two profiles simultaneously. Two torch blocks are provided for the cutting of one profile; one is for horizontal, and the other for vertical use. Each torch block has two cutting torches. It can also carry out bevel cutting as well as normal cutting.

Features:

1) Applicable to both angle steel and T-shaped steel.
2) For bevel cutting, I-shaped, V-shaped, inverted V-shaped, and Y-shaped cuttings are possible. In curved cutting, the uniformity of the bevel angle can be controlled.
3) When bevelling for welding purposes, a special device is fitted to prevent any excess cutting of the corners of the profile.

4) Curved marking for the bending process in addition to various basic line markings is also possible.
5) For vessels of the 20,000-ton class, the man-hours can be reduced by about 3,000 hours.

Fig. 9 Marking and cutting machine with clamping device

(3) MULTI-TORCH AUTOMATIC STEEL PLATE BENDER (Fig. 10)

Ordinarily, there are two uses for linear heating. One is the application of steel plates as they are, while the other is the use of plates after primary processing by means of a cold press and bending roller. In conventional methods, only one torch is manipulated per worker. However, when the new bender is used, linear heating is carried out automatically and by a single operator manipulating several torches at a time.

The machine operates in the following manner: plural lines are marked by chalk on the plate surface prior to heating; the torches then heat these lines, which are optically traced by a detector attached to the torches. All the torches are loaded on a bogie; each torch can travel independently of the others at right angles to the bogie's travelling direction. This means that several heating lines of different curves can be heated simultaneously.

Mitsubishi has also developed an improved model of this automatic bending machine which comes with a numerically controlled recording device. In the case of this model, its burners are first made to run, without being kindled, in order for the machine to memorize the desired heating lines. Upon the completion of this procedure, the torches are kindled simultaneously to start the bending work on the basis of the memorized data. Data regarding the curves of the lines are recorded on a paper tape after heating, so that from the second plate of the same curvature, the plates can be bent fully automatically.

Moreover, when symmetric steel plates on both sides of the center line of the hull are processed, the steel plates of one side can be automatically made using the data obtained in processing the steel plates of the other side.

Features:

1) Simultaneous mainpulation of several torches by a single operator for greater efficiency.
2) The mechanically regulated travelling speeds of the torches make possible the accurate control of the heating temperatures applied to steel plates. The latter are thus protected from undesirable effects of heating at incorrect temperatures.
3) Simple operation relieves the operator from uncomfortable working postures.
4) Heating work requires no experience.
5) A smaller surface plate for plate bending will suffice.

Fig. 10 Multi-torch automatic steel plate bender

(4) TRIPLE-ROW BENDING PRESS (Fig. 11)

This high-efficiency press, equipped with three rows of presses, is used for the three-dimensional bending of shell plates by a cold process. By feeding in the data for the necessary spring-back adjustment, shell plates are quickly bent as required.

This press, incidentally, comes with an automatic transfer device for the transfer of material.

Features:

1) Compared to the conventional manual bending method of the line-heating type, efficiency is increased fivefold.
2) The employment of the cold process protects the wash primer from damage and makes unnecessary any repair or treatment of the surface prior to coating. Furthermore, as gas for heating can be economized, it is highly effective in the conservation of material as well as in the reduction of manpower.
3) As data concerning the pressing of a plate are recorded, the pressing of the symmetrical plate is automatically carried out. This means that, in constructing the second ship, all pressing work can be automated.
4) While an automatic line-heating device may prove to be more convenient, budget-wise, in factories where production capacities are small, this triple-row bending press can be used effectively in factories with a relatively large production output.

Fig. 11 Triple-row bending press

(5) LATTICE FRAME ASSEMBLING DEVICE (Fig. 12 and Fig. 13)

According to the conventional frame-assembling method, a loose slit has to be cut on each transverse member so it can be assembled with the longitudinal members into a lattice frame. Then, at each point where the transverse and longitudinal members come in contact, a filler-plate is fitted and welded. In order to avoid the work of the filler-plate fitting, the loose slit would have to be made into a key-hole shape, into which the longitudinal members could be inserted.

Under the method, we at Mitsubishi have developed, the transverse members are held in fixed positions by a holding device, while the longitudinal members, laid out on trolleys beforehand, are inserted into the slits consecutively by means of an inserting device.

Mitsubishi has also developed another device. According to this device, the required number of longitudinal members are lined up at specified intervals; the transverse members are then inserted from one end of the longitudinal rows.

Features:

1) The number of workers required for frame assembly and welding can be reduced by about 30 percent, because the slits are of a key-hole shape, making filler-plates unnecessary.
2) The device for holding the transverse members in position can be adjusted in accordance with the length of, and the interval between the members, which means that the device can be readily used for the construction of ships of any size.
3) The smooth and speedy insertion of longitudinal members is possible by means of the movable guide roller placed in front of each slit.

Fig. 12 Lattice frame assembling device

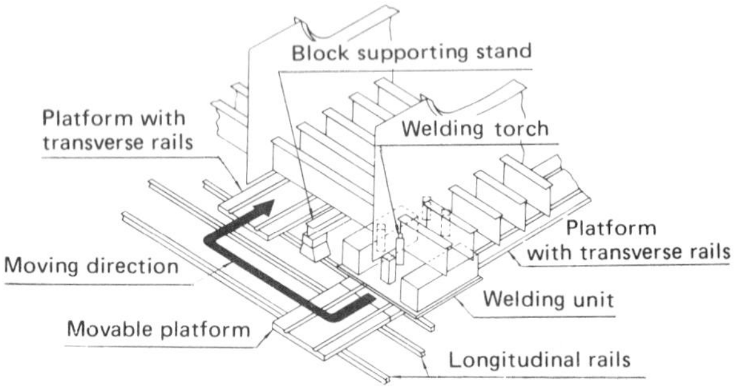

Fig. 14 Transfer method of the automatic welding unit

Fig. 13 Longitudinal frame insertion

Fig. 15 Automatic vertical fillet-welding unit in framework assembly

(6) AUTOMATIC VERTICAL FILLET WELDING IN FRAMEWORK ASSEMBLY (Fig. 14 and Fig. 15)

This system is used in a welding process of putting longitudinal frames and transverse webs together into a lattice. After the welding unit is initially set at the lower end of a tacked lattice, it performs upward welding while automatically detecting the positions to be welded, moving the welding heads up and down, and tracing the lines of weld.

Equipped with a leg-length channel-switching device, the system can change its leg-length over a very wide range.

When the welding of one part of a transverse member is completed, the welding machine automatically moves on its rails to the next part.

When all the joints of a transverse member have been welded, the machine travels to the end of the transverse and moves to the position of the next transverse member by means of longitudinal rails which are laid at the end of transverse rails. The machine thus carries out the welding continuously.

Features:

1) As it does the welding fully automatically, the system requires no skilled operator.
2) Since the system works in a non-gas arc vertical upward welding process, it gives more satisfactory and qualitatively uniform joints than does the conventional downward manual-welding method.
3) As it allows each operator to handle four torches at a time, the working efficiency is so high that the manhours required for welding can be reduced by 55 percent.
4) Unlike conventional methods in which workers have to move over a lattice, under this system the workers need not move over the lattice, ensuring safer operation.

(7) LATTICE ROBOT WELDER SYSTEM (Fig. 16 and Fig. 17)

Intended for use in panel shops, this system carries out, in a fully automatic process, the horizontal fillet welding of frame lattices, composed of longitudinals and transverses, to shell and/or bulkhead panels. The system is an epoch-making welding and moving robot in the shipbuilding field. Following instructions from the control board, the transferring unit sets several welding machines in each of the squares of a lattice. The machine works on its own along the frame members and automatically welds the four sides. When this is done, the machine is automatically transferred to the next square to continue the welding process. Scallops and serrations on a weld line are automatically detected, and the welding machine automatically by-passes them and continues welding. U-shaped, L-shaped, or straight weld lines at the edges of a lattice can also be automatically welded in a continuous process, and the welding leg-length can be set in advance.

Features:

1) No skilled operator is needed, and it allows a single operator to take charge of several welding machines.
2) Repairings are reduced by 50 percent in comparison with gravity welding.
3) The leftover of the weld, which is inevitable in gravity welding or fine-wire submerged-arc welding (usually about 10 percent of the total weld line) is eliminated.
4) Compared to various fillet-welding methods, the system is highly efficient.

Fig. 16 Lattice robot-welder system

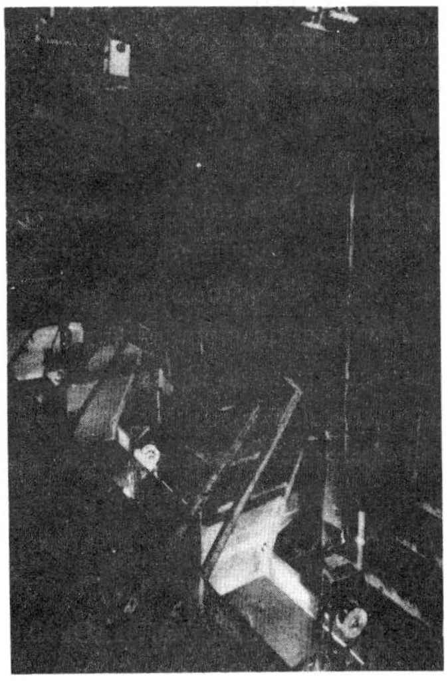

Fig. 17 Automatic welding machine

(8) OPTICAL CHECKING SYSTEM FOR HULL BLOCK ACCURACY (Fig. 18 and Fig. 19)

In shipbuilding, the overall efficiency is considerably improved if the volume of work to be done in the erection stage can be reduced. Since the volume of work, in turn, depends largely on the accuracy of blocks, the assembling of blocks with a high accuracy is required so that blocks can be checked prior to block erection in order to make any further post-erection adjustment unnecessary. This system was developed for such a purpose.

Under this system, reflexive films are attached onto which laser rays are projected. Accurate measurements are taken of the distance to each of these points by means of a control unit which is attached to the system. In the same manner, accurate measurements are also taken of the horizontal and elevation angles at each of these points. The measured results are recorded on a cassette tape by means of a data recorder connected to the system. The distance to each measureing point is obtained by comparing the phases of the transmitted wave and reflected wave.

The accuracy of the block is checked in the following manner: from one position, several points are measured; then, from another position, several points, including the same two points of the former several points, are again measured; on the basis of these measurements, a special network of the measured points is formed. The results, recorded on a cassette tape, are fed into the main computer through an input unit installed near the work site; the computer operates in accordance with a prescribed program to figure out the correlation between the points. Data concerning each measuring point are digitally indicated on a display unit as soon as they become available, so that the person in charge of the measurement can check the figures as he continues his work.

Fig. 18 Measuring instruments

Fig. 19 Data input to computer

Features:

1) The correlation among all the points in a structure can be analyzed, regardless of their positions relative to each other.
2) Since accuracy is controlled on a block-by-block basis, the post-erection adjustment of the blocks by cutting becomes unnecessary.
3) Weighing only 40 kilograms in all and operated by storage batteries, the measuring instruments can be taken wherever required.
4) The distance between the measuring points can be detected within a difference of 2 mm.

(9) AUTOMATICALLY CONTROLLED WAREHOUSE FOR OUTFITS (Fig. 20 and Fig. 21)

This automatically controlled warehouse operates in the following manner. Piping components, electrical outfits, and smaller outfit items for the deck and engine departments are placed on storage pallets as they are delivered to the warehouse by manufacturers; as soon as their identification numbers and quantities have been fed into the control system, a stacker crane automatically places each pallet in an unoccupied space in the rack warehouse. Then, when an item is to be taken out, its storage pallet can be automatically located and brought out by giving the control system appropriate instructions stating the identification number and the quantity required.

Features:

1) The concentrated storage of outfits, which were previously divided by department, such as deck, engine, and electric, contributes to rationalized control.
2) The multi-level storage of outfits means improved storing efficiency and greater utilization of the warehouse space.
3) Since the receiving and delivery of outfits are computerized as well as rack handling the new warehouse needs only about half as many attendants as a conventional warehouse of the same scale would.

Fig. 20 Automatically controlled warehouse for outfits

Fig. 21 Automatically controlled warehouse for outfits

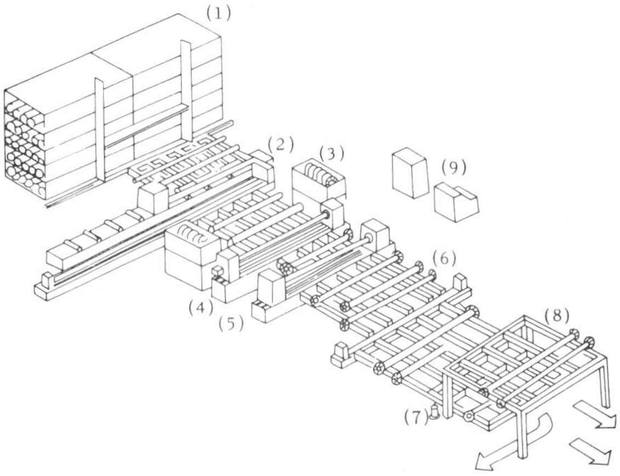

1 Pipe racks
2 Pipe-cutting machine
3 Flange-supply machine
4 Flange temporary fitting machine
5 Flange-welding machine
6 Flange-finishing table
7 Pipe-classifying device console
8 Pipe skids
9 Control console

Fig. 22 Centrally controlled pipe processing system

(10)CENTRALLY CONTROLLED PIPE-PROCESSING SYSTEM (Fig. 22 and Fig. 23)

This system centrally controls as well as automates various phases in pipe shops, such as the fabrication, assembly and handling of small and medium-sized straight pipes.

Pipes to be fabricated are taken out of pipe racks where pipes of various kinds are stored, and cut into the required lengths. After the selection of the required flanges from the flange racks, the positions of the bolt holes in the flanges are adjusted; then, prior to permanent welding, the pipes and flanges are tack-welded. When finishing work on the flange surfaces has been completed, the pipes to be bent are separated from the others.

The system includes a minicomputer which centrally controls the operational-information inputs to the system and the controllers of the individual processing machines.

Features:

1) This system can stock processing pipes in spaces between processing machines and greatly improve efficiency by means of the parallel operation of the machines. The processing capacity is about 200 pipes per day.
2) Only one operator is required except for the finishing work of the flange faces. Since all phases of work are fully automated, special skill or judgement on the part of the operator, indispensable in conventional manual processing methods, is not necessary.

Fig. 23 Centrally controlled pipe-processing system

(11) N/C PIPE BENDER (Fig. 24 and Fig. 25)

This is a hydraulic pipe bender designed to be installed on processing lines for small pipes. It can cold-bend pipes most efficiently and accurately.

Bending a pipe with this machine is accomplished in the following manner: the bending angle and feed distance are supplied as input information; appropriate buttons on the control board are pressed; the pipe is loaded in a predetermined sequence and set in the prescribed position for bending; flange holes are sought for and adjusted; the pipe is then clamped; the bending form starts revolving and stops when the desired bending angle is reached; the clamp is released, and the pipe is pushed out.

In bending pipes with this machine, it is recommended that each group of pipes be of the same outer diameter, thickness, and bending radius as far as the fabrication schedule will permit.

When a pipe has to be bent in two or more positions, consecutive bending can be achieved if the distance data between the first bending and the next bending are determined in advance. When two or more bendings are to be carried out on different planes, the input of the twist angle (angle of rotation), will have to be made additionally.

In the case of special pipes, the quantity of springback on the bending angles has to be pre-set manually.

Features:
The use of this machine dispenses with the marking of the bending positions on pipes. Automatic positioning reduces the number of operators from three (for a conventional hydraulic bender) to one, and makes possible the precision bending of pipes safely be this single operator.

Fig. 24 N/C pipe bender

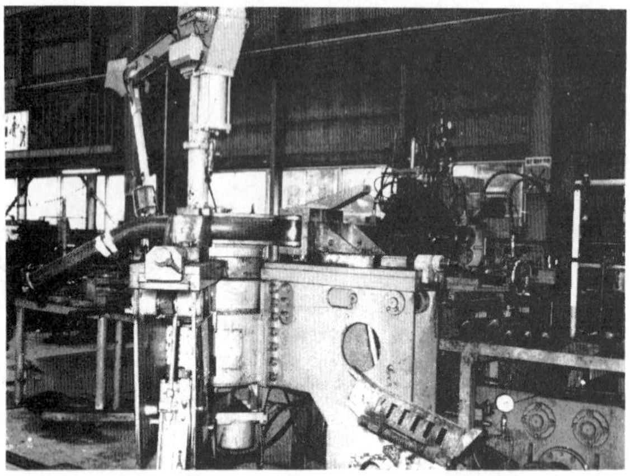

Fig. 25 Front view of N/C pipe bender

(12) AUTOMATIC WELDING MACHINE FOR LARGE BRANCH PIPES (Fig. 26 and Fig. 27)

This machine is for the highly efficient and accurate welding of the joints of branch pipes which connect to main pipes at right angles. By pre-setting the pipe diameter, the center of the main pipe and the chuck can be automatically matched.

In order to determine the locus by means of digital control, the welding conditions and actual diameters of the main and branch pipes are pre-set. Welding is then done automatically.

If the cross-section of a pipe is not a perfect circle, the bevelling of the weld joints is likely to be inaccurate. Under this system, however, the welding conditions and welding torch targets can be easily adjusted by hand, so no skilled worker is required.

Features:

1) The welding torch is directed downwards over the whole circumference of the weld for uniform welding.
2) After about one week of training, the operator can achieve bead shapes that are more uniform than the bead shapes achieved in hand welding, by skilled and well-experienced workers.
3) This machine shortens both the welding time, including the preparation time, and the cutting time by about 50 percent, as compared with manual methods.

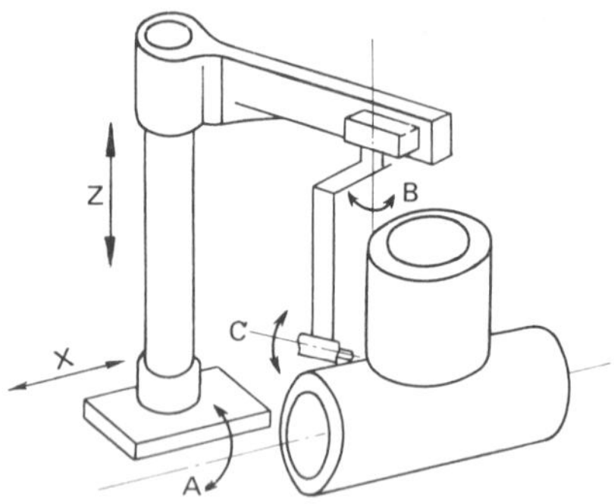

Fig. 26 Movement of torch for branch-pipe welding

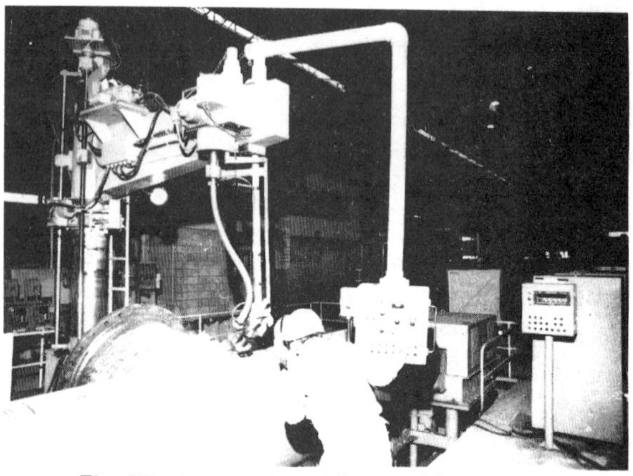

Fig. 27 Automatic welding machine for large branch pipes

3. INFORMATION–CONTROL TECHNIQUES IN OTHER AREAS OF OUR PRODUCTION

We have thus far described our techniques in the shipbuilding area. In other areas of production also, similar technology is used from design through production. Let us briefly describe a few such instances.

(1) AUTOMATIC DESIGN AND DRAWING SYSTEM OF CRANES (Fig. 28 and Fig. 29)

It is important to establish a designing system of various cranes to comply with customers' diverse requests due to the modernization of handling facilities, demanding increasingly larger capacities.

To realize such a system, Mitsubishi has made step-by-step studies of new techniques to make it possible for this system to do, totally or partially, the automatic design and optimum lay-out of various cranes by means of computer programs adopting standard patterns systematically derived from the conventional norms and techniques. This system is designated "Total System of Organized Crane Program Design" (abbreviated TOP-D).

Features:

1) Each computer program for the girders and end-ties, travel mechanism, grab frame, grab machinery (hoist, cross-travel, etc.), and other structures (footway, stairway, etc.) of overhead cranes was developed individually, and then all were organized comprehensively for automatic design. The configurations of the TOP-D is shown in Fig. 28.

2) The sub-programs of TOP-D are:
   a) structure design program.
   b) grab-machinery layout program
   c) machine-design program
   d) automatic-drawing program

   An automatic drawing of the individual machines, as calculated by the automatic layout program of the TOP-D is shown in Fig. 29.

(2) DIRECT NUMERICAL CONTROL SYSTEM OF NC MACHINE TOOLS (Fig. 30, Fig. 31, and Fig. 32)

A direct numerical control system of NC machine tools by means of a computer is used at the Machine Tools Department, Hiroshima Shipyårds & Engine Works, of our company.

Designed from the user's standpoint, this direct numerical control system is suitable for use in factories. It is capable of controlling many NC machine tools (at present, 22 sets) of different kinds simultaneously, also, it is so designed that each function is performed conversationally from several CRT display units. (Fig. 31)

Features:

1) Different NC machine tools connected together (up to 22, currently) can be controlled simultaneously.
2) With a CRT display unit installed for every two or three machine tools, in-shop correction and variety of information processing are facilitated. That is, the on-line operation is all via conversation by means of CRT display units in shop and computer room. (Fig. 32)

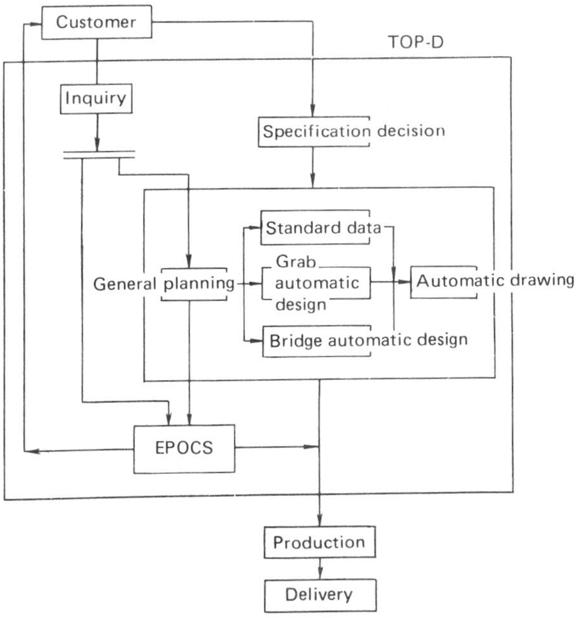

EPOCS: Estimate Programs Of Crane System

Fig. 28 Configuration of the TOP-D system

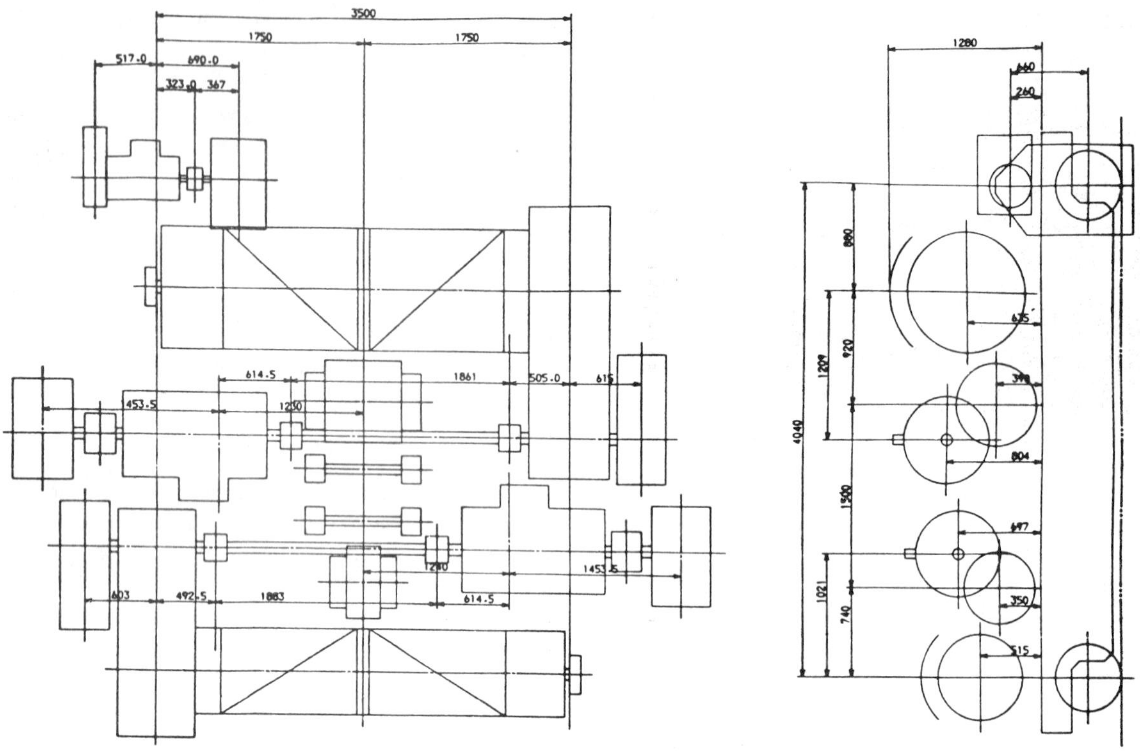

Fig. 29 Drawing of lay-out of trolley equipments by plotter

3) The central computer is connected with the communication circuit, so that APT processing is on-line.
4) It is a shop-dependent system, based on user's needs, thus, raising the operation rate of the machine tools.
5) The configuration of the system is shown in Fig. 30.

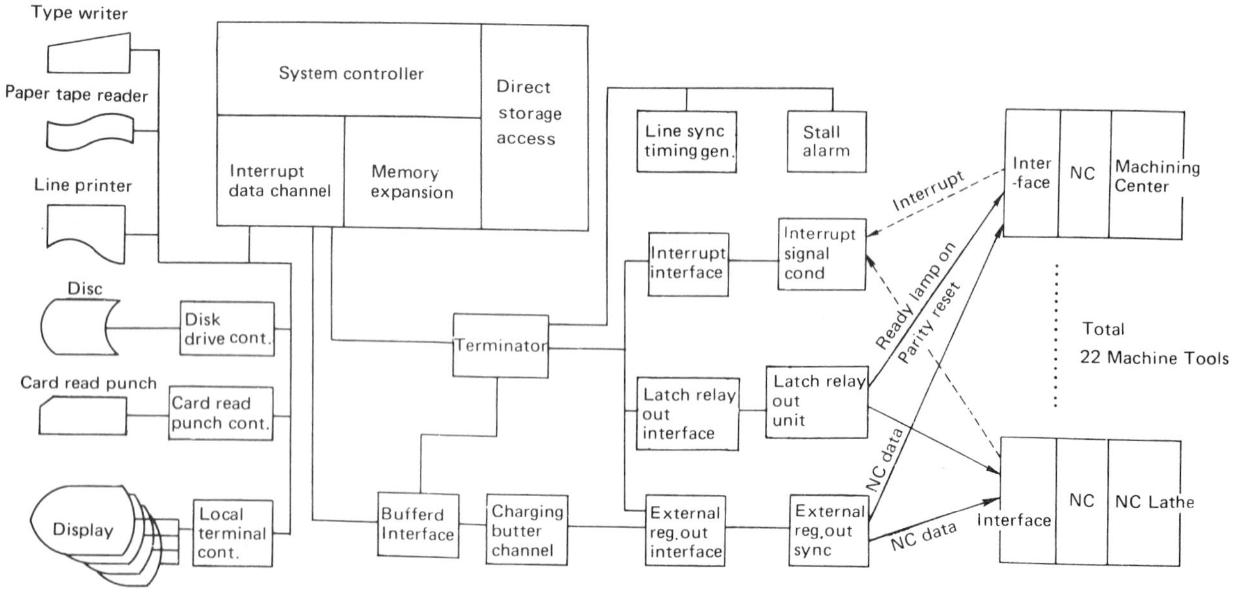

Fig. 30 System configuration

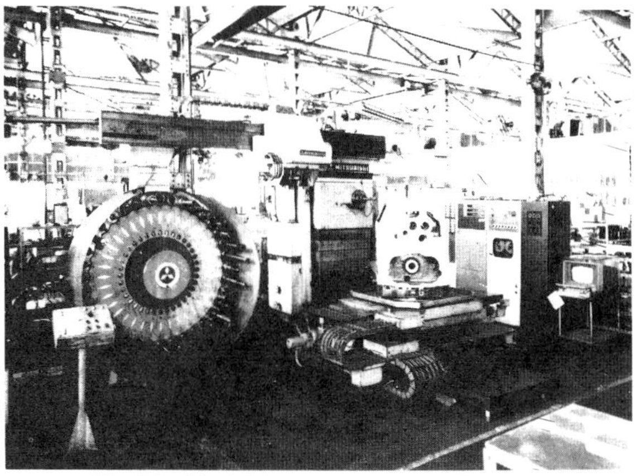

Fig. 31 Machining center and CRT display

Fig. 32 Central computer room

(3) INDUSTRIAL-ROBOT APPLIED TO THE AUTOMATIC MACHINING SYSTEM (Fig. 33, Fig. 34, and Fig. 35)

In most mass-production machine shops, it is very common to see quite a few automation system installations; however, in other types of machine shops, where various types of products of rather small quantities are handled, such an automation system is seldowm found, but the so-called group technological layout of NC machining centres is generally found. This is perhaps due to economic reasons, even if the technological solution exists.

Among the varieties of machine parts, a cylindrical configuration such as a rotating machinery shaft is one of the most suitable parts to which an automatic system can be applied.

We would like to introduce such a automation system which utilizes two sets of RC Module Robots (ROBITUS) as the automatic material handling means to join six universal machine tools together. The system handles various sizes and configurations of shafts of such rotating machinery as hydraulic pumps and motors.

Features:

1) Brief description of the line.
   a) types of shafts : 10
   b) material weight : 5 – 30 kg
   c) lot size : a couple of ten to hundred repeated every month and every other month.
2) Advantages of this system
   a) Manpower saving from 5 to 1
   b) Reduction of the in-process material volume
   c) Doubling of the production capacity
   d) Protection of the operator from the weight-lifting problem.

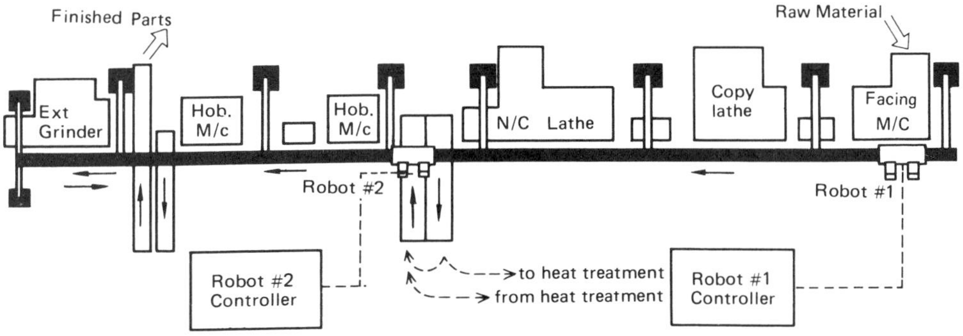

Fig. 33 Layout of the system

Fig. 34 General view of the industrial Robot

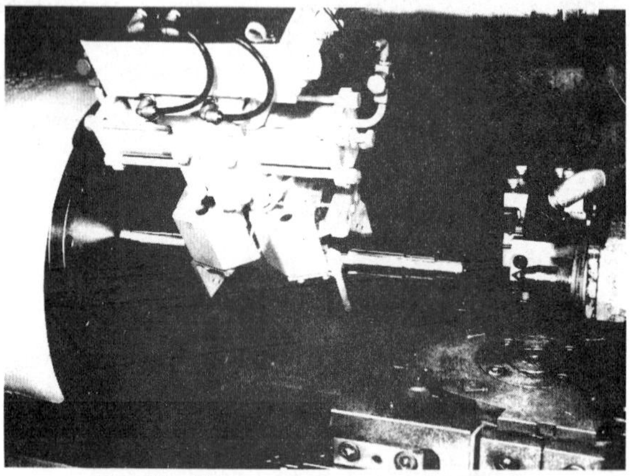

Fig. 35 Gripper of the Industrial Robot

(4) WELDING SYSTEM OF AUTOMATIC WELDING IN TUBE-TO-TUBE SHEET JOINT OF THE HEAT EXCHANGER (Fig. 36 and Fig. 37)

In our company, tube-to-tube sheet welding technique has been applied in the feed-water heater of the boiler drum, and in the steam generators in nuclear plants and various kinds of chemical plants.

As the results of these valuable experiences, in 1972 Mitsubishi set out to develop an automatic tube-to-tube sheet welder with an automatic setting by means of programming control. Mitsubishi has thus obtained more productivity and quality in tube-to-tube sheet welding.

Features:

1) The products which can thus be welded are mentioned below.
   Diameter of tube : 16mmϕ, 20mmϕ, 25mmϕ
   Tube pitch : 21mm, 26mm, 32mm
   Wall thickness of tube : 1 ~ 3mm
   Diameter of tube sheet : 500mmϕ ~ 1800mmϕ

2) Our system can operate 6 series of operation depending on 2 kinds of tube thickness ($t > 1.5$, $t < 1.5$), 2 kinds of welding grooves (projection and recess), and 2 kinds of welding positions (horizontal and flat), as is shown in the following Table.

Table

Series of operations		A	B	C	D	E	F
Wall Thickness of Pipe		> 1.5 mm				<1.5 mm	
Welding	Flat	○		○			○
Position	Horizontal		○		○	○	
Joint	Projection	○			○		
Type	Recess		○	○		○	○

3) Programmed welding-location control
   a) Specifications
   Number of control axes : X—axis (right and left directions)
   Y—axis (upper and lower directions)
   Minimum control unit : 0.1mm (X and Y axes each)
   Maximum feeding pitch : 99.9mm
   Detection method of position : Pulse-count method by means of magnetic flux chopping
   b) Operation mode
   This machine can control the following 4 mode types of program, selected by operating switches:

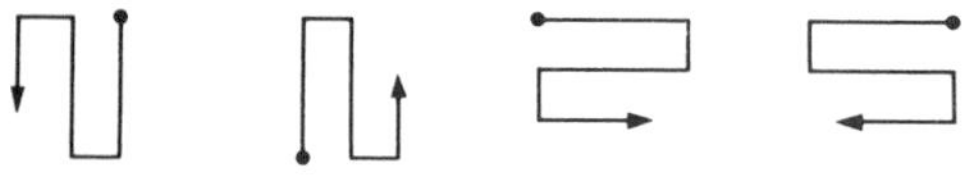

This programmed welding location control with 4 mode types of program does not cover the 10% tube hole, because the arrangement of the tube hole in the circular tube sheet has specific areas comprising tube holes located in the periphery of the arrangement.

(5) REAL-TIME CONVERSATIONAL ON-LINE PROCESSING SYSTEM FOR FACTORY TESTS OF COMPRESSORS AND DRIVING TURBINES (Fig. 38, Fig. 39, and Fig. 40)

Automation and rationalization by computer have been promoted in machine shops. However, it has been quite difficult to perform automatic testing at factories, because test patterns are complex and variable, particularly for order-made products.

A real-time conversational system, employing a mini-computer and character display (C/D), capable of measuring and calculating quickly and accurately for compressors and driving turbines, has been developed by our company.

Fig. 36 Appearance of welding machine

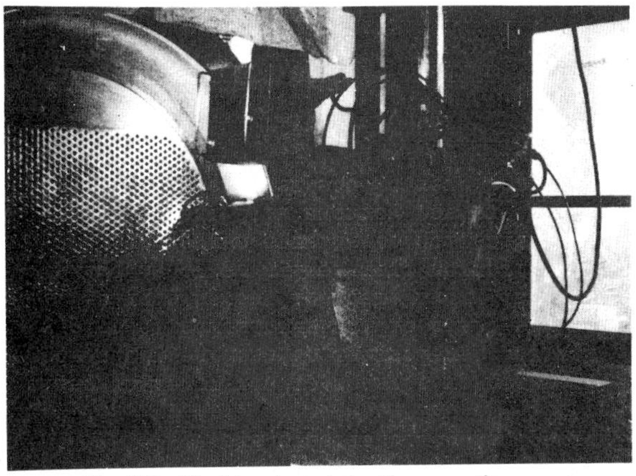
Fig. 37 Machine in automatic operation

Features:

1) The compressor types and test patterns are standardized and programmed.
2) Adopting a conversational system by menas of character display (C/D), tests are conducted in a conversational-like manner. Since, in this method, each test flow and the measurement instructions are all displayed on C/D screens, the operator and workers need only to obey the instructions, thus saving labour as well as preventing erroneous actions and measurements.
3) By containing various physical properties necessary for tests and performance calculations, and also calibration values within a magnetic disk, test and computation times are shortend and the accuracy is improved.
4) By virtue of this system, for instance, in the case of cc npressor-performance-tests the measuring men nine in a shift, are replaced with one or two operators; thereby the data arrangement and performance calculation work, that needed "one person/one week", is finished when the test ends. Furthermore, since it is possible to determine the next work's components after one test is over, tests can be work's components after one test is over, tests can be carried out efficiently.
5) The gases employed for performance tests are in general as follows:
   a) Nitrogen
   b) Carbon dioxide
   c) Freon
   d) Helium
   e) Atmosphere
   f) Mixed gas of 3 kinds at most, including the atmosphere.
6) The physical properties required for performance tests and calculation are as follows:
   a) Compressibility factor
   b) Absolute viscosity
   c) Entropy
   d) Enthalpy

Fig. 38 Compressor and turbine

Fig. 39 Pressure transmitter

Fig. 40 Mini computer

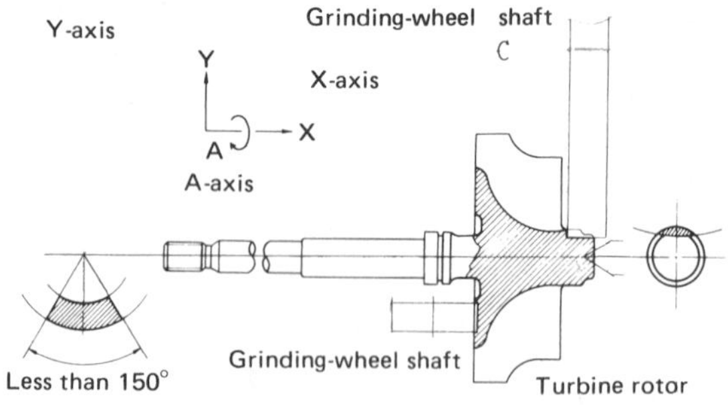

Fig. 41 Turbine rotor

(6) SMALL–SUPERCHARGER TURBINE ROTOR UNBALANCE–CORRECTING MACHINE (Fig. 41, Fig. 42, and Fig. 43)

High-speed Diesel engines of from several tens to several hundreds horsepower and their auxiliary superchargers are manufactured in our company. With the unbalance-correcting machine, the unbalance of the small-supercharger turbine rotor is measured and grinding-eliminated automatically in the inspection stage of manufacturing.

The mechanism is as follows: On the basis of information for each turbine rotor obtained by means of a balance tester (unbalance weight between front and rear faces and the index angle), specific arithmetic is first carried out with a microcomputer. Then, through control of the X-Y-A axes and of two grinding-wheel shaft motors, the work is so done that the correction is done in a single stage. The unbalance-elimination time per rotor with this machine is about 1/5 that in the conventional manual system.

Features:

1) With a microcomputer as the heart of control, the computerized NC, with its few discrete parts, is highly reliable.
2) With a status No. display function as man/machine communication, handling instructions are given to the worker and any abnormality is indicated.
3) Control logical functions, such as the generation of a pulse rate to determine the feed rate and of instruction signals for reduction and stop points, are handled with software, so adjustment and specification-modification are facilitated.
4) The working sequence originates in the microcomputer, without the use of tape.
5) By the self-diagnostic function, any system abnormality is detected.

Fig. 42 Turbine rotor

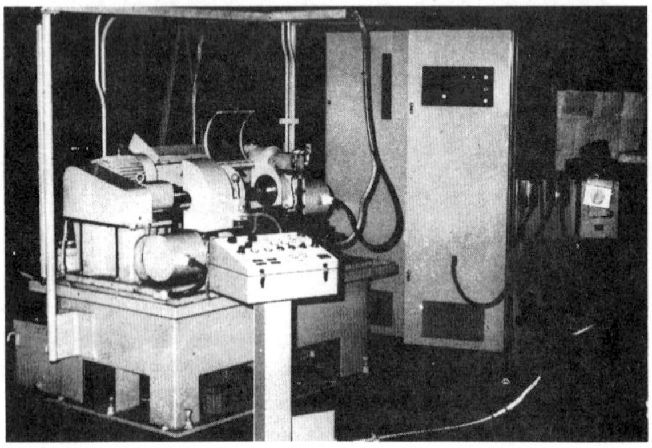

Fig. 43 General view of unbalance-correcting machine

4. CONCLUSION

The first instances of information-control technology in manufacturing industries as early as 1960, were CAD (computer-aided design) systems and line-balancing systems with in-shop computers to produce different types of automobiles efficiently. Subsequently there has emerged CAD/CAM (computer-aided manufacturing) systems utilizing computers to raise efficiency from design through production. Studied in a variety of enterprises, it is now being used practically.

This so-called CAD/CAM system has, however, been developed and realized toward the needs of each enterprise or of the manufacture of each product. Therefore, it comes in a great variety of forms. In conceiving an information-control system for manufacturing, there are two major alternatives. In one, a through system from design to inspection (or including also inquiry and delivery) is first studied; then follows the information-control, either partially or individually. In the other, on the contrary, individual or partial information-control is first studied; these then follows the consolidation into several stages of the process or the overall process. Further, there are such problems as aspects impossible to automatize and phases better handled by man.

Within Mitsubishi Heavy Industries itself, there are some differencies between our respective works in the method of adopting information-control techniques of design and production, and also in the scope of application, Therefore, there are frequent interchange and dissemination of technology among our respective works in the effort to develop better production systems and techniques suitable for each division.

We have explained Mitsubishi's manufacturing technology in part, hoping that it will contribute somehow to your studies, although it may not quite suitable to the themes of this symposium.

NEW FLEXIBLE MANUFACTURING SYSTEMS FROM THE G.D.R.

Günter Kleditzsch

Research Centre of the Machine Tool Industry, 90 Karl-Marx-Stadt, German Democratic Republic

All the activities of the nearly 70,000 workers in the machine tool industry of the G.D.R. are aimed at the development and manufacture of highly productive manufacturing equipment for the rationalization of the metal working industry of the G.D.R. and for meeting the requirements of the commercial partners.

The production programme of the machine tool industry of the G.D.R. includes problem solutions for machining rotationally symmetrical and prismatic workpieces as well as sheet metal parts at different automation level and machining centres for the small and medium series production as well as integrated manufacturing equipment for medium, large-scale and mass production.

In addition to the supply of highly productive products also the conditions are created for the supply of the adequate application documents as software in high quality for the effective use of the goods with the user. The available development results ready for application in the field of the machine programming of NC machine tools, machining centres and machine systems, characterized by the SYMAP programming systems - SYMAP being a symbol language for the machine programming - reveal the fact that also in this field the machine tool industry of the G.D.R. can offer record achievements to the users.

The coordinated and purposive work of the industrial groups of the G.D.R. machine tool industry (in German "Kombinate"), the vast experience and traditions in the field of the manufacture of machine tools as well as extensive scientific investigations form the basis of this high performance.

INTRODUCTION

For the complete machining of a workpiece or a parts family there is an increasing trend to link several NC machines or machining centres and to control them through process computers.

Such manufacturing installations are called flexible, computer controlled machine systems. The need and the use of flexible machine systems are becoming more relevant.

NEW COMPUTER CONTROLLED MACHINE SYSTEMS OF THE G.D.R.

In the G.D.R. up to now eleven machine systems have been developed and manufactured. They are all computer controlled and used successfully in the different branches of industry of the G.D.R. The sale into other countries has begun.

PRISMA 2 MACHINE SYSTEM

The first example of a computer controlled machine system is that built by VEB Werkzeugmaschinenkombinat "Fritz Heckert" in Karl-Marx-Stadt, the so-called Prisma 2 system. The Prisma 2 system allows the fully automatic machining of prismatic parts made of grey cast iron and steel measuring up to 60" x 40" x 35". This system can economically machine small to medium series on different milling and drilling machines. It also comprises working stations for measuring, cleaning and cooling the workpieces.

The system shown is being used in the factory "Fritz-Heckert"-Werk in Karl-Marx-Stadt for manufacturing parts of machine tools. It represents the latest state of technology in the field of manufacturing engineering in the series production sphere.

Machine castings are fed into the system and then completely milled, drilled, broached, cleaned and measured. A particular advantage follows from the close connection of the measuring technique, manufacture and quality control.

The main task relating to the measuring technology consists in the scanning of two shape elements:

- surface (horizontal, vertical or inclined)
- bore (horizontal, vertical, in certain cases open at the sides).

At the measurement, which can be carried out in three coordinate directions, two coordinates each are pre-set for tracer positioning, the third is scanned and stored as a measured value together with the real values of the tracer positioning. The scanning of the surfaces is accomplished in a dot screen, the bores are scanned through eight measuring points at the bore periphery, as a rule in two differently deep measuring levels. The data recording is performed through two scanning heads carrying the tracers corresponding to the task and used optionally for an axial and side scanning task, respectively.

The two CMKeZ 1250 measuring machines used in the system are new developments of the factory VEB Mikromat Dresden incorporated in the Industrial Group Werkseugmaschinenkembinat "Fritz Heckert".

Their concept is characterized by the following functions:

- command reception by process computer (PRS)
- workpiece scanning by means of two measuring heads adapted to the measuring tasks
- measuring data read-out
- measurement accuracy of the 1/2 8 B TGL 15 041 class which corresponds to the workpiece tolerance.

Both the positional real values and the recorded measurement values are transmitted into a central process computer PRT and evaluated for

- either the optimum control of the grinding process (PRS)
- or the quality assessment of the workpieces at intermediate and final inspection (PRT)

The measuring technology contains the whole of the mathematical rules for computing, according to which the measurement values are converted into operands compared with the predetermined parameters and tolerances on the workpiece:

- From the single measuring points of the dot screen of a scanned surface first of all a compensating plane is determined arithmetically, which includes position parameters and direction factors for three directions (x, y and z).
- The measuring points of a bore are used for calculating the centre point of the bore and the bore axis, respectively, including position and direction factor.

The arithmetically determined compensating planes and bore axes, respectively, with their parameters are used in consequence of the mathematical relations according to their mutual communication. Thus, for instance, position errors of the coaxiality, inclination, rectangularity and parallelism can be determined. By comparing single real values for the compensating plane form errors and for the desired diameter dimensional variations, respectively, are determined.

In this way it is possible to calculate 18 different quality parameters at the workpiece from the measuring values and to compare the numerical value gained in each case with the present tolerance.

With the computer print out a high-quality product, which can not be absolutely influenced subjectively, is available for each workpiece.

On the theoretical basis of the mathematical rules for computing included in the measuring technology an inspection rule with those parameters inherent in the workpiece is worked out for every workpiece to be machined in the system. This inspection rule is transformed by the machine into a programme through a compiler, through which the whole workpiece measuring sequence is initiated beginning with the mechanical scanning up to the outprint of the evaluation result (production-engineering NC programme).

On the basis of the measuring technology for the machine system a computing programme package for the used PRT process computer was prepared, which contains the automatical quality surveillance in the system as well as the supply of information for the grinding process optimization.

During the measuring process the three coordinates of each measuring point are transmitted into the PRT process computer by the PRS measuring machine control (CNC computer) and stored there. After realizing the last measuring point of a surface (bore), the "fundamental evaluation" computing programme is started, the result of which is a field of results including all information which is sufficient for the evaluation methods of the measuring technique to be realized.

For the both form elements "surface" and "bore", respectively such a field of results contains different information:

surface:

- surface No for identification (from the production-engineering programme)
- kind of the surface (parallel to the plane, inclined)
- position of the surface in the coordinate system
- coefficients of the compensating plane (approximation from the measuring point coordinates according to the least squares method)
- minimum and maximum form error (relative to the compensating plane)
- corner points of the surface (approximately, because the measuring points are positioned only in the near of the true corner points)
- minimum and maximum measuring value (selection from all measuring values).

bore:

- bore No for identification (from the production-engineering programme)
- kind of the bore (open, closed, one or two diameter planes)
- position in the coordinate system (direction of the bore centre line)
- minimum and maximum diameter (selection from several calculated diameters)
- centre point coordinates (calculation from the measuring values)

All the fields of results are restored on the disk memory. After finishing the measuring process the PRT process computer receives together with the so-called evaluation records further all information from the measuring machine control (PRS) which is required for carrying out the evaluation methods proper, for instance, what parameters are to be checked on what form elements in what way, reference lengths, allowable errors. After recognizing the last evaluation record, these given evaluation methods are worked off by the computing programme. For this purpose in each case the appertaining fields of results of the basic evaluation as well as the corresponding evaluation routine are recalled by the disk memory. Thus always only one evaluation routine is located in the core memory (segmenting). In this way all evaluation records are worked off. Every evaluation method includes a tolerance comparison forming the basis for the qualitative assessment of the test sample. In the case of exceeding the tolerance the workpiece is retained automatically for the further machining and the command is given for removing the part from the system.

In addition to the pure quality control the computing programme realizes the supply of information for desired value determination, if a subsequent grinding operation is provided.

In addition to the automatic evaluation of the quality control (tolerance comparison) for the further run of the workpiece through the machine system a measuring record for documentation purposes is printed out via the parallel printer of the process computer.

The workhandling system represents a new solution. The handling of the workpiece is performed by air-supported pallets, the motion of which is realized through linear motors controlled by the process computer.

For controlling the system two process computers are used. One computer controls the handling system and in DNC operation the machining centres. The computer is equipped with disk memories for programme administration. The other computer controls the measuring machines in CNC operation.

M 250/02 MANUFACTURING SYSTEM

The M 250/02 manufacturing system is designed for the five-side machining of prismatic workpieces with 400 mm edge length and was built by VE Werkzeugmaschinenfabrik Auerbach, a factory of the "Fritz-Heckert" -Kombinat.

Two C 250/01 and C 250/02 NC machining centres as well as the tool and workpiece flow are controlled by a process computer through two selection units of the CONCEMA DNC-CNC system. The CONCEMA system is a system of direct computer control of a number of different machine tools, which was developed in the GDR and used for computer controls. The handling system consists of two pallet changing mechanisms and a loop conveyor. A third pallet changing mechanism is connected with a work store. The design of the work handling system permits the connection of further NC machine tools and machining centres. By the use of this manufacturing system with direct computer control an increase of labour productivity up to 300% will be obtained compared with the machining on individual machines.

ROTA F 125 NC MANUFACTURING SYSTEM

This manufacturing system for machining chucking components comprises four NC lathes, two NC milling machines and one NC grinding machine arranged under an annular workpiece storage magazine. The workpieces, which may be removed from the storage rings by means of elevators, are immediately fed to the machine tools for machining.

The capacity of the storage consisting of nine rings is 540 workpieces. There is an additional clamping and unclamping station where the workpieces are received in the chuck and after having been machined will be cleaned and released. The control of these machines is achieved in off-line operation, i.e. an external computer produces the control tapes for the machines and optimizes the capacity of the system and hence the sequence of motion of the workpieces. The following data show exactly the economic advantages of the system.

- Output: 135,000 workpieces per year
- Assortment: 400 parts with 1,300 NC programmes
- Savings: T_S (production time per piece: 50%
  T_A (start-up and shut-down time): 80%

ROTA FZ 200 MANUFACTURING SYSTEM

The Rota FZ 200 manufacturing system of the VEB Werkzeugmaschinenkombinat "7 Oktober" Berlin is designed for soft machining spur gears up to 4 module, comprising turning, hobbing, deburring, shaving including cleaning as an intermediate operation. Besides three DF 200 NC chucking lathes of VEB Werkzeugmaschinenfabrik Magdeburg, which are computer controlled by the CONCEMA control system, two gear hobbers, one tooth edge chamfering and deburring machine, one gear shaving machine and a work cleaning installation are used, which operate under programme sequence control.

At a pallet loading station, the workpieces are loaded onto pallets in three storeys, temporarily stored at the entrance and exit of storage locations and transported to the machine. A stacking crane, which is provided with a target control device and receives its commands from a KRS 4100 minicomputer of 12 bit and 12K words capacity, carries out the transport.

The computer is also connected with all the machines, the washing station and the pallet loading station.

During setting-up operations or in the event of a computer failure the system can be controlled from a manual control panel. By means of this system about 200,000 spur gears per annum can be produced with an assortment of about 2,000 gears comprising 64 prototypes. The average lot size amounts to 40 pieces.

1. The parts assortment should be arranged so that the various operations on the individual workpieces take similar times. This allows a high rate of utilization of all machines, or

2. Certain operations can be performed on parallel machines permitting an optimization of their capacity, and finally

3. To some extent single-purpose machines can be additionally used in order to avoid bottlenecks in overloaded universal machines.

As a result of the parallel machining on various machines the number of pieces in a manufacturing system is reduced considerably. However, by way of ensuring a good economy the following four principles should be observed:

1. High numbers of pieces per annum of a component family must be provided.

2. Many different, but very similar workpieces must be comprised in the component family.

3. A high flexibility and reliability of the manufacturing system must be granted.

4. In large factories a centralized manufacturing must be considered.

THE ECONOMY OF MACHINE SYSTEMS

If factories take the use of a machine system into consideration, they should be aware of it that they are concerned with a new manufacturing theory which, if it is to be successful, needs the assistance of the whole staff. The main difficulty is the organization of a management system representing the completion of a machine system with tremendous possibilities.

There are direct and indirect advantages connected with machine systems:

From our experience in using such systems in the GDR the following direct advantages have become apparent:

- The labour productivity has been increased by 300-500% compared with the traditional manufacture.
- The savings in manpower amount to 70-80%. We were able, for instance, to reduce the number of manpower by more than 100 men by means of the Prisma 2 system and we are still manufacturing the same number of workpieces.
- The space requirement is reduced by 50% or more according to the type of the system.
- The lead times were reduced by 2/3 and others.

Indirect economic effects are:

- Creation of advance of six to eight years for the development of machine tools and in the field of the automation technique
- General improvement of the enterprise organization from designing to shipping
- qualification of a large number of engineers and workers with the manufacturer and user of the machine systems and others.

CERTAIN FACTORS FOR THE ECONOMY

1. Guaranty of three-shift utilization of the machine systems including

Saturday and Sunday in order to justify the high investment cost.

2. High reliability of the machines and other equipment.

3. Use of automatically operating error detection and checking equipment. Thus the Prisma 2 machine system is permanently supervised by means of more than 200 control points, one of the existing process computers being used for this. The experience shows that nearly 90% of the repair time is required for the determination of errors and the remaining time for the elimination of faults. Diagnostic monitoring points influence this ratio very positively.

4. Good enterprise organization, prophylactic maintenance as well as a clearly arranged and comprehensive wearing stock. A well qualified maintenance and servicing staff is another important condition.

Our experience in using machine systems in the GDR shows that under consideration of these points of view an availability of machine systems of more than 80% can be achieved.

SUMMARY

A high-quality machining of workpieces in the field of small and medium series is only possible by means of automatic, very flexible manufacturing equipment.

NC machine tools and machining centres are especially suitable for it. Flexible computer controlled machine systems are at present the highest form of the product design for the complete machining of workpieces in small batch production.

True to system, linkable machines and machining centres are the basis for designing machine systems of different forms of construction.

MAJOR PROJECTS ON CONTROL SYSTEMS FOR DISCRETE PARTS MANUFACTURING IN THE FEDERAL REPUBLIC OF GERMANY

Ingward Bey

Gesellschaft für Kernforschung mbH, Projekt PDV, Postfach 3640, D 7500 Karlsruhe 1
Federal Republic of Germany

Abstract:

The major recent applications of computer control of flexible manufacturing systems for short-run production, which are in development today in the Federal Republic of Germany, are presented; including a flexible manufacturing cell for turning parts, more complex industrial systems with linked machines for gear parts and armature production for electric motors. Furthermore some special requirements and problems which arise in information processing when such systems are built up, are described. Specially the process and experiment realtime automation language PEARL which will have a major impact on implementing these systems, is described in more detail.

1. Introduction: Increase in productivity in parts manufacturing by means of flexible manufacturing systems (FMS)

In the field of discrete parts manufacturing the evolution which began in the early sixties with the marriage between the old good machine-tool and the data processing machine called computer is still going on. The trend started with the numerically controlled (NC-) machine-tool and continued with the DNC* and CNC** concepts. It is leading us presently to the flexible manufacturing systems. Eventually it may end with the unmanned factory.

In the Federal Republic of Germany economical reasons are forcing us to increase productivity to build and operate machine tools. This means there will be more computerized automation in the discrete industrial process of parts batch production. In this context, we feel that attention must not be paid primarily to automation of a single machining unit - we have today already very sophisticated examples of computer controlled machining centers with automatic tool changing, etc. - but it is quite necessary to concentrate one's efforts on integrating such units into larger systems and into factory organization.

* Direct Numerical Control
** Computerized Numerical Control

One important approach to achieve this is given by the Flexible Manufacturing Systems (FMS), which can be characterized as follows:

- system configuration with several working stations linked together by automated transport and storage devices
- parts run through the system in an arbitrary order
- automatic control of the whole system including material flow and information processing
- automatic tool and workpiece changing

In the Federal Republic of Germany the development and application of FMS is at the very beginning. The main reason for this lies in the structure of the machine-producing companies. The nearly 400 firms affiliated to VDMA - German assocation of machine-tool producers - have an average of 300 employees with an average turnover of $ 6 million a year (figures for 1973). The relatively small factory size and low productivity have definite influences: There are a great variety of products, short-run production, low budgets for capital investment and the subsequent difficulties in doing research and accepting the financial risks of introducing new manufacturing systems.

The Federal Ministry of Research and Technology has taken this situation into consideration and is actually funding several industrial projects supporting different application programs to realize computerzed manufacturing systems.

2. Computerized Parts Manufacturing Systems in Development in the Federal Republic of Germany

From several industrial systems which are in the planning, development or installation stage the main features of the most important systems will be shown. A summary is given in Table 1.

2.1 Flexible manufacturing cell for turning operation

A team formed by the machine-tool producer Gildemeister AG and the Institut für Werkzeugmaschinen und Fertigungstechnik, Technical University of Berlin (Prof. Spur) is developing a fully automated, single machining unit, capable of producing around the clock turning parts up to 300 mm in diameter with negligible set-up and idle time. The system was conceived to be used initially as a highly automated "flexible manufacturing cell" in a conventionally operated factory. With this approach it is intended to overcome the difficulties and the high risk of introducing a complete new complex system. [1,2]

Figure 1 shows this flexible manufacturing cell. Its main components are a machine-tool, a handling and storage system and a control and supervisory system. Located in the center of the cell is the NC-lathe. By integrating the handling system it was possible to eliminate the need for an independent industrial robot. This saves space and increases positioning accuracy. Transportation of parts is carried out by a conveyor, an elevator and a storage device located next to the machine-tool. The cell can be connected to the central automated material transport system of a factory.

Information processing within the flexible cell includes the control of approximately one hundred different functions; more than a half of them are one-bit, the others multi-bit or analog functions. To perform these operations, a CNC with a 16 K - 16 bit minicomputer is used. The internal hardware structure and the software architecture are shown in figure 2. In both cases, modularity will result in lower design, service and maintenance costs. Many control functions otherwise executed in conventional hardware are replaced by software. The complete process control logic is included in the main operating program, which is stored in the main memory.

The above described flexible cell will be ready for industrial use at the end of 1978. It will first be used at Gildemeister's own production plant. In a second stage this automated unit will be integrated into complex systems with a number of similar or identical cells linked to each other.

Such an advanced system will be described in the next paragraph.

2.2 Flexible manufacturing system for rotatory parts

At Zahnradfabrik Friedrichshafen AG, Lake Constance, a FMS is being developed since 1976. It consists of ten different manufacturing cells and it is suitable for short-run production of cylindrical/disk like workpieces in gear manufacturing. Each cell includes a machine-tool, an industrial robot, positioning aids, other auxiliary devices and a computerized numerical control (CNC-)unit.

Workpieces will be transported as single parts or in magazines from the storage area to the corresponding CNC machine-tools and viceversa by an automatic transport and handling system. A central process control computer will control the overall operation of the system including short-term scheduling, tool selection, material flow and supervisory functions. The manufacturing process will be organized for lots of 50 to 5000 workpieces. The system will be built up successively and introduced step by step into a conventional factory. Industrial production is planned to start in 1980.

2.3 FMS for armature production for electric motors

Another flexible manufacturing system is being planned to be in operation in 1979 at AEG-Telefunken-Elektrowerkzeuge, Winnenden (near Stuttgart). This will modernize armature fabrication in a plant for small electric tools, where production reaches a total number of about 1 million armatures a year. There it will be tried to make the existing system flexible enough to produce with a high degree of automation 150 types of armatures in lots of 100 to 5000 parts with only very short set-up time. Armature production involves 30 different machining operations by nearly 70 processing units, which in this case are not numerically controlled machine-tools. A completely new system for automated transportation, handling and storage, including universal magazines for blanks and finished workpieces have yet to be developed.

Also in this case a hierarchical system architecture was chosen for realtime data processing. One important characteristic is the busline for information transmission between the central process control computer and peripheral control units, processors, displays, keyboards, sensoring elements, etc. This serial data transmission system will correspond most probably to the "PDV-Bus", a development which is being conducted since 1974 by a number of institutes and firms (including AEG).

3. Common aspects and information control problems concerning flexible manufacturing systems

The Federal Republic of Germany has little experience with FMS. In other industrialized countries, i.e. Japan or the U.S.A. several systems exist which are operating under industrial conditions. These units demonstrate that the concept of FMS is sound. However, it can be noticed that broad application of FMS as state of the art in manufacturing technology is far from reality.

One important obstacle is the lack of standarization: most of the systems which are actually in operation or are being planned are individual solutions with their high unit development costs and high application risks for the user. The consequence: although producers are able to build FMS they find no or only a very restricted market for them.

Information flow and control play a major role in these problems. These subjects have an impact on systems realization, operation and integration into the organization of a factory. In the same manner, modularity and standardization of hardware and software components are necessary requirements and will be helpful aids for both, manufacturers and users of FMS.

If one considers first one important aspect of the hardware of information control systems, it will be necessary to overcome problems related to the conventional solutions by new bus-line concepts with standardized interfaces for decentralized systems. In the Federal Republic of Germany, one important step in this direction is given by the development of the serial data transmission system called "PDV-Bus". The characteristic features are described in detail in [3] .

It permits the communication between different computerized and/or non-computerized devices over a length of 3000 m at a max. transmission rate of approximately 500 Kbaud. Interfaces and transmission procedures will be standardized and coupling/decoupling of new participants will easily be done without disturbing the actual process. Initial installation costs are low. Details of the system are discussed also at an international level at the Purdue Workshop Technical Committee "Interfaces and Data Transmission". The first bus prototype will be available at the end of 1977 and it is expected that it will give an answer to all requirements of FMS applications.

Although specific operation goals may differ substantially from one FMS to another, in most cases the information processing functions to be implemented will be identical. They could be classified roughly by a matrix structure as shown in figure 3, independently of their realization in software or hardware. Functions like NC-data management, machine operation, scheduling, job control, material flow control (including workpieces, tools, coolant supply, chip disposal), process data acquisition, etc. are common to almost all FMS.

Therefore, from the point of view of software engineering, system analogy and similarity of functional requirements, it is necessary to clearly delimit and describe each single functional block within the whole application program. This will permit under certain conditions multiple use of common parts of programs.

This technique is well known, but its application is very difficult today, when one considers the conventional assembly programming languages, which do not allow program portability. Better basic software tools are needed, i.e. the development, implementation and market introduction of a high level realtime programming language. To solve this problem, in Germany there was created and implemented the Process and Experiment Automation Realtime Language PEARL [4 , 5] . Compilers for several process control computers were shown in operation at the INTERKAMA-International Exhibition and Congress for Instrumentation and Automation, Düsseldorf, October 1977.

In the next chapter more emphasis will be given to this subject because PEARL will contribute to the efforts which are being made to improve information processing. Thus such an easy to handle tool would also be of advantage in case of FMS.

4. Short description of PEARL

PEARL is a high level general purpose realtime programming language suitable to formulate structure, algorithms, timing and input/output instructions for realtime programs. In comparison with assembly programming its main advantages are a high degree of self documentation of programs, the possibility of applying methods of structured programming and providing a standard interface to computer operating systems. This leads to greater program and programmer portability, easy methods of learning, higher reliability of programs, less testing and debugging efforts and last but not least a significant cost reduction.

4.1 PEARL Data Types

As in other programming languages it is possible to declare

- problem data: fixed, floating denotations; bit and character strings; durations, clocktime
- algorithmic and scheduling instructions: procedures, functions, operators, labels
- I/O-instructions: files, formats, devices.

Beyond that, PEARL permits to declare

- structured objects: arrays, structured data types
- realtime features: tasks, interrupts
- extensions, i.e. new operators may be defined by the user.

Names for procedures or other program elements can be freely designated by the programmer.

4.2 Main Realtime Feature: Task

In programs to be used for automatic control of industrial processes it is, in general, not possible to order all required actions into a single chronological sequence. E.g., interrupts arising asynchronously from the process require immediate response whereas current activities must not be terminated. In consequence, PEARL provides a set of language elements to organize such parallel activities. The basic unit hereto is the task, the corresponding program segment has to be designated with the task name. The task declaration has static character; task execution can be activated, suspended or terminated immediately, periodically or accordingly to certain process events or clocktime by PEARL program statements without using a special job control language.

4.3 Program Structure

A PEARL program consists of one or more modules. These modules may be compiled separately or simultaneously and then linked either to a new or to an already running program system. Items declared in one module may be linked to corresponding items in other modules. In general, a module contains two divisions:

- system division, which describes at a language level the hardware configuration and serves to replace manufacturer specific device names by freely defined identifiers used in the
- problem division, in which is declared independently of hardware configuration the actual process control program with all actions to be performed.

This strict separation is a very important step to obtain portability of application program.

4.4 Current Status of PEARL

There are two language descriptions available: one is called Full PEARL [4]and the other Basic PEARL [5]. The existing implementations for German process computers are subsets of Full PEARL and contain at least the features of Basic PEARL. The language is on the way to become a national standard for industrial process automation programming in Germany. It is planned to apply PEARL to the above mentioned flexible manufacturing systems, as soon as they will enter the software preparation and programming phase. The development was funded by the Federal Ministry for Research and Technology since 1972 through the Project PDV (computerized control of industrial processes) with the amount of approximately 24 Million DM.

5. Conclusion

With this paper I tried to give an overview on the current activities in the Federal Republic of Germany in flexible manufacturing systems and information control technology, the two principal topics of the present IFAC Symposium. The flexible manufacturing system is one of the most challenging possibilities to obtain an advanced manufacturing technology. But there will be no significant progress on this subject without improving information control as one of the central tools to improve automation. Being successful in the task of reducing risks and the "complexity-complex" from the users point of viev, i.e. by offering better and more standardized tools, I think the market for such advanced technology as FMS will grow substantially in the near future.

References:

1 K. Rall, "Flexible manufacturing cells for rotatory simmetric parts", Proceeding of the 8th Machine-Tool Congress Budapest, October 1976, 37-49

2 G. Spur, H.P. Mattle, W. Prehn, "Computer Control of a Flexible Manufacturing Cell", Proceedings of the Ninth CIRP International Seminar on Manufacturing Systems, Cranfield/Bedford UK, July 1977.

3 E. Buxmeyer, G. Hausmann, P. Mielentz, H. Walze, "Serial Line Sharing System for Industrial Real-Time Applications (PDV-Bus)", PDV-Report KFK-PDV 70, Gesellschaft für Kernforschung mbH, Karlsruhe, May 1976

4 "Basic PEARL Language Description", PDV-Report KFK-PDV 120, Gesellschaft für Kernforschung mbH, Karlsruhe, June 1977

5 "Full PEARL Language Description", PDV-Report KFK-PDV 130, Gesellschaft für Kernforschung mbH, Karlsruhe, October 1977

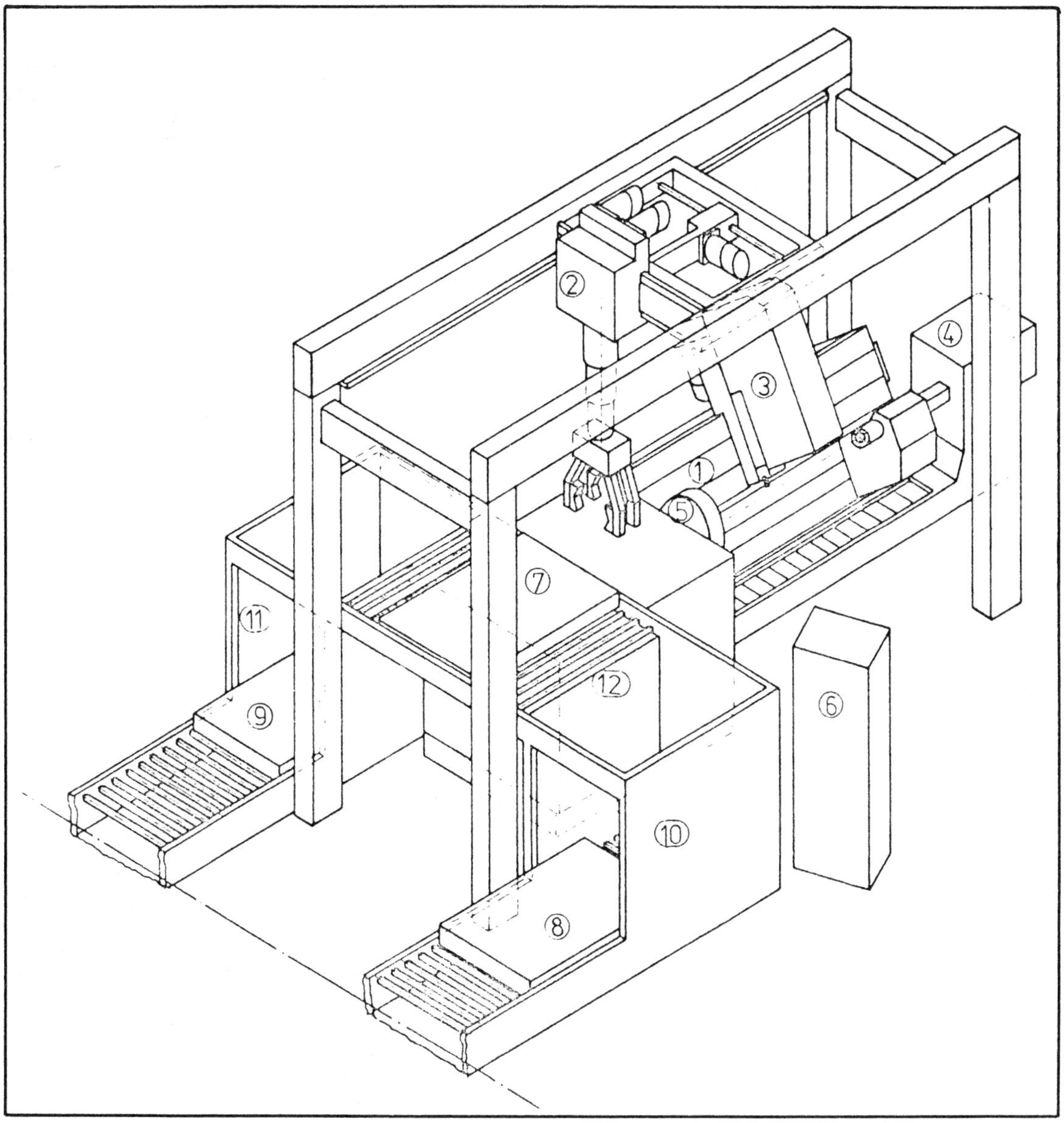

Fig. 1: Flexible manufacturing cell for turning operation

1) NC-turning machine
2) Integrated robot system
3) Automatic tool changer
4) Automatic chip disposal
5) Chuck changing device
6) Computerized numerical control
7) Palet
8) Palet with blanks
9) Palet with finished parts
1o) 11) Elevators
12) Transportation device

Source: Gildemeister AG

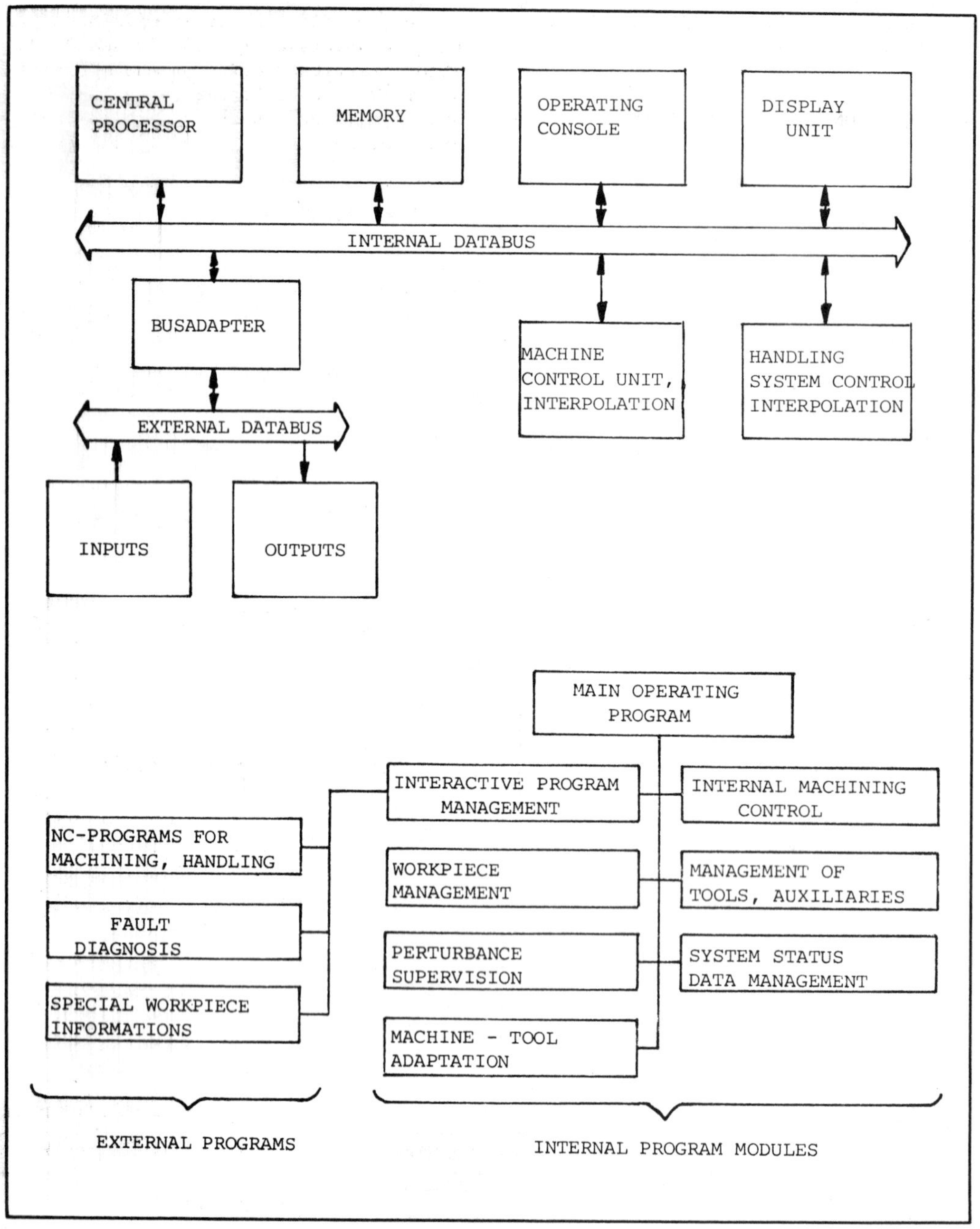

Fig. 2: Modular Hardware and Software Configuration of Flexible Manufacturing Cell Control. (Source: Gildemeister)

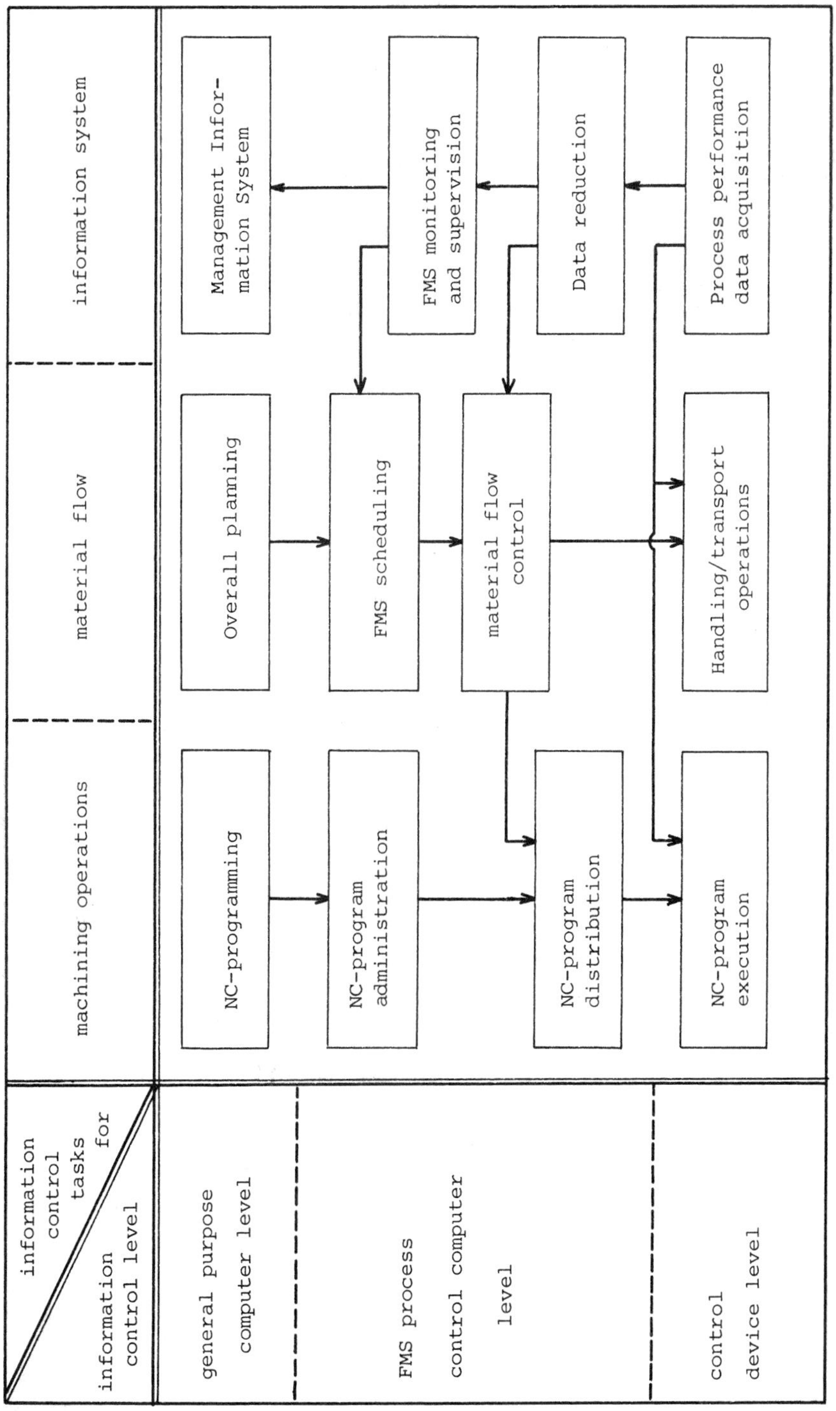

Fig. 3: Information processing functions related to flexible manufacturing system operation.

Table 1: Main funded projects on FMS in the Federal Republic of Germany

	1	2	3	4	5
System application	Research and development	R and D	gear parts fabrication	armatures for small electric motors	manufacturing cell
User	University Stuttgart	Technical University Berlin	Zahnradfabrik Friedrichshafen	AEG-Telefunken	Gildemeister AG
Workpieces	prismatic	rotatory	Cylindric, gear parts	shaft parts 20 mm ∅	rotatory parts up to 300 mm ∅
batch size	--	--	50-5.000	50-10.000	100
machine-tools	4 NC milling m.	1 NC-turing m. 1 NC-milling/ drilling m.	10 different NC machines	30 diff. conventional machines	1 NC-turing m.
transport system	stack transport device	elevated track palet transport	elevated track magazine transport	magazine transport	elevators, roller conveyors
handling	automatic palet handling	robots	robots, integrated handling devices	handling aids	integrated handling device
parts storage	stacker crane	elevated hanging system	elevated hanging system	high-bay storage	integrated in transport
DNC operation	X	X	X	--	X
process control computer for system control and monitoring	X	X	X	X	X
Status	Operation starting	in Operation	planned	planned	planned

SYSTEMS OF SENSITIZED ROBOTS SUPERVISIORY CONTROL

S. I. Novatchenko, V. A. Pavlov, N. S. Teleshev and E. I. Jurevich

Leningrad Polytechnical Institute, 195251, Leningrad, USSR

ABSTRACT

The paper exhibits the question of an organization of the sensitized robots supervisory control. The various approaches to the synthesis of robots control algorithms are described. The Algorithmic Robot Control System has been developed in Leningrad Polytechnical Institute to control the actions of Robots. The robot control language ROCOL and the built-in program support aids have been developed to make a dialogue interface between a man and a robot. The operators of this language are described in the paper. The examples of the systems of supervisory control of the industrial and underwater robots which are developed in the Leningrad Polytechnical Institute are given.

INTRODUCTION

A great work on the production preparation is necessary to use the first generation industrial robots. Its purpose is to minimize the uncertainty of the environment. First of all it is caused by the reason that the first generation robots have no ability for adaptation. An enlargement of a robot application sphere depends on their adaptation possibilities greatly.

To function in the uncertain environment a robot must have a well developed sensory system and its control system must include a computer. During its functioning a robot must perceive and recognize the external medium and independence upon the state of the latter, to construct the tactics and strategics of its own behaviour to fulfil the assigned task. An automatization of all control processes of a robot with a complex behaviour, including recognition, planning and decision making, is a complicated problem that has not yet solved completely and its modern partial solutions are commercially inexpedient. The compromise decision for this problem is a supervisory control, i.e. a computer control under supervision of a man who performs the highest level of control in the hierarchical structure of a system (Ref. 1). In case of a supervisory method of a robot control the functions of a man-operator are: recognition of visual information, strategic (and sometimes tactic) planning, target designation, delivery of the directives to a computer that provides its fulfilment by robot.

SUPERVISORY CONTROL

The supervisory control allows to combine both the advantages of a computer that can solve formalized tasks successfully and man's intellectual capabilities and efficiency to solve complex unformal tasks. A development of supervisory methods of a robot control - is a complex problem that requires the solution of a set of interconnected tasks; it is necessary to distinguish the following ones among them:

1) General system tasks of functional determination of a man - computer interaction, man - robot programming interface, study of a man - operator in supervisory control system loop.

2) Problems of a kinematic synthesis of the "hand-eye"

systems.

3) Problem of a sensory equipment of robots.

4) Problems of adaptive control algorithms development.

It is possible to separate robots supervisory control systems in dependence upon a degree of control processes automatization, i.e. on a degree of a man's participation in a robot control process. A control function distribution between a man and a computer, and accordingly a definition of a degree of robot behaviour autonomy, is one of the most important stages of a robot supervisory control system development. To do this, we must rely on the real problems of definite robot design taking into account all specific technical considerations and constraints and of course commercial factors.

For example, to distribute the control functions of the underwater robot manipulator it is expediently to entrust with a computer an execution of simply formalized repeating operations such as removal of a tool to an object chosen by an operator, movement of a tool along the given trajectory, lifting and carrying of samples, holding of a tool over the work object under robot disturbed motion. A man-operator in this case has to plan operations, choose the targets and make the running check of the task execution.

CONTROL ALGORITHMS

The control algorithms of such robots must secure, firstly, a performation of typical robot motions and, secondly, a correction of robot actions in accordance to the information from the sensory devices of the robot.

One can distinguish two types of the first group algorithms:

1) algorithms of a direct calculation of characteristic robot coordinates;

2) algorithms of optimization.

Geometric correlations between links and characteristic coordinates of a robot arm are used in the direct calculation algorithms. Characteristic coordinates are calculated in unique form for the arm with three degrees of freedom only, when the robot hand moves to the assigned point. One must put some restrictions to avoid an exessiveness and to solve this task for an arm with more than three degrees of freedom. For instance, one can use the hand orientation, that is necessary to perform the assigned task, as such restriction.

A calculation of characteristic coordinates of a robot in the target point during one iteration is the main advantage of the algorithms of this type. Disadvantages of these algorithms are an application of the developed algorithm for the concrete robot kinematics only and a nonoptimality of the calculated trajectory of a hand movement.

Another method of the calculation of characteristic robot coordinates is the utilization of optimization algorithms. In this case, one can regard a disconcordance between the initial and assigned positions of a hand as a target function that is minimized during the process of a robot control. It is necessary to minimize the disconcordance functional between three points of a hand and a target at least to secure a hand removal to the target point with the assigned orientation. The latter condition can be lead to the minimization of the disconcordance functional between the current hand position and the target point under the restriction on the hand orientation.

A calculation of optimal trajectory of the joints movements during the robot motion is the main advantage of the optimization methods. But a large number of iterations and a large calculation time reduce this advantage greatly.

Now we consider methods of the realization of robot adaptation possibilities in accordance with the information from the sensory devices. The first method is a utilization of a modular principle. In accordance with this principle a special module corresponds to every combination of readings of the robot sensors. This module realizes necessary adjusting motions.

Practically, this method can be used to control the robot that possesses a few sensors only. Accordingly, adaptation possibilities of such a robot are small.

An application of optimization methods allows to take into consideration the information from sensory devices by means of restrictions very simply. In this case the minimization of the disconcordance functional is realized by the penalty functions method. A value that is inversly proportional to a distance square from the hand to the restricted plane is taken as a penalty function. The restricted planes are built in every step of optimization. They are parallel or perpendicular to the hand in dependence upon the sensors readings. An application of the penalty functions method allows to change a structure of the motion control algorithm in dependence upon operation performance conditions that leads to the optimization of the robot control process.

ALGORITHMIC ROBOT CONTROL SYSTEM

The Algorithmic Robot Control System has been developed in the Leningrad Polytechnical Institute to realize the robots supervisory control and to research the above-mentioned principles of the control algorithms construction (Ref. 2).

This is a specialized software system that controls the robots actions. Design considerations of the Algorithmic System include a number of requirements that used to present in the most of such systems. Particularly, it is necessary to provide a flexible and multi-purpose robots control, to perform a control process in real time, to provide possibility of a dialogue between a man and a robot, to develop a flexible, easily expanded and modified structure of the Algorithmic System itself and so on. In this case the robot should be regarded as a complex system of interacting subsystems. The connection of all subsystems together and subordination of their functioning to the achievement of a general goal - are the tasks that the software system of the control computer has to solve.

The Algorithmic System consists of the system routines which provide the functioning of the System itself, and of the applied routines which provide the functioning of a robot. System routines control the work of the applied ones and have no contacts with the external (with respect to computer) world, i.e. have no external links. In distinction to the system routines, the applied routines have both internal and external links.

Generally speaking, the Algorithmic System must control actuators of a robot, process an information from the sensors and associate with a man simultaneously. In other words, one must organize a regime multiprogramming in the computer controlling the robot actions. One of the basic requirements to the robots control systems is providing a fast response of the system on the variations of external (and sometimes - internal) world of the robot. This information is transferred to the control computer via interrupt system that is based on the priority principle. A dialogue regime of a man's contact with a robot has been also made on the base of the interrupt system. In accordance with this, the computer software system has to be regarded as the time-sharing.

The principles of the modular programming (Ref. 3, 4) are in the base of the Algorithmic System structure. When decomposing of a system into modules each of them is logically and physically independent. The modules form an hierarchical structure. Each hierarchically organized group of modules accomplishes one logical function over one class of data. All program modules of the Algorithmic System are separated into five groups in accordance with their functions: 1) Monitor of the Algorithmic System; 2) Interpreter of the System input language; 3) Routines of the robot movement control; 4) Routines of the sensors information processing; 5) Auxiliary Routines. Currently the Algorithmic System includes 15 basic program modules.

Data exchange between the modules is made via buffer files organized on a cyclic principles. The system of priorities is used to perform the program modules control. Each module has a priority in accordance with an importance of its function and a necessity of a fast response on the request to activate this module.

ROBOT CONTROL LANGUAGE

To facilitate the process of the robots programming, the special programming language-ROCOL (Robots Control Language) and various aids for a programming automatization have been developed. The input of the robot functioning program having been written in ROCOL into the computer is fulfilled in a dialogue form. ROCOL includes three types of operators: basic operators, editing operators and control operators (Ref. 5).

The basic operators of ROCOL are used to describe robot functioning program logics. The directive is the basic meaning element of the developed language; it is a set of basic operators which specify an execution of a definite action. Each directive when input in the computer for the first time is labelled by the set of symbols - by the name. All consecutive calls of the directive for the execution are using this name. Furthermore, the name of the directive is the macro definition of the language using which we can insert this robot functioning program into any assigned place of other directives.

The basic operators of ROCOL are divided into three groups. The first group includes operators that perform arithmetic and logic operations with data files and operations of conditional and unconditional jumps in a program. The second group consists of the operators that secure a performance of various robot specific actions. For instance, the opening and closing of hand fingers, the removal of a hand in space,etc. The operators of the third group secure the communication between a man and a robot. This group includes the operators of the interrogation of a robot control desk and an automatic target designation system and the operators of the message printing. Each basic operator is described by a set of parameters which are set during the directive input into the operator informative field. The filling of the informative field is fulfilled in a dialogue regime.

The editing operators allow to carry out the transformations of the object ROCOL code in the computer memory. Furthermore, the special operators of this group perform the input of the robot functioning program to the computer.

The control operators of ROCOL are used to specify the working regimes of the robot and of the control computer. We may perform an operative interaction with a robot during its functioning with the help of operators of this group.

APPLICATIONS

An application of the developed Algorithmic System is its using to control the assembly robots. During the assembly such robot has to do following typical operations: taking of parts and movement of them to the assembly zone, mutual orienting of the assembling parts, joining of the parts in the assembly, securing of the parts in the assembly,moving of the erected assembly to the zone of the next operation execution. Such operations can be written in ROCOL. The language structure allows to use the information from the sensory devices of the robot. The ROCOL code consists of the basic and correcting parts. The basic part of the program prescribes the execution of the typical operations which must be done by the robot during the assembly under given functioning conditions. The correcting parts of the program are used to take into account the variations in the environment. The Algorithmic System structure also provides for the control of more than one robot.

The study of taking of the non-oriented parts, of moving

of parts to the assembly zone and of parts orienting has been done at the experimental robot LPI-2 of the Leningrad Polytechnical Institute. The TV target designation system is used to plot the coordinates and the orientation of the parts in space. A man-operator designates the part's coordinates and its orientation in space on the screen of the video-control device by the request of the Algorithmic System.

The Algorithmic System is based on the computer model ACBT M-6000. It occupies about 8K of memory (16-bit words). When the robot functioning program is input into the computer the automatic test is fulfilled. This test allows to minimize the syntactic errors.

Another example of the simple system of the supervisory control by the target designation is the system of the deep water robot manipulator control. It consists of the specialized control desk and the board computer. The control desk includes the target designation device with the screen and the directive assignment device. The board computer realizes the following functions: the choice of the regime, the control of the scanning search, the movement of the tool to the target and the sampling.

The control system secures the execution of the following operator directives: take the object pointed out by the operator, move the object to the TV camera, to the bunker, to the assigned point, search the object in the assigned zone (the automatic obstacles detour is provided). The board computer has the overall dimension 0.23 x 0.18 x 0.09 m, the mass - 1.6 kg, the energy consumption - 20 wt. The control desk has the overall dimension 0.2 x 0.11 x 0.045 m, the mass - 0.3 kg, the energy consumption - 5 wt.

The system tests showed that it is considerably shortens the operations execution time in comparison with the manual control. So, the time of the manipulator grip movement to the object is 1 - 2 minutes with the manual control, and it is only 20 - 40 seconds with the automatic control. The time of taking, lifting and moving of the object to the assigned place is about 5 minutes and more with the manual regime, and it is only 1-1.5 minutes with the automatic one. The automatic regime also reduce the operator's load essentially because to control the manipulator he must transmit just the single commands - the directives.

The extension of this design is a system of a deep-water robot manipulator supervisory control intended for sampling when a non-rigid robot stabilization over the working object and a translatory motion of the robot over a bottom take place. The manipulator tool stabilization over the working object is fulfilled independently from the robot motion regime due to using of the natural manipulator exsessiveness.

REFERENCES

(1) N.S. Teleshev, E.I.Jurevich, Supervisory control of underwater robots. Proc. of the All-Union symposium "Man-machine problem in the sea vessels" (1975) (in Russian).

(2) V.V. Nickiphorov, S.I. Novatchenko, V.A. Pavlov, E.I. Jurevich, Modular software system of integral robot. J.Control systems and computers, 5 (1976) (in Russian).

(3) J. Rhodes, Management by module, "Data Systems", 8-12 (1971).

(4) D.L. Parnas, On the criteria to be used in decomposing systems into modules, CACM, 12 (1972).

(5) V.V. Nickiphorov, S.I. Novatchenko, V.A. Pavlov, ROCOL-language for the robot control. Robototechnica(1976), LPI, Leningard (in Russian).

THE ROLE OF NUMERICAL CONTROL USED FOR THE MANUFACTURING PROCESS IN MACHINING ON MAIN INDUSTRIES IN JAPAN

M. Soeda, H. Yonaiyama and E. Yamaguchi

Department of Administrative Engineering, Tokai University, Hiratsuka City, Japan

Abstract. We have set out a questionnaire in order to try to survey the benefit of the N/C machine tool and have obtained information on many items. The discussion and data below are the result of the summation of replies and of dealing with the information, in some cases we have investigated from door to door. The benefit regarding N/C, as a whole, is expressed more strongly than presented in many books or papers. A large number of N/C or N/C applications have been installed specially in large factories and middle-scale factories and for the years following the oil crisis in Japan. The most typical example is that which exists in many ship-building yards. Roughly speaking, the ratio of a numerical control N/C machine to a conventional machine is approximately 20% for a recent year. From this viewpoint, it is significant to know how the N/C machine is operated in machining and how the N/C meets the demands that are expected of it, and to find how N/C reduces or eliminates labour and what profit increase can be expected.

1. INTRODUCTION

In Japan numerical control machine tools were introduced from about 1950 by personnel in universities or laboratories.

Since then several big enterprises have tried to develop N/C and machine tools or have attempted to use imported N/C combined with the machine tool as a sample machine.

But generally speaking in Japan, small- to medium-sized enterprises have made more effort to increase the efficiency of working by hand as opposed to large enterprises.

However, in the development of expansion and in the rationalization of industry and modern developments in the elimination or reduction of labor, large enterprises have made more effort than have small- or middle-sized enterprises.

Behind the above facts, certain reasons are shown for the case of small- or middle-sized enterprises

(a) Shortage of funds.

(b) The small lot size of the products.

(c) Intrinsic difficulty of the above-mentioned production process.

The same tendency exists today in the case of N/C; however, N/C has been popularized in small- to middle-sized enterprises gradually

Up to 1976, about 18,000 N/C machine tools have been installed, and the ratio of numeric machine tool to conventional machine tool has been about 20%.

Meanwhile, most textbooks or papers concerning N/C machine tool, however, express generally the advantages of it.

We would like to know the actual advantage or disadvantage according to how they are used, especially in relation to the profit of the investment, and for this reason we tried to survey the above problem for the first time for typical workshops, such as shipbuilding, electrical machinery, construction machinery and machine tool makers, etc.

Figures 1 and 2 show one of the results of this survey.

2. THE RATIO OF N/C MACHINES TO CONVENTIONAL MACHINES (FOR EACH KIND OF MACHINE)

The result of our research shows that the ratio of the N/C machine to the conventional machine is generally similar to that of the data shown by the Statistics Bureau run by the Prime Minister's Office, except for the machining center. Compare Fig. 3 with Fig. 4.

In this investigation machining centers are included elsewhere because they are very few.

Outlines of these results show that less than 40 of lot-size occupied 77.5% of the sum total.

In addition to this, the high growth of economy allowed Japan to invest more and more fiercely in many works.

Consequently, the high growth of economy made Japan become short of labour, especially the skilled workers.

Consequently, N/C have been expanded at a much higher rate in big enterprises and companies such as shipbuilding, electrical machinery, the construction of machinery, machine tool makers and so on.

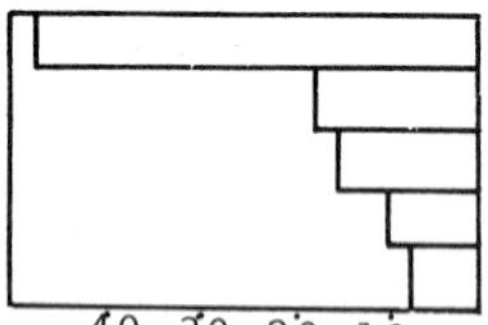

Fig. 1. The rate of spread of the N/C machine in each field.

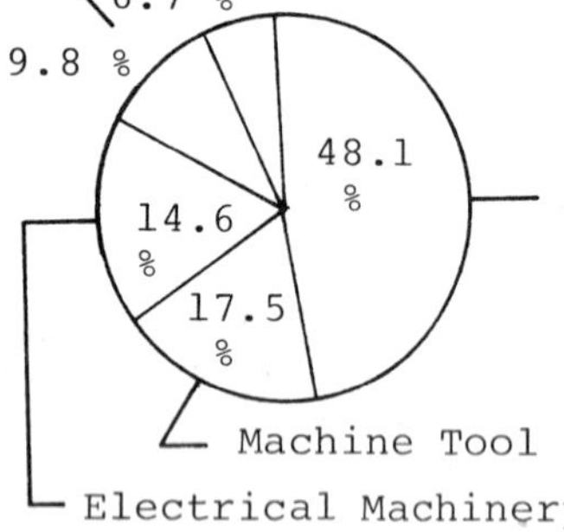

Fig. 2. The rate of spread of the N/C machine in industries.

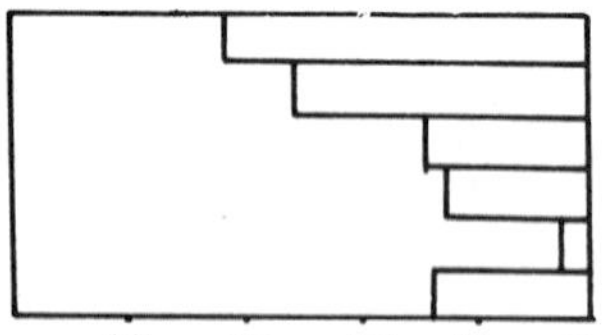

Fig. 3. The rate of spread of each N/C machine.

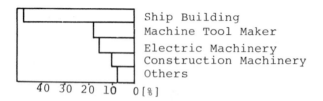

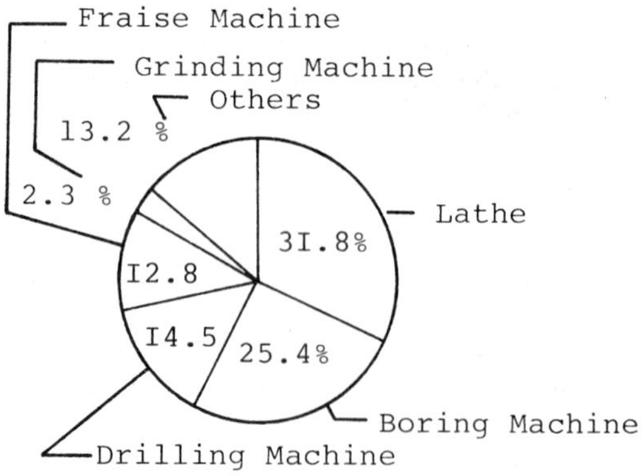

Fig. 4. The rate of spread of the N/C machine.

3. THE EXAMPLES OF THE REDUCTION OF MACHINING

An example of the rate of reduction of manpower (operator) for each machine is shown in Table 1.

The result of our questionnaire on the subject of the rate of manpower reduction for each N/C machine is as follows.

The rate means the number of N/C machines which can be handled by one operator.

On the whole, one operator handling two machines was not often seen in our survey.

The above values in Table 1 will be advanced, when the reliability (which is not shown here) of the overall machine, including the controller, is improved, and when, at the same time, some new method of dealing with scrap metal is developed.

The values shown in the table differ from machine to machine and from machine shop to machine shop. (See page the analysis of idle time in machining in relation to the improvement of operating time.)

TABLE 1. THE NUMBER OF N/C MACHINES HANDLED BY ONE OPERATOR

The sort of machines	Machine/ man
Lathe	1.43
Drilling machine	1.31
Fraise machine	1.43
Machining center	1.57

4. THE MERIT OF THE N/C LATHE

We attempted an analysis of the operation time and the investigation of the relation between the rate of decrease of defective products and the ratio of the N/C machine to the conventional machine.

The rate of decrease of the defective product:

$$A = \frac{[\text{The number of the defective products by the formar lathe}]}{[\text{The number of total products by the formar lathe}]} \quad (1)$$

$$B = \frac{[\text{The number of the defective products by the N/C lathe}]}{[\text{The number of total samples machined by the N/C lathe}]} \quad (2)$$

$$A\text{-}B\text{-} [\text{The rate of decrease of defective products}] \quad (3)$$

The rate of increase of operation time:

$$C = \frac{[\text{The real production by the formar lathe}]}{[\text{The theoretical production by the N/C lathe}]} \quad (4)$$

$$D = \frac{[\text{The real production by the N/C lathe}]}{\text{The theoretical production by the N/C lathe}} \quad (5)$$

$$C\text{-}D = \text{The rate of increase of operation time} \quad (6)$$

The parts of the data calculated by the above formulae are shown in Table 2.

This regression line is

$$Y = (0.247X + 0.03).$$

This diagram indicates that N/C machines have many advantages, such as in precision machining, the uniformity and equality of the products. Moreover, the above functions cause less fatigue to the worker, consequently, there is no need to machine extra products.

Namely, N/C machines prevent the production of defective products.

TABLE 2. THE EFFECT OF N/C-IZATION

The rate of N/C-ization* (%)	The rate of decrease of defective products (%)	The rate of increase of operation time (%)
4.0	0.0	0.3
27.4	0.8	0.8
7.7	0.1	0.2
25.4	0.5	0.3
16.4	0.4	0.2
7.1	0.5	0.3
7.8	0.2	0.2
0.7	0.0	0.5
10.3	0.7	0.0
15.4	0.2	0.5
. . . .	. . . .	. . . .

*This means the ratio of N/C machines to conventional machines.

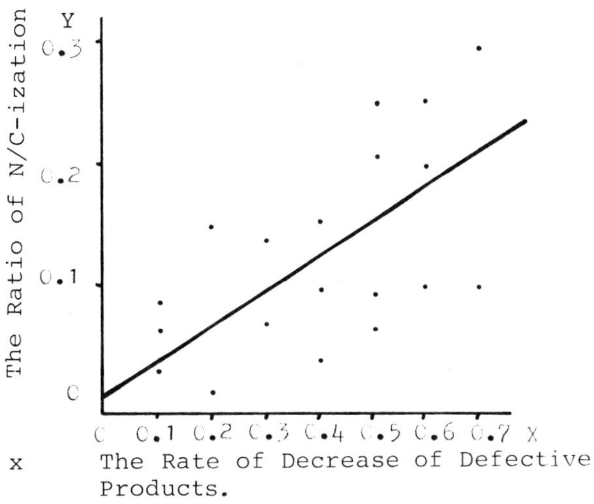

Fig. 5. Correlation between N/C-ization and decrease of defective products.

4.1. Correlation between the Rate of N/C-ization and Increase of Operation Time

Strictly speaking, when we name the specific character of the N/C, it would seem that the rate of operation time increases. However, the relation between the operation time and N/C-ization is weak.

This would indicate that there are doubts on what parts the N/C machine removes from the total process, and this rate is affected by any other factor.

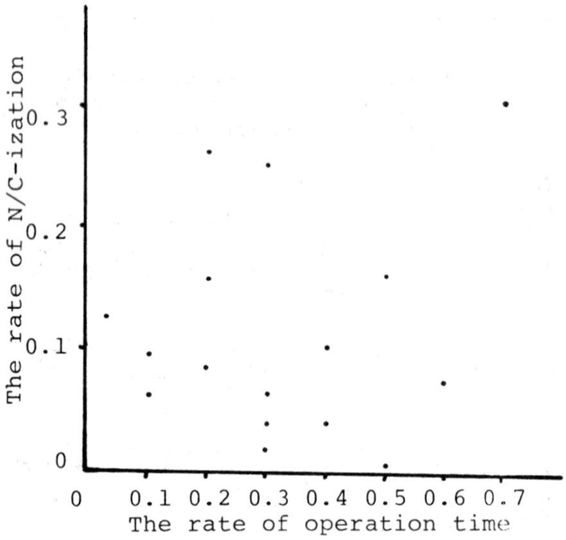

Fig. 6. Correlation between N/C-ization and operation time.

5. LOT SIZE

When we plan to install N/C machines, we expect some advantageous factors. One of the most important factors is to be able to deal with *various kinds, but also to the too-small lot-size effectively.*

The results of our questionnaire are shown in Table 3.

Roughly speaking, the result shows that less than forty of lot-size occupies 77.5% of the sum total.

It also becomes clear that not many factories are using N/C machines fully under the best conditions, by displaying their own characteristic feature of N/C.

From this standpoint, it is necessary to plan to make the investment profitable giving due consideration to the demands to be processed and the total stock.

It is worthwhile considering the development of some software for operation of the N/C machines with the economical lot size.

6. AN EXAMPLE OF DEPRECIATION FOR THE N/C LATHE

Since the installation cost of the N/C lathe is negligible, about 1% of the total cost, it is ignored in this paper.

It should be understood that the annual depreciation is nearly 4,070,000 yen for the amount of 17,000,000 yen of investment; therefore, the investment of this machine is depreciated over four or six years.

TABLE 3. THE RATE OF LOT-SIZE

Lot-size	Below 19	20 - 39	40 - 59	60 - 99	> 100
Lathe	14.3%	10.9%	2.7%	4.1%	1.3%
Fraise machine	9.5%	6.8%	2.0%	1.3%	2.7%
Drilling machine	10.2%	4.8%	2.0%	2.7%	2.0%
Boring machine	12.2%	3.4%	0.0%	0.0%	0.6%
Grinding machine	2.7%	2.7%	0.6%	0.0%	0.0%
Total	48.9%	28.6%	7.3%	8.1%	6.6%

TABLE 4. AN EXAMPLE OF DEPRECIATION OF THE N/C LATHE

The Average Price of the N/C Lathe (Yen)	The Rate of Depreciation/ Year (%)	Depreciation/ Year (Yen)
17,000,000	23.9	4,063,000

Our results concerning the price of N/C lathe of 17,000,000 yen correspond closely to the data shown in Table 5, from the statistical machinery reports of the Ministry of International Trade and Industry.

Therefore, we have made the calculations, on our side, by using equation (7). The results of the trial calculation are shown below.

Accordingly, in the case of the facility investment that the price of the N/C lathe is 17,000,000 yen, the amount of annual profit is about 4,400,000 yen when the depreciation is over 4 years, and the amount of annual profit is about 3,000,000 yen when the depreciation is over 6 years.

This result, from Table 6, is:

$$I = \frac{R_1}{(1+i)} + \frac{R_2}{(1+i)^2} + \cdots\cdots + \frac{R_n}{(1+i)^n} \qquad (7)$$

I: The amount of investment (Unit: Yen)
i: The rate of interest
n: Passage years
R: Profit per year
I: 17,000,000, i=10%, n=4 to 6

TABLE 6. ANNUAL PROFIT OF THE N/C LATHE

The Average Facilities Investment (Yen)	Presumed Number of Depreciation Year (Year)	Presumed Profit/ Year (Yen)
17,000,000	4 to 6	Between 3,000,000 and 4,400,000

7. TOOL COST FOR THE N/C MACHINE TOOLS VS. JIG AND TOOL COST FOR THE CONVENTIONAL MACHINE TOOL

The repliers to our questionnaire concerning the above title were few.

Table 7 shows the results of data dealt with by only six replies.

However, it would be interesting to know the results arising from many more replies being received.

The cost of jigs for the N/C machine is not included in the data because in this respect the N/C machine does not differ basically from the conventional machine.

The results of our questionnaire gave us insufficient information to comment on the cost of tool and jig.

TABLE 5. AN EXAMPLE OF DEPRECIATION FROM THE STATISTICAL MACHINERY REPORT

	1970		1971		1972	
	A	B (Yen)	A	B (Yen)	A	B (Yen)
Lathe	576	1450	588	1700	580	1530
Fraise machine	226	1330	264	1390	190	1600
Boring machine	118	680	95	1040	112	970
Grinding machine	16	1560	14	2100	16	3060
Machining cent.	323	1750	277	2150	325	2240

A: The quantity of production B: The price of machine (unit: ten thousand yen)

For reference, let us compare the N/C lathe with the conventional machine concerning tooling operation. See Fig. 7.

TABLE 7. COMPARISON OF COST BETWEEN N/C MACHINE TOOLS AND THE CONVENTIONAL MACHINE

	N/C machine	Conventional machine
Lathe	757,500	867,500
Fraise machine	1,361,300	1,285,000
Drilling machine	356,000	542,800

(Unit: Yen)

For the N/C lathe:

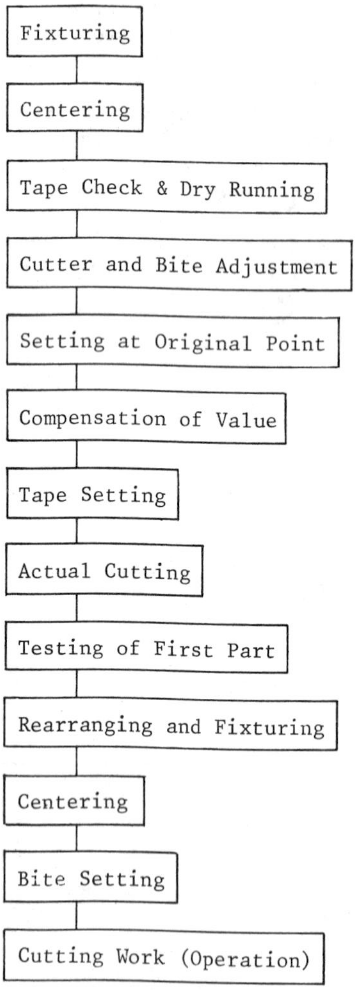

Fig. 7. Working order of the N/C lathe.

For the conventional lathe:

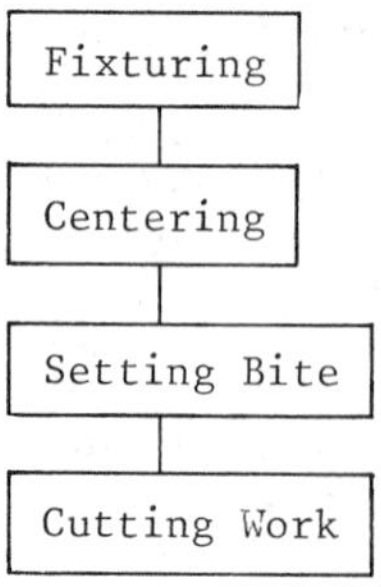

Fig. 8. Working order of the N/C and the conventional lathe.

Fig. 8 is an example from a certain factory and could be roughly associated with most shops. The cost of keeping and servicing tools for the N/C is greater than that of conventional machines - such as various preset equipments and devices or special tool holders.

8. THE ECONOMICAL VALUE OF THE LATHE

The economical profit for the lathe was considered by using three methods. The value is calculated by the cost accounting, Simple Annual Cost Method of Comparison and Hourly Cost Method of Comparison. However, the results of these comparisons are not always accurate, since the products of the same kind are not machined under the same conditions by the N/C and the conventional machine. The results treated by the three methods on trial are shown below.

8.1 The Cost Accounting

The formula of the cost accounting is shown as below:

$$X = \{(K_m + K_t)/60\}(T_c + T_e + T_p/n) + K_u \qquad (8)$$

X: Manufacturing cost per one product,

n: Lot size,

T_c: Actual cutting time,

T_e: No cutting time,

T_p: Programming time,

K_m: (Machine cost per hour) = (Purchase machine cost) { (The rate of depreciation)+(The rate of interest) +(The rate of tax)}/ (The total work time for a year).

K_m calculated according to this formula is

2025 = 22,150,000 x (0.184-0.08-0.064)/3588.

The work time for a year is, 13x23x12 = 3588 (hour) with 13 (hour) a day (two shifts) and 23 days a month.
k_t = operating cost per hour,
= labor cost + tool cost + miscellaneous cost,

T_c: 15 min. T_e: 6 min.
n : 20 to 40 products.

K_u: Preparation cost per product
= programming cost of tape/total products (K_u: 50 yen).

The values of x are calculated for every five products ranging from 20 to 40.
(i) When this N/C lathe is operated by one person, the results of manufacturing cost per product are as follows:

If n = 20, X = 1516 (yen)
n = 25, X = 1504
. .
. .
. .

(ii) When this N/C lathe of two machines is operated by one person, the result of manufacturing cost per product is shown as below. In case of a personnel labor cost is supposed to be 750 yen.

(iii) The cost for formar lathe.

K_m: zero yen,

K_t: 1500 + 96 + 408 = 2004 yen,

T_c: 16 min. Te: 35 min.,

T_p: 20 min. n: 20 to 40 products,

K_u: as the jig cost, 20,000 yen, 20,000/600 = 33 yen.
On the assumption, total products are 600.

8.2. Simple Annual Cost Methods of Comparison

The equation is as follows:

$$C = [\, aA+bq+X\{t(1+Z+K)+Sp\}] /x \quad (9)$$

where

A: Total cost of equipments (let this be 22,150,000 yen),

a: Depreciation factor.

TABLE 8. COMPARATIVE COST PER PRODUCT OF LOT SIZE

Lot Size	Conventional lathe (yen)	N/C lathe (yen) One machine /man	N/C lathe (yen) Two machines /man
20	1769	1516	1242
25	1763	1504	1232
30	1759	1496	1226
35	1755	1490	1221
40	1753	1486	1219

[$1: about 280 yen]
[1000 yen: about $3.6]
[Lot size means number of parts to be cut for one process time]

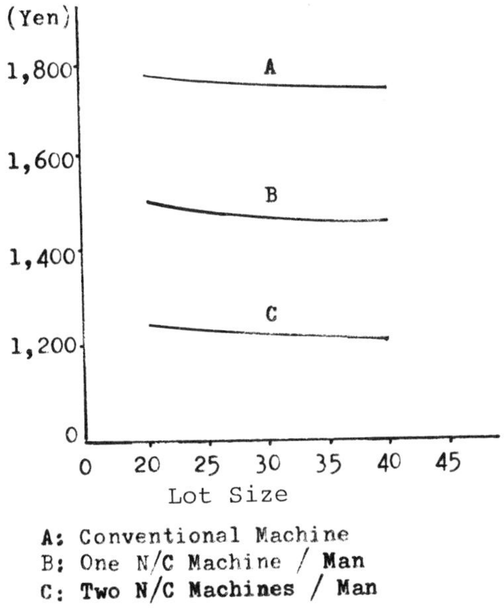

Fig. 9. Machining cost/product.

$$a = d + \frac{2}{3}i + W \quad (10)$$

d: the rate of depreciation,

i: interest rate,

w: the ratio of mending cost vs. A,

$$a = 0.184+\frac{2}{3}x0.1+\frac{185,000}{22,150,000} = 0.26,$$

b: The cost of a unit area (let this be 42,000),

c: hourly cost,

q: total area need for the equipment (let this be 28 m^2),

t: hourly wage (let this be 1200 yen),

p: total electric power consumption (let this be 15 kW/h),

X: operation time (let this be 1793 H),

Z: the ratio of incidental expense (let this be 0.09),

S: electric power cost per 1 kWh (let this be 7.7 yen),

K: 0.25.

In the case of a single operator for a N/C machine: Let C be 5590 yen.

In the case of a conventional machine: similarly let the above value be as follows:

A: 9,980,000 yen	a: 0.26
b: 2000 yen	X: 1140 H
q: 27 m^2	t: 1200 yen
s: 7.7 yen	Z: 0.09
p: 14 kW/h	C = 4987 yen

As far as the cost accounting method is used, even one N/C machine is, in some degree, cheaper than a conventional machine. When two N/C machines are operated by one operator, it clearly costs less.

TABLE 9. COMPARISON OF THE COST FOR N/C VS. CONVENTIONAL MACHINES

		Hourly Cost (Yen)
N/C Machine	One Machine/ man	5590
	Two machines/ man	4786
Conventional machine		4987

According to The Simple Annual Cost Method of Comparison, on the contrary, the hourly conventional machine cost is a little cheaper than the N/C machine, so long as one operator handles one machine.

Thereby, from reasons discussed here, we can conclude that so long as two N/C machines are operated by a single operator, the N/C machine is more advantageous than the conventional machine, regardless of the cost accounting methods.

8.3. The Hourly Cost of Comparison

On the other hand, let us try to survey the operation cost for an hour in connection with costs of installation, housing, wages, air-conditioning, repair, jig and tool and electric power, etc. In addition to this, when cutting velocity is also considered, the results become as shown in Table 10.

TABLE 10. COMPARISON OF THE HOURLY COST

	N/C machine (Yen/H)	Conventional machine (Yen/H)
Installation	498	234
Housing	108	60
Wages	1002	1002
Air-Conditioning	102	102
Overhaul	42	6
Repair	78	12
Jig & Tool	-------	156
Electric Power	-------	-------
Total	1830	1572

In some instances, the machining costs for a part which is to be cut are as follows. Let the cutting time be 0.2 hour for the case of the N/C machine and 0.3 hour for the conventional machine, respectively.

For the N/C lathe: 1830 x 0.2 = 366 [yen/hour].
For the conventional: 1572 x 0.3 = 477 [yen/ hour].

These results show that the conventional machine tool is more advantageous than the N/C machine, from the cost per hour point of view. On the other hand, the N/C machine has advantages over the conventional machine when the machining time is considered.

This result derives from calculations of information from a certain factory which we investigated privately.

In order to obtain this result, it is better to deal with as much information as possible.

9. ACTUAL VARIATION OF ECONOMICAL VALUATION OF N/C MACHINE INSTALLATION

TABLE 11. VALUATION OF AN N/C MACHINE

The Method	A	B	C	D	E	F	Total
Capital recovery method		4				1	5
Simple annual cost method of comparison	1	2				1	4
Payout method	1	2	1				4
Average return method	1	2				1	4
Permissible amount of investment method		1					1
Machinery & allied institute						1	1
Minimum cost rule		1					1
The rate of simple return method						1	1
Annual expense method		1					1
Annual expense method of comparison		1					1

A: Very useful B: Useful, depending on the condition

C: Few useful D: Almost useless

E: Quite useless F: No reply

As the replies for each item in the questionnaire are extremely few, the value of N/C-ization may not be in a position to evaluate the economical position effectively.

10. PROGRAMMING COST

Auto-programme including APT, ADAPT AUTOSPOT, ADAPT, EXAPT I,II, etc., are mostly used in big factories such as shipbuilding, electric machinery, large-scale machinery, etc. About 60 per cent of total repliers to our questionnaires have been using autoprogramme together with manual programme. Roughly speaking, APT and EXAPT are used most effectively in shops which have several N/C machines. As far as programming cost is concerned, we cannot obtain accurate data because it is difficult to assess clearly its cost. However, it is calculated that the programming cost will range on average from 20,000 to 30,000 yen. After treatment of two or three examples, programming cost becomes about 21,000 yen for one tape which has about 62,000 steps, for example, namely it costs 124 yen per step.

11. ANALYSIS OF IDLE TIME BECAUSE OF SHORTENING OF OPERATING TIME

The object of the questionnaire is to investigate the amount of idle time that will become available for additional jobs as the result of improvement of the machining operation by using N/C.

Questions:

(1) Is there some improvement regarding the rate of machine operation?

(2) Is this idle time better available for the purpose of other work?

(3) What reasons are there in case of no utilization?

Reasons:

(a) In order to watch the operation of machines.

(b) On account of too short a period.

(c) Owing to having to deal with cutting scrap.

(d) Instead of a loader or unloader.

(e) For the purpose of safety of the operation.

(g) On account of difficulty in preparing another job.

(h) For the purpose of lubrication.

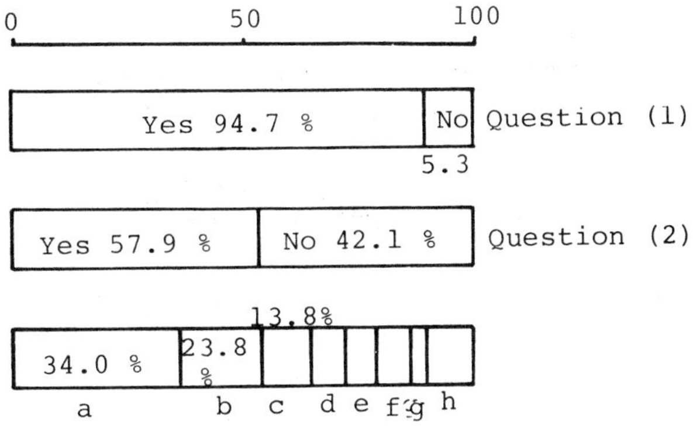

Fig. 10. Analysis of idle time.

According to this result, it can be understood that the equipment is needed to be more reliable and some useful loaders or unloaders are expected to be developed.

In addition to this, it is desirable to do further study on the subject of improvement of the controller. Consequently, one operator is able to operate two or more machine tools.

12. THE INTRODUCTORY REASON AND THE VALUE AFTER INTRODUCTION OF AN N/C MACHINE

Items of the questionnaire:

(A) To be an object of economy in the production of many small quantity items.

(B) The quicker processing and increased reliability.

(C) To meet the need for processing of complicated items.

(D) To be out of date for the formar machines.

(E) To locate another factory and in the development of new goods.

(F) To increase production.

(G) To meet the need for providing facilities with versatility and with new functions.

(H) To purchase because of shortage of skilled workers.

(I) To assist in dealing with the amount of excess orders and using inside production instead of outside production.

(J) To improve safety of work.

(K) To introduce a new line.

(L) The nearness of the date of delivery.

The most numerous reasons of purchase of these items were three, as follows:

(A) To be an object of economization for the many kinds of small quantity production.

(B) The improvement and stability of exact processing.

(C) To need processing for the complicated form.

Resultantly, we can get five items shown below after the introduction and actual use.

(A) To be an object of economy in the production of many small quantity items.

(B) The quicker processing and increased reliability.

(D) To be out of date for the formar machines.

(F) To increase production.

(G) To meet the need for providing facilities with versatility and with new functions.

According to the above reasons, most of the enterprises expect N/C machines to be profitable as the reason of installation.

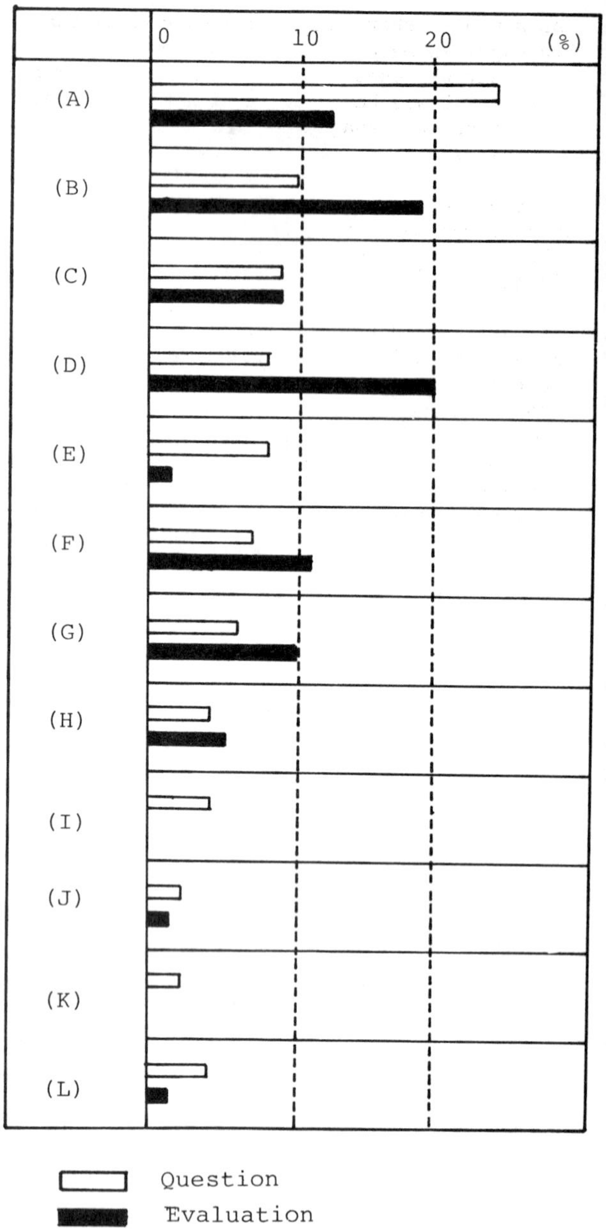

Fig. 11. Expectation and value of N/C machine.

CONCLUSION

Up to now the advanced big companies and factories in Japan have been using several kinds of N/C machines in fabrication and in machining jobs. In most cases, shipbuilding and electric machinery take the top rank of these fields.

One of the most interesting items in our survey is to estimate the profit of installation of N/C machine tools.

Consequently, it becomes necessary to know how many machines are operated by one operator all the time and at the same time to know if the operators are also able to work on other jobs.

As a whole, there are great economical advantages in machining, especially for the big user who uses a large number of N/C machines which are kept in good condition or by improving the management system regarding use of the N/C.

On the contrary, for smaller companies vice-versa. One more thing needed to be known is the realistic lot size of workpieces in machining.

It can be said that N/C machines are explicitly more profitable than conventional machines so long as two N/C machines are operated by an operator.

Needless to say, when the installation of N/C machines is being considered, it is necessary to compare them with the conventional equipment.

ACKNOWLEDGEMENTS

This paper has been greatly improved by the help of many people among whom are members of several electrical machinery and ship-building companies, etc., and also students, especially Miss. H. Takahagi, in finalizing the data in our seminar.

Lastly we also express our great appreciation to the applicants or repliers to our questionnaire.

REFERENCES

"*Numerical Control*", R.M. Dyke, KENPAKUSHA.

"*Numerical Control*", NILSO, OLESTEN, WILEY.

INFORMATION STRUCTURE, DYNAMIC TEAM DECISION, AND AN ECONOMIC APPLICATION

H. Myoken

Faculty of Economics, Nagoya City University, Mizuhoku, Nagoya 467, Japan

ABSTRACT

The dynamic team decision problem specified by the decentralized control system with linear information structure and quadratic cost function is considered in this paper. We derive a linear decentralized control scheme that follows person-by-person-satisfactory(PBPS) team decision for given information sharing pattern. An illustrative example is presented based on the aggregate firm model of production planning in manufacturing industry.

I. INTRODUCTION

In recent years, a great deal of attention has been paid to decentralized control systems that possess limited and non-identical information sets on the states of the system, inputs and its structure(see [1],for instance). Different information sets under consideration play a central role in team(or organization) decision problem, the difficulty of which also arises from the specific information pattern. Such situations present themselves in various forms of realistic economic systems. The construct of team decision developed first by Marschak and Radner[2] provided a useful framework for the conceptualization and evaluation of information within organizations. Team decision problems are the area of mutual interests to control scientists and economists.

The so-called linear-quadratic-Gaussian(LQG) problem with classical information structures results in a linear optimal decision rule. However, the famous Witsenhausen counter-example[3] showed that for non-classical information structure optimal decision rules need not be linear. The recent works of Ho and Chu[4] demonstrated that linear optimal decision rules also result if the information structure is partially nested: the dynamic team decision problem is reduced to an equivalent static problem by Marschak and Radner [2].

Further contributions have been made by many authors(see for example [5,6,7,8,9,10,11, 12,13]). Chong and Athans[5] considered a constrained optimal control problem of continuous-time linear stochastic system with two control agents that do not exchange information and attempted to determine the optimal values of coefficient parameters, where the structures of agents were assumed to be linear. Then they derived necessary conditions for optimal parameters and showed that the separation theorem does not hold in such a case. Following to Chong and Athans[5], Yoshikawa[6] derived the same necessary conditions that are satisfied in the discrete-time case, and, in addition, he obtained sufficient conditions for the problem to be weak separable by introducing an extended concept of the separation theorem. Myoken[13] modified the results given by Yoshikawa[6] in some ways to apply for dynamic economic systems. The papers[8,9,10,11,12] dealt mainly with the derivation of the optimal controller for the LQG one-step-delay sharing information pattern problem. For example, Sandell and Athans[8] performed a valuable service by showing that, in the LQG stochastic control problem case, the team decision can be solved by means of multistage decision approach.Also, Kurtaran[12] considered the control of discrete-time nonlinear stochastic systems under an n-step-delay sharing pattern. However, it should be noted that the studies along these lines emphasis on the theoretical and analytical aspects of the optimal control solution to nonclassical LQG stochastic decision problem. Consequently, it becomes exceedingly difficult to analytically solve the problem under consideration, which is given by numerical solution or by suboptimal control solution.

This paper is concerned with the dynamic team decision specified by the decentralized control of a discrete-time linear stochastic system with two control agents. These two agents try to minimize the same quadratic cost function and are assumed to be able to exchange their control vectors. The decentralized control scheme obtained follows the person-by-person-satisfactory(PBPS') team desion under information structure assumption. Many investigations of the production planning problems have been undertaken by economics and management scientists. In this paper a more general aggregate production problem consisting of inventory, sales and finance sectors is cast in a form amenable to solution by discrete-time optimal control theory. Then we present an analytical framework of a wide spectrum of production planning policies applicable to the method proposed in the present paper.

2. THE MODEL AND PROBLEM STATEMENT

Any realistic models including economic systems are generally nonlinear. Sometimes we can treat nonlinear dynamic equations directly. However, very often we must resort to approximately linearizing the model in some small neighborhoods about the equilibrium point or about some specified reference time path, i.e., about tentative path as will be seen in Section 4. In this paper we assume the linearized approximation of nonlinear dynamic systems.

Consider a linear time-invariant system dynamics and observation equations described by

$$(2.1)\quad x(k+1) = Ax(k) + B_1u_1(k) + B_2u_2(k), \quad k = 0, 1, 2, \ldots$$

$$(2.2)\quad y_i(k) = C_ix(k) + \eta_i(k), \quad i = 1, 2; \quad k = 1, 2, \ldots$$

where $x(k)\in R^n$ in the state vector, $u_i(k)\in R^{p_i}$, the control vector applied by agent i, $y_i(k) \in R^{q_i}$, the observation signal available to agent i. The noises $\eta_i(k)$, i = 1,2 are taken to be mutually independent, their density distributions are

$$p(\eta_i(k)) = N(0, R_i), \quad i=1,2;\ k=1,2,\ldots.$$

It is assumed that agent i has his own prior distribution with mean α_i and covariance Σ_i, where Σ_i, i=1,2 are symmetric nonegative definite matrices and known. Furthermore it is assumed that a priori information on x(0) for each agent is different and is unknown to the other.

Most of economic models characteristically become proper, since they have much large sampling intervals, and since the impact multiplier often is not zero matrix in policy implementation[14]. Thus the direct part Du(k) is added to the observation equation. However, now define

$$\Delta u(k) \triangleq u(k+1) - u(k)$$

where $\Delta u(k)$ is the input, y(k) is the output. Then the model becomes strictly proper.

The performance measure is given by

$$(2.3.1)\quad J = \sum_{k=1}^{N} F(x(k), u_1(k-1), u_2(k-1))$$

where

$$(2.3.2)\quad F = x^TWx + u^TP_1u + \eta^TP_2\eta$$

where $F\geq 0$ is real valued. The performance criterion in economic systems may be specified by

$$(2.3)'\quad J' = \sum_{k=1}^{N} [x(k)-\bar{x}(k)]^TW(k)[x(k)-\bar{x}(k)]$$

where $\bar{x}(k)$ is the desired value for the state vector x(k). Now let $\bar{u}(k)$ denote the desired control vector for u(k). When u(k) becomes a part of state variables, we can express the system involving $\bar{x}(k)$ and $\bar{u}(k)$. In such case, the usual tracking problem can be formulated for the decentralized system by (2.1), (2.2) and (2.3)'. (For the discussion regarding this, see [15].)

In this paper it is assumed that agents exchange their control values. Different informations under consideration play an important role in the decentralized systems. Let $I_i(k)$ be denoted as the information set available to the control agent i at time k. In this paper we consider the information sets defined as

$$(2.4.1)\quad I_i(k) = \{I_i(k-1),\ y_i(k),\ u_1(k-1),\ u_2(k-1)\}, \quad i = 1, 2.$$

A priori information of agent i consists of

$$(2.4.2)\quad I_i(0) = \{A, B_1, B_2, C_1, C_2, {}_i, R_1, R_2\}$$

Various information sets may be considered: for examples, the case with information exchange on control and observation variables with one-time delay, or the case with information exchange on control laws used by the other, etc..

This paper derives the PBPS team decision rules under the information structure assumption (2.4). The results obtained are compared with these of informationally centralized control systems. Following to Marschak and Radner[2], a team decision rule is defined to be PBPS if it cannot be improved by changing one of its components. A pair of decentralized control laws is PBPS if the expected cost cannot be reduced by changing any single agent's control law.

3. PBPS TEAM DECISION RULES

The optimal control vector at the last time period under the centralized information assumption is given by

$$(3.1)\quad u_{N-1} = -(p+B^TWB)^{-1}B^TWAE\{x(k-1) \mid I_1(N-1)\cup I_2(N-1)\}$$

where

$$B = (B_1, B_2), \quad u_{N-1} = \begin{pmatrix} u_1(N-1) \\ u_2(N-1) \end{pmatrix},$$

$$P = \mathrm{diag}\ (P_1, P_2)$$

Let

$$(3.2)\quad \gamma_i(N) = E\{F_N \mid I_i(N-1)\}, \quad i = 1, 2$$

where $\gamma_i(N)$ stands for the cost observed by control agent i. For agent 1, (3.2) can be written as

$$(3.3)\ \gamma_1(N) = ||\hat{x}_1(N)||^2_W + ||u_1(N-1)||^2_{P_1} + ||\hat{u}_2(N-1)||_{P_2} + l_1(N)$$

where

$$(3.4)\ \hat{x}_1(N) = E\{x(N)\,|\,I_1(N-1)\} = A\mu_1(N-1) + B_1u_1(N-1) + B_2\hat{u}_2(N-1)$$

$$(3.5)\ \mu_1(N-1) = E\{x(N-1)\,|\,I_1(N-1)\}$$

$$(3.6)\ \hat{u}_2(N-1) = E\{u_2(N-1)\,|\,I_1(N-1)\}$$

and where

$$(3.7)\ l_1(N) = E\{||x(N) - \hat{x}_1(N)||^2_W + ||u_2(N-1)\ \hat{u}_2(N-1)||^2_{P_2}\,|\,I_1(N-1)\}$$

since $l_1(N)$ is independent of $u_1(N-1)$. For $E\{F_N|I_2(N-1)\}$, we obtain a similar expression.

The unique PBPS decision rules at the last stage are obtained by the solution of

$$(3.8)\quad \min_{u_i(N-1)} \gamma_i(N-1), \quad i = 1, 2$$

Then the problem (3.8) is equivalent to solving

$$(3.9)\ \frac{\partial\gamma_i(N)}{\partial x_i(N)} \cdot \frac{\partial\hat{x}_i(N)}{\partial u_i(N-1)} + \frac{\partial\gamma_i(N)}{\partial u_i(N-1)} = 0, \quad i = 1, 2$$

where recall that F_N is quadratic in all its arguments, and where

$$(3.10.1)\ \hat{x}_1(N) = A\mu_1(N-1) + B_1u_1(N-1) + B_2E\{u_2(N-1)\,|\,I_1(N-1)\}$$

$$(3.10.2)\ \hat{x}_2(N) = A\mu_2(N-1) + B_1E\{u_1(N-1)\,|\,I_2(N-1)\} + B_2u_2(N-1)$$

Therefore, the PBPS decision rules at the last stage are the solution of

$$(3.11.1)\ M_{11}u_1(N-1)_1 + M_{12}\hat{u}_2(N-1) = G_1\mu_1(N-1)$$

$$(3.11.2)\ M_{21}\hat{u}_1(N-1) + M_{22}u_2(N-1) = G_2\mu_2(N-1)$$

where

$$M_{ii} = R_i + B_i^TWB_i, \quad M_{12} = B_1^TWB_2,$$

$$M_{21} = B_2^TWB_1, \quad G_i = -B_i^TWA, \quad i = 1, 2$$

and are given by

$$(3.12.1)\ u_1(N-1) = L_1(N-1)\mu_1(N-1)$$

$$(3.12.2)\ u_2(N-1) = L_2(N-1)\mu_2(N-1)$$

if the following equations are satisfied:

$$(3.13.1)\ \hat{\mu}_1(N-1) = \mu_2(N-1)$$

$$(3.13.2)\ \hat{\mu}_2(N-1) = \mu_1(N-1)$$

where

$$\begin{pmatrix} L_1 \\ L_2 \end{pmatrix} = M^{-1}\begin{pmatrix} G_1 \\ G_2 \end{pmatrix}$$

In his paper[7], Aoki observed that the PSPB decision rules have a certain correction terms due to the well-known optimal proportional feedback control signal obtainable under the information centralization assumption. As indicated in the results (3.11) and (3.13), they do not rely on the information structure, so that the PBPS decision rules under given information sharing pattern (2.4) are the same as that of the centralized systems. The estimates under consideration are the conditional means that are determined using Kalman filter, and then the equations (3.13) are satisfied.

We can also deal with the PBPS decision rules for the case where the agents share the control law with each other. In this case, an infinite-dimensional filter would be required, when computing the conditional expectations (3.4), (3.5) and (3.6). Approximations to conditional expectations must be considered, from the practical point of view. For this purpose, a useful method may be found in the guaranteed cost synthesis approach proposed by Chang and Peng[16] and Jain[17, 18]: The PBPS decision rules will be given so that the control law minimizes an upper bound on the performance cost function.

4. THE FIRM DECISION MODEL AND THE CONTROL SIMULATION METHOD

4.1 The Basic Model

Much of the model formulations appeared in the literature on aggregate production planning has its origins in Holt et al.[19]. Very recently, considerable attention has paid to the application of discrete optimal control theory to production planning policy. (see [20],[21], for instances.) However, most of the previous models have in large part neglected the impact of policy decision under informationally decentralization. In this section, we present a dynamic simultaneous model that considers the interaction between the sectors of a firm. The firm model developed here is a sound basis for the investigation of control scheme of informationally decentralized systems.

Production sector on firm behavior interdependently is associated with other sectors consisting of at least inventory, sales and finance sectors. (see Fig.1.)

Fig.1: A Simultaneous Firm Model

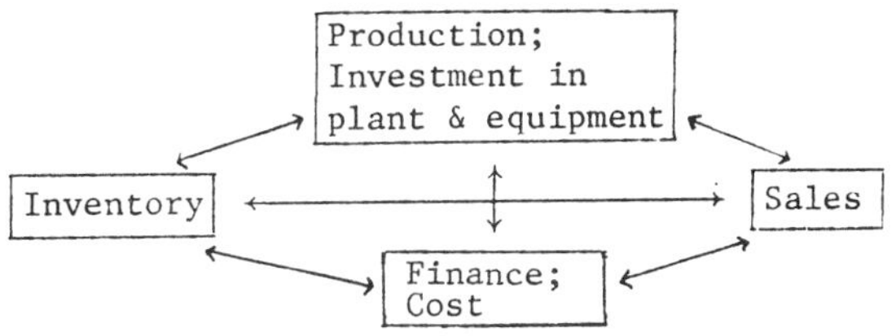

Naturally, it is also possible to consider micro-aspects of firm behavior such as research development and labor management sectors. However, the model presented here devotes itself to the derivation of empirically testable hypotheses regarding macro-aspects of firms' activities on aggregative economic variables. The symbols in this model are as follows:

Symbols

- Q: the desired production capacity(i.e. potential for production)
- q: change in production capacity
- O: production
- η: capacity utilization ratio
- C1: cost of investment in plant and equipment
- C2: cost of production
- I: inventory
- S: sales
- C3: cost of inventory
- a: advertising cost
- p: price
- C4: marketing cost
- C: total cost
- T: total sales amount
- π: profit
- e: the gap between supply and demand
- d: demand forecasts

(i) Production and Investment in Plant and Equipment Sector

(4.1) $Q(k) = Q(k-1) + q(k-1)$

(4.2) $\eta(k) = O(t)/Q(k)$

(4.3) $C1(k) = C1(q(k))$

(4.4) $C2(k) = C2(Q(k), O(k), \eta(k))$

In a manufacturing concern the management wants to determine how much the present capacity for production is to be changed in order to obtain the desired capacity for production. The capacity for production during period k indicates the relation with one time delay as shown in (4.1). Since Q(k) and O(k) are the fixed cost and the variable cost, respectively, $\eta(k)$ stands for the explainning factor regarding the adjustment cost.

(ii) Inventory Sector

(4.5) $I(k) = I(k-1) + O(k-1) - S(k-1)$

(4.6) $C3(k) = C3(I(k))$

Equation (4.5) indicating the amount of inventory at beginning of period k can be expressed by the relation between one time delayed inventory, production, and sales, where a conservation of the number of unit items is assumed.

(iii) Sales Sector

(4.7) $S(k) = S(a(k-1), P(k), S(k-1), a(k-2), S(k-2))$

(4.8) $C4 = C4(S(k))$

Sales during period k is assumed to be a function of the price during the same period, advertising cost and sales during time lagged period. This relation is a reasonable assumption.

(iv) Identities

(4.9) $C(k) = C1(k) + C2(k) + C3(k) + C4(k) + a(k)$

(4.10) $T(k) = P(k)S(k)$

(4.11) $\pi(k) = T(k) - C(k)$

(4.12) $e(k) = d(k) - S(k)$

It should be noted that the demand forecast for the commodity is estimated in connected with macroeconometric model that is set up outside the model considered. d is generally expressed as

$$d(t) = d(\mu, D(k), \dots)$$

where μ is the market share; D is the total demand forecast for the commodity estimated in the firm world. Thus d is assumed to be given as the data variable,which is exogenous in the sense that it is determined by the relation(i.e., macroeconometric model) outside the model. (On the other hand, the variables which are determined by the model are called endogenous variables.)

The variables used in this model are partitioned as:

Endogenous variables $y = (Q, \eta, I, S, e, T, C1, C2, C3, C4, C, \pi)$

Control varaibles $u = (q, O, a, P)$

Data variables $z = d$

State variables (= the number of predetermined variables − the number of exogenous variables)

$$x = (Q(k-1), I(k-1), S(k-1), q(k-1), O(k-1), a(k-1))$$

where the predetermined variables are also classified as:

- predetermined variables
  - lagged endogenous variables
  - exogenous variables
    - control variables*
    - data (or interaction) variables

$* \begin{cases} \text{current control variables} \\ \text{lagged control variables} \end{cases}$

The basic model is represented by the following vector form:

$$(4.13)\quad y(k) = \alpha(y(k), x(k), u(k), z(k))$$

which is of the structural form. Economic systems generally are nonlinear in structure, but very often we must resort to some approximations. Now let us be

$$\hat{y}(k),\ \hat{x}(k),\ \hat{u}(k),\ \hat{z}(k)$$

where superscript "^" indicates tentative paths. Then we can approximate the model (4.13) about tentative paths as follows:

$$(4.14)\quad y(k) = F(k)x(k) + G(k)u(k) + h(k)$$

where

$$(4.15)\quad [F(k),\ G(k)] = [I - \frac{\partial\alpha}{\partial y(k)}]^{-1}[\frac{\partial\alpha}{\partial x(k)},\ \frac{\partial\alpha}{\partial u(t)}]$$

$$(4.16)\quad h(k) = \hat{y}(k) - F(k)\hat{x}(k) + G(k)\hat{u}(k)$$

Equation system (4.14) is called the reduced form or the output equation.

Since the state variables are defined by the endogenous and control variables, we have

$$(4.17)\quad x(k+1) = Ly(k) + Mu(k)$$

where elements of the matrices L and M may be supposed to be zero or to be unity. Substitution of (4.14) into (4.17) yields

$$(4.18)\quad x(k+1) = A(k)x(k) + B(k)u(k) + W(k)$$

where

$$A(k) = LF(k)$$

$$B(k) = M + LB(k)$$

$$W(k) = Lh(k)$$

We call (4.18) the state equation system, which expresses the dynamics of the model. The dimensions of the vectors in the model under consideration are as follows:

x: NX = 6

u: NU = 4

y: NY = 12

z: NZ = 1

As indicated in the above examples, the dimensions of observable variables y are greater than these of state variables x. Very often this case appears in the usual economic systems. However, since the system dynamics can be experssed by the state variables(= the number of predetermined variables - the number of current exogenous variables), the state variables are done without a great number of variables. In addition, all they can be computed using (4.17).

Boundary Conditions: Next we suppose that several variables used have some upper and lower limits:

$$(4.19)\quad \underline{q}(k) \le q(k) \le \overline{q}(k)$$

$$(4.20)\quad \alpha(k) \le 1.2$$

$$(4.21)\quad i_0 S(k) \le I(k) \le i_1 S(k)$$

$$(4.22)\quad S(k) \le I(k)$$

$$(4.23)\quad C(k) \le \overline{C}(k)$$

$$(4.24)\quad \underline{P}(k) \le P(k) \le \overline{P}(k)$$

Performance Cost Function: Finally, we suppose that the firm wishes to regulate production so to minimize the sum of the gap between supply and demand, total cost, and capacity utilization ratio deviated from a reasonable value over some fixed time interval [1, NN]. We can then write this performance criterion function as

$$(4.25)\quad \phi = \sum_{k=1}^{NN} \{\omega_1(k)e^2(k) + \omega_2(k)C^2(k) + \omega_3(k)(\eta(k) - 1.0)^2\}$$

where ω_1, ω_2, and ω_3 are, respectively, the weights assessed against the gap, total cost, and the deviated capacity utilization ratio for the period. We first consider a control problem with the cost function (4.25), where the constraints are subject to (4.1) through (4.12) and (4.19) through (4.24). Then the optimal paths are computed when obtaining the solutions so as to minimize the performandce criterion cost in (4.25). We call this computation or the operation the control simulation.

4.2 Optimal Control Simulation

The model (4.1) through (4.12) is generally nonlinear, and the boundary conditions (4.19) through (4.24) involve the state and control variables. Thus the optimal solution and the optimal path are obtained employing the iterative operation by the linearized approximation procedure. (For the discussions in details regarding this method, refer to [22].)

Suppose now the optimal paths indicating superscript "*" are given using the method as

$$x^*(k),\ u^*(k),\quad k = 1, 2, \ldots, NN$$

The linearized approximations of the model in the neighborhood of optimal paths are as follows:

$$(4.26)\quad x(k+1) - x^*(k+1) = A(k)(x(k) - x^*(k)) + B(k)(u(k) - u^*(k)) + W(k)(z(k) - z^*(k))$$

The data variables for the period are assumed

to be given, i.e.,

$$z(k) = \hat{z}(k) = z(k),\ i = 1, 2, \ldots, NT$$

The performance criterion function is minimized by regarding the optimal paths as the target variables, i.e.,

$$(4.27)\quad \phi = \sum_{k=1}^{NK} \{\|x(k+1) - x^*(k+1)\|^2_{\Gamma(k+1)} + \|u(k) - u^*(k)\|^2_{\Lambda(k)}\}$$

The weighted coefficients are defined as

$$(4.28)\quad \Gamma(k) = \frac{1}{x^*(k)} \quad (\neq 0)$$

$$(4.29)\quad \Lambda(k) = \frac{1}{u^*(k)} \quad (\neq 0)$$

In doing so, each term in (4.27) is the squared error for each variable. Therefore, (4.27) is expressed as the squared sum of error. The optimal control solutions so as to minimize (4.27) subject to (4.26) are given as

$$(4.30)\quad u(k) = u^*(k) - \Xi(k)(x(k) - x^*(k))$$

where the state variables $x(k)$ (= the number of predetermined variables - the number of current exogenous variables) are defined by (4.17) and perfectly observable.

5. MULTI-ITEM PRODUCTION PLANNING AND CONTROL SIMULATION APPROACH TO TEAM DECISION

5.1 A Multi-Item Decision Model for Manufacturing Concerns

A considerable portion of the aggregate production planning problem can be traced to the traditional framework done by Holt-type model [19]. The model presented in Section 4 is in some part different from the aggregate Holt model: For examples, we first treat the production planning by inventory and sales as a typical problem of stochastic optimal control, the impact of the resultant cost or finance flows for each sector is considered, and the firm model is developed in combination of macroeconometric model. Kriebel[23] investigated the quadratic team decision problems to the Holt-type model on optimal linear decision rules for aggregate planning. As Bergstrom and Smith[24] pointed out, however, because of the aggregate nature of this formulation, it is not possible to solve directly for the optimal production rates for individual products: Therefore in situations where no natural dimension for aggregate exists, the breakdown of an aggregate production plan into individual item plans may result in a schedule which is far from optimum. In this case, specification of an aggregate production planning neglects the most interesting question. In this section, we extend the model presented in Section 4 to a multi-item formulation which solves directly for the optimal production, inventory, and sales for individual items in the future periods. Also, in doing so, it may be easier to observe the practical significance and the empirical validity of the PBPS team decision rules for the aggregate production planning. We proceed to the model formulation.

The plants and equipment allocated to the production for each commodity are transfered to these for another commodity, according to the supply and demand for each commodity. It is assumed that the sales amount for each commodity is also influenced by the sales and advertisement for another commodity. In this case, increase in the sales amount for another commodity does not necessarily become positive. If it is a substitute, we have a negative effect. We now extend the basic model (4.1) through (4.12) used in the previous section to a multi-item formulation.

$$(5.1)\quad Q_i(k) = \sum_{j=1}^{N} \Delta_{ij}(k-1)Q_j(k-1) + q_i(k-1)$$

where Δ_{ij} stands for the transfer from the plants and equipment for the jth commodity to these for the ith commodity.

$$(5.2)\quad \eta_i(k) = O_i(k)/Q_i(k)$$

$$(5.3)\quad C1_i(k) = C1_i(q_i(k),\ \Delta_{ij}(k)) \qquad j{=}i;\ j=1,2,\ldots,N$$

$$(5.4)\quad C2_i(k) = C2_i(Q_i(k),\ O_i(k),\ \eta_i(k))$$

$$(5.5)\quad I_i(k) = I_i(k-1) + O_i(k-1) - S_i(k-1)$$

$$(5.6)\quad C3_i(k) = C3_i(I_i(k))$$

$$(5.7)\quad S_i(k) = S_i(a_i(k-1),\ P_i(k),\ S_i(k-1),\ a_j(k-2),\ S_j(k-2)) \qquad j=1,2,\ldots,N$$

$$(5.8)\quad C4_i(k) = C4_i(S_i(k))$$

$$(5.9)\quad C_i(k) = C1_i(k) + C2_i(k) + C3_i(k) + C4_i(k) + a_i(k)$$

$$(5.10)\quad T_i(k) = P_i(k)S_i(k)$$

$$(5.11)\quad \Pi_i(k) = T_i(k) - C_i(k)$$

$$(5.12)\quad e_i(k) = d_i(k) - S_i(k)$$

Similarly, the boundary constraints (4.19) through (4.24) can be also rewritten in connection with multi-item formulation. Individual optimization is implemented using submodels (5.1) through (5.12), and after exchange of some values for interaction variables, the optimal design is made in such a way as the iterative operation is repeated until the optimal paths converge. Also, the submodels are set up as one firm model together, and then the optimal planning may be designed employing this model. Assuming that the determination of the optimal planning is made using the model involving many establishments, the decision-making for each establishment implemented according to the firm plan frame. (See Fig.2.)

The model for the ith establishment (that is charge of the ith commodity) is

(5.13) $y_i(k) = \alpha_i(y_i(k), x_i(k), u_i(k), z_i(k))$

Suppose that the optimal paths are given by the firm plan frame as

$$y_i^*(k),\ x_i^*(k),\ u_i^*(k),\ z_i^*(k) \qquad k = 1, 2, \ldots, NN$$

It is apparent that

(5.14) $y_i^*(k) = \alpha_i(y_i^*(k), x_i^*(k), u_i^*(k), z_i^*(k))$

The linearized approximation of (5.13) in the neighborhood of optimal paths "$*$" can be written in the state equation form as

$$(5.15)\quad x_i(k+1) - x_i(k+1) = A(k)[x_i(k)-x_i^*(k)] + B_i(k)[u_i(k) - u_i^*(k)] + C_i(k)[z_i(k) - z_i^*(k)]$$

Unless otherwise stated the subscript "i" is deleted.

The performance measure assumed is given by

$$(5.16)\quad = \sum_{k=1}^{NN}\{\|x(k+1) - x^*(k+1)\|^2_{\Gamma(k+1)} + \|u(k) - u^*(k)\|^2_{\Lambda(k)}\}$$

which indicates a reasonable specification form implementing the optimal control. (see (4.27), also.)

5.2 The Practical Control Simulation for Determining Optimal Planning

Assuming that the data-interaction variable vector

(5.17) $z(k) = z^*(k), \quad k = 1, 2, \ldots, NN$

we consider the minimization of the performance cost in (5.16) subject to (5.15). The control solutions are then given as

(5.18) $u(k) = u^*(k) - F(k)A(k)[x(k) - x^*(k)]$

where

$$(5.19)\quad F(k)=[\Lambda(k)+B^T(k)\pi(k+1)B(k)]^{-1}B^T(k)\pi(k+1), \quad k = 1, 2, \ldots, NN$$

(5.20) $\pi(NN) = \Gamma(NN)$

$$(5.21)\quad \pi(k)=\Lambda(k)+A^T(k)\pi(k+1)[I-B(k)F(k)]A(k), \quad k = 1, 2, \ldots, NN-1.$$

However, we here note that there are the two problems encountered. First, it is rarely the case that $z(k) = z^*(k)$, $i=1,2,\ldots,NN$. Second, it is very difficult to obtain the realized values for $x(k)$ and $z(k)$ at period k. Furthermore, it may be not possible to generally treat these problems. Therefore, more realistic situations must be assumed as follows.

It is possible to obtain the realized values for $x(k)$ and $z(k)$ at one time period before, but their values at current period are obliged to forecast. Accordingly, we use

$$(5.22)\quad x(k|k') = \begin{cases} x(k),\ k \leq k'-1: & \text{the realized values} \\ x(k|k),\ k = k': & \text{the forecasting values} \end{cases}$$

$$(5.23)\quad z(k|k') = \begin{cases} z(k),\ k \leq k'-1: & \text{the realized values} \\ z(k|k),\ k = k': & \text{the forecasting values} \\ z^*(k),\ k \geq k'+1: & \text{the forecasting values} \end{cases}$$

to carry out the rivision of (5.18). Then we have

$$(5.24)\quad u(k|k) = u^*(k) - F(k)[A(k)[x(k|k) - x^*(k)] + C(k)(z(k|k) - z^*(k))]$$

$$(2.25)\quad x(k+1|k+1) = x^*(k+1) + A(k)[x(k) - x^*(k)] + B(k)[u(k) - u^*(k)] + C(k)[z(k) - z^*(k)]$$

where it is clear that

(5.26) $u(k) = u(k|k) = u(k|k+1)$

and where in (5.24) through (5.26), $x(k|k)$, $z(k|k)$ and $u(k|k)$ are the forecasting values; the realized values are given by $x(k)$, $z(k)$ and $u(k)$. Fig.3 describes the procedure for the implementation of the planning made in the interaction between the head office and individual establishment or branch in manufacturing concerns.

6. CONCLUDING REMARKS

Most of studies on the decentralized control problems from a team decision approach have been prescriptive and very formal rather than empirical. The main point of this paper is to suggest a new practical and empirical method by illustrating the well-known aggregate production planning problem within the framework of the dynamic team decision under informationally decentralization. In particular, it is verified that the team decision of multi-item extension is one certain convenient framework for detailing the normative evaluation. In the realistic multi-item firm model, the information available at the various control agents on which decision are to be made is different. On the other hand, this multi-item model, indicates a multiple person situation in which no conflict of interest exists among members.

The optimal team decision rules are generally bound to be nonlinear and comples, so some possible results are given in the linear solution case only. The computational device and its applicability are emphasized in order to hold an empirical validity of promise for integrating and extending our knowledge about information and decision. The approach proposed here may be a useful method adapted to analyze various aspects of decision problems in this direction.

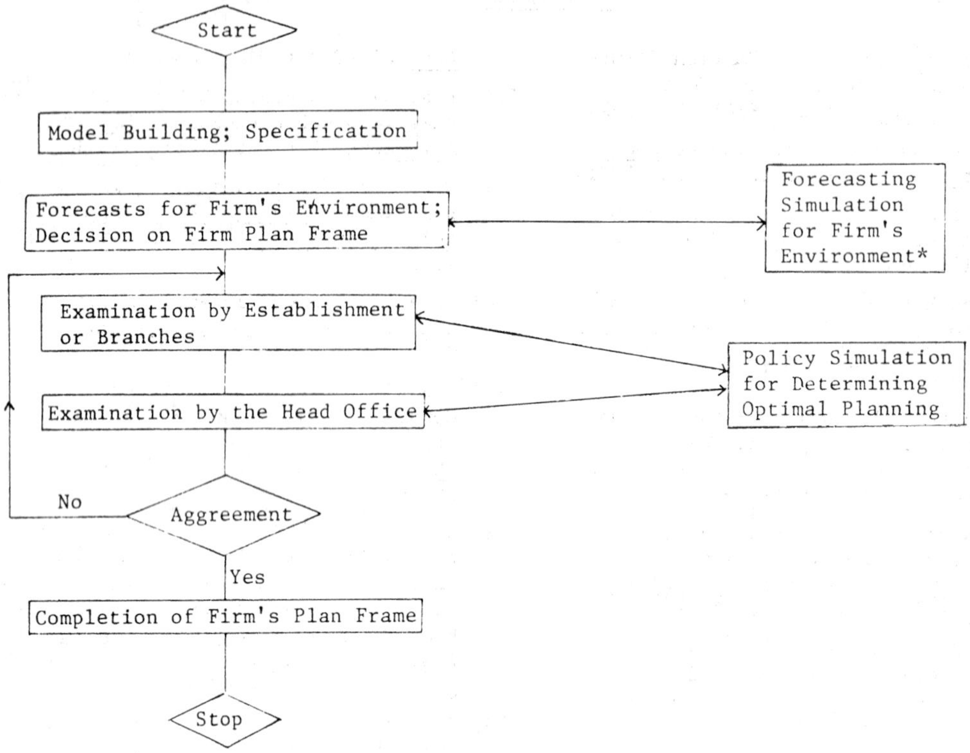

* The course of the development of the firm's environment including demand forecast for the commodity is estimated in the combination of macroeconometric model.

Fig. 2: The Procedure for the Firm Plan Frame

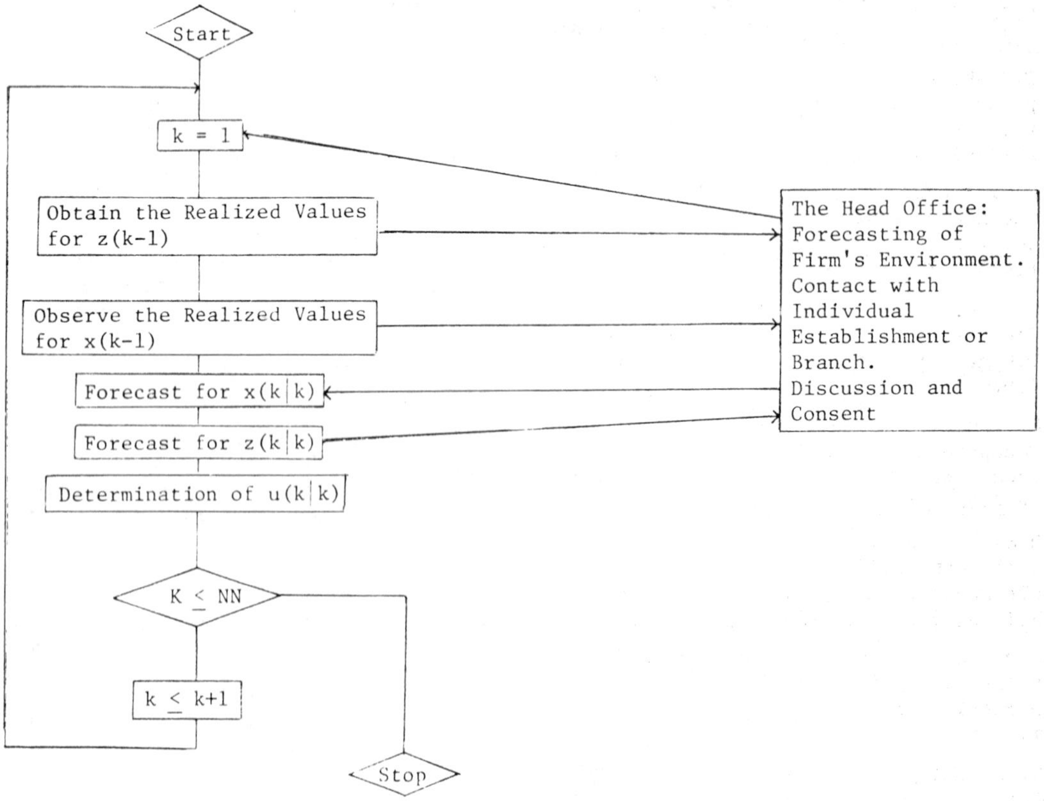

Fig. 3: Procedure for the Planning Implementation for Individual Establishment or Branch

REFERENCES

[1] Y.C.Ho and K.C.Chu: Information Structure in Dynamic Multi-Person Control Problems, Automatica 10(1974), 341-351.

[2] J.Marschak and R.Radner: The Economic Theory of Teams, Yale Univ. Press, 1971.

[3] H.Witsenhausen: A Counter-Example in Stochastic Control, SIAM J. Control 6 (1968), 131-147.

[4] Y.C.Ho and K.C.Chu: Team Decision and Information Structure in Optimal Control Problems, IEEE Trans. Aut. Control AC-17 (1972), 15-22.

[5] C.Y.Chong and M.Athans: On the Stochastic Control of Linear System with Different Information Sets, IEEE Trans. Aut. Control AC-16(1971), 423-430.

[6] T.Yoshikawa: Decentralized Control of Discrete-time Stochastic Systems in Proc. 3rd IFAC Symp. Sensitivity, Adaptivity, and Optimality, 444-451, 1973.

[7] M.Aoki: On Decentralized Linear Stochastic Control Problems with Quadratic Cost, IEEE Trans. Aut. Control AC-17 (1973), 15-22.

[8] N.R.Sandell and M.Athans: Solution of Some Nonclassical LQG Stochastic Decision Problems, IEEE Trans. Aut. Control AC-19(1974), 108-116.

[9] B.Z.Kurtaran and R.Sivan: Linear Quadratic Gaussian Control with One Step-Delay Sharing Pattern, IEEE Trans. Aut. Control, AC-19(1974), 571-574.

[10] T.Yoshikawa: Dynamic Programming Approach to Decentralized Stochastic Control Problems, IEEE Trans. Aut. Control AC-20(1975), 796-797.

[11] B.Z.Kurtaran: A Concise Privation of the LQG One-Step-Delay Sharing Problem Solution, IEEE Trans. Aut. Control AC-20 (1975), 808-810.

[12] B.Z.Kurtaran: Decentralized Stochastic Control with Delayed Sharing Information Pattern, IEEE Trans. Aut. Control AC-21 (1976), 576-581.

[13] H.Myoken: Optimal Control Problem of Decentralized Dynamic Economic Systems, Proc. the VIII th International Congress on Cybernetics, Namur, 1975.

[14] H.Myoken and Y.Uchida: A Minimal Canonical Form Realization for a Multivariable Econometric System, Int. J. Systems Sci. 8(1977), 801-811.

[15] H.Myoken: Controllability and Observability in Optimal Control of Linear econometric Models, Kybernetes 6(1977), 1-13.

[16] S.S.L.Chang and T.K.C.Peng: Adaptive Guaranteed Cost Control of Systems with Uncertain Parameters, IEEE Trans. Aut. Control AC-17(1972), 474-483.

[17] B.N.Jain: Guaranteed Error Estimation in Uncertain Systems, IEEE Trans. Aut. Control AC-20(1975), 230-232.

[18] B.N.Jain: Bounding Estimators for Systems with Coloured Noise, IEEE Trans. Aut. Control AC-20(1975), 365-368.

[19] C.C.Holt, F.Modigliani, F.Muth, and H.A.Simon: Planning Production, Inventories, and Work Force, Prentice Hall, 1960.

[20] L.Taylor: The Existence of Optimal Distributed Lags, R. Econ. Studies, 37(1970) 95-106.

[21] P.R.Kleindorfer and K.Glover: Linear Convex Stochastic Optimal Control with Applications in Production Planning, IEEE Trans. Aut. Control AC-18(1973), 56-59.

[22] H.Myoken, H.Sadamichi and Y.Uchida: Decentralized Stabilization and Regulation in Large-Scale Macroeconomic-Environmental Models, and Conflicting Objectives: Proc. IFAC Workshop on Urban, Regional & National Planning: Environmental Aspects, Pergamon Press, 1977.

[23] C.H.Kriebel: Quadratic Teams, Information Economics, and Aggregate Planning Decisions, Econometrica 36(1968), 530-543.

[24] G.L.Bergstrom and B.E.Smith: Multi-item Production Planning — an Extension of the HMMS Rules, Management Science 16 (1970), 614-629.

ASSEMBLY LINE CONTROL MODELS IN AUTOMOTIVE INDUSTRY

J. Hampl and P. Skvor

INORGA - Institute for Industrial Management Automatization, Letenská 17, 11 806 Prague 1, Czechoslovakia

1. INTRODUCTION

The paper deals with assembly line model within the framework a production control and information computer system consisting of five basic functional areas. These areas and their mutual interactions are being briefly reviewed including the proposed computer hardware and communications equipment.

A more detailed attention is paid to the description of the production control area where the problem of finding an optimum sequence of different vehicle types and options that are to be completed assembly line was solved.

The relevant mathematical model is based on the daily vehicle schedule and considers assembly timing data of different vehicle types, loading of each work center and technológical restrictions. The control of movements of selected parts and conveyor control are integral parts of the algorithm.

2. BASIC CONCEPTS AND FUNCTIONS OF THE PRODUCTION CONTROL AND INFORMATION SYSTEM

The total system problem area was divided according the nature of various production, planning and control activities into the following main functional areas:

(1) Production planning,
(2) Production scheduling,
(3) Production monitoring and reporting,
(4) Production control,
(5) Quality control.

2.1 Production planning

The plan is formed generally for three planning periods ahead, the first period plan being compulsory, the other two periods data being of perspective nature. As a planning period one calendar month was chosen. For this plannnig period necessary parts, subassemblies and assemblies to be manufactured are calculated for different work centers and shops.

The planning of manufacuture of parts and subassemblies and/or assemblies differs for batch (rota cycle) production and flow line production, respectively.

Considering current stock levels of finished manufactured parts and bought out items, lead times and delivery times and other planning standards are determined the process of calculations of requirements is based on the vehicle build requirement given by volume of basic type of vehicle ordered, volume of spare parts and parts for supplies for reject and direct takings from production process.

2.2 Production scheduling

Similar approach to that of planning process is applied for production scheduling in metallurgical shops, press shops, mechanical and assembly shops but contrary to the planning process a time period shorter than one month is used. The production scheduling process for the area body shop - paint shop - final assembly line follows up the calculated one month vehicle build plan and sales subsystem requirements (one month order file). Due to the nature of production process in this area no optimatization techniques were applied the calculation of schedules.The vehicle build schedule represents disjunction of the required volume of vehicles to be built and manufactured and/or bought out items delivery restrictions prevailing in the production process. The production schedule is formed by succesive sorts of considered monthly order book. Using production planning standards and bill of material explosion tables the daily schedules for different work centers and successive shops are formed out of the three days vehicle built schedule file. The three days file at the same time permits to decide allocation of substite orders in case of paint shop failure. The requirements for material and transfers to the lines are derived from the three days order file.

2.3 Production monitoring and reporting creates a necessary feedback for the production scheduling and control. In the body shop - paint shop - assembly line area the production monitoring a reporting system provides the collection and processing of data on real number of parts and subassemblies manufactured, number of bodies produced and number of painted bodies (in different body type breakdown). The order follow up is carried out along the assembly line area (including body number tracking) from the order allocation point to the finished car shipping area. The collection of production data on trims, wheels, engines, transmissions and axes of different types is provided as well as processing of these data into the form necessary for production control and (i.e. necessary accumulations, explosions, deriation calculations and reporting and failure signalling are carried out).

The production monitoring and reporting data records will be also utilized for the payroll calculations.

2.4 Production control

Assignement of orders to painted bodies in the body shop - paint shop - assembly line is done by the use of the created three days order file. This order assignment is based on the line capacity possibilities, such that all different work stations be maximum utilized. The algorithm applied is described in more detail in Part 4 of this paper. The order assignment procedure takes into consideration the material status on conveyor and inventory carrying sections. This function is linked with the successive shop control, the preparation of vehicle documentation and preparation of documents for inventory carrying section automatic take down. Out of other interesting control functions the assignments of colours before actual spraying can be mentioned. As a part of production control process in this area also production reporting and distribution of control information to selected work stations in shops is performed.

2.5 Quality control function provides monitoring of quality in manufacturing shops, work and adjustment centers, material and parts stock yards and warehouses and guarantee analysis and follow up.

This functional area objective is to collect information and data for production and preproduction management on the defectivity of parts so as to permit design and technological modification.

3. INFORMATION SYSTEM HARDWARE EQUIPMENT

Some of the above mentioned functions have been at the present time partially implemented in A.Z.N.P. works using the IBM 360/30 computer.

To provide computing and communication facilities for further functions in other areas two control computer systems IBM S/7 are installed with the data installed with the data collection terminals 2790 scattered directly in work shops.

As a result, part of the system functions described above will be processed by the control computers IBM S/7, the latter part will be processed by the central IBM 360/30 computer.

The mutual interaction in the processing of outputs and data retransmittion between IBM 360/30 and IBM S/7 computers will be ensured by the magnetic tape data files exchange.

4. GENERAL FORMULATION OF MULTIPRODUCT ASSEMBLY LINE CONTROL PROBLEM

In this part of the paper a detailed description of a mathematical model of multiproduct assembly line is presented. This part belongs to an important area of production control in automotive industry, featuring problems that have not been solved in Czechoslovakia by use of a process control computer so far.

An assembly line is defined as an organization of technological process during which course assembly of components (parts, subassemblies) into a final, finished product is performed. Due to organizational and technological reasons the assembly line is usually divided into a number of work stations. These will be assumed as elementery units of assembly process.

A work station (area) is usually defined by a particular location and position in technological sequence. According to its work objective the work station is equipped by necessary tools, materials and work force of required professional qualifications. Let us assume an assembly line divided into $\underline{m}$ work areas, each of them being of length l_j ($j = 1,2,\ldots\ldots , m$).

Generally, the work stations may be of different size, but for the sake of simplicity let us assume l_j, the work station length, being expressed as an integer number; its practical interpretation may be for example a certain number of positions of main transfer conveyor. In our case this number denotes number of products assembled simultaneously in the j-th work station.

The other parameter of each work station is D_j, the number of workers assigned to the j-th work station.

The transfer of products between different work stations along the line is usually performed by a transport conveyor, which also sets rhythmical rate of output. The time interval between the arrival of two succesive products to the work station is usually called line work (denoted by symbol t). This is the time necessary for the assembled product to proceed by a step, i.e. by one conveyor position.

The work capacity of j-th work station may be obtained using the work station area length l_j and the number of workers D_j as

$$K_j = D_j \cdot l_j \cdot t \qquad (1)$$

This is the model of the situation on the assembly line derived from the length and work force level of particular work area.

Further on, an opposite variable K_j (PLAN) will be introduced, representing work capacity derived from the production plan, i.e. work capacity required to assemble the planned volume of products.

The succession of assembly activities on the line are given technological sequencing requirements, i.e. by a compulsory sequence of prescribed manufacturing operations (i.e. elementary work unit tasks). These operations have been assigned to particular work areas and their volume is characterized by the length of their performance times. The usual way how to express the volume of work is to specify the <u>number of standard performance minutes</u> required. As mentioned above, technological operations at one work station area may be performed by one or more (D_j) workers. If the assembly line is designed only for one type of product the technological time for j-th work station area is denoted by T_j (j = 1, 2 ...., m). The sum of performance times of all work tasks performed on the whole assembly line is usually called the <u>product performance time.</u> Methaphorically, the term <u>performance time</u> could also be used for the variable T_j of j-th work station area.

An assembly line need not to be used for assembly of a single product exclusively but may be used for simultaneous production of several products, or rahter several types (modifications) of one product. However, approximately same sequence of technological operations and line design (including the division into work stations) must remain unchanged - this must hold but the performance times of different types may vary, of course. Hence, in our further explanations a multiproduct assembly line, technologically designed for simultaneous assembly of <u>n</u> different types (modifications) of a certain product will be considered. Let us denote different modifications by index i (i = 1,2, ... n) and assume that technologically required performance time of different assembly operations expressed by a number of performance minutes required will be specified in a form of a matrix

$$(T_{ij}) \text{ for all } \quad i = 1,2, \ldots, n \quad j = 1,2, \ldots, m$$

The next term to introduce is variable V_j which represents the level of loading (utilization) of j-th work station. V_j will be obtained by summing up technological performance times of all different products that are to be formed during a certain time interval in the j-th work area;

$$V_j = \sum_{k=1}^{l_j} V_{jk} \qquad (2)$$

where index k denotes the relative position of the product in j-th area and the auxiliary variable V_{jk} represents a part of work load (utilization) of j-th work area capacity by k-th product.

The relative position index k of work area j may obtain values k = 1,2, ..., l_j. If k = 1 then the product is just incoming to the 1st position of the appropriate work area it follows that k = l_j. Similarily it means that the product is located on the last position of j-th work area, i.e. it will move into the immediately following (j+1) work station during the next step (move) of the assembly line conveyor.

The decisive factors of performance timings for calculation of changes in work area loading are the timings in both extreme positions, i.e. the quantities $V_{j,1}$, V_j, l_j, respectively. The loading of the j-th work area is increased by the quantity $V_{j,1}$ at the arrival time of the product into the 1st position. At the same time the j-th work station area is being left by a product with relative position index k equal to l_j. As a result the loading of area is decreased by quantity $V_{j},_{l_j}$. Hence the resulting loading after this step will be

$$V'_j = V_j + V_{j,1} - V_{j,\,l_j}. \qquad (3)$$

From (3) it follows that if the difference

$$V_{j,1} - V_{j,\,l_j} > 0$$

then

$$V'_j > V_j \qquad (4)$$

$$V_{j,1} - V_{j,\,l_j} < 0$$

then

$$V'_j < V_j\ . \qquad (5)$$

This means practically that by arrival of a product of higher performance time then that of the departing one the work station loading in the appropriate step becomes increased and vice versa. Hence, if the products coming to the assembly line have different performance timings (as given by technological time matrix (T_{ij}) the loading of different work stations fluctuates. The objective of production process control is to achieve minimum fluctuations, i.e. maximum loading evenly balanced with the work area capacity.

The difference between the real work capacity of the area and area loading (utilization) according to (3) will be called slack capacity. This quantity is consequently used for decision making as to which of n possible product types (modifications) will be put to the assembly line. This decision is made under the constraint that the total loading V_j must not exceed the j-th work area real capacity, i.e.

$$K_j \geq V'_j\ . \qquad (6)$$

for all j=1,2, ..., m.

As the product´s arrival time to the multiproduct assembly line (i.e. i-th modification arrives to 1st position of 1st work station area) the value $T_{i,1}$ is put for

$$V_{1,1} = T_{i,1} \qquad (7)$$

and more generally for a vector

$$V'_{j,k} = V_{j,k} - 1 \ . \qquad (8)$$

for $k = 1, 2, \ldots\ldots, l_j$.

This calculation can be performed consecutively for all work areas $j = 1, 2, \ldots, m$ in the cycle. The sequence model does not consider the product arrival time to the work area station. It was proved that it is sufficient to know the sequence of products of performance timing length max $l_{\bar{j}}$ and this verifies the performance timing of each modification for all work stations.

Using the values of technological performance timings in j-th row of (T_{ij}) matrix the capacity requirement for j-th work area for scheduling interval x may be calculated from expression

$$K_j \text{ (PLAN)} = (l_j / P_{TOTAL}(x)) .$$

$$. \sum_{i=1}^{n} T_{ij} \cdot P_i (x) \ . \qquad (9)$$

By simple comparison of real work capacity K_j from the relation (1), with capacity requirements derived from K_j (PLAN) according to relation (9) the possibility of fulfillment of the appropriate time period x production schedule may be evaluated. Also critical work stations, that are not in position to fulfil the plan, can be found. The production schedule can be fulfilled under existing work capacities if holds the following unequality:

$$K_j \geq K_j \text{ (PLAN)} \ . \qquad (10)$$

5. PRACTICAL TESTS OF ALGORITHM

The above described model of multiproduct assembly line control was applied in a decision making algorithm during experimental control of assembly line of Škoda cars in A.Z.N.P. works in Mladá Boleslav.

The production control experiment was carried out in A.Z.N.P. works enabled practical operational verification of the mathematical model of assembly line control including the related functions of information system (recording of bodies coming to the assembly line, operator´s activities by system initiation and/or failure, control of conveyor´s stockage branches according to the required options of sub-assemblies, etc.). The fact that the systems people and shop floor management could test and verify beforehand the use of process control computer for the actual assembly line control contributed significantly to the possibility of planned early information system implementation.

TECHNICAL PAPER DISCUSSIONS

PLENARY SESSION

REMOVING BARRIERS TO THE APPLICATION OF AUTOMATION IN DISCRETE PART BATCH MANUFACTURING

Author: J. M. Evans

Discusser: Y. Morita

Affiliation: Tokyo Institute of Technology, JAPAN

Discussion:

I congratulate you on your good summary. Two points I want you to make clear.

1. You mentioned the correction of inherent errors of a measuring machine by measuring them and storing them to be made use of in a dynamic operation. This is understandable. But you also added that the same technique can be applied to a machine tool. I think this is not so simple because a machine tool consumes far greater power than a measuring machine, and eventually ejects heat. Could you explain a bit further on this point?

2. "The mirror surface has a flatness two orders of magnitude better than you are able to measure," you said in your lecture. How do you know it if you are not able to measure?

Author's Reply:

1. Yes, you must compensate for the thermal error also. In general, the correction will be a function of position, temperature, and applied forces.

2. You can measure the optical quality of the surface with optical techniques. This is beyond the mechanical measurement capability of stylus instruments. So there really is a measurement made.

Discusser: A. Kuisma

Affiliation: Innotec Ltd, FINLAND

Discussion:

How widely are HP-Bus Standard (IEEE488) and different types of CAMAC systems nowadays used in USA?

Author's Reply:

Before this year, practically no one used the HP Standard except Hewlett Packard. As of this year, several other scientific instrument manufacturers have adopted this standard. CAMAC has been used in nuclear instrumentation and discussed for process control applications; I see little additional application beyond what now exists. I expect ADCCP (ISO HLDC) to become the most attractive interface standard because of its low cost and wide support.

Discusser: A. Nomoto

Affiliation: Tokyo Agricultural and Technological University, JAPAN

Discussion:

You have figured out the increase of productivity due to NC to be about 300% or a factor of three. Let me ask if this is normally accepted measure in industry.

Author's Reply:

Productivity is something that is often argued about. This is data reported in many studies and confirmed in our own experience. This is factor for both labor productivity (output per man hour) and total factor productivity (cost reduction). For integrated systems, labor productivity may be thousands of percents, while cost reduction is only 50-70%, quite a different figure.

AUTOMATION RESEARCH IN GERMANY AND ITS ROLE REGARDING NATIONAL PRODUCTIVITY

Authors: U. Rembold and I. Bey

Discusser: H. Sato

Affiliation: University of Tokyo, JAPAN

Discussion:

It is very interesting to know how the national projects in Germany is carried on. I would like to know the situation of the evaluation for these projects.

This might not be directly related with your presentation, however, it seems to me that we are facing with some conflicts as for the international trade problems as the results that we have made an effort to increase the productivity and Germany is doing good in this feature. I would like to learn your comments if you have any on these problems

Authors' Reply:

In general, it is very difficult to get quantitative figures. In addition, the economical situation in the country will change during a funding program is executed by means of other, "funding independent" influences. But there are some figures which will be an answer to your question, e. g. the number of process control computers in the F. R. of Germany increased substantially in the year and surpassed 17,000 installations in 1977. In small business computers and process control computers German manufacturers also get a greater market there within Germany.

Projects are evaluated by an advisory board consisting of industry, government and research people who are experts in the field. The results are evaluated in a similar manner. However, this usually is a very difficult job. We look at computer sales figures, computer usage, number of similar installations installed etc. Such figures are very readily available in Germany. Also the word usually gets very quickly around on good computer installations. It thus can be noticed that competitive companies are doing the same thing.

The Federal Republic of Germany has a similar problem with trade imbalance as Japan. The frequent re-evaluation of the German Mark had to be done due to this problem. The German government is watching this problem very carefully. With a positive trade balance export will be falling off. I also would like to add that automation may increase unemployment. However, economists say that it will not. In any case, we do have to watch this problem very carefully.

SESSION 1: RESEARCH PROJECTS SPONSORED BY GOVERNMENTS

NEW FLEXIBLE MANUFACTURING SYSTEMS FROM THE G. D. R.

Author: G. Kleditzsch

Discusser: D. E. Whitney

Affiliation: C. S. Draper Lab., USA

Discussion:

What are the plans of the GDR for building more ROTA or PRISMA Systems?
I was interested especially in machine systems for domestic use within GDR.

Author's Reply:

In these days, we are mounting a second machining system similar to the first, but with 50% higher capacity. For another system like FZ200, we have finished the whole project and there is no problem for building up others.
Activities in this direction are planned.

Discusser: J. Chiba

Affiliation: R & D Div., Komatsu Ltd., JAPAN

Discussion:

I think that the most important thing in such as no man controlled manufacturing system is to minimize down times or to shorten the time of repairing system. Please let me know how to monitor the system activity on an actual line, and how to keep and educate the machines.

Author's Reply:

The weekly maintenance is 8 hours for the FMS in GDR. The repairing of the System-Elements (machines, measurement-machines) goes on each time with a service-team.
In the FMS are Diagnostic-Elements.

MODELING AND SIMULATION OF AUTOMATED MANUFACTURING PROCESSES

Authors: H. J. Warnecke and E. Gericke

Discusser: D. Whitney

Affiliation: C. S. Draper Lab., USA

Discussion:

Have you made direct mathematical models of FMS behavior to supplement your simulation models?

Authors' Reply:

No, we think that mathematical models are too sophisticated and expensive when the structure of the FMS is getting more complex, for instance having 6 working stations as in our simulation case study. We are going to summarize the results in rules of thumb for the designer.

Discusser: T. Sata

Affiliation: University of Tokyo, JAPAN

Discussion:

What is the purpose of building the physical model of a flexible manufacturing system?

Authors' Reply:

There are several purposes. One is for teaching students, the others are for supporting design and selling such systems. It is good to simulate and see the performance not only on paper but to see it really before implementation the original system.

CONCEPTUAL DESIGN OF INTEGRATED PRODUCTION CENTER

Authors: F. Honda and H. Takeyama

Discusser: J. M. Evans

Affiliation: National Bureau of Standards, USA

Discussion:

In your figures, robots are shown in several places. Are the parts always free, and located and handled by robots, or are they moved on pallets to maintain part orientation?

Authors' Reply:

Parts come to the assembling machine on pallets properly oriented, and the robot depalletizes the parts to execute programmed activities while maintaining or identifying the coordinates of the parts.

Discusser: U. Rembold

Affiliation: Universität Karlsruhe, FRG

Discussion:

How high is the software cost on this project as percentage of the total cost?

Authors' Reply:

We have not figured out the software cost precisely, but according to a rough estimation it is more than three times of the hardware cost.

Discusser: H. J. Warnecke

Affiliation: University of Stuttgart, FRG

Discussion:

The project "Unmanned Factory", how is it going on here in Japan and by how much money is it sponsored by government?

Authors' Reply:

The project of a so-called "Unmanned Factory" has been modified into "Integrated Production Center" which is of smaller scale compared to a "Factory" mainly because of the limited funds. The budget is approximately 12 billion yens (= 46 million dollars) for seven years and the project is planned to be sponsored by the Government.

Discusser: H. J. Warnecke

Affiliation: University of Stuttgart, FRG

Discussion:

In merging processes and designing high integrated manufacturing center, is there not the risk of losing flexibility and bad use of all the investment when there are changes in the design of work pieces and products?

Authors' Reply:

Flexibility of the system and effectiveness of machines or unit utilization depend upon the industrial structure to a large extent, but this is not a matter to discuss here. Apart from this, the pattern of products to be manufactured by a definite factory is usually fixed. If so, limited types and number of modular units can manage the required activities although special operations inherent in the specific products should be trusted to the special purpose equipments.

Discusser: D. Whitney

Affiliation: C. S. Draper Lab., USA

Discussion:

Please list all the National Big Projects.

Authors' Reply

The National Big Projects range to a wide variety, and at the moment no big project is going on except for this Project "High Quality, Laser-Applied Integrated Manufacturing System", as far as the field of production engineering is concerned.

MAJOR PROJECTS ON CONTROL SYSTEMS FOR DISCRETE PARTS MANUFACTURING IN THE FEDERAL REPUBLIC OF GERMANY

Author: I. Bey

Discusser: T. Sata

Affiliation: University of Tokyo, JAPAN

Discussion:

1. Are the last three flexible manufacturing systems listed in Table 1 of your paper going to be developed on the commercial base?

2. What is the relation between the development of the flexible manufacturing systems and that of the PEARL programming language?

Author's Reply:

1. Yes, that's right. They are planned to operate economically at normal industrial conditions.

2. PEARL will be applied to program the real time operation of FMS, i.e. the system listed in Table 1, column 4 is developed for an AEG - Telefunken plant, where an AEG process control computer with PEARL compiler implemented by AEG will be used.
   On the INTERKAMA Exhibition October 77 at Duesseldorf a Fischer-Technik-Model of a FMS was shown running with a PEARL program.

Discusser: D. E. Whitney

Affiliation: C. S. Draper Lab., USA

Discussion:

When will PEARL be available for US Computers?

Author's Reply:

This is no my competence. All that I can say is that German software houses are developing PEARL compilers for US computers, too.

Discusser: J. M. Evans

Affiliation: National Bureau of Standards, USA

Discussion:

1. Does robot shown in Fig. 1 do tool changing and part loading?

2. What is the accuracy of parts on pallets?

3. Does this require sensors?

4. Are there any sensors in the system?

Author's Reply:

1. The final version most probably will contain two independent handling devices for tool changing and part loading.

2. I can't tell you this exactly, there is no experience with the system. I think, positioning accuracy will be something like 1 mm.

3. This will require some kind of gripping force sensors.

4. Yes, i.e. for the quality control measurement. The specification is not yet finished.

SESSION 2: AUTOMATIC ASSEMBLY AND INSPECTION (I)

ON-LINE SYSTEM FOR MEASURING THICKNESS OF ULTRA-THIN NON-METALLIC LAYER ON STRIP SURFACE

Authors: A. Izumidate, H. Yamamoto, S. Shiki, M. Motomura and Y. Nomura

Discusser: J. Aseltine

Affiliation: United Nuclear Corp., USA

Discussion:

What type of computer was used in the on-line computation?

Authors' Reply:

INTEL 8080 was used for computing the quantity of the oil film of ET or the hydrated chromium oxide of TFS.

PRACTICAL APPLICATION OF DIAGNOSTIC SIGNATURE ANALYSIS TO TESTING OF ROTATING MACHINES

Authors: T. Usami, T. Koizumi, T. Inari and E. Ohno

Discusser: A. Oledzki

Affiliation: Warsaw Tech. University, POLAND

Discussion:

1) In your paper you took into account only basic sources of noise which may cause failure of a simple equipment like a ventilator. Does your system give a proper answer in case, when the source of noise is of random kind? We know, that very often a perfectly good object (from mechanical point of view) can produce a tremendous amount of noise, and very often of random kind, which source is very difficult to locate (Example - A film-projector).
2) In Europe, equipment is used made by BRIUEL & KJAER for similar diagnostic purposes (But not so sophisticated!). I could not find any information in references of your paper. If you try it, by the chance, could you kindly express your opinion? (As far as I know the system of B&K gives no answer in the form: "GOOD" or "BAD".)

Authors' Reply:

1) In my lecture, I mentioned the sound noises and to give an example out of numerous cases I cited only two defects of a ventilator. Well, I'm not sure of the exact answer because I don't know what feature the random noise of the film-projector you gave as an example has. However, I think it is possible to detect the random noise using our system if you try to modify our system for the noise you wish to detect.
2) It is quite difficult to answer your question right now. That is because I don't have enough information to compare the BRUEL & KJAER with our system, unfortunately. Therefore, I promise to write to you in Warsaw on the examination of that BRUEL & KJAER System at our laboratory.
However, I think our system is superior to the BRUEL & KJAER System, which can find each defect by the noises and give a "GO!" or a "NO GO!" signal.

APPLICATION OF LASER HOLOGRAPHY TECHNIQUE TO MICRO PATTERN POSITIONING IN INTEGRATED CIRCUITS MANUFACTURING

Authors: Y. Oshima, N. Mohri and Y. Isogai

Discusser: A. Izumidate

Affiliation: Nippon Steel Corp., JAPAN

Discussion:

Has this technique any limitation with scanning area?

Authors' Reply:

In principle there is no limitation with respect to the size of the object, but as a matter of course there occurs the limitation from the viewpoint of the size of the optical system and the intensity of the laser. We are going to apply this technique to positioning of the IC wafer with the size of several ten millimeters. We can not say the limitation quantitatively because we do not have any experience with respect to the objects with bigger size.

PROFILE PATTERN RECOGNITION SYSTEM FOR MACHINE PARTS

Author: H. Kono

Discusser: A. Niemi

Affiliation: Helsinki Univ. of Tech.,FINLAND

Discussion:

How do you make a distinction between a slightly curved contour and a corner?

Author's Reply:

In the developed pattern recognition system, the profile pattern is recognized as a polygon. Therefore, if a slightly curved contour portion is to be recognized, only the corners which change the corner angle extremely are detected. The recognition limit of the corner angle change to be recognized is from greater than 45° to less than 135°.

SESSION 3: AUTOMATIC ASSEMBLY AND INSPECTION (II)

STUDY ON AUTOMATIC VISUAL INSPECTION OF SHADOW-MASK MASTER PATTERNS

Authors: Y. Nakagawa, H. Makihira, N. Akiyama, T. Numakura and T. Nakagawa

Discusser: A. Kuni

Affiliation: Hitachi Ltd. JAPAN

Discussion:

Have you ever investigated the use of the laser hologram for the inspection of such repetition patterns?

Authors' Reply:

We have discussed whether or not we can use the technique of hologram or optical Fourier transformation. But we didn't dare to use this technique.
The emulsion thickness on the shadow mask master plate is not constant all over the plate surface. But in an optical Fourier transformation, the variation of the emulsion thickness can detected with high sensitivity. But it doesn't necessarily mean that the variation is a defect. For this reason we could not use this method.

Discusser: A. Niemi

Affiliation: Helsinki Univ. of Tech., FINLAND

Discussion:

Is the amount of illumination of the plate a limiting factor to the speed of operation?

Authors' Reply:

Yes, it is a limiting factor to the speed of operation. The scanning speed of the photodiode array depends on the intensity of illumination. In this machine, we use the halogen-lamp (150w) for illumination.
If we can use the lamp which has higher intensity, we can get higher speed of inspection. But in this case, the shadow-mask master plate is damaged by the heat of the light. So we couldn't use the lamp which has much higher intensity than this one.

Discusser: A. Izumidate

Affiliation: Nippon Steel Corp., JAPAN

Discussion:

Does the magnitude of the reflected light vary depending on the flatness of the surface ? It means that threshold level must vary depending on the flatness of the surface.
Namely, threshold level must vary depending on both magnitude of the injected light and the flatness of the surface.
Don't you think that this may limit the accuracy of this system?

Why is not area-array applied to this system?

Authors' Reply:

The flatness doesn't influence the magnitude of the transmitted light, but the roughness of the glass plate does. The surface of the glass plate is so smooth that the roughness doesn't influence the magnitude of the transmitted light. When the magnitude of the injected light varies, the threshold level should be varied. This machine has the adaptive thresholding ability in which the thresholding level varies in response to the detected signal level.

In an area-array, a certain area is detected. In the case that a large area must be detected, the shadow-mask plate should be driven in a step and repeat motion. During the detection, the shadow-mask plate has to keep the position without any motion.
But, in a linear-array sensor, a row of patterns is detected, during the shadow-mask plate is being driven. In this case, the driving control is very easy and speed is very high. Every time after the longitudinal plate driving, the detecting head is driven transverse, step by step, so the sensor can detect a new row. A linear-array sensor has little distortion, high detection speed and small detector size. In these points of view, we used the solid-state linear image sensor as a detector.

SESSION 4: ROBOTICS AND MATERIAL HANDLING (I)

CLASSIFICATION OF GRASPED OBJECT'S SHAPE BY AN ARTIFICIAL HAND WITH MULTI-ELEMENT TACTILE SENSORS

Author: G-I Kinoshita

Discusser: C. A. Rosen

Affiliation: SRI, USA

Discussion:

Have you considered using lateral inhibition to enhance the contrast of your multiple sensors? This would sharpen up discontinuities.

Author's Reply:

I think it is important that for extracting the feature of objects, enhancing the contrast of multiple sensors should be considered.

Discusser: H. Asada

Affiliation: Kyoto Univ., JAPAN

Discussion:

1) What sequence do you use to let the robot hand grasp the object?
2) Do you have any experiments to verify the Eq. (2.3) for practical materials?

Author's Reply:

1) Thumb is opposed to the index, middle, ring, and little finger. And each finger is controlled sequentially.
2) This problem is now under consideration.

Discusser: I. Bey

Affiliation: Ges. für Kernforschung, FRG

Discussion:

Is the system planned to be applied in industry- if yes, where and when will that be?

Author's Reply:

We have no plan, now. We want to apply in industry.

A ROBOT HAND WITH ELASTIC FINGERS AND ITS APPLICATION TO ASSEMBLY PROCESSES

Authors: H. Hanafusa and H. Asada

Discusser: G. Kinoshita

Affiliation: Chuo Univ., JAPAN

Discussion:

1) You proposed the rigidity matrix Q. I understand the physical meaning of the diagonal elements in the matrix Q. But the non-diagonal elements are not clear. Would you please explain the meaning?
2) Is your robot's hand able to adjust the handling force arbitrarily for various shapes of objects?
3) How much is the clearance of the parts mated in your experiments?

Authors' Reply:

1) The handling force can be written as follows:

$$\begin{bmatrix} F_x \\ F_y \\ M \end{bmatrix} = \begin{bmatrix} p_x \\ p_y \\ p_\theta \end{bmatrix} + \begin{bmatrix} * & q_{xy} & * \\ * & * & * \\ * & * & * \end{bmatrix} \begin{bmatrix} \Delta x_a \\ \Delta y_a \\ \Delta\theta_a \end{bmatrix}$$

I explain by an example. The element q_{xy} means the ratio between F_x and Δy_a. Thus the row diagonal elements mean the interactions between the components of the handling force and the object deviation in different directions.
2) The possibility to adjust B and C to construct desired P and Q is determined from det R, and the fact that each finger force has the limit to generate, such as $0 < f_i <$ Max f_i. The details are discussed in Chapter 4 of the paper.
3) The clearance between the block and the fixture is less than 0.1mm.

TASK-ORIENTED VARIABLE CONTROL OF A MANIPULATOR AND ITS SOFTWARE SERVOING SYSTEM

Author: K. Takase

Discusser: H. Asada

Affiliation: Kyoto Univ., JAPAN

Discussion:

You introduced H-variables. How do you apply H-variables to the task shown in the film?

Author's Reply:

For example, when the manipulator saws a board, H-variables are determined in the space where the sawing task is carried out, as shown in the Figure.

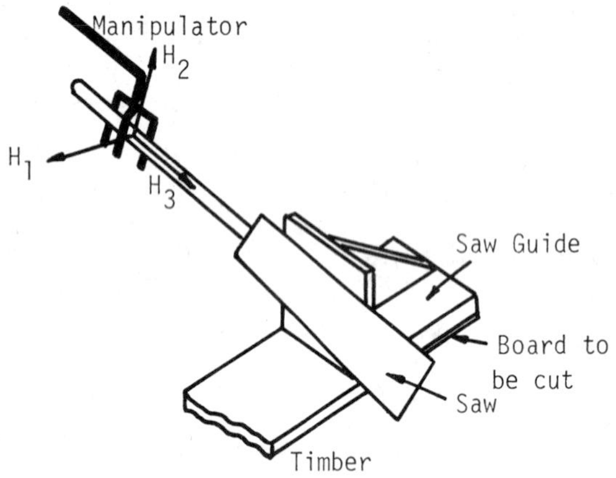

H_1 is set to zero by 3-D position feedback control. The position of H_2 is decided by the environmental constraint, and a downward force is applied. Control of H_3 realizes the reciprocating motion for cutting.

SESSION 6: AUTOMATIZATION OF MATERIAL PROCESSING (I)

ADVANTAGES AND CONDITIONS FOR A DIRECT MEASUREMENT OF THE WORKPIECE-GEOMETRY ON NC-MACHINE TOOLS

Authors: T. Pfeifer and A. Fürst

Discusser: T. Sata

Affiliation: Univ. of Tokyo, JAPAN

Discussion:

How do you take into account thermal deformation of the machine-tool?

Authors' Reply:

The system I introduced here is not running yet, but in a planning status. We hope to get first experiences at the end of the next year. Coming back to the question, I've plan to build up a calibration-point for all three axis of the machine-tool. The position of the calibration-point is very precise measured while the machine-tool is under good thermal conditions. Before measuring the workpiece geometry with the special probe, the probe has to be checked at the calibration-point, to see if there is any deviation from the given value coming, for instance, from thermal deformation of the machine-tool.

PROPOSAL OF THE MULTILAYERED CONTROL OF MACHINE TOOLS FOR FULLY AUTOMATED MACHINING OPERATIONS

Authors: T. Sata and K. Matsushima

Discusser: T. Watanabe

Affiliation: Kyoto Univ., JAPAN

Discussion:

In your system, the identification of the parameters functions well in Fig. 9. There are four parameters in Eq. 9. Therefore, I think these parameters are decided after collecting four measured values.
How long does it take to determine these parameters?

Authors' Reply:

The control system on the first level starts to control the cutting variables by using the parameters assumed in advance. After getting a simple datum of the tool wear, the system is able to evaluate the parameters by using equation (17).
From an economical point of view it is advisable to perform such a computation after getting several data of the tool wear, unless the system recognizes a considerably large error in the predetermined parameters. So I would like to say that the computation is performed every half day, for example. The real computing time by a minicomputer is much shorter than 1 second.

Discsser: H. -J. Warnecke

Affiliation: Univ. of Stuttgart, FRG

Discussion:

Much research work has been done world-wide in the adaptive control field, the response in industry and application is in comparison rather poor. Where do you see the reason and have you already done some cost-value-analysis for your system?

Authors' Reply:

The reason why the adaptive control of a machine tool does not attract the interests of the industrial people, lies in the fact that the function of the simple adaptive control system is not enough to take an operator away from the side of the machine tool, resulting in little contribution to cost reduction. Our research on the multilayered control of a machine tool does not reach to the level to be able to make exact economical evaluation on the merit brought by the system.

Discusser: M. Soeda

Affiliation: Tokai Univ., JAPAN

Discussion:

What kind of merit or profit can be expected by using that system?
Please list up the items, for example:
1. saving the operator
2. making the cutter life longer
3. .....
4. .....
.
.
.

Authers' Reply:

If we will be successful to realize a fully automated machining operations, many advantages would be expected.
These are:
1) to increase productivity even in batch production,
2) to reduce machining cost due to saving of the labour cost and
3) to give workers better working environment.

Discusser: G. K. Hutchinson

Affiliation: Univ. of Wisconsin, USA

Discussion:

How was the overhead cost (Mc) in eq. 1 determined?

Authers' Reply:

The overhead cost in equation (1) is the conventional one which includes depreciation of the machine tool, the labour cost and others.

THE ROLE OF NUMERICAL CONTROL USED FOR THE MANUFACTURING PROCESS IN MACHINING ON MAIN INDUSTRIES IN JAPAN

Authors: M. Soeda, H. Yonaiyama and E. Yamaguchi

Discusser: H. J. Warnecke

Affiliation: Univ. of Stuttgart, FRG

Discussion:

Especially the NC machine being expensive it seems to me that the number of shifts is of great influence to the machining cost, more for instance than the number of operators per machine. Am I right in this assumption?

Authors' Reply:

The cost of man power will be increased proportionally, or over proportionally, with increasing of number of shift. By this reason, cost/product is not so much changed as we expect, so long as shift is concerned. But depreciation period is largely changed toward advantageous condition.
Judging from the above factor, I presume the cost may be decreased in some degree depending on conditions. This condition will be left to study further.

SESSION 7: AUTOMATIZATION OF MATERIAL PROCESSING (II)

A METHOD OF TOOL PATH DISTRIBUTION ON A CNC

Author: M. Kiyokawa

Discusser: T. Pfeifer

Affiliation: Werkzeugmaschinenlabor, Aachen, FRG

Discussion:

How is running your method when there is only a few material to be cut? That means, when the rough-part is very similar to the finished-part-geometry.

Author's Reply:

The method mentioned here is for cutting bar-stock on a lathe. There is no special consideration on the amount of material to be cut. The cutting area can be calculated by this method according to the information of the shape and allowance to be finished.

MULTIMICROPROCESSOR CONTROL SYSTEM FOR SPECIAL PURPOSE MACHINE TOOLS

Author: A. Kuisma, K. Mäkelä and E. Rasi

Discusser: T. Watanabe

Affiliation: Kyoto University, Japan

Discussion:

1. In Fig.5, the microprocessor controls many servo systems. Do you need the priority interrupt system?

2. How much are the maximum feed rate and spindle speed of the machine controlled by your system?

Author's Reply:

1. We have only one program that is executed every 1/200... 1/50 second. It is doing all the control of slide units one after another and it is also checking some limit switches for safety etc. So no interrupt signals from the slide units are used.

2. The maximum feed rate, we have used in our design, is 12 m/min. The sampling speed is in that case 1/200 s.
We are controlling the spindle drives in an open loop manner, so we just send a command value to the drive system.
The only problem is the command value resolution, which can be fairly high in some cases.

AN ADAPTIVE CNC SYSTEM OF A MILLING MACHINE TOOL

Author: T. Watanabe

Discusser: Y. Morita

Affiliation: Tokyo Institute of Technology, Japan

Discussion:

Would it be possible to measure the temperature of the tool tip? Some of the radiation sensitive instruments are capable of detecting the temperature of a spot having very small diameter, say 70 μm.

Author's Reply:

Of course, it is possible to measure the tool tip temperature directly. I think that there are three representative methods. The first method is to use a thermocouple consisting of the tool and work. But, the value measured by this method indicates the mean temperature over the total tool-work interface as mentioned in this presentation.
The second method is to use a thermocouple constructed by the thin wire set in the tool tip and the work material. But, in the case of using a milling cutter, it is difficult to set the thin wire in the tool tip.
The third method is to use radiation sensitive instruments as is advised from you. But, this method has some problems. Firstly, the temperature of the tool tip, while contacting with the work, can not be measured. Secondly, the chip and the cutting fluid disturb the measurement. Thirdly, the mutual positions between the tool and the work vary widely in milling, therefore, the instrument must be moved.
We think it is practical to compute the temperature at the flank wear of the tool tip theoretically, because it can be done easily by a minicomputer and it is not affected by the chip and the cutting fluid.

CNC APPLICATIONS

Author: R. Nozawa

Discusser: T. Sata

Affiliation: University of Tokyo, Japan

Discussion:

1. I would like to know how the output of the measuring device is connected with CNC to compensate the setting error of a large workpiece.

2. Is the simulater to find the mulfunction of the machine tool the hardwired one or the softwired one?

Author's Reply:

1. The probe is moved to a workpiece by the jog or manual pulse generator capability of the CNC. The CNC updates the position and store the final position (position of workpiece) in the memory.

2. The simulater in the check system is realized by a hardware.

CNC APPLICATIONS

Author: R. Nozawa

Discusser: T. Pfeifer

Affiliation: Werkzeugmaschinenlabor, Aachen, FRG

Discussion:

What type of probe do you use for identifying the actual workpiece position on the table of the CNC machine-tool?

Author's Reply:

The same probe with tracer control is used for detecting actual work positions.

SESSION 8: AUTOMATIZATION OF MATERIAL PROCESSING (III)

CONTROL SYSTEM OF NC MACHINE TOOL FOR HIGH WORKING ACCURACY

Author: N. Nishiwaki

Discusser: M. Kiyokawa

Affiliation: Mitsubishi Electric Corp., Japan

Discussion:

Are there any problems on the optical fiber sensor, which may be influenced by the vibraton of tool?

Author's Reply:

If there is any vibration of the tool during cutting, it will be recorded by the optical fiber as a noise signal as shown in Fig.6(b). Since the signal obtained through this sensor is used to investigate the surface roughness as well as the chatter behaviour, the vibration of tool is not suppcsed to create any problem.

EXTRA-CYCLIC PASSAGES OF GRAY CODES AND THEIR APPLICATIONS FOR NUMERICAL CONTROL DESIGN

Author: H.J. Leskiewicz

Discusser: T. Watanabe

Affiliation: Kyoto University, Japan

Discussion:

1. What is the cause of generating the hazard phenomena in the NC system in the case of using the ordinary method?

2. For which part of a NC system, is your Gray code available?

Author's Reply:

1. The hazard may take place in going from one state to another when two or more letters are changed simultaneously in the two coding expressions of those states. This should be avoided by proper coding, although this is not always possible.

2. The method presented in the paper explains first if such a proper coding is possible, and where this is so, gives all codes protecting from hazard from which the designer may choose. The application of the method is as wide as the problem of proper coding of any states which do not form a cycle of states which appear only once in this cycle.

SESSION 9: PRODUCTION CONTROL (I)

AN ANALYSIS OF WATER SUPPLY AND STORAGE CAPACITY

Author: T. Odanaka

Discusser: G.K. Hutchinson

Affiliation: The University of Wisconsin, USA

Discussion:

Has the control theory you developed been applied to the original water supply control problem?
With what results? (i.e. What would the plot for one week, like figures 2 & 3, look using your optimal control?)

Author's Reply:

Yes, I have applied my control theory to the original water supply control problem, and given the theoretical background.
Simulation excersises have been carried out and some numerical results have been obtained.

INFORMATION STRUCTURES, DYNAMIC TEAM DECISION, AND AN ECONOMIC APPLICATION

Author: H. Myoken

Discusser: G. Hutchinson

Affiliation: The University of Wisconsin, USA

Discussion:

Could you tell us where you expect to go with your interesting work from this point in time?

Author's Reply:

As mentioned in this paper, most of studies on the decentralized control problems from a team decision approach have been prescriptive and very formal rather than empirical.
This paper presents a new practical and empirical method in order to hold an empirical validity of promise for integrating and extending our knowledge about information and decision.
As an illustrative example, the realistic multi-item firm model is considered, and then we explain in details regarding the procedure of the practical control simulation for determining optimal planning.

SESSION 10: PRODUCTION CONTROL (II)

IMPLEMENTING AN INFORMATION CONTROL SYSTEM FOR MANUFACTURING

Author: J.A. Aseltine

Discusser: J. Talavage

Affiliation: Purdue University, USA

Discussion:

Did you consider, in the design stages, the use of a decentralized network of, say, minicomputers?

Author's Reply:

The state of the art in software requires the use of a central computer for efficient data base handling. However, we do use about 10 minicomputers for automated inspection, the data being sent to the large computer for inclusion in the data base.

IMPLEMENTING AN INFORMATION CONTROL SYSTEM FOR MANUFACTURING

Author: J.A. Aseltine

Discusser: M. Terao

Affiliation: University of Tokyo, Japan

Discussion:

Was there a problem with the time-sharing use of many CRT's on the factory floor?

Author's Reply:

We expanded core memory as terminals and data base expanded to keep response time to about 10 seconds in max. Incidentally, we had no difficulty in training manufacturing personnel to use the terminals-due, I think, to their interest in obtaining data so efficiently.

"PASS" AN INTERACTIVE ONLINE SIMULATOR FOR PREDICTIVE PRODUCTION CONTROL

Author: K. Tabata

Discusser: G.K. Hutchinson

Affiliation: The University of Wisconsin, USA

Discusser:

What resources were required to develop PASS?

Author's Reply:

18 months with one and a half persons were required to develop PASS.

ERRATA

Page	Column	Line or Equation	For	Read
42	left	9	place	plane
42	left	Eq.(1)	$u = ae^{j(wt - kz)}$	$u = ae^{j(kz - wt)}$
42	right	Eq.(3)	$u(\alpha)$	$u(\alpha,\beta)$
43	left	Eq.(5)	$2\Sigma_{(m,1)} \cos(c_m - c_1)$	$2\Sigma_{(m,1)} \cos\beta(c_m - c_1)$
43	right	7	lagging	leading
43	right	18	$\chi_o = \int F(x)e^{-j\frac{k}{f_1}\alpha x}\,dx$	$\chi_o = C_1\int F(x)e^{-j\frac{k}{f_1}\alpha x}\,dx$
43	right	Eq.(10)	$L(p) = \int_{\Pi}\chi 2(a)I(\alpha)e^{-j\frac{k}{f_2}\nu\alpha}\,d\alpha$	$L(p) = \int_{\Pi}\chi 2(\alpha)I(\alpha)e^{-j\frac{k}{f_2}p\alpha}\,d\alpha$
44	left	9	1f $\Delta x = 0$	1f $\Delta x \neq 0$
44	right	Eq.(12)	$\sin(\theta_1 - \theta_2) -(\sin\theta_1 + \sin\theta_2)$	$\sin(\theta_1 - \theta_3) -(\sin\theta_1 + \sin\theta_3)$
45	left	Eq.(16)	$-(\sin\theta_1 + \sin\theta_2)y$	$-(\sin\theta_1 + \sin\theta_3)y$
46	right	11	diviation	deviation
46	right	5 from bottom	Photo 4	Photo 5
47	left	21	Photo 5	Photo 4
47	right	26 from bottom	inverse Fourier	Fourier
48	left	3 from bottom	Q_o to P	T to P

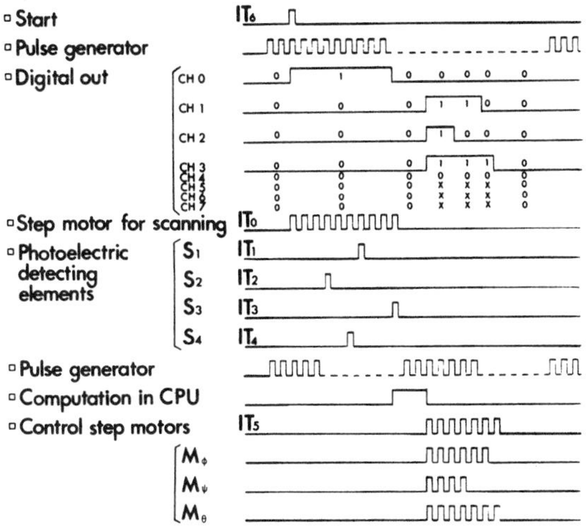

Fig.17. Timing chart

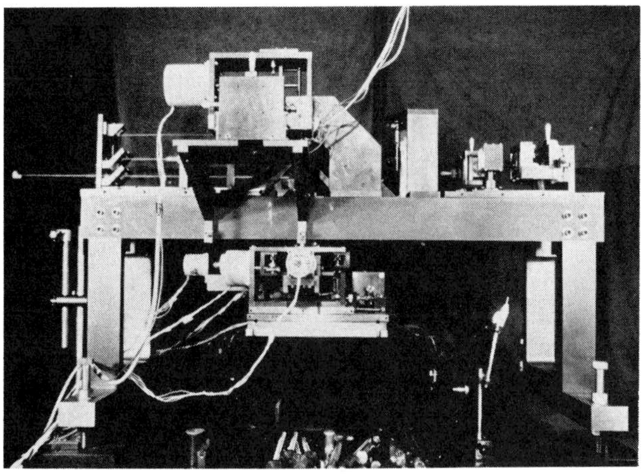

Photo 5. Exterior view of total system

AUTHOR INDEX